House Church *and* Mission

House Church and Mission

The Importance of Household Structures in Early Christianity

ROGER W. GEHRING

House Church and Mission: The Importance of Household Structures in Early Christianity
© 2004 by Roger W. Gehring
Hendrickson Publishers, Inc.
P. O. Box 3473
Peabody, Massachusetts 01961-3473

ISBN 978-1-59856-375-7

House Church and Mission, written and translated by Roger W. Gehring, is a translation of Roger W. Gehring, *Hausgemeinde und Mission* © Brunnen Verlag Giessen 2000, Bibelwissenschaftliche Monographien (BWM) Band 9.

All rights reserved. No part of this book may be reproduced or transmitted in any form or by any means, electronic or mechanical, including photocopying, recording, or by any information storage and retrieval system, without permission in writing from the publisher.

Printed in the United States of America

First Printing, Softcover Edition — February 2009

All Scripture quotations, unless otherwise indicated, are taken from the HOLY BIBLE, NEW INTERNATIONAL VERSION ®. NIV ®. Copyright © 1973, 1978, 1984 by International Bible Society. Used by permission of Zondervan. All rights reserved.

Cover Art: The houses of Nazareth. Detail from The Return from Egypt to Nazareth. Byzantine mosaic in the Exonarthex. 14th C.E. Hora Church (Kariye Camii), Istanbul. Photo Credit: Erich Lessing / Art Resource, N.Y. Used by permission.

Library of Congress Cataloging-in-Publication Data

Gehring, Roger W.
   [Hausgemeinde und Mission. English]
   House church and mission : the importance of household structures in early Christianity / Roger W. Gehring.
      p. cm.
   Includes bibliographical references and indexes.
   ISBN 1-56563-812-3 (alk. paper)
   1. Church—Biblical teaching.   2. Church history—Primitive and early church, ca. 30–600.   I. Title.
   BS2545.C5G45 2004
   225.9′5—dc22
                             2004005915

For my wife Claudia

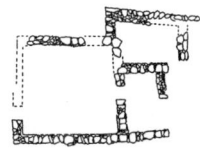

Table of Contents

	PREFACE TO THE ENGLISH EDITION	xi
	ABBREVIATIONS	xiii
CHAPTER ONE	INTRODUCTION	1
	The House Church: A Subject with a Long History	1
	Before and after F. V. Filson (1939)	1
	Renewal of Interest (1980s)	5
	Consensus, Dissonance, and Further Research	17
	Consensus	17
	Dissonance	19
	Moving Forward	26
CHAPTER TWO	THE USE OF HOUSES BEFORE EASTER	28
	Jesus' Use of Houses	28
	A House in Capernaum	31
	Jesus and the House of Peter	35
	Galilean House-to-House and Village-to-Village Outreach	42
	Conclusions	46
	The Disciples' Pre-Easter Use of Houses	48
	The Mission Discourse	48
	House-to-House and Village-to-Village Missional Outreach	53
	Conclusions	60
CHAPTER THREE	THE POST-EASTER USE OF HOUSES IN THE PRIMITIVE JERUSALEM CHURCH	62
	Jerusalem Houses in the Book of Acts	62
	Acts 1:12–15	63
	Excursus: ὑπερῷον	65
	Acts 12:10b–17	69
	Acts 2:42–47 and 5:42	74
	Idealizing Summaries	76
	Historical Reliability of the Passages in Acts	78

	Everyday Life in Jerusalem House Churches	79
	The Worship Service	79
	Excursus: A Plurality of House Churches in Jerusalem	86
	Missional Outreach from House to House	89
	House Church Leadership Structures in Jerusalem	95
	From Jerusalem to Antioch	105
	The Missional Outreach of the Hellenists	105
	The Missional Outreach of Peter	107
	The Missional Outreach of the Church of Antioch	109
	From Jesus to Paul through the Hellenists	113
	Conclusions	116
CHAPTER FOUR	THE USE OF HOUSES IN PAULINE MISSIONAL OUTREACH	119
	A Literary and Historical Analysis of House Church Passages	119
	Paul	119
	Acts 16:14–15	121
	Acts 16:29–34	123
	Acts 17:1–9	124
	Acts 18:1–4, 7–8	128
	Cities with Demonstrable House Churches	130
	Philippi	131
	Thessalonica	132
	Corinth	134
	Cenchrea	142
	Ephesus	143
	Rome	144
	Colossae	151
	Laodicea	154
	A Plurality of House Churches within the Whole Church at One Location	155
	Preliminary Questions on Language Usage and Text Criticism	155
	Paul's Ecclesiological Assertions	160
	Social Strata in Pauline House Churches	165
	Roman Society	166
	Pauline House Churches	167
	The Worship Services in Pauline House Churches	171
	A Separation of the Service of the Word and the Celebration of Communion	171
	The Celebration of Communion in the Corinthian House Churches	173
	The Service of the Word in Pauline House Churches	178
	The House in the Pauline Mission	179
	Center and Coworker Missional Outreach	179
	Missional Outreach from House to House	182

	Leadership Structures and Organizational Formation	190
	The Sociohistorical Approach	190
	References to Leadership Structures in Pauline House Churches	196
	Excursus: Leadership Responsibilities of Women	210
	Conclusions	225
CHAPTER FIVE	THE CONTINUING INFLUENCE OF *OIKOS* STRUCTURES	229
	Household Code in Colossians as *Oikos* Order	229
	The Present State of Research (Col 3:18–4:1)	229
	The Household Ethic: A Regression	230
	Structural Analysis of Col 3:18–4:1	233
	Exegetical Analysis of Col 3:18–4:1	234
	Household Code in Ephesians as a Rule of Order	243
	Structural Analysis of Eph 5:21–6:9	243
	Exegetical Analysis of Eph 5:21–6:9	244
	The Development of Household Ethics from the Christian Oikos	247
	House Church, Local Church, and Church Order in Colossians and Ephesians	257
	Christian *Oikos*, Church, and Leadership Structures in the Pastoral Epistles	260
	Oikos Order as Church Order	260
	Leadership Structures	268
	Excursus: House Churches in 2 and 3 John	281
CHAPTER SIX	THE ECCLESIOLOGICAL AND MISSIONAL FUNCTION AND SIGNIFICANCE OF HOUSE CHURCHES	288
	Function and Significance from Jesus to Paul	288
	The House as a Building (Architectural Significance)	288
	The House as a Community (Socioeconomic Significance)	291
	The House as a Church (Ecclesiological Significance)	295
	The House Church Model for Today	300
APPENDIX	FLOOR PLANS AND RECONSTRUCTIONS	313
	Floor Plan of St. Peter's House in Capernaum	313
	Isometric Reconstruction of St. Peter's House in Capernaum	314
	Floor Plan of the Church House in Capernaum	315
	Isometric Reconstruction of the Church House in Capernaum	316
	Floor Plan of the Roman Villa at Anaploga	317

	Reconstruction of the Roman Villa at Anaploga	318
	Reconstruction of the House Plan (Dura) before Adaptation	319
	Reconstruction of the Church House in Dura	320
	BIBLIOGRAPHY	321
INDEXES	MODERN AUTHORS	383
	SUBJECTS	387
	ANCIENT SOURCES	397

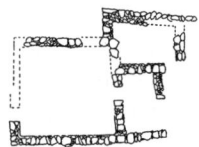

Preface to the English Edition

THE FOLLOWING STUDY IS THE TRANSLATION of an earlier German work, which was accepted in December 1998 by the Protestant theological faculty of the Eberhard-Karl's University in Tübingen as the Inaugural dissertation toward a ThD degree in New Testament Studies with the title *Hausgemeinde und Mission—Von Jesus bis Paulus*. It was then published by Brunnen Verlag in Giessen, Germany in the year 2000. For that publication I was able to include only some of the literature written after 1998 and for the English translation I have not considered any literature published since the German edition appeared. Where German-language publications are quoted in English throughout this book, the translations are my own. If published English editions are available, the footnote citations and bibliography reflect the English-language version. Scripture translations are taken from the NIV unless otherwise noted.

The completion of a doctorate is always something for which one is very thankful. First, I would like to thank my supervisor and "Doktorvater" Professor Peter Stuhlmacher for the scholarly and stimulating assistance he provided during my research. He was selfless and available, truly as a father, not only with advice and encouragement, but with concrete support as well. I would also like to thank Professor Rainer Riesner (Dortmund) for all his important counsel throughout my work on this project and for his willingness to take on the task of the second reader in grading my dissertation. It was a special honor for me personally and an important inspiration for my research as well to co-lead a graduate level seminar with Dr. Rainer Riesner at the University of Tübingen (Winter Semester 1993/94) on the topic "The House Church in the New Testament and the Early Church."

I would also like to thank Professor Hans-Josef Klauck (Munich/Chicago), Dr. Werner Neuer (Gomaringen), Dr. Wiard Popkes (Hamburg) and Dr. Bruce Winter (Tyndale House, Cambridge) for their competent advice and valuable insights. Further I'm very grateful for the work of a number of theology students: Uli Adt, Detlef Garbers, Kerstin Graap, Volker Krüger, Martin Spindler, and Robert Wiens. They were helpful in locating and copying literature as well as in proofreading my German manuscripts. Heinrich Ottinger provided all-important assistance with computer issues. The Verein zur Förderung missionarischer Dienste, Stuttgart; the Arbeitskreis für

Evangelikale Theologie; good friends from the Free Evangelical Church, Giessen (Hans-Joachim Dernbecher, Fritz Hain, Dr. Magdalene Höfner, Helmut Jablonski, Andrea Katz); and my own ministry fellowship Campus für Christus, Germany, all contributed very generous scholarship funds to offset the formatting and printing costs of the manuscript.

Most importantly, I would like to thank my wife Claudia for her willingness to sacrifice and her patient support during the entire doctoral program. Without her this project would not have been possible—it is in deep appreciation that I dedicate this book to her.

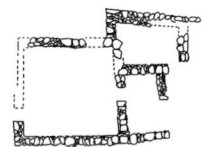

Abbreviations

General

ad loc.	*ad locum,* at the place discussed
b.	Babylonian
bk.	book
cf.	*confer,* compare
ch(s).	chapter(s)
col(s).	column(s)
ed(s).	editor(s), edition
e.g.	*exempli gratia,* for example
esp.	especially
ET	English Translation
fig.	figure
LXX	Septuagint (the Greek OT)
m.	meter(s)
m.	Mishnah
NF	Neue Folge
n(n).	note(s)
no(s).	numbers
n.p.	no page, no publisher
n.t.	no translator
NT	New Testament
OT	Old Testament
repr.	reprinted
rev.	revised
sec.	section
sq. m.	square meter(s)
t.	Tosefta
v(v).	verse(s)
y.	Jerusalem

Apostolic Fathers

Barn.	*Barnabas*
1 Clem.	*1 Clement*

| Did. | Didache |
| Ign. *Pol.* | Ignatius, *To Polycarp* |

Dead Sea Scrolls

1QM	Milḥamah or *War Scroll*
1QS	Serek Hayaḥad or *Rule of the Community*
1QSª	*Rule of the Congregation* (Appendix a to 1QS)

Early Christian Literature

Clement of Alexandria
    Strom.   *Stromata*
Eusebius
    Onom.   *Onomasticon*
Jerome
    Epist.   *Epistulae*
    Sit.   *De situ et nominibus locorum hebraicorum (Liber locorum)*
Justin
    1 Apol.   *Apologia i*
    Dial.   *Dialogus cum Tryphone*
Origen
    Cels.   *Contra Celsum*
Paulus Orosius
    Hist.   *Historiae adversus paganos*

Josephus

Ag. Ap.	*Against Apion*
Ant.	*Jewish Antiquities*
J.W.	*Jewish War*

Mishnah, Talmud, and Related Literature

B. Bat.	*Baba Batra*
B. Qam.	*Baba Qamma*
Bek.	*Bekorot*
Ber.	*Berakot*
Giṭ.	*Giṭṭin*
Ketub.	*Ketubbot*
Mak.	*Makkot*
Meg.	*Megillah*
Menaḥ.	*Menaḥot*
Šabb.	*Šabbat*

Sanh.   *Sanhedrin*
Šeqal.   *Šeqalim*

Non-Christian Literature

Apuleius
    Metam.   *Metamorphoses*
Aristotle
    Eth. nic.   *Ethica nichomachea*
    [Oec.]   *Oeconomica*
    Pol.   *Politica*
Columella
    Rust.   *De re rustica*
Diogenes Laertius
    Clar. phil.   *De clarorum philosophorum vitis*
Juvenal
    Sat.   *Satirae*
Martial
    Epigr.   *Epigrammata*
Musonius Rufus
    Or.   *Oratio*
Philostratus
    Gymn.   *De gymnastica*
Plutarch
    Ant.   *Antonius*
    Conj. praec.   *Conjugalia praecepta*
    [Lib. ed.]   *De liberis educandis*
    Lyc.   *Lycurgus*
    Mar.   *Marius*
Seneca
    Ira   *De ira*
Strabo
    Geogr.   *Geographica*
Suetonius
    Claud.   *Divus Claudius*
Xenophon
    Oec.   *Oeconomicus*

Old Testament Pseudepigrapha

3 Bar.   *3 Baruch (Greek Apocalypse)*
1 En.   *1 Enoch*
Pss. Sol.   *Psalms of Solomon*

Papyri

P.Ryl.	Ryland papyrus
P.Tebt.	Tebtunis papyrus

Philo

Hypoth.	*Hypothetica*
Legat.	*Legatio ad Gaium*
Mos. 2	*De vita Mosis* II
Prob.	*Quod omnis probus liber sit*
Somn. 2	*De somniis* II
Spec. 2	*De specialibus legibus* II

Secondary Literature

AB	Anchor Bible
ABD	*Anchor Bible Dictionary.* Edited by D. N. Freedman. 6 vols. New York: Doubleday, 1992
AnGr	Analecta gregoriana
ANRW	*Aufstieg und Niedergang der römischen Welt: Geschichte und Kultur Roms im Spiegel der neueren Forschung.* Edited by H. Temporini and W. Haase. New York: de Gruyter, 1972
ASNU	Acta seminarii neotestamentici upsaliensis
ATANT	Abhandlungen zur Theologie des Alten und Neuen Testaments
AzTh	Arbeiten zur Theologie
Bauer[5]	Bauer, W. *Griechisch-deutsches Wörterbuch zu den Schriften des Neuen Testaments und der übrigen urchristlichen Literatur.* 5th ed. Berlin: de Gruyter, 1971
Bauer-Aland[6]	Bauer, W. *Griechisch-deutsches Wörterbuch zu den Schriften des Neuen Testaments und der frühchristlichen Literatur.* Edited by K. and B. Aland, 6th fully revised ed. Berlin: de Gruyter, 1988
BBB	Bonner biblische Beiträge
BBET	Beiträge zur biblischen Exegese und Theologie
BDAG	Bauer, W., F. W. Danker, W. F. Arndt, and F. W. Gingrich. *Greek-English Lexicon of the New Testament and Other Early Christian Literature.* 3d ed. Chicago: University of Chicago Press, 2000
BDF	Blass, F., A. Debrunner, and R. W. Funk. *A Greek Grammar of the New Testament and Other Early Christian Literature.* Chicago: University of Chicago Press, 1961.

BETL	Bibliotheca ephemeridum theologicarum lovaniensium
BEvT	Beiträge zur evangelischen Theologie
BFChTh.M	Beiträge zur Förderung christlicher Theologie 2. Reihe, Sammlung wissenschaftlicher Monographien
BFCT	Beiträge zur Förderung christlicher Theologie
BHH	*Biblisch-historisches Handwörterbuch: Landeskunde, Geschichte, Religion, Kultur, Literatur.* Edited by B. Reicke and L. Rost. 4 vols. Göttingen: Vandenhoeck & Ruprecht, 1962–1979
BHT	Beiträge zur historischen Theologie
BiJer	Bible de Jérusalem
BiSe	Biblical Seminar
BJS	Brown Judaic Studies
*BL*²	*Bibel-Lexikon.* Edited by H. Haag. 2d ed. Einsiedeln: Benziger, 1968
BNTC	Black's New Testament Commentaries
BRL2	*Biblisches Reallexikon.* 2d ed. Edited by K. Galling. HAT 1/1. Tübingen: Mohr, 1977
BU	Biblische Untersuchungen
BWA(N)T	Beiträge zur Wissenschaft vom Alten (und Neuen) Testament
BWM	Bibelwissenschaftliche Monographien
BZNW	Beihefte zur Zeitschrift für die neutestamentliche Wissenschaft
CBET	Contributions to Biblical Exegesis and Theology
CII	*Corpus inscriptionum iudaicarum.* Edited by J. B. Frey. 2 vols. Rome: Pontificio istituto di archeologia cristiana, 1936–1952
CIL	*Corpus inscriptionum latinarum*
ConBNT	Coniectanea neotestamentica or Coniectanea biblica: New Testament Series
CRINT	Compendia rerum iudaicarum ad Novum Testamentum
CThM.PT	Calwer theologische Monographien Reihe C, Praktische Theology und Missionswissenschaft
CSEL	Corpus scriptorum ecclesiasticorum latinorum
CwH	Calwer Hefte
DACL	*Dictionnaire d'archéologie chrétienne et de liturgie.* Edited by F. Cabrol. 15 vols. Paris: Letouzey et Ané, 1907–1953
DTV WR	*Deutscher Taschenbuch Verlag Wissenschaftliche Reihe.* Munich: Deutscher Taschenbuch, n.d.
EAEHL	*Encyclopedia of Archaeological Excavations in the Holy Land.* Edited by M. Avi-Yonah. 4 vols. Jerusalem: Prentice-Hall, 1975
EdF	Erträger der Forschung

EEPSTh	Epistēmonikē epetēris tēs Philosophikēs Scholēs tou Panepistēmiou Thessalonikēs
EHS.T	Europäische Hochschulschriften Reihe 23, Theologie
EK	*Evangelische Kommentare*. Stuttgart, 1968–
EKKNT	Evangelisch-katholischer Kommentar zum Neuen Testament
ESt	Eichstätter Studien
EThS	Erfurter theologische Schriften
EThSt	Erfurter theologische Studien
ETS	Erfurter theologische Studien
EvT	*Evangelische Theologie*
EDNT	*Exegetical Dictionary of the New Testament*. Edited by H. Balz and G. Schneider. Translated from the 1st German ed. by J. W. Medendorp, D. W. Stott, J. W. Thompson, and V. P. Howard. 3 vols. Grand Rapids: Eerdmans, 1990–1993
FB	Forschung zur Bibel
FRLANT	Forschungen zur Religion und Literatur des Alten und Neuen Testaments
GBL	*Das Grosse Bibellexikon*. Edited by H. Burkhardt et al. 3 vols. 2d ed. Giessen, Germany: Brunnen, 1990.
GCS	Die griechische christliche Schriftsteller der ersten [drei] Jahrhunderte
GNS	Good News Studies
GNT	Grundrisse zum Neuen Testament
GTA	Göttinger theologischer Arbeiten
HerBü	Herder-Bücherei
HMT	Handbuch der Moraltheologie
HNT	Handbuch zum Neuen Testament
HNTC	Harper's New Testament Commentaries
HRCS	Hatch, E., and H. A. Redpath. *Concordance to the Septuagint and Other Greek Versions of the Old Testament*. 2 vols. Oxford, 1897. Suppl., 1906. Repr., 3 vols. in 2, Grand Rapids: Baker Books, 1983
HTKNT	Herders theologischer Kommentar zum Neuen Testament
HTS	Harvard Theological Studies
ICC	International Critical Commentary
IG	*Inscriptiones graecae*. Editio minor. Berlin: de Gruyter, 1924–
ISBE	*International Standard Bible Encyclopedia*. Edited by G. W. Bromiley. 4 vols. Grand Rapids: Eerdmans, 1979–1988
IVP NT	InterVarsity Press New Testament Commentary Series
JAC.E	Jahrbuch für Antike und Christentum, Egänzungsband

JSHRZ	Jüdische Schriften aus hellenistisch-römischer Zeit
JSNTSup	Journal for the Study of the New Testament: Supplement Series
KAV	Kommentar zu den apostolischen Vätern
KBANT	Kommentare und Beiträge zum Alten und Neuen Testament
KEK	Kritisch-exegetischer Kommentar über das Neue Testament (Meyer-Kommentar)
KIG	Kirche in ihrer Geschichte
KlPauly	*Der kleine Pauly: Lexikon der Antike.* Edited by K. Ziegler and W. Sontheimer. 5 vols. Stuttgart: A. Druckenmüller, 1964–1975
KNT	Kommentar zum Neuen Testament
KStTh	Kohlhammer-Studienbücher Theologie
KT	Kaiser-Taschenbücher
KuM	Kerygma und Mythos
LAW	*Lexikon der alten Welt.* Edited by C. Andresen et al. Zurich: Artemis, 1965
LCL	Loeb Classical Library
MAAR	Memoirs of the American Academy in Rome
MBTh	Münsterische Beiträge zur Theologie
MM	Moulton, J. H., and G. Milligan. *The Vocabulary of the Greek Testament.* London: Hodder & Stoughton, 1930. Repr., Peabody, Mass.: Hendrickson, 1997
MNTC	Moffatt New Testament Commentary
MThS.S	Münchener theologische Studien: Systematische Abteilung
NAC	New American Commentary
NBL	*Neues Bibel-Lexikon.* Edited by M. Görg and B. Lang. 3 vols. Zurich: Benzinger, 1988–2001
NCB	New Century Bible
NCBC	New Century Bible Commentary
NEAEHL	*The New Encyclopedia of Archaeological Excavations in the Holy Land.* Edited by E. Stern. 4 vols. Jerusalem: Israel Exploration Society, 1993
NEB.NT	Neue Echter Bibel: Kommentar zum NT
NIBCNT	New International Biblical Commentary on the New Testament
NICNT	New International Commentary on the New Testament
NIGTC	New International Greek Testament Commentary
NTAbh	Neutestamentliche Abhandlungen
NTD	Das Neue Testament Deutsch
NTL	New Testament Library
NTOA	Novum Testamentum et orbis antiquus
OBO	Orbis biblicus et orientalis

ÖBS	Österreichische biblische Studien
ÖTK	Ökumenischer Taschenbuch-Kommentar zum Neuen Testament
PEFQS	Palestine Exploration Fund Quarterly Statement
PG	Patrologia graeca
PGrLa	Papiri greci e latini
PL	Patrologia latina
PSBF	Pubblicazioni dello Studium Biblicum Franciscanum, Jerusalem
PSBF.Mi.5	Pubblicazioni dello Studium Biblicum Franciscanum, Jerusalem: Collectio minor
PThMS	PTMS Pittsburgh Theological Monograph Series
PuP	Päpste und Papsttum
PW	Pauly, A. F. *Paulys Realencyclopädie der classischen Altertumswissenschaft.* New revision by G. Wissowa, W. Kroll, et al. Stuttgart: Metzler, 1893–. 2d series, 1914–
PWSup	Supplement to PW
QD	Quaestiones disputatae
RAC	*Reallexikon für Antike und Christentum.* Edited by T. Kluser et al. Stuttgart: Hiersemann, 1950–
RE	*Realencyklopädie für protestantische Theologie und Kirche.* Edited by J. Herzog and A. Hauck. 24 vols. 3d ed. Leipzig: J. C. Hinrichs, 1896–1913
RGG	*Religion in Geschichte und Gegenwart.* Edited by K. Galling. 7 vols. 3d ed. Tübingen: Mohr, 1957–1965
RGG²	*Religion in Geschichte und Gegenwart.* Edited by K. Galling. 7 vols. 2d ed. Tübingen: Mohr, 1927–1931
RMP	*Rheinisches Museum für Philologie*
RNT	Regensburger Neues Testament
RS	Religion and Society
SANT	Studien zum Alten und Neuen Testaments
SAOC	Studies in Ancient Oriental Civilizations
SB	*Sammelbuch griechischer Urkunden aus Aegypten.* Edited by F. Preisigke et al. Vols. 1–Strasbourg: K. J. Trübner, 1915–
SBAB	Stuttgarter biblische Aufsatzbände
SBEC	Studies in the Bible and Early Christianity
SBF.CMa	Studium biblicum franciscanum: Collectio major
SBF.CMi	Studium biblicum franciscanum: Collectio minor
SBLDS	Society of Biblical Literature Dissertation Series
SBLMS	Society of Biblical Literature Monograph Series
SBLSBS	Society of Biblical Literature Sources for Biblical Study
SBLSP	Society of Biblical Literature Seminar Papers

SBS	Stuttgarter Bibelstudien
SD	Studies and Documents
SG	Sammlung Göschen
SGKA	Studien zur Geschichte und Kultur des Altertums
SIG	*Sylloge inscriptionum graecarum.* Edited by W. Dittenberger. 4 vols. 3d ed. Leipzig: S. Hirzelium, 1915–1924
SIGC	Studien zur interkulturellen Geschichte des Christentums
SJLA	Studies in Judaism in Late Antiquity
SNT	Schriften des Neues Testaments
SNTSMS	Society for New Testament Studies Monograph Series
SNTSMS	Society for New Testament Studies Monograph Series
SPAW	Sitzungsberichte der Preussischen Akademie der Wissenschaften
SPLi	Studia patristica et liturgica
Str-B	Strack, H. L., and P. Billerbeck. *Kommentar zum Neuen Testament aus Talmud und Midrasch.* 6 vols. Munich: Beck, 1922–1961
SUNT	Studien zur Umwelt des Neuen Testaments
TANZ	Texte und Arbeiten zum neutestamentlichen Zeitalter
TB	Theologische Bücherei: Neudrucke und Berichte aus dem 20. Jahrhundert
TBLNT	*Theologisches Begriffslexikon zum Neuen Testament.* Edited by L. Coenen, E. Beyreuther, and H. Bietenhard. 9th ed. Wuppertal: Brockhaus, 1993
TDNT	*Theological Dictionary of the New Testament.* Edited by G. Kittel and G. Friedrich. Translated by G. W. Bromiley. 10 vols. Grand Rapids: Eerdmans, 1964–1976
TEH	Theologische Existenz heute
Teubner	Bibliotheca scriptorum graecorum et romanorum teubneriana
ThF	Theologische Forschung
THKNT	Theologischer Handkommentar zum Neuen Testament
ThW	Theologische Wissenschaft
TNT	Texte zum Neuen Testament
TNTC	Tyndale New Testament Commentaries
TRE	*Theologische Realenzyklopädie.* Edited by G. Krause and G. Müller. Vols. 1–. Berlin: de Gruyter, 1977–
TSK	*Theologische Studien und Kritiken*
TUGAL	Texte und Untersuchungen zur Geschichte der altchristlichen Literatur
UB	Urban-(Taschen-)Bücher
UNT	Untersuchungen zum Neuen Testament

UTB.W	Uni-Taschenbücher für Wissenschaft
VIMW	Veröffentlichungen des Instituts für Missionswissenschaft der Westfällischen Wilhelms-Universität Münster
VKHSM	Veröffentlichungen aus dem Kirchenhistorischen Seminar München
WBC	Word Biblical Commentary
WdF	Wege der Forschung
WMANT	Wissenschaftliche Monographien zum Alten und Neuen Testament
WTB	Wissenschaftliche Taschenbücher
WUNT	Wissenschaftliche Untersuchungen zum Neuen Testament
YCS	Yale Classical Studies
ZBK.NT	Zürcher Bibelkommentare: Neues Testament

CHAPTER ONE

Introduction

ON ONE POINT NEARLY ALL NT SCHOLARS presently agree: early Christians met almost exclusively in the homes of individual members of the congregation. For nearly three hundred years—until the fourth century, when Constantine began building the first basilicas throughout the Roman Empire—Christians gathered in private houses built initially for domestic use, not in church buildings originally constructed for the sole purpose of public worship.

As elementary as this insight might appear, all the more astonishing is the observation that for many years the subject "house church" generated little or no interest among NT scholars. Only in the last twenty-five years has research begun to focus more closely on the architectural setting of early Christian gatherings and on its corresponding social and theological implications. Since 1980 we have seen a flood of popular and scholarly publications on the subject. Here again it appears most scholars are in agreement: the fact that early Christian communities met in homes is of great sociohistorical, ecclesiological, and missional significance. Therefore, it would seem more than appropriate to take a fresh and yet critical look at the research efforts of the last two decades.

THE HOUSE CHURCH: A SUBJECT WITH A LONG HISTORY

Before and after F. V. Filson (1939)

The insight that early Christians met in homes is not new. As early as 1694 C. Vitringa argued that the primitive church patterned itself after house synagogues.[1] In 1832 N. C. Kist quoted Vitringa in support of his own argument that early Christians met in the homes of its affluent members, who in turn acted as its initial leaders.[2] F. C. Baur (1835) and H. Weingarten

---

[1] C. Vitringa, *De synagoga vetere*, bk. 1, part 1, 145–47, 257–58; bk. 1, part 3, 429–31.

[2] N. C. Kist, "Über den Ursprung," 47–90, here 54–56. For Kist, however, these house churches are not churches in the full sense. For my definition of "house church" in the full sense, see pp. 27–28.

(1881) offered similar arguments.[3] At the turn of the century, W. Sanday and A. C. Headlam drew attention to house churches at Rome.[4] J. P. Kirsch made cursory note of the fact that Christians gathered originally in houses, without drawing any conclusions regarding their significance.[5] A. Hauck observed this as well and concluded that the size of the inner rooms of these ancient homes would have limited the number of possible community members to only a few dozen unless they made use of the atrium (inner courtyard).[6] In 1906 F. Wieland concluded in his research on the development of the altar that Christian liturgy was already being practiced in private homes during the ministry of the apostles. Of particular interest for our research is his reference to a plurality of house churches in the primitive church in Jerusalem as well as in Corinth and Rome.[7] In his two-volume work of 1912 entitled *Das Christentum in den ersten drei Jahrhunderten*, H. Achelis dealt with the topic of house churches in a single paragraph.[8] J. Weiss treated the subject just as briefly in his book *Das Urchristentum*, written in 1917.[9] In 1924 the fourth edition of A. von Harnack's monumental description of the social history of early Christianity appeared.[10] Harnack delved deeper than any other scholars before him and recognized that house churches were a factor in the rapid growth, the diversity, and the triumph of the early Christian movement.[11] Nevertheless, he neglected to clearly spell out in what specific manner the house church contributed to the expansion of Christianity. For a rather long time following Harnack, relatively little was done to develop his observations.[12]

It was not until the discovery of the house church in Dura Europos[13] that F. V. Filson (1939) published an article in which he attempted to demonstrate that primitive Christianity would be better understood "if more attention were paid to the actual physical conditions under which the first Christians met and lived. In particular, the importance and function of the house church should be carefully considered."[14] Whenever the question of

---

[3] F. C. Baur (*Pastoralbriefe*, 83–84) mentions "small Christian associations" as well as "small Christian congregations" but does not refer explicitly to house churches; Weingarten ("Umwandlung," 444–48) does not refer directly to house churches but rather to the organization of the early church in "family groups."

[4] W. Sanday and A. C. Headlam, *Romans* (1895), 420–21.

[5] J. P. Kirsch, "Cultusgebäude," 6–8. Kirsch was more interested in first-, second-, and third-century church buildings.

[6] A. Hauck, "Kirchenbau," 10:774–76.

[7] F. Wieland, *Altar*, 29–33.

[8] H. Achelis, *Christentum* (1925), 96–97.

[9] J. Weiss, *Earliest Christianity*, 1:620.

[10] A. von Harnack, *Mission*.

[11] Ibid., 1:457, 2:611–18.

[12] Cf. also H. Leclercq, "Églises," 4:2279–2349, for his reference to house churches.

[13] Cf. the appendix, p. 319, for Dura Europos floor plans.

[14] F. V. Filson, "Significance," 105–12, here 105.

the significance of the physical conditions for the setting of early Christian gatherings is raised, almost all scholars point to Filson's seminal article.[15] For that reason it seems quite appropriate to briefly summarize his catalogue of observations in order to better evaluate the development of NT research on the house church since 1939.

In his article, Filson listed five areas that needed to be considered more carefully in order to deepen our understanding of the early church:

1. The house church "enabled the followers of Jesus to have a *distinctively* Christian worship and fellowship from the very first days of the apostolic age."

2. "The large part played by the house churches affords a partial explanation of the great attention paid to *family life* in the letters of Paul and in the other Christian writings. It must not be forgotten that in both Jewish and Gentile life religious observance had been largely centered in the home."

3. "The existence of several houses in one city goes far to explain the tendency to *party strife* in the apostolic age."

4. "A study of the house church situation also throws light upon the *social status* of the early Christians."

5. "The development of *church polity* can never be understood without reference to the house churches. The host of such a group was almost inevitably a man of some education, with a fairly broad background and at least some administrative ability. . . . The house church was the training ground for the Christian leaders who were to build the church after the loss of "apostolic" guidance, and everything in such a situation favored the emergence of the host as the most prominent and influential member of the group."[16]

In spite of Filson's challenge that scholars ought to focus more on the research of house churches in early Christian missions, very little attention was given this issue for a considerable period of time. As late as 1954, O. Michel criticized scholarship's neglect in this area and implied that further research needed to be done in order to recognize more fully the importance of the household in the early Christian community.[17] Not until the 1960s was the topic was taken up again.[18] In 1960 and 1961 E. A. Judge published

---

[15] E.g., cf. White, "Domus," 45; Klauck, *Hausgemeinde*, 12 (all citations are to the 1981 printing); Meeks, *First Urban Christians*, 52; H. Maier, *Social Setting*, 5 (all citations are to the 1991 reprint); Theissen, *Social Setting*, 56 n. 62 (all citations are to the 2d ed.); Hainz, *Ekklesia*, 203; Elliott, *Home*, 169–70; Crosby, *House*, 32; Verner, *Household*, 8; Blue, "In Public," 2; Vogler, "Bedeutung," 786 n. 2; indirectly, Dassmann, "Hausgemeinde" (all citations are to the 1984 article); Laub, "Sozialgeschichtlicher Hintergrund," 261; Harder, "Hausgemeinde."

[16] Filson, "Significance," 109–12 (italics added).

[17] Michel, "οἶκος," *TDNT* 5:130 n. 42.

[18] Until then we see only cursory treatment of the subject. In 1945 Dix (*Shape of Liturgy* [all citations are to the 1978 edition], 16–18, 63) notes that the Eucharist was celebrated in private homes and was therefore characterized by a family-like,

a short monograph and two articles.[19] These, as well as subsequent articles of his, made a seminal contribution in sociohistorical research of the NT.[20] Judge, apparently independent of Filson,[21] drew attention to the significance of the house in early Christian missions. In contrast to Filson, rather than focusing on the physical conditions, he pointed out the social importance of the house. In particular, he demonstrated that the ancient institution of the family played a crucial role in the expansion of Christianity.[22] In addition, Judge questioned the generally accepted assumption of Adolf Deissmann[23] that early Christians came primarily from, and were dominated by, the lower social classes. Judge countered this position by arguing, "Far from being a socially depressed group, then, if the Corinthians are at all typical, the Christians were dominated by a socially pretentious section of the population of big cities. Beyond that they seem to have drawn on a broad constituency, probably representing the household dependents of leading members."[24]

A few years later Willy Rordorf wrote an article focusing on Christian worship facilities in the time prior to Constantine.[25] Rordorf observes, "In general it would be safe to say that the first three centuries belonged to the house church."[26] Up until the fourth century, Christians met for worship not in church buildings erected solely for that purpose but, rather, primarily in rooms of houses already in existence.

The 1970s ushered in a renewal of sociohistorical research in NT studies that continues through the present.[27] G. Theissen, widely recognized today as one of the most prominent NT scholars in the field of social history, attempted to identify Christians of a higher social status in the Pauline churches in particular. Inspired by Judge, he considered ownership of a home in which the rest of the congregation gathered to be one of the most important criteria for determining higher social status.[28] One of Theissen's

---

exclusive, and specifically Christian understanding. Farrer ("Ministry," 147–48) argued that the early Christian heads of the household were also church bishops. In 1949 J. Wagner researched the significance of the domestic house in connection with the development of the Eucharist (unfortunately his findings were not published until 1993 in *Altchristliche Eucharistiefeiern*, 25–102). Apparently neither Dix, Farrer, nor Wagner knew of Filson's article.

[19] Judge, *Social Pattern;* "Early Christians." Cf. also his later article "Social Identity."

[20] Cf., e.g., Schöllgen, "Probleme," 23 n. 5: "E. A. Judge ... has played a seminal role for sociohistorical research of the New Testament during the postwar period."

[21] Nowhere in the footnotes of these three documents does he mention Filson.

[22] Judge, *Social Pattern*, 35–39.

[23] Deissmann, *Licht vom Osten*, 115. Deissmann referred to Matt 11:25 and 1 Cor 1:26–31 as proof texts for his hypothesis.

[24] Judge, *Social Pattern*, 60. "Christianity was a movement sponsored by local patrons to their social dependents" (Judge, "Early Christians," 8).

[25] Rordorf, "Was wissen wir?" Rordorf does not mention Filson either. For discussion of house churches and tituli in Rome, cf. Petersen, "House-Churches."

[26] Rordorf, "Was wissen wir?" 111 (citations are to the 1964 printing).

[27] Cf. from this period S. Williams, "Household."

[28] Theissen, *Studien*, 10 n. 25; *Social Setting*, 69, 73.

most valuable contributions to the sociohistorical research of the NT was to call attention to the significance of social status in Pauline house churches.

Renewal of Interest (1980s)

The year 1980 represents a watershed for the publication of literature on the topic of the house church. In *Social Aspects of Early Christianity* (1977), A. J. Malherbe observed that up until that time "no major work has been devoted to the New Testament house church."[29] Then suddenly at the beginning of the 1980s, five exegetic sociohistorical studies on the topics "family," "house," and "house church" in early Christianity appeared independently of one another. And by the time Malherbe's book was reprinted in 1983, one of the most substantial and significant works in the Anglo-Saxon world on the subject of the house church had been completed by his pupil L. M. White.[30] It would appear that, beginning in 1980, the time had fully come for scholars to tackle the issues relating to the house church. Since then a relatively large number of books and articles have been published on the subject.[31] The following pages summarize the main findings of seven studies.

D. von Allmen

D. von Allmen, *La famille de Dieu: La symbolique familiale dans le paulinisme* (1981), is a purely literary and exegetic-theological investigation of the metaphorical language of family in Paul's epistles. The author's intent is primarily to demonstrate that Paul does not see family as *the* organizing idea of his ecclesiology and that the concept "family of God" is present in Paul's writings only in a limited, indirect sense. H. J. Klauck criticized Allmen for failing to demonstrate in what way Paul's family metaphor is or is

---

[29] Malherbe, *Social Aspects*, 61. He remarks, however, that some scholars had begun to give more, although brief, attention to the house church. In pp. 60–91 he summarizes the present state of research, focusing in particular on Theissen's work.

Klauck, *Hausgemeinde*, 12, also observes that exegetical literature on the house church was "relativ dünn gestreut" ("scattered somewhat sparsely") at the time he wrote his book, and he lists all that of which he was aware (cf. p. 12), including these not yet mentioned in our study: F. Maier, *Paulus*, 27–29; Hainz, *Ekklesia*, 195, 199–203, 345–48; Schreiber, *Gemeinde*, 130–34; Grimm, *Untersuchungen*, 194–211; Provencher, "Vers une théologie"; Coyle, *Empire and Eschaton*, 35–94.

One year after Klauck's book was published, Vogler's article "Bedeutung," appeared with a number of insightful observations relating to the house church. (Vogler apparently knew only of Filson and Stuhlmacher at the time he wrote his article.)

[30] White, "Domus."

[31] Granted, one explanation for this renewal beginning in the 1970s is the interest in social and sociohistorical study in general, growing out of and characteristic of the period following the student revolts during the 1960s. Cf. Riesner, "Soziologie," esp. 214. Nevertheless, one can observe a certain aversion to "mere theology" in the work of some of these exegetes—an aversion that, unfortunately, can lead to the substitution of theology with sociology (cf. the discussion of this issue in Meeks, *First Urban Christians*, 2–4).

not connected with the concrete life of the community, which was integrally intertwined with a very real family. Such a family was in turn foundational for the development of each house church as human "building material," as support and as living space.³² This quite commendable study could have been improved considerably by including a more sociohistorical approach. In fact, in his sociohistorical study of the function of family language in Paul's letters, L. A. Lewis has come to quite a different conclusion, and that totally independent of Allmen: "The language of family determines the nature of several Pauline churches."³³

R. Banks

R. Banks, *Paul's Idea of Community: The Early House Churches in Their Historical Setting* (1980), paints a picture of virtually every aspect of community life in Pauline congregations.³⁴ Unfortunately, the extensive treatment of the sociohistorical context of Pauline house churches one would expect on the basis of the subtitle is realized only in a limited sense. Technically, apart from a few cursory comments elsewhere, the house church becomes the central focus of discussion merely in chapter 3 (pp. 26–36), and the church as "family" is dealt with in chapter 5 (pp. 47–57). In both these chapters Banks demonstrates his exegetical ability and makes a number of keen insights regarding the subject. His observation that the house of Gaius was the gathering place of the whole church in Corinth, in contrast to smaller groups coming together as "church" at other times (p. 32), and his insight regarding a plurality of house churches in Rome (32–33) are of particular importance for our study. The analogies for the house church in the Jewish and Hellenistic world are given only cursory attention (43–46).

J. H. Elliott

J. H. Elliott, *A Home for the Homeless: A Sociological Exegesis of 1 Peter, Its Situation and Strategy* (1981), examines the entire sociological context of the Christian community of 1 Peter in light of the opposition between οἶκος and παροικία.³⁵ As 1 Peter is outside the parameters of our study, it is primarily chapter 4, in which Elliott deals with function of the οἶκος in the Roman, Hellenistic, and Jewish worlds, that is of greatest interest to us. Of fundamental importance is Elliott's insight that "households thus constituted the focus, locus and nucleus of the ministry and mission of the Christian movement."³⁶

D. C. Verner

D. C. Verner, *The Household of God: The Social World of the Pastoral Epistles* (1983), attempts to illuminate the social setting and strategy of the

---

³² Klauck, "Neue Literatur," 292.
³³ Lewis, "'As a Beloved Brother,'" ii.
³⁴ Citations are to the 1994 ed., however.
³⁵ For a convincing rebuttal of Elliott's thesis, cf. Chin, "Heavenly Home."
³⁶ Elliott, *Home*, 188.

Pastoral Epistles from a sociohistorical perspective.³⁷ According to Verner, the metaphor οἶκος θεοῦ contains the ecclesiological blueprint of the author of these letters, which is in itself quite consistent, and the statement in 1 Tim 3:15 ("so . . . you will know how people ought to conduct themselves in God's household") constitutes the key to understanding the author's perspective. For Verner this concept of church as the "household of God" incorporates two aspects: (a) the house or family is the fundamental unit of the church, and (b) the church is a social structure patterned after the household.³⁸

One of Verner's contributions is certainly his suggestion that the Greek and Roman household tradition be applied in the interpretation of the Pastoral Epistles. Apart from the question whether Verner's sociohistorical exegetical thesis is convincing, his description of households in the Hellenistic-Roman world³⁹ and his attempt to understand the ecclesiology of the Pastoral Epistles in terms of the "house of God" deserve our attention.⁴⁰

H. J. Klauck

H. J. Klauck, *Hausgemeinde und Hauskirche im frühen Christentum* (1981), ranks to this day as the most significant German work on the house church.⁴¹ The book examines the history of early Christian house churches from the beginning up into the fourth century and offers an overview of possible models from the environment surrounding early Christianity. Klauck summarizes the findings of his examination thus: The house church served as a building block and building center of the church at any given location, as a support base for missional outreach, as a gathering place for the Lord's Supper, as a sanctuary for prayer, as a classroom for catechetic instruction, and as an opportunity to experience and exercise Christian brotherly love. In its early beginnings the church established itself "in a houselike manner."⁴²

In his first chapter Klauck analyzes the word pair οἶκος/οἰκία by examining the classical texts, inscriptions, and papyri as well as the LXX and NT

---

³⁷ Verner's work is characterized by a *formgeschichtliche* approach applied to the household codes.

³⁸ Cf. Verner, *Household*, 1–2, 127. Lips, *Glaube-Gemeinde-Amt*, 106–49, draws similar conclusions.

³⁹ This applies even though certain nuances in his description of the Jewish family are missing (cf. the critique by Quinn, book review, 178–79). In addition, the fruit of continued research of family life in the Greco-Roman world since the publication of his book would obviously supplement his presentation.

⁴⁰ For a critical examination of Verner's overall thesis, cf. Karris, book review, and Wagener, *Ordnung*, 38–43.

⁴¹ The importance of this work is also highly appreciated in Anglo-Saxon scholarship. Cf., e.g., H. Maier, *Social Setting*, 5: "Hans-Josef Klauck, in what is becoming the authoritative work on the house church in the New Testament, provides a fruitful account of the impact of the household on the earlier church."

⁴² Klauck, *Hausgemeinde*, 102. Klauck translated Paul's idiomatic expression ἡ κατ' οἶκον ἐκκλησία as "die sich hausweise konstituierende Kirche" ("the church that establishes itself in a houselike manner"), probably inspired by Stuhlmacher, *Philemon*, 71. Cf. also Rordorf, "Was wissen wir?" 117.

and comes to the following conclusion: The two Greek words for house, οἶκος and οἰκία, have a double meaning that can be observed in all of classical Greek, even in the colloquial.[43] The two words mean (a) house in the sense of living quarters, inhabited building, and (b) house as in family, extended family, clan. Οἶκος is used more often to mean "house" in an architectural sense, and οἰκία "house" in a sociological sense (i.e., household). At any rate, the term οἶκος is to be understood much more broadly than our two English terms "house" and "family." In its *sociological* meaning οἶκος includes not only father, mother, and children but slaves, clients, and property as well. The house in ancient times was, granted, the point of origin of the family but should not be confused with the term "family" in the modern sense. In its *architectural* sense οἶκος has the physical nature of the house in view. With regard to the Christian usage, it can be observed that in particular the LXX prepared the way for an assimilation of the two terms.

The LXX uses οἰκία as well as οἶκος (more often) for בית without distinguishing clearly between the two.[44] This insight is significant for us, among other reasons, because this usage, typical for the LXX, is continued in the NT. Depending on whether οἶκος/οἰκία is translated as "house" or as "household," both of which are linguistically possible, the result is a different nuance, whereby the two connotations need not be seen as mutually exclusive.[45] Klauck comes to the conclusion that in the NT the context is decisive in determining the meaning of the word pair as well as who or what an οἶκος or an οἰκία comprises.

Even though Klauck's analysis is a sound rendering of the present state of lexical research,[46] a number of scholars are inclined to question his results, particularly regarding the classical Greek. This could have implications for NT exegesis of the word pair. First, it is apparent that some scholars come to precisely the opposite conclusion regarding the meaning of the word pair. For J. H. Elliott, for example, οἰκία is literally "house" or "building" and οἶκος means "groups of persons." "The distinction was, however, not rigid."[47] As a

---

[43] Cf. Klauck, *Hausgemeinde,* 15–20.

[44] A classic example is Jos 24:15 (quoted by Klauck, ibid., 17): codex A, οἶκος; codex B, οἰκία. Cf. HRCS 969–70, 973–82; Weigandt, "Zur sog. 'Oikosformel,'" 50–63.

[45] E.g.: (a) Even though οἶκος appears 112 times and οἰκία 94 times in the NT, we encounter οἶκος 4 times in connection with ἐκκλησία (Rom 16:5; 1 Cor 16:19; Phlm 2; Col 4:15) and οἰκία not once. (b) In 1 Corinthians the two terms appear in 6 places: οἰκία in 1 Cor 11:22; 16:15; and οἶκος in 1 Cor 1:16; 11:34; 14:35; 16:19. Paul switches, e.g., from οἰκία in 1 Cor 11:22 to οἶκος in 11:34. In 1 Cor 16:15 he uses οἰκία, but οἶκος in 1:16 and 16:19. (Most exegetes see this as an indication that Paul uses the two terms synonymously. Cf. Theissen, *Social Setting,* 87.) (c) In Phil 4:22 οἰκίας appears rather than οἴκου (cf. also John 4:53).

[46] Cf., e.g., Michel, "οἶκος," *TDNT* 5:119–34; Bauer-Aland⁶, 1130–31, 1135–37 (BDAG 698–99).

[47] Elliott, *Home,* 188 nn. 110–12; 252 n. 112. Cf. also Crosby, *House,* 33, and the discussion between Jeremias and Aland regarding the so-called *Oikosformel*

result of this lack of clarity, White has suggested that "on the terminology of 'house' and 'household' new lexicographical work needs to be done."[48] An examination of these issues would lead beyond the parameters of our study. In light of the present state of scholarship, we need to leave the question open.[49] For our study we can abide by Klauck's results. We will determine the meaning of the word pair on the basis of the respective context of each.

In the second and longest chapter, Klauck discusses the significance of the house church in the NT. His methodological approach can essentially be characterized as descriptive sociohistorical. At the same time, he demonstrates a healthy reluctance to attempt sociological explanations (cf. below). Here again he shows his exegetical expertise as he tackles the decisive issues and offers cutting-edge solutions. Some of the most significant results are (a) proof that, in addition to the gathering of the whole church (Rom 16:23; 1 Cor 14:23), we find a plurality of smaller house churches in Corinth and (b) the demonstration of a probable plurality of house churches in Rome (Rom 16). Klauck, however, does not consider whether a plurality of house churches existed in the primitive church in Jerusalem, nor does he examine if and how Jesus and his disciples used houses in their pre-Easter ministry.

This is an important issue with far-reaching implications for our study. On the one hand, it appears as if a consensus might have been emerging among scholars concerning the plurality of house churches, particularly in a number of Pauline mission churches.[50] In recent years, however, a few scholars have contested this position.[51]

---

in the NT. In this discussion it becomes apparent that there is considerable disagreement on the precise understanding of the terms. Cf. Jeremias, *Kindertaufe,* and *Nochmals,* 9–27; Aland, *Säuglingstaufe,* 60–67.

[48] White, "Domus," 568 n. 195. The tentative result of his preliminary examination of the documentary evidence is that οἰκία means "domestic edifice" and οἶκος "may be used for almost any kind of building, including a domestic house." In a book review of Klauck, *Hausgemeinde,* commenting on Klauck's treatment of the semantic nuances of οἶκος/οἰκία, White points out, "The standard assumptions of Moulton-Milligan, which Klauck tends to follow, need to be reexamined" (White, book review, 288). Cf. Judge, "Social Identity," 216: "Hundreds of new inscriptions may be published in a year, while the volume of documentary papyri published has probably increased fivefold since the work of Deissmann and of Moulton and Milligan was done early this century, with the rate of new publications currently at a higher level than ever before."

[49] Cf. also the latest research results of Dassmann and Schöllgen, "Haus II," esp. 802–3, 806, and our discussion on p. 195.

[50] Cf. Käsemann, *Römer,* 395; Hainz, *Ekklesia,* 195 n. 4, 346; Schreiber, *Gemeinde,* 132 n. 55; Theissen, *Social Setting,* 89; Gnilka, *Philemonbrief,* 17–33; O'Brien, *Colossians, Philemon,* 257; Dunn, *Romans,* 2:910–11.; Stuhlmacher, *Römer,* 225; Meeks, *First Urban Christians,* 75–76; Branick, *House Church,* 22–27; Lampe, *Stadtrömischen Christen,* 161, 301–10; Weiser, "Evangelisierung im 'Haus,'" 74–75; Banks, *Paul's Idea,* 31–36.

[51] Cf. Gielen, "Zur Interpretation," 109–25, here 110–12. In agreement with Gielen are Schöllgen, "Hausgemeinden," 78; and Wagener, *Ordnung,* 36–38.

Klauck also demonstrates convincingly that the historical context of NT texts can be better understood once we have considered the house church setting of the early Christian community. For instance, he entertains the idea that a multiple number of house churches in any one location, together with the dominant personalities in each, could lead to competition between the different groups and that this would be a possible explanation for the formation of the different and conflicting parties observable in Corinth.[52]

The last two chapters, covering pre-Constantine Christianity and models from the environment for the house church, are more or less a survey. They offer a useful overview of the state of research at that time. The third chapter intends to show that the entire development in later centuries built upon the foundational elements of the house church in form and theology. The review of the possible models from the environment (ch. 4) supplies quite a number of archaeological and documentary examples and proposes, in conclusion, that the Jewish synagogue is the only analogy that comes into question as a direct model after which the house church could have been patterned.

L. M. White

L. M. White, "Domus Ecclesiae—Domus Dei: Adaptation and Development in the Setting for the Early Christian Assembly" (1982), continues the research by examining the environmental models in the ancient world for the house church.[53] In his dissertation White undertook the massive task of collecting and cataloging the entire archaeological, literary, and documentary data and sources for early Christian gathering places during the first three centuries. In his study he examines all of the data and sources.[54] His primary focus, however, is on the architectural development of general patterns for the construction of early Christian assembly places, paying particular attention to their religious and social setting (e.g., in the *oikos*) from the Pauline house churches up until the Constantinian basilica. The point of departure for White's study is the acknowledgment of two landmarks in the architectural development of the setting for early Christian meeting places: (a) by the middle of the first century, the first Pauline Christians began gathering in small groups in the private homes belonging to individual members of the congregation; (b) in contrast to this "primitive" period, 250 years later we

---

[52] Here and elsewhere we see the influence of Filson, which Klauck does not hesitate to acknowledge. Cf. Achelis also (above).

[53] This dissertation has been revised, expanded, and published as White, *The Social Origins of Christian Architecture,* composed of vol. 1, *Building God's House,* and vol. 2, *Texts.*

[54] D. Smith, book review, 255, comments on *Building God's House,* "When used with the collection of data in the companion volume *[Texts],* it should emerge as the most important analysis of the development of early Christian architecture since Krautheimer." White's dissertation is criticized by Finney, "Early Christian Architecture." White responded to this criticism in *The Social Origins of Christian Architecture.*

find that a basilical or monumental architecture had become normative (early fourth century in particular, after Constantine).[55]

His history of the scholarship shows first of all that the old assumption of a genetic evolution from Roman houses to Christian basilicas is no longer tenable.[56] Recent studies attempt to demonstrate that basilical architecture was supported and/or implemented by Constantine quite abruptly in the years directly after he introduced religious freedom with the Edict of Milan.[57] The key to the development of Christian architecture into the basilica is not some normative type of structure evolving from the pre-Constantinian house church but rather a process of architectural adaptation and accompanying social factors. In other words, it was not some abstract floor plan that served as a general guideline for the architectural development of Christian communal worship space during the first three centuries, but rather the social and religious needs of the particular group along with the local physical conditions relating to the type of ancient house in question.

White's thesis regarding the abrupt transition from house church to monumental basilical architecture at the time of Constantine is not new but rather originates from the research of Krautheimer and Ward-Perkins,[58] and it has, however, been disputed. Without referring directly to Krautheimer and Ward-Perkins, P. Maser has questioned the thesis of an abrupt transition.[59] According to Maser, Christian architecture could have originated from a basilical pattern similar to that which was used quite early (cf. Jas 2:2–3) in building the synagogue.[60] In addition, P. Richardson, apparently independent of Maser, is challenging the thesis as well. He believes "that there was a transitional period in the third century during which the example of Jewish synagogues was a critical factor."[61]

---

[55] Cf. White, *Texts*, 9–10; *Building God's House*, 3–5.

[56] White, "Domus," 11–25; *Building God's House*, 11–17. White ("Domus," 45–46; *Building God's House*, 141) clearly states that his work is best understood as an answer to Filson's challenge that scholarship would benefit by paying more attention to the "actual physical conditions under which the first Christians met and lived."

[57] White, "Domus," 18–25; *Building God's House*, 17–19. This architecture "was based on the standard forms of monumental public architecture at Rome. Derived from civil halls, imperial palaces, or classical hypostyle architecture, it was self-consciously adapted to the social position of the Christian Church under imperial patronage" (*Building God's House*, 18).

[58] Krautheimer, "Beginnings" and *Early Christian*; Ward-Perkins, "Constantine." It appears that most scholars take this view. Cf., e.g., Snyder, *Ante Pacem*, 67.

[59] Maser, "Synagoge."

[60] Apparently White is not aware of this article from Maser; at least he does not include it in the bibliography of *Texts*, nor, to my knowledge, does he discuss it anywhere else.

[61] Richardson, "Architectural Transitions." The discovery of a building in Aqaba (southern Jordan) that is possibly the oldest known Christian sacred structure (ca. 290–305 C.E.) could, as a "rectangular transitional basilical church," support the view taken by Maser and Richardson. Cf. Parker, "Brief Notice"; Keys, "Wunder"; Weintraub, "Unearthing"; "Oldest Church Found."

The first Christians were not the only religious community in the Greco-Roman world that adapted and renovated private domestic houses for the purpose of communal worship. White refers to the well-known example of Dura Europos, where not only the oldest house church but also a synagogue as well as a Mithraeum were found, all three of which were renovated private homes.[62] In the second part of his dissertation, White examines the Roman cult of Mithras and Diaspora Judaism.[63] At the conclusion of his study, he comments, "A common thread for the diffusion of Jewish groups in the Diaspora, as with other foreign religious associations, was to move into private quarters which over time were gradually adapted more to the peculiar needs of religious use in accordance with social circumstances of the community."[64] In this manner, White places the architectural history of the early church in its larger social context. In the first three centuries Christians adopted a pattern of architectural development found in other, similar religious groups of that period and at the same time responded to the social and liturgical needs unique to their own group by adapting or renovating private domestic structures to meet those needs.

As already mentioned, White builds his case upon the research results of Krautheimer. Krautheimer drew upon a hypothesis borrowed from Ward-Perkins, which his own research then confirmed: The first formal Christian architecture for early Christian assembly came into existence with Constantine.[65] It was implemented rather abruptly around 314 C.E. with the Lateran basilica.[66] On the basis of his research, Krautheimer suggests an approximate periodization of the architectural development of houses used for Christian assembly from the NT era up until the basilica at the beginning of the fourth century (50–314 C.E.) in four phases:[67]

---

[62] White, *Texts*, 10–22. Cf. floor plans and discussion of Dura, 123–34.

[63] The six most important synagogue excavations sites (Dura, Sardis, Priene, Delos, Stobi, Ostia) are discussed in White, "Domus," ch. 4, 248–326; ch. 5, 437–74 (White, *Building God's House*, 26–101; *Texts*, sec. 3, 272–397). Also there is a detailed description of floor plans, discussed in connection with the documentary, literary, archaeological, and social evidence and implications. Interestingly, White, after an extensive examination of these synagogues, comes to this conclusion: "It is significant, then, that all of the synagogues from the Diaspora were renovated from existing buildings, and five of the six were houses or private *insulae* of some sort" (*Texts*, 29).

[64] White, *Building God's House*, 101; cf. also "Domus," 469–74. Similar observations can be made regarding the cult of Mithras. Cf. *Building God's House*, 26–59.

[65] Ward-Perkins, "Constantine," 80.

[66] Krautheimer, *Early Christian*, 15–17; cf. also Krautheimer et al., *Corpus basilicarum*, for an impressive collection (five volumes) of archaeological evidence for Christian architecture. In this *opus magnum* Krautheimer does a thorough archaeological analysis of Roman church buildings with special focus on the findings that are considered to be from the pre-Constantinian substrata.

[67] Krautheimer, *Early Christian*, 1–15.

In the first phase (ca. 50–150 C.E.), Christians met for worship in private homes of wealthy members of the congregation—in other words, in "house churches" (cf. the Lukan example in Acts).[68] Such assemblies would have included a common meal and, for that reason, most likely took place in the living or dining rooms of these houses.

During the second phase (ca. 150–250), while some (poorer) congregations might have continued to meet in private homes, others structurally altered their homes and used them (primarily as property of the community) either in part or exclusively for their worship.[69] Because of the radical changes in social position and in the personal composition of the Christian movement, new, specialized structural needs arose regarding the place of assembly.[70] Such specific needs could no longer be accommodated by an unaltered private house or apartment. Krautheimer adopts the term *domus ecclesiae* ("house of the church") as a technical designation for this type of building (cf., e.g., Dura Europos, tituli Byzantis and Clementis).[71] The *domus ecclesiae* is not the only architectural form in use during this period, but it is the dominant form.

In the third phase (ca. 250–313), the *domus ecclesiae* pattern is continued, but a gradual transition toward ever larger buildings and halls becomes apparent.[72] The main example for this phase is the titulus S. Crisogono.[73]

The fourth phase (313 and beyond) begins with the Constantinian revolution and the introduction of the Lateran basilica.

White adopts Krautheimer's periodization of the development of the house church up until the basilica, however, merely as a *heuristic* model. In addition, White makes several revisions and focuses in particular on the transitional periods. In doing so, he makes significant progress in three ways:

---

[68] Ibid., 1–3.

[69] Ibid., 3–12.

[70] Krautheimer lists three general areas of alteration and expansion: (1) The development of a set liturgy: in particular, the separation of the actual meal, which was taken around a table in the dining room, from the celebration of the Eucharist, which more often took place in a hall, had an effect on the room size, design, and arrangement. (2) The development of the organization and administration of the liturgical gathering: a formalization of the seating order (separation of clergy from laity) and the introduction of certain pieces of furniture (pulpit, podium, etc.) necessitated the enlargement of the meeting room. (3) The remodeling and/or extension of certain areas in the building for other functions, e.g., for baptism or instruction (*Early Christian*, 6).

[71] This is the terminology used in the third century for this phenomenon. Krautheimer borrowed the term from Adolf von Harnack, *Mission*, 2:610–12. Floor plans and discussion of the tituli Byzantis and Clementis by White, *Texts*, 209–18, 219–28.

[72] Krautheimer, *Early Christian*, 12–15.

[73] Floor plans and discussion of the titulus S. Crisogono by White, *Texts*, 233–40. According to Krautheimer and White, however, such large buildings are to be distinguished from the architecture of the Constantinian basilica, as they were neither basilical in form nor monumental in size (cf. White, *Building God's House*, 20).

1. He differentiates the developmental phases more precisely and offers a more exact definition of the terminology. The *house church* from the first phase is defined as a private domestic house that remained unaltered architecturally and was used by a local Christian community for worship.[74] "By definition, these house churches would not have had any distinguishing features since there was no architectural adaptation. For the most part they were houses which remained in domestic use while also serving as the place of Christian assembly."[75] In contrast, the *domus ecclesiae* of the second phase is defined as any building (primarily as property of the community) specifically adapted or renovated by Christians partially or totally for social or religious use. White draws attention as well to additional transitional categories for all three phases: the partial adaptation or renovation of a home or building in successive stages. This is imaginable for the first phase, even though there is no concrete archaeological evidence. In the second phase Lullingstone and the tituli Clementis and Byzantis provide evidence for structures that were partially adapted or renovated for Christian use while the unaltered part of the house continued to be used for private domestic purposes.[76] For the third phase White suggests the term *aula ecclesiae* as the technical designation for the larger, more formal hall, which is seen as the transitional form between the *domus ecclesiae* and the basilica.[77] "Though probably nothing like the scale of monumental basilicas, it [the *aula ecclesiae*] had progressed quite beyond the domestic triclinium as a setting for assembly."[78] Architecturally characteristic for the *aula ecclesiae* is the tendency toward standardization of the rectangular form of a hall.[79]

2. White underscores as well that the development was not consistent in all areas at all times,[80] and consequently argues for the necessity of an approach regarding this issue in terms of the local history. Overall, his examination of the archaeological, literary, and documentary evidence yielded a complex and diverse set of results.[81] For instance, even though certain groups met in public halls during the later phases, Christians elsewhere continued to gather in the private home or *domus ecclesiae*. This coexistence of architectural types can be observed for the period

---

[74] White, "Domus," 27, 479–86; *Building God's House*, 21.

[75] White, "Domus," 483; cf. also *Building God's House*, 21; *Texts*, 25.

[76] White, "Domus," 35–36, 486–88; cf. *Building God's House*, 20–25. White, however, does not suggest any technical designation for this type of house church.

[77] White, "Domus," 29–30 n. 53, 510; cf. *Building God's House*, 22 n. 49. This technical term is adopted by White following the suggestion *Saalkirche* from Harnack, *Mission*, 2:615.

[78] White, "Domus," 507; cf. also *Building God's House*, 22–23.

[79] White, "Domus," 518; cf. *Building God's House*, 22.

[80] Krautheimer saw this in essence (*Early Christian*, 15). White simply emphasizes it more and offers an additional number of convincing examples as proof ("Domus," 32; *Building God's House*, 24–25).

[81] "The body of data is annoyingly diverse and does not readily admit architectural systematization" (White, "Domus," 36; cf. *Building God's House*, 24).

characterized by monumental basilicas after the Constantinian revolution.[82] White therefore revises Krautheimer's periodization on the basis of the insights mentioned above and advocates that the chronological outline not be taken too rigidly. He underscores or relativizes the outline with additional archaeological examples and with literary and documentary evidence.[83]

3. As White illumines the social history surrounding the development of religious architecture, he focuses in particular on the phenomenon of patronage, and in doing so confirms the earlier insight of Judge (see above). White emphasizes, "Access to property through patronage and donation was perhaps the sine qua non for the architectural development from house church to domus ecclesiae."[84] "The ability to attract such individuals [patrons] in greater numbers was probably a significant factor in the social 'triumph' of Christianity. These individuals provided the network of social relationships and economic capabilities that made possible growth, expansion, acquisition, and adaptation."[85]

B. B. Blue

B. B. Blue, "In Public and Private: The Role of the House Church in Early Christianity" (1989), is the next extensive work on the house church. Along with White, Blue wants to take up Filson's challenge to examine more closely the "physical conditions under which the early believers gathered" as well as the social factors and the theological implications connected with them. On the basis of Acts, he attempts (ch. 3, pp. 72–93) to prove his most important thesis, that Luke distinguishes between *public* and *private* in the following manner: In Acts 5:42 (cf. 3:11–12, 48; 17:17, 22; 19:9) Luke differentiates between public evangelistic proclamation and the domestic church life.[86] Missional proclamation takes place in the public arena of the temple, the hall of Solomon, the marketplace (agora), and Mars Hill (the Areopagus) or the hall of Tyrannus. In contrast, the life of the church (the Lord's Supper, instruction, prayer) takes place in the private sphere of individual houses. Blue summarizes, "If we have rightly understood the Lukan presentation of early Christianity, both in Palestine and the Greco-Roman world on the whole, the Gospel was first proclaimed in the publicly acceptable places. Subsequently, those who had responded were drawn into house gatherings. Luke *never even suggests that during these private meetings of believers the Gospel message was preached for the purpose of converting the hearers.* On the contrary, for Luke, these private house meetings were for the benefit of

---

[82] White, "Domus," 28, 31–32; *Building God's House*, 23–24.
[83] White, "Domus," 479–86; *Building God's House*, 20–25.
[84] White, *Building God's House*, 146.
[85] White, "Domus," 615; *Building God's House*, 57, 101, 144–47.
[86] Cf. Klauck, *Hausgemeinde*, 47–48, and, earlier, Rordorf, "Was wissen wir?" 111–12. Neither Klauck nor Rordorf, however, elevates it into a schematic program for the entire book of Acts.

the Christian community alone."[87] According to Blue, there are only two exceptions to this programmatic pattern in Luke: Acts 10:1–3 and 28:16–18. He attempts to give an explanation for each, but neither attempt is convincing.[88] The question must also be asked whether Blue has convincingly made a case for his overall thesis.

Nevertheless, an article of Blue's published later on the house church in Acts is of great importance for our study, particularly regarding his discussion of the most important passages in Acts referring to house churches and his useful description of ancient houses.[89] Unfortunately, Blue neglects to examine the historical reliability of each of these texts.

Since the appearance of Klauck's book and these two studies by White and Blue, there has been a whole series of contributions that concentrate either directly or indirectly on the topic of the house church. We will refer to these monographs,[90] articles,[91] and commentaries[92] at the appropriate time in our discussions.

---

[87] Blue, "In Public," 84. Contra Blue, Stowers, "Social Status," 59–82; and Hock, "Paul's Tentmaking."

[88] Cf. Blue, "In Public," 87. In reference to Acts 28:16–18, Blue emphasizes "the public character of Paul's open door policy." Nevertheless, Paul evangelizes in the context of his private apartment (cf. also 1 Cor 14:23–25). In reference to Acts 10:1–3: "Despite the house setting for the forum, the meeting is public." Here also, however, the same is true: a private home is used evangelistically. There is no indication in the story that only the public part of the house is used for the meeting (that a part of a house could, in fact, be used for public purposes is seen on pp. 37–42, 79–86, and 137–55).

[89] Blue, "Acts." Blue no longer argues for the distinction between public and private in this article.

[90] Meeks, *First Urban Christians;* for a critique of Meeks, cf. Schöllgen, "Was wissen wir?"; Lampe, *Stadtrömischen Christen,* esp. 124–53, 156–64, 301–45; for a critique of Lampe, cf. Schöllgen, "Probleme"; Crosby, *House,* esp. 21–36; Branick, *House Church,* a synthesis of Banks and Klauck; Murphy-O'Connor, *St. Paul's Corinth;* Gielen, *Tradition;* Kidd, *Wealth;* H. Maier, *Social Setting;* Reck, *Kommunikation,* esp. 235–37; Klauck, *Gemeinde,* 11–36, 95–113; Pöhlmann, *Der Verlorene Sohn;* Campbell, *Elders;* Sandnes, *New Family;* Wagener, *Ordnung;* Hirschfeld, *Palestinian Dwelling;* Schmeller, *Hierarchie;* Matson, *Household Conversion;* Osiek and Balch, *Families;* Perdue, Blenkinsopp, Collins, and Meyers, *Families.*

[91] Lührmann, "Wo man nicht mehr"; Lampe, "Zur gesellschaftlichen und kirchlichen Funktion," 533–42; Gnilka, "Neutestamentliche Hausgemeinde"; Lohfink, "Christliche Familie"; Elliott, "Philemon"; Gielen, "Zur Interpretation"; Lorenzen, "Christliche Hauskirche"; White, "Social Authority"; Schöllgen, "Hausgemeinde"; Klauck, "Urchristliche Hausgemeinde" and "Hausgemeinde als Lebensform"; Covolo, "'Domus Ecclesiae'"; Weiser, "Evangelisierung im antiken 'Haus'" and "Evangelisierung im 'Haus'"; Noordegraaf, "Familia Dei"; Jewett, "Tenement Churches and Communal Meals" and "Tenement Churches and Pauline Love Feasts"; Osiek, "Family"; Reumann, "One Lord"; Krentz, "Order"; Osiek, "Women"; and Richardson, "Architectural Transitions."

[92] The house church has become a topic for an increasing number of commentators. E.g., cf. R. Brown, *Epistles of John,* 676, 728–39, 743–48; Gnilka, *Philemonbrief,* 17–33; O'Brien, *Colossians, Philemon,* 257; Roloff, *Der erste Brief,* 169–78;

Consensus, Dissonance, and Further Research

Consensus

The insight that the *oikos* was of fundamental importance for society and economy in the ancient world is gaining ever more acceptance among scholars.[93] D. Lührmann summarizes that the ancient *oikos* "is not just one social and economic form among others but rather *the* basic social and economic form not only for the ancient world and the New Testament but presumably for every pre-industrial sedentary culture as well."[94] Scarcely anything determined daily life more than the *oikos* with its network of relationships. It was an all-encompassing social structure with legal, economic, and biological implications.[95] By belonging to an *oikos*, each individual gained a sense of identity within society as a whole; it provided them an "inside" and an "outside," not only a dwelling place but also a home.[96] This small "*oikos* fellowship" provided a basic building block for the entire society as well. It was from this point outward that individuals entered into relationships with one another, building the πόλις and, with that, the entire political system (see Judge below). With this in mind, the significance of the *oikos* for the establishment and organization of early Christian church life can hardly be overemphasized. Even though there appears to be a consensus in this regard among scholars, opinions tend to differ when it comes to more clearly determining the importance of the house church. Moreover, an extensive scholarly examination of the significance of the *oikos* for the formation and organization of the house church has yet to be done.

An insight from White also deserves our attention at this point: "Housing patterns, of course, varied considerably across the Empire. The Italian villa, the Greek peristyle, the Hellenistic-oriental multistoried *insula*, apartments, and others had their own local stylistic traditions. We must expect . . . considerable diversity from place to place depending on the local circumstances."[97] For many years much of scholarship has assumed that the physical dimensions of a house in Pompeii, Herculaneum, Ostia, or Corinth

---

Stuhlmacher, "Exkurs: Urchristliche Hausgemeinden," in *Philemon*, 70–75 (see Stuhlmacher's extended list of literature); Klauck, *Zweite und dritte Johannesbrief*, 65–67.

[93] Cf. Filson, "Significance," 109–11; Judge, *Social Pattern*, 49–61; Finley, *Antike Wirtschaft*, 8–10; Stuhlmacher, *Philemon*, 74; Laub, *Begegnung*, 19–31, esp. 20, and "Sozialgeschichtlicher Hintergrund," 253–58; Lührmann, "Neutestamentliche Haustafeln," 84–90; Verner, *Household*, 27–81; Elliott, *Home*, esp. ch. 4; Bieritz and Kähler, "Haus III," 14:478–92; Dassmann and Schöllgen, "Haus II"; Meeks, *First Urban Christians*, 75–78; Gielen, *Tradition*, 68–103, esp. 84–99; White, *Building God's House* and *Texts*.

[94] Lührmann, "Neutestamentliche Haustafeln," 87. Cf. also Rostovtzeff, *Hellenistische Welt;* O. Brunner, "Das 'ganze Haus'" (1956), 33–61.

[95] Cf. Bieritz, "Rückkehr?" 115.

[96] Cf. Bieritz and Kähler, "Haus III," 14:478.

[97] White, *Building God's House*, 107.

would supply data that could be generally applied to the houses of all Pauline house churches, with the argument that they, too, were located in Greco-Roman cities.[98] This conclusion was based on the assumption that a general blueprint existed that was typical for Roman houses throughout the entire Roman Empire. Archaeological discoveries since the late nineteenth century have proven this assumption false.[99]

The methodological consequence of this for our study is that in order to approximate the architectural dimensions of houses used as meeting places on the Pauline mission, we need to take an approach in terms of local history.[100] This entails gathering the archaeological and sociohistorical data from each individual city or area in which the specific church that interests us was located, in order to give the most accurate possible description of that church. It means that Palestinian, Greek, and Roman types of private houses come into question for the period of early Christian missions. We need to be aware, however, that wherever most or all of the members of a synagogue joined the new messianic faith, a public building, for example, the synagogue, might have been available as an assembly place for worship (Maser). On the other hand, if this synagogue met in a private home, we are dealing again with the above-mentioned types of houses.[101] During our examination, rather than simply assuming the reader's knowledge of the architectural dimensions of such ancient homes, we will attempt to interject it at the appropriate times.

In addition, we consider it prudent to adopt the *architectural* technical terminology with definitions suggested by Krautheimer and White. As mentioned, White distinguished three basic possibilities: (a) The *house church* was defined as a private domestic house that remained architecturally unaltered. This house was used by a local Christian group for public worship and by the owner (and his/her family) for private domestic purposes. (b) A *church house* (Krautheimer and White's *domus ecclesiae*) is a private domestic house that was physically altered and adapted in order to meet the social and/or religious needs of the group. It was used by Christians—in some cases as property of the congregation, in other cases as private property—exclusively for social and religious purposes.[102] (c) A *hall church* (their *aula ecclesia*) refers to a larger, more formal, rectangular (private or public) hall that

---

[98] Cf., e.g., Murphy-O'Connor, *St. Paul's Corinth*, 161–75.

[99] Cf. White, "Domus," 18–19; Krautheimer, "Beginnings," 144–45; McKay, *Römische Häuser*.

[100] This term is adopted from the German *lokalgeschichtlich*. This applies not only for architectural but for sociohistorical research as well. This methodological insight seems to be gaining more and more acceptance among scholars. Cf. Schöllgen, "Probleme," 23; and Lampe, *Stadtrömischen Christen*, xi; Judge, "Social Identity," 216.

[101] The possibility that synagogue communities met in homes is a phenomenon discussed below (see p. 30, n. 106).

[102] White draws attention to the partial adaptation of a private home that was used only in part for Christian purposes and belonged in most cases to a private individual. As he did not suggest a technical term for such a case, it will be called a church house as well.

was used by Christians exclusively for social and religious purposes. It denotes the transition from church house to basilica. The two forms b and c were, for the most part, considered church buildings.

I have also decided to adopt the periodization suggested by Krautheimer and White as a heuristic model for our study; we will remain primarily within the parameters of the first phase (50–150) and within the context of the NT. Our exegetical examination will not begin, however, with the year 50; instead our point of departure will be prior to Easter, with the ministry of Jesus and his disciples. By so doing, I hope to gain a broader geographical and historical perspective. It was precisely at this point that my research uncovered a deficit in scholarly research on our topic. Up until now, most studies of early Christian house churches have begun with the Pauline missions. This is most likely due to the assumption of many scholars that we do not find ourselves on solid historical footing in the NT until we examine the undisputed Pauline Epistles.[103]

Dissonance

Models from the Religious, Intellectual, and Social Environments

In his summary of the state of research up until that point on the potential models for the house church, Klauck lists house and private cults, voluntary associations, the Sarapis cult and mystery religions, Orphism, and the synagogue.[104] For Klauck only the synagogue comes into question as a direct model.[105] This position appears even more plausible if we consider that a large portion of the Christians up until the year 100 came from Judaism and the setting surrounding the synagogue and if we can be sure that house synagogues were already fairly widespread during the NT period.[106] As early as

---

[103] Cf. White, *Building God's House,* 103, as an example of this approach: "Like the early Pharisees, we may imagine the followers of Jesus and other teachers of the time gathering occasionally for fellowship, prayer, and study. This practice is depicted both in the gospel narratives regarding Jesus and in the traditional picture of Acts. In Acts 2–5 the earliest disciples at Jerusalem reportedly met 'from house to house' or just 'at home,' while also attending to traditional Jewish observance at the Temple. *Beyond this little more can be said*" (italics added). Cf. also Klauck, *Hausgemeinde,* 49; Gnilka, "Neutestamentliche Hausgemeinde," 231–32; Schöllgen, "Hausgemeinde," 79; Vogler, "Bedeutung"; Meeks, *First Urban Christians,* 26–27.

[104] Klauck, *Hausgemeinde,* 83–99. Cf. also Klauck, *Stadt- und Hausreligion,* 1–128; for a discussion of the different models, Meeks, *First Urban Christians,* 75–84; Verner, *Household,* 6–9.

[105] So also Stuhlmacher, *Philemon,* 72–73; Blue, "In Public," 127, 144–46; Laub, "Sozialgeschichtlicher Hintergrund," 270; Vogler, "Bedeutung," 787. This assumption is confirmed by reports in Acts. Cf. Acts 2:46; 5:42; 12:12; 16:13–15, 30–34; 18:1–8. For the position that the early Christian worship service was patterned after that of the synagogue, cf. Wiefel, "Synagogengottesdienst"; Salzmann, *Lehren,* 450–79.

[106] This is, however, disputed. See our discussion on p. 30.

the nineteenth century, however, scholars pointed out that the first Christians imitated associations or *collegia*.[107] Although this thesis found only limited support at the time, a number of scholars in the second half of the twentieth century advocated that the association be reconsidered as a model for the house church.[108] The possibility that Pauline house churches were patterned after schools of philosophy or a combination of a *collegium* and a philosophical school have also been considered.[109]

Scholars have also attempted to apply our relatively new knowledge of the Qumran community to the early church in Jerusalem, in particular, suggesting that the primitive church was patterned at least to some degree after the Essene model, which may have included two different community forms: the first, a more rigorous one, of those who led a celibate lifestyle in a strict community of goods without private ownership of property; the second, of those who were scattered throughout the countryside and did not practice celibacy or a community of goods in the strict sense.[110] This form was organized with families' private homes, usually focused on one specific house.[111]

Filson and others have emphasized the importance of the household for the social structure of the house church.[112] "The community life of early Christians was patterned in many ways after the *oikos* model.... In terms of the *oikos* structure, these gatherings were neither the club meeting of a *collegium* nor the assembly of a philosophical Thiasos but instead merely the private invitation of a host to fellow Christians in his area of the city: the private hospitality of the head of the household."[113] Malherbe raises the question whether more light would be shed on the social structure of the early church if we were to examine more closely the relationship between house-

---

[107] G. Heinrici, "Christengemeinde," 465; building upon Heinrici is Hatch, *Organization*, 26–55.

[108] Judge, *Social Pattern*, 40–48; Malherbe, *Social Aspects*, 87–91; not to be overlooked is the thorough research done by Schmeller, *Hierarchie*, a sociohistorical comparison of Pauline congregations and Greco-Roman associations.

[109] Judge, "Early Christians." Wilken, "Collegia," combines elements from Judge and Hatch.

[110] Capper, "PANTA KOINA." Cf. also the summary of his dissertation, "Community of Goods of the Jerusalem Church," and "Palestinian Cultural Context." Cf. also Schwartz, "Non-joining Sympathizers," who independently confirms some of Capper's findings. This fairly widely accepted view has been contested. For a discussion, cf. Klauck, "Gütergemeinschaft," 57–68; Mealand, "Community of Goods at Qumran."

[111] Klauck, *Hausgemeinde*, 94. Josephus reports that they gathered in a special building, a house, for consultation and worship (*J.W.* 2.129, 132). For further discussion of the findings of Capper and Klauck, cf. Gehring, *Hausgemeinde*, 150–55.

[112] Filson, "Significance," 109–12; cf. also Michel, "οἶκος," *TDNT* 5:119–34; Judge also points to the significance of the household, in particular the patronage, for the social structure of Pauline house churches, *Social Pattern*, 75.

[113] Lampe, *Stadtrömischen Christen*, 314–16. So also Lührmann, "Neutestamentliche Haustafeln," 93.

hold communities and associations.[114] The two models do not necessarily exclude one another. We know of examples in which an association was formed in close connection with a specific household (cf. the Dionysus association in Pompeia Agrippinilla or the Agdistis cult in Philadelphia).[115] W. A. Meeks points out that the Pauline congregations resemble the philosophical schools only "to the extent that they take the form of a modified household or voluntary association."[116] Still, the philosophical schools offer ideas, language patterns, and a social model that can be meaningfully compared with those of early Christians.

It is also possible that Hellenistic associations had an indirect influence on the early Christian house churches by way of the Jewish synagogue.[117] If the Diaspora synagogue was organized like an association, this would provide an explanation for the fact that elements of the association can be seen in the organization of a house church.[118] One must distinguish between the theological self-understanding of the early Christian house churches, on the one hand, and the sociological and legal form of organization or outward appearance, on the other. It could be that the house churches were organized like a house synagogue (that is, like an association or household) and yet understood themselves theologically not as an association but as an *ecclesia* or the family/house of God, which in turn would suggest a theological connection between the house church and the house synagogue.

One therefore could ask whether all of the above-mentioned scholars are at least partially right. White observed that each of the four models (philosphical school, association, synagogue, household) demonstrates a similarity to one aspect or another of early Christianity and continues, "In one sense, however, each of these 'models' is a variation on a larger process of expansion; each 'group' is one configuration of social networks. The historical evidence shows that all of them have overlapping organizational schemes ... especially at two key points of social structure: (a) they use and adapt private, often domestic, settings; and (b) they depend on patronage for

---

[114] Malherbe, *Social Aspects*, 90–91.

[115] Meeks, *First Urban Christians*, 31 n. 143; 77 n. 17; White, *Building God's House*, 45 n. 70.

[116] Meeks, *First Urban Christians*, 84–85.

[117] I thank R. Hermann for pointing this out to me (cf. "Das antike Vereinswesen"; see n. 120). Hengel, in particular, has drawn attention to the concrete influence of Hellenistic associations on their Jewish counterparts (*Judentum und Hellenismus*, 1:243–45). It can be asked whether the synthesis between Judaism and Hellenism can be demonstrated in concentrated form here in the synagogue—in other words, patterned after the organization of a voluntary association yet Jewish in self-understanding.

[118] Cf. also Stuhlmacher, "Evangelium-Apostolat-Gemeinde," esp. 37, where he makes the point that anyone who wanted to establish a mission church anywhere in the Mediterranean had to do it in the context of Roman law. This meant that early Christians had to organize themselves either as a voluntary association or as a corporation of foreigners.

ongoing expansion.... If the house church is related to these models it is because it, too, was operating within similar social networks."[119]

In summary, scholarly research still has not reached a consensus concerning possible models for the early Christian house church in its environment. One problem is that we simply do not know enough about the house synagogues and house churches in relation to the organization of associations in order to determine satisfactorily any direct or indirect dependence. The present state of research appears to indicate that none of the models surveyed above is identical with the house church although all offer useful analogies. All are examples of contemporary groups that tackled similar problems that Christians also encountered and attempted to solve. It is not the objective of this study to do an extensive examination of the religious, social, and intellectual background of the early Christian house churches. Others have already undertaken this task.[120] Nevertheless, I would like to follow up on suggestions made by Lampe and White in that this study intends to examine to what degree the social life, the organizational and leadership structures, and the ecclesiological self-understanding of early Christians were patterned after the household model (Lampe). White's insight applies here as well: all analogies to the house church are characterized by two overlapping structures of social organization, both of which are dimensions of the ancient *oikos*—the private domestic house and patronage. Accordingly, this study will focus more on both of these sociohistorical phenomena in the hope that this will contribute to a better understanding of early Christian house churches.

Judge has drawn the attention of NT sociohistorical research to the importance of patronage for the entire Greco-Roman world. He considers it misleading to picture ancient society, in which Christianity originated, as one united entity and yet divided into horizontal social-class lines. This is not to say that there were no social strata but rather that the dimensions and the dynamics of these strata can only be fully comprehended if and when specific "institutions" are brought into the picture. Judge suggests that the world of the Hellenistic republics be understood as a series of overlapping and yet not systematically related circles: "the small republican *state* . . . secondly the far-reaching *household* organization of life on a household basis . . . and thirdly the unofficial *associations*."[121]

The key to understanding the structure of Roman society is patronage:

> The republic recognized not only the sweeping powers the Roman *pater familias* enjoyed over his personal family, bond and free alike, but also the rights and duties imposed by the relationship of *clientela*. Freedmen, who had formerly been members of a household through slavery, retained their link

---

[119] White, "Adolf Harnack," 120.
[120] Cf. Schmeller, *Hierarchie*, and the studies from Claussen, *Versammlung, Gemeinde, Synagoge*, and Hermann, "Das antike Vereinswesen."
[121] Judge, "Social Identity," 202 (italics added).

with it, and in some respects their obligations, as its clients. Others also freely associated themselves with it for their mutual benefit. Loyalty to the household interest was expected, though the authority of the patron was grounded in his trustworthiness, which guaranteed that the material and social needs of the client's family were met.[122]

Judge's views, of course, have not remained undisputed. Nevertheless, a growing number of scholars are beginning to recognize the profound importance of patronage for the early Christian community.[123] The significance of patronage for early Christian missions has as yet not been sufficiently researched.[124] One question in particular is of central importance for our study: how is the ancient *oikos,* a hierarchically composed social phenomenon centered around the head of the household, related to the social organization of the early church as it came into existence?

It thus becomes clear that our study will need to take not only an exegetical-theological but also a sociohistorical approach. A few clarifying words regarding the definition of methodology will have to suffice. In the Anglo-Saxon world, scholarship has distinguished between "social" and "sociological." By this it means—somewhat simplified—that "social" research focuses on a mere description of the social facts whereas "sociological" research attempts to explain the facts it describes, generally with sociological models (often originating with Durkheim or Weber).[125] Some scholars maintain that the two are not mutually exclusive—sociological explanation builds upon the social description of facts. It has also been suggested that, particularly in the case of the NT, the social data are so sparse that one is compelled to make use of hypotheses or heuristic models in order to fill in the gaps. Others caution against taking preconceived models developed in the nineteenth or twentieth century in the context of modern society and arbitrarily applying them to an ancient setting. In doing so, we are in danger of obscuring the actual conditions of the ancient world and merely securing results

---

[122] Judge, *Social Pattern,* 31.

[123] Cf. Meeks, *First Urban Christians,* 74–84; Schmeller, *Hierarchie,* 33–53, 56–75; Winter, *Seek the Welfare,* 11–78; for my discussion, see pp. 193–96.

[124] Kidd, *Wealth,* 74: "The texture of relationships as conditioned by cultural notions of obligation, reciprocity, and the like, appears to be a field of study as yet relatively unexcavated." Some work has been done in recent years; cf. Sampley, *Pauline Partnership;* Danker, *Benefactor;* Chow, *Patronage;* P. Marshall, *Enmity;* A. Clarke, *Secular and Christian.* Cf. the criticism of the studies of Chow and Clark by Schmeller, *Hierarchie,* 9–10, 94–96. From secular research, the book by Saller, *Personal Patronage,* also should be mentioned.

[125] Cf. J. Smith, "Social Description"; Scroggs, "Sociological Interpretation"; Judge, "Social Identity"; Malina, "Social Sciences"; Malherbe, *Social Aspects,* 113–22; Meeks, *First Urban Christians,* 1–8; White, "Adolf Harnack," for an Anglo-Saxon discussion of types, problems, limitations, and opportunities of the sociohistorical approach to early Christianity; for the German-speaking world, cf. Schöllgen, "Probleme"; Theissen, *Social Setting,* 175–200; *Social Reality,* 1–29, 231–56.

predetermined in advance by our model. Our study therefore intends to take primarily a sociodescriptive approach but will work with the *oikos* model, which is developed directly from the ancient world rather than from modern society. At the same time, we will need to be content with building our case on the unambiguous examples found in the social data, and we will resist the temptation to fill in the gaps.

One caution regarding the ancient *oikos* as it is described in the household literature: the sociological approach is an important supplement to social- and literary-historical methodology, but it dare not be given absolute status.[126] It has been pointed out that some scholars are guilty of the questionable tendency to reduce literary texts to mere reflection of a social reality understood as being free from contradiction.[127] In contrast, sociohistorical exegesis has shown that social reality tends to be more contradictory, complex, and open-ended than the "ideological" description of that reality known to us in literary form (e.g., the *oikos* society of the ancient world in contrast to the household literature written by Aristotle et al.).[128] Voluntary associations, for instance, that were not simply organized according to patriarchal *oikos* structures did exist in the ancient world. Most associations, however, attempted to find a wealthy patron who provided the group with finances, rooms for assembly, and so forth. In that we again see the hierarchical *oikos* structures. No one disputes the central economic and social significance of the *oikos* for the ancient world.[129] Therefore, it is legitimate to speak of an "*oikos* society" in this differentiated sense.[130]

A Plurality of House Churches within the Whole Church at Any One Location

One further question that our study will need to address is the possible plurality of house churches alongside the whole church at any one location in early Christian missions. My history of scholarship indicated that a majority of NT scholars tend to agree regarding this issue. Yet several scholars have contested this relative consensus. The discussion has focused on the following key issues.

Within the *corpus paulinum* the stock phrase ἡ κατ' οἶκον ἐκκλησία appears four times.[131] Some exegetes prefer translating the Pauline expres-

---

[126] Cf. Wagener, *Ordnung*, 35–37, 64. She follows Thraede, "Ärger"; "Frau"; and "Zum historischen Hintergrund."

[127] Wagener, *Ordnung*, 35; Wagener criticizes esp. Laub, "Sozialgeshichtlicher Hintergrund."

[128] Wagener, *Ordnung*, 36.

[129] One needs to consider, however, that there is a difference between a pure *oikos* society and one in combination with a temple state (e.g., Palestine with its temple in Jerusalem).

[130] Cf. Lührmann, "Neutestamentliche Haustafeln," 84, 88–90; Laub, "Sozialgeschichtlicher Hintergrund," 261, who both speak of the ancient *Oikosgesellschaft* (see also Judge).

[131] Rom 16:5; 1 Cor 16:19; Phlm 1–2; Col 4:15.

sion with "the church that establishes itself in a houselike manner."[132] Many NT scholars believe that both forms—small house churches and the whole church as a unit at that location—existed side by side in early Christianity.[133] M. Gielen and G. Schöllgen, however, have contested this position.[134] Gielen is of the opinion that for Paul ἡ κατ' οἶκον ἐκκλησία and ἡ ἐκκλησία ὅλη do not stand in opposition to one another; instead, he uses ὅλη in both cases (Rom 16:23; 1 Cor 14:23) for text-pragmatic reasons only.[135] Gielen is convinced that the expression ἡ κατ' οἶκον ἐκκλησία refers to local churches, that is, to the whole church at that location or in that town and so all passages that are held by other scholars to refer to so-called house churches refer in reality only to houses.[136] They would thus not be house churches in the full sense but merely household fellowship groups. The findings of her exegetical examination do not indicate in any way that house churches existed separate or along side the local church in any given city.[137]

One important task for our study will be to address this issue regarding the possible plurality of house churches alongside the whole church at any one location in early Christian missions. This issue has far-reaching implications concerning the social relationships of believers one to another, for the leadership structures and for the ecclesiology of the early Christian church. The smaller the churches, the less they would have distanced themselves from the household unit, the more closely they would have been intertwined with *oikos* structures, and the greater the potential would have been for the ancient *oikos* to influence the social reality of the community. The ability of the early Christian house churches to integrate outsiders would thus be directly related to the dynamic *oikos* model. If it is true that the social reality of the community was closely patterned after the *oikos* model, then it would also be possible to explain the development of church leadership structures and offices within that context. According to household literature, the οἰκοδεσπότης provided leadership to the ancient household. If the first house churches understood themselves essentially as the "house of God," it appears consistent to assume that they were led by the head of the household, that is, by *one* overseer. From there it is one small step to suggest that the early Christian understanding of leadership was predisposed to develop into the office of the monarchical bishop. In the same context, a convincing demonstration of the plurality of house churches would provide a plausible explanation for a plurality of bishops at one location (cf. Phil 1:1).

---

[132] Klauck, *Hausgemeinde,* 21.

[133] For my discussion, see pp. 155–62.

[134] Gielen, "Zur Interpretation," 109–25, here 110–12; Schöllgen, "Hausgemeinden," 78; and also Wagener, *Ordnung,* 36–37.

[135] Gielen, "Zur Interpretation," 110–18.

[136] E.g., Acts 2:46; 12:12–14; 16:15; 18:2–4; 20:8–10, 20; 21:8; 1 Cor 11:17–19.

[137] Gielen, "Zur Interpretation," 118. In agreement with her on all points is Schöllgen, "Hausgemeinde," 74–90, here 78–79, 89.

In addition, the proof of a plurality of house churches alongside the whole church at one location would shed light on the controversial issue regarding the clarification of the relationship between the individual churches and the whole local church, and between the local church and the universal church.[138]

One problem connected with this issue is that as yet no clear *ecclesiological* definition has been formulated on what the term "house church" means.[139] Only after we agree on a precise definition of the house church in its full sense can we determine if one really exists. Klauck differentiates between house churches and the assembly of the whole church. He then points out that the same content regarding the worship service can be assumed for the house church as for the assembly of the whole church.[140] Lampe also offers a definition: a house church consists of the assembly for worship in a house.[141] As already noted, Gielen distinguishes between house churches and household groups without clearly defining the difference between the two.[142] Schöllgen suggests at least a partial definition: a plurality of house churches alongside the whole church in a given location can be assumed if the existence of house churches with regular gatherings and their own clearly developed religious life as a substructure to the whole church can be convincingly demonstrated.[143] But the question remains: what exactly did "their own religious life" encompass?

Moving Forward

In order to promote further progress on this issue, I would like to suggest a working definition of the house church in the full sense. Our objective is to formulate a description that is neither exhaustive nor too rigid or static. It seems fitting, though, that we at least list the essential elements of the house church so that during our study we have the criteria for distinguishing

---

[138] See pp. 160–62 for an extensive discussion of Paul's theological definition of these terms.

[139] See White's architectural definition of "house church," etc., above.

[140] Klauck, *Hausgemeinde,* 36–39. There he refers to the contents of the worship service: evangelistic sermon, catechetical instruction for baptism, teaching, the meal, celebration of the Lord's Supper, and celebration of baptism. He emphasizes, however, that our understanding of the transition from house church to whole church needs to be kept as open as possible.

[141] Cf. Lampe, *Stadtrömischen Christen,* 319–20. In addition, he points out that we do not have to wait until positions of office are clearly recognizable to consider a group of Christians in assembly a house church.

[142] Gielen, "Zur Interpretation," 118, 121, 125. By "household group" Gielen most likely means the ancient *oikos* with its social dimensions and not a Christian "home Bible group." The difference between the two, however, remains unclear. Cf. 118 n. 37 also, where she gives a list of the elements of a so-called house church, which she found in Gnilka, "Neutestamentliche Hausgemeinde," 234.

[143] Schöllgen, "Hausgemeinden," 77, 79.

a house church from what is not a house church. Most scholars would agree that the following elements constitute a house church. (a) A group exists that has developed its own religious life, including regular gatherings for worship. (b) The content of these regular gatherings for worship includes evangelistic and instructional proclamation, the celebration of baptism and communion, prayer, and fellowship. (c) Elements such as (unclearly defined) organizational structures can be considered further indications of a house church in the full sense. The more these elements are evident in the gatherings of a certain group, the more certain we can be that we are dealing with a house church.

It would also be advisable to briefly clarify the general ecclesiological terminology to be used in our study. It will suffice to define the terms in the following manner: A *house church* is a group of Christians that meets in a private home. A *local church* consists of all the Christians that gather at a geographically definable location (e.g., town or city). The terms "local church" and "house church" refer to the same group only if there is just one single house church gathering at that specific location. We will use the term "whole local church" or "whole church at one location" to refer to the whole church in one locality. This term already implies a plurality of individual house churches for that location. The term "universal church" will, as usual, be reserved for the worldwide body of Christians.[144]

---

[144] For possible meanings of the terms "missional" and "mission" respectively, cf. Bosch, *Transforming Mission*, 1–3.

CHAPTER TWO

The Use of Houses before Easter

JESUS' USE OF HOUSES

It has often been suggested that a certain connection exists between multiple references to houses in the Gospel of Mark and house churches in early Christianity.[1] In general, scholarship assumes that the references to houses in Mark are actually in connection with the post-Easter situation of the Markan congregation in Galilee (or Rome).[2] Most of the geographical references in the Gospels are to locations within Galilee. According to the above assumption, these references do not inform us regarding the actual pre-Easter history of Jesus but rather regarding the history of post-Easter congregations that met, evangelized, composed, and handed down traditions at these locations. Obviously, redaction-historic analysis of the different ways in which the authors of the Synoptic Gospels accent their subject matter is entirely legitimate. It must also be considered methodologically legitimate to pursue our investigation of the use of houses back to the time before Easter.[3] After all, no one involved in NT scholarship contests the fact that the historic Jesus preached and taught—and he obviously did this at specific, concrete locations.[4]

The Synoptic Gospels create a very clear impression of Jesus as an itinerant preacher. For this reason most exegetes describe Jesus as such.[5] Even

---

[1] Trocmé, *Formation*, 162–63; Best, *Following Jesus*, 226–27; Klauck, *Hausgemeinde*, 56–61; Vogler, "Bedeutung."

[2] Cf., in addition to Trocmé, e.g., Klauck, *Hausgemeinde*, 56–61; Best, *Following Jesus*, 226–27; Vogler, "Bedeutung," 787.

[3] Cf. Schürmann, "Die vorösterlichen Anfänge." Schürmann's main arguments have been accepted by a number of scholars. Cf. Trocmé, *Jesus;* Stanton, "Form Criticism"; Riesner, *Jesus als Lehrer*, 74 (see there a list of additional scholars).

[4] Even though Jesus did not complete any kind of higher education, his parents, visits to the synagogues in Nazareth and the surrounding area, and regular pilgrimages to Jerusalem would have given him the biblical knowledge and training necessary to teach and make disciples of his followers. All four gospels record quite clearly and intentionally the memory of the earthly teaching ministry of Jesus. Cf. Normann, *Christos Didaskalos*, 1–32, 45–54; Meye, *Jesus*, 30–60; Hengel, "Jesus als messianischer Lehrer," 148; Riesner, *Jesus als Lehrer*, 246–64, 298–344, 353–57, 408–40, 476–87, 507; France, "Mark."

[5] Cf. Bousset, *Kyrios Christos*, 117; for present-day scholarship, cf. Bornkamm, *Jesus;* Theissen, *Social Reality*, 33–59.

though almost every other aspect of Jesus' life and ministry has been critically questioned, surprisingly the itinerant character of his ministry has almost never been disputed.[6] The Synoptic Gospels relate that Jesus taught not only in open-air settings but in synagogues and houses as well. A number of scholars, however, maintain that he only taught in the synagogue[7] or in the open.[8] Nevertheless, it is most likely, for a number of reasons, that Jesus practiced at least a sporadic, if not a regular, teaching ministry in houses.

According to the Gospels, Jesus' ministry can be divided into two periods: his public ministry and, following that, a period of time when Jesus, more or less in the role of a fugitive because of persecution, was forced to minister more in private, most likely, at least in part, in domestic houses. Even during the first period of his public ministry we can assume that Jesus went into a house to instruct his disciples, particularly at night or whenever it was cold or rainy.

The assumption that Jesus used houses for his teaching ministry as well as for other activities is supported by three additional insights. First, in the ancient Jewish, Christian, and Hellenistic world, a private home often provided the meeting place for religious and intellectual dialogue and instruction. Particularly in the Jewish and Christian setting, domestic houses were viewed as "die Urzelle der Zusammenkünfte von Meister und Jüngern."[9] Even though it would be exaggerating to suggest that Jesus was a rabbi, it cannot be contested that he taught like a Jewish "teacher." Jewish teachers at the time of Jesus were known to make journeys, but for the most part they remained at home and led a fairly sedentary lifestyle.[10] Their followers came to them. The Gospels report quite often, too, that individuals or groups came or were brought to Jesus as the news of his presence in a town or village spread into the surrounding area.[11] Even though a sedentary and an itinerant lifestyle are not mutually exclusive, this evidence does imply that Jesus' ministry was at times more sedentary than often assumed.

Second, as we consider the central economic and social significance of the *oikos* in the ancient world generally and in Palestine or Galilee specifically, it should not surprise us to discover that houses played a central role in the life and ministry of Jesus.[12]

---

[6] Cf. the (one-sided) exception, Borsch, "Jesus."
[7] Bultmann, *Jesus* (1988), 43–44.
[8] Hengel, *Nachfolge*, 59–60; Loffreda, *Heiligtümer;* Dalman, *Orte,* 167–68; Riesner, *Jesus als Lehrer,* 353–54.
[9] Gevaryahu, "Privathäuser," 5 ("the basic cell for the assemblies of the master with his disciples"); cf. Rengstorf, "μανθάνω," TDNT 4:390–92; Hengel, *Judentum und Hellenismus,* 148–49.
[10] Borsch, "Jesus," 55.
[11] Cf. Mark 1:28, 32, 40, 45; 3:8; 6:33; 8:1; 9:17; 10:13; Matt 8:34; 9:26, 28, 31–32; Luke 4:14.
[12] Cf. Safrai, "Home"; R. Horsley, *Galilee,* 195–201, 203–7; Hirschfeld, *Palestinian Dwelling,* 21–107, 289–95.

Third, synagogues may well have been widespread in 70 C.E. and earlier, not only in the Diaspora but in Palestine as well,[13] primarily in the form of house synagogues, that is, private homes that served with or without architectural alteration as the place of assembly for a synagogue community.[14] We can assume, particularly for the poorer areas in Galilee, that these were house synagogues rather than the pompous structures we are familiar with from the third to sixth centuries C.E.[15] Such house synagogues probably existed even in relatively small Jewish villages.[16] Accordingly, the Gospels presuppose a multiplicity of them for Galilee as well.[17]

All of this is evidence that Jews of the first century were accustomed to meeting for worship in private homes, which in turn would apply also to Jesus and his disciples.[18] Therefore, it appears reasonable to assume that Jesus would have used houses at least for his teaching ministry and possibly for other activities as well. The question, then, is whether we can support this hypothesis with reliable tradition from the Gospels.

---

[13] References by Josephus, *J.W.* 2.229 (presumes synagogues in villages in the surrounding area of Jerusalem); Philo, *Spec.* 2.62; *Mos.* 2.216; *Legat.* 132. The rabbinical sources (possibly exaggerated), stating that Jerusalem had 480 (*y. Meg.* 73d), 460 (*y. Ketub.* 35c), or 394 (*y. Ketub.* 105a) "houses of instruction," Bethar had 400 (*y. Giṭ.* 58a), and Tiberias had 13 (*y. Ber.* 8a; 30b), confirm the impression given by the NT (see Str-B 4/1:117 for a list of the synagogues mentioned in the NT) that the synagogue was a widespread phenomenon.

This view, however, is contested. Cf. Kee, "Transformation," 1–24, here 8, and "Early Christianity in the Galilee," esp. 3–14. Kee follows the findings of Neusner, *Formative Judaism,* 75–83. For a rebuttal of Kee's arguments by means of extensive literary, inscriptional, and archaeological evidence, cf. Oster, "Supposed Anachronism." Cf. Kee's response to Oster in "Changing Meaning." For a criticism of Kee's response to Oster, cf. Riesner, "Synagogues," esp. 179–87. Cf. Levine, "Second Temple," 7–31, here 7, for an extensive and balanced discussion of the very diverse evidence. Levine believes that "by the end of the Second Temple period, the synagogue had become a central institution in Jewish life."

[14] Hengel, "Synagogeninschrift," 175 n. 98; Klauck, *Hausgemeinde,* 95–97; Wilkinson, "Christian Pilgrims," 75–101, here 77; White, *Building God's House,* 60–101; G. Foerster, "Ancient Synagogues," 300–301; Riesner, "Synagogues," esp. 186. Similarly Neusner, *Formative Judaism,* 75–83; Kee, "Transformation," esp. 13–14. For Neusner and Kee, however, the house groups prevalent at this time were not house synagogues. Cf. also Oster, "Supposed Anachronism," esp. 192–93 n. 55.

[15] Schwank, "Qualis erat forma?"; Ma'oz, "Synagogue," 35; Levine, *Ancient Synagogues,* 19–35, 52–59; and Riesner, "Synagogues," esp. 184–87. Cf. the Theodotus inscription from Jerusalem, Masada, Gamla, Herodium, and Capernaum(?). Cf. Strange and Shanks, "Has the House Been Found?" esp. 29–30.

[16] Schrage, "συναγωγή," *TDNT* 7:812–13; Gowan, *Bridge,* 279–80; Safrai, "Synagogue," 909–10; Avi-Yonah, "Synagogues," 4:1129.

[17] Matt 4:23/Mark 1:39; Matt 9:35; Luke 4:14–15.

[18] This is not to say that they, as Jews, attended and/or held worship services in a private home that was not declared a synagogue. They most likely attended and/or held such services in a (house) synagogue.; cf. Luke 4:16, 43–44; 5:17–26; 6:6–11; 7:1–10; 13:10–17.

A House in Capernaum

After an extensive tradition- and redaction-historical examination of sixteen passages in which the Gospels refer to Capernaum, W. Bösen concludes, "The Capernaum tradition rests on a solid foundation. . . . Capernaum is . . . securely associated with Jesus."[19] Capernaum appears to be embedded in the text in at least seven places, in three different streams of tradition: the sayings source Q (Matt 8:5–13/Luke 7:1–10; Matt 11:20–24/Luke 10:13–15); the Gospel of Mark (Mark 1:12; 2:1); and the pre-Johannine tradition (John 2:12; 4:46; 6:17).

Not all of the twenty-nine references to houses in the Gospel of Mark are of significance for our study; we will focus on the verses that refer to the house of Peter in Capernaum (Mark 1:29, 33; 2:1; 3:20; 9:33).[20] Since the work of K. L. Schmidt, it has become customary for NT scholarship to view quite negatively the historical value of the topographical and chronological framework connecting the individual Gospel narratives to one another.[21] In the meantime, however, Schmidt's negative judgment of the Gospel framework has undergone serious criticism.[22] G. N. Stanton has convincingly countered Schmidt's position by arguing that the framework is most often not secondary but, rather, integrally intertwined with the original narratives. In fact, according to Stanton's findings, "the framework of Mark emerges with strong claims to historicity."[23]

Apart from that, though, even in Schmidt's opinion the references to the house of Peter in Capernaum in four out of five of the verses of interest to us (1:29, 33; 2:1; 3:20) originate from reliable pre-Markan tradition.[24] In 1:29–31 he sees "in its present state the result of a transposition of a report from Peter in the first person plural into the third person plural."[25] According to Schmidt, Mark has conserved the old report and changed it very little. Other exegetes take a similar position.[26] The pericope involving the

---

[19] Bösen, *Galiläa als Lebensraum*, 87. "Die Kafarnaum-Tradition ruht auf festem Fundament. . . . Kafarnaum ist . . . fest mit Jesus verbunden" (pp. 83–87).

[20] I do not plan to discuss all twenty-nine references to houses in Mark. For a list and discussion of *all* the passages in Mark, cf. Best, *Following Jesus*, 226–28; and Klauck, *Hausgemeinde*, 56–62. Cf. also Ravarotto, "Casa." He sees the house of Peter in Capernaum in six of twenty-nine references to a house in Mark (2:1; 3:20; 7:17; 9:28–29, 33; 10:10).

[21] K. Schmidt, *Rahmen*.

[22] Stuhlmacher, *Evangelium und die Evangelien*, 7.

[23] Stanton, "Form Criticism," 13–27, here esp. 15–18; quote, 15.

[24] K. Schmidt, *Rahmen*, 55–58, 78–79, 120, 229–30.

[25] Ibid., 56.

[26] Cf. Zahn, *Einleitung*, 2:251–52. Cf. also Lohmeyer, *Markus*, 40; V. Taylor, *Mark*, 178; Jeremias, *Jesus' Promise*, 91 n. 2; and with them Lane, *Mark*, 76–77; Riesner, *Jesus als Lehrer*, 353; Hengel, "Probleme," 252–57. Hengel argues convincingly that Petrine authority stands behind the Markan report and that the author of Mark is dependent on Peter.

disciples' dispute gives the impression of being very old as well, so that the mention of a house in Capernaum (9:33) can also be considered part of an old, reliable tradition. As in 1:29, 33 and 3:20, this verse is to be understood as a reference to the house of Peter.

Passages unique to Matthew refer twice—once certain reference and another probable—to a house in Capernaum that was available to Jesus for use in his ministry. The mention of a house in which two blind men were healed (9:27), a scene that the author obviously believed took place in Capernaum (cf. 9:1), cannot be explained away as stemming from the redactional intent of the author.[27] In the narrative about the temple taxes (17:24–27), an instructional dialogue takes place between Jesus and his disciples. The house mentioned here must have been Peter's, as the tax collectors came to Peter for the two-drachma tax (17:24). Even though scholars tend to doubt the historical reliability of these two miracle narratives,[28] it can be asked if the two stories reflect at least knowledge of the (pre- and post-Easter?) significance of the house of Peter. At any rate, we are struck with the fact that here pre-Matthean tradition is in agreement with reliable Markan tradition (Mark 1:29, 33; 2:1; 3:20).

The exegetical findings that at least some of the Markan references to the house of Peter in Capernaum are historically reliable are also supported by archaeological evidence. In Tell Hum (Capernaum), studies draw attention to the existence of local tradition about the house of Peter as early as the second half of the first century. In her pilgrimage journal (late fourth or early fifth century) Egeria tells of a church in Capernaum that was constructed from the house of Peter.[29] This information has been confirmed by findings of archaeological excavations beginning in 1968 and led by Virgilio C. Corbo and Stanislao Loffreda.[30] A church building dating from the fourth century was discovered under an octagonal Byzantine basilica from the fifth century. Both structures are centered over a private house from the first century C.E. that has a number of features distinguishing it from all other buildings from the early Roman period as yet found in Capernaum (see floor plans in appendix). For example, fragments from ornaments and inscriptions indicate that this domestic house was used earlier than the third century by Jewish Christians for the purpose of worship.[31] Two inscriptions with the name

---

[27] Cf. Roloff, *Kerygma,* 132.

[28] For the exception regarding Matt 17, 24–27, cf. Horbury, "Temple Tax"; regarding Matt 9:27–31, cf. Blomberg, *Matthew,* 162–63.

[29] "In Capharnaum autem ex domo apostolorum principis ecclesia facta est, qui parietes usque hodie ita stant, sicut fuerunt," *Itinerarium Egeriae* (CSEL 34, 112–13). Tell Hum has been identified as Capernaum; cf. Kopp, *Heiligen Stätten,* 215–30.

[30] Corbo, *House; Edifici;* and "Church"; Loffreda, *Recovering Capharnaum,* 50–68. Cf. also Mancini, *Archéologie,* 78–82; Murphy-O'Conner, *Holy Land,* 225; more cautiously, White, "Domus," 165–69.

[31] Cf. an inscription that presumably refers to a Jewish-Christian addition to the apocalyptic book *3 Baruch (Greek Apocalypse)* (*3 Bar.* 4:9–15).

Peter are indication of a special relationship between this house and the apostle. Multiple restorations of the beaten lime floor in the living room of the house as early as the second half of the first century imply that the house already had special significance back then. In addition, numerous fragments of oil lamps were found, which could indicate that the home was used as the place of assembly for a house church.[32]

For the existence of a Jewish-Christian group in Capernaum after Easter, Mark (14:28; 16:7–8 par.) and John (21:1–14) provide indirect evidence.[33] It is possible that this group of Jewish Christians preserved a local tradition and formed the community that constituted this house church. According to a rabbinical reference, a relatively large number of Jewish Christians were present in Capernaum in the fourth century.[34]

Joan E. Taylor, however, has strongly contested this view.[35] She is not convinced that it really is the house of Simon Peter that was discovered in Capernaum.[36] Her argument is based on the contention that the chronology suggested by the excavators is in need of correction. According to their view, a house church met in the house of Peter as early as the end of the first century and a church house in the fourth century.[37] A central issue in the discussion regarding the dating of the so-called insula 1 in level 1 (according to the excavators, the house church in the house of Peter) is the significance of the beaten lime floor in room N, which the excavators date to the second half of the first century.[38] This date was calculated based on the analysis of twenty fragments of Herodian oil lamps, two pot rims, and one jug rim A 1,[39] all of which were found between the thin layers of lime collected in small beds of black earth, with a terminus post quem based on the ceramic found in the prior layer B and the following layer A.[40]

It is this dating of the floor and with it the excavators' entire chronology that Taylor radically questions. "It is unclear when precisely the

---

[32] Cf. Acts 20:7–8.

[33] It is unknown precisely when this house church came into existence (see pp. 31–32).

[34] *Qoh. Rab.* 7:27, 38a. The passage *Qoh. Rab.* 1:8, which used to be considered a reliable reference to the existence of a Jewish-Christian group in Capernaum at the turn of the second century, is now disputed. Cf. J. Maier, *Jüdische Auseinandersetzung*, 119–20; J. Taylor, *Christians*, 26. Str-B 1:159–60 can no longer be considered authoritative. Cf. regarding *Qoh. Rab.* 1:8, however, Freyne, *Galilee from Alexander*, 347–48; and Blenkinsopp, "Literary Evidence," esp. 203: "While the term mîn can denote more than one type of sectarian or apostate, these particular mînîm and sinners . . . were almost certainly Christians of Jewish origin."

[35] Cf. J. Taylor, "Capernaum"; *Christians*, esp. 269–94; and "Critical Investigation." For a rebuttal of her arguments, cf. Loffreda, "Tradizionale casa."

[36] Cf. J. Taylor, "Capernaum," 26.

[37] See our definition of "church house," pp. 18–19.

[38] The "living room." Cf. illustration 1 by Loffreda, "Tradizionale casa"; or fig. 4, "Area b," by Corbo, *Edifici*, 78.

[39] Registration nos. 5477–5496, 5497–5498, and 5499 respectively.

[40] Corbo, *Edifici*, 80.

intermediate beaten lime floors were laid; they may have been put down as late as the middle of the fourth century, or as early as the beginning of the third. There is insufficient evidence to be conclusive. They did *not*, however, come from the first century."[41] But how are we to explain the fragments of Herodian lamps present in the thin black beds of earth between the two layers of lime-plastered floors?

Taylor offers the following hypothesis as her explanation. The fragments "could have been embedded in the mix *if* it was made in a refuse dump outside the city (a probable place for lamp burning)."[42] Apart from the fact that Taylor is forced to take refuge in an unsubstantiated hypothesis,[43] she has also made the following mistake: The fragments were not found in the lime layer as she suggests. Its thickness is thinner than the respective fragments. Instead they were found in an in-between layer of black earth.[44] In addition, there is one more piece of evidence used by the excavators to determine the date and fully overlooked by Taylor: the existence of an entire pot (no. 4653) from the first century, standing with its bottom directly on top of the beaten lime floors in question.[45]

Taylor suggests as well that S. Loffreda's dating of the ceramic that was found in rubble floor B in room N.1 is in need of correction:[46] "Bed B was laid in the middle of the first century or the beginning of the second and continued to be used . . . until at least the third century."[47] According to Loffreda, however, this floor cannot have been in use much longer than the middle of the first century because the kinds of ceramic typical for Capernaum in the late first century are totally missing.[48]

Taylor questions the dating of the *domus ecclesiae* in layer 2 as well. Central to her argument is the suggestion that the polychrome floor of the *domus ecclesiae* that the excavators date to the fourth century on the basis of coin and ceramic findings was installed as late as the mid-fifth century.[49] This puts it in the period in which, according to V. Corbo, the octagonal church was erected. But this is in contradiction to a prior assertion made by Taylor: "A fifth-century dating of the octagonal structure (Corbo, 1975, 56) seems reasonably sure on the basis of coins from the first two decades of the fifth

---

[41] J. Taylor, "Capernaum," 18.
[42] Ibid. (italics added).
[43] Loffreda, "Tradizionale casa," 54: "Does Taylor really believe that she can correct the chronology of the excavators by almost three hundred years by simply making use of a hypothesis that is ultimately supported by nothing more than a feeble crutch called 'if'?"
[44] Ibid.
[45] Corbo, *Edifici*, photo 41; Loffreda, *Ceramica*, fig. 2:2 and photo 2:2.
[46] Loffreda, "Tradizionale casa," 55, fig. 16:1–7; *Ceramica*, 116–17, fig. 39:1–7.
[47] J. Taylor, "Capernaum," 17.
[48] Loffreda, "Tradizionale casa," 56.
[49] J. Taylor, "Capernaum," 18.

century found beneath the mosaic pavements (1975, 54) and from pottery." If the date for the construction of the octagonal church (layer 3) in the middle of the fifth century is "reasonably sure," how can it also apply to the installation of the floor of the *domus ecclesiae* (layer 2)?[50]

We are therefore forced to conclude that Taylor's contention that the chronology of the excavators needs to be corrected is unsubstantiated.[51] In conclusion, it can be assumed that the numerous references to Jesus' presence in the house of Peter in Capernaum are reliable. This is based on the well-founded assumption that Mark was familiar with Petrine tradition, so that the framework in Mark 1:29, 33; 2:1; 3:20; 9:33 does not contain secondary but, rather, original information regarding Capernaum. As our investigation has demonstrated, this assumption is supported by the available archaeological data. Now, using the criteria of coherence, we can ask whether there is further traditional evidence that would confirm the above-mentioned critical minimum.[52]

Jesus and the House of Peter

It has often been observed that Capernaum seems to be a special point of concentration in the Gospels.[53] All the Gospels agree that once Jesus began his public ministry, Capernaum appeared to be his preference for place of residence.[54] Many of the significant events in the life and ministry of Jesus took place in the town of Capernaum.[55] It seems as if the story line always returns to Capernaum.[56]

Luke 10:15/Matt 11:23 also support the view that much in the life of Jesus took place in Capernaum. Here it is implied that Capernaum experienced more of the "ultimate" than any other Galilean town or city. With the "elevation" of Capernaum, the Q material is referring to the ministry of

---

[50] Loffreda, "Tradizionale casa," 58, 60–61.

[51] Ibid., 56: "The chronological upheaval suggested by Taylor is based on a disregard for the most elementary rules of ceramic science . . . and on hypothetical structures born of fantasy that accomplish nothing in archaeology."

[52] Cf. Riesner, *Jesus als Lehrer,* 92. In order to determine the historic reliability of a passage, Riesner suggests a number of criteria. The criterion of coherence is met when a text or combination of texts (the critical minimum), whose reliability has already been demonstrated on the basis of evidence secured through other criteria, coheres, i.e., agrees with other traditions or sets of tradition in terms of content and form.

[53] Gnilka, *Markus,* 1:78; Ernst, *Markus,* 63; Bishop, "Jesus," 431; Meyers and Strange, *Archaeology,* 126; Trilling, *Das wahre Israel,* 132 (citations are to the 1964 ed.). Cf. also Bösen, *Galiläa als Lebensraum,* 90.

[54] Mark 1:2; 2:1; 9:33; Matt 4:13; 11:23 par.; Luke 10:15; John 2:12; 6:17–59.

[55] Particularly in Mark it is partially coincidental and therefore cannot be attributed to the redactional interest of the author. This may not be the case for Matthew. Cf. Bishop, "Jesus."

[56] Cf., e.g., Mark 1:21, 29; 2:1, 15; 3:20, 31–32; 9:28, 33.

Jesus at this location.[57] This elevation is all the more understandable if Jesus actually lived in Capernaum temporarily and as a result ended up ministering more there than in the other cities.[58]

On the basis of Mark 2:1;[59] Matt 4:14,[60] and Matt 9:1,[61] one could form the impression that, after Nazareth, Capernaum became *the* residence for Jesus.[62] That Capernaum was Jesus' residence is implied by Matt 17:24–27. While Jesus was living in the house of Peter, the men who collected the temple tax came to him. According to numerous references regarding Jewish temple taxes, if a man was not able to deliver his taxes to the temple, he was allowed to do so at his place of residence.[63] Matthew reports that it was Peter who paid the taxes for Jesus and himself. It follows that at least temporarily Jesus made his residence in the house of Peter in Capernaum (if only from Matthew's perspective).[64]

---

[57] So correctly Schniewind, *Matthäus*, 148; Grundmann, *Matthäus*, 313–14; and *Lukas*, 211; Percy, *Botschaft*, 112–13; Neuhäusler, *Anspruch*, 201; S. Schulz, *Spruchquelle*, 366. Contra Wellhausen, *Matthaei*, 54–55; Bultmann, *Geschichte*, 119–20; E. Klostermann, *Matthäusevangelium*, 100.

[58] Clearly Capernaum has the leading role in this triangle of villages (A. Schlatter, *Evangelist Matthäus*, 380; S. Schulz, *Spruchquelle*, 365; Pesch, *Markusevangelium*, 1:120). Bösen views Jesus' lamentation in these two passages as a strong indication that Jesus elevated the city of Capernaum to the center of his Galilean ministry. Nowhere else did he preach as impressively, and nowhere else did he do more miracles. For Bösen, Capernaum was therefore a kind of center for the messianic ministry of Jesus (*Galiläa als Lebensraum*, 94). Cf. also Luke 4:23 as a confirmation of our view.

As with most sayings of Jesus in the Synoptic Gospels, the historic reliability of Luke 10:13–15 and Matt 11:21–24 is disputed. Cf. S. Schulz, *Spruchquelle*, 362 n. 257, for a discussion. For many good reasons, the following scholars support the reliability of the passages at least in their core: Kümmel, *Verheissung*, 30; Hahn, *Verständnis*, 27, 34; Kopp, *Heiligen Stätten*, 214; Jeremias, *Jesus' Promise*, 50 n. 1; Trilling, *Fragen*, 103; Schniewind, *Matthäus*, 147; Grundmann, *Lukas*, 211; Ernst, *Lukas*, 336; G. Schneider, *Lukas*, 1:239; Mussner, "Gab es?" 244; Laufen, "Doppelüberlieferung," 276. Hoffmann, *Studien*, 303, esp. n. 53; Pesch, *Markusevangelium*, 1:120.

[59] The prepositional expression ἐν οἴκῳ can be translated "in a house" or "at home." The latter is to be preferred here (Bauer-Aland[6], 1136; BDAG 698)—i.e., "at home, in the house that was usually available to him."

[60] It is reported here that Jesus left his original home, Nazareth, and he "came and lived in Capernaum."

[61] "and came to his *own* town."

[62] Schweizer, *Matthäus*, 145; Gevaryahu, "Privathäuser," esp. 9; Loffreda, "Tradizionale casa," 38; Bösen, *Galiläa als Lebenraum*, 90–92; Blinzler, "Heimat Jesu," esp. 18–20; Kennard, "Was Capernaum?"; Str-B 1:493–94.

[63] References collected by Str-B 1:760–73. Cf. esp. *m. Šeqal.* 1:1, 3; 2:1; and Ex 30:13 and Neh 10:32–33 LXX; Josephus, *J.W.* 3.194–196; 7.218; *b. Bek.* 50b; *b. B. Qam.* 36b. Cf. Garland, "Matthew's Understanding," esp. 190–95; Horbury, "Temple Tax"; Kadman, "Temple Dues."

[64] Cf. Grundmann, *Matthäus*, 409; Blinzler, "Heimat Jesu," 19; and Loffreda, "Tradizionale casa," 38. Cf. also Kopp, *Heiligen Stätten*, 214.

The House of Peter as a Place of Assembly, Instruction, and Healing

The five historically reliable verses (Mark 1:29, 33; 2:1; 3:20; 9:33) clearly demonstrate that Jesus' healing and teaching ministry took place in and around the house of Peter in Capernaum. The two narratives from the passages unique to Matthew are historically disputed. Nevertheless, they are in agreement with the picture portrayed by the above-mentioned verses (critical minimum) and therefore can be considered to confirm their perspective.

In Mark 1:29–31, Jesus enters the house of Peter and heals the mother-in-law's fever. That evening all the sick and demon-possessed are brought to Jesus in front of the same house: "the whole town gathered at the door." Many of the sick and possessed are healed or liberated from their possession (1:33). In the same house in Capernaum, Jesus heals a paralytic (2:1). Matthew also reports that Jesus exercised his gift of healing in the house of Peter. The "house" in the story of the two blind men (Matt 9:27–31) is, according to Matthew, in Capernaum (9:1) and the very same house of Peter.

Directly after the appointment of the Twelve, it is reported that Jesus went into a house (from the context most likely the house of Peter). After that a crowd gathered, so that he and his disciples could not eat. At this point nothing is said of either a healing or a teaching session. It is safe to assume, however, that the crowd gathered with a certain expectation—possibly in hopes that Jesus would heal or teach again? At any rate, it is reported that the crowd gathered inside and outside the house. Here the house of Peter with its courtyard served as a gathering place or as a meeting room for the followers of Jesus.[65]

The teaching ministry of Jesus is much more clearly documented in Mark 9:33. Once again in Capernaum and "at home" Jesus has an instructional discussion with his disciples evolving out of their argument over who was the greatest. Jesus' teaching ministry is also confirmed in a gospel parallel. In the narrative about the temple tax (Matt 17:24–27), a master-disciple conversation, that is, an instructional discussion, takes place in the house of Peter in Capernaum.

In light of the above observations, one wonders if the Markan representation of the esoteric instruction of the disciples, which very often took place in a house, is quite plausible as well.[66] It could be that this scheme has its origin in early Christian catechism and that it is the situation of the Markan congregation reflected here. It is just as likely, however, that Jesus

---

[65] This is all the easier to imagine when one has the results of the excavation in Capernaum as well as the reconstruction of the floor plans and isometrical illustrations of the insula (see appendix, below). Cf. Loffreda, *Recovering Capharnaum*, 50–67. For the significance of the courtyard in the private, everyday life of a Palestine family, see p. 45.

[66] Of course, not always in the house of Peter; cf. Mark 7:14–15, 17, 18–23; 9:14–27, 28–29; 10:2–9, 10–12. Cf. also the passages in Mark without direct connection to a house, e.g., Mark 4:10, and also in Matt 13:36.

himself actually taught "catechism" in houses.⁶⁷ We have already demonstrated that it is historically quite likely that Jesus taught not only in the open or in synagogues but also in houses (see above), and on the basis of what we have observed here, we can be certain that Jesus taught at least in the house of Peter.

The House of Peter as the Operational Base for Jesus' Missional Outreach

The observations that Jesus made his home in Capernaum and at the same time was active as an itinerant preacher are not mutually exclusive.⁶⁸ The image of Jesus as itinerant preacher, however, needs to be revised slightly in that "at least temporarily he had a fixed, stable home base."⁶⁹ There are good reasons to believe that Jesus concentrated on the area surrounding Capernaum, Chorazin, and Bethsaida (cf. Matt 11:21/Luke 11:13–15). During this period of residency in Capernaum, the house of Peter was available to Jesus as a center of operation for his ministry and outreach in the area surrounding the Sea of Galilee.⁷⁰

It has often been observed that the area surrounding these three neighboring villages became the major focus for Jesus' ministry.⁷¹ Indeed, in German scholarship the term "evangelical triangle" *(das evangelische Dreieck)* was coined to describe this phenomenon. The three villages are only one to two hours by foot from one another. The location of Capernaum at the time of Jesus has been identified with the modern-day Tell Hum on the bank of the Sea of Galilee about 2.5 miles west of the mouth of the Jordan.⁷² Chorazin is mentioned only once in the Gospels (Luke 10:13), but we find several references to it in post-NT Jewish sources. In this early Jewish literature, Chorazin is described as a medium-sized town (*t. Mak.* 3:8) that was known for its

---

⁶⁷This position is quite common among today's scholars. Cf., e.g., Klauck, *Hausgemeinde*, 62.

⁶⁸Summaries in Matt 4:23/Mark 1:39/Luke 4:44; Matt 9:35; Luke 4:14–15, 43; 13:33; Mark 1:21–39. Cf. Jeremias, *Proclamation*, 92; *Drei-Tage-Worte*, 83, esp. n. 10; *Sprache*, 234; Schürmann, *Lukasevangelium*, 1:256.

⁶⁹Riesner, *Jesus als Lehrer*, 439 ("es für ihn wenigstens eine zeitweilige stabilitas loci gab"); cf., for a different view, Theissen, *Sociology*, 10. This *stabilitas loci* is different, however, from that of the rabbinical scribes, who were tied to the house where they taught (cf. Hengel, *Origins*, 61–62). Indeed, Jesus' *stabilitas loci* in Capernaum was temporary.

⁷⁰Gnilka (*Markus*, 1:78) believes that Capernaum was a special "support base" for Jesus' ministry and outreach. For Ernst (*Markus*, 63), the assumption that Jesus set up his "fixed quarters" in Capernaum during his ministry in Galilee needs to be taken seriously. Bishop ("Jesus," 431) calls Capernaum a "centre"; Overman ("Who Were the First?" esp. 168), a "center" and "base"; Meyers and Strange (*Archaeology*, 126), a "headquarters"; Bösen (*Galiläa als Lebensraum*, 92), "a center for the messianic ministry" of Jesus. For Trilling (*Das wahre Israel*, 131), Capernaum is the "theater" ("Schauplatz") for Jesus' ministry.

⁷¹Cf. Kopp, *Heiligen Stätten*, 243–46; Grundmann, *Lukas*, 210; Riesner, *Jesus als Lehrer*, 353.

⁷²Corbo, "Capernaum"; Kopp, *Heiligen Stätten*, 215–30; Finegan, *Archeology*, 50–56; Tzaferis, "New Archaeological Evidence."

wheat production (*b. Menaḥ.* 85a).[73] Its identification by C. W. M. Van de Velde in the mid-nineteenth century with the modern-day Khirbet Kerazeh about 1.5 miles north of Tell Hum is still generally accepted.[74] There is presently not much that can be said with certainty about its size and appearance during the NT period.[75] Whether Bethsaida is to be identified with the present-day Khirbet el Araj (ca. 45 m from the bank of the Sea of Galilee, a little east of the mouth of the Jordan) or with et Tell (ca. 1.7 miles northeast of el Araj and ca. 2.5 miles from Tell Hum) is still disputed.[76] Both are near Capernaum, however, and so they would have been easily and quickly accessible for Jesus from Capernaum.[77] It can be assumed that Jesus ministered in Chorazin even though there is no record of such a visit in the Gospels. That Jesus visited Bethsaida is documented in Mark 8:22 and Luke 9:10.[78]

From a missional-strategic perspective, Capernaum had at least three advantages as a base of operations for Jesus' Galilean outreach:

First, according to the latest investigations, we can assume that during the time of Jesus Capernaum was a town with a relatively large population and thus a substantial target group for Jesus' message of the coming kingdom of God.[79] At the time of Jesus, Capernaum was in all probability already an economically flourishing[80] as well as a politically and militarily important

---

[73] Cf. also Eusebius (*Onom.* 174.23) and Jerome (*Sit.* 194).

[74] Yeivin, "Ancient Chorazin," 22–36, here 24.

[75] Yeivin, "Chorazin," 1:301–4.

[76] Bethsaida is often mentioned by Josephus, Pliny the Elder, and Ptolemy, and later by Eusebius and Jerome; cf. Strange, "Beth-Saida," 1:692. The excavation findings speak ever more clearly for et Tell. Cf. H. Kuhn, "et-Tell (Betsaida)"; H. Kuhn and Arav, "Bethsaida Excavations"; Pixner ("Searching" and *Wege des Messias,* 127–41, and esp. 391–93) considers it possible that el Araj was a suburb of et Tell; cf. also Strange, "Beth-Saida."

[77] The reconstruction of the Roman road system by Avi-Yonah, "Development," shows to what degree the road system in Lower Galilee had been developed for travel and commerce. Overman, "Who Were the First?" 160–61; Edwards, "First Century" and "Socio-economic."

[78] For a discussion of the three villages, cf. Kopp, *Heiligen Stätten,* 215–46; Finegan, *Archeology,* 50–60; Yeivin, "Ancient Chorazin," 22–36; Urman, *Golan;* Loffreda, *Recovering Capharnaum;* Strange, "Beth-Saida"; Corbo, "Capernaum"; R. W. Smith, "Chorazin."

[79] Just how large the population of Capernaum was is disputed. Cf. Loffreda, *Recovering Capharnaum,* 18, and *Visit,* 20. He and others estimate ca. 1,000 at the time of Jesus. Cf. Laughlin, "Capernaum," 57. Meyers and Strange, *Archaeology,* 58, estimate 12–15,000. Kee goes as high as 25,000 in "Import of Archaeological Investigations," quoted by Reed, *Population,* 1–19, esp. 3, 11, 15; with him R. Horsley, *Galilee,* 194.

That Jesus wanted to reach the entire town of Capernaum through word-and-deed proclamation and had at least partial success is implied by Mark in 1:33, "the whole town" gathered at the door; 1:37, "everyone is looking for him"; 2:2, "so many gathered that there was no room left, not even outside the door."

[80] Laughlin, "Capernaum," 55; Loffreda, *Recovering Capharnaum,* 18–19, 68–69; Overman, "Who Were the First?" 162. Agriculture, fishing, and commerce

Galilean border and garrison town.[81] According to the Gospels, it had barracks (cf. the non-Jewish centurion, Mark 8:5/Luke 7:1–2), a synagogue (Luke 7:5), and a customs office (Mark 2:13–15; Matt 9:9). The ruins of Tell Hum include a large area in which an impressive synagogue from the second/third or from the fourth/fifth century and, east of the house of Peter, a Roman bathhouse from the second/third century were excavated. It is possible that beneath the synagogue lies an older (house?) synagogue and under the Roman bathhouse an older bathhouse, both from the first century.[82] The building material used to construct the buildings under the synagogue and the basilica indicate that the town had greater financial means than is usually assumed.[83] Capernaum also had a marketplace.[84] Archaeological investigations also indicate that it had access to a fairly large port[85] on the bank of the Sea of Galilee as well, which underscores its significance for the Romans, as relatively high duties were charged for fish.[86] All of this is a clear indication that at the time of Jesus Capernaum was not a typical small Galilean village but an important, centrally located town or small city.

Second, Capernaum was centrally located on an important trade route between Damascus and Caesarea with connections to Tiberias and Ptolemaïs.[87] This was not only an advantage economically.[88] Capernaum's

---

were the main sources of income; cf. Wuellner, *Meaning*, 61–62. According to Weullner, fishing in the Sea of Galilee was "big business." Cf. in this context the reference to the sons of Zebedee, who earned enough through their fishing business to afford hired men (Mark 1:20).

[81] Bösen, *Galiläa als Lebensraum*, 76; Kopp, *Heiligen Stätten*, 215; Avi-Yonah, *Holy Land*, 138.

[82] Cf. Loffreda, "Ceramica ellenistico-romana"; Corbo, "Resti"; Strange and Shanks, "Synagogue" and "Has the House Been Found?" esp. 29–30. Laughlin, "Capernaum," 61: "The archaeological evidence, while not conclusive, points to the existence of a . . . synagogue and a Roman bathhouse, all in operation in the first century."

[83] Strange, "Capernaum," 65–74.

[84] Reed, *Population*, 17.

[85] Tzaferis, "New Archaeological Evidence," 198–204, here 201; Nun, *Sea of Galilee*, 40–42.

[86] For duties charged to the fishing industry in Galilee, cf. Wuellner, *Meaning*, 43–44, 62.

[87] Reicke, *Neutestamentliche Zeitgeschichte*, 87; Pixner, "Wege Jesu," 3–9. A Roman milestone from Hadrian (117–138 C.E.) implies that in the second century a Roman road came past Capernaum that most likely followed an already existing route. Cf. Loffreda, *Visit*, 23–24, and *Recovering Capharnaum*, 18–20, 68. Cf. somewhat differently Schwöbel, "Verkehrswege"; Avi-Yonah, "Development"; Bösen, *Galiläa als Lebensraum*, 76, 89.

[88] Bishop, "Jesus," 431: "Capernaum became the first busy centre of the Christian evangel, as it had been, and still was, the centre of marketable produce." Meyers and Strange, *Archaeology*, 59; Overman, "Who Were the First?" 162 (he describes Capernaum as "the Gateway to Gaulanitis").

Recent studies indicate the need to change our view of Galilee back then as being rural, backward, and isolated from culture and commerce. Meyers, "Galilean

central location made it an ideal center for the missional outreach of Jesus and his disciples.

Third, Capernaum was located far enough from the larger centers such as Sepphoris, Tiberias, and Jerusalem that Jesus was able to spread the message of God's kingdom at least initially without having to directly confront the political and religious leaders located in those cities.[89]

How it came about that Jesus took up residence in this house in Capernaum is not reported in the Gospels. An interesting observation in this context is that some of Jesus' closest followers, Peter and Andrew, came from Bethsaida and yet lived in the house of Peter in Capernaum.[90] We can assume that initially Peter (or his father- or mother-in-law?) was the owner and head of this household. E. Ravarotto draws attention to a biographical aspect of Peter's life that is generally unknown: as the head of the household and a fishing businessman, he had a secure and strong economic position in Capernaum. "This allowed him to provide ongoing hospitality not only to Jesus but to all of the disciples as well."[91] That would mean, in calling Peter as his follower, Jesus gained the head of a household and with him the entire household for his cause, a household that was then available to him as an operational base for his missional outreach.

Jesus was not only active as an itinerant preacher. He also led a sedentary life at least temporarily in Capernaum (as guest and friend of Peter).[92] Consequently, we again see that taking up residence in a house at one location and exercising an itinerant ministry are not mutually exclusive but, rather, complementary. The house becomes in this case a base of operation for the itinerant ministry, from which Jesus went out on evangelistic trips and to which he again returned. In light of this we suggest that even before Easter a complementary relationship existed between the stationary household of Peter in Capernaum and the itinerant preacher Jesus. In this scenario Jesus is seen as the healing, teaching "head" of a following in this house and

---

Regionalism: a Reappraisal"; Meyers, Strange, and Groh, "Meiron Excavation"; Meyers and Strange, *Archaeology*, 31–47; Meyers, "Galilean Regionalism as a Factor" and "Cultural Setting"; in agreement, Overman, "Who Were the First?"; and Edwards, "First Century" and "Socio-economic." More cautiously, R. Horsley, *Galilee*, 158–85, 193 n. 10.

[89] Freyne, *Galilee, Jesus*, 140: "Jesus' avoidance of the main Herodian centres of Galilee is best explained, therefore, in the light of a conscious decision not to become directly embroiled in a confrontation with Herodian power. The fate of the Baptist must have been a salutary warning (see Mt 14,13)." Overman, "Who Were the First?" 167–68: "Their [Sepphoris's and Tiberias's] absence appears as less of an oversight and more of a strategy."

[90] Mark 1:29. According to John 1:44, Peter and Andrew came from Bethsaida. Cf. Borsch, "Jesus," 58, for possible explanations.

[91] Ravarotto, "'Casa,'" 419.

[92] Here one can ask whether Jesus was a member of this family in a sociological sense (not only in a theological sense), not as a biological son but rather as a φίλος or *amicus* (or as a house teacher), i.e., as a member of the extended *oikos*.

household of Peter. Perhaps D. L. Dungan is on the right track when he suggests that even before Easter "some sort of already-formed community with Jesus at its head" existed.[93] And as such, the house of Peter became the social and material basis for Jesus' missional ministry. It was the *social basis* of Jesus' ministry as a source of coworkers (Peter, Andrew) and quite possibly as a "network" of relationships that provided a source of evangelistic contacts—for example, the extended family of the *oikos* (Peter's mother-in-law and wife), including friends of the family. It was the *material basis* in that it provided a meeting place for ministry activities such as preaching and healing and enabled mission journeys as well as ministry on the home front. According to E. Haenchen, Jesus was "obviously dependent upon the hospitality of those who had a house, an income, and a job."[94]

Galilean House-to-House and Village-to-Village Outreach

As we have seen, Jesus performed missional outreach in the "evangelical triangle" (Capernaum, Chorazin, Bethsaida). Is there any reason not to assume that Jesus preached in other villages and was offered hospitality by houses outside this triangle during his Galilean itinerant ministry?[95] We have already shown that the central location and importance of Capernaum as well as the well-developed system of roads and trade connections in Lower Galilee facilitated Jesus' missional outreach. One saying of Jesus refers to his itinerant preaching from Capernaum outward into the surrounding villages and towns (Mark 1:38–39). According to Mark 6:6, Jesus went around to the villages neighboring Capernaum and taught. It is possible that Jesus stayed in one or several villages for a time as the guest in someone's home. Mark reports as well that Jesus and his disciples visited the region of Gerasenes/Decapolis (Mark 5:1; Mark 7:31; cf. Matt 8:28 par.), the area surrounding Tyre and Sidon,[96] Gennesaret (Mark 6:53), and the villages near Caesarea Philippi (Mark 8:27). There is no reference here to houses in which Jesus stayed. But Mark gives the impression with this geographical breadth that the entire region of Galilee and beyond was reached by the itinerant ministry of Jesus and his disciples, and it happened from village to village (which implies from house to house).

---

[93] Dungan, *Sayings*, 57.
[94] Haenchen, *Weg Jesu*, 109.
[95] This is not to insinuate that Jesus never spent the night outside. Cf. Matt 8:20/Luke 9:57b–60. These references appear to negate the notion that Jesus stayed overnight in a house at all. But they need not be understood as a literal description of Jesus' situation; rather they could be a general reference to his relative poverty (cf. Borsch, "Jesus," 51).
[96] Mark 7:24; cf. Mark 3:8. Mark 7:24 even says that he entered a house. This, as well as the trip to Tyre, is often classified as Markan redaction (cf. Kertelge, *Wunder*, 151; Schenke, *Wundererzählungen*, 254–55; and some commentaries, e.g., Gnilka, *Markus*, 1:290). But for Pesch (*Markusevangelium*, 1:387) the reference to a house is not Markan redaction but a necessary part of the original narrative.

If our perspective here is correct, it follows that Jesus may have undertaken a Galilean village-to-village (or house-to-house) mission, in which houses, households, and sedentary followers of Jesus played a role similar to that which they played in Capernaum (Mark 6:1, 6, 56; 8:27; 9:30). All three Synoptic Gospels report unanimously that Jesus had a larger circle of followers extending beyond the twelve disciples.[97] Among them were followers who stayed at home.[98] Such sedentary followers and sympathizers are reported to have lived in Galilee (Mark 1:29–31), Judea (Matt 24:16/Mark 13:14/Luke 21:21; 26:6/Mark 14:3; Luke 19:1–10), and in the Decapolis (Mark 5:19–20/Luke 8:37–39). We even know some by name: Mary and Martha, Lazarus (Luke 10:38–39; cf. John 11:1, 18), and Simon the leper (Matt 26:6/Mark 14:3), all of whom were residents of Bethany on the Mount of Olives.[99]

At this point it must be asked if the house of Martha in Bethany might not be considered the counterpart to the house of Peter in Capernaum even though, according to record, it did not enjoy the same prominence. Like Capernaum, Bethany had a central location. It was close enough to Jerusalem (cf. John 11:18; Mark 11:1) and easily accessible for Jesus from there; at the same time, it was far enough away to provide the necessary distance from his enemies.[100]

Mark reports that Jesus often came back from Jerusalem to Bethany (Mark 11:1, 11, 12, 15, 27; cf. Matt 21:17) and creates the impression that Jesus stayed there for a time (probably living with his sedentary followers under one roof). Jesus along with his disciples enjoyed the hospitality of Martha in Bethany during his last stay in Jerusalem.[101] She opened her home to them and gave them a place to stay (Luke 10:38–39; cf. John 11:1, 18).[102]

---

[97] Minear, "Audience Criticism," "Jesus' Audience," and "Disciples."

[98] This is supported by the observation that, inspired by Theissen, Riesner, *Jesus als Lehrer,* 488–89, asks if the historicity of some Jesus sayings needs to be reappraised. A whole series of sayings that are normally suspect appear to have a Sitz im Leben within the pre-Easter sedentary circle of followers. Cf. Matt 5:23, directed at an audience that brings sacrifices on a regular basis, e.g., sedentary followers of Jesus; Matt 6:1–4, directed toward followers who still own and have a say about their property, as opposed to the itinerant disciples. Some followers were able to retreat into their own houses in order to pray (Matt 6:5–6). Cf. also Matt 24:4–5 par.; 24:23–25 par.; 24:26–27 par.; 7:15; 23:2–3. Cf. Riesner, *Jesus als Lehrer,* 488–89, and Theissen, *Sociology,* 18–22, for additional passages.

[99] Joseph of Arimathea (Mark 15:42–47) and the women in Luke 8:2–3 (possibly those in Mark 15:40–41 as well) all belonged to those who supported Jesus materially.

[100] Bethany is 1.7 miles (ca. twenty to thirty minutes by foot) from Jerusalem.

[101] Martha appears in Luke 10:38–42 in the role of the hostess. She was presumably a widow (Easton, *Luke,* 173) and, as such, a homeowner and head of the household (Schürmann, *Lukasevangelium,* 2:154; I. H. Marshall, *Gospel of Luke,* 451).

[102] Many texts add a variation at the end of 10:38: εἰς τὴν οἰκίαν (+ αὐτῆς) or εἰς τὸν οἶκον αὐτῆς. The shorter text is considered the more original, as there is no

This indicates that Martha's house must have been relatively large, as there was room for Jesus and (some of) his disciples. The house in Bethany also appears to serve as a meeting and teaching facility (John 11:19, 31; 12:1–9; Luke 10:38–42).[103]

Another interesting question is how those who led a sedentary lifestyle became followers of Jesus. It can be assumed that many of those who came to hear Jesus in Capernaum returned home as his followers. One would also expect that, as a result of the itinerant ministry of Jesus, a large number of people would have come to faith through his preaching. It is reasonable to believe that they then would have remained in their vocations and at home with their families in expectation of the coming kingdom.[104]

This perspective has recently found the support of a number of scholars.[105] In particular, R. A. Horsley would like to revise the broadly accepted view of Theissen, who perceives the Jesus movement as led primarily by radical itinerants.[106] In Theissen's reconstruction, the sedentary sympathizers of Jesus play a secondary role. On the contrary, Horsley argues that the Jesus movement behind Q consisted mainly of local communities[107] in which the itinerant preachers lived, who then left home, property, and family for the most part temporarily—and all of this post-Easter as well.[108]

Theissen, however, considers it misleading to speak of "communities" or "churches" in this context.[109] These groups, according to Theissen, remained completely within the parameters of Judaism and did not intend to start "the church."[110] This is supposed to be true initially for the entire Christian movement. The question is whether from the very beginning even

---

recognizable motive for deleting the expression "in her house." "On the other hand, the bold and bare ὑπεδέξατο αὐτόν seems to call for some appropriate addition, which the copyists supplied in various forms" (Metzger, *Textual Commentary*, 129).

[103] When Mary (Luke 10:39) "sat at the Lord's feet listening to what he said," she took the same position as a pupil or disciple would have in the presence of his or her elementary teacher or scribe. Cf. references, Str-B 2:763–65.

[104] Jeremias, *Proclamation*, 167; Kretschmar, "Ein Beitrag," 27–67, here 48–49; with him Theissen, *Sociology*, 17–23.

[105] R. Horsley, *Sociology*; Kee, *Community*; Kelber, *Oral and Written Gospel*.

[106] The work of Horsley represents one of the most thorough and convincing criticisms of the reconstruction of Theissen and is one of the best attempts to offer a supplemental but also corrective alternative; R. Horsley, *Sociology*, esp. 43–64, 111. Horsley is not the first to criticize Theissen. For an extensive list of Theissen's critics, cf. Gehring, *Hausgemeinde*, 84–85 n. 157.

[107] R. Horsley, *Sociology*, 106–11. Independent of Riesner, Horsley comes to a similar conclusion: many of the sayings of Jesus presuppose a sedentary lifestyle.

[108] Ibid., 117. For Horsley, leaving home here is, in contrast to the Cynics, not a lifestyle for the itinerant preacher but rather an unavoidable but coincidental secondary phenomenon, necessary because of the commission to evangelize. The main proof texts for his view are 1 Cor 9:5; Mark 10:28–30. Cf. "fields": the prerequisite for receiving a field back is at least a part-time sedentary life. Cf. ibid., 123.

[109] Cf. ibid., 17.

[110] Here Theissen follows Kretschmar, "Ein Beitrag," 27–67, here 41–42.

among Palestinian Christians a sectarian consciousness grew, which led to a separation between them and the rest of the people of Israel—a consciousness that enabled them to form a "distinctly Christian worship and fellowship."[111] Wherever people became committed to the kingdom of God, a separate group within the people of Israel came into existence. In addition, there is good reason to believe that Jesus intended to start the church in the form of a new people of God.[112] But even if one contends that Jesus did not want to found the church but rather only intended to renew Israel, one must assume that even before Easter a new community within Israel came into being through the proclamation of, and as a response to, the coming of the kingdom of God.[113] If not fully Christian, it was at least distinct. According to Filson, houses and their physical dimensions played the key role in making this possible.

We do not dare imagine these groups to be very large, however. According to references in rabbinical texts, the dimensions of a living room in a typical house in the rural regions in Palestine at this time were about five meters square.[114] The results of archaeological investigations show that the average size of a living room was between four and five meters square.[115] Nevertheless, one should keep in mind that the courtyard was an essential part of any Palestinian home and provided room for somewhat larger meetings at least during the warmer seasons.[116] "The courtyard was an integral part of the house.... During the summer months, the family often ate in the courtyard ... the courtyard had the important function of serving as a barrier between the public and private domains.... It seems that no one in the country, members of the lower classes as well as the upper classes, renounced the virtues and pleasure of having a private courtyard inside or beside his house."[117]

The social setting of the Jesus movement, then, appears to have consisted of small house communities in villages and towns. Horsley understands these "local communities" as a kind of missing link between the

---

[111] Cf. Filson, "Significance," 109; Dungan, *Sayings*, 57.

[112] Cf. Stuhlmacher, "Kirche," esp. 304.

[113] Cf. Lohfink, *Jesus and Community*, 55–56; also Borsch, "Jesus," 60; Sanders, *Jesus*, 147 and 222.

[114] *m. Ber.* 8:12c; 3:6d; *Gen. Rab.* 31:11.

[115] Cf. Hirschfeld, *Palestinian Dwelling*, 21–107, 260; cf. esp. his presentation of several Palestinian houses from our period: e.g., a "wall house" in Gamala (second century B.C.E. to first century C.E., with a triclinium ca. 5×5.5 m.), 28; a "farmhouse" 1.9 miles east of Umm Rihan (first century B.C.E. to first century C.E., with a triclinium ca. 7×2.5 m.), 40–41; "farmhouses" in Qasr e-Leja and Kalandiya (both second century B.C.E. to first century C.E., with triclinia ca. 57.5 sq. m. and 5×9.5 m. respectively), 52–54; a "triple courtyard house" in Capernaum (first to second century C.E., with a triclinium ca. 4×3 m.). Cf. also Dar, *Landscape*, 1:80–85, for additional illustrations of houses from our area and period.

[116] See the appendix, below, for sketches of the house of Peter with courtyard.

[117] Cf. Hirschfeld, *Palestinian Dwelling*, 290–92.

earthly ministry of Jesus and the more highly developed Christian churches after Easter.[118] The existence of these groups, however, can only be assumed; they cannot be documented in our texts. In Acts we have a record only of the primitive urban church in Jerusalem and its missional outreach. Galatians 1:22 hints at a broader perspective. Here Paul speaks of Christian churches, that is, a multiple number of churches outside Jerusalem. Nevertheless, one wonders whether it would have been possible for Jesus to develop a relatively large number of well-structured local communities during his earthly ministry within the short time available to him (three years at most). Still, we can point with certainty to the families in the house of Peter in Capernaum and the siblings Martha, Mary, and Lazarus in Bethany,[119] who had already formed local communities before and possibly after Easter.[120]

Conclusions

Our observations lead us to the following conclusions: Jesus' missional approach consisted of finding a house and a household willing to commit themselves to his kingdom message. With this house as a social and material basis, he, along with his newly recruited followers, attempted to reach the entire town of Capernaum and from there the surrounding area within and beyond the "evangelical triangle" by traveling from house to house and village to village.

During his itinerant ministry in Galilee, the house of Peter in Capernaum appears to have been the temporary residence of Jesus as well as the base and center of operations for his missional outreach. We can also assume that it was a place for Jesus and his disciples to cultivate their personal domestic faith life (e.g., prayer, fellowship, spiritual formation). It served also as a meeting room and a place of healing and instruction.

Our study demonstrates that there are good reasons to believe that, already in the pre-Easter period, the house of Peter served as a kind of prototype of a house church with most of the key elements included in our definition of a house church in the full sense of the word.[121] Prayer, fellowship, and missional and instructional proclamation are all elements of a full-fledged house church. But assuming that Jesus and his disciples, as good Jews, most likely attended a synagogue as their main form of public worship, it would be premature to speak of the pre-Easter house of Peter as a house church in the complete sense. The house of Peter before Easter was a place where the first core group of disciples gathered around Jesus in a house

---

[118] R. Horsley, *Sociology*, 111.
[119] Luke 10:38–39; cf. John 11:1, 18. See my discussion above.
[120] Cf. Mark 3:20–21, 31–35 in connection with Mark 10:29–30 and the mission discourse (Luke 10:1–12).
[121] See the definitions on pp. 27–28.

community that can be described as a kind of house church in embryonic form, the "cradle of the ecclesia in its early formation."[122]

We can be sure that, in the view of the post-Easter primitive church (at the latest with the writing of the Gospel of Mark; cf. Mark 3:20–21, 31–35), even before Easter this house appears not only as the house of Peter and the home of Jesus but as the house of the new family of God as well. If we take into consideration that the pre-Easter core of disciples undoubtedly formed a community and that one of its main characteristics was to bond together into a new family,[123] then we can assume that the point of view taken here by the primitive church as it has been handed down to us in Mark 3:20–21, 31–35 is of pre-Easter origin.[124]

This corresponds well with the observation that the image for the new people of God, which Jesus preferred, was the eschatological *familia Dei*.[125] It is the substitute for the earthly family, which is left behind by the itinerant preacher (Mark 10:29–30 par.). In this family God is the father (Matt 23:9). Jesus is the head of the household, and his followers are members of the household (Matt 10:25). The older women that follow him are his mothers, and the men his brothers (Mark 3:34 par.). Together they are all children even though adults in real life.[126]

This image of the *familia Dei* was Jesus' favorite most likely because it best communicated the theological essence of what Jesus was trying to impart. He wanted to gather together the new eschatological people of God, in which the love of God reigns just as it does in the intimate relationship between Jesus and the Father. What the family of God meant and how it differed from the ancient understanding of the *oikos* was illustrated by Jesus all the more clearly because he was often in or in front of the house of Peter as he taught on the subject. Everyone could see how he and the disciples lived together. Jesus not only spoke theoretically of this new family of God; he called real people together and he "lived

---

[122] Loffreda, "Tradizionale casa," 38. One should keep in mind that at the time of Jesus the house of Peter had only a small living room, which would have constituted a gathering space for only a small number of people. Even in a later phase, once the house was being used as a church house and the living room had perhaps been enlarged by partially removing a dividing wall, the room was only 7 x 6.5 m (Corbo, *House*, 42); see our definition of "church house," pp. 18–19.

[123] Roloff, *Kirche*, 40; cf. also Lohfink, *Jesus and Community*, 47–50.

[124] Lohfink, *Jesus and Community*, 48–50. For the historicity of this tradition, Mark 3:33–35 itself is strong evidence. The primitive church would not have been interested in fabricating a saying of Jesus in which he undermines the fourth commandment (cf. Pesch, *Markusevangelium*, 1:222–24; Hengel, *Nachfolge*, 14–15). If the early church had created such a saying, they would have been strongly criticized by the Jews for destroying the family. It is much more likely that this passage originated with Jesus' own behavior and teaching.

[125] Schniewind, *Markus*, at Mark 3:31–32; so too Jeremias, *Proclamation*, 169.

[126] Matt 11:25; Mark 10:24; cf. 2:5; 5:35. Cf. Michel, "μικρός," *TDNT* 4:648–59, esp. 650–56.

among them." Nowhere was this more evident than in the house of Peter in Capernaum.[127]

This overall perspective finds support in the observation that Jesus trained his disciples to do house-to-house and village-to-village outreach as well. This is particularly apparent in his mission discourses. These instructions correspond almost entirely to what we have just discovered regarding Jesus' own approach. If it can be convincingly demonstrated that Jesus trained his disciples to do house-to-house evangelism, by inference we can confirm that he also followed this approach. As a result of the analysis of the mission discourse in the sayings source (Luke 10:1–12), we gain not only a clearer picture of the disciples' approach to missional outreach but more clarity regarding Jesus' outreach methods as well. The precondition for all this, however, is that the mission discourse contain historically reliable information. Our next step, then, is to address these questions by examining the missional instructions given by Jesus to his disciples.

THE DISCIPLES' PRE-EASTER USE OF HOUSES

Now that we have examined Jesus' pre-Easter use of houses, we can ask if his disciples patterned their ministry after his. This seems likely considering the central significance of the house in the ancient world in general. It becomes even more probable if one considers that a master functions as an example for his pupils and this can be demonstrated for Jesus in his relationship to his disciples.[128] We ask again, "Do reliable texts confirm that the disciples used houses for ministry activities like Jesus, and if so, for which ministry activities?"

The Mission Discourse

The mission discourse in the sayings-of-Jesus tradition is very important for our investigation.[129] In contrast to the reservations of the "formgeschichtliche Schule," H. Schürmann extended the perspective regarding the Sitz im Leben of the Q tradition back to the time before Easter. His thesis

---

[127] For this reason, Trilling called Capernaum the "Schauplatz des Wirkens Jesu" (the theater or showcase for the works or ministry of Jesus). Cf. *Das wahre Israel*, 131.

[128] Rengstorf, "μανθάνω," *TDNT* 4:444–50; Larsson, *Christus*, 38–40; A. Schulz, *Nachfolgen*, 252–70; Daube, "Responsibilities"; Gerhardsson, *Memory*, 182–88; Meye, *Jesus*, esp. 9–113, 198–99.

[129] Luke 10:1–16 (17–20); cf. also Luke 9:1–6; Matt 9:37–38; 10:7–16; Mark 6:6b–11. That the mission discourse of Jesus was of central importance in the context of the early Christian house church has already been noticed by Schierse, "Zelle," 111–28, here 120; following him, Vogler, "Bedeutung," 785–94, 787; cf. also Gnilka, *Markus*, 1:240; Klauck, *Hausgemeinde*, 56–57.

that this tradition had a pre-Easter origin has found wide acceptance even internationally.[130] Today an overwhelming majority of scholars are in agreement: that the disciples were sent out to engage in their own preaching ministry can be considered one of the most certain facts in the entire history of Jesus.[131] There are many good reasons to support this.

All three Synoptic Gospels tell of at least one mission charge (Matt 10:1–40; Mark 6:7–13, 30; Luke 9:1–6, 10; 10:1–20). In addition, in the context of 1 Cor 9 a considerable number of similarities with the mission discourse in Luke 10:1–20 can be observed.[132] The connection between 1 Cor 9:14 and Luke 10:7 leads one to believe that Paul is referring to a Jesus saying related to the one in Luke. This means that, by the time of the composition of 1 Corinthians (ca. early 55), a fairly extensive mission discourse tradition must have existed.[133] Added to this is the observation that post-Easter christological content is totally missing in the mission discourse tradition.[134] Moreover, several of the ascetic regulations in the pre-Easter mission instructions were untypical for the post-Easter early Christian mission (Matt 10:9–10/Luke 9:3; Matt 10:4; cf. Mark 6:8–9; Luke 10:4, 7).[135] Finally, without a mission charge the disciples of Jesus would lose any discernible purpose for existing.[136]

R. Pesch summarizes, "That *the Twelve*, . . . who were sent out by Jesus to do mission two by two with a charge to preach repentance, to exorcize, and to heal, actually supported his missional efforts is historically credible."[137] The question remains, however, whether the details in the mission discourse regarding houses are historically reliable.

In general, scholars are in agreement that Luke 10:2–12 can be considered the oldest reference to the mission discourse.[138] Only a brief glance at

---

[130] Schürmann, "Die vorösterlichen Anfänge" (1960), 342–70. Before Schürmann, H. E. W. Turner, *Jesus*, 137; Davies, *Setting*, 421–34, and those scholars mentioned by Schürmann in Supplement, ibid., 64–65 and those mentioned by Riesner, *Jesus als Lehrer*, 74 n. 26.

[131] Hahn, *Verständnis*, 40; Hengel, *Nachfolge*, 82–89; Kasting, *Anfänge*, 125; Bornkamm, *Jesus*, 131; Testa, "Discorsi"; Ellis, "New Directions," 303; Schweizer, *Markus*, 71–72; Manson, *Sayings*, 73; Gnilka, *Markus*, 1:241; Trautmann, *Zeichenhafte Handlungen*, 168–233; the historicity of the mission charge is rejected by Bultmann, *Geschichte*, 155–56; Haenchen, *Weg Jesu*, 223; Hoffmann, *Studien*, 262. Cf. J. Vincent, *Disciples*, 65 n. 39, for additional exegetes pro and contra.

[132] Fjärstedt, *Synoptic Tradition*, 64–77. Following him, Allison, "Pauline Epistles." Contra, Tuckett, "Paul."

[133] Beyschlag, *Clemens Romanus*, 34.

[134] Hengel, *Origins*, 62.

[135] Ibid.

[136] Hengel, *Nachfolge*, 82–83.

[137] Pesch, *Markusevangelium*, 1:331.

[138] Even Wellhausen (*Lucae*, 48–49), Bultmann (*Geschichte*, 351), but also Schürmann (*Traditionsgeschichtliche Untersuchungen*, 147–49) have seen in Luke 10:5–12 the original Q text. Hahn (*Verständnis*, 33–34), Kasting (*Anfänge*, 125 n. 5), and Lührmann (*Redaktion*, 59) assume that Luke preserved the original Q text in

the present state of research, however, shows that forming an opinion regarding specifics is much more difficult.[139] The literary-critical attempts to divide Luke 10:2–12 into two or more layers have resulted in a great variety of complicated hypotheses without leading to any kind of consensus. This demonstrates the limitations of the literary-critical method and encourages caution regarding judgments on whether individual verses originally belonged to Q. As a result, we are forced to look for other criteria to determine historicity.

F. Hahn has pointed out that both mission discourses, Luke 10:2–12 and Matt 9:37–10:16, are constructed according to the same scheme. "The basic form consists first of the mission charge, then the regulations regarding equipment and outfitting, further the instructions regarding behavior in houses, and finally the instructions relating to behavior in the town/village."[140] The parallel introductory expressions in verse 5a (house) and in verses 8a, 10a (town) are also indications of a uniform composition.[141] This is not to say that there are no traces of Lukan redaction, but they are minimal.[142] Individual missional instructions need to be distinguished,[143] and there are obvious tensions that have often been observed in the text.[144] For the most part, however, these tensions can be resolved by assuming that the

---

10:2–12; also Hoffmann (*Studien*, 267–87) and S. Schulz (*Spruchquelle*, 408–19) categorize the text as Q.

[139] Cf. the discussion by Gehring, *Hausgemeinde*, 95–96. Apart from Schürmann, most exegetes assume a post-Easter origin for Q. In contrast, Hahn (*Verständnis*, 34–36), Hengel (*Nachfolge*, 84–85), and Lührmann (*Redaktion*, 59) are of the opinion that the mission discourse in Luke (esp. 10:8–9, 10–11) gives us insight into very old tradition that most likely originated with the historical Jesus.

[140] Hahn, *Verständnis*, 34.

[141] Ibid.; I. H. Marshall, *Luke*, 414. Against Schürmann (*Lukasevangelium*, 2:72), who sees this as Lukan harmonization.

[142] Jeremias (*Sprache*, 184–89) remarks on Luke 10:1–20, "Except for the introductory verses 10:1–2a, the pericope is almost free of redactional intervention" (189) and to be considered tradition.

[143] But they should not be totally separated. S. Schulz (*Spruchquelle*, 409) considers extremely improbable the assumption that these individual instructions were originally in circulation separately from one another. Cf. Schweizer, *Markus*, 68, for a different view.

[144] Early on, Wellhausen (*Lucae*, 48–49) pointed to tension in the sequence of events: In the present sequence, the entrance into a city and the reception in it are mentioned after the delegation has already entered the houses. In addition, the food rule appears in the house (7b) as well as in the city instructions (8b) and is seen therefore as a bothersome doublet (e.g., Schürmann, *Lukasevangelium*, 2:71; cf. Manson, *Sayings*, 74). For some scholars, these tensions as well as a few others justify separating the house and city instructions into two different layers; e.g., Manson, *Sayings*, 73–74; Roloff, *Apostolat*, 151; Hoffmann, *Studien*, 268–83; Schürmann, *Traditionsgeschichtliche Untersuchungen*, 137–49, esp. 147–49 (but with totally different conclusions regarding the oldest layer). In contrast, S. Schulz (*Spruchquelle*, 409) sees a uniform composition from the very beginning of the pericope's tradition history.

instructions were originally more extensive and that in the present form in Luke we have an abridged summary of pre-Lukan tradition.[145]

The question is whether Matthew summarizes the two instructions (house and city rules) into one or Luke created two instructions out of one by interjecting 8a. In spite of the arguments made by P. Hoffmann for the latter, it appears that there is more to support the former.[146] Hoffmann even admits that his arguments are not compelling.[147] The proximity of Luke 10:8a and Matt 10:11a is an indication of origin from a mutual source. The suggestion that verse 9 (without 8) was added very early to the house instruction in 10:5–6, and 10:7a, b, is based on the dubious assumption that verses 8a and 10 originally did not mention the city mission.[148] Even Hoffmann in the end is forced to presuppose the "city" in the second source as well.[149] It makes more sense if the change from house to town takes place in 8a.

There are numerous details that also appear to speak for the antiquity, and so the historicity, of the report in Luke 10:1–12. In it many archaic features have been preserved: 10:1, the disciples are sent out in pairs;[150] 10:4, the greeting prohibition[151] and the rigorous nature of the rules regarding equipment and outfitting;[152] 10:5–6, the expression "peace" and "son of peace"[153] as well as the notion of rest and peace returning;[154] 10:5–7a, the combination of coming and staying;[155] 10:7a, the instruction to stay, eat, and

---

[145] I. H. Marshall, *Luke*, 421.
[146] Hoffmann, *Studien*, 276–83.
[147] Ibid., 282.
[148] Ibid., 288, 298.
[149] Ibid., 280–81.
[150] Jeremias, "Paarweise Sendung," 134–35.
[151] Easton, *Luke*, 160; with him I. H. Marshall, *Gospel of Luke*, 418: "The command to dispense with them [the greetings] is so unusual that it must be original."
[152] This rule is documented in Q and in Mark (I. H. Marshall, *Gospel of Luke*, 31–32, 352–53). For Marshall, Matthew and Luke had different versions of Q available to them. Therefore, Luke 10:4 needs to be supplemented with the staff prohibition in 9:3 and Matt 10:10. Cf. also Percy, *Botschaft*, 29; Laufen, "Doppelüberlieferung," 265; Hahn, *Verständnis*, 36; Hengel, *Nachfolge*, 84, all of whom consider the instruction authentic. Hengel points out that it is "unthinkable that the early church would have created such a tradition, because the instructions contradict the real missional conditions of the post-Easter period." Against Hoffmann, *Studien*, 312–31; S. Schulz, *Spruchquelle*, 409, 414–15.
[153] Cf. Hoffmann, *Studien*, 297. With the peace greeting, the messengers of Jesus proclaim "the coming of the kingdom; their appearance belongs then to the events of the end times, just as Jesus' appearance did (cf. Luke 10:23f/Matt 13:16f)." The union of the Beatitudes (Luke 6:20–21; Matt 5:1–2 = Q) with the peace message of the end-time prophets according to Isa 52:7 and Nah 2:1 points to an origin in Jesus himself. Cf. Stuhlmacher, *Vorgeschichte*, 147–49.
[154] Εἰρήνη as the designation for salvation in the full eschatological sense and the Semitism υἱὸς εἰρήνης, which occurs in the NT only here, are pre-Lukan. The absence of the copula in the peace greeting must also be classified as a pre-Lukan Semitism. Cf. Jeremias, *Sprache*, 21, 76, 185.
[155] The instructions regarding the peace greeting, the sons of peace, and staying with them belong to the earliest stage in the tradition-building process because

drink;[156] 10:7b, the worker and his wages;[157] 10:8b, the instruction "to eat what is set before you";[158] 10:9, 11, the reference to healing and the kingdom of God;[159] 10:11, the eschatological tension and the intense earnestness;[160] and lastly, 10:17, the return of the disciples to Jesus[161] after their outreach.[162]

---

the instructions on entering the houses and the greeting demand a continuation in order to make a statement with adequate content (against Hahn, *Verständnis*, 36, who sees v. 7 entirely as a secondary extension). Cf. also Hoffmann, *Studien*, 296.

[156] Luke 10:7a must be considered old tradition because of the doublet in Mark 6:10b (Klauck, *Hausgemeinde*, 57 n. 99). In addition, according to Jeremias, *Sprache*, 185, the very rare poetic form ἔσθω occurs only three times in prose in the NT: Mark 1:6; Luke 22:30, and our passage. This speaks for the pre-Lukan origin of the expression ἔσθοντες καὶ πίνοντες, which used to be included in the older editions of Nestle, *Novum Testamentum Graece*. Cf. also Hoffmann, *Studien*, 297. According to Hoffmann, this instruction originates, in all probability, with the earthly Jesus.

[157] According to Dalman, *Worte Jesu*, 210, this saying is not documented as a proverb in Jewish literature; this goes against an assumption of Bultmann (*Geschichte*, 107) that it was such a proverb that the early church included in an instruction speech that the church itself created. The often observed connection of 10:7b to 1 Cor 9:4–18 and 2 Cor 11:7–13 can be understood not only as a thought taken from the apostolic policy regarding issues of support and subsistence and inserted into the mission discourse (cf. Schürmann, *Lukasevangelium*, 2:70; Klauck, *Hausgemeinde*, 57) but also from the opposite direction as well. If Paul is referring to Luke 10:7b in 1 Cor 9:14, which has often been assumed (cf. Tuckett, "Paul"; Harvey, "Workman," esp. 218–19; Fjärstedt, *Synoptic Tradition*, 64–77; Beyschlag, *Clemens Romanus*, 34), then this instruction regarding the worker and his wages was known quite early as a missional rule of the Lord, and we know of no better traditional context for Luke 10:7b than the mission discourse of the Q material, specifically Luke 10:5–7.

[158] This does not fit well with the post-Easter Palestinian church, but very well with Jesus' attitude regarding dietary policy (Hengel, "Ursprünge," 36). Cf. Paschen, *Rein*, 177; with him Pesch, *Markusevangelium*, 2:379. According to Luke 10:8b, Jesus liberates the messengers from the concern whether the food given to them is allowed to be eaten according to the Jewish (pharisaic) dietary policy (Rengstorf, *Lukas*, 137; D. Schlatter, *Evangelium des Lukas*, 277). Thus v. 8b is not simply a repetition of v. 7b; v. 7b is not yet referring to the dietary policy, as v. 7c demonstrates (Schürmann, *Lukasevangelium*, 2:69, 73). For the time of Jesus in Palestinian territory, one would need to interpret the passage in the following way: "Don't pay any attention to *pharisaic* dietary policy."

[159] Hahn, *Verständnis*, 35–36: "The charge to proclaim the kingdom of God approaching and to perform miracles as Jesus did . . . is to be viewed as authentic." With him, Hengel, *Nachfolge*, 84–85; Lührmann, *Redaktion*, 59. Cf. also Hoffmann, *Studien*, 299. The connection of healing and of the presence of the kingdom is documented in the authentic Jesus word of Luke 11:20/Matt 12:28, and there it is also transferred over to the ministry of the disciples (Luke 11:23/Matt 12:30).

[160] Cf. Schweizer, *Markus*, 68.

[161] Cf. also Luke 9:10. Here the mission charge to the disciples is temporary. After Easter the return to Jesus was no longer possible. This is obviously a pre-Easter situation. In this context the double transmission needs to be pointed out. In the second edition by Mark 10:7–16, the disciples no longer return to Jesus, which reflects the post-Easter situation.

[162] Here the discussion regarding the historic value of the mission charge in Luke 10:2–12 is discontinued in order not to overburden this study with excessive

In summary, with Schürmann we are confident that, on the basis of the historicity of the mission charge itself, the pre-Easter origin of a large part of the sayings material and, in particular, the mission discourse in Luke 10:2–12 can be assumed.[163] According to Hahn, M. Hengel, and Lührmann, Luke 10:2–12 gives us insight into very old instructions most likely originating with Jesus himself.[164] The radical charge to enter into mission without equipment and outfitting, to renounce all belongings, and thus to be dependent on the hospitality of houses surely corresponds with the attitude and practice of Jesus.[165] Therefore, Luke 10:2–12 can be seen as dependable pre-Easter tradition originating with Jesus, even though the question of the unity of the pericope as such remains open and the possibility of minimal Lukan redaction is to be expected. We can thus assume that the equipment, house, and town instructions in Luke 10:2–12 originate with the earthly Jesus and were passed on by him to his disciples before Easter.

House-to-House and Village-to-Village Missional Outreach

It seems likely that in his mission discourse Jesus instructed his disciples to use houses in a manner similar to the way he did: as fixed quarters and a base of operations for his mission.[166] What can we learn from the mission discourse in Luke 10:1–12 about Jesus' instructions regarding the use of houses and about the disciples' actual use of houses in the context of their missional outreach?

The first thing that strikes us is that Jesus sends his disciples out in pairs. The origin of this practice can be found in OT witness regulations. According to these rules, a testimony that was confirmed by two or three witnesses was considered authenticated.[167] The implication of this in our context is that, sent out in pairs, the disciples saw themselves as authenticated missionary witnesses giving testimony regarding the coming of God's kingdom.

In addition, the two stages in the mission discourse—house (5a) and town (8a)—have been mentioned above. These two stages correspond to the

---

detail. For additional arguments for the historicity of the mission discourse tradition, cf. Gehring, *Hausgemeinde*, 93–103.

[163] Schürmann attempts to demonstrate the probable need to separate Luke 10:3–7 from 10:8–11 and assigns Luke 10:3, 4, 5–7a to a pre-Markan and pre-Easter layer of tradition.

[164] See n. 139.

[165] Hahn, *Verständnis*, 36; Schürmann, *Lukasevangelium*, 1:71; cf. also Theissen, *Social Reality*, 45; with him Klauck, *Hausgemeinde*, 56–60. Theissen assumes the authenticity and thus the pre-Easter origin of the radical itinerant tradition.

[166] Ravarotto, "'Casa,'" esp. 405.

[167] Jeremias, "Paarweise Sendung," 134–35. This statute, documented in Deut 17:6; 19:5; Num 35:30, appears again in the NT quite often: Matt 18:16; 26:59–60; John 8:17; 2 Cor 13:1; 1 Tim 5:19; Heb 10:28.

steps of an old mission strategy as follows.[168] Missional outreach began with a house, that is, with a family, which probably meant with the head of the household (see below). It spread from there in ever larger circles, reaching its climax once the entire town had been exposed to the message of the coming kingdom. Seen in this light, the house and household were the immediate mission objective; the house fellowship was the starting and gathering point for the final objective, which was reaching the entire town or city.[169] House-to-house missional outreach, as the first stage of proclamation, was actually person-to-person. The second stage involved citywide outreach; at this point it is not entirely clear whether this stage involved reaching the town/city person-to-person, house-to-house, or via open-air or public proclamation (e.g., in the streets, at the marketplace, or in the synagogue).[170]

At any rate, the predominant theme is undoubtedly seen in the progression of the mission from house to city. Apparently, this is the view of Luke, who in so writing reflects the missional approach of his own congregation (or the Q community?).[171] Nevertheless, it is also quite possible that Luke at the same time not only wanted to[172] but in fact did pass on reliable historic information and that Jesus really did give such missional instructions to his disciples. After all, Jesus took this same approach, as can be clearly demonstrated at least for Capernaum and the "evangelical triangle" (see above).

As previously mentioned, these stages from house to city have often been noticed in the past. Most exegetes, however, see them as an old *post-Easter* early Christian mission strategy, which is more developed than would have been possible before Easter, in part because the instructions attempt to solve problems that were characteristic for a later period. The assumption being made here is that such problems could not and did not exist during the time of Jesus. But in reality there is no reason to view the house and city instructions as a later development other than because of an a priori reluctance to go back beyond the Easter cutoff. Scholars have also attempted to separate the house and city instructions from one another in order to support the "later development" argument. This was done, however, not with historical but primarily with literary-critical arguments.

Our interest is primarily in the first stage of this old missional approach, the "house missional rule"[173] (Luke 10:5–7), as we find here most of

---

[168] F. Hauck, *Lukas*, 139–40. For him, this is more formal than the content of the original is. Grundmann, *Lukas*, 209; Ernst, *Lukas*, 334; Klauck, *Hausgemeinde*, 57.

[169] Actually we are dealing here with villages or towns for the most part, but because Luke uses the term πόλις, we will continue to use the word "city," at least intermittently.

[170] For the latter, cf. F. Hauck, *Lukas*, 140. The three are not, however, mutually exclusive. As we have seen, Jesus was involved in all of the above: he preached publicly in synagogues and in the open but also in houses.

[171] Hoffmann, *Studien*, 278; with him Ernst, *Lukas*, 334.

[172] Schürmann, *Lukasevangelium*, 2:70–71, 73–74.

[173] Klauck, *Hausgemeinde*, 57.

the references to the house, the focus of our study. The house mission rule needs to be seen in the overall context of the mission discourse of the Q material (Luke 10:1–12). The lifestyle of the itinerant missionary, as it is described in Luke 10:4 and 10:5–6, had a negative side (radical asceticism and poverty, 10:4a) and a positive side (the promise of hospitality, 10:7a, b), which are to be understood as parallel and complementary to one another. This harsh requirement to live in radical poverty is softened by the promise of hospitality, the temporary nature of the charge, and the geographical conditions in Galilee. The radical lifestyle of the messengers of Jesus is, in contrast to the Cynics, not an end in itself but the unavoidable and yet coincidental side effect, a necessary consequence of their charge to do missional outreach.[174]

Initially, the "house rule" is concerned with regulating the issue of room and board necessary for the intended town outreach. After arriving in a certain location, the disciples, who were sent out by Jesus as itinerant missionaries for a limited time (Luke 10:4; 9:2, 3; Mark 6:7–9), were to look for a house at random. The house into which the disciples enter is to be given the peace greeting.[175] If a child of peace is there, peace will rest upon him or her. The disciples are then to stay in this house (7a), without moving from house to house (7d), and they are to eat and drink whatever they are given.[176] In other words, they are supposed to accept the customary hospitality of this household.

The question of quarters is thus clarified: the messengers are to move into quarters provided by the host and are to remain there until they leave town (cf. Luke 9:4 and Mark 6:10).[177] A change of houses is not allowed; the messengers are to occupy fixed quarters. This house is to become a starting point, a kind of headquarters, a center and base of operations for the following stage of the mission, reaching the entire town. In addition, the question of board is also regulated: the missionaries are to allow the host to feed them; they are to sit at the table of the *oikos* not as beggars but as guests.

What is implied here is the messengers' right to room and board on the basis that they serve the one whose hospitality they enjoy.[178] They offer the host something of high value and as a result are entitled to be treated as guests. As "wages" for their spiritual assistance they receive material

---

[174] Cf. R. Horsley, *Sociology*, 123.

[175] Nowhere in the ancient East was a person allowed simply to enter a house. The initial encounter always took place in front of the house, outside the house at the front door. Only in large cities was this not the case.

[176] Verse 7a has a parallel in Matt 10:11 and Mark 6:10/Luke 9:4, but v. 7d is without parallel. It is therefore not clear if it was already in Q (cf. Schulz, *Spruchquelle*, 406) or if Luke added it as clarification.

[177] In contrast to the instructions in *Did.* 11:5, here a longer-lasting stay in one house is prescribed.

[178] Schürmann, *Lukasevangelium*, 2:69; Polag, *Christologie*, 68; Hoffmann, *Studien*, 301.

assistance. The instructions exclude the observance of any specific dietary rules. At the same time, the messengers are to be content with whatever is given to them. They have no claim to any kind of special menu. Acceptance of them concerns not only these outward details; it presumes the household's spiritual acceptance of the itinerant's message as well. The messengers are "thus accepted into the house community of faith—and that may be the primary intention of these simple instructions. The meal documents the fellowship that exists between the hosts and the messengers."[179] Eating and drinking are to be understood as an act of table fellowship secured by the household's acceptance of the peace greeting.[180] Here we see, within an already existing sociological house fellowship, the formation of a spiritual (ecclesiological-theological?) house fellowship between the family in the house and the messengers. In this way the first community focal points of the Jesus movement come into existence, in which the house serves as the assembly place for the new converts.

In this context we might wonder to whom the peace greeting was given and what its content was. Unfortunately, verse 5 does not reveal much regarding the content of the greeting (but cf. 1:9). The greeting formula is quite simple: εἰρήνη τῷ οἴκῳ τούτῳ, "Peace to this house." A greeting upon entering a house was common at that time (Luke 1:28–29, 40–41), including this exact formula.[181] Nevertheless, most scholars agree that this greeting is more than just a polite yet empty phrase, that it is pregnant with meaning.[182] It appears that Jesus filled the greeting with new content: εἰρήνη does not only include a person's outward well-being; it embraces "the eschatological salvation *[Heilsein]* of the whole person."[183]

The expression "son/child of peace" is of central significance in our passage and, as such, key to understanding the house instructions. The

---

[179] Hoffmann, *Studien,* 297; with him Klauck, *Hausgemeinde,* 57.

[180] The tension between the implicit instructions to evangelize numerous houses and the explicit command not to go from house to house has often been noted (I. H. Marshall, *Gospel of Luke,* 421). This tension is accentuated if we assume that Hoffmann is correct in suggesting that they enjoyed table fellowship. This table fellowship would need to be offered to every household that was willing to accept the message of the kingdom. The suggestion here that the instructions intend the first house to become a base of operation from which the other houses could be reached would resolve this apparent tension. We can assume that the instructions were originally longer, perhaps dealing with issues such as this. In that case Luke 10 would be a compressed version of the older instructions.

[181] John 20:19, 21, 26; Luke 24:36; W. Foerster, "εἰρήνη," *TDNT* 2:408–17, here 412. In Semitic usage, greeting and peace are expressed with the same word; cf. *m. 'Abot* 4:15b; Str-B 1:380–85.

[182] Some scholars assume that Luke filled the term with new content. Cf. Schürmann, *Lukasevangelium,* 2:69. Others assume that it was Jesus himself who filled it with new content, which is also the view taken here; cf. Grundmann, *Lukas,* 209; I. H. Marshall, *Gospel of Luke,* 419.

[183] Schlatter, *Evangelium des Lukas,* 276–77. Cf. also Acts 10:36.

person who is receptive to this peace is designated "child of peace."[184] "To rest in/upon" is an OT expression and has to do with the Spirit resting in or upon a person (Num 11:25; 2 Kings 2:15). As such, the peace greeting is to be understood as a transfer of spiritual power, which can return to the greeter if the person greeted is not receptive.[185] The peace greeting therefore contains the power of salvation; this peace is *the* salvation gift offered to all.[186]

This instruction is to be understood within the context of the kingdom proclamation of Jesus. The disciples are Jesus' coworkers and are actively engaged in his ministry in that they participate in spreading the kingdom message.[187] With the peace greeting the messengers proclaim the coming of the *basileia tou theou*.[188] This implies that the peace greeting is integrally connected to the proclamation of the kingdom of God. In Luke 10:9 the content of the peace greeting is more clearly defined.[189] The mission charge of the messengers is to heal and proclaim the presence of the reign of God just as Jesus did. Anyone who accepts the messengers and their peace greeting also accepts Jesus' message of the coming reign of God (10:9, 11).[190] It thus becomes unmistakably clear that the peace greeting is all about mission, more specifically about mission from house to house.[191] The assumption that it is a matter of house mission is supported by the observation that apparently both Mark and Matthew also have missional outreach from house to house in

---

[184] Str-B 1:476–78; 2:166. The idiomatic phrase occurs in classical and Hellenistic Greek as well as in the Semitic languages (cf. Danker, "υἱός Phrases"; Schweizer, "υἱός," *TDNT* 8:363–65) and can describe someone who has peace or someone who has been appointed or is qualified to receive peace. The latter is most likely the intent in the context of this passage. See Hoffmann, *Studien*, 296. Cf. also Ernst, *Lukas*, 333.

[185] Schürmann, *Lukasevangelium*, 2:68. Rabbis also understood the greeting to be so real that they saw a (prohibited) interest payment in it (references in Str-B 1:383i).

[186] Luke 1:79; 2:14; 6:20–21; Matt 11:5; Isa 52:7, Nah 2:1. Against Schürmann, *Lukasevangelium*, 2:68, and with Grundmann, *Lukas*, 209; Hoffmann, *Studien*, 297; Ernst, *Lukas*, 333; I. H. Marshall, *Gospel of Luke*, 420.

[187] Cf. Hengel's understanding of discipleship in *Nachfolge*, 80–82.

[188] Manson, *Sayings*, 257: "It [the greeting] is a manifestation of the kingdom of God in word . . . an announcement that 'the kingdom of God has come nigh to you.'" Cf. also Hoffmann, *Studien*, 297. The kingdom message cannot be reduced, however, to the proclamation of a contemporary political peace, as Hoffmann suggests (307–11), but concerns rather the eschatological peace with God.

[189] Cf. Mark 1:15; Matt 4:17; Luke 11:20 (Q).

[190] Schürmann, *Lukasevangelium*, 2:69. Cf. also 10:16.

[191] Cf. Hoffmann, *Studien*, 297. Cf. W. Foerster, "εἰρήνη," *TDNT* 2:400–417, esp. 413–14; Grundmann, *Lukas*, 209. I. H. Marshall, *Gospel of Luke*, 420, notes that Luke 10:5–6 "does not refer to finding a house in which there are already disciples, but to offering salvation to those who are willing to receive it." Against Schürmann, *Lukasevangelium*, 2:68; *Traditionsgeschichtliche Untersuchungen*, 147–48; and with him Uro, "Sheep," 138–39; neither believes that Luke 10:5–6 refers to a house mission.

mind (Mark 6:10; esp. Matt 10:12, 13).[192] Remaining in a house only makes sense if, beyond the initial confrontation with the salvation message, the messengers are allowed to stay to further nurture and establish a faith community. Today many scholars are in agreement that the house church was the starting point for church development in post-Easter early Christian missions. The mission instructions indicate that the pre-Easter house mission, as Jesus and his disciples practiced it, was likely the embryonic form of house-to-house missional outreach and church development practiced after Easter.

But the question remains: How did house missional outreach actually function? Who is the one who is greeted and accepts or rejects the peace greeting? It is reported in Luke 10:5 that the house is to be greeted. Obviously this is intended in a sociological and not an architectural sense: the *oikos* addressed here is the household, that is, the family.[193] As previously mentioned, a Jewish household even in Galilee consisted of father, mother, children, and servants.[194] Surely the messengers would not have greeted the slaves, and most likely not the mother or children either. In the Palestinian setting the only conceivable person to receive the greeting would have been the head of the household.[195] He alone would have been able to accept the greeting and offer an invitation. Only with his permission would the messengers have been able to stay in the house. He alone was able to make a religious decision, a decision that the entire household would customarily embrace.[196] When the head (and his household) accepted the peace greeting and provided hospitality for Jesus' messengers, he proved himself to be a "son of peace." The peace of God had already begun its work within his heart and mind, and he and his entire household were prepared and ordained for further gifts of grace.[197]

Does this mean that house-to-house missional outreach already at the time of Jesus consisted initially of winning the head of the household for the cause of Christ? Are the disciples being instructed here to reach the householder and with him his entire household for Christ and in this way establish

---

[192] Cf. Gnilka, *Markus,* 1:239–40, and *Matthäusevangelium* 1:368.

[193] I. H. Marshall, *Gospel of Luke,* 419.

[194] Cf. Gaudemet, "Familie"; Sandnes, "A Family in Antiquity," ch. 6 in *New Family,* 47–55; Dassmann and Schöllgen, "Haus II"; and most recently R. Horsley, *Galilee,* 195–201, 203–5; Perdue, Bleukinsopp, Collins, and Meyers, *Families,* for a discussion of the significance of the household at this time.

[195] Cf. Schürmann, *Lukasevangelium,* 2:68–70.

[196] Granted, houses existed at the time of Jesus in which a woman was the head of the household, even though this was the exception (cf. R. Horsley, *Galilee,* 195–201). It is therefore possible that a woman as head of the household could have accepted the peace greeting. We have already seen one likely NT example of a woman as householder: the house in Bethany with Martha as its head (cf. Luke 10:38, 42; John 11:1); cf., however, John 12:2, where one gets the impression that Lazarus exercises the function of the head of the household: while he sits at the table with Jesus Martha serves them the meal.

[197] Schürmann, *Lukasevangelium,* 2:68.

a base of operations for reaching the rest of the town? Unfortunately, we are not able to define the role of the household head with final exegetical certainty. The mission discourse does not give us enough unambiguous information on the matter. But our above exegetical examination does seem to indicate that the disciples practiced a kind of "householder evangelism." This seems all the more likely when we consider that Jesus evidently took this approach himself (see above). In addition to the house of Peter in Capernaum, we know of sedentary followers of Jesus in Bethany and even the names of householders there: Martha (or Lazarus) and Simon.[198] In Jericho we know of a certain Zacchaeus, the head of a household who became a sedentary follower of Jesus (Luke 19:1–10). It could be that Jesus originally won at least some of these people for his kingdom message through house-to-house missional outreach as it is described in Luke 10:5–6.

The flow of the mission discourse with its progression in two stages—house mission and city mission—points in the direction of householder evangelism as well. As we will see, this approach was also a pattern observable in early Christian outreach, particularly in the Pauline mission. It also fits well with our sociohistorical knowledge of the ancient world as an "*oikos* society." One is inclined to ask if it would have been advisable to take any other approach in an *oikos* society.

Returning to the instructions on house-to-house mission, upon closer examination we notice that two different lifestyles are implied in these instructions. On the one hand, we see disciples sent out for duty as itinerant preachers for a limited period of time. Patterned after Jesus, as his followers they practice an ethos temporarily renouncing home, family, and belongings.[199] On the other hand, this lifestyle implies that there was a second that from the very beginning was every bit as legitimate and even a necessary precondition for the first lifestyle. The outreach of the itinerant missionaries with the renouncement of all belongings would not have been possible without the existence of household heads and their families who made their houses, their belongings, and their hospitality available to the itinerants and their sedentary followers. "The missionaries could not have existed in a vacuum. For clothing as well as room and board, they were dependent on the houses, which provided them a solid platform in the villages and towns."[200]

This dual movement—the renouncement of one's own home, family, and belongings, on the one hand, and the recovery of all of these in the form of a spiritual household community (later as a house church), on the other—

---

[198] See discussion, pp. 43–44, nn. 101 and 102.
[199] Luke 9:58 par.; Mark 6:4; 3:21; Matt 8:21–22 par.; 10:37 par.; Cf. Hengel, *Nachfolge*, 16–17, 96, who considers the itinerant ethos of the disciples to have originated with Jesus because of its break with the family (Matt 8:21–22). For a somewhat different position, cf. Theissen, *Sociology*, 8–23, and *Social Reality*, 33–59; with him for the most part is Klauck, *Hausgemeinde*, 57–59.
[200] Klauck, *Hausgemeinde*, 58.

is clearly illustrated in the authentic words of Jesus in Mark 10:29–30: "no one who has left home or brothers or sisters or mother or father or children or fields for me and the gospel will fail to receive a hundred times as much in this present age (homes, brothers, sisters, mothers, children and fields . . .)."[201] Mark 10:29–30 can also be understood in connection with 3:20–21, 31–35 as a confirmation of the mission instructions of Luke 10:2–12. In Mark 10:29–30 the existence of a second lifestyle complementary to the itinerant style is implicitly assumed: sedentary followers made their house and home, their belongings and goods available to the mission, the missionaries, and the group of followers who emerged from their missional outreach.

We can assume that these new houses, the new families with their relatives mentioned in Mark 10:29–30, were pre-Easter house communities of faith that came into existence through the missionary work of Jesus' disciples. Analogous to the establishment of a faith community in the house of Peter in Capernaum (cf. Mark 3:20–21, 31–35),[202] we see the formation of community through the proclamation of the kingdom of God. The disciples continued what Jesus had begun in Capernaum as they met together with their new faith companions in various houses. Throughout the countryside sedentary cell-like house communities came into existence, communities that, along with Jesus and his disciples, were experiencing and expecting the coming of the kingdom.

These houses offered Jesus' disciples, who as itinerant missionaries had left their homes for a time, not only quarters with a roof over their heads, not only room and board, not simply the material necessities for their existence, but also a family community and a home. These houses became in a figurative sense "a home for the homeless."[203] It is thus confirmed once again that houses played a very important role in making pre-Easter missional outreach possible.

Conclusions

The house formed a necessary precondition for missional outreach even before Easter. This is evident in the instructions given in the commissioning of the twelve. It served as fixed quarters for the missionaries, as a source for room and board, as a place for (table) fellowship with new believers and thus as a gathering place of the new faith community. In addition, the house was the immediate objective (with the town as the final objective) as

---

[201] It is of note that nothing is reported regarding wives. Some apparently did participate in the itinerant lifestyle of their missionary husbands (cf. 1 Cor 9:5); Klauck, *Hausgemeinde,* 59.

[202] See the discussion of Mark 3:20–21, 31–35 on pp. 47–48.

[203] Cf. Elliott, *Home,* who uses this expression for the house churches he sees in 1 Peter—differently, however, than I am using it here.

well as a starting point for missional outreach to a town or city. In light of the missional approach of Jesus in Capernaum and in the "evangelical triangle," it can be assumed that the disciples, after winning a household in a given village or town, attempted to reach the surrounding countryside from it. There are also good reasons to believe that house missional outreach consisted of reaching the head of the household first and thus the rest of his house. The missionaries were thereby able to establish a base of operations for missional outreach to the rest of the town and the surrounding area. The picture of Jesus and his disciples as engaged exclusively in a "shotgun" missional approach needs to be revised.[204] Even before Easter they practiced "regional mission" from a central operational base in one village or town out to the surrounding area.[205]

Characteristic for the pre-Easter mission of Jesus and his disciples was the double movement consisting of the renouncement of one's own house and home, on the one hand, and the recovery of a spiritual household community/family, on the other. This presupposes that complementary to the itinerant lifestyle a second option for following Jesus existed, every bit as legitimate and in fact necessary. This sedentary lifestyle was the material and financial prerequisite for the existence of itinerant missionaries. Both lifestyles were very closely intertwined; both were integral elements of pre-Easter missional outreach.

---

[204] A "shotgun" approach ("Durchreisemission") is mission understood as itinerant missionaries traveling from location to location without staying long, preaching their message, and then moving on without building solid faith communities or establishing churches that were able to stand on their own.

[205] In my opinion, it cannot be said that Jesus did not establish communities as a part of his itinerant mission; the proclamation of the coming of the kingdom of God in itself led to community formation. Wherever the householder and the rest of his household became followers of Jesus, a new fellowship or faith community emerged. Against Ollrog, *Paulus*, 150–61.

CHAPTER THREE

The Post-Easter Use of Houses in the Primitive Jerusalem Church

AS NOTED, JESUS MADE USE OF HOUSES in various ways in his missional outreach, and he instructed his disciples to take the same approach. Can it be demonstrated that houses played a significant role in the missional efforts of the primitive church in Jerusalem? This is to be expected considering the importance of the *oikos* in the ancient world[1] as well as its significant role in pre-Easter missions. It is all the more surprising to discover that until recently the household setting for assembly in the context of the Jerusalem church has been a neglected topic of Acts research.

JERUSALEM HOUSES IN THE BOOK OF ACTS

Apart from a few indirect allusions in the Pauline Epistles, the book of Acts is our only source of information on the use of houses in the primitive church in Jerusalem. With this, however, we are confronted with a problem. To this day an overwhelming majority of scholars consider the historical information given in Acts to be unreliable. This is especially true of the report on the Jerusalem church because Luke projected his own ideal image into it. Historians and exegetes must be aware of the overall literary and theological concept behind Luke's two-volume work as they read and interpret the book of Acts. But it needs to be pointed out that in the last twenty years a new trend in scholarship can be observed when it comes to assessing the historical reliability of the book of Acts.[2] In the following exegetical analysis, the most

---

[1] Cf. the history of scholarship, pp. 1–16.
[2] Stuhlmacher even speaks of an apparent turning point in the assessment of the reliability of Acts, *Grundlegung*, 227. The turning point is, to a large extent, due to the fact that scholars are returning to an older view held by the early church with all its historical implications: that Luke actually was a coworker and travel companion of Paul. Cf. the study by Thornton, *Zeuge*. Regarding reliability in general, cf. Hengel, *Zur urchristlichen Geschichtsschreibung*, 11–61; Winter, *Book of Acts;* Hemer, *Acts;* I. H. Marshall, *Luke: Historian*, 13–76; F. F. Bruce, *New Testament Documents*, 80–92. Cf. also Harnack, *Beiträge*, vols. 1–4; Wikenhauser, *Apostelgeschichte;* E. Meyer, *Ursprung*, vol. 3.

important references to houses in the context of the primitive church in Jerusalem will be examined for their historical reliability.

Acts 1:12-15

> Then they returned to Jerusalem from the hill called the Mount of Olives, a Sabbath day's walk from the city. When they arrived [in the city], they went upstairs into the [upper] room where they were staying. Those present were Peter, John, James and Andrew; Philip and Thomas, Bartholomew and Matthew; James son of Alphaeus and Simon the Zealot, and Judas son of James. They all joined together constantly in prayer, along with the women and Mary the mother of Jesus, and with his brothers. In those days Peter stood up among the believers (a group numbering about a hundred and twenty) and [spoke]. (Acts 1:12-16)

Pre-Lukan Tradition and Lukan Redaction

The text in 1:12-14 is not a Lukan "summary." It contains an older tradition used by Luke in Luke 24:52-53.[3] The biblical form Ἰερουσαλήμ, which occurs twice in our text, is an indication that tradition is being used here;[4] the reference to the Mount of Olives with the name Ἐλαιών without an article is unique (cf. Josephus, *Ant.* 7.202; 20:169; *J.W.* 5.70); the information regarding the distance of the Mount of Olives from the city is to be considered tradition, as it is a Semitic expression ("a Sabbath day's walk") and exact distances are usually not offered in Luke or in Acts;[5] the assembly place of the group is conspicuously emphasized (cf. the determined expression τὸ ὑπερῷον),[6] also an indication of tradition: it shows that the transmitters and receivers of this tradition were quite familiar with this place.[7] The

---

Regarding sources for the primitive church, cf. Hengel, "Ursprünge," 15-38, here 24-25, and "Zwischen Jesus und Paulus." Regarding the problem of the primitive church in general, cf. Reicke, *Glaube*; S. E. Johnson, "Jerusalem Church," 131; Daniélou, *Dead Sea Scrolls*, 39; Klauck, "Gütergemeinschaft"; Stuhlmacher, *Grundlegung*, 197-221, esp. 206; Roloff, *Apostelgeschichte*, 89-91; Riesner, "Das Jerusalemer Essenerviertel"; *Formen*, 26-36; and *Jesus als Lehrer*, 66-68; Capper, "Community of Goods of the Jerusalem Church" and "Palestinian Cultural Context"; Reinhardt, *Wachstum*.

[3] Pesch, *Apostelgeschichte*, 1:78. Here ὑποστρέφω is most likely Lukan, as it is one of his favorite words.

[4] Cf. Bachmann, *Jerusalem*, 46-47.

[5] Cf. also Luke 22:41; Luke 24:13 from pre-Lukan tradition, according to Wanke, *Emmauserzählung*, 123. Hemer, *Acts*, 108, points out that Acts 1:2 implies the knowledge of Jerusalem's topography. Cf. also Hengel, "Historiker Lukas."

[6] Cf. BDF §252.

[7] So already Zahn, *Apostelgeschichte*, 1:44; also Conzelmann, *Apostelgeschichte*, 23; Mussner, *Apostelgeschichte*, 18; with Mussner Riesner, "Jesus," esp. 202; also Lüdemann, *Das frühe Christentum*, 35. The determined article and the absence of any explanation of the upper room is indication that the author had a very well known place in mind.

connection προσκαρτεροῦντες . . . τῇ προσευχῇ is traditional (cf. Rom 12:12; Col 4:2).[8]

The list of the eleven is also a tradition adapted by Luke; it is neither Markan nor from Q but should rather be categorized as unique to Luke.[9] The mention of Mary, the mother of Jesus, and his brothers, cannot be explained as Lukan redaction.[10] In contrast to the "women," Luke did not have Jesus' mother and brothers follow him to Jerusalem. The fact that the reader knows the individuals mentioned in Acts 1:14 from Luke's gospel is not a sufficient argument for Lukan redaction.

Acts 1:15 is also almost entirely pre-Lukan tradition. Only ἀναστὰς . . . εἶπεν and ὡσεί are Lukan.[11] The temporal connector (1:15a, ἐν ταῖς ἡμέραις ταύταις) is pre-Lukan, since it is only seldom used by Luke in this form.[12] Acts 1:15b also needs to be classified as pre-Lukan tradition for the following reasons: The expression ἐπὶ τὸ αὐτό is old.[13] The narrative sections 1:15, 23–24a, 26 are connected six times throughout with καί. These sections "give concrete information in compact sequence and are not composed in typical Lukan style."[14] Together they form a unit—a short report on the election of Matthew. It can therefore be assumed that 1:15 is also pre-Lukan tradition, which could have been connected with 1:12–14 from the very beginning.[15]

Content Analysis

Right at the beginning of his narrative (Acts 1:12–14), Luke reports that after the ascension the disciples return from the Mount of Olives to Jerusalem, enter a house, and go up into the upper room.[16]

---

[8] With Lüdemann, *Das frühe Christentum*, 35.

[9] Pesch, *Apostelgeschichte*, 1:78–79; cf. also Jervell, *Apostelgeschichte*, 120; Lüdemann, *Das frühe Christentum*, 35.

[10] Pesch, *Apostelgeschichte*, 1:80, and *Simon Petrus*, 71–74; Jervell, *Apostelgeschichte*, 118. Against G. Schneider, *Apostelgeschichte*, 1:199 n. 13; Lüdemann, *Das frühe Christentum*, 33.

[11] Luke probably interjected the introduction in 1:15 with Peter's comments in 1:16–22 in mind. The word ὡσεί is typical of Lukan usage (cf. Acts 2:3, 41; 6:15; 10:3; 19:7).

[12] Cf. Acts 1:15; 6:1; 11:27 with the temporal connector always at the beginning of the appointment narratives.

[13] For a demonstration of this, cf. p. 86 and Gehring, *Hausgemeinde*, 168–69. Whether Luke found this idiomatic phrase in this context and then used it in 2:44, 47 independently (so Dömer, *Heil Gottes*, 143), or the other way around, or he found it in both contexts, which has good support (cf. below), is no longer possible to determine.

[14] Pesch, *Apostelgeschichte*, 1:84.

[15] Ibid.

[16] Cf. Thurston, "τὸ ὑπερῷον."

Excursus: ὑπερῷον

The use of the term ὑπερῷον is very common in the Hellenistic period[17] and signifies the upper (second or third) floor of a house,[18] for example, an additional room with windows on the flat roof of larger houses that was accessible only via an outside stairway. In the East the upper room was the most ventilated and best-furnished room of the house.

Such a room was quite common in ancient architecture and was utilized in a variety of ways. In contrast to the lower, large-sized living room, upper rooms were not normally used for everyday activities (sleeping, cooking, eating, etc.).[19] They were a place for rest and relaxation. Even as early as OT times they occasionally had a certain religious significance (1 Kgs 17:19–21; 2 Kgs 4:10–11; Dan 6:11). For this reason they became the preferred assembly place for scribes.[20] Scholars used them not only as meeting rooms (*m. Šabb.* 1:4; *y. Sanh.* 21b) but as study rooms (*b. Šabb.* 13b) and prayer rooms as well.[21] In light of this ancient and Jewish usage, it appears quite plausible that the primitive church in Jerusalem would make use of an upper room as a gathering place just as Luke indicates in Acts 1:12–15.

Our text implies a fairly large meeting room (1:14–15). In this context the question as to where a group of this size could have met is seldom asked in NT scholarship.[22] The suggestion that a private upper room that could accommodate over a hundred people would be unimaginable for that period[23] can be refuted on the basis of archaeological evidence.[24] Excavations in Jerusalem clearly demonstrate that such facilities were available; however, a capacity of 120 would have been the upper limit.[25]

---

[17] Cf. Bauer-Aland⁶, 1678 (BDAG 1034).

[18] Grenfell and Hunt, *Oxyrynchus Papyri*, part 1, 76:I, i. Cf. G. Dalman, *Orte*, 296–97. The Aramaic עיליתא is used similarly (cf. *b. B. Bat.* 133b).

[19] They were apparently reserved by the homeowner as guest rooms or as separate quarters for a widowed daughter or a newly married son. Cf. Safrai, "Home and Family," esp. 730–32.

[20] Str-B 2:594–95.

[21] Peterson, "Geschichtliche Bedeutung."

[22] Cf. Stuhlmacher, *Grundlegung*, 204; Pesch, *Apostelgeschichte*, 1:77–79, as exceptions.

[23] Thurston, "τὸ ὑπερῷον," considers a hall in the temple. That Luke, when referring to a hall, explicitly uses a different term goes against this. Cf. "hall of Solomon" (Acts 3:11; 5:12; cf. John 10:23; Josephus, *J.W.* 5.185); cf. Riesner, "Das Jerusalemer Essenerviertel," 26.2:1840 n. 308.

[24] Pesch, *Apostelgeschichte*, 1:81.

[25] Cf. Stuhlmacher, *Grundlegung*, 204. Cf. also Blue, "Acts," esp. 140–44, 198–204, and Hirschfeld, *Palestinian Dwelling*, 21–107, for examples of Palestinian houses from this period, including descriptions and floor plans; cf. also Broshi, "Excavations"; Avigad, "How the Wealthy Lived"; *Discovering Jerusalem*, 83–137; and "Jerusalem"; Murphy-O'Connor, "Cenacle," esp. 318–21. Regarding Palestinian architecture for private houses in general, cf. Safrai, "Home," esp. 730–35.

For Luke and his readers, the upper room was already well known. He appears to present this house as "a prototype of an early Christian place of worship."[26] It was there that the disciples experienced community with one another (1:14) and prayed together (1:14; 4:31). There they gathered continually as the church, not only the Twelve and those with them but all together over 120 believers at one place (ἐπὶ τὸ αὐτό).[27] They probably met in this house on Pentecost[28] and then later used it as the church for worship services.[29] It was most likely there as well that they gathered together for the breaking of bread and for teaching and preaching (2:46; 5:42).

This leads to the following intriguing observation: all of the above-mentioned characteristics are elements of a house church. One preliminary result of our examination, then, is that according to our definition (see pp. 27–28) the upper room appears to be an example of a house church in the fullest sense.[30]

Much has been written about the actual historical location of the upper room. Tradition has identified the upper room in Acts 1:13 with the room of the Last Supper, which in Mark 14:14/Luke 22:12 is referred to as ἀνάγαιον[31] and is located on present-day Mount Zion (the southwest hill of Jerusalem).

---

[26] Cf. Riesner, "Essener," 68, who draws attention to the fact that the Greek word occurs only four times in the NT and then only in Acts. It always appears in contexts in which a room is used primarily for worship purposes (cf. also Acts 9:37, 39; 20:7–8). Luke reports that important events took place in this upper room: waiting for the Holy Spirit to come, the election of Matthew (Acts 1:13–14, 15–17), the pouring out of the Holy Spirit on Pentecost (2:1–3), and additional worship assemblies later (4:23–25, 31).

[27] Haenchen, *Apostelgeschichte*, 159 n. 3: ἦσαν καταμένοντες means staying or gathering continually. See p. 86 for a discussion of the meaning of ἐπὶ τὸ αὐτό.

[28] Acts 2:1–2. Acts 2:1–4 certainly contains pre-Lukan tradition that was only slightly adapted (so Kremer, *Pfingstbericht*, 78–79; Pesch, *Apostelgeschichte*, 1:99; Barrett, *Acts*, 110; against G. Schneider, *Apostelgeschichte*, 1:387–88, and Lüdemann, *Das frühe Christentum*, 44). Here it is assumed that "all" (2:1, 4a) are gathered "at one place" (compare with 1:15). This means that not only the Twelve (cf. 1:26; 2:14–15) but also the 120 people mentioned in 1:15 gathered in the "house" whose upper room is referred to in 1:13 as a meeting place. So Pesch, *Apostelgeschichte*, 1:102–3; also Barrett, *Acts*, 112, considers it possible. So Chrysostom and also Jerome, *Epist*. 103, "The same Spirit that was poured out upon the one hundred and twenty in the upper room on Mt. Zion"; cf. also Origen, *Cels*. 8.22. Roloff, *Apostelgeschichte*, 38, 41 takes a different view.

[29] Acts 4:23–25, 31. Even though it cannot be demonstrated with certainty, we can assume the "their own" (compare v. 23 with v. 32) refers to the church here and that the "place" (v. 31) where they gathered was the upper room.

[30] For an extensive proof, see pp. 79–86.

[31] This seems to correspond with Luke's understanding in spite of the fact that he, along with Mark 14:15, also uses the synonym for "upper room" (Luke 22:12). Cf. Zahn, *Apostelgeschichte*, 1:43–45. Also according to Cadbury and Lake, *Acts*, 4:10, in Luke's opinion the upper room is identical with the ἀνάγαιον in Luke 22:12. Cf. also Mussner, *Apostelgeschichte*, 18; Pesch, *Wie Jesus*, 103–4; F. F. Bruce, *Acts*, 105; Riesner, "Das Jerusalemer Essenerviertel," 26.2:1854–1859, here 1859.

Chapter 3 / The Post-Easter Use of Houses in the Primitive Jerusalem Church • 67

Literary and archaeological evidence would indicate that the site of the first center for the primitive church was indeed on the southwest hill of Jerusalem.

On the basis of old sources, Eutychius, patriarch of Alexandria (first half of the tenth century), reports that in the fourth year of Vespasian (72/73) a remnant of the primitive Jerusalem church came back from East Jordan to the Holy City and erected a church there.[32] This is confirmed by a note from Bishop Epiphanius of Salamis (315–403), who reports of Hadrian's exploratory trip and his visit to Jerusalem (130 C.E.), "he found the temple of God trodden down and the whole city devastated save for a few houses and the church of God, which was small, where the disciples, when they had returned after the Savior had ascended from the Mount of Olives, went to the upper room. For there it had been built, that is, in the portion of Zion which escaped destruction, together with blocks of houses in the neighborhood of Zion."[33]

Numerous scholars have taken these literary testimonies seriously.[34] After examining archaeological findings in support of this literary evidence, R. Riesner follows P. Benoit's lead in concluding that the local tradition regarding the location of the first center for the primitive Jerusalem church on the southwest hill deserves our confidence.[35] According to Riesner, there are good reasons to assume that "in Jerusalem there was a Jewish-Christian presence up until the fourth century with only very short interruptions" that could have guaranteed a reliable local tradition from the apostolic period on.[36] In his opinion, the Jewish-Christian synagogue near David's tomb is not to be identified with the NT building (the house with the upper room in Acts 1:13), but it keeps the memory of such a local tradition alive. J. Murphy-O'Connor has come to similar conclusions independent of Riesner: "Textual and archaeological data suggest the existence of a Christian building on Mount Zion in the 2nd century. The difficulty of access and the proximity of suspicious Roman sentries preclude invention of a Christian holy place at that period. The tradition of veneration must go back to the 1st century."[37]

Murphy-O'Connor points out that the first center of the primitive church was located on Mount Zion in a wealthy quarter of Jerusalem. After the earthquake of 31 B.C.E. (Josephus, *Ant.* 15.121–122), this area was

---

[32] Eutychius, *Annales* (PG 111:985).

[33] Epiphanius, *Treatise* (Dean), 30.

[34] Cf. Zahn, *Einleitung,* 2:200, 211–13, 243–45; with him Rordorf, "Was wissen wir?" 113. Cf. also Bagatti, *Church,* 117–18; Riesner, "Essener"; extensive archaeological and historical detail in Riesner, "Das Jerusalemer Essenerviertel"; Murphy-O'Connor, "Cenacle"; Blue, "Acts," 135–36.

[35] Benoit, "Prétoire," esp. 177.

[36] Riesner, "Essener," 69. Cf. also Riesner, "Das Jerusalemer Essenerviertel," esp. 26.2:1831–59, for an extensive historical proof on the cutting edge of present-day scholarship. The presence of a Gentile-Christian community in *Aelia Capitolina* could also have guaranteed the continuity of a local tradition. Cf. Riesner, "Das Jerusalemer Essenerviertel," 1844–45; Murphy-O'Connor, "Cenacle."

[37] Murphy-O'Connor, "Cenacle," 303.

rebuilt with two- and three-story buildings with barrel-vaulted cisterns. According to M. Broshi, *fresco secco* art, mosaic floors, and architectural elements "leave no doubt that this Quarter was occupied by the more affluent residents of Jerusalem."[38] Consequently, if the first center of the primitive church truly was located in the quarter, the owner of the building "must have had significant financial resources."[39]

Murphy-O'Connor's view, however, is not totally free of problems. In particular, because the present-day Cenacle is located between this affluent quarter and an area (the so-called Essene quarter) in which more modest houses were excavated, it is very difficult to determine with any kind of certainty to which of these areas it belonged.[40] Unfortunately, Murphy-O'Connor does not address the results of these excavations in his article.

In summary, even though this thesis is still disputed, and at this point we cannot know for certain, there seems to be good indication that the center of the primitive church was located on Mount Zion in one of the most affluent quarters in Jerusalem.[41]

As yet there is no certain archaeological evidence for Christian places of assembly in Jerusalem, such as the house of Mary, mother of John Mark, or the house with the upper room. Excavations of private homes in Jerusalem can, however, assist us in reconstructing Palestinian living conditions.[42] They also serve as illustrations of what the homes of the more affluent looked like. The literary references in the book of Acts to at least one such house owner (Mary, mother of John Mark), with her relatively large house, and the assumption that the house with the upper room served as the first center for the primitive church on Mount Zion in a wealthy quarter in Jerusalem allow us to safely assume that at least some of the early Christians there could very well have owned or rented relatively large houses with an architectural design common in Palestine during that period. Unlike the house of Mary, we do not know the name of the owner of the house with the upper room. It is possible, however, that wealthy individuals such as Joseph

---

[38] Broshi, "Excavations," 83–84.

[39] Murphy-O'Connor, "Cenacle," 313–21, here 319.

[40] Cf. Riesner, "Das Jerusalemer Essenerviertel," 1825: "Sowohl vor der Dormitio-Abtei . . . wie beim ehemaligen Nigrizia-Haus . . . wurden Spuren sehr einfacher Häuser aus der Zeit des Zweiten Tempels gefunden."

[41] J. Taylor has also criticized this viewpoint in *Christians*, 207–20. Cf. Murphy-O'Connor, "Cenacle," for his rebuttal of her position. Cf. also Gehring, *Hausgemeinde*, 137 n. 48, for a summary discussion and additional arguments against Taylor.

[42] Cf. Hirschfeld, *Palestinian Dwelling*, 21–107, particularly the excavations in the Jewish quarter: the "Herodian house," first century B.C.E.; the "palatial mansion," first century C.E.; and the "burnt house," first century C.E. (see p. 65 n. 25). They testify to living conditions enjoyed by a very wealthy social class in Jerusalem. Even more important than these luxurious houses for our study are the more modest and yet substantial houses found in the excavations of Broshi, "Excavations." Cf. also Avigad, *Discovering Jerusalem*, 83–137, esp. 95.

of Arimathea,[43] a council member, or Joanna, the wife of Chuza, one of Herod's administrators (Luke 8:3), were willing to make space for assembly available to the first Christians in Jerusalem even after Easter.

Acts 12:10b–17

> When they had walked the length of one street, suddenly the angel left him. Then Peter came to himself and said, "Now I know without a doubt that the Lord sent his angel and rescued me from Herod's clutches and from everything the Jewish people were anticipating." When this had dawned on him, he went to the house of Mary the mother of John, [with the surname] Mark, where many people had gathered and were praying. Peter knocked [on the door of] the outer [gatehouse], and a servant girl named Rhoda came to answer the door. When she recognized Peter's voice, she was so overjoyed she ran back without opening it and exclaimed, "Peter is at the door!" "You're out of your mind," they told her. When she kept insisting that it was so, they said, "It must be his angel." But Peter kept on knocking and when they opened the door and saw him, they were astonished. Peter motioned with his hand for them to be quiet and described how the Lord had brought him out of prison. "Tell James and the brothers about this," he said, and then he left for another place. (Acts 12:10b–17)

Pre-Lukan Tradition and Lukan Redaction

Peter's reencounter with, and departure from, the church in the house of Mary is essentially based on historical facts and on tradition that originated in the primitive church in Jerusalem.[44] Conzelmann observes, "Local tradition shows through; it is assumed that the house is well known."[45] The following details are additional indications of local tradition. The narrative contains biblical Palestinian coloration—for example, the expression "angel of the Lord" and the notion of a guardian angel as the heavenly image of a person (12:7, 11, 15; cf. Str-B 2:707–8). In addition, the story includes some illustrative, narrative-enriching, topographical (12:10), personal (12:12, 13), and architectural (12:13–14) details as well as the specific description of gestures (12:17).[46] The abrupt mention of the

---

[43] Matt 27:57, 60; Mark 15:43, 45–46; Luke 23:50–52; John 19:38, 40–42.
[44] Pesch, *Apostelgeschichte*, 1:360–62. Cf. also Weiser, *Apostelgeschichte*, 286; Radl, "Befreiung," esp. 85; and Jervell, *Apostelgeschichte*, 338, who views vv. 12–17 as tradition but vv. 4–17 as a whole as a personnel legend.
[45] Conzelmann, *Apostelgeschichte*, 79; with him Ollrog, *Paulus*, 48. Cf. also Lüdemann, *Das frühe Christentum*, 152, who considers the note regarding the house of Mary in Jerusalem a historical fact.
[46] Cadbury and Lake, *Acts*, 4:138: "However skeptical one may be about the details in the prison, it is impossible to deny the convincing nature of the behavior of Rhoda and the family." See Pesch, *Apostelgeschichte*, 1:361; F. F. Bruce, *Acts*, 239. Hemer, *Acts*, 207–8, 227, 345, points out that many of these details in the narrative do not have any theological function and therefore should be considered historically reliable. The name Rhoda is well documented. Cf. the following

Lord's brother James (the first occurrence in Luke-Acts) also indicates a pre-Lukan origin of Peter's message.[47]

Content Analysis

Some scholars have attempted to prove that the upper room was located in the house of Mary, the mother of John Mark (Acts 12:12).[48] This hypothesis, however, does not hold up under scrutiny. There is no indication of this in any of the Gospels or in any other reliable tradition. One isolated tradition identifies the upper room with the house of John Mark, but not until 530 C.E.[49] Numerous scholars consider it more likely that the house with the upper room is identified with the residence of James, the Lord's brother (12:17; 20:18). The following are some of the important arguments presented by different scholars in support of this position.

Filson drew attention to the fact that, in addition to the group gathered in the house of Mary, Acts 12:17 makes reference to a second group of Christians in Jerusalem.[50] After Peter tells about his miraculous escape from prison, he says, "Tell James and the brothers about this." According to this, James and the brothers connected with him were not present at the assembly in the house of Mary. Instead it appears that they gathered elsewhere. Rordorf concludes from this reference in Acts that "at least one other house must have served as a meeting place."[51] For H. J. Cadbury, it is obvious that the house of Mary in 12:12 cannot be identical to the one with the upper room, "for from the context it is plain that this house was not the headquarters of 'James and the brethren.'"[52] The implication, according to Cadbury, is that James and the brothers were gathered that night in the center for the primitive church. Whether the center was located in the house

---

inscriptions: *IG* 22, 12570 (Athens, Roman period) and 12571 (Athens, fourth century B.C.E.). Also some examples from burials far away from home: *IG* 22, 9864 (no date) and 9865 (second century C.E.), both Milesians in Athens; *SB* 1:392, a Mysian woman in Alexandria, Egypt (third century B.C.E.); *IG* 22 8274 (first century B.C.E.), an Antiochene woman in Athens.

[47] Pesch, *Apostelgeschichte,* 1:366.

[48] Cf., e.g., Zahn, "Dormitio," esp. 406–9, and *Einleitung,* 2:213, 244; following him, Rordorf, "Was wissen wir?" As early as the fifth and sixth centuries, scholars speculated regarding the owner of the house. There were at least three candidates, John Mark, Mary, and James; cf. Wilkinson, *Jerusalem Pilgrims,* 66, 84, 171–72.

[49] Theodosius, *De situ terrae sanctae* 7; Baldi, *Enchiridion,* 483; Cadbury and Lake, *Acts,* 4:136–37. Cf. also Kopp, *Heiligen Stätten,* 382 (correctly contra Zahn, "Dormitio," 406–9), and F. F. Bruce, *Men,* 28, 88; following them, Riesner, "Essener," 69, and "Das Jerusalemer Essenerviertel," 1840; Burkitt, "Last Supper," esp. 296; Gibson, "House." Mark 14:14 implies a male householder (οἰκοδεσπότης) for the room for the Last Supper, which most likely took place in the upper room.

[50] Filson, "Significance," 106.

[51] Rordorf, "Was wissen wir?" 114.

[52] Cadbury and Lake, *Acts,* 4:137.

Chapter 3 / The Post-Easter Use of Houses in the Primitive Jerusalem Church • 71

with the upper room Cadbury does not say. K. Lake, however, is very clear about this: "Acts xii suggests that this house [the house of Mary] was not the same as that in which James was living. If either of these houses contained the upper room, it is perhaps more likely that it was the house of James."[53] F. F. Bruce points out as well that verses 12 and 17 both imply at least two distinct places of assembly. The message of Peter to James suggests that "James and the brethren associated with him met in a different place from Peter's company—that they belonged, to use Pauline language, to a different house-church."[54]

Klauck makes a few additional exegetical observations in support of this thesis. First, gathered in the house of Mary in prayer were "many" (ἱκανοί) but not all of the believers, which is again a reference to at least two groups. Second, in light of the possibility that at least two organizational forms existed in the Jerusalem church, namely, the Aramaic-speaking "Hebrews" originating from Palestinian Judaism and the Greek-speaking "Hellenists" who had converted to Christianity and were residing in Jerusalem (6:1–7),[55] Klauck supposes that, as with the synagogue, the two groups could have had different meeting places.[56] "It is possible that for this reason James, a Palestinian, was not present (Acts 12:12) in the house of Mary, a Hellenist."[57]

Riesner sees the situation similarly and develops the thesis somewhat further.[58] For him 12:12–17 implies that in Jerusalem around 43/44 C.E., in addition to the "upper room" in which the Aramaic-speaking Christians (Ἑβραῖοι; cf. 6:1) gathered around James, the Lord's brother, there existed another meeting place in the house of Mary, mother of John Mark.[59] If one follows closely the Lukan narrative up to this point, according to Riesner, there can be no mistake that by the house with the upper room the residence of James is intended. Acts 1:13–14 emphasizes that it is in this room that the relatives of Jesus were present. It can be assumed that James was among those who later were to assume a leading role in this center. This bit of information was most likely added for James's sake. In the house of Mary, the

---

[53] Ibid., 5:477.
[54] Bruce, *Men*, 88 (cf. also 28).
[55] Cf. Hengel, "Zwischen Jesus und Paulus." The assumption that from the beginning the primitive church in Jerusalem consisted of two separate ideological groups, Hebrews and Hellenists, is not new. This view was first articulated by Baur (cf. "Die Christuspartei," esp. 114, and *Paulus*, 1:42–43; cf. also Neudorfer, *Stephanuskreis*). This view is disputed, however. Cf. the fundamental criticism of it by C. C. Hill in *Hellenists*.
[56] As former Jews, the first Christians would have been accustomed to meeting in separate groups, each with their own countrymen, as was somewhat common in the synagogue at that time (cf. Hengel, "Zwischen Jesus und Paulus," 178–79).
[57] Klauck, *Hausgemeinde*, 49.
[58] Riesner, "Essener," 69, and "Das Jerusalemer Essenerviertel," 26.2:1840–41.
[59] For Riesner, however, the building with the upper room was possibly a synagogue ("Das Jerusalemer Essenerviertel," 1839–41).

Greek-speaking Jewish Christians gathered together. John Mark can be identified as Greek-speaking (Ἑλληνιστής) from his surname.[60] Because of his family's connection with Peter, it can be assumed that they belonged to the Hellenists known for their openness to the Gentile mission (cf. 13:5, 13; 15:37).[61]

The following can be said regarding the view that the residence of James is to be identified with the house with the upper room. It appears certain that the building that contained the upper room was also the center for the primitive church in Jerusalem initially under Peter's leadership. It is possible that the Jerusalem church continued to use this house as its center after Peter's departure. We can also be certain that the house with the upper room was not identical with the house of Mary and that in both houses early Christian groups gathered together for worship.[62] We can be quite sure as well that the residence of James was not in the house of Mary. The interpretation of 12:17 as a reference to a house church under James's leadership, however, is disputed.[63] It is clearly documented that James, particularly after the departure of Peter between 41 and 44 C.E., became the leader of the Jerusalem church (see below).[64] In light of this, it could be that primarily Aramaic-speaking Jewish Christians gathered for worship in the house with the upper room and those mostly Greek speaking in the house of Mary.

Still, on the basis of the texts available, this cannot be determined with certainty.[65] Mixed groups could have assembled in both houses. The family of Mary, however, most likely did not belong to the Hellenists critical of the law because as such they would have been expelled from Jerusalem.[66] In spite of this, it can be asked whether their family belonged to the Hellenists who were supportive of the Gentile mission. Barnabas was active later as a mediator between both parties. John Mark accompanied Barnabas and Paul on a mission journey. In addition, he had connections with Peter, who was

---

[60] Cf. also Hengel, *Studies*, 45–53.

[61] Peter's special relationship with the Greco-Palestinian John Mark speaks in favor of the connection between Peter and the house of Mary. For a discussion of John Mark's connection to Peter and his authorship of the second Gospel, cf. Hengel, "Probleme," esp. 242–57, and "Entstehungszeit."

[62] Hengel, "Historiker Lukas," 147–83, here 161–62, also distinguishes between the house of Mary and the upper room.

[63] Cf., however, Pesch, *Apostelgeschichte*, 1:366, and Bauckham, "James," 440 n. 79, for similar positions in disagreement with mine. Bauckham: "The idea that James was the leader of a specific group in the Jerusalem church, distinct from Peter's group, is quite dubious. It certainly cannot be supported from Acts 12:17"; "Peter's words in 12:17 refer to all the members of the Jerusalem church not present in Mary's house."

[64] Hengel, "Jakobus," esp. 98–104. Cf. Gal 1:18; 2:1, 9; Acts 12:17; 15:13–21.

[65] Cf., e.g., Blue, "Acts," 136 n. 62: "We should not conclude that the group meeting in Mary's house was a group of Hellenists and that James and the brethren represent another group (Hebrews)."

[66] Schmithals, *Paulus und Jakobus*, 72 n. 6.

also supportive of the Gentile mission. Barnabas and John Mark, however, went along with Paul only up to a certain point before they separated from him (because some of Paul's convictions regarding the Gentile mission were too radical?). At any rate, regarding this question we must carefully differentiate. The Greek and Hebrew double name of John Mark implies that he was bilingual. This meets the linguistic prerequisite for the possibility that in the house of Mary worship assemblies were held in Greek. Aramaic-speaking Jewish Christians could have participated in the services as well. On the other hand, it is extremely unlikely that those who spoke Greek as their first language would have all been expelled from Jerusalem. At least some would have remained behind, and thus a need for both Greek- and Aramaic-speaking worship services would have existed. We know of at least two houses in Jerusalem in which the first Christians met: the house of Mary and the house with the upper room. According to all that we know about them, it makes the most sense to assume that the Greek-speaking services were held in the house of Mary.

The view that James provided leadership to the Aramaic-speaking community (or later the whole Jerusalem church) from the original center of the primitive church, that is, the house with the upper room, appears historically quite plausible. It is by all means possible that the residence of James is to be identified with the house that contained the upper room, but at this time we cannot be certain.

What can we learn from Acts about the house of Mary and the faith community that met in her home?[67] The description of the building indicates a relatively large, distinguished home including a gatehouse (πυλών). The gatehouse was accessible directly from the street and as such served as a buffer between the street, the courtyard, and the rooms in the house. The absolute ἱκανοί in 12:12 refers to a considerable number of people (cf. 14:21; 19:19; 1 Cor 11:30) and implies a larger house. The specific mention of the servant girl is also an indication that this household with "employees" belonged to the more affluent in Jerusalem. Mary's social background points in this direction as well. She apparently came from a Levite family (according to Col 4:10, John Mark was cousin to Barnabas, a Levite from Cyprus, Acts 4:36–37) and therefore belonged to the circle of Diaspora Jews from Cyprus, who could have afforded comfortable homes. After a period of time out of the country, these Diaspora Jews had become quite wealthy and were then able to purchase property and resettle in Jerusalem.[68] Quite early on, then (43/44 C.E.), there existed in Jerusalem well-to-do Christians who were able to make their houses available as meeting places for larger groups

---

[67] It is no longer possible to determine the location of this house. Cf. the proximity to the prison in Acts 12:11–12. Where this prison was located is also unknown. Some commentators suggest the fortress of Antonia as an option; e.g., Cadbury and Lake, *Acts*, 4:136.

[68] Stuhlmacher, *Philemon*, 71.

of believers (cf. Acts 1:13; 21:15–18). Mary's house and the relatively large group that was meeting there that night in order to pray for Peter had apparently become quite well known in the primitive church. "The matter-of-fact manner in which both persons [Mary and John] are introduced into the narrative implies that those for whom the story was first told were very well acquainted with them."[69] Quite obviously, Peter knew of this house. After escaping from prison, he searched for the house, knowing that he would find Christians there because it was Passover (12:3–4).[70] One can conclude from this not only that this portion of the primitive church in Jerusalem met there that evening for prayer because of Peter's imprisonment, but that they also gathered on other occasions for worship in the house of Mary.[71]

Acts 12:12 says that many came together in this house and prayed (cf. 5b). Fellowship and prayer are two elements of worship that belong to the characteristics of a house church in the full sense. It can be assumed that the Christians who met there also celebrated the Lord's Supper with one another—after all, we can be relatively certain that they met there on Passover night, most likely for this very purpose. Teaching and preaching probably took place there as well (2:46; 5:42). Therefore, the house of Mary can be considered a full-fledged house church according to our definition.[72]

Acts 2:42–47 and 5:42

> They devoted themselves to the apostles' teaching and to the fellowship, to the breaking of bread and to prayer. Everyone was filled with awe, and [the apostles did] many wonders and miraculous signs. All the believers were together and had everything in common. Selling their possessions and goods, they gave to anyone as he had need. Every day they continued to meet together in the temple courts. They broke bread in their [individual houses] and ate together with glad and sincere hearts, praising God and enjoying the favor of all the people. And the Lord added to their number daily those who were being saved. (Acts 2:42–47)

> Day after day, they never stopped proclaiming Jesus as the Christ in the temple and teaching in the individual houses. (5:42; author's translation)[73]

---

[69] Weiser, *Apostelgeschichte*, 1:290.
[70] So already Zahn, *Einleitung*, 2:244. It can also be assumed that Peter sympathized with the group that met in the house of Mary (see above).
[71] Many scholars have already suggested that a house church met in the house of Mary. Cf. Rordorf, "Was wissen wir?"; Pesch, *Apostelgeschichte*, 1:366; Klauck, *Hausgemeinde*, 49; Stuhlmacher, *Philemon*, 70; Blue, "Acts," 136.
[72] See the research report on pp. 27–28 and 79–86 for extensive proof.
[73] This translation of 5:42 attempts to acknowledge an observation made by Klauck, *Hausgemeinde*, 50, that in Greek the central terms have been aligned in a chiastic sequence: the temple with public proclamation and the private houses with teaching. Cf. the expression of the same content through the use of parallelism in Acts 20:20.

Pre-Lukan Tradition and Lukan Redaction

Luke most likely found 2:42–47, the first summary report, in his source and possibly revised it slightly.[74] The short, concise style (esp. vv. 42–43) and some non-Lukan expressions speak for the traditional character of the report. In particular, κοινωνία (v. 42) does not occur otherwise in Luke-Acts; it does appear, however, in some of Paul's letters (1 Cor 1:9; 2 Cor 8:4; 9:13) and in pre-Pauline tradition as an idiomatic phrase (1 Cor 10:16). As a result, we can assume that the term κοινωνία is old and was handed down to Luke via his tradition source.[75] The expressions κλάσις τοῦ ἄρτου and ἦσαν ἐπὶ τὸ αὐτό are also old.[76] "Breaking bread" (Acts 2:46) occurs in 20:7, 11 (in a Pauline church in Troas) and also in Paul (1 Cor 10:16); "being together" (Acts 2:44) occurs in Paul (1 Cor 11:20; 14:23).[77] The set phrase κατ' οἶκον appears to be old as well, as it is also used by Paul (cf. 1 Cor 16:19; Phlm 2; Rom 16:5).

Whether Acts 5:42 is pre-Lukan tradition or Lukan redaction is difficult to determine; that will be left open here.[78] Even if one takes the position that the summary in verses 41–42 was created by the hand of Luke, we can assume that his description is historically accurate. After all, on the basis of historically reliable tradition, he had previously reported in 2:42–47 that the first Christians gathered together in the temple and in individual houses.

---

[74] Pesch, *Apostelgeschichte*, 1:129–30. Jervell, *Apostelgeschichte*, 155, sees tradition in v. 42; Roloff, *Apostelgeschichte*, 65–66, sees it in 42–43; and Weiser, *Apostelgeschichte*, 102–3, sees it in 46–47. There is most likely tradition in 42–43 as well as in 46–47 (with Pesch). Cf. Stuhlmacher, *Grundlegung*, 203–7, esp. 204. Against Lüdemann, *Das frühe Christentum*, 53.

A series of exegetes see good reasons to assume that a very old, reliable, Semitic tradition originating in Jerusalem lies behind the first summary report of Luke in Acts 2:42–47. Similarly, Torrey, *Composition*; Vazakas, "Acts I-XV. 35?" Wilcox tried to demonstrate two Semitisms in 2:44, 47 that reflect Qumran terminology (*Semitisms*, 93–100, esp. 96, 99–100). Cf. also Black, *Aramaic Approach*, 10; and Capper, "Community of Goods of the Jerusalem Church," 26.2:1737–39.

[75] Because of this observation and the doublet of v. 42 in vv. 44–47, a number of exegetes have attempted to literary-critically dissect this summary and thereby reconstruct the written source used by Luke, which they concluded was v. 42. For H. Zimmermann, "Sammelberichte," 71–82, here 75, the development was just the other way around: v. 42 originated from Luke and summarized the rest. In contrast, cf. Haenchen, *Apostelgeschichte*, 192–94. As yet, however, no consensus has been reached by applying this type of literary-critical approach.

[76] With Roloff, *Kirche*, 73.

[77] For further arguments in favor of the assumption that ἐπὶ τὸ αὐτό is an old expression, cf. p. 86.

[78] Cf., on the one hand, Barrett, *Acts*, 298, "There can be little doubt that Luke composed this short summary, which is in his style, is based on the stories he has already told, and serves a literary purpose"; Lüdemann, *Das frühe Christentum*, 77, "The verses are totally Lukan in terms of both language and content"; and also Roloff, *Apostelgeschichte*, 99–101. On the other hand, cf. Pesch, *Apostelgeschichte*, 1:210–13, esp. 213.

Idealizing Summaries

In an attempt to explain the relationship between the three summaries (2:42; 4:32–35; 5:11–16), a number of relatively complicated source-critical hypotheses have been suggested.[79] As yet no convincing solution, however, has been found. The counterattempt to prove that the summaries originated from the pen of Luke, who created them without relying on any traditional sources whatsoever (e.g., E. Haenchen), also leaves questions unanswered. It cannot explain the tensions, repetitions, and linguistic irregularities in 2:42–47, for instance.[80] Haenchen's view is questionable for another reason as well. Luke's use of summaries from Mark for his own gospel demonstrates that he is willing to use such material from his sources.[81] A number of scholars are of the opinion that the summaries in which references to house churches are embedded contain reliable details about the primitive church in Jerusalem.[82]

In his presentation in the book of Acts, Luke has often been accused of projecting his own ideal image of the church back into the early Christian community in Jerusalem. This is considered true of his summaries in particular. It cannot be contested that Luke viewed the primitive church in Jerusalem as an example for his own congregation and that he describes it as such in his summaries. In this sense, it is true that he draws an ideal picture of the early church in Jerusalem. This is no reason, however, to conclude that his portrayal is historically misleading. Regarding 2:42, C. K. Barrett comments,

> In this verse Luke gives an idealized picture of the earliest church—idealized but not for that reason misleading. That it is not misleading appears at once if negatives are inserted: they ignored the teaching of the apostles, neglected the fellowship, never met to take a meal together, and did not say their prayers. This would be nonsense. The idealizing is in the participle προσκαρτεροῦντες ("continuing faithfully," "remaining constant"), and that Luke did not intend it to be understood as unmarked by exceptions is shown by his story of Ananias and Sapphira (5:1–11).[83] There is no ground for doubting the outline of Luke's account; if he had not given it we should doubtless have conjectured something of the kind.[84]

---

[79] Cf., e.g., Dibelius, Cadbury, Jeremias, and Benoit.

[80] Cf. Roloff, *Apostelgeschichte*, 65. See Haenchen, *Apostelgeschichte*, 194–97; H. Zimmermann, "Sammelberichte"; Lindemann, "Beginnings."

[81] Mark 1:28 = Luke 4:14b, 37; 7:17; Mark 9:32 = Luke 9:45; 18:34. Cf. Cadbury, *Style*, 108–11.

[82] Pesch, *Apostelgeschichte*, 1:77–80, 99, 129–30, 173–75, 211–13; Roloff, *Apostelgeschichte*, 89–91; following him Stuhlmacher, *Grundlegung*, 204; Capper, "Palestinian Cultural Context"; cf. also Jervell, *Apostelgeschichte*, 157–58, who considers the summaries of Luke old tradition originating in the primitive Jerusalem church.

[83] For an additional exception to, or weakness of, the Jerusalem version of community of goods, cf. Acts 6:1–3 (my note).

[84] Barrett, *Acts*, 166; cf. also 60; Roloff, *Apostelgeschichte*, 89–91, and his comments regarding the connection between "ideal" and "historic reality."

Chapter 3 / The Post-Easter Use of Houses in the Primitive Jerusalem Church • 77

It has also been suggested that Luke projected Hellenistic utopian ideas back into the primitive church by describing its community life, using terms such as κοινωνία (2:42) and κοινός (2:44; 4:32).[85] The frequent use of the term יחד in the "community rule" of Qumran demonstrates that, at the latest since the discovery of the rule, the mere occurrence of Hellenistic notions regarding the community-of-goods ideal in the description of a Jewish group can no longer serve as proof that this group, whether Essene or Christian, did not actually practice a community of goods.[86]

It is also quite plausible that at least some of the early Jerusalem Christians had "everything" in common in light of the expectation of the imminent return of Christ.[87] It appears that they initially made little or no financial provision for the future and lived quite intentionally from hand to mouth, as Jesus himself had commanded.[88] This did have consequences, though. The version of community of goods practiced by the primitive church in Jerusalem was apparently not capable of providing a solid, long-term basis for survival.[89]

In the early days at least two different forms of community organization appear to have been practiced in the primitive church in Jerusalem. Upon closer scrutiny it becomes clear that the community of goods was

---

[85] Plümascher, *Lukas*, 16–18; W. Stegemann, "Nachfolge." For a discussion of the Hellenistic literature, cf. Klauck, "Gütergemeinschaft," 47–52; Mealand, "Community of Goods and Utopian Allusions"; Capper, "Palestinian Cultural Context," 324–25 nn. 3–6.

[86] Stuhlmacher, *Grundlegung*, 204–5; Capper, "Community of Goods of the Jerusalem Church," 26.2:1737. Dombrowski, "היחד," demonstrated as early as 1966 that the term djy is an equivalent of the Greek τὸ κοινόν and in the Qumran literature probably represents the attempt to translate τό κοινόν into Hebrew. Since then, many scholars have recognized this—cf. literature in Schwartz, "Non-joining Sympathizers," esp. 554 n. 22; Weinfeld, *Organizational Pattern*, 13–14.

"At the latest" refers here to the thesis of W. Bauer that in reality no Essene community practiced a community of goods because in Philo's and Josephus's descriptions of the Essenes, Hellenistic utopian ideas can already be observed (cf. Philo, *Prob.* 76–77, 85–87; *Hypoth.* 11.14–13; Josephus, *Ant.*18.20–22; *J.W.* 2.122–127). Since the discovery of the *Rule of the Community* in Qumran, which gives us clear insight into the internal affairs of the Essenes regarding the organizational form of their community of goods, Bauer's thesis has been abandoned (cf. Segert, *Gütergemeinschaft*, 66–73).

[87] Stuhlmacher, *Grundlegung*, 206; cf. also Hengel, "Zwischen Jesus und Paulus," 181 n. 111.

[88] Mark 1:16–18 par.; 10:17–19, 28–30 par.; Luke 9:3; 10:4; 11:3 par.; Matt 6:25–34; and Hengel, "Zwischen Jesus und Paulus," 181–82, and *Eigentum*, 31–36, 39–42.

[89] Later the primitive church in Jerusalem did develop economic difficulties critical enough that at least some of the believers there became dependent on the charity of other congregations. This is documented in Acts 11:27–29, which reports the necessity for a collection in support of the saints in Jerusalem (cf. Acts 15:26 as well). For a different view, cf. Capper, "Community of Goods of the Jerusalem Church" and "Palestinian Cultural Context."

considered voluntary (cf. 5:4; 12:12). At least some of the members of the community must have kept their homes—otherwise the congregation would not have had a place of assembly. In the beginning, then, we see a dual structure in the Jerusalem church: the practice of the community of goods, on the one hand, and on the other, the organization of the community into house groups.

Historical Reliability of the Passages in Acts

The results of our examination suggest that it was not a Lukan exaggeration that the community organization practiced by the first Christians in Jerusalem consisted of the mutual material support of one another, provided in the form of the community of goods and in the form of *oikos* structures. In light of practical considerations inherent to their situation and in view of later literary evidence referring to the bread-breaking celebration, the report in Acts indicating that the first Jerusalem Christians gathered together to break bread in the homes of well-to-do members of the congregation should not be doubted. It is also safe to assume that they met in houses for other activities such as prayer, fellowship, and instruction.[90]

Another reason for taking seriously the information regarding the primitive church handed down to us by Luke in his summaries is that he evidently knew Jerusalem from personal experience.[91] According to the "we" report in Acts 21:15–18, he visited the city at least once (ca. 57/58 C.E.), perhaps only briefly, and met with James, the Lord's brother, at his place of residence.[92] This has significance for the historical reliability of the Lukan portrayal of the early church in Jerusalem for two reasons. First, it would have been possible for Luke to gather reliable oral and written tradition for his report. For instance, he could have become familiar with the tradition about the life of the Jerusalem church—for example, the community of goods, their approach to missional outreach and their evangelistic successes, the breaking of bread in individual houses, and the temple gatherings of the first Christians. Second, at that time he could have come to know the city and the situation of the primitive church firsthand and so would have been in a position to report all the more reliably. In this light, the references to the upper room become more credible. The unusual use of the article to determine "upper room" (see above) implies that Luke knew this room and its location from firsthand experience. The reference to James and the brothers (12:17) as a separate group of believers not present in the house of Mary is strengthened in its historical reliability if Luke had actually seen James's residence in person.

---

[90] Stuhlmacher, *Grundlegung*, 203–10; Barrett, *Acts*, 162.

[91] Cf. Hengel, "Historiker Lukas," esp. 161–62, 182–83; before Hengel, Pixner, "Lukas."

[92] Hengel, "Historiker Lukas," 161–62. For the "we" reports in general, see below, ch. 4.

As a result, we can assume that the primitive church in Jerusalem did indeed gather together in the house containing the upper room initially and then later in other houses throughout the city. One of the best-known of these houses was the house of Mary, the mother of John Mark. As we will see shortly, Christians met as well in the temple (courts) for activities such as teaching and preaching.[93]

Everyday Life in Jerusalem House Churches

The Worship Service

What happened in such a house church? What did the worship life of one of these house churches look like? Is it really theologically legitimate to call them house *churches*? Even though Luke does not directly comment on the social and worship setting of the primitive church in Jerusalem, a substantial amount can be indirectly gleaned from Acts 2:42–47 as well as from 4:32 and 5:12–16.

Whether the list in 2:42 (teaching, fellowship, breaking bread, and prayer) indicates the program agenda for an early Christian worship service or simply a description of the life of the church in general is contested in present-day scholarship. Of particular interest is the debate between J. Jeremias and E. Haenchen.[94] This issue is also very important for our study. If it can be demonstrated that the four elements mentioned above truly are a part of a worship service, perhaps even indicative of a sequence, that is, a kind of worship service schedule, this would simultaneously be proof that the worship service took place in individual houses.[95] The only other place of assembly mentioned in our text is the temple, and it is unthinkable that a

---

[93] Cf. Luke 24:52; Acts 2:46; 3:1–3; 5:42 (the temple in general); Acts 3:11; 5:12 (the hall of Solomon). With Salzmann, *Lehren,* 32–33. Cf. Hengel, "Historiker Lukas," esp. 152–60. For 3:11 Haenchen (*Apostelgeschichte,* 203) suggests that the reference to the hall of Solomon is a Lukan creation in order to give his report more local coloration and thus credibility, but this hall stood outside the Nicanor Gate. He concludes therefore that Luke obviously had no personal knowledge of the temple. Hemer, *Acts,* 224 n. 10, demonstrates convincingly that Haenchen is wrong here on all points.

[94] Jeremais, *Abendmahlsworte,* 111–14, 112 n. 3; cf. Schürmann, "Gemeinde," 61–73, esp. 65. Haenchen, *Apostelgeschichte,* 192. Following Haenchen are Pesch, *Apostelgeschichte,* 1:130–31, and Salzmann, *Lehren,* 32–37. Cf., however, Barrett, *Acts,* 162, who points out that the opposition between the worship service of the primitive church in Jerusalem and the life of the church appears to be an unreal alternative. "In an ideal community . . . the church meeting constitutes a particular focus of the whole of the community's life, so that each consists of the same elements." Similarly Goppelt, *Apostolische und nachapostolische Zeit,* 28.

[95] Haenchen does not contest that they are part of a worship service, even though he speaks out against the interpretation of Acts 2:42 as an example of an early Christian worship service. (cf. *Apostelgeschichte,* 192).

worship service consisting of all four of these elements could have taken place there. Consequently, it would be theologically legitimate to call the house groups mentioned here house churches in the full sense.

In this context it is important to note that the report in 2:42–47 focuses specifically on the worship life of the church. At the beginning as well as at the end (vv. 42 and 46), the two series of statements are joined with the catchword προσκαρτεροῦντες, which is typical worship terminology. The phrase ἦσαν ἐπὶ τὸ αὐτό is also worship service terminology (see p. 86). The worship service character of the report also fits well with the overall context.[96]

Jeremias is correct in suggesting that the interpretation of our texts must proceed from the participle προσκαρτεροῦντες. Particularly in Acts, προσκαρτερεῖν can be translated "to regularly take part in worship service" (cf. 2:46; 1:14; 6:4). From 2:42 it can be concluded that the four elements following προσκαρτεροῦντες and joined together as pairs with καί form "the program or agenda for an early Christian worship service."[97] The analogy of early Christian assemblies in general can also be cited in support of this view. There is reason to believe that the worship service began with instruction and ended with prayer.[98] This can be deduced from 2:46–47 (cf. the indirect reference in 12:12) and can be confirmed for the liturgical history of the entire early church.[99]

The objection raised by Haenchen[100] that the first Christians taught in the temple court and took part in prayer in the temple does not exclude the possibility that the teachings of the apostles regularly took place at the beginning of the worship meetings or that the bread-breaking celebration ended with prayers of thanksgiving. With Jeremias we can conclude, then, that the sequence in 2:42 represents that of an early Christian worship service. There it is reported that the primitive church in Jerusalem gathered together in houses for the teachings of the apostles, for fellowship, to break bread, and for prayer.

That the first Christians broke bread in houses has already been demonstrated and is repeatedly documented in our texts.[101] We can be sure that they also had fellowship with one another in individual houses. Κοινωνία signifies here the close connection or relationship among community members, their mutual support of one another, and the empathy and participation in each other's lives.[102] This includes spiritual as well as material

---

[96] Compare 2:41 with 2:42. Jeremias, *Abendmahlsworte*, 112–13.
[97] Ibid., 112 ("den Verlauf eines urchristlichen Gottesdienstes").
[98] Cf. direct references to the instruction: Acts 20:7–9; Justin, *1 Apol.* 67.4; *Acts of John* 106–110. Indirect: Rom 16:16; 1 Cor 16:20; 2 Cor 13:12; 1 Thess 5:26; 1 Pet 5:14. Communion, preceded by the holy kiss, followed directly after the reading of the apostle's letter, which took the place of instruction.
[99] With Jeremias, *Abendmahlsworte*, 112.
[100] Haenchen, *Apostelgeschichte*, 192.
[101] Cf. esp. 2:42, 46 and also 5:42.
[102] Bauer-Aland⁶, 892–93 (BDAG 552–53): in Acts 2:42 κοινωνία (only here in Acts; cf. κοινός in 2:44 and 4:32, however) means brotherly cohesiveness. Cf. also

considerations.¹⁰³ Κοινωνία implies a God-given unity of heart and mind among the first Christians, an often recurring theme in the first chapters of Acts (1:14; 2:46; 4:32). This unity manifests itself in a concrete way in a willingness to share material with one another (cf. 2:44–45; 4:32–37). Sharing with one another certainly took place during the worship service in the individual houses, particularly during the common meal¹⁰⁴ and the breaking of bread. This sharing began, however, with the householder's willingness to make his or her home available to the group as a meeting place and, in many cases, to provide major portions of the common meal. Even though the individual members of the congregation offered what they could, the more affluent homeowners would have carried the main burden.

In 2:42, αἱ προσευχαί occurs in the plural. For this reason many exegetes have assumed that here Luke is referring to prayer times in the temple or prayers in the synagogue.¹⁰⁵ This does not exclude the possibility that the bread-breaking celebrations ended in prayers of thanksgiving. Thus 2:42 clearly documents that prayer was a part of the worship assembly, which took place in individual houses.¹⁰⁶ This is unambiguously confirmed in other texts as well.¹⁰⁷ None of this should surprise us, as prayer was an integral part of the household life of most Jewish families. The Jewish-Christian families certainly would have continued this practice during the meetings that took place in their homes.

With the teachings of the apostles (2:42) we encounter a more complex problem. Without entering into an extensive discussion of the issues, it can be said that these teachings at least contained rudimentary elements of a

---

F. Hauck, "κοινωνία," *TDNT* 3:809. Already Calvin, *Acts*, 1:85: "Mutual association, alms, and other duties of brotherly fellowship"; this meaning of κοινωνία is supported by the use of djy in the Qumran writings. Cf. Barrett, *Acts*, 164, 163–66; Goppelt, *Apostolische und nachapostolische Zeit*, 33 (Gal. 2:9–10.; 1 John 1:3, 6–7).

¹⁰³ Two main ways of interpreting κοινωνία in 2:42 have been suggested: first, as the financial collection during the worship service, whose main elements are listed in v. 42 (Reicke, *Diakonie*, 25–28; Jeremias, *Abendmahlsworte*, 111–15; and our n. 104); Lohse, *Grundriss*, 64); second, as the fellowship of the believers between one another (Seesemann, *Begriff* ΚΟΙΝΩΝΙΑ, 87–90; Haenchen, *Apostelgeschichte*, 192; H. Zimmermann, "Sammelberichte," 75).

¹⁰⁴ On such sharing, see Haenchen, *Apostelgeschichte*, 192; cf. also Reicke, *Diakonie*, 25: "Because κοινωνία appears in the context of worship and is very closely connected with the ritual act of breaking bread, we must assume that here this word also takes on worship service connotations." On the common meal, cf. Jeremias, *Abendmahlsworte*, 113–14. For him it might be more accurate to translate the word κοινωνία with "(table) fellowship," referring to the love feast or common meal.

¹⁰⁵ Ibid., 111; Pesch, *Apostelgeschichte*, 2:130; Haenchen, *Apostelgeschichte*, 149; F. F. Bruce, *Acts*, 73; cf. Acts 3:1; 6:4; also Luke 24:53.

¹⁰⁶ Cf. also Cullmann, *Gebet*, 24–26, 143–45.

¹⁰⁷ Acts 1:14, 24–25; 4:24–30; 10:9; 12:12; Pesch, *Apostelgeschichte*, 1:130. Haenchen, *Apostelgeschichte*, 192, concedes that it is possible that the primitive church had its own prayers and prayer times, which were distinct from those of the Jewish community.

confessional tradition, the teachings of Jesus and a christological interpretation of the Holy Scriptures along with the end-times fulfillment in Christ.[108]

The analogy to the (house) synagogue also supports the view that instruction and prayer were common components of the house church meetings. Worship assemblies took place in synagogues even before 70 C.E., in which Torah instruction and most likely prayer were integral elements.[109] The focal point of instruction in the house churches, however, was not only the Torah but also the teachings of the apostles.

It can also be assumed that, from the very beginning, instruction took place with the breaking of bread. The primitive church thereby followed the Jewish pattern of teaching in the context of sacred meals.[110] The Jewish-Christian head of the household would have taught during the bread breaking, just like the Jewish householder during the Passover meal or the Essene community meal. Paul's description of the farewell worship assembly in Troas (20:7–12) shows that in house meetings teaching was associated quite early with bread breaking. In addition, the central terms in 5:42 are best understood in chiastic connection: evangelistic proclamation took place primarily in the temple, and catechetical instruction for the most part in the individual houses, though this observation cannot be elevated to a rigid scheme applying to the whole of early Christianity.[111] All of these arguments speak against the recently suggested view that the teaching of the apostles took place only in the temple (hall of Solomon) and not in houses because it was only in the temple that everyone could have heard the apostles as they taught.[112]

It can be inferred from our text that the primitive church gathered for two different types of worship services,[113] which can be distinguished from one another on the basis not only of their locality but of their organizational

---

[108] Stuhlmacher, *Grundlegung*, 203; Goppelt, *Apostolic and Post-Apostolic Times*, 43–45.

[109] On instruction, see Levine, "Second Temple." On prayer, cf. Schürer, *History*, 2:448–50. With a different view, D. Falk, "Jewish Prayer." Cf. also the balanced discussion in Levine, "Second Temple," esp. 17–22.

[110] Acts 20:7. At Passover: Str-B 4:67–69, and perhaps at the community meals in Qumran. Cf. Goppelt, *Apostolic and Post-Apostolic Times*, 45–47.

[111] On the chiatic connection, with Klauck, *Hausgemeinde*, 47–48; following him, Roloff, *Kirche*, 71 n. 33; cf. also Rordorf, "Was wissen wir?" 111–12. The first Christians gathered in the temple, in the hall of Solomon, for large evangelistic meetings. Cf. Luke 24:52; Acts 2:46; 3:1–3; 5:42 (the temple); Acts 3:11; 5:12 (the hall of Solomon). Early Christians also taught in the temple (Acts 4:2; 5:12, 21, 25) and did evangelism in individual houses (Acts 10:1–2, 22; 24:24, 26; 28:30). Against Blue, "In Public," 72–93.

[112] Salzmann, *Lehren*, 32–37, esp. 34.

[113] Ibid., 33–35. Even though it is unlikely that they took part in the sacrificial cult (with a different view, Roloff, *Kirche*, 71–72), they prayed regularly and participated in the worship services in the temple (with Stuhlmacher, *Grundlegung*, 203; cf. Acts 2:46; 3:1).

arrangement as well.[114] The main emphasis in the houses was on bread breaking. The first Christians likely took part in the temple prayers held in the temple courts, and from there they went into the hall of Solomon for a gathering of the whole congregation, with the emphasis on missionary proclamation and biblical instruction.[115]

This view is supported by the observation that ὁμοθυμαδὸν ἐν τῷ ἱερῷ in 2:46 does not signify a mere emotional unity but the unity of individuals in their corporative totality. "The meaning is approximately 'in corpore,' and the expression stands in opposition to the following phrase 'in the [individual] houses.'"[116] As such a publicly visible unit, the primitive church gathered in the temple. Separately and privately its members gathered for the holy breaking of bread in individual houses. That is, the primitive church in Jerusalem came together in the temple in a large meeting as the *whole church,* and in private homes as individual church bodies in small groups as *house churches.*[117]

The community life of the Jerusalem church was experienced most intensively and was continually renewed in the joint celebration of the bread breaking in individual houses. Scholars have reflected on and written a great deal about the character of these communion celebrations. In general, it is assumed that these celebrations certainly entailed a common meal.[118] We can be sure that the community of goods described by Luke in Acts included common meals together.[119] The expression "breaking bread" also implies a meal: it is the designation for the act of tearing the bread, which, in addition to the word of blessing, forms the opening rite at the beginning of Jewish meals (27:35).[120] Moreover, Luke also places "bread breaking" in the context of the worship service elsewhere in Acts.[121]

At this point the question must be asked whether here the common meal and the bread breaking are synonymous with the Lord's Supper. The following seems to speak in favor of this view. If we focus first on Luke's use of language, it directs our attention from 2:42, 46 to 20:7, 11. This would indicate a connection between the primitive church in Jerusalem and the Pauline church in Troas as well as with the church in Corinth (1 Cor 10:16;

---

[114] Cf. Roloff, *Kirche,* 71.

[115] Christian participation in prayer in the inner courts was possible provided one was not a Gentile. Cf. Roloff, *Apostelgeschichte,* 69; Haenchen, *Apostelgeschichte,* 199; Hengel, "Historiker Lukas," 154–57; Salzmann, *Lehren,* 37.

[116] Reicke, *Glaube,* 60–62. Following him, Barrett, *Acts,* 89.

[117] This does not mean that every member of the whole church in all of Jerusalem was gathered in the temple.

[118] Acts 2:42, 46. Esp. μεταλαμβάνειν τροφῆς in v. 46 speaks in favor of this position.

[119] Acts 6:1–3 clearly demonstrates this.

[120] Jeremias, *Abendmahlsworte,* 113–14 nn. 2 and 4.

[121] Acts 20:7, 11; 2:42, 46. In our context it is clear that the breaking of bread has the character of a worship service. In Acts 2:46 it is mentioned parallel to the temple visit (Goppelt, *Apostolic and Post-Apostolic Times,* 45).

11:23–25) and thereby to the Lord's Supper (κυριακὸν δεῖπνον—1 Cor 11:20), which was also celebrated as a common meal in Corinth.[122] In addition, we know that Jesus was addressed as the exalted κύριος in the μαραναθά in Jerusalem at this early date.[123] The Aramaic prayer cry מרנ אתא, "Our Lord come!" is documented as one of the central elements in the Lord's Supper. All this demonstrates that it is not at all anachronistic to suggest that the Lord's Supper was celebrated in the primitive church in Jerusalem from the earliest days.[124] Moreover, "breaking bread" in Acts 2:42, 46 is most likely the designation for the Lord's Supper as an integral part of a common meal.[125] There is a connection as well in the opposite direction, from the primitive church in Jerusalem back to Jesus (Luke 24:13–35; Mark 14:22–25). "The 'breaking of bread' and the Lord's Supper (in the Pauline letters) originate from a common source leading back to the Last (Passover) Supper Jesus celebrated with his disciples in Jerusalem."[126]

We can thus conclude that the celebration of the Lord's Supper stood at the center of the worship assemblies held in the house churches of Jerusalem.[127] The observation that the Lord's Supper was celebrated in Jerusalem house churches weekly (Acts 20:7), on the day of the Lord's resurrection, and possibly even daily underscores as well the central significance of bread breaking for the primitive church.[128]

In summary, it has been demonstrated that all four elements (teaching of the apostles, bread breaking, fellowship, and prayer) possess the character

---

[122] Stuhlmacher, *Grundlegung*, 206–7. For Corinth and the situation there, cf. Hofius, "Herrenmahl," in dispute with Klauck (*Herrenmahl*, 291–97), Pesch (*Abendmahl und Jesu Todesverständnis*, 44–45, 62–64), and Stuhlmacher ("Neutestamentliche Zeugnis").

[123] Stuhlmacher, *Grundlegung*, 183–85.

[124] Compare 1 Cor 16:22 with 11:26; Rev 22:20. Cf. H. P. Rüger, "Aramäisch," *TRE* 3:607.

[125] Also for Roloff, *Kirche*, 73, "bread breaking" in Acts 2:46 means the Lord's Supper.

[126] Stuhlmacher, *Grundlegung*, 207. Cf. also Jeremias, *Abendmahlsworte*, 111–14; I. H. Marshall, *Last Supper*, 76–140. Against Lietzmann, *Korinther*, 55–60.

[127] So also Pesch, *Apostelgeschichte*, 1:130; Roloff, *Kirche*, 72–73; Stuhlmacher, *Grundlegung*, 204; J. Wagner, *Altchristliche Eucharistiefeiern*, 38; Dix, *Shape of Liturgy*, 16–17, 63. Dix considers two things certain: "(1) that some sort of Eucharist was held corporately in the Jerusalem church from the earliest days; (2) that it was held in private houses."

[128] Acts 2:46: καθ' ἡμέραν. That the bread breaking took place daily is the common interpretation. For Haenchen, *Apostelgeschichte*, 193, καθ' ἡμέραν in 2:46 also belongs with κλῶντες. Διακονία καθημερινή in 6:1 speaks in favor of Haenchen's suggestion. Cf. also Kretschmar, "Abendmahlsfeier I," 1:238; Salzmann, *Lehren*, 37. With a different view, Roloff, *Kirche*, 74. Cautiously, Pesch, *Apostelgeschichte*, 1:132. The daily breaking of bread can also be assumed simply because of the daily need for nutrition. As we have demonstrated, bread breaking and the Lord's Supper were one and the same meal. Thus, it would be logical to conclude that the Lord's Supper was celebrated daily.

of a worship service. They were an integral part of the worship assemblies held in individual houses in Jerusalem. Consequently, it is legitimate to call these house groups house *churches* according to the definition agreed upon at the beginning of our study (see pp. 27–28).

One more aspect of the importance of the house church for early Christian missions has also become apparent. House churches enabled early believers to have distinctly Christian worship and fellowship from the earliest days.[129] Proclamation and instruction as well as partial fellowship could be more or less performed and experienced in the temple. But the celebration of the Lord's Supper would have been unthinkable in the Jewish community. This was only possible for Jerusalem Christians in their own homes.

It has often been pointed out that the first Christians, even after their conversion to Jesus the Messiah, continued to worship with their countrymen and countrywomen in the temple. This was confirmed by our examination. It would be incorrect, however, to conclude on this basis that the first Christians did not in any way distinguish themselves from the rest of Judaism. It cannot be contested that they initially remained within the Jewish community and attempted to win their fellow Jews for Jesus' message of the coming kingdom. But the creative and determining aspects of their faith and community life were precisely what distinguished them from their Jewish countrymen.[130] For instance, they celebrated a meal together according to the words of institution, a meal that was "totally unique in their world, as unique as everything central to the primitive Christian faith, which was called into existence through the Easter event."[131] It was the hospitality of numerous householders who, in the context of their own homes, enabled the celebration of the Lord's Supper, a Christian worship service focused on the word, the practice of Christian prayer, and the empowering and missionally effective κοινωνία fellowship.[132] In this sense the house church provided a setting from the very beginning in which the first Christians could effect a certain inner distance (in the beginning partially subconscious?) from the

---

[129] Filson, "Significance," 109; cf. also Dix, *Shape of Liturgy*, 16–18.

[130] Filson, "Significance," 109, 112. Luke actually uses the word αἵρεσις (a Jewish separatist group) in Acts 24:5 and 28:22 for Christians. A αἵρεσις distinguishes itself in that it combines old and new religious elements with one another.

[131] Goppelt, *Apostolic and Post-Apostolic Times*, 47: "The notion of a sacramental 'communio' is foreign to both Judaism and the Essenes."

[132] On the word, in that "the teachings of the apostles—not the scribe as for all Jewish separatist groups—are normative for the first Christians; they proclaim that for them the Torah is superseded in terms of a fulfillment through Jesus; the scribe of all persuasions represents and proclaims the Torah, whereas the apostles represent and proclaim a person, namely Jesus" (ibid., 29). For the distinctly Christian practice of prayer (Jesus' unique manner of addressing the Father in prayer, "Abba, Father!" [cf. Mark 14:36 par.] and the very old prayer form "Maran atha"), cf. Goppelt, *Apostolic and Post-Apostolic Times*, 48. Christians would not have been allowed to pray in this way in the Jewish faith community. On the fellowship, cf. Stuhlmacher, "Weg," 114.

rest of the Jewish community until later the complete separation became outwardly visible.

Excursus: A Plurality of House Churches in Jerusalem

Now that it has been demonstrated that the passages examined in Acts refer to house churches in the full sense according to the agreed-upon definition, we can address the question concerning a plurality of house churches in the primitive church in Jerusalem. We have discovered two houses that served as meeting places for the first Christians: the house of Mary and the house containing the upper room. Thus the question whether the first Jerusalem Christians met for worship in only one place has already been answered.

The expression ἐπὶ τὸ αὐτό, however, seems to imply a gathering of the congregation all in one place. The expression does not necessarily need to be understood locationally. In light of the Hebrew term יחד, the expression appears to be quite old and can be translated more or less in a social sense.[133] Although ἐπὶ τὸ αὐτό is very difficult to interpret, scholars tend to agree that it can be understood differently depending on its context.[134] Generally the phrase means "the church gathered (at one place) for worship and fellowship."[135] It is clear that Luke intentionally uses the expression in each specific context in Acts for the gathered community (at one place)[136] or for the Christian church as a whole (cf. Acts 2:47).

It cannot be assumed, however, that the Jerusalem Christians only met in these two houses, as Luke reports that the church grew quite rapidly (cf. Acts 2:41, 47; 4:4; 5:14; 6:7). Even if his figures of three thousand (2:41) and five thousand (4:4) were exaggerated, these two houses alone would not have had adequate space for even a tenth of these numbers of individuals.[137]

It can be asked if Luke exaggerated his figures as is commonly assumed. The main argument against the historical reliability of the Lukan account regarding the size of the primitive church is seen in its alleged incompatibility with the assumed population of the city of Jerusalem at the time of Jesus. Most commentators today still accept the research results in an older work of Jeremias as authoritative. He estimated the population of Jerusalem to be about 25,000–30,000.[138] Recent investigations arrive at a much higher re-

---

[133] Cf. Wilcox, *Semitisms*, 94–98; Cadbury, "Luke—Translator or Author?"; Rordorf, "Was wissen wir?" 114; Metzger, *Textual Commentary*, 265.

[134] A brief look at the interpretation history demonstrates the difficulty. For a good, well-balanced overview, cf. Ferguson, "When You Come Together"; Gehring, *Hausgemeinde*, 168–69.

[135] Cf. Pesch, *Apostelgeschichte*, 1:87: "am gleichen Ort; zur Gemeinde versammelt," with a reference to 1QS 5:12; 8:12.

[136] Acts 1:15; 2:1 (1 Cor 11:20; 14:23). In Acts 2:44 the expression must be understood as the gathered community in different locations.

[137] Cf. Ysebaert, *Amtsterminologie*, 87.

[138] Jeremias, *Jerusalem*, 96–98, and "Einwohnerzahl."

sult for the population of Jerusalem in the first century on the basis of demographic studies of ancient cities and the examination of many factors that influenced population density.[139] W. Reinhardt, after examining the latest research, comes to the conclusion that a population of 60,000–120,000 (more likely in the direction of 120,000) would be a much more realistic estimate.[140] He emphasizes, "The dominant argument against the historical plausibility of Luke's figures—the alleged small population of Jerusalem at the time—can no longer be considered valid."[141]

Certainly, the numbers given by Luke are not intended to be precise in a strict sense (cf. often ὡσεί).[142] It would be just as erroneous, however, to dismiss them as pure fiction, for they preserve at least the memory that the early church grew quite rapidly beyond the capacity of one single meeting place.[143] Nor need we assume that there were three thousand personal decisions for Christ, which implies radical conversion to a new religion in every single case.[144] We must remember that Palestine at that time represented an "*oikos* society" and that we are most likely dealing with "house conversions" here in Acts. With this in mind, it is much more plausible that the primitive church could have grown at such a very rapid rate.[145]

Above all, the intense form of κοινωνία experienced among the members of the community and their communion celebrations κατ' οἶκον in 2:42, 46 imply the existence of a plurality of house churches.[146] First, the phrase κατ' οἶκον (2:46; 5:42) is further evidence for a plurality of meeting places because it is used here in a distributive rather than a locational sense, and this means that Christians met in a number of different homes.[147] Second, both the

---

[139] Cf. the summary in Reinhardt, "Population Size." This article is the translation of the fourth chapter of his dissertation, "Das Wachstum des Gottesvolkes." Cf. also *Wachstum*.

[140] Reinhardt, "Population Size," 263–65.

[141] Ibid., 238.

[142] Cf. Acts 1:15; 2:41; 4:4 [ὡς]; 19:7). Cf. also Barrett, *Acts*, 96: "We are not dealing with a period in which precise numerical records were made and kept."

[143] Cf. ibid., 159, 162: "The number may be traditional; there is no reason why a considerable number should not have accepted—in addition to a foundation in Jewish religion which may be assumed—the Messiahship of Jesus, and done so to the accompaniment of a good deal of religious excitement."

[144] With Barrett, ibid., 159.

[145] Acts 2:41 reports nothing regarding this view. On the other hand, it does not exclude the possibility. If we can assume an evangelistic approach targeting heads of households, assuming that an average of 10–20 members (their wives, children, friends, and clientele) lived in one *oikos,* the scenario is conceivable that if 150 householders made a commitment to Christ, we would be at 1,500–3,000. That 150 householders in a city the size of Jerusalem, with a population of 120,000, could have converted to Christianity is not fantasy.

[146] Cf. Wieland, *Altar,* 30.

[147] For κατ' οἶκον, Bauer-Aland⁶, 825, has "in den einzelnen Häusern" ("in individual houses"). BDAG 512 has "from house to house," which in our opinion is not as good as the German rendition in Bauer-Aland. White, *Building God's House,*

external conditions for, and the intimate character of, the communion celebration required private space, for example, the inner rooms of a house.[148] The prerequisite for celebrating the Lord's Supper combined with a common meal is access to a kitchen, a living or dining room, and in some cases a table and so forth. In addition, scholars agree that, among other things, κοινωνία here means the close, personal fellowship of the individual members of the community. The precondition for this kind of intimate fellowship is a small group, in which it is possible to develop close personal relationships. All of these requirements would have been met in a house church setting.

The assumption of a plurality of house churches in Jerusalem is also supported by the following observations:

1. In Acts 8:3 Saul forcefully enters the houses of Jerusalem Christians in order to arrest them.[149] We can assume that Saul did not randomly choose some houses but, rather, precisely the houses in which he suspected Christian assemblies, in hopes of catching them in flagrante delicto.[150] At any rate, this is evidence that a plurality of house churches existed in Jerusalem even before the conversion of Paul (32/34 C.E.).

2. So many Greek-speaking Jews were won for Christ in the first one to two years in Jerusalem that it was necessary for them to start their own worship services (Acts 6:1–3).[151] This can be seen as evidence for at least two house churches: one with services in Greek and the other in Hebrew.

3. Even if the above literary evidence were not available, we would also expect the existence of a plurality of Christian house churches on the basis of religious-historical analogy with the organization of the Jewish community in Jerusalem in house synagogues. In those days such house meetings were presumably not uncommon for Jerusalem Judaism, for this was a

---

103 n. 7, suggests "at home," which would be more of a locational understanding of the term. This translation "would be more consistent with the inferred customary action in Acts 12:12 as well as with the Pauline usage.... This seems to be more in keeping with the distinction being made in Acts between the private gathering 'at home' versus the public worship 'in the Temple.'" Nevertheless, the necessity of a plurality of house churches in Jerusalem remains. White also sees this (cf. *Building God's House,* 104). Cf. also pp. 155–62 regarding the existence of a plurality of house churches alongside the whole church in one location. Codex D gives the plural in 2:46: κατ' οἴκους.

[148] Wieland, *Altar,* 29: "Just as the Passover celebration was a family meal, so was the Christian agape meal."

[149] Regarding the historicity of Paul's persecution of Christians, cf. his own testimony: 1 Cor 15:9; Gal 1:13, 23; Phil 3:6. In Gal 1:22 the Jewish-Christian churches in Judea outside Jerusalem are meant. So Pesch, *Apostelgeschichte,* 1:266; cf. also Hengel, "Ursprünge," 24 n. 35; Burchard, *Der dreizehnte Zeuge,* 26–31, 169–70, esp. 30 n. 23; Roloff, *Apostelgeschichte,* 130; against Haenchen, *Apostelgeschichte,* 288–89.

[150] Rordorf, "Was wissen wir?" 114; so also Barrett, *Acts,* 393. Here we see that meeting in a private home did not always provide absolute protection against persecution.

[151] Hengel, "Ursprünge," 30–31.

period of rapid growth for synagogue communities. Even before 70 C.E. we can assume the existence of a plurality of synagogues in Jerusalem, perhaps predominantly in the form of house synagogues.[152] As the majority of the believers in Jerusalem came from a Jewish background, it is safe to assume that they would have organized their community in a similar manner, namely, as house churches. It is also quite possible that Jewish-Christians who had made their houses available as meeting places for the synagogue community would now, as followers of Christ, act as patrons of house churches, allowing Christians to assemble in their homes.[153] Mary, the mother of John Mark, could be an example of such a patroness.

It has become clear, then, that in the earliest days of the primitive church, a plurality of house churches existed alongside the local church as a whole in Jerusalem. At least some of the believers gathered together in the temple as the local church body. To begin with, a house church met in the upper room. Very soon after that (most likely directly after Pentecost) this house became too small to accommodate all of the believers, and so they had to find other houses in which they could assemble. In addition to the house church in the upper room, at least one other house church was established in the house of Mary the "Hellenist." Besides these two, we can assume that a whole series of additional house churches were established whose exact number can no longer be determined.[154]

Missional Outreach from House to House

Our next focus is on the significance of house churches in the missional outreach of the Jerusalem church. In the past it has been customary for scholars to follow the view of early Christian missions first put forth by J. Jeremias in his 1956 work *Jesu Verhiessung für die Völker*. Recently, however, P. Stuhlmacher has seriously questioned this perspective.[155] On the basis of a diachronic and synchronic analysis, Stuhlmacher demonstrates convincingly that in 28:16–20 Matthew includes old Jewish-Christian tradition

---

[152] In rabbinical sources it is reported that Jerusalem had 480 (*y. Meg.* 73d), 460 (*y. Ketub.* 35c), or 394 (*b. Ketub.* 105a) synagogues and that Bethar had 400 houses of instruction (*b. Giṭ* 58a). Even though these figures may be exaggerated, they illustrate "the significance of the new movement to gather together in small groups" (Roloff, *Kirche*, 72). Most scholars agree that the synagogue was a widespread phenomenon by the beginning of the first century C.E. in the Diaspora as well as in Palestine. As already mentioned, this view is contested; cf. the dispute between Kee and Oster on p. 30, n. 13. Regarding historical evidence for house synagogues, see p. 30, n. 14.

[153] Blue, "Acts," 136.

[154] Even if we were extremely conservative in estimating the size of the Jerusalem church at the time at ca. five hundred and the average size of a house church at ca. twenty to thirty members, there would have been between fifteen and twenty-five house churches.

[155] Stuhlmacher, "Matt 28:16–20."

and develops it as the programmatic conclusion to his gospel. This traditional passage takes as its point of departure Jesus' exaltation as the Son of Man and embraces the expectation that defined the Jewish Feast of Tabernacles: that the messianic Son of Man will restore greater Israel in the end times (cf. Ps 80) and that the Gentile peoples will one day accept Zion as their mother (cf. Ps 87). The disciples of the exalted Christ are sent out to prepare the way for this restoration by proclaiming the gospel of the kingdom of God to all nations, including Israel (cf. Matt 24:14). According to Stuhlmacher, Matthew included this tradition, which had been transmitted faithfully in Jerusalem, because this old missional charge was important to him and it remains binding for the Christian church today.

During his pre-Easter ministry Jesus sent his disciples particularly to the lost sheep of Israel (Matt 10:5–6, 23).[156] According to the view set forth by Jeremias, only this commission is renewed after Easter.[157] Thus Peter and the Twelve continued Jesus' work of gathering Israel (compare Matt 15 with Luke 15:3–7) in Jerusalem, the Holy City, where the Son of Man was expected (soon) to return.[158] For them it was self-explanatory that they should begin their mission in Jerusalem, the focal point where the nation of Israel came together for the great pilgrimage festivities.[159] They took it for granted as well that they should concentrate exclusively on the Jewish population until the Messiah's return.[160]

According to Jeremias's view, the Gentiles would participate in salvation in the end times when the nations made their pilgrimage to Zion.[161] For these reasons the mission to the Gentiles would not have been an issue for the disciples in the early days in Jerusalem. This view, however, is partially based on the conviction that Matt 28:16–20 did not take place before the beginning of all post-Easter missions. Redaction criticism has placed it late (after 70 C.E.), at a time when the mission to the Jews was believed to have failed and the Gentile mission was considered the main task of the church. The results of Stuhlmacher's study mentioned above indicate, however, that this view needs to be revised. If Matt 28:16–28 belongs before the commencement of all missionary activity, and we agree with Stuhlmacher that it did, then it follows that the disciples would have had the Gentiles in view

---

[156] Cf. Luke 10:1–12 and Mark 6:6–13 par. Cf. Hengel, "Ursprünge," 34–37.

[157] Cf. 1 Cor 15:5–7; Pesch, "Voraussetzungen," 17–45, esp. 30–31; Stuhlmacher, *Grundlegung,* 211–12; Hengel, "Ursprünge," 32–34.

[158] Paul confirms that between the years 35 and 40 the Galilean Apostles were usually still in Jerusalem (Gal 1:18; 1 Cor 15:5; cf. Acts 1–6; 10–11; 12). So also Goppelt, *Apostolic and Post-Apostolic Times,* 35.

[159] Cf. Hengel, "Zwischen Jesus und Paulus," 174, and "Ursprünge," 31–32.

[160] Cf. Isa 56:1–8; Hengel, "Ursprünge," 37; Stuhlmacher, "Weg," esp. 112–15.

[161] Jesus independently adopted this view. Compare Matt 8:11–12 with Mic 4:1–4; Isa 2:2–4; *1 En.* 57; 90:33; *Pss. Sol.* 17:32–35; *4 Ezra* 13:13. Cf. also Jeremias, *Jesus' Promise,* 46–48.

from the earliest days of their post-Easter missional outreach. However one might view this issue, our task at this point is to examine the function of houses in the context of early missional outreach in the primitive church in Jerusalem.

The term "mission" has a broad spectrum of meanings. Without entering into an extensive missiological discussion of the issues involved, it will suffice for our study to define "mission" (or "evangelism"), as we will use the term, in the following way: the active effort to lead nonbelievers to faith in Jesus Christ.[162] Three dimensions of missional outreach should be noted: mission proclamation or preaching; mission through personal conversation; mission through lifestyle (missional outreach through living the Christian life). In this context it is clear that structural differences exist between a mission, on the one hand, in which people are sent out to take the initiative to proclaim the gospel and, on the other hand, the personal magnetism and attraction of a group of people living in community with one another who more often than not wait for others to come to them and to ask why they are the way they are.[163] Our study is interested in the question whether and in what way houses played a role in these three dimensions of missional outreach.

Frankly, we have very little exact knowledge on the post-Easter missional activities of the Twelve as a whole. Only regarding Peter and John, son of Zebedee, do we have concrete information. Initially they preached publicly in Jerusalem.[164] In the context of these public messages, private houses do not play any role whatsoever, at least not in the available texts on the primitive church in Jerusalem. It is documented in Acts 5:42 that the apostles preached evangelistically in houses, but because these messages took place in the context of a private home, they cannot be characterized as "public" in the pure sense.

Even if it is not specifically documented for the Jerusalem church, it can be assumed that the first Christians were evangelistically active in and through their houses. The assembly of the primitive church, as Luke portrays it (Acts 2:46; 3:1–10; 5:42), testifies to a strong missional initiative on the part of the apostles.[165] The strongest impulse for spreading the faith is embedded in the message itself. Initially it was a matter of reaching all of Israel (4:10), which could only be saved through this message (4:11–12).[166] Later the whole world became the objective (Matt 28:16–28). The rapid expansion that Luke implies was certainly accomplished (to a large extent) through public preaching. The expansion was also accelerated, however, by the fact

---

[162] For a discussion of the issues, cf. Bosch, *Transforming Mission*, 1–11.
[163] Cf. Harnack, *Mission and Expansion*, 1–101.
[164] Acts 2:1–41; 3:1–10, 11–13. Acts 5:42 reports, however, that the "apostles" did not stop preaching the gospel every day in the temple.
[165] Cf. Hengel, "Ursprünge," esp. 30.
[166] Cf. Goppelt, *Apostolic and Post-Apostolic Times*, 56–57, 73.

that many believers became evangelistically fruitful in their immediate surroundings through personal conversations and through an attractive Christian lifestyle.[167]

At this point it is appropriate to mention Hengel and his dispute with M. Dibelius and E. Haenchen. Haenchen adopted the view first put forth by Dibelius that the early Jerusalem Christians did not evangelize publicly but rather "led a quiet and, in the Jewish sense, 'pious' life."[168] The spreading of the gospel occurred exclusively "in the quietness of personal encounters from person to person." Not until the conflict with the Hellenists did the situation change. In contrast Hengel says, "This view can be easily disproved by pointing out the simple fact that in only a short period of time, one or two years, the first Christians were able to win so many Greek-speaking Jews for Christ that they had to establish their own worship service. This would not have been possible through quiet conversations one at a time but rather only through genuine missionary activity."[169] In my opinion, the two are not mutually exclusive.[170] Surely public proclamation and personal conversations, combined with an attractive lifestyle, all contributed to the rapid spread of the gospel.

Missional Outreach as a One-on-One Conversation

Presumably this missional attitude, to which every Christian felt called, became particularly fruitful in the social setting provided by the environment in and around the house and household.[171] The ancient *oikos* with its network of relationships provided a very favorable opportunity for evangelistic contacts. In this setting it would have been quite natural to pass on the Christian message from person to person (from householder to householder, from slave to slave, etc.).[172] For example, an invitation to a meal in the home would have created an opportunity to cultivate contacts and deepen relationships. The first Christians certainly would have engaged in conversations about the faith in their homes—in a certain sense, evangelism from house to house.[173] Some of those who came to Christ through Peter's message may have been householders. It is quite possible that they would have invited one

---

[167] Acts 4:29b, 31c could be understood in this way. Cf. 2:18 also.

[168] Haenchen, *Apostelgeschichte,* 190–91, 252; cf. 221; here Haenchen quotes Dibelius, *Aufsätze,* 109.

[169] Hengel, "Ursprünge," 30–31. By "genuine missionary activity" Hengel apparently means the public preaching of the gospel by official missionaries.

[170] The fact that public preaching by the first Christians is documented in reliable texts goes against Dibelius and Haenchen (see n. 164). Hengel's argument that the prerequisite for the rapid expansion of Christianity is *public* proclamation does not hold up in the history of missions (cf. the rapid growth of the Christian church in China in spite of the impossibility of preaching publicly after the communist seizure of power).

[171] Similarly Goppelt, *Apostolische und nachapostolische Zeit,* 60.

[172] So also Haenchen, *Apostelgeschichte,* 252.

[173] Goppelt, *Apostolische und nachapostolische Zeit,* 23.

of the apostles or an evangelist to come to their home so that their entire household could hear the good news of the gospel; this, of course, would have been a kind of house evangelism as well. For the development of this reconstruction, however, we are entirely dependent on our social-historical *oikos* model, and the result is admittedly somewhat speculative. There is no concrete evidence in the texts that would document such an approach by the first Christians in the primitive church in Jerusalem. On the other hand, the story in Acts 10:23–48 offers an analogy. If Peter could be invited by Cornelius into his home to give an evangelistic message to the entire household in Caesarea, then it is not unthinkable that something similar could have happened in Jerusalem as well.

Missional Outreach as Community Lifestyle

The first Christians in Jerusalem also had an evangelistic impact in and through their house churches simply by living in community with one another, which the following observations will illustrate. As we have already seen, members of the primitive church in Jerusalem remained in close fellowship (ἐν κοινωνίᾳ) with one another (Acts 2:42). This had an inward impact. Practically speaking, the precondition for realizing this intimate fellowship was the possibility of gathering in small groups (see below). In a church that was continually growing larger, the house churches offered a personal, family-like setting.[174] In a house church consisting of about ten to twenty people, it was possible to get to know one another, to grow close and connect on a deeper level. Only in such a setting was it possible to become "one in heart and mind" (Acts 4:32) in a practical sense. Only in this way could early Christians go beyond the superficial, cultivate deeper personal relationships, and support one another in a very concrete way, even in material matters.

This fellowship as experienced in the house churches in Jerusalem also had an outward impact. One of the prerequisites for this impact was again the *oikos,* in which the attractive elements of this fellowship became visible to those outside the faith. An integral part of this scenario was not only the architectural features of a house, its living room, kitchen, and so forth, but also its sociological features, the family, the real people living in community with one another. Both the architectural and the sociological features play a necessary role in making this fellowship visible to outsiders. "The way Christians lived in community with one another in spite of their social differences, the fact that they made the needs of one the concern of all . . . all of this generated a power that flowed out from their community, requiring and producing a response . . . Moreover, these (house) groups were compellingly attractive, drawing others into their midst."[175] The close connection between

---

[174] Regarding the family-like character of the NT house churches, cf. Rordorf, "Hausgemeinde."

[175] Vogler, "Bedeutung," 788–79; cf. esp. Acts 2:42–47; 5:14; Lorenzen, "Christliche Hauskirche," 333–52, here 336–37, esp. n. 13.

intensive community life and church growth is illustrated in Acts 2:47, which, after a description of koinonia fellowship, says, "they had the favor of all the people. And the Lord added to their number daily those who were being saved."

The attractive community life of the first Christians drew others into their midst. The draw was not only because of the (God-given) human attractiveness of these early Christians. It was also rooted in the truth of the teachings of the apostles: the crucified Jesus is the exalted Christ and the returning Lord of the universe (2:36).[176] The teachings of the apostles certainly included the Decalogue and the instructions of Jesus, for which the double commandment to love God and neighbor (Mark 12:28–34 par.) and the commandment to love your enemies (Luke 6:27–36/Matt 5:38–48) were typical examples. These commandments, along with the series of sayings on serving one another (Mark 10:42–44), outline the community life of the primitive church in Jerusalem. They stand in striking contrast to customary religious life otherwise encountered at the time, and ultimately this is one of the main reasons the first Christians were so attractive to others around them.[177]

The preliminary conclusion from these findings is that house churches were significant for the missional outreach of the primitive church in Jerusalem in a dual sense. They were a training ground for Christian koinonia fellowship inwardly and a showplace of Christian fellowship outwardly. This missional expansion of the gospel was due not so much to the mission-strategic initiatives of individuals as to the powerful attraction of a Christian community actively practicing koinonia fellowship.

It must be emphasized again, however, that we have no direct evidence for such a house mission advance (by way of either conversation or lifestyle) in the primitive church in Jerusalem. We have no direct textual evidence that the first Christians in the primitive church in Jerusalem practiced this style of evangelism. An indirect reference can be seen in the fact that the missional outreach of the Jerusalem church took place not only in the city but in the surrounding area as well (Acts 5:16).[178] This is understandable especially in

---

[176] Stuhlmacher, *Grundlegung*, 202–3.

[177] Lohfink, *Jesus and Community*, 149–63, 181–85. Only the Essenes would have been able to give the Christians competition in this regard. This is all the more likely in the case of an Essene presence in Jerusalem at the time of Jesus (cf. Riesner, "Das Jerusalemer Essenerviertel," 1777–1831; following him, Capper, "Community of Goods of the Jerusalem Church," 26.2:1760; both are of the opinion that literary and archaeological evidence appears to support the view of an Essene presence in Jerusalem at the time of Jesus). This could have been a motivating factor for the primitive church. "For evangelistic reasons alone, the primitive church could not afford to live a lifestyle ethically less attractive than that of its neighbors" (Riesner, "Essener," 76).

[178] This can be concluded from Matt 10:23 and Acts 9:31–43 (cf. Pesch, "Voraussetzungen," 48). Acts 11:1, 29; Gal 1:22; and 1 Thess 2:14 inform us as well regarding the existence of Judean congregations. Mark 13:14 also implies Judean churches in the surrounding area of Jerusalem.

light of the fact that members of the primitive church lived outside the city (e.g., Bethany, Emmaus, Jericho).[179] It is possible that their homes became bases of operation for the missional outreach of the Jerusalem church to the surrounding areas.

In addition, we need to keep in mind that Luke instead emphasizes the public ministry of the apostles and the rapid growth of the Jerusalem church through mass conversions. He is known to be an author who simply leaves some things untold. C. Weizsäcker suspected long ago that the primitive church in Jerusalem did practice the evangelistic approach described above, for the reason that the barriers there, such as fear of officials, would have been even greater than elsewhere.[180] Not all Christians would have been as courageous as Peter and John. Rather than preaching publicly, they would have preferred to share their faith from person to person in the private spheres of their homes.[181] This applies as well before 32/34 C.E. because of the persecutory activities of Paul in Jerusalem (Acts 8:1–3).

The fact that both before and after Easter (during the ministry of Jesus and in the Pauline missions) houses played a significant role in missional outreach leads us to believe that they made an important contribution in the primitive church as well. Hence, there is good reason to assume that evangelistic activities of the Jerusalem church were also performed in the private setting of domestic houses.

House Church Leadership Structures in Jerusalem

We know very little about the development of leadership structures in the Jerusalem church or about the practical and theological ideas behind them. Here the NT scholar is dependent on a few almost incidental references in Acts and in the Pauline Letters. Inferences can be made from these references in an effort to reconstruct the developmental process of leadership structures in the primitive church. The objective of this section is not to piece together an extensive reconstruction of the situation.[182] The intention is much more modest: to attempt merely to determine the significance of Jerusalem houses in the development of these organizational structures. One general observation regarding our context can be made: the history of the primitive church in Jerusalem can be divided into two periods—one under the leadership of Peter and the other under the leadership of James, the Lord's brother.

---

[179] These names are explicitly mentioned in Mark 14:3–9, 10:46–52, and Luke 24:13–35. With Pesch, "Voraussetzungen," 48. Cf. also Luke 10:38–42; John 11:1–3; 12:2.

[180] Weizsäcker, *Das apostolische Zeitalter*, 25–26.

[181] In addition, we need to ask whether some have the calling to preach publicly and others to missional outreach by way of personal conversations and lifestyle. One can get this impression from the texts. Cf. Stuhlmacher, "Weg," 115.

[182] Cf. Roloff, *Kirche*, 75–82, for an extensive reconstruction.

Under the Leadership of Peter

The circle of the Twelve was established by Jesus before Easter and chosen as the twelve regents of the eschatological Israel with Peter as their leader. Thus Peter together with the Twelve had a position of preeminence in the Jerusalem church. From the very beginning, the Twelve were responsible for the leadership of the primitive church (Acts 1–12 passim; cf. also Gal 1:18) with its center in the house with the upper room. Peter was simultaneously the head of the entire Jerusalem church and leader of the house church in the upper room. In none of our texts, however, is he described as head of the household or as owner of this house.

Nevertheless, it would have been quite natural for Peter to take on the role of the housefather by presiding over the bread-breaking celebration in the house with the upper room. It would have been just as natural for the actual homeowner to retain this function for himself. Unfortunately, the texts do not give us an answer to this question. In this regard the position of Peter is ambivalent—at one point he is in Jerusalem and leader of the primitive church, and later he is under way as an itinerant preacher. He in fact takes on the role more of a church planter. At any rate, Peter was certainly not a typical housefather figure in the sense required by our *oikos* model. It is clear that this house church does not fit neatly into the *oikos* scheme, whereby the house owner is also patron and/or leader of the house church. To some extent the concept of the Twelve collides with *oikos* structure here.

An interesting observation is that the householder of the house containing the upper room is not once mentioned by name.[183] We can assume that someone was its owner (Joseph of Arimathea?) and made it available to the congregation as a meeting place, but we do not know whether this person had a leading role, if any, in this house church. We can assume on the basis of the *oikos* model that this person did have an important function, even if it was merely the role of a patron to the congregation meeting in his or her house. Here again the texts are silent.

After the Twelve had left house and home in Galilee and moved to Jerusalem, we can assume that they did not become house owners in Jerusalem. For this reason they do not come into question as householders who emerged from the *oikos* setting as house church leaders. What function they did have, if any, in the organization of the Jerusalem house churches is difficult to determine. We only know that during the early days John, son of Zebedee (Acts 12:2),[184] and presumably his brother James (12:16) also had prominent positions, though somewhat lower than Peter in the Jerusalem church.

---

[183] Cf., however, Mark 14:14. Here a householder is implied for the house, which contained the room of the Last Supper. This would be significant if the house with the upper room (Acts 1:13) can be identified with the house containing the room of the Last Supper (Mark 14:15). See n. 48.

[184] Acts 1:13; 3:1, 3, 4, 11; 4:1, 3, 7, 13, 19, 23; 8:14, 17, 25.

It was under the leadership of Peter that the events involving the Hellenist seven led by Stephen (6:5) took place. In 6:1 Luke tells of a conflict centered on the food distribution for the Hellenist widows. Because the distribution network organized by the Hebrew congregation did not cover the Hellenists adequately, they were confronted with the necessity of establishing their own system of distribution. "The organizational structure that they then selected remained within customary Jewish parameters. The group of seven corresponded to the leadership structure in a local synagogue with a council of seven elders as the leaders of the congregation. The task of the group of seven was also analogous: they were to represent the congregation outwardly in the public arena and to look after the organization of the inner life of the community."[185]

There are many NT scholars who, along with J. Roloff, assume that the Hellenists formed a leadership council in the Jerusalem church analogous to the synagogue.[186] The question, however, is how it came about that precisely these men were considered qualified for such a leadership task. Where did they gain the experience needed to carry out the responsibilities of such an office? Even though it cannot be demonstrated with certainty, at least some of the seven may well have been homeowners and/or leaders of, or teachers in, house churches before they were selected for this office.[187] Some of the seven had teaching gifts and leadership abilities that match those a Jewish housefather would have acquired from his education and experience as a householder (see ch. 4).

The following scenario is certainly within the realm of possibility. In the house churches some or all of the seven were able to develop their leadership skills and grow into maturity, proving themselves reliable, capable leaders. As a result, their leadership ability came to the attention of the Hellenists as a whole, and they were then elected as the leaders for the Hellenists in 6:1–6. If this is an accurate description of the events as they happened, then it would be a very early example of how house churches served as training grounds for future leaders of the church as a whole.[188]

Two things should be kept in mind, however, in this regard. First, the number seven had symbolic significance in the primitive church in Jerusalem. We therefore need to exercise caution here. We are not suggesting that there were precisely seven Hellenist house church leaders available who then

---

[185] Roloff, *Kirche,* 77. On the correspondence, cf. Str-B 2:641.
[186] Hengel, "Zwischen Jesus und Paulus," 175, 180, "das Führungskollegium"; Schürmann, "'... und Lehrer,'" 137; Goppelt, *Apostolic and Post-Apostolic Times,* 53. The hypothesis that the synagogue served as a model here assumes that Schürer, Krause, and, following them, Schrage have accurately described the Jewish synagogue and its leadership structures for that time. This, however, is disputed (cf. Rajak and Noy, "ARCHISYNAGOGOI").
[187] Goppelt, *Apostolic and Post-Apostolic Times,* 51, 53, considers this a possibility without, however, reflecting further on the matter.
[188] Filson, "Significance," 111–12.

in some miraculous way became the seven leaders of the whole Hellenist community. The exact number of house churches that existed in Jerusalem at the time of the events of 6:1–6 is not known. Second, neither is it being suggested that the seven could only have proven their leadership skills as homeowners and/or leaders of, or in, house churches.[189] Some of them were charismatic preachers, teachers, or evangelists (cf. Stephen and Philip)[190] who could have developed and proven their leadership ability either partially or totally independent of the house church structure (e.g., in the synagogue, in the temple, at the marketplace, or as a house guest and teacher in someone else's home).[191]

The following consideration regarding leadership structures in the primitive church in Jerusalem also belongs to the period of Petrine leadership. In the narrative of Ananias and Saphira (5:1–11), it is implied that the congregation is divided into younger and older groups, which apparently took on different tasks.[192] The νεώτεροι are responsible for burials. The spectrum of opinions among NT scholars varies, with some referring the term ecclesiologically to "office," others sociologically to "station" or "rank," and yet others chronologically to "designation of age."[193]

Discussing the ransom saying of Jesus, J. Jeremias addresses the relationship of Mark 10:54 to Luke 22:25–27.[194] According to Jeremias, the Lukan version of the saying regarding Jesus' serving (Luke 22:27) is grecized.[195] Luke 22:26–27 represents a Gentile version (free from Semitisms and avoiding all that would be foreign to Hellenists), and Mark 10:45 a Jewish-Christian version, of the sayings. In the context of 22:26–27, *Gemeindesprache* also occurs.[196] An example of this *Gemeindesprache* is νεώτεροι in verse 26. Seen in this way, the young men, as a station or rank, stand in contrast to the older ones (elders).[197] In 22:26 the νεώτερος is juxtaposed to the

---

[189] If Str-B 2:641 is correct in assuming that the seven were a kind of "Ortsvorstand" ("local council"), then it would not have been necessary for every one of them to have led a house church. They could have had honorary positions in these house churches (see below).

[190] Acts 6:1–3, 10, 13; 7:2–53; 8:5, 26–40; 21:8.

[191] It was quite common in the ancient world for a householder to hire a house teacher or invite a specialist in rhetoric to stay in the house for longer periods. Cf. Lynch, *Aristotle's School*, 174–75; Hock, *Social Context*, 53–55; following them, Blue, "In Public," 225–26; Osiek and Balch, *Families*, 68–70, 220.

[192] The "older" group is not explicitly mentioned.

[193] For office, see Bauernfeind, *Apostelgeschichte*, 86–87; Cadbury and Lake, *Acts*, 4:51. For station or rank, see Jeremias, *Abba*, 226. For age, see Haenchen, *Apostelgeschichte*, 233; Roloff, *Apostelgeschichte*, 94; F. F. Bruce, *Acts*, 106; Pesch, *Apostelgeschichte*, 1:200; Conzelmann, *Apostelgeschichte*, 45 (νεώτεροι was not intended as "office"); following him, G. Schneider, *Apostelgeschichte*, 1:375; Barrett, *Acts*, 268.

[194] Jeremias, *Abba*, 226.

[195] Ibid., 225.

[196] With this term Jeremias is referring to "language created by the church."

[197] Cf. besides Acts 5:6 also Titus 2:6, οἱ νεώτεροι = young men as a rank in the community; 1 Tim 5:1; 1 Pet 5:5, as in contrast to πρεσβύτεροι.

μείζων. If Jeremias is correct in his analysis of Mark 10:42–45 in relation to Luke 22:25–27, then compared with Mark 10:42–44 the Lukan version is a Hellenist form of tradition that appears to originate partially from Luke himself.[198] With the νεώτεροι he probably had a group (of young men; cf. Acts 5:10) in the congregation in mind who were expected to perform (lower or higher) services. Acts 5:6 is to be understood in the same way. It is striking, however, that πρεσβύτεροι do not appear in any of our texts; instead, the νεώτεροι are juxtaposed only to the μεγάλοι or to Peter himself. If the presbyters were not office holders but instead merely persons of honor or respect, it would by all means be plausible to say that the νεώτεροι in Luke 22:26–27 and Acts 5:6 correspond to the πρεσβύτεροι.[199] Acts 5:6 would then be a reference demonstrating that at least Luke reckoned with presbyters from the earliest days in the primitive church in Jerusalem. The factual use of νεώτεροι in 5:6 allows us to conclude that even as early as the leadership of Peter, μείζονες, perhaps also honored as πρεσβύτεροι, could have stood opposite the νεώτεροι. Actually, μεγάλοι must be understood in the sense of status. Because they were influential, πρεσβύτεροι could have come to be called μεγάλοι exclusively. In light of this, the μείζονες or the πρεσβύτεροι could have acted as leaders of individual house churches. This, of course, cannot be proven with certainty. In light of 1:21–26,[200] they would have at least been treated as respected, diversely qualified, leading members of the congregation.

The reference to the house of Mary, mother of John Mark (12:12–14), lies between our two time periods. This house church existed during the period of Peter's leadership but continued to play an important role in the Jerusalem church under the leadership of James (cf. 12:17).

Here, interestingly enough, it was a woman who made her home available to the church as a place of assembly. We can thus assume that she also played an important role with a possible leadership function in the group that met in her house. In our context we need to distinguish between *oikos* structures in general and patriarchal structures in particular. If Mary had influence in the church that met in her home, it was most likely due to her position as householder within the *oikos*.[201] In this case not patriarchal but rather ancient *oikos* structures would have been influential in the formation of leadership within her house church.

But exercise of authority in such a household setting can happen in many different ways. The question whether the householder presided over

---

[198] Jeremias, *Sprache*, 290.

[199] On πρεσβύτεροι as a designation of honor, see pp. 102–5.

[200] From this passage we get the impression that a whole group of respected men with leadership ability was available who were considered candidates for election to the circle of the Twelve.

[201] Cf. Philostratus, *Gymn.* 272.30–31, for a reference to a woman as head of a household (after the death of her husband).

only part or all of the worship service that took place in his or her house will need to be answered differently from situation to situation. In the case of Mary, we know too little about the actual leadership structures of the house church that met in her home. Presumably Mary exercised some sort of patronage toward the congregation. Our texts do not indicate whether she presided over the worship service.[202] We know for certain that Mary is one of the first examples of the concrete involvement of a woman in a house church setting in the history of Christianity. It is possible, on the basis of all that we know about the *oikos* in the ancient world in general and about Palestine in particular, that John Mark took on the role of the head of the household in his mother Mary's home. We need to bear in mind, however, that he was often gone on missionary trips with Peter, Paul, and Barnabas even if it was only for short periods.

Under the Leadership of James, the Lord's Brother

Scholars assume that, because of the persecution of the primitive church in Jerusalem by Agrippa I (Acts 12:1–3), particularly after the execution of James, son of Zebedee, Peter felt compelled (41/42 C.E.) to give up the leadership of the church and at least temporarily leave the city.[203] Drastic changes in the Jerusalem church followed. The circle of the Twelve was no longer supplemented by special elections. Instead of Peter and the Twelve as the decisive figures in the leadership of the church (1:12–14; 6:2), now a distinct group of apostles appear in leading roles (15:3, 22), and the elders, along with James as their head,[204] appear as the body giving leadership to the Jerusalem church.[205]

It was also necessary to leave behind some of the practices from the period of enthusiasm. The church began at this point to organize itself more stringently. By this time, James, the Lord's brother, had already established himself as leader of the church. This also implies that the organizational structures of the church had become more stable. Matthew 18:15–17 could be an indication of firmer structures in the primitive church. Here we find a rigorous regulation that suggests a three-stage procedure in case a member of the congregation transgressed basic norms of the ἐκκλησία. This regulation appears to be very constant in early Christianity and to be in effect for all congregations, including those in the Pauline and Johannine missions.[206] Matthew probably obtained it from an

---

[202] This kind of involvement is much more apparent in the Pauline house churches for quite a number of women, a topic taken up later in this study (see pp. 210–25).

[203] Regarding chronology, cf. Riesner, *Frühzeit*, 104–8. For possible reasons for the departure and the permanent exclusion of Peter from the city, cf. Hengel, "Jakobus," 101–2.

[204] Cf. Roloff, *Kirche*, 80–82.

[205] Cf. Riesner, *Frühzeit*, 71–104, here 91; Roloff, *Kirche*, 80–82.

[206] Cf. Luke 17:3; 2 Thess 3:6, 14–15; Rom 16:17; 1 Cor 5:9–13; 6:1–11; 2 Cor 13:11; Gal 6:1; 1 Tim 5:19–20; 2 Tim 4:2; Titus 3:10; 1 John 5:19–20.

older Jewish-Christian tradition with pre-Easter roots.[207] All this supports the view that this tradition could also have a Sitz im Leben in the primitive church in Jerusalem.[208]

The leadership of the primitive church in Jerusalem passed over to James, and from this time on he and a council of elders oversaw the congregation.[209] This presbyterial organization of the church proved to be stable and lasted at least until 62 C.E. (the martyrdom of James).[210]

In the earliest days of the Jerusalem church, we hear virtually nothing regarding elders.[211] Not until the later years under the leadership of James does the situation develop in that direction. The question is what factors led to this development and whether house churches played a role in any significant way. Generally, the origin of the office of elder in the Jerusalem church, as recorded in other documents from the apostolic and postapostolic periods, is explained by NT scholars in the following manner:[212] Sometime during the first ten to fifteen years, the "office" of elder was created and patterned after the Jewish synagogue. Either these elders succeeded the Twelve after their departure from Jerusalem to preach the gospel elsewhere or they functioned in the church as administrative assistants to the apostles from the very beginning.[213]

A. E. Harvey has pointed out, however, that this view has a number of weaknesses and needs to be revised.[214] First, this understanding of the general way in which the term "the elders" was used in the ancient world is open to question. Both in the Greco-Roman and in the Jewish worlds the term connoted respect, honor, and prestige rather than office or rank.[215] The designation was indefinite, representative, and rooted in the ancient *oikos*. The "elders" in the ancient world were most often householders and they "owed

---

[207] On its provenance, cf. the discussions of Roloff, *Kirche,* 167; I. H. Marshall, *Gospel of Luke,* 642. K. Schmidt, "ἐκκλησία," *TDNT* 3:518–26, considers it possible that the saying containing the rebuke of the brother in Matt 18:15–17 is pre-Easter. The context would then be the local synagogue community. Regarding the Jewish background, cf. Str-B 1:789–92.

[208] Cf. Dodd, *New Testament Studies,* 57–58.

[209] Acts 15:2, 4, 6, 22–23; 21:18. Also 11:30 points to this time. Cf. Riesner, *Frühzeit,* 120.

[210] Cf. Josephus, *Ant.* 20.200.

[211] Cf., however, the discussion of νεώτεροι on pp. 98–99.

[212] Lightfoot, *Philippians,* 179–81; cf. Pesch, *Apostelgeschichte,* 1:357; Roloff, *Kirche,* 81; G. Schneider, *Apostelgeschichte,* ad loc..

[213] F. F. Bruce, *Acts,* 231 n. 44; Farrer, "Ministry," 115–82, 133–42. Cf. Bauckham, "James," for a discussion and his view of the matter, a third position.

[214] Harvey, "Elders." Campbell further develops Harvey's thesis in *Elders,* 159–61. Cf. also Karrer, "Ältestenamt."

[215] Campbell, *Elders,* 160; cf. also his extensive examination of the term "elder" in the ancient world, pp. 20–96. Cf. also Krauss, *Synagogale Altertümer,* 143; Leon, *Jews,* 181.

their position in society to the power of their family, and their position in the family to their relative seniority."[216]

Second, the thesis that the office of elder in the Jerusalem church was patterned after the Jewish synagogue is also problematic. As many scholars have already noticed, the synagogue did not have an office of elder as such. There were, granted, men in the synagogue with this title who exercised authority in the synagogue community as a whole, but they did not have an office.[217] Neither were elders officially appointed; they existed independent of any kind of appointment on the basis of their seniority and social position in the community.[218] The elders were not the ones who presided over the daily or weekly worship services in the synagogue.[219] Who took on such leadership functions in the synagogue is disputed. For many years scholars assumed that office holders or clerics (e.g., the ἀρχισυνάγωγος or the ὑπηρέτης) had this function.[220] On the basis of recent research, scholars are beginning to get the impression that not even the ἀρχισυνάγωγος was an office holder or the leader of the synagogue community.[221]

Even though scholars have noticed that the synagogue did not have the office of elders in the sense often assumed and that elders were not responsible for running the internal affairs of the synagogue, this insight is rarely applied to the elders in the Jerusalem church.[222] The logical consequence would be that early Christians could not have patterned their organizational structures, specifically the office of elder, after the Jewish synagogue because no such office existed there.[223]

---

[216] Campbell, *Elders*, 95.

[217] This also depends on the definition of the term "office." See pp. 197–210. It is also important to distinguish between the synagogue as the community in a village, town, or city and the synagogue as the congregation of faith that gathers for prayer and study of the word. In some Jewish communities a leadership council existed, some of whose members were called elders. But the term "elders" as a designation of office is not documented for the synagogue congregation of faith. Cf. Campbell, *Elders*, 112.

[218] Harvey, "Elders," 331: "There can be no question of appointing people to be elders: elders exist already."

[219] Campbell, *Elders*, 111–12; cf. also 44–54. Here Campbell is able to refer to a series of scholars also in support of his view: Harvey, "Elders"; Sobosan, "Role"; Powell, "Ordo"; Karrer, "Ältestenamt," 159; M. MacDonald, *Pauline Churches*, 215; Banks, *Paul's Idea*, 147. Against Bornkamm, "πρέσβυς," *TDNT* 6:662–63.

[220] "The elders . . . did not themselves hold office, but their corporate judgment probably decided who did, namely the ἄρχοντες." Thus, "the elders ran the synagogues, but it was not as the elders of the synagogue that they did so. They ran the synagogues because they ran the community, and they did so not by virtue of an office they held but because of the honour they enjoyed as senior men from traditionally powerful families" (Campbell, *Elders*, 54).

[221] Cf. the results of the study by Rajak and Noy, "ARCHISYNAGOGOI."

[222] Cf. as an exception Karrer, "Ältestenamt," 159, and Campbell's criticism of Karrer's view in *Elders*, 161–62.

[223] This does not mean that the synagogue played no role at all as a model for the formation of the Christian understanding of elders.

If R. A. Campbell's analysis of the term "elders" as it was used in the ancient world and specifically in the synagogue is accurate, this implies that we should not look for a separate group of office holders who bore this title in the Jerusalem church.[224] Instead we need to ask to whom such a title of honor or respect could have naturally been applied.

Campbell suggests an intriguing answer to this question.[225] First of all, he observes that the majority of scholars now agree that, from the primitive church in Jerusalem through the Pauline mission and beyond, householders provided early Christianity with a meeting place and the protection of their patronage.[226] Campbell suggests therefore that it was inevitable that the patriarchal structures of the ancient household would partially and in some respects largely determine the leadership structures of the church. Because so much points in the direction that the first Christians in Jerusalem met primarily in private homes, Campbell assumes that leaders existed there at the house church level. It would have been quite natural even in the earliest days for the house owner and host of the church meeting in his house to assume that leadership role.[227]

In addition, Campbell suggests that the overseer of the Aramaic-speaking house churches in Jerusalem was called *mebaqqer* (מבקר) and later in the Greek-speaking house churches ἐπίσκοπος. Collectively, however, it would have been quite natural to call them זקנים or πρεσβύτεροι. After all, they were the "senior men in the community, heads of the leading families within it, . . . informal, representative and collective,"[228] which fits well with the general understanding of elders in Judaism and in the ancient world as a whole. The term was both flexible and vague—it neither refers to office holders in particular nor excludes them.[229] It was also rooted in the ancient *oikos* and therefore easily understandable not only for those from an OT background but also for those in the contemporary social setting.

Campbell's thesis is quite attractive, and he has made a number of points worthy of consideration. His overall proposal, however, dead-ends in an age-old dilemma: there is no mention either of "house fathers" (see above) or of overseers or ἐπίσκοποι in the pertinent Lukan texts on the Jerusalem church. As already observed, the householder of the house with the upper room is not referred to by name. In the house of Mary it can only be assumed that she herself was the householder. In Acts 1–14 not one single

---

[224] Regarding elders, the question is whether we know enough about the Diaspora synagogue in order to make definitive statements about its structures of office.

[225] Campbell, *Elders*, 151–63.

[226] See ch. 4, for an extensive discussion of Pauline house churches. For additional literature, see pp. 1–16.

[227] Campbell is not the first to suggest this. Cf. also Dassmann, "Hausgemeinde," 82–97, esp. 89–90. So also Filson, "Significance," 111–12; following him, Vogler, "Bedeutung," 792; Klauck, *Hausgemeinde,* 32.

[228] Campbell, *Elders*, 65.

[229] Cf. also Rajak and Noy, "ARCHISYNAGOGOI," who also point out the flexibility of the titles used in Jewish synagogues.

householder in the Jerusalem church is mentioned (10:1–3 refers to Cornelius, however, in Caesarea). Not until the writings of Paul does this change (cf., e.g., Phlm 1–3). Neither are Christian ἐπίσκοποι mentioned until later.[230] Campbell is aware of this, of course. He attempts to fill the gaps left in Luke's report on the Jerusalem church in Acts by drawing analogous inferences about the church in Jerusalem on the basis of what we know about the Pauline house churches and the sociohistorical model of the ancient *oikos*. It is precisely for this reason that it is worth considering Campbell's thesis that the first Christians met in private homes and that therefore we can assume leaders automatically emerged from the structure of the ancient *oikos* for those house churches, but it nevertheless remains a conjecture.

In particular, patriarchal *oikos* structures were perhaps not as prominant in the formation of leadership structures as the sociohistorical *oikos* model would require.[231] First, the line between the Jerusalem church and the Pauline mission was probably not as continuous as Campbell portrays it. Second, as we have seen, at least in the beginning up until the death of James, son of Zebedee, that is, after the concept of the Twelve was no longer in effect, a tension existed between the circle of the Twelve and *oikos* structures regarding leadership structures in the Jerusalem church. It can be asked whether James, the Lord's brother (also given the surname "the just"), who then became leader of the primitive church in Jerusalem, subsequently exercised a kind of housefather function from his residence in the house with the upper room (Acts 21:18). It seems to make sense to imagine him being more sedentary and in a household setting—we have no indication in our texts that he was active as an itinerant preacher. It is by all means possible that when the Jerusalem church gathered (in his residence), he often presided as housefather over the breaking of bread. But again, the texts testify neither to this nor to any other patriarchal tasks that James might have performed.

Likewise, Campbell's thesis that the leaders in the Aramaic-speaking house churches were called מבקר is certainly attractive but, again, not documented in the texts.[232] Harvey and Campbell would appear to be on the mark, however, with their suggestion that the synagogue elders did not bear that "office." In the Jerusalem church, πρεσβύτερος was most likely, at least in the beginning, an honorific title that had a fairly flexible range of connotations. It is also within the realm of possibility that, analogously to the synagogue, some of the Christian elders in the Jerusalem church grew out of a collection of householders or house church leaders.[233] Also, the elders mentioned in Acts

---

[230] Cf. Acts 20; Phil 1:1; 1 Tim 3:2. See pp. 205–10 and 268–81 for discussion.

[231] Cf., e.g., Gaudemet, "Familie," esp. 299–300, 302–38; Z. W. Falk, "Jewish Private Law," esp. 513–18; Safrai, "Home," esp. 748–73; Klauck, *Hausgemeinde*, 15–18; Campbell, *Elders*, 20–96; Verner, *Household*, 44–47.

[232] Campbell clearly admits this (*Elders*, 155, 158).

[233] "Analogously" here is meant in the sense that the elders of the synagogue were given this honorific precisely because they were senior men from traditionally powerful families and thus homeowners and heads of households.

15 may well have been men who had originally led house churches. But again, this cannot be proven with certainty from the texts at our disposal.

The book of Acts appears to indicate that the title "elder" indeed became a designation for office with the passage of time (cf. esp. 15:4, 6, 22, 41; 16:4; 21:18). In that case, we have the Christian use of office terminology that is not derived from the synagogue. Accordingly, we must assume a stronger early Christian contribution to the formation of the office of elder than is normally assumed, something that went unnoticed by Campbell.[234] We will revisit some of these issues again in chapter 4 in the context of the Pauline house churches, as the texts there give us additional information toward formulating a more comprehensive perspective.[235]

From Jerusalem to Antioch

This section traces the path of the gospel from the Jerusalem church to the congregations known to us from the Pauline Epistles and thus the transition to the Gentile mission, with particular consideration given to the significance of the house church for this development.[236] This transition should not be imagined as a one-time event but rather as a process in several different stages and at various locations.[237]

The Missional Outreach of the Hellenists

There are indications that the Hellenists took courageous steps quite early in a boundary-breaking, parameter-transcending direction. The so-called seven, the group of Hellenists formed around their most prominent member and leader, Stephen (Acts 6:1–6), was of great significance in the missional history of the Christian movement from the earliest days.[238] Initially Stephen and the other members of the seven engaged in a fairly organized outreach to the Hellenistic synagogues of Jerusalem among their Greek-speaking fellow Jews (6:8–10).[239] Stephen's criticism, contained in

---

[234] He concludes that the title "elder" was used in the Jerusalem church analogously to its use in the synagogue as an honorific, but not as a designation of office (see Campbell, *Elders*, 190).

[235] Esp. in late Pauline literature (cf. the household codes and the Pastoral Letters), *oikos* structures become predominant.

[236] Regarding early Christian missions in general, cf. Hahn, *Verständnis*, 37–48; Hengel, "Ursprünge"; Stuhlmacher, "Weg"; Kertelge, *Mission*, esp. Pesch, "Voraussetzungen"; Ollrog, *Paulus*; Riesner, *Frühzeit*, 95–110; Stuhlmacher, "Matt 28:16–20."

[237] Hengel, "Zwischen Jesus und Paulus," esp. 197, and *Zur urchristlichen Geschichtsschreibung*, 63–70; B. Meyer, *Early Christians*, 67–83; Löning, "Stephanuskreis"; Pesch, "Voraussetzungen"; Riesner, *Frühzeit*, 96–97.

[238] Stuhlmacher, *Grundlegung*, 204.

[239] Ollrog, *Paulus*, 155 n. 195; Hahn, *Verständnis*, 49–50. Regarding the Greek-speaking Diaspora synagogues in Jerusalem, cf. Str-B 1:661–63 and the Theodotus inscription, *CII* 2:1404.

his missional messages (6:14), of the temple cult and the revealed authority of the Torah became an offense fatal for him and his Hellenistic countrymen. Because of this "blasphemy" his angry audience stoned Stephen to death, and his followers were driven out of Jerusalem (7:59–8:3). Ironically, as a result of the Hellenists' expulsion from Jerusalem, the spread of the Christian message was significantly accelerated.[240]

One of the expelled was a member of the seven by the name of Philip. He carried the gospel beyond the previous boundaries of Judaism to the God-fearers and to the Samaritans (8:4–13, 26–40).[241] The Palestinian coastal range with its predominantly Gentile cities, such as Gaza (8:26), Asdod, and Caesarea (8:40), played a central role in his mission. It is most likely that Philip and other Hellenists progressively altered their approach to missional outreach, adapting it for the Gentiles by making it "law-free," that is, by not holding the Gentiles accountable to the demands and restrictions of the law.[242]

Although it cannot be documented with certainty, there seems to be some indication that Philip proceeded as an itinerant missionary from house to house like the approach that Jesus took.[243] In 21:8–9 we learn that Philip was a homeowner in Caesarea. It was probably there that he earned the title "evangelist" (21:8). With Hengel, I suggest that in his missional outreach Philip strategically concentrated on a specific area by setting up residence in Caesarea and then targeting the above-mentioned cities in the surrounding countryside.[244] The house of Philip apparently played an important role in his mission efforts. His house was possibly the meeting place for a house church. It is well known that the Jewish Christians who came from a Greco-Roman background were generally more affluent than those from a Judean origin.[245] The information that he was able to offer Paul and his companions his hospitality and take them into his home is an indication that his house might have been large enough to serve as an assembly place for a house church. Along with the house of Cornelius, this could have been a second house church in Caesarea and so an indication of a plurality of house churches there.

In addition to Caesarea, Damascus appears to be another Hellenist center (9:1–19).[246] The congregation there was presumably a filial church of

---

[240] Hengel, "Zwischen Jesus und Paulus," 151–206.

[241] For a nationalistic Jew, the Samaritans were worse that the Gentiles. Cf. Str-B 1:538–40; 2:525; 3:313, 1183; Jeremias, *Jerusalem*, 387–89; Hengel, *War Jesus Revolutionär?* 19, 38–39.

[242] Hengel, *Zur urchristlichen Geschichtsschreibung*, 70, and "Historiker Lukas," 164–69.

[243] Acts 8:40: "he traveled about and preached the gospel in all the towns" (cf. also 8:5–7, 26–28).

[244] Hengel, *Zur urchristlichen Geschichtsschreibung*, 69. Cf. Mark 7:24, 31; 8:27. See p. 42.

[245] Kasher, "Diaspora," *TRE* 8:714.

[246] Hahn, *Verständnis*, 49. Alexandria and possibly Rome as well belonged to the Hellenist centers. Cf. also F. F. Bruce, *Men*, 60.

the Hellenists, or at least under the influence of the theological ideas of Stephen and the seven; otherwise Paul would not have wanted to persecute the church there (9:2). After his conversion Paul stayed in the house of Judas (9:11, 17). Luke reports that Paul was baptized there (in this house?) and "stays a few days with the disciples in Damascus." During this time he probably received instruction in the faith in the house of Judas from "the disciples in Damascus," and this was likely combined with training on how to live the Christian life.[247] Concrete memories of the conversion of Paul before Damascus, the disciple by the name of Ananias (9:10–19a), the explicit mention of the house of Judas on Straight Street (9:11), and the large number of disciples in Damascus (9:2, 19) are all reasons to believe that a fairly large congregation might have existed there that could have met in the house of Judas.

The Missional Outreach of Peter

One indication of the boundary-breaking missionary activity of Peter in the Jewish town of Joppa is handed down to us in Acts 9:36–43. After many came to faith through his healing ministry there, Peter stayed on for some time in the house of Simon the tanner. Unfortunately, the text does not inform us how Simon came to faith. One thing is certain: here we have clear evidence of a householder who extended Peter his hospitality and in doing so supported his missional outreach in the area.[248]

Interestingly, Acts informs us of another boundary-breaking, parameter-transcending incident, in which Peter again takes a house mission approach. Presumably because he considered this to be in agreement with Jesus' own example and teaching, Peter took a life-endangering step and began missional outreach to Gentiles.[249] His approach is clearly different from the pre-Easter mission instructions (Luke 10:1–12). In contrast to the itinerant setting of the mission tradition in Luke, Peter does not go randomly from house to house. Instead he is instructed by the Spirit of God to accompany into Cornelius's house the messengers sent by him. One

---

[247] Cf. Vogler, "Bedeutung," 789. Cf. Rom 1:3–4; 1 Cor 11:23b–25; 15:3b–5, in which it can be observed that Paul received such instruction. This kind of early Christian catechumenical instruction and lifestyle training for new converts in a household setting is further evidence of the significance of the house church in early Christian missional outreach. Such instruction and training in the Christian life were only possible in a house church because at that time it was not possible to live as a Christian anywhere other than in such household communities.

[248] A house church could have met in Simon's house. Where else would the many who came to faith through Peter's healing ministry have gathered for worship?

[249] Compare Acts 9:43 (accommodations in the house of Simon the tanner is indication of a freedom from pharisaic laws that is reminiscent of Jesus); 10:1–3 (Peter's administration of baptism to Cornelius without demanding circumcision) with Matt 8:5–13 par.; 15:21–28 par.; John 4:1–42 (Jesus' unorthodox involvement with Gentiles); Stuhlmacher, "Weg," 115, and esp. "Matt 28:16–20."

other post-Easter modification can also be observed: the content of the message has been slightly revised (compare Acts 10:36, 39–41 with Luke 10:5–7).

As early as 40/41 C.E. (Acts 10:1–48), then, we have a clear example of a house mission approach in the home of Cornelius in Caesarea.[250] A God-fearing householder invites Peter into his house[251] and gives him shelter (10:22–23). There the family, relatives, and closest friends of Cornelius are waiting for Peter to preach the gospel. All of those gathered accept the word of God (10:44; 11:1). At this point both a difference and a parallel to the pre-Easter mission situation can be observed. Through the proclamation of God's word, Cornelius and his entire household come to faith; through the peace greeting and the proclamation of the kingdom of God, the peace of God rests on the son of peace and his household (Luke 10:5–7; Matt 10:12–13). After this Peter is invited to stay a few days (compare Acts 10:48 with Luke 10:7). Many exegetes view Acts 10:1–48, among other things, as the story of the establishment of a house church and thus the history of the founding of the church in Caesarea.[252] From all we know, this view appears to be quite convincing. It is by all means possible that this house became a base of operations for the outreach to the city and surrounding area of Caesarea. Here again, however, the text does not inform us of further developments regarding the house of Cornelius.

As we have already seen, after Easter the Twelve initially continued Jesus' work of gathering of Israel, starting in Jerusalem. In particular, the texts report on the public preaching ministry of Peter and John (Acts 2:1–41; 3:1–26). Not until later did they begin an itinerant ministry, and then they preached the gospel "in many Samaritan villages" (Acts 8:25; cf. also 9:32). Peter and John presumably carried out their mission in accordance with pre-Easter mission instructions.[253] In Acts 3 John and Peter appear together as witnesses of Jesus. They are without belongings and combine proclamation with healing (cf. Luke 10:4, 9). The content of their proclamation, however, is no longer the kingdom of God drawing near in Jesus but rather Jesus as Messiah and returning Lord.[254] As itinerant preachers, they traveled from village to village, which implies from house to house, missionizing two by

---

[250] See the chronological classification of the Cornelius episode in Riesner, *Frühzeit*, 102, 110.

[251] See Matt 10:11–12 par. and the discussion of the pre-Easter householder mission on pp. 53–60. There it is observed that Luke 10:5–7 also implies the invitation of missionaries into the house by the householder.

[252] Klauck, *Hausgemeinde*, 56. Regarding the historical reliability of the report, cf. Hengel, *Zur urchristlichen Geschichtsschreibung*, 79–84; for some of the problems concerning historicity, cf. Lüdemann, *Das frühe Christentum*, 130–39, and a response in Gehring, *Hausgemeinde*, 201 n. 318.

[253] See pp. 48–60. Cf. Acts 9:32–43 and Pesch, "Voraussetzungen," 26–28, 48.

[254] Cf. Stuhlmacher, "Weg," 115.

two like the instructions given in Luke 10:1–3.[255] And here as well are the beginning stages of a planned missional outreach that was also cutting-edge in the sense that it was outside the boundaries of Judaism (Acts 8:4–25).[256]

The Missional Outreach of the Church of Antioch

The cutting-edge missional perspective of the Hellenists becomes even more clearly visible in the city of Antioch on the Orontes. In Antioch a planned centrifugal mission is initiated with the explicit objective of reaching out to Gentiles.[257] After fleeing Jerusalem, some of the members of the company formed around Stephen established a church there, which soon became the focal point of a worldwide mission.[258] From this "mother church" they engaged in missional outreach not only in Antioch but out into the surrounding area as well (Acts 11:20–30; 13:1–3; 15). This regional or "mission journey" type of outreach is illustrated particularly well by the activities of the main figures of Antioch's missional enterprise. Members of this group are, first of all, Barnabas (4:36–37), who "moved" from Jerusalem to Antioch presumably for this purpose, and, second, Paul, who is recruited by Barnabas and brought from Tarsus to be a part of Antioch's missional outreach (11:19–26). After one year of missional ministry in the city, Barnabas and Paul set out together on the first great mission journey via Cyprus into southern Asia Minor and then back to Antioch (13:4–14:28).

The book of Acts reports concrete details regarding the missional practice of the Antioch church.[259] Some of her members were sent out on mission journeys after fasting, prayer, and the laying on of hands. The missionaries returned to the church after completing their task and gave an accountability report (14:26–27; cf. Luke 10:17–20). At the very least, it can be inferred from this information that the church sent out some of its members on missional outreaches and, upon completion of their task and their return, it evaluated their missional ministry.[260]

Particularly in the reports on the trips of Barnabas and Paul, we get a clear picture of the practice of the itinerant or partner mission and its

---

[255] "From house to house" does not exclude the possibility that they went into synagogues, on the streets, and to the marketplaces in order to evangelize.
[256] Hengel, *Zur urchristlichen Geschichtsschreibung*, 68–69.
[257] Pesch, "Voraussetzungen," 45.
[258] Hahn, *Verständnis*, 49.
[259] Luke's report regarding Antioch's mission enterprise (esp. Acts 13:2–3; 14:26–27) is confirmed by two of Paul's remarks: the first is a reference to his mission spanning several years in Syria and Cilicia (Gal 1:21), and the second is that he undertook mission trips with Barnabas from Antioch (Gal 2:1–3; 1 Cor 9:6). Cf. Liechtenhan, *Urchristliche Mission*, 54–56; Schweizer, *Gemeinde*, 189; Georgi, *Gegner*, 47; Schnackenburg, "Lukas," 240–41; Kasting, *Anfänge*, 105; Filson, *Geschichte*, 226–27; against Merklein, *Das kirchliche Amt*, 253.
[260] Ollrog, *Paulus*, 157.

connection with some elements of the radical itinerant ethic as we observe it in Jesus' mission instruction tradition (Luke 10:1–12 par.) and as it was evidently practiced in the Antioch church.[261] Both Paul and most likely Barnabas renounced their right to marry, to own personal property, and to have a permanent residence (cf. 1 Cor 7:7; Phil 4:11–13; 2 Cor 6:10; 11:27; Acts 5:36–37). On the first mission trip (Acts 13 and 14) Paul and Barnabas appear as exorcists and healers.[262] Jesus' instructions for radical itinerants, however, were observed by Paul, Barnabas, and other missionaries at the time not rigidly but in a post-Easter modified form.[263] For instance, both men attempted to provide for themselves so as not to be a financial burden on the churches that they themselves had established (compare 1 Cor 9:6, 12–18 with Matt 10:9–10).

On the first mission trip, Gentiles came to faith through the mission efforts of Barnabas and Paul and were then baptized without being circumcised. Some of the Jerusalem Jewish Christians strongly objected to this practice. This conflict led then to the "council of the apostles" (compare Gal 2:1–24 with Acts 15:1–15).[264] At this council Barnabas and Paul receive confirmation of their missional approach from the three "pillars" (Gal 2:9). From the perspective of the history of missions, this was a decisive breakthrough. As a result, the path was cleared for a Gentile mission without circumcision and the establishment of an independent Gentile church. The foundation for this enterprise can be traced back to the mission church in Antioch established by the Hellenists (Acts 11:20).

In Antioch there are also indications that a church organizational form with charismatic leadership was practiced in contrast to the presbyterial structure we saw under James in Jerusalem (Acts 13:1–2).[265] The Antioch church apparently had already developed relatively firm organizational forms by the 40s C.E. Prophets and teachers are distinguished from the congregation as a whole (cf. also 14:27).[266] The list of names in 13:1b is evidence that these men belonged to the leadership of the Antioch church for an extended period of time; otherwise they would not have deserved mention. Acts 11:29–30 mentions an organized form of charity. In 11:26 the members of the Antioch church are referred to as Χριστιανοί, which is an indication of community forms distinct from those of the synagogue. Our next chapter will show that the organizational structures of the Antioch church as well as

---

[261] We can assume with Ollrog, ibid., 156 n. 197, that Paul and Barnabas were not the only ones who made such mission journeys (cf. Acts 15:38–40; 13:1).

[262] Compare also 2 Cor 12:12; Rom 15:19 with Luke 10:29 par.

[263] Cf. Stuhlmacher, "Weg," 118.

[264] Regarding the relationship between Gal 2 and Acts 15 and the different views among scholars, cf. Pesch, *Simon Petrus*, 77–78; Ramsay, *Galatians*, ad loc.; Gunther, *Paul*, 15–16; Hemer, *Acts*, 251–70; Bauckham, "James."

[265] For the good reasons in favor of the historicity of this old list in Acts 13:1, cf. A. Zimmermann, *Die urchristlichen Lehrer*, 118–35.

[266] Cf., e.g., Roloff, *Apostelgeschichte*, 193; Streeter, *Primitive Church*, 75.

the Jerusalem model had a lasting effect on Paul and his mission outreach (cf., e.g., 1 Cor 12:28).

In Antioch the transition was made, then, to gathering God's people from the Jews *and* the Gentiles. Everything seems to indicate that this gathering was done in small house groups. At least in this instance, one can speak of continuity between the primitive church in Jerusalem and the mission church in Antioch. That the church in Antioch met κατ' οἶκον in the private domestic houses of affluent members as in Jerusalem is probable simply because this was the case for the overwhelming majority of all believers in the early Christian movement for the first three centuries (see the history of scholarship on pp. 1–16). Since a relatively large number of Jews as well as a good share of God-fearers and proselytes lived in Antioch at that time,[267] since many in this group had acquired a certain affluence,[268] and since the Christian missionaries converted primarily God-fearers,[269] we can assume that at least some of the wealthy homeowners made their homes available to the congregation as assembly places. That the Antioch church was capable of participating so heavily in the financial contribution to the Jerusalem church is also evidence in support of this view (Acts 11:27–30).

A number of the individuals in the Antioch church mentioned by name in Acts 13:1 may be affluent homeowners. The fact that they are called teachers and prophets and therefore had "charismatic" leadership responsibilities in the church does not necessarily exclude the above possibility. As childhood companion or possibly trusted friend of the tetrarch Herod Antipas, Menahem can be assumed to have grown up in a noble family (probably Greek-educated lay aristocracy in Jerusalem or Galilee) and surrounded by princes.[270] The text does not reveal anything regarding the status of Simeon and Lucius, but the mere mention of their names could be an indirect indication of a higher social position.[271] Nicholas the proselyte from Antioch could also be counted in the group of potential house owners (6:5).

The mention of these men at least implies that the church had grown beyond the initial phase of development, where the congregation consisted of merely one house church or perhaps only a few. A citywide organization of the church had become necessary. It is possible that, just as in Jerusalem,

---

[267] Cf. Kraeling, "Jewish Community," esp. 136, 147, who estimates the Jewish segment of the population of Antioch at the time of Augustus at ca. 45,000 and points to "the attraction to the Jewish synagogue of a 'multitude of Greeks,'" or rather God-fearers and proselytes (cf. Josephus, *J.W.* 7.45). Cf. also Meeks and Wilken, *Jews and Christians,* 8; Norris, "Antiochen I," 3:101. Socially, God-fearers often belonged to the more affluent (cf. Gülzow, *Christentum,* 13–14).

[268] Kraeling, "Jewish Community," 147; Acts 11:27–30.

[269] Dunn, "Incident," esp. 30.

[270] Pesch, *Apostelgeschichte,* 2:17; Haenchen, *Apostelgeschichte,* 379; Meeks and Wilken, *Jews and Christians,* 15; Hengel, *Zur urchristlichen Geschichtsschreibung,* 63–64.

[271] Theissen, *Social Setting,* 179–80; Pesch, *Apostelgeschichte,* 2:17.

some of these men were leaders of house churches and as such formed a sort of leadership council for the church as a whole in Antioch. But we cannot be certain about any of this.

In addition, we can assume a plurality of house churches in Antioch. Acts 11:26 is not only a reference to the fact that the Christians in Antioch had attracted the attention of their social environment as a distinct group and were therefore called "Christians." The fact that they attracted attention indicates that they were a group of considerable size—the residents of the city of Antioch would not have noticed one relatively small house church.[272] Apart from that, as the third (or fourth) largest city in the empire and the capital of the province of Syria and with a large segment of the Jewish population being proselytes, Antioch was fruitful soil for the Jewish and Gentile mission.[273] The cosmopolitan character of the city, with its stable Roman government, also speaks for the rapid growth of the Christian community in Antioch.[274]

Galatians 2:11–14 also suggests a multiple number of house churches in Antioch. At first, Peter enjoyed common meals with Gentile Christians. When the men sent by James came, he withdrew and had table fellowship exclusively with the Jewish Christians. It is safe to assume that these Gentile and Jewish-Christian meals took place in separate house churches. At the latest, with the Antioch conflict we can observe a multiple number of house churches alongside the church as a whole at that location (for definitions, see pp. 27–28).[275] Galatians 2:14 seems to indicate the possibility for an assembly of the whole church in Antioch. The dispute that Paul describes here took place "in front of them all," which implies that the whole church was gathered at one place.[276] From Acts 13:1–3 one could conclude that,

---

[272] Cf. Conzelmann, *Geschichte*, 51. Similarly Meeks and Wilken, *Jews and Christians*, 15–16; with them Riesner, *Frühzeit*, 99. This note from Luke is generally considered historically reliable today. Cf., e.g., Roloff, *Apostelgeschichte*, 177; G. Schneider, *Apostelgeschichte*, 2:274; Lüdemann, *Das frühe Christentum*, 143; Zingg, *Wachsen*, 226–27. Cf. also Corwin, *St. Ignatius*, 189.

[273] Norris, "Antiochien I," 3:101; Corwin, *St. Ignatius*, 49; Downey, *History*, 278. Cf. Acts 11:19–21. Cf. also Hengel, *Zur urchristlichen Geschichtsschreibung*, 84–85. The population of Antioch in the first century C.E. was somewhere between 150,000 and 600,000 inhabitants; cf. Riesner, *Frühzeit*, 98.

[274] In spite of the rapid growth of the church in Antioch, we do not dare imagine it to be too large. Most of the Christian groups in various cities throughout the Roman Empire were relatively small: cf. Wilken, *Christians*, 31.

[275] Cf. Klauck, *Hausgemeinde*, 35, 40 n. 64; Downey, *History*, 278; Corwin, *St. Ignatius*, 49, 76–77, 85–86. Meeks and Wilken (*Jews and Christians*, 24) and Andresen (*Von den Anfängen*, 3) assume a plurality of house churches in Antioch. Hengel (*Zur urchristlichen Geschichtsschreibung*, 8) dates the Antioch conflict to ca. 48 C.E. after the council of the apostles. Others date it much earlier (cf. Stählin, *Apostelgeschichte*, 206, 209–10; Zahn, *Apostelgeschichte*, 2:539–40). Cf. also F. F. Bruce, *Acts*, 282–85 n. 9.

[276] If we assume a rapid growth of the whole church in Antioch and at the same time the capacity of a house at its upper limit of even a hundred, it would be difficult

even before the first mission journey of Barnabas and Paul, a worship service was held with the whole church present.[277]

In view of the rapid growth of the Antioch congregation, it can be assumed that the plurality of house churches came into existence before the conflict came to a head. Whether these house churches were separated according to ethnic background, as was the custom with the synagogue, is difficult to determine. The assumption that they were not ethnically divided before the conflict is supported by two observations. First, the conflict appears to take place in front of the entire congregation, obviously made up of both Jewish and Gentile Christians—here a communion meal with everyone is implied, as in 1 Cor 11:17–26.

Second, even if we do not know with certainty precisely what it was like in the individual house churches, the Antioch baptism and communion tradition (Gal 3:26–28/1 Cor 11:23–25) seems to speak against house church assemblies that were divided ethnically. Such a separation would tear the body of Christ in two. According to this tradition, in the Christian church, not only the social but also the ethnoreligious barriers are to be overcome in Christ. The Antioch church held fast to this tradition, not only theologically, but practically as well. Before the conflict it appears as if the Antioch church practiced a community life that made no distinction between Jews and Gentiles (Gal 2:12–13). Whether after the conflict there existed in Antioch house churches divided according to ethnic background can no longer be determined.

From Jesus to Paul through the Hellenists

As we have observed, NT history shows that missiologically the Hellenists played a significant role in the development of early Christian outreach. I wholeheartedly concur with Hengel, who believes that the Hellenists represent *the* connecting link between the primitive church in Jerusalem and the Pauline mission congregations.[278] We can thank "the virtually unheard-of 'Hellenists,' Jewish Christians associated with the company of seven with Stephen as their head, and the Greek-speaking congregation that they established in Jerusalem, for bridging the gap between Jesus and Paul."[279] They

---

to imagine a meeting place large enough for the whole church. Here one needs to ask if "in front of them all" means in front of everyone who attended the meeting.

[277] Pesch, *Apostelgeschichte*, 2:17; Campbell, *Elders*, 165. Cf. Acts 13:1–2.

[278] Hengel, "Zwischen Jesus und Paulus," 151–206, here 201; cf. also "Ursprünge."

[279] Hengel, "Zwischen Jesus und Paulus," esp. 201, 204: "Although the time span of the congregation's active ministry was relatively short, its impact was immense. The Hellenists were the 'eye of the needle' through which the early Christian kerygma and, inseparably associated with that, the message of Jesus Christ found its way to the Greco-Roman world."

translated the Jesus tradition into the Greek language and conveyed it to the Greek-speaking population in Jerusalem. Through their criticism of ritual law and the (OT) sacrificial cult, they prepared the way for the Pauline message of freedom from the law, and they carried the gospel of Christ from Jerusalem to Damascus, Caesarea, and Antioch.

Our study, however, raises the question whether the Hellenists were responsible for the transmission of yet another element of early Christian missional outreach. Bearing in mind that Jesus and his disciples both practiced, at least in its preliminary stage, the community organizational form built upon the foundation of the family and the private domestic houses of sedentary followers as well as a fairly well developed house-missional approach, one could ask whether the Hellenists were also the connecting link through which at least some, perhaps numerous, components of the house-missional approach were passed on from Jesus via Jerusalem and Antioch to the Pauline mission and from there to all the churches in the Greco-Roman world. Can a connection be demonstrated not only between Hellenists and Paul but between them and Jesus as well?

The following general observations appear significant. The similarities of the Pauline mission with the house-to-house, itinerant, and regional missional approach of Jesus and his disciples can best be explained by assuming some kind of connecting link through which elements of the tradition of the mission discourse were transmitted from Jesus to Paul. The Hellenists, who, as we have seen, practiced such a house mission approach, seem the most likely to have been that link.[280] In addition, a number of factors indicate that the Hellenists were conceivably more receptive than the Hebrew segment of the Jerusalem church to the Jesus tradition with its criticism of the ritual and cultic law. They were perhaps more open as well to the tradition of the mission discourse and to the forms of community organization and the house mission practices associated with it. First, some of the Hellenists, particularly those who had come from the Diaspora to Jerusalem, were more flexible in their thinking and thus more capable of absorbing new ideas and customs because of their experience abroad. Second, they appear to have oriented themselves quite closely to Jesus and his teachings. Apparently they felt a special attraction to the uniqueness of his proclamation. Presumably there was a group of Hellenistic followers of Jesus in Jerusalem even before Easter.[281] There they could have encountered, among other things, the content of the mission discourse tradition firsthand from Jesus and his disciples. If not before Easter, this would certainly have been possible after Easter through the contact they would have had with the disciples. Third, the early persecution, which forced the Hellenists to leave the sedentary life they enjoyed in Jerusalem and take on, at least temporarily, more of an itinerant existence, could have been a fac-

---

[280] Paul also had contact, however, with Peter and James, the Lord's brother in Jerusalem, and so did not depend on the Hellenists alone for the transmission of this tradition.

[281] Hengel, "*Hellenization*," 18.

tor as well. By then at the latest, one would expect that they started putting the mission discourse instructions into practice; all the evidence indicates that this is precisely what they did, albeit in modified form.

We noted in our reconstruction of the Hellenists' missional outreach that their approach was very similar to that of Jesus. Capernaum was the temporary residence of Jesus, with Peter's house an operational base for his local as well as his village-to-village mission. One could say that Jesus practiced regional or "mission journey" outreach on a small scale in Capernaum and the "evangelical triangle." Granted, it was not as organized and as extensively developed as in Antioch and certainly not as in the "center" missional approach of Paul (see ch. 4). Nevertheless, in Jesus' ministry we see elements of the sedentary lifestyle (with a temporarily fixed local residence), the itinerant missional outreach with its radical ethic, the partner mission, and the house, village/city, and regional or "mission journey" approaches to mission all integrated with one another.

Our sources give the distinct impression that Peter, who was open to the mission to the Gentiles and had relations with the Hellenists, and Philip, the other Hellenists, and finally Barnabas (and along with him even Paul) all adopted and practiced the mission discourse tradition in one form or another. The mission style of Philip comes the closest to the pre-Easter approach of Jesus, at least in its structure. Philip traveled in Samaria from city to city like Jesus and his disciples. It appears that he developed his mission strategy around his house in Caesarea and from there to the surrounding area, using elements of an itinerant style combined with one that was simultaneously (temporarily) sedentary.

The parallels between the mission structures in Antioch and those of Jesus are even more clearly documented in our texts. The common elements of itinerant, partner, sedentary, and planned missional outreach along with structures for sending and accountability upon return are all observable, even though with certain Easter modifications and post-Easter developments that take us noticeably beyond what we have detected in the missional outreach of Jesus in Capernaum and the surrounding area. In Antioch, for instance, we encounter a *church* that saw itself responsible to select congregational members as missionaries and to send them out on missional outreach to the region surrounding the city. Before Easter there was no church as such in Capernaum but a house community with Jesus as its head. Not this house community but Jesus himself was responsible for sending members of this fellowship out to do mission work.

Certainly Antioch but also Caesarea can be categorized as cities, large urban areas that differ considerably from the more rural, small-town setting of Capernaum.[282] The near surroundings of Antioch were presumably more

---

[282] Capernaum, however, was probably no small village but rather a very vital, dynamic town or even city with well-developed means of transportation and a system of commerce in the surrounding regions (see pp. 31–35).

urbanized also. As a result, the situation there and in the large metropolitan areas targeted in the Pauline mission demanded a modified, in some cases a fairly different, approach. It is for these megacities that Paul develops his "center" missional outreach, which is, though related and containing some similar elements, much more developed and in many aspects unlike the concept Jesus realized in Capernaum.

Another similarity to the pre-Easter mission of Jesus can be seen in practice of community formation around a core family in private domestic houses. As we have observed, this was a pattern in Jerusalem, presumably in the house of Philip in Caesarea, and surely in the house churches of Antioch. Houses served as community centers for the life of the church and as operational bases for missional outreach; as such they were a powerful force for the mission enterprise in all these places. In light of the missional zeal of the Hellenists, it seems only fitting that they too would have continued this approach and would have utilized houses in a similar way in the missional outreach of the various Hellenistic centers, such as Caesarea and Antioch. This assumption is supported by the observation that, as for the primitive church in Jerusalem as a whole, the house churches there also had a certain exemplary character for the church in these Hellenistic centers, particularly in Antioch (see above).

In summary, the missional practice of Hellenists reflects a number of at least structural similarities to that of the pre-Easter house mission approach of Jesus and his disciples, even though certain modifications and innovations are certainly evident. The transition from a Jewish to a Gentile missional approach called for adaptations. Moreover, the gospel had to be taken from the fairly rural setting of Palestine into the more urbanized Greco-Roman world. The early Christian missionaries (including initially the Hellenists) were faced with the challenge of reaching Jews and Gentiles in the Hellenistic (metropolitan) cities. Obviously, the instructions found in the mission discourse alone were not sufficient, and so the missionaries found it necessary to innovate. The establishment of house churches meant not only confrontation with the respective cultural circumstances but also the necessity to evaluate the individual social conditions in the ancient *oikos* and then to either adopt or (partially) reject them. As we will see, the criterion used in this evaluation was in concurrence with the (Antiochene) baptismal form and confession found in Gal 3:28. The Pauline Epistles reflect an ongoing struggle with this very issue.[283] Our next chapter will investigate how Paul and his churches dealt with and resolved this problem.

Conclusions

The private domestic house served as the foundation for missional outreach and community formation in the primitive church in Jerusalem, just as

---

[283] Compare Gal 3:26–28 with, e.g., 1 Cor 11:1–16 or Col 3:18–25.

it did in the ministry of Jesus and his disciples. Because of the small size of house churches, it was possible to maintain a family-like atmosphere and practice brotherly love in a very personal and concrete way. Thus they became very attractive to outsiders. Even though the evidence is not as conclusive for the primitive church in Jerusalem as it is for the Pauline communities, here as well we can assume that the ancient *oikos* served as a source of evangelistic contacts, with its built-in network of relationships reaching far beyond the immediate family to servants, friends, clientele, and business associates.

Also, alongside meetings of the whole church in the temple for prayer and instruction, we find a plurality of house churches in Jerusalem. Because of the rapid growth of the primitive church, from the very beginning a multiple number of house churches sprang into existence. We know for certain of two concrete examples: one that met in the upper room and another that met in the house of Mary. In addition, we can assume that there were many more house churches that met in the private homes of wealthier members of the congregation. These homes also served as meeting places for worship, prayer, instruction, community formation, and the celebration of the Lord's Supper, all elements that, by definition, need to be present for qualification as a house church in the full sense (see pp. 27–28). They hereby enabled early Christians in Jerusalem to hold distinctly Christian worship services, something that would not have been possible in the synagogue or the temple.

Further, at least in the use of houses for community formation and missional outreach, an organic transition can be observed from the Jerusalem church to the mission church in Antioch. In both Jerusalem and Antioch the first Christians met in homes. There is also evidence for a plurality of house churches within the church as a whole in Antioch.

There seems to be some indication that house churches already played a significant role in the development of leadership even in the primitive church in Jerusalem. The homeowners, as the heads of the household and hosts of the house church, may well have had more authority and influence, because of their social position, in the group that met in their house. After all, the community met in *their* home, which was more that just a building. They met in the social context of the *oikos,* that is, the extended family with its built-in authority structures. We can assume that some of the hosts became the leaders of the church that met in their home. Also, before their election, some of the elders mentioned in the context of the primitive church in Jerusalem or some of the seven mentioned in Acts 6 might have served as house church leaders. In that case the house church would have served as a kind of training ground for future leaders of the church even in the earliest days in Jerusalem. Here again, however, the evidence is not totally conclusive.

The book of Acts gives the impression that, with the passing of time, the title "elder" became the designation for office in the Jerusalem church

(15:4, 6, 22, 41; 16:4; 21:18). In that case, assuming as well that Harvey and Campbell have accurately described the ancient usage of the title of "elder" as an honorific, we have the Christian formation of the office of elder, which was not patterned after the synagogue model. This is especially true if in fact there was no office of elder in the synagogue. This would mean that early Christians were much more instrumental in the independent formation of this office than is generally assumed. This issue will receive further attention as we continue our investigation of the Pauline house churches.

CHAPTER FOUR

The Use of Houses in Pauline Missional Outreach

THAT HOUSES PLAYED A DECISIVE ROLE in the Pauline mission is to be expected, not only in light of the central significance of the *oikos* in the ancient world but particularly because of the important role they played in Jesus' pre-Easter mission and in the Jerusalem and Antioch churches. Can this be historically demonstrated for Pauline congregations?

A LITERARY AND HISTORICAL ANALYSIS OF HOUSE CHURCH PASSAGES

Paul

Among the most important passages on the household setting of Pauline churches are four greetings, in which Paul explicitly mentions house churches, that is, Christian fellowship groups that were formed in and/or around an *oikos*:

1. Paul writes to the Corinthians from Ephesus, "The churches in the province of Asia send you greetings. Aquila and Priscilla greet you warmly in the Lord, and so does the church that meets at their house" (1 Cor 16:19).

2. Approximately three years later, Paul writes to Rome, "Greet Priscilla and Aquila, my fellow workers in Christ Jesus. Greet also the church that meets at their house" (Rom 16:3, 5; cf. also 16:14–15, 23).

3. From prison Paul writes a note to his friend Philemon most likely in Colossae. Paul begins his letter in his normal style with the following greeting: "Paul, a prisoner of Christ Jesus, and Timothy our brother: to Philemon our dear friend and fellow worker, to Apphia our sister, to Archippus our fellow soldier and to the church that meets in your home" (Phlm 1–2; cf. also 21–22).

4. In the Epistle to the Colossians, Nympha in Laodicea near Colossae is greeted: "Give my greetings to the brothers at Laodicea, and to Nympha and the church in her house" (Col 4:15).

In contrast to the pre-Easter and Jerusalem church situation, these and several other indirect references to house churches (especially in Corinth;

see below) are fortunately in the undisputed Pauline Letters and so are generally considered historically reliable.[1] We can thus readily assume the factual existence of these house churches without any further historical investigation. Nevertheless, two text-critical questions need to be addressed:

First, was Rom 16 an original part of the Letter to the Romans or a secondary addition? The answer to this question has clear implications for our study. Only after its clarification can we determine the location of the house church of Prisca and Aquila mentioned there. This problem has occupied the attention of scholars for many years, yet to this day the discussion has not led to any kind of consensus.[2] Recent studies advocate the inclusion of Rom 16 as an original part of the letter.[3] From a review of these studies and others, there appears no convincing reason not to view Rom 16 as an original part of the book of Romans; it is the position taken in this study.[4]

Second, Col 4:15 contains another text-critical problem. Νύμφαν is ambivalent; it can be considered either feminine or masculine.[5] The gender of the possessive pronoun in connection with "house" does not help clarify the matter because of inconsistency in the manuscripts. B 6 1739 1881, a portion of the Syriac and the Coptic translations, and Origen read "in her [αὐτῆς] house"; D (F G) K Ψ, the majority of the Koine text manuscripts, lectionaries, and translations, and several of the Fathers read "in his [αὐτοῦ] house." The reading "in their [αὐτῶν] house" (א A C P 33 and several other witnesses) is surely secondary and probably worded analogously to Rom 16:5; 1 Cor 16:19. The editors of *Novum Testamentum Graece* (27th ed.) and many exegetes have decided that Νύμφαν is the name of a woman and opted for the translation "in her house."[6] The main argument is the age and

---

[1] In order not to burden our investigation of the Pauline house churches with a discussion of the issues of authenticity, it appears advisable to limit our use of Pauline literature primarily to the undisputed epistles of Paul (Romans; 1 and 2 Corinthians; Galatians; Philippians; 1 Thessalonians; Philemon). For practical reasons, Col 4:15 will be taken up in this chapter. The question concerning the authorship of Colossians is addressed in Gehring, *Hausgemeinde,* 385–86.

[2] For an overview, cf. Ollrog, "Abfassungsverhältnisse."

[3] Lampe, *Stadtrömischen Christen,* 124–34, and "Roman Christians," 216–30; Klauck, *Hausgemeinde,* 25–26; Schlier, *Römerbrief,* 440; Wilckens, *Römer,* 1:24–27, 3:132; Stuhlmacher, *Römer,* 215–16; Malherbe, *Social Aspects,* 65; Donfried, "Short Note" and *Romans Debate,* lxx: "Romans 16 . . . is now viewed by the majority as being an integral part of Paul's original letter." Cf. also the foundational work of Gamble, *Textual History.*

[4] For a more extensive treatment of the issues with arguments in support of this position, cf. the discussion in Gehring, *Hausgemeinde,* 221–23. Cf. also Stuhlmacher, *Römer,* 216; Lampe, *Stadtrömischen Christen,* 124–31, here 125–26. The above-mentioned studies (cf. esp. Lampe) demonstrate convincingly as well that the literary-critical objections against Rom 16 are not at all compelling.

[5] Regarding the textual problem, cf. Klauck, *Hausgemeinde,* 44–45.

[6] F. F. Bruce, *Colossians, Philemon, Ephesians,* 309; Pokorný, *Kolosser,* 164; Lohse, *Kolosser und Philemon,* 244–45; Gnilka, *Kolosserbrief,* 244; Gielen, "Zur Interpretation," 109–25, here 109; Stuhlmacher, *Philemon,* 71; O'Brien, *Colossians, Philemon,* 256; Klauck, *Hausgemeinde,* 44–45.

reliability of B versus D. Apparently a woman as a possible house church leader seemed offensive to later copyists, and so they changed the text accordingly.

In addition to the letters of Paul, the book of Acts provides a valuable source of references to the use of houses in the Pauline mission.[7] In the following we will attempt to distinguish pre-Lukan tradition from Lukan redaction in the main texts in Acts in an effort to determine their historical reliability.

Acts 16:14–15

> One of those listening was a woman named Lydia, a dealer in purple cloth from the city of Thyatira, who was a worshiper of God. The Lord opened her heart to respond to Paul's message. When she and the members of her household were baptized, she invited us to her home. "If you consider me a believer in the Lord," she said, "come and stay at my house." And she persuaded us. (Acts 16:14–15)

Pre-Lukan Tradition and Lukan Redaction

Verses 14–15 are embedded in the prelude (16:11–15) of a larger narrative (16:11–40) telling of the missional outreach in Philippi, a Roman colony in Macedonia—according to Luke, the first attempt to spread the gospel on European soil. We can be fairly certain that this section of the story (11–15), which is told in the "we" style, was taken almost word for word from an old travel diary,[8] most likely from the itinerary notes of the narrator himself.[9] "It is characterized by a sober chronicle-like narrative style, which does without any story telling accessories and is limited to the mention of locations, persons, and facts."[10] First Corinthians 1:16 demonstrates that the so-called *oikos* formula in 16:15 was not initially created by Luke and that quite early Paul had developed a habit of baptizing individuals along with their entire house, as Luke reports in Acts 16:14–15.[11] The story of a non-Jewish woman by the name of Lydia (Lydian = originating from the region or country of Lydia), a purple trader from the city of

---

[7] On the historical reliability of Acts, see p. 62, n. 2.
[8] Roloff, *Apostelgeschichte,* 243; following him, Pesch, *Apostelgeschichte,* 2:103–4. Even stronger is Thornton, *Zeuge,* 275–80: "The Lydia episode (16,13–15) belongs without a doubt to the source," 278; Following him, Jervell, *Apostelgeschichte,* 428 n. 130.
[9] Roloff, *Apostelgeschichte,* 243; Pesch, *Apostelgeschichte,* 2:104. Cf. also Pilhofer, *Philippi,* 204–5, who emphasizes that in this section Luke "portrays the local realities in Philippi quite graphically and with remarkable precision."
[10] Roloff, *Apostelgeschichte,* 243. Also Weiser, *Apostelgeschichte,* 421, assumes reliable tradition here.
[11] Cf. 1 Cor 16:15 and the pre- or non-Lukan tradition in John 4:53. With Klauck, *Hausgemeinde,* 53; following him, Gielen, *Tradition,* 83–84; Campbell, *Elders,* 153.

Thyatira who now lives in Philippi and has joined the synagogue community there, has a ring of historic plausibility.[12]

Historical Reliability

Even though the historical reliability of the Lydia narrative has recently been questioned,[13] C. J. Thornton has argued convincingly that Luke, the author of Acts, was at the same time the coworker and travel companion of Paul. If this is the case, then we can be certain that the companion of Paul implied in these and other "we" sections in Acts is not simply the literary figment of some author's imagination but, rather, Luke himself.[14] This means that Luke was an eyewitness of the events reported in 16:11–15 and so the author of the "itinerary notes" mentioned above, and this clearly increases the reliability of his report.[15] In his undisputed letters Paul also confirms this pattern of establishing a Christian community in a private home as an integral element of his missional outreach (see below).

There is thus no reason to doubt the reliability of the statements made in Acts 16 regarding the house and family of Lydia and what occurred in her house. Here is evidence for the formation of a church in the house of a God-fearing woman at a very early stage of the Pauline mission. Understood in this way, the story in Acts 16 is a "church origins" report based on very old tradition that portrays how a household nucleus became a house church in the city of Philippi.[16]

---

[12] Cf. Pilhofer, *Philippi*, 174–82; Wikenhauser, *Apostelgeschichte*, 410; Hemer, "Lydia" and *Acts*, 114; G. Horsley, *New Documents*, 2:27–28, 30.

Lüdemann, *Das frühe Christentum*, 189, also sees the name Lydia, the specific mention of her origin, and her baptism as indications of the traditional character of this piece. Lydia most likely grew up as a Gentile in Thyatira, in Asia Minor southeast of Pergamon, one of the centers for purple dye. Cf. Hemer, "Lydia" and *Acts*, 114. Excurse: "The name 'Lydia' is attested both as a regular and as an alternative name" (cf. also 114 n. 32: "The name is also now attested of women of apparently high social prestige"). Cf. Pilhofer, *Philippi*, 234–40.

[13] Cf. Abrahamsen, "Rock Reliefs," 18.

[14] Thornton, *Zeuge*, 341–67, esp. 363–67; cf., following him (cautiously), Stuhlmacher, *Grundlegung*, 227–28, and Jervell, *Apostelgeschichte*, 428 n. 132: "Luke knew about the conversion of Lydia as recorded in his own notes as well as from the local tradition in Philippi." Cf., even before Thornton, Hengel, *Zur urchristlichen Geschichtsschreibung*, 60.

[15] Cf. Jervell, *Apostelgeschichte*, 431. According to Thornton, it was certainly not Luke's intent to underscore the reliability of his report by claiming autopsy for himself. If he had wanted to do that, he would have referred to himself explicitly, as would have been the custom for historians back then (Thornton, *Zeuge*, 364). Just the same, his autopsy has this effect for us de facto. In addition, Thornton (pp. 275–77) gives good reasons in support of the view that the "we" sections were based on notes written shortly after the events.

[16] Similarly Klauck, *Hausgemeinde*, 56, and "Hausgemeinde als Lebensform," 7–8 (citations are to the 1981 printing). Cf. also Pilhofer, *Philippi*, 249; Hengel, *Zur urchristlichen Geschichtsschreibung*, 40.

Acts 16:29–34

The jailer called for lights, rushed in and fell trembling before Paul and Silas. He then brought them out and asked, "Sirs, what must I do to be saved?" They replied, "Believe in the Lord Jesus, and you will be saved—you and your household." Then they spoke the word of the Lord to him and to all the others in his house. At that hour of the night the jailer took them and washed their wounds; then immediately he and all his family were baptized. The jailer brought them up into his house and set a meal before them; he was filled with joy because he had come to believe in God—he and his [entire household]. (Acts 16:29–34)

Pre-Lukan Tradition and Lukan Redaction

The narrative contains an unusually high number of concrete details, which is an indication that it is based on reliable historical recollection:[17] for example, the jailer's call for torches to produce light, as it is midnight; his trembling (16:29); the cleansing of the wounds (16:33); and the reference to the house and table. The sequence of the narrative (30–34) is quite appropriate given the situation:[18] the jailer brings them out of the prison, he receives faith instruction[19] from the missionaries, he takes them and cleans their wounds, he is baptized and then takes them up into his house for a celebration meal.[20] The mention of the jailer's entire household should also be considered a part of the original tradition.[21] As with 16:14–15, we can also argue that the *oikos* formula here is very old (31–34). Verses 29–34 are a part of a larger mission narrative (11–40) that reports the activities and experiences of Paul in Philippi; however, it is not a part of the "we" report.[22] Some have argued against the reliability of the report by suggesting that Luke molded and conventionalized the tradition available to him in order to emphasize a point.[23] That Luke has stylized the report here should not be disputed. But this cannot be used as an argument against the historicity of his portrayal. One must distinguish between stylization and invention. Proof of the former is not automatically proof of the latter.[24]

---

[17] Roloff, *Apostelgeschichte*, 243; cf. also Pilhofer, *Philippi*, 250–51.

[18] With Pesch, *Apostelgeschichte*, 2:112. Against Kratz, *Rettungswunder*, 487.

[19] Paul and Silas proclaim here "the word of the Lord." Τὸν λόγον λαλεῖν is mission terminology of the early church (cf. Acts 4:29, 31; 8:25; 11:19; 13:46; 14:25; 16:32; Phil 1:14; Heb 13:6).

[20] According to Kratz, *Rettungswunder*, 487, this celebration meal belongs to the conversion context.

[21] Ibid.; following Kratz is Pesch, *Apostelgeschichte*, 2:112.

[22] Cf. 16:18–20; after that, "we" disappears. Cf. Thornton, *Zeuge*, 278–79. F. F. Bruce (*Acts*, 316) considers 16:25–34 an "independent narrative, inserted by Luke into the record of events at Philippi. . . . But we may be glad that Luke did add it at this point: it enriches his account of Paul's Philippian ministry."

[23] Cf. White, "Visualizing," esp. 252–61

[24] In support of the reliability of the report, cf. also Giesekke, "Zur Glaubwürdigkeit." Cf., however, Haenchen (*Apostelgeschichte*, 484–86), who points out

Historical Reliability

In this narrative the representatives of Roman power, portrayed quite negatively by Luke, confront the Pauline mission team for the first time. This in itself is already an indication of the reliability of the report because in general Luke tries to put the Roman political powers, in particular their behavior toward early Christian missions, in a more positive light.[25] The details in the narrative also fit well with what we know of the character of the city of Philippi.[26] It was a Roman colony inhabited by non-Greeks and ruled by Roman officials according to Roman law. "With the exception of the portrayal of Athens, no other report in the book of Acts has the *genus loci* so deeply imprinted upon it as this report on the events that took place in Philippi. Indeed, if one were to delete the Roman components from the report, there would be nothing of significance left."[27] The information in 1 Thess 2:2 that Paul and his coworkers were mistreated and suffered can also be seen as confirmation of the Lukan report in Acts 16:25–29.[28] In addition, in several of his undisputed letters, Paul himself confirms our view that this practice of establishing house churches was an integral part of his missional approach.[29]

At this point, then, there is no reason to doubt the reliability of the report in 16:29–34 regarding houses and the events that took place in them. In addition to the Lydia narrative, we thus have a second "church origins" report of a house church in Philippi whose nucleus consisted of an *oikos* (house and household).

Acts 17:1–9

> When they had passed through Amphipolis and Apollonia, they came to Thessalonica, where there was a Jewish synagogue. As his custom was, Paul went into the synagogue, and on three Sabbath days he reasoned with them from the Scriptures, explaining and proving that the Christ had to suffer and rise from the dead. "This Jesus I am proclaiming to you is the Christ," he said. Some of the Jews were persuaded and joined Paul and Silas, as did a large number of God-fearing Greeks and not a few prominent women. But the Jews were jealous; so they rounded up some bad characters from the marketplace, formed a mob and started a riot in the city. They rushed to Jason's house in search of Paul and Silas in order to bring them out to the crowd. But when

---

inconsistencies between Philippians and Acts and sees a series of improbabilities and contradictions in the Lukan narrative. Similarly White, "Visualizing," 245–51.

[25] Roloff, *Apostelgeschichte*, 243.
[26] Pilhofer, *Philippi*, 159–65.
[27] Elliger, *Paulus*, 32; cf. also 54–55.
[28] O'Toole, "Philippian Jailor," 5:318.
[29] White, "Visualizing," esp. 245–51. He considers the report of the establishment of a house church here to be historically reliable because this is "a pattern reflected in Pauline epistolary address and central to the situation of several of the letters."

they did not find them, they dragged Jason and some other brothers before the city officials, shouting: "These men who have caused trouble all over the world have now come here, and Jason has welcomed them into his house. They are all defying Caesar's decrees, saying that there is another king, one called Jesus." When they heard this, the crowd and the city officials were thrown into turmoil. Then they made Jason and the others post bond and let them go. (Acts 17:1–9)

Pre-Lukan Tradition and Lukan Redaction

This report describes the second establishment of a church on European soil, namely, in Thessalonica, the capital of Macedonia. This report has often been considered a Lukan construction:[30] Luke supposedly had at his disposal only itinerary notes and an anecdotal narrative that was in circulation in the Thessalonian church.[31] There is no question that this Lukan report on Paul's church-founding visit to Thessalonica is stylized, but again stylization cannot be equated with invention (see above).[32] It is also possible that Luke had a source at his disposal that reported on the second mission trip, which originated with Timothy.[33] R. Pesch believes that in 17:1–15 Luke adapted a coherent report that he found in his tradition source.[34]

In fact, there are a number of things that speak for the traditional origin of the narrative. For instance, the verb ὀχλοποιέω is a hapax legomenon. The name Jason is introduced abruptly.[35] The expression λαβόντες τὸ ἱκανόν is so specific that it must be viewed as traditional.[36] The note regarding the success of the Pauline proclamation among Gentiles must be classified as traditional as well.[37] This is demonstrated by our historical discussion in connection with 1 Thess (see below). The expression προαγαγεῖν εἰς τὸν δῆμον is judicial terminology[38] and indicates that the author had concrete political knowledge of the situation. The formation of a mob for the purpose of a demonstration is a typical element of the life in a Hellenistic city.[39] These points alone may not be enough to convince some, but the next two

---

[30] The most radical in this direction is perhaps W. Stegemann (*Zwischen Synagoge und Obrigkeit*, 226–37), who, on the basis of linguistic considerations, classifies the entire narrative as a Lukan creation that historically reflects the experiences of Christians at the time of Domitian.

[31] G. Schneider, *Apostelgeschichte*, 2:223–24; Roloff, *Apostelgeschichte*, 249.

[32] Cf. the three-part outline: Acts 17:1–4, 5–7, 8–9.

[33] Pesch, *Apostelgeschichte*, 2:120–21.

[34] Ibid., 121. Cf. also Schille, *Apostelgeschichte*, 352–53; following him, Lüdemann (*Das frühe Christentum*, 194), who sees a traditional piece in vv. 5–9. Cf. also Jervell, *Apostelgeschichte*, 435: Luke was able to build on solid mission and church tradition.

[35] Here even W. Stegemann (*Zwischen Synagoge und Obrigkeit*, 228 n. 141) assumes pre-Lukan tradition.

[36] Lüdemann, *Das frühe Christentum*, 195.

[37] Ibid., 194–95.

[38] So Conzelmann, *Apostelgeschichte*, 103; cf. Judge, "Decrees," 2.

[39] Cf. Judge, *Social Pattern*, 26–27.

arguments appear even stronger. First, the political circumstances in Thessalonica, the capital of Macedonia, described in 17:1–9 reflect credible local coloring (especially the mention of πολιτάρχαι, documented in inscriptions particularly in the Macedonian region).[40] Second, the intentional political formulation of the accusation (17:6–7) is reported in a very straightforward manner.[41] This is conspicuous because Luke normally attempts to avoid politics in his portrayal. Here he obviously found it in his sources and apparently did not want to repress it.

Historical Reliability

Fortunately, in this case we are able to compare the Acts report on the founding of the Christian church in Thessalonica with statements made by Paul about the Thessalonian church, particularly in 1 Thessalonians.[42] Indeed, the most recent treatments of Acts 17:1–9 almost all conclude that Luke's report is at least partially, if not completely, reliable.[43] Luke and Paul agree that the route the missionaries took was from Philippi to Thessalonica. From there Paul was forced to depart because of persecution (Acts 16:16–40; cf. 1 Thess 2:2). First Thessalonians 2:15–16 confirms that in Thessalonica Paul was obstructed by the Jews from doing missionary work among the God-fearers and the Gentiles and that as a result he was forced to discontinue his work there. Paul probably learned from Timothy (1 Thess 2:14; 3:1–6)[44] or from messengers who traveled to Beroea in order to visit Paul[45] that their fellow citizens persecuted the Thessalonian Gentile Christians after Paul's departure. The apparent tension between the time men-

---

[40] Cf. Elliger, *Paulus*, 91–94; following him, Lüdemann, *Das frühe Christentum*, 194. Cf. also Kanatsoulis, *Politarchen*, 155–79, esp. 120–29, 151–61, 171–72; Schuler, "Macedonian Politarchs"; G. Horsley, *New Documents*, 2:34–35, and "Politarchs." Cf. also Robert, "Inscriptions," 207–12; Helly, "Politarchs"; Papazoglou, "Politarques"; Hemer, *Acts*, 115; F. F. Bruce, *Acts*, 324–25; Cadbury and Lake, *Acts*, 4:205–6; following them, Haenchen, *Apostelgeschichte*, 488 n. 9. Cadbury and Lake and Haenchen offer only older, somewhat outdated evidence.

[41] On its political formulation, see Elliger, *Paulus*, 95–96. Cf. also Judge, "Decrees." Similarly Donfried, "Cults." Following Elliger and Judge is Pesch, *Apostelgeschichte*, 2:123–24; following Judge, F. F. Bruce, *Acts*, 325 nn. 13, 15; Riesner, *Frühzeit*, 316. Against G. Schneider, *Apostelgeschichte*, 2:225.

[42] For an extensive list of the most important scholars since Lightfoot who have engaged in the discussion on the relationship between Acts 17:1–9 and 1 Thessalonians, cf. Riesner, *Frühzeit*, 301–2 n. 27.

[43] The exception is W. Stegemann, *Zwischen Synagoge und Obrigkeit*, 226–37. For a criticism of his view, however, cf. Riesner, *Frühzeit*, 303. For at least partial reliability, in addition to the above-mentioned studies, cf. Molthagen, "Die ersten Konflikte"; Botermann, "Heidenapostel," 79–81. For complete reliability, in addition to the above mentioned studies, cf. Tajra, *Trail*, 30–44; F. F. Bruce, *Acts*, 369–75; J. Gillman, "Paul's εἴσοδος," 39–49; Binder, "Paulus," 87. Cf. Riesner, *Frühzeit*, 301–28, for the most current, extensive, and convincing proof.

[44] Perhaps Timothy stayed in Thessalonica, as he did in Philippi, after the expulsion of Paul and Silas.

[45] Pesch, *Apostelgeschichte*, 2:126.

tioned in 17:2 and that in Phil 4:16 can be explained by assuming that the report in Acts 17:1–9 has only the beginning and the end of the missional outreach in perspective. About what happened between the founding of the church and the persecution Luke says nothing.[46] Philippians 4:16 allows us to supplement the Lukan report.[47] In addition, the stereotyped quality of the narrative (cf. also Acts 13:46–50; 18:5–17; 16:12–40; 19:8–41) could imply that the house of Jason is to be seen as a base of operation, established after persecution by the synagogue community, for the Pauline mission to the Gentiles, like the house of Titius Justus in Corinth (Acts 18:6–7). In that case, the Titius report could be cited as a supplement to the Jason report.[48]

Whether the Jason mentioned in Acts 17:6, 9, who provided Paul quarters in Thessalonica, is identical with the one mentioned in Rom 16:21 is difficult to determine. Nevertheless, it is quite likely that both are references to the same person: Sopater, who is also mentioned directly after Jason in Rom 16:21, is from Beroea, which is a neighboring town to Thessalonica.[49] If this is correct, it means that both were Jewish Christians who were with Paul in Corinth as collection delegates from their home church at the time of the writing of Romans.[50] Nothing speaks against the assumption that a Jew by the name of Jason in Thessalonica came to faith through the Pauline mission there and then became the host and patron of a house church at that location.[51] "The report of an uproar surrounding Jason is also quite credible. First Thessalonians implies that their fellow citizens embroiled the Gentile Thessalonians in conflict (1 Thess 2:14). In particular, the reference to the

---

[46] Haenchen, *Apostelgeschichte*, 491. Cf. Malherbe, *Paul*, 13–15, who also considers the narrative historically reliable. He points out that grammatically nothing implies, much less compels, the conclusion that Paul stayed only three weeks in Thessalonica.

[47] Here we learn that Paul received financial support from the congregation in Philippi twice or maybe even more often: Bauer-Aland[6], 160–61, 401 (BDAG 97, 252); cf. however F. F. Bruce, *Acts*, 349 n. 23. This implies a longer stay in Thessalonica. Cf. also Haenchen, *Apostelgeschichte*, 491–92. For other possible interpretations, cf. Riesner, *Frühzeit*, 321–23; Morris, *Thessalonians*, 16–17; I. H. Marshall, *1 and 2 Thessalonians*, 1983, 5.

[48] With Malherbe, *Paul*, 13–14.

[49] For the identification, also Lüdemann, *Das frühe Christentum*, 194. So also early church tradition (cf. Pölzl, *Mitarbeiter*, 230). Cf. also Wilckens, *Römer*, 3:146; Gillman, "Paul's εἴσοδος," 40; Riesner, *Frühzeit*, 307.

[50] So Pesch, *Apostelgeschichte*, 2:126; Lüdemann, *Das frühe Christentum*, 195–96; Wikenhauser, *Apostelgeschichte*, 194.

[51] Against Cadbury and Lake, *Acts*, 4:205, who doubt that Jason became a Christian. One should not wonder why the host of Christian missionaries who also allows other Christians to meet in his home would be depicted as a Christian; with Haenchen, *Apostelgeschichte*, 488. Jason was a common name (in Thessalia and elsewhere) that Jews used as a Greek name in addition to Joshua (= Jesus); Cadbury and Lake, *Acts*, 4:205, and, following them, Haenchen, *Apostelgeschichte*, 488. Cf. also BDF §53,2d; W. Foerster, "Ἰησοῦς," *TDNT* 3:286–87; Hengel, "Zwischen Jesus und Paulus," 175.

posting of a bond speaks for the reliability of the tradition."[52] In addition, the reason mentioned for the Jews' jealousy—the Christian missionaries converted and enticed a number of God-fearers and prominent women away from the Jewish community—is understandable and historically plausible.[53]

In light of all this, we can assume that the report in Acts 17:1–9 is reliable. We thus have clear documentation of a house and its householder named Jason, both playing a significant role in the Pauline mission in Thessalonica.[54] We can, then, also assume that a Christian community continued to gather in the house of Jason even after Paul's departure and that this led to the formation of a house church.

Acts 18:1–4, 7–8

> After this, Paul left Athens and went to Corinth. There he met a Jew named Aquila, a native of Pontus, who had recently come from Italy with his wife Priscilla, because Claudius had ordered all the Jews to leave Rome. Paul went to see them, and because he was a tentmaker as they were, he stayed and worked with them. Every Sabbath he reasoned in the synagogue, trying to persuade Jews and Greeks. (Acts 18:1–4)

> Then Paul left the synagogue and went next door to the house of Titius Justus, a worshiper of God. Crispus, the synagogue ruler, and his entire household believed in the Lord; and many of the Corinthians who heard him believed and were baptized. (Acts 18:7–8)

Pre-Lukan Tradition and Lukan Redaction

The narrative is constructed with four progressive scenes.[55] All four were most likely in Luke's source originally.[56] The following all indicate that

---

[52] Lüdemann, *Das frühe Christentum*, 195. Cf. also Sherwin-White, *Roman Law*, 96.

[53] Roloff, *Apostelgeschichte*, 250; following him, Pesch, *Apostelgeschichte*, 2:122–23. The emphasis on prominent feminine members of the congregation is undoubtedly a Lukan motif (Luke 8:2–3; Acts 13:7–12; 17:34; cf. Meeks, *First Urban Christians*, 61). This emphasis may also be based, however, on the historic reality regarding the position of women in Macedonian society (cf. F. F. Bruce, *1 and 2 Thessalonians*, xxv). The inscription evidence also confirms Luke's portrayal (also in Acts 17:4–6); cf. Horst, *Ancient Jewish Epitaphs*, 102–13, and "Das Neue Testament," esp. 171.

[54] This is the view of almost all commentators. Even Jewett, *Thessalonian Correspondence*, 116–17, finds no reason to doubt this. Ollrog, *Paulus*, 30, also views this as the historical core of the narrative.

[55] Acts 18:1–4, 5–8, 9–11, 12–17. So Haenchen, *Apostelgeschichte*, 516–17; Roloff, *Apostelgeschichte*, 269; Pesch, *Apostelgeschichte*, 2:146.

[56] Pesch, *Apostelgeschichte*, 2:146. Acts 18:5b, 6, and 9–10 are not clearly Lukan redaction. With a different view, Roloff, *Apostelgeschichte*, 269. Cf. also Schmithals, *Apostelgeschichte*, 166–69; Jervell, *Apostelgeschichte*, 463, who assumes that Luke had extensive material from a mission report on Corinth available for the writing of Acts 18:1–17.

Luke's portrayal of Paul's ministry in Corinth is essentially based on the information he found in his tradition source: the accumulated references to names (Aquila, Priscilla, Titius Justus, Crispus, Gallio, Sosthenes), concrete locations (the synagogue, the house of Titius Justus, the court of Gallio), and contemporary events (the expulsion of the Jews from Rome by Claudius, the proconsul Gallio in the province of Achaia).[57] In addition, the news that Paul is taken in by Aquila and Priscilla because they had the same profession rather than because of their mutual faith is not tendentious and a singular bit of information.[58] The references to Aquila's origin in Pontus (cf. 2:9), to Paul's teaching in the house of Titius Justus, and the conversion of Crispus, the synagogue ruler, are all nontendentious as well. For historical reasons (see below), the conversion of the entire household of Crispus also should be considered a part of the original tradition.

Historical Reliability

The note in 18:1–2 is confirmed by a reference in Suetonius as well as by statements of Paul regarding his own ministry.[59] In many cases the information given throughout the report in 18:1–17 finds confirmation in the letters of Paul.[60] As was observed in 16:14–15 and 16:31–34, 1 Cor 1:16 proves that the *oikos* formula occurring in 18:8 is very old.[61] Moreover, in 1 Cor 1:14 Paul confirms the report in Acts, in that he indicates that he himself baptized Crispus. Paul, however, does not mention the conversion of the entire house of Crispus. Still, the account in Acts can be considered historically credible. In the ancient *oikos* society, the conversion of the entire household as a consequence of the conversion of the head of the household was no rarity but, rather, a social and religious commonplace. We notice as well that Paul never calls Crispus a synagogue ruler. Nevertheless, the note in Acts 18:8 can be considered reliable. The high standing of a synagogue ruler can be seen as a plausible explanation for why Paul, in contrast to his common practice not to baptize new converts, nevertheless did so in this case.[62] The mention in 18:8b that *many* Corinthians heard about this, believed, and

---

[57] Cf. Hemer, *Acts*, 119, on the reliability of the references to Claudius, Gallio, and the synagogue.

[58] With Lüdemann, *Das frühe Christentum*, 206 (against Roloff, *Apostelgeschichte*, 270).

[59] Cf., e.g., 1 Thess 2:5, 9; 1 Cor 9:16–18; 2 Cor 11:7–10. Suetonius, *Claud.* 25.4: "Iudaeos impulsore Chresto assidue tumultuantes Roma expulit." Compare with Paulus Orosius, *Hist.* 7.6.15–16 (CSEL 5 451,7–13; ca. 417 C.E.); cf. Ollrog, *Paulus*, 24–27; Roloff, *Apostelgeschichte*, 272–73; Pesch, *Apostelgeschichte*, 2:152–53. Cf. also, however, the new approach of Lüdemann (41 C.E.), *Studien*, 183–95; the response of Riesner, *Frühzeit*, 139–80, who considers 49 C.E. most likely.

[60] Compare 18:2 with 1 Cor 16:19; 18:5 with 1 Thess 3:6; 18:5 with 2 Cor 1:19; 18:18 with Rom 16:1; 18:19 with 1 Cor 16:19; 18:27 with 1 Cor 1:12; 3:6; 4:6; cf. Hemer's comment on the topic (*Acts*, 187).

[61] With a different view, Klauck, *Hausgemeinde*, 53.

[62] Cf. Theissen, *Social Setting*, 73–74.

were baptized appears to be credible as well. It is quite likely that the conversion of a synagogue ruler would have had this kind of ripple effect in Corinth.[63]

The traditional reference to the reception of Paul into the home of Titius Justus (18:7) is neither confirmed nor disputed in the Pauline Letters. Still, it can be considered reliable, as Paul would have needed a suitable place for his teaching and preaching ministry. Moreover, the close proximity to the synagogue would have been mission-strategically advantageous. Besides, no convincing reason comes to mind for why the name Titius Justus would have been invented in this context.[64] In addition, the reference to the house of Titius Justus "next door to [συνομοροῦσα] the synagogue" under the leadership of an ἀρχισυνάγωγος fits well with what we know about the socio-historical world at that time.[65]

Our passage is embedded in a report (18:1–17), which scholarship generally considers historically reliable, on the beginnings of the Corinthian church.[66] G. Bornkamm comments that 18:1–17 is indisputably reliable.[67] Roloff writes that the narrative informs us about the Corinthian church in an "unusually precise" manner and it is "as a whole . . . historically reliable. It is therefore an important supplement to the letters, as its report focuses on the beginning of the church prior to the great upheaval and conflicts that followed."[68]

In light of all this, we can consider the references to houses and their use in the Pauline mission to be reliable. For Corinth, at least three houses are documented (those of Aquila, Titius Justus, and Crispus), all of which played a significant role in missional outreach and church formation in that city.

CITIES WITH DEMONSTRABLE HOUSE CHURCHES

As we have already observed, the book of Acts reports on Christian house meetings in the Pauline mission in the cities of Philippi, Thessalonica, Corinth, and lastly Troas (20:7–12). In his letters Paul also mentions such groups in Ephesus (1 Cor 16:19), Rome (Rom 16:3, 5), Colossae (Phlm 1, 2, 21–22), and Laodicea (Col 4:15) and implicitly in Corinth (1 Cor) and Cenchreae (Rom 16:1–2). This section will examine the textual references to house churches in these cities; the main focus will be on

---

[63] Lüdemann, *Das frühe Christentum,* 211.
[64] With Lüdemann, ibid., 211.
[65] White, "Visualizing," 256, and "Delos Synagogue," 133–38; Kraabel, "Social Systems."
[66] Pesch, *Apostelgeschichte,* 2:153.
[67] Bornkamm, *Paulus,* 85. Cf. also Ollrog, *Paulus,* 24–25 n. 88–89; Klauck, *Hausgemeinde,* 21. Even according to Haenchen, *Apostelgeschichte,* 515–20, esp. 520, "we can view the report as a whole as trustworthy."
[68] Roloff, *Apostelgeschichte,* 269. Cf. also Hemer, *Acts,* 119–20.

Corinth and Rome for the simple reason that we are best informed on the circumstances there.

Philippi

Because of the scarcity of source material, relatively little can be said about the house church situation in Philippi.[69] Nevertheless, the little that we can glean from our texts gives us interesting information regarding house churches. From our historical analysis it became evident that the two narratives (Acts 16:11–15, 25–34) offer reliable reports on house churches in the house of Lydia and in the house of the jailer. The Pauline mission team arrived in Philippi on the Sabbath and went to the river, where they entered into conversation with a group of women gathered there for prayer. Among those who heard Paul's message was a God-fearing woman by the name of Lydia, a dealer in purple cloth from Thyatira. As a result of hearing the message, Lydia came to faith. She and her whole household were baptized. After this she invited the missionaries into her home and offered them her hospitality for an undetermined period of time. Her house thus became a place where table fellowship was enjoyed, a meeting place for worship, and a base of operations for the Pauline mission as well.[70] Later it is reported that the new faith community gathered there to hear the missionaries' words of encouragement (16:40). Παρακαλέω appears elsewhere in Acts as proclamation, particularly in a Christian context (cf. 11:23; 14:22; 15:32; 20:1–2, 12).[71] Here we have an example of a businesswoman to whom Luke draws attention as the first patroness in the Pauline mission in Europe and who offered Paul her hospitality and served him and one of his mission churches with house and home.[72]

This woman appears to be relatively wealthy. In the ancient world, purple was considered a luxury item. At any rate, she was doing so well financially that she could afford to either own or rent a house that was large

---

[69] For background information on the city of Philippi at the time of Paul, cf. Jones, *Cities*; Elliger, *Paulus*, 23–77; Borchert, "Philippi"; S. E. Johnson, *Paul*, 74–76; Riesner, "Philippi"; Hendrix, "Philippi." Cf. esp. Pilhofer, *Philippi*; Bormann, *Philippi*.

[70] The word μένω implies table fellowship in Luke's writings (cf. Luke 1:56; 9:4; 10:7; 19:5; 24:29). In light of the significance of this word in early Christian missions, we can assume that the missionaries celebrated communion with Lydia in her house. Certainly Luke wanted to insinuate this (compare Acts 16:15— παρεβιάσατος, εἰσελθόντες, μένετε—with Luke 24:29–30). Cf. Matson, *Household Conversion*, 148–49; he follows Just, *Ongoing Feast*, 222, 236–53.

[71] F. F. Bruce, *Acts*, 252, observes that λόγος παρακλήσεως is a technical term for the synagogue sermon (cf. Acts 13:15; Heb 13:22).

[72] Schüssler Fiorenza, *Zu ihrem Gedächtnis*, 228, sees in Lydia the leader of the house church in her house. See pp. 210–25, the excursus on leadership responsibilities of women in Pauline house churches. For Lydia's significance in the Pauline mission, cf. Pilhofer, *Philippi*, 234–40.

enough to accommodate not only her own household but a number of guests as well.[73] Her home was large enough that the "brothers" were able to assemble there. Also the fact that Luke depicts her as a σεβομένη τὸν θεόν could imply a higher status (see p. 138, n. 109).[74]

In addition to the Lydia narrative, we have a second report on the establishment of a house church in Philippi (16:25–34). The original core of this church consisted of the house and household of the jailer. We know very little about him; not even his name has been passed down to us. As the overseer of a prison in a Roman colony, he most likely belonged to the Roman military and so was a soldier, perhaps a veteran.[75] Apparently he lived in a relatively large two-story house.[76]

Unfortunately, the Pauline Letters do not inform us any further regarding these two house churches. Philippians 1:1 mentions several ἐπίσκοποι, which can be taken as an indication that there were several house churches in Philippi at the time (see pp. 190–210). Acts 16, however, reports on two house churches, and therefore we can assume a plurality of house churches for Philippi.

Thessalonica

Also relatively little can be said about house churches in Thessalonica.[77] As we have seen above, Acts 17:1–9 contains a reliable report on the important role that a house and its householder, Jason, played in the Pauline missional outreach. By the time Jason appears in the narrative, we already know of the existence of a Christian group in connection with

---

[73] The mission team at that point included at least Paul, Silas, Timothy, and most likely also Luke (the author of Acts; cf. the "we" report). Cf. Polhill, *Acts,* 349: "Lydia's invitation to the four missionaries to stay in her home in itself indicates that she had considerable substance, such as guest rooms and servants to accommodate them adequately."

[74] Cf. Schüssler Fiorenza, *Zu ihrem Gedächtnis,* 228, who assumes Lydia was a freed slave rather than a wealthy woman from a distinguished family. Regarding the term "status" in general, see the section on social stratification in Pauline house churches (pp. 165–71).

[75] F. F. Bruce, *Acts,* 315. From the time of Julius Caesar on, soldiers settled in Roman colonies. This was considered a kind of reward for their faithful service to Rome.

[76] Cf. 16:34: ἀναγαγών. Precisely how we should picture this house is difficult to determine. Was the prison in the basement of the house or completely separate? Where did Paul preach the gospel to the jailer, and where were he and his family baptized—in his house or in the courtyard of the prison? Unfortunately, the text does not give us adequate information to answer any of these questions.

[77] For background information on the city of Thessalonica at the time of Paul, cf. Reicke and Suhl, "Thessaloniki," 3:1968–69; Elliger, *Paulus,* 78–113; Meeks, *First Urban Christians,* 46–47; T. Holtz, *Der erste Brief,* 9–23; Jewett, *Thessalonian Correspondence,* 118–32; Riesner, "Thessalonisch" and *Frühzeit,* 297–301; Hendrix, "Thessalonica."

his house (17:6, 10); this implies that Paul and his mission team had done prior missional outreach there—after all, it is Paul for whom the masses were searching.

According to the information given by Paul at the time of the composition of 1 Thessalonians, only a few months after the foundation of the church in Thessalonica a Christian community existed there composed primarily of Gentiles (1 Thess 1:9; 2:14; 4:15).[78] On the basis of indirect evidence, we can deduce a number of points about the social circumstances of the group. It is Luke's tendency to draw attention to the conversion of distinguished individuals; in this case it is "not a few prominent women" (Acts 17:4). At first glance, this paints a one-sided picture of the social level of the Thessalonian church. Upon closer examination, however, it can be observed that Luke does not suggest anywhere that the higher classes are in the majority.[79] The treatment of the topic of manual labor in 1 Thessalonians implies that Paul was writing to members in the congregation who belonged to the working middle or lower classes.[80] Nor does his letter exclude the possibility that there were a number of wealthy, higher-class individuals in the church. It is likely that the κοπιῶντες ἐν ὑμῖν καὶ προϊστάμενοι ὑμῶν mentioned in 1 Thess 5:12 should be classified at a high social level. This is particularly true if it can be assumed that the social levels in the Thessalonian church were analogous to other Pauline churches, for example, Corinth.[81] As we will see, those mentioned in 5:12 were most likely patrons (and leaders?) of the house churches in Thessalonica (see p. 138, n. 109).[82] According to 5:27, it can also be assumed that more than one group existed in Thessalonica, and this would indicate a plurality of house churches here as well.[83] It appears to be confirmed by the plurality of προϊστάμενοι in 5:12.

The social levels suggested above and the existence of such house church leaders also seem to be confirmed by Luke's report. First, Jason provides hospitality to Paul and his coworkers (Acts 17:7, ὑποδέδεκται). Second, he makes his house available to the brothers as a meeting place (17:6, 9). Together Jason and the brothers assume the legal responsibility for

---

[78] Cf. Hultgren, *Paul's Gospel*, 140–42; Jewett, *Thessalonian Correspondence*, 118–19.

[79] In support of the historical plausibility that such distinguished women would have belonged to the church in Thessalonica, see p. 128.

[80] Cf., e.g., 1 Thess 4:11; also 2:9–12; 2 Thess 3:6–12.

[81] See the section on the social stratification of the Pauline churches in general (pp. 165–71).

[82] Cf. Jewett, *Thessalonian Correspondence*, 103.

[83] Because of the special emphasis placed on πᾶσιν, we can assume that Paul has meetings in different house churches in mind rather than the assembly of the whole church in one place. With Gnilka, *Philemonbrief*, 27; Malherbe, *Social Aspects*, 70; following him, Klauck, *Hausgemeinde*, 35. With a different view, Chapple, "Local Leadership," 205, 273 n. 116.

the activities of the Pauline mission team by posting bond. All this indicates that Jason must have been "a man of means."[84] His role as patron of the church corresponds with that of other householders discussed below—for example, Phoebe from Cenchreae (Rom 16:2) and Gaius from Corinth (Rom 16:23).

Corinth

The city of Corinth as Paul knew it was a Roman colony founded in 44 B.C.E. by Julius Caesar and built upon the ruins of the ancient Corinth of Greece, which was destroyed during the Roman conquest.[85] Because of its favorable location, the city flourished through trade, banking, and bronze handicrafts. The city was also characterized, however, by a steep social curve—a very wealthy minority and a very poor majority. The Corinthian church reflects a similar social constituency: a few who were from the affluent upper class, some from the middle class, and the majority from the lower social levels (1 Cor 1:26–28).[86] From the texts in 1 Corinthians it is possible to glean indirect information about well-to-do individuals and their relationship to the Corinthian church.

From reliable tradition in the book of Acts we know that the Jewish-Christians Priscilla (Paul calls her Prisca) and Aquila were expelled from Rome as a result of the Jewish edict issued by the emperor Claudius (49 C.E.) and were already in Corinth before the arrival of the apostle.[87] The edict affected not only Jews but Jewish Christians as well. It is highly probable that Priscilla and Aquila were already Christians at the time they were forced to leave Rome. This is confirmed by Paul's reference to Stephanas and his house as the firstfruits of Achaia (1 Cor 16:15) rather than to them.[88]

Originating from the Roman province of Pontus on the Black Sea, Aquila appeared in Corinth as a tentmaker or leather craftsman and opened a shop there.[89] Paul presumably took advantage of this natural setting con-

---

[84] Malherbe, *Paul*, 15; Meeks, *First Urban Christians*, 61–62.

[85] For background information on the city of Corinth, cf. Elliger, *Paulus*, 200–250; Murphy-O'Connor, "Corinth" and *St. Paul's Corinth*; Riesner, "Korinth," 2:816. Meeks, *First Urban Christians*, 47–50.

[86] Judge, *Social Pattern*, 59–60; following him, but he adds nuances and proofs, cf. Theissen, *Social Setting*, 94–96. Cf. also 2 Cor 8:14; 1 Cor 16:1–4; 6:1–11 as indications of the social makeup of the Corinthian church. Regarding terms such as "upper," "middle," and "lower" class, together with their meaning and (difficult) application to the ancient society, cf. the section on social strata (pp. 165–71).

[87] Acts 18:1–9. For proof, see pp. 128–30. The exact date of the event is disputed (see p. 129, n. 59).

[88] Additional reasons are listed by Haenchen, *Apostelgeschichte*, 511 n. 4; with him Klauck, *Hausgemeinde*, 22; Ollrog, *Paulus*, 25. Cf. also F. F. Bruce, *Acts*, 347.

[89] For a discussion of Aquila's vocation, cf. Lampe, *Stadtrömischen Christen*, 156–58.

sisting of Aquila's colleagues and customers to develop evangelistic contacts.[90] "The citywide missional outreach spread out from this focal point, and this led to the formation of a house church with Paul and this couple as its nucleus."[91]

In recent times it has often been asked in what kind of house Priscilla and Aquila lived. Unfortunately, the texts do not give a clear answer to this question. On the other hand, from analogies in the surrounding environment, there are only a limited number of possibilities. The term οἶκος can imply an atrium house, a villa, a peristyle house, an insula, or a house with a built-in workshop. Each one of these models is documented archaeologically and would have been a possibility in any one of the three cities in which a "house" belonging to this couple is mentioned (Corinth, Ephesus, Rome). With Aquila's vocation in mind, the most likely model for his house would have been the workshop, which was available to craftsmen for rent. In recent years both Lampe and Murphy-O'Connor have advocated this view.[92] Lampe points out that Aquila could have rented his workshop-style house. Nowhere in our texts is it explicitly stated that Aquila was the owner of his home—κατ' οἶκον αὐτῶν ἐκκλησία does not necessarily imply house (or slave) ownership. For Murphy-O'Connor, this idiomatic expression means that "Prisca and Aquila controlled access to their dwelling. They were not workers residing on their employer's property, but were owners or, more probably, tenants of a workshop."[93]

In Corinth such *tabernae* have been excavated.[94] In a row of small workshops north of the southern stoa there are fourteen *tabernae* altogether about 44 meters long. This results in a width of 3 meters per workshop. Their length was just below 4 meters. In the row of workshops on the western side of the forum there is a series of larger workshops, which are approximately 4.5 by 6 meters in size. This results in a shop area of 27 square meters. The work was done in the lower level of the shop. The living, dining, and bedroom was either in the back of the shop or in a loft above it, lit by an unglazed window centered above the shop entrance. The loft was accessible by a series of steps in stone or brick, continued by a

---

[90] Ibid., 156; Branick, *House Church*, 61; Meeks, *First Urban Christians*, 29–32.

[91] Klauck, *Hausgemeinde*, 23. Acts 18:1–9 does not explicitly mention a house church in the couple's home in Corinth. In spite of this we can assume that they did here what they had previously done in Ephesus and Rome; cf. 1 Cor 16:19; Rom 16:5 (see pp. 143–51). So also Murphy-O'Connor, "Prisca and Aquila," 49.

[92] Lampe, *Stadtrömischen Christen*, 161; Murphy-O'Connor, "Prisca and Aquila."

[93] Cf. Murphy-O'Connor, "Prisca and Aquila," 49.

[94] Cf. Waele, "Roman Market"; Finley, *Atlas*, 154–56. Apparently there was virtually no difference between such shops in the East and the West (cf. Murphy-O'Connor, "Prisca and Aquila," 49: "A generic description is valid for all major towns throughout the empire"). Cf. also K. Schneider, "Taberna."

wooden ladder located in one of the back corners of the shop.[95] In such a room or in the shop itself, about twenty believers could have assembled for a house church meeting.[96]

The attempt to determine the social status of this couple has also generated much discussion among NT scholars without a consensus being reached. Recent scholarship in particular has tended to ascribe to them a higher status.[97]

We know relatively little about Prisca; interestingly, the NT generally mentions her name before her husband's, which was quite unconventional for the ancient world.[98] We can therefore assume that this was intentional, indicating that she was in some way more important than her husband. But in what way? Was it based on a spiritual criterion of some kind—for example, because she came to faith before her husband or because of her special significance in the early Christian movement?[99] Or does it originate from a secular concern, for example, Prisca's higher social status?[100] On the basis of Acts 18:26, it can be presumed that Prisca was well educated, which would indicate a higher status. The fact that she did manual labor in the same profession with her husband (18:3) implies, however, that Prisca was neither of higher status than Aquila nor independently wealthy.[101]

Most scholars assume that Aquila was a well-to-do craftsman engaged in the trade industry and a homeowner who performed services of patronage and took mission journeys for the Pauline missional outreach.[102] Theissen

---

[95] There was no running water and no toilet. For a description of the "living room," cf. Juvenal, *Sat.* 3.203–207; Martial, *Epigr.* 12.32; Apuleius, *Metam.* 9.24–25.

[96] Lampe, *Stadtrömischen Christen*, 161, envisions the situation in the following way: "Some of Aquila's Christian guests would therefore have sat on stacks of tent canvases for their worship meetings." For further description including drawings, cf. Murphy-O'Connor, "Prisca and Aquila," 49.

[97] Ollrog, *Paulus*, 26–27 n. 105; Wilckens, *Römer*, 3:134; Hengel, *Eigentum*, 46; with a nuanced view, Meeks, *First Urban Christians*, 59. Also with a different view, E. and W. Stegemann (*Urchristliche Sozialgeschichte*, 252–54) and Klauck (*Hausgemeinde*, 23), who leaves the question open.

[98] Cf. Acts 18:18, 19, 26; Rom 16:3; 2 Tim 4:19; the opposite sequence in Acts 18:2; 1 Cor 16:19.

[99] Harnack, *Mission*, 1:85. With him Ollrog, *Paulus*, 25; Klauck, *Hausgemeinde*, 26; Murphy-O'Connor, "Prisca and Aquila," 42; in Rom 16:3 Paul refers to Prisca as a "coworker."

[100] Judge, "Early Christians," 129; Branick, *House Church*, 61; F. F. Bruce, *Acts*, 348.

[101] Murphy-O'Connor, "Prisca and Aquila," 42: "A woman of noble birth would not know how to do the heavy needle-and-palm work of tentmakers, nor would her hands be adapted to it, and a woman of independent means would not need to work." On Prisca, cf. also Harnack, "Probabilia," esp. 33–35.

[102] Ollrog, *Paulus*, 26–27 n. 105, speculates that Aquila owned a business in Rome that was run by one of his slaves in his absence after his expulsion due to Claudius's edict. He owned a house not only in Rome but also in Ephesus according to Wilckens, *Römer*, 3:134. Aquila was director of an industrial business with different branches, in which not only Paul was employed according to Hengel, *Eigentum*,

lists a set of criteria that enable us to determine the social status of an individual: office, home ownership, services for the church, mission journeys. He concludes that most of the Corinthians mentioned by name, including Prisca and Aquila, fulfilled a number of these criteria and therefore were probably of higher social status. They were, however, craftsmen and Jews from the eastern provinces, and as such they would not have belonged to the local aristocratic upper class.[103] Lampe addresses all these issues and comes to the opposite conclusion: Aquila belonged to the lower class in his vocation, owned neither house nor slaves, and did not employ hired help.[104] Neither are Aquila's documented journeys certain evidence of a higher status.[105] Our study can leave this issue undecided. Decisive for us is not the status of the couple or their home ownership but the fact that they made their house available in various ways to the Pauline mission effort, be it a Roman atrium house or a workshop apartment. It is not exaggerating to suggest that as co-workers of Paul this couple truly made a significant contribution to the furtherance of the Pauline missional outreach by unselfishly offering their own services as well as those of their house and household. This applies not only to their mission journeys and services but to their willingness to provide Paul a place of employment and the church a meeting place. It applies in particular to the special service that Paul mentions in Rom 16:4: "They risked their lives for me." Somewhere (Corinth or Ephesus?) at some time they saved Paul's life. Perhaps it was in connection with his term in prison in Ephesus that they gave him their protection as patrons, much as Jason did in Thessalonica.[106] We cannot know this with certainty. One thing for sure is that their support of the Pauline mission enterprise was so extensive that Paul is moved to praise them in 16:4: "Not only I but all the churches of the Gentiles are grateful to them."

After a time Paul moved into the house of Titius Justus, a worshiper of God, next door to the synagogue (Acts 18:7). It is assumed that Aquila and Prisca were not able to set up their business in a location that was best suited for an evangelistic ministry and that Paul moved into the house of Titius Justus because it was near the synagogue and strategically better positioned for missional outreach to the Jews but particularly to God-fearers. It is also

---

46. Initially Prisca and Aquila traveled from Rome to Corinth. From 1 Cor 16:19 we know that they accommodated a church in their house in Ephesus. Later, as we will see, they returned to Rome and led a house church there.

103. Theissen, *Social Setting*, 73–74, 94–96.

104. Lampe, *Stadtrömischen Christen*, 156–64.

105. As Theissen admits, documented travel alone is not sufficient proof for a higher status. Lampe does not consider journeys to be a criterion at all in determining social status; cf. *Stadtrömischen Christen*, 162–64. Cf. also Schöllgen's criticism of Lampe and Meeks in "Probleme"; "Was wissen wir?" Part of the problem is due to different definitions of the term "status." These and other issues concerning the social level of early Christians in general will be addressed later (see pp. 165–71).

106. For proof of Paul's prison term in Ephesus, cf. Ollrog, *Paulus*, 27 n. 114.

possible that the couple's house was not large enough to accommodate a sufficient audience for Paul's preaching and teaching. In contrast, the triclinium in the house of Titius Justus was perhaps larger and therefore more suitable.[107] That Titius Justus was a God-fearer insinuates that he already sympathized with Judaism but was not yet ready to submit to circumcision and to fully convert. In other words, the conversion of God-fearers to Christianity was prepared for and made easier by their prior contact with the Jewish synagogue. Titius Justus also appears to be a good candidate for leadership in the early church, as he demonstrated courage in his rejection of paganism,[108] he was presumably well educated,[109] and he owned a house that was large enough to provide Paul a venue for his evangelistic preaching ministry. This assumption is supported by the observation that Titius Justus appears still firmly embedded in the memory of the church many years later as Luke began gathering tradition sources and writing the book of Acts.

Acts 18:8 mentions another potential house owner. As we have seen, Crispus, the synagogue ruler, came to faith with his entire house. In his case, private home ownership and higher status are quite certain, as synagogue rulers were often fairly wealthy individuals.[110] Their title usually implied that they had helped finance the building of the synagogue or its maintenance.[111]

Stephanas, the first convert in Corinth, was baptized "with his house" by Paul (1 Cor 1:16). As the first convert, he probably had a unique position in the Corinthian church (16:15). The group was supposed to submit themselves to him, his family, and all their coworkers (16:16). Stephanas along with Fortunatus and Achaicus (members of his household? his slaves?) traveled to visit Paul in Ephesus (16:17). His property and his mission journeys imply that Stephanas was a wealthy person.[112] Such status, coupled with his

---

[107] Cf., e.g., Lampe, *Stadtrömischen Christen*, 160; Murphy-O'Connor, "Prisca and Aquila," 49. Also in Ephesus (see pp. 143–44), was it the case that Aquila's apartment did not come into question as a meeting place for Paul's preaching ministry (cf. Acts 19:9) because there, too, it was too small?

[108] So Filson, "Significance," 112. Acts does not specify clearly whether Titius Justus became a Christian, but from the context it is safe to assume he did (cf. the general openness of God-fearers toward the Christian message and the acceptance of Paul into his house). We can assume he became a Christian particularly if he is to be identified with Gaius in Rom 16:23 and 1 Cor 1:14. So Ramsay, *Pictures*, 205; Goodspeed, "Gaius Titius Justus." Meeks (*First Urban Christians*, 63 n. 75) leaves the question open.

[109] K. Kuhn and H. Stegemann, "Proselyten," point out that God-fearers in the Diaspora were generally of higher status than proselytes and as a result were better educated (cf. also Gülzow, *Christentum*, 13–14; Siegert, "Gottesfürchtige"; Radin, *Jews*, 149–62).

[110] Theissen, *Social Setting*, 87 and 94; with him Meeks, *First Urban Christians*, 57; Klauck, *Hausgemeinde*, 33; Blue, "Acts," 176–77.

[111] For a list of the inscriptions that confirm this, cf. Brooten, *Women Leaders*, 23 n. 93; cf. also Theissen, *Social Setting*, 73–74.

[112] Theissen, *Social Setting*, 94. Stephanas fulfills three of the criteria.

exceptional service in the group, indicates the existence of a house church under his leadership, although his exact function is difficult to determine (see pp. 190–210).

In his Letter to the Romans (16:23) Paul sends greetings from individuals in the Corinthian church, Gaius and Erastus (see below). Paul describes Gaius as his host and host of the entire church (ὁ ξένος μου καὶ ὅλης τῆς ἐκκλησίας).[113] Many commentators see Gaius's role as simply extending hospitality and lodging to Paul and other believers (especially those traveling through) on behalf of or by order of the Corinthian congregation, but not as providing a meeting place for the congregation.[114] Patristic exegesis, however, understood Gaius to be the owner of a home in which the entire church gathered for worship.[115] Along with Klauck, I tend to favor this interpretation of the text, for the following reasons.[116] First, nowhere in the text is there an indication that Gaius acted on behalf of, or on an order from, the congregation. Second, according to 1 Cor 14:23, we can assume a gathering of the whole church from that location. This would mean that at some point the house of Gaius became the regular meeting place for the whole church in Corinth, perhaps for the simple reason that his house was the only one large enough to accommodate the entire group. This is supported by 14:23 and 11:20. It is quite probable that Paul praises Gaius because he made his triclinium and atrium available to the whole Corinthian church as a place of assembly. Apparently his living room was quite large.[117] Acts 18:10 preserves the memory of "many" Christians in Corinth. We must assume therefore that at that time the whole church in Corinth was relatively large[118] and consisted of not less than thirty and probably from fifty to ninety members.[119]

---

[113] He is presumably identical with the Gaius mentioned in 1 Cor 1:14.

[114] Käsemann, *Römer*, 401; Schlier, *Römerbrief*, 451; Lietzmann, *Römer*, 128; Wilckens, *Römer*, 3:146.

[115] Origen, *Röm Kommentar in der freien lateinischen Übertragung des Rufin*, PG 14:1289C; cf. also Theissen, *Social Setting*, 56 and 89.

[116] Klauck, *Hausgemeinde*, 34.

[117] All this information is an indication that Gaius enjoyed a relatively high status in Corinthian society. Cf. also E. and W. Stegemann, *Urchristliche Sozialgeschichte*, 254.

[118] Theissen, *Social Setting*, 89.

[119] Branick, *House Church*, 64: "the whole church of Corinth" had "no less than thirty people." Thirteen are mentioned in the NT. Cf. the list made by Theissen, *Social Setting*, 94–95. On the basis of archaeological considerations, Murphy-O'Connor (*St. Paul's Corinth*, 164–66) estimates that the total number in the Corinthian church was between thirty and fifty people (more likely in the direction of fifty). Cf. Banks, *Paul's Idea*, 35: "A meeting of the 'whole church' may have reached forty to forty-five people—if the meeting spilled over into the atrium then the number could have been greater, though no more than double that size." According to Blue ("Acts," 175 n. 219), including those in congregations in the surrounding area, such as Cenchreae, one hundred total members would have been possible.

At this point it would be helpful to get a clearer picture of the architecture of ancient houses that come into question for Pauline house churches.[120] Included are a Roman atrium house or villa; a Roman city insula, that is, a multistory rental building with business shops on the ground floor; a Greek peristyle house; and a Hellenistic hybrid with courtyard and adjacent rooms or a house with workshop. The floor plans for such houses give us helpful data for estimating the potential size of house churches. Archaeology can provide information in this regard even though the evidence is somewhat limited. Unfortunately, no archaeological evidence for Christian house churches has been discovered in Corinth itself.[121] Up until recently it was assumed that the physical conditions of houses in Pompeii, Herculaneum, Ostia, or Corinth could be determined and then generalized for all Pauline house churches on the basis that they were all located in Greco-Roman cities. This conclusion was based on the assumption that a floor plan existed that was typical for houses throughout the entire Roman Empire.[122] Investigations of the archaeological discoveries since the late nineteenth century have demonstrated that this assumption is false, making an approach in terms of the local history necessary for research in this context.[123] "Housing patterns, of course, varied considerably across the Empire. The Italian villa, the Greek peristyle, the Hellenistic-oriental multistoried *insula*, apartments, and others had their own local stylistic traditions. We must expect ... considerable diversity from place to place depending on the local circumstances."[124] The consequence of this insight for our study is that in order to determine the architectural conditions of the houses used for Pauline house churches, we must utilize archaeological data from the specific city or region in which the house churches in question were located.

Fortunately, in this case there are sufficient examples of Corinthian private homes for our time period that offer analogies to the houses that were

---

[120] For ancient houses in general, cf. D. Robertson, *Handbook*, esp. ch. 17, "Greek and Roman Houses and Palaces"; Carcopino, *Daily Life*, esp. ch. 2, "Houses and Streets"; Kraus, "Haus"; McKay, *Römische Häuser*; Boethius and Ward-Perkins, *Etruscan* and "Notes"; Hermansen, *Ostia*; Wallace-Hadrill, "Houses" and *Houses*; J. Clarke, *Houses*; Osiek and Balch, *Families*, 5–35, 201–3.

[121] This applies also for all other cities (Ephesus, Philippi, Thessalonica, etc.) in which Paul established churches. For evidence of house churches elsewhere and in other times, cf. White, *Building God's House*, 12–25, 62–75, 103–10, and "Domus," 545–53; Petersen, "House-Churches, 267–72; Kraeling, *Christian Building*, 129–34; Rordorf, "Was wissen wir?"; Klauck, *Hausgemeinde*, 77–81; Branick, *House Church*, 38–42.

[122] Cf., e.g., Murphy-O'Connor, *St. Paul's Corinth*, 161–78; following him Branick, *House Church*, 39. Cf. White, *Building God's House*, 190 n. 29: "By contrast note the assumptions of homogeneity in housing" by Murphy-O'Connor, *St. Paul's Corinth*, 161–78.

[123] White, "Domus," 18–19; Krautheimer, "Beginnings," 144–45; McKay, *Römische Häuser*.

[124] White, *Building God's House*, 107.

most likely used for Christian house churches.[125] In Anaploga near Corinth, for instance, an atrium house contained a series of rooms surrounding a courtyard (atrium; 35 square meters) with a small pool (impluvium), a living room (triclinium) measuring 41.25 square meters. Such a living room would have accommodated nine people on the couches placed along the walls, and in the courtyard there would have been room for several more.[126] If all of the couches were removed, there would have been room for about twenty people total. If the courtyard were used for extra space, the capacity could have been expanded to about forty to fifty. This can serve as a helpful guideline for determining the hypothetical size of Pauline house churches at least in Corinth.[127]

As a possible house owner, Ersatus also needs be considered. He was a city official (οἰκονόμος τῆς πόλεως) in Corinth (Rom 16:23). There are two ways of interpreting this vocational designation. Either he was an unimportant slave serving in the area of financial administration, or he was involved in city administration at a fairly high leadership level as quaestor and later as aedile. Only in the latter case could he have been a house owner. Interestingly, a Corinthian inscription has been found that documents an aedile by the name of Erastus.[128] Although it would be quite an unusual coincidence for the Erastus mentioned in Rom 16 to be identical with the one in the inscription, the possibility must be left open. A number of scholars consider the two identical.[129] Regardless of whether the two can be identified, however, there is additional evidence that indicates a higher status of the Christian Erastus. For instance, mission travel by Erastus can be documented (Acts 19:22; 2 Tim 4:20).[130] In addition, Paul mentions the secular status of a

---

[125] For ancient houses in Corinth, cf. Shear, *Roman Villa;* Wiseman, "Corinth and Rome"; Weinberg, *Southeast.*

[126] See floor plan and drawing in the appendix, below.

[127] Cf. Murphy-O'Connor, *St. Paul's Corinth,* 161–78, with archaeological data for a number of houses from the first century in and around Corinth. The measurements of the villa at Anaploga appear to be representative. Cf. also Branick, *House Church,* 39.

[128] Text in Kent, *Inscriptions,* no. 232. An exact dating is not yet possible, but an origin in the first century C.E. is possible.

[129] Positively, Theissen, *Social Setting,* 83; Winter, *Seek the Welfare,* 195; Kent, *Inscriptions,* 100. Evidence for identification is that Erastus is not a common name and we know of no other Corinthian city official by this name. So V. P. Furnish, "Corinth," 20. For Klauck (*Hausgemeinde,* 33), Elliger (*Paulus,* 230), and Meeks (*First Urban Christians,* 58–59), the identification is a plausibility about which we cannot be certain. Negatively, Cadbury, "Erastus." For E. and W. Stegemann, *Urchristliche Sozialgeschichte,* 253, the Erastus mentioned in Rom 16 was at least a lower-level city official in Corinth. As such, he was on the staff of the highest level of city officials.

[130] It is disputed, however, whether the Erastus in Acts 19:22/2 Tim 4:20 can be identified with the one in Rom 16:23. In support of an identification are Theissen, *Social Setting,* 75–83; Redlich, *S. Paul,* 231–32; negatively, Cadbury, "Erastus," 45; Hemer, *Acts,* 235; U. Wilckens, *Römer,* 3:146.

member of the church only here in Rom 16:23. It can be assumed that Paul intentionally mentioned Erastus's special status because his position was remarkable and quite high.[131] It is possible to establish linguistically that οἰκονόμος τῆς πόλεως is indeed an expression for a high and honorable position. A. D. Clarke has convincingly demonstrated that Erastus had a high position, whether he can be identified with the Erastus of the inscription or not. "Regardless of any direct connection between these Erasti, there is the firm probability that in the Erastus of Romans 16.23, there is a figure who was one of the established people of Corinth, and was in a position to offer hospitality to the whole church of Corinth. . . . It is reasonable to argue back from the circumstances suggested in Romans 16:23 that this particular οἰκονόμος τῆς πόλεως was a position not of a public slave, but one of considerable honour. Here is one figure who certainly belonged to the οὐ πολλοὶ δυνατοί of 1 Corinthians 1.26."[132] Everything appears to support the view that Erastus was another affluent individual with a high city office, and who, as a homeowner, served as host to a house church in Corinth.

If our conclusions are correct, then in Corinth there existed a plurality of house churches, which gathered quite often in different homes, alongside the whole church at that location, which met less often but regularly.[133] How many house churches existed in Corinth is difficult to determine. At any rate, the groups that met in the house of Gaius and in the house of Aquila and Prisca can be counted as house churches.[134] If Titius Justus should not be identified with Gaius, then the group that gathered in his home would be an additional house church in Corinth. In addition, it is possible that house churches met in the homes of Stephanas, Erastus, and Crispus. The church that met in the home of Phoebe in the harbor town of Cenchreae can be considered an additional house church in or near Corinth.

Cenchreae

In Rom 16:1–2 we are introduced to Phoebe, an important person for our study. Paul refers to her as "our sister Phoebe, a servant [διάκονον] of the church in Cenchreae."[135] Phoebe apparently served the church in Cenchreae by offering her home as a meeting place.[136] The text does not explicitly mention a house, but verse 2 implies one. There Paul calls Phoebe a προστάτις,

---

[131] Theissen, *Social Setting*, 75–76.

[132] A. Clarke, *Secular and Christian*, 46–56.

[133] Jülicher, *Römer*, 331, holds that the conditions in a large city allowed for a gathering of the whole church at most once per week on Sunday (1 Cor 16:2).

[134] Even if the whole church at that location came together at Gaius's house, it still would have been a house church.

[135] This was a church branch in one of the port cities of Corinth and most likely established by the Corinthian congregation (cf. Klauck, *Hausgemeinde*, 30). For background information on the city of Cenchreae, cf. Riesner, "Kenchreä."

[136] Cf. Klauck, *Hausgemeinde*, 30–31.

which, among other things, can mean "patron" or "protector."[137] Accordingly, Phoebe would have been an affluent patroness who made her property available for service to Paul and the other Christians.[138] As such, she played the role of hostess to the local church in Cenchreae.[139] The verb διακονέω appears often in the context of table service.[140] The name Phoebe originates from mythology; back then such names were given to slaves.[141] Her ability to offer such service and to afford travel is an indication, however, that Phoebe gained her freedom and a position of relative wealth.[142] Recently E. W. and W. Stegemann have even suggested that Phoebe belonged to the upper class in Cenchreae, on the basis of Paul's reference to her as προστάτις.[143] Her slave name therefore does not necessarily exclude the possibility that she was an affluent patroness of a house church in Cenchreae.

Ephesus

Approximately one year after the conclusion of his mission outreach in Corinth, Paul began the mission in Ephesus.[144] As far as we know, his stay there was longer than in any other city. The book of Acts preserves the tradition that Prisca and Aquila traveled with Paul from Corinth to Ephesus, where they gave the Alexandrian Apollos Christian instruction in their home (Acts 18:18–19b, 26)—one further reference to a house used

---

[137] Judge ("Early Christians," 128–29) suggested that προστάτις is to be understood here as a synonym for the Latin *patrona* (in the sense of "protector"), which was common language for areas with strong Roman influence. Following him, Meeks, *First Urban Christians*, 60; similarly Klauck, *Hausgemeinde*, 31. Exegetes as early as Stigel and Bengel saw Phoebe as patroness and protector of the Christians in Cenchreae; cf. G. Heinrici, *Der zweite Brief*, 414.

[138] The fact that a woman as widow had the *materna potestas* was not uncommon. Cf. Thraede, "Frau," 8:198.

[139] With leadership responsibility? See pp. 210–25, the excursus on women's leadership responsibilities in the Pauline churches.

[140] Mark 1:13, 31; Luke 10:40; John 12:2; Acts 6:2

[141] Cf. Lietzmann, *Römer*, 126, for an extensive excursus on the topic.

[142] Theissen, *Social Setting*, 87–89, 91–93; following him, Klauck, *Hausgemeinde*, 31.

[143] E. and W. Stegemann, *Urchristliche Sozialgeschichte*, 254. For them, this is theoretically possible because of Phoebe's designation as patroness.

[144] For background information on the city of Ephesus, cf. Elliger, *Ephesos*; Oster, "Ephesus"; E. Green and Hemer, "Ephesus." Domestic houses have been discovered in Ephesus; two insulae with private houses on the hillside of Bülbüldag (Mt. Koressos) are almost completely excavated. But they are primarily upper-class peristyle houses and probably not the type of house that would come into question for the Pauline churches. On the second and third levels, however, smaller living units have been excavated in an insula on the east side. Owners or renters of these apartments would have been from the "middle class" (cf. McKay, *Römische Häuser*, 151–57, esp. 156). For the most thorough discussion, cf. Akurgal, *Ancient Civilizations*, 142–44, 378–80. Cf. also Thür, "Ephesos."

for instruction in early Christian missions.[145] From Ephesus Paul sent greetings from Prisca and Aquila, again with the idiomatic expression σὺν τῇ κατ' οἶκον αὐτῶν ἐκκλησίᾳ—"along with the church in their house" (1 Cor 16:19). Apparently, Aquila and Prisca had established a house church there as well.

Not much can be said about house churches in Ephesus. The greeting from "all the brothers" (1 Cor 16:20) points to other Christians in Ephesus who did not meet at Aquila's home. This, along with the relatively large size of the church in Ephesus, suggests a plurality of house churches there, but we cannot be certain.

It is assumed that after the Jewish edict was repealed (55 C.E.), a number of the members of this congregation traveled with Aquila and Prisca to Rome. If Aquila and Prisca were in fact well-to-do craftspeople, it is possible that they employed independent workers and/or slaves in their operation who in turn traveled with them and would have belonged to the inner core of their house church.[146] For instance, it is possible that Epaenetus and Mary (Rom 16:5–6) were servants and belonged to the house church of Prisca and Aquila in Ephesus.[147]

Rome

In the long list of greetings in Rom 16 we encounter Prisca and Aquila again, this time in a request with the stock formula ἡ κατ' οἶκον ἐκκλησίαν: "Greet Prisca and Aquila . . . and greet also the church that meets in their house [καὶ τὴν κατ' οἶκον αὐτῶν ἐκκλησίαν]" (Rom 16:3, 5). It can therefore be assumed that, after stations in Corinth and Ephesus, Prisca and Aquila returned to Rome, their earlier place of residence, established a house church there again, and were perhaps prepared to receive Paul on his planned visit

---

[145] 1 Cor 16:19 confirms Prisca and Aquila's move to Ephesus. The continuing existence of a church in Ephesus cannot be convincingly denied (cf. Acts 20:4; 1 Cor 16:1–4; Rev 2:1–7; Acts 19:1–3; 20:17–19; 1 Tim 1:3; 2 Tim 1:18; 4:12); against Schille, *Urchristliche Kollegialmission*, 51. Cf. Ollrog, *Paulus*, 32–34, 58–61. Particularly the size of the staff team, the many trips of Paul as well as his coworkers in this area, and the length of the stay in Ephesus all speak in favor of a relatively large congregation.

In comparison to Acts 18:1–17, the opinion of exegetes regarding historic reliability is not as consistent here. Cf. Ollrog, *Paulus*, 33 n. 142, 143; 37–39, esp. nn. 164, 167, for a discussion of the tension between Lukan and Pauline texts. For Pesch, *Apostelgeschichte*, 2:154, vv. 18–19b are not Lukan additions.

[146] Klauck, *Hausgemeinde*, 23; with Ollrog, *Paulus*, 38 n. 164. Following them, Branick, *House Church*, 73.

[147] The structure of the greeting list in 16:3–16 implies this; Epaenetus and Mary are greeted in a preferred manner. This would also explain why others from Ephesus are present in Rome. In the same text Epaenetus is called the "first fruit" of Asia Minor, and thus he would have been the first to be baptized in the area of Ephesus.

to Rome.¹⁴⁸ We thus have references to the house churches of this couple for three different locations of the Pauline mission: Corinth, Ephesus, and Rome. For Corinth the expression ἡ κατ' οἶκον αὐτῶν ἐκκλησία is not documented. Nevertheless, the evidence indicates that initially a house church was established in the couple's home, even though Paul later moves to the house of Titius Justus.¹⁴⁹

It appears that traces of two additional house churches can also be observed in Rom 16:14, 15: "Greet Asyncritus, Phlegon, Hermes, Patrobas, Hermas *and the brothers with them*" and "Greet Philologus, Julia, Nereus and his sister, and Olympas *and all the saints with them.*"¹⁵⁰ These names represent "the members of two house churches, to which an undetermined number of additional Christians belong,"¹⁵¹ some relatives, others slaves or emancipated slaves.¹⁵²

In addition, in Rom 16:10 those "who belong to (the household of) Aristobulus" and in 16:11 those "in (the household of) Narcissus" are greeted by Paul. These individuals are most likely groups of Christian slaves within extended households whose householders do not appear to be Christian.¹⁵³ These groups do not constitute house churches, but rather some sort of house fellowship groups that belonged to house churches somewhere else in the city.

Here again there exists a plurality of house churches, in some cases house fellowships. Indeed, our examination has revealed five different Christian groups in the city of Rome. One of them is with certainty a house church—namely, the one that met in the home of Prisca and Aquila (Rom 16:5).¹⁵⁴ It is highly probable that the two groups in Rom 16:14, 15 are also

---

¹⁴⁸ So Ollrog, *Paulus*, 26–27. For background information on the city of Rome, cf. Lampe, *Stadtrömischen Christen;* Alföldy, *Römische Sozialgeschichte;* Garnsey and Saller, *Roman Empire;* Rostovtzeff, *Social and Economic History* (1926), esp. 125–79; Hall, "Rome."

¹⁴⁹ It is possible that Aquila moved so often for strategic reasons because of his commitment to Paul and his mission objectives (cf. Ollrog, *Paulus*, 27: "These rapid changes in location cannot have benefited the development of his own business"). Similarly Murphy-O'Connor, "Prisca and Aquila."

¹⁵⁰ Gielen, "Zur Interpretation," 121, points out, however, that neither of these two texts attributes the status of church to the groups mentioned. It can also be asked why Paul does not use the stock expression here: was it because they were not house churches but instead merely house fellowship groups? See pp. 155–62 for further discussion.

¹⁵¹ Käsemann, *Römer*, 395; also Branick, *House Church*, 69–70; Klauck, *Hausgemeinde*, 27–28; Stuhlmacher, *Philemon*, 71. But cf. Banks, *Paul's Idea*, 39–40, for the opposite view that the groups were not house churches but Christian "domestic or work groups."

¹⁵² Lietzmann (*Römer*, 126–27) shows in an excursus that some of the names point in this direction. Cf. also Lampe, *Stadtrömischen Christen*, 135–51.

¹⁵³ Klauck, *Hausgemeinde*, 28.

¹⁵⁴ Evidently this house church enjoyed a certain independence, as Paul normally calls a local church ἐκκλησία (cf. Rom 16:1, 23; 1 Cor 1:2; 11:18; 14:23;

house churches. Two additional groups were noted in Rom 16:10, 11. If we assume that the other fourteen individuals mentioned in Rom 16 did not belong to any one of these five groups, and that it is unlikely that they all belonged to one group, this results in at least seven different groups.[155] It is interesting to observe, first, that the fractionalization of the first-century Roman Christian church as a whole into separate groups corresponds with the historical discovery that at that time Christians in Rome were geographically dispersed in the different districts throughout the city.[156] Second, we encounter the same phenomenon of geographical fractionalization when we examine the origins of the Roman *tituli*.[157] After a thorough examination of the *tituli*, Lampe comes to the following conclusion: "In the pre-Constantine period the urban Christians of Rome gathered fractionalized—in premises made available by private individuals dispersed throughout the cosmopolitan city. In principle we can observe a continuity between the structure implied in Rom 16 and the *tituli* network in Rome (even though a continuity between an individual house church of the first century and a specific *titulus* from the third century cannot be documented)."[158] Third, in light of the organization of the Jewish community in Rome in a series of individual (house) synagogues (documented with inscriptional evidence) also without any recognizable urban suprastructure (see below),[159] one would be inclined to assume the existence of separate house churches in Rome even if there were no textual evidence.[160]

There does not appear, however, to be any evidence for a physical center for the house churches that were scattered throughout the city. Nowhere in the Letter to the Romans is the church as a whole in Rome called ἐκκλησία, not even in 1:7, where it would normally be expected in a Pauline epistle. Nowhere is there mention that the local church in Rome gathered as a whole church in a citywide assembly.[161] This could be connected with the

---

2 Cor 1:1; 1 Thess 1:1). Only in Ephesus and in the Lycos valley is a house church otherwise designated an ἐκκλησία: 1 Cor 16:19; Phlm 2; Col 4:15 (cf. p. 8, n. 45 and p. 137).

[155] Lampe, *Stadtrömischen Christen*, 64–65, reflects on the possible existence of an eighth house church in Rome, where Paul gathered believers together for instruction in a rented apartment (Acts 28:30–31).

[156] Cf. the extensive study by Lampe, ibid., 10–35.

[157] Cf. our n. 166 for the references to a whole series of studies on the topic, esp. the foundational article by Petersen. Scholars generally agree that Roman Christians were organized in house churches until well into the third century

[158] Lampe, *Stadtrömischen Christen*, 305.

[159] Wilckens, *Römer*, 1:35–39; Klauck, *Hausgemeinde*, 26; Lampe, *Stadtrömischen Christen*, 306. Cf. Leon, *Jews*, 135–94 (p. 193: "no good evidence for a body exercising supervision over Roman Jewry as a whole"); Wiefel, "Jüdische Gemeinschaft."

[160] Klauck, *Hausgemeinde*, 26–28, 35, 40 n. 64; Andresen, *Von den Anfängen*, 3; Branick, *House Church*, 25.

[161] This observation is confirmed by Justin ca. one century later (cf. *Martyrium Justini* 3.1, 3). Cf. Klauck, *Hausgemeinde*, 69–70, for an extensive discus-

size of the city of Rome: it was by far the largest in the empire (presumably about a million).[162]

In recent times the view of house churches presented in this study, particularly concerning Rome but also concerning the other Pauline cities, has been challenged by R. Jewett.[163] According to Jewett, in addition to the "traditional" house churches, there is evidence for the existence of "tenement churches," which gathered in the work and living space of insulae without the assistance of householders or patrons. He also claims to be able to demonstrate that it led to a different leadership structure and community lifestyle in the groups that gathered in such space.

In support of his thesis, Jewett points out that only very few Christians lived in their own houses. In accordance with the structure of Roman society in general, the overwhelming majority of Christians found housing in small urban insulae, that is, in tenement houses—rented, very small, barrackslike apartments.[164] This leads to the question whether the Pauline Christians "conducted their services within the *insulae* itself, either using one of the workshop areas on the ground floor or using space rented by Christian neighbors in upper floors, clearing away the temporary partitions between cubicles to create room for the meeting. In either case the church would not be meeting in space provided by a patron but rather in rented or shared space provided by the members themselves."[165] The results of archaeological research supposedly demonstrate that Christians gathered in such rooms in later periods.[166] There is also evidence, according to Jewett, for "tenement churches" in the Pauline Epistles, particularly in Rome. Jewett points to the work of Lampe, who, on the basis of his research, locates the overwhelming majority of the first Roman Christians in the poorest districts of the city (Trastevere and Via Appia/Porta Capena) and places them accordingly in the lower social strata.[167] Corresponding to this is the result of his analysis of the social background of the individuals mentioned in Rom 16: "Out of thirteen persons about whom it is possible to make a judgment, with all probability over one-third have a slave origin."[168] Because it can be demonstrated that the names that are mentioned in both of the groups in Rom 16:14 and 16:15

---

sion. Independently of Klauck, Lampe, *Stadtrömischen Christen*, 306, comes to the same conclusion (for further literature, cf. ibid., 368).

[162] Cf., e.g., Packer, "Housing."

[163] Jewett, "Tenement Churches and Communal Meals"; "Tenement Churches and Pauline Love Feasts."

[164] Jewett, "Tenement Churches and Communal Meals," 25–26.

[165] Jewett, "Tenement Churches and Pauline Love Feasts," 49–50.

[166] Cf. some of the tituli, esp. Titulus Byzantis, and Krautheimer, "Beginnings"; Rordorf, "Was wissen wir?" 119–20; Petersen, "House-Churches," 266, 270; Kirsch, *Titelkirchen*, 21, 26–29, 39–40, 42–44; White, "Domus," 188–210, 232–38; Finney, "Early Christian Architecture."

[167] Lampe, *Stadtrömischen Christen*, 10–52.

[168] Ibid., 153; Lampe is dependent on Solin, *Die Griechischen Personennamen*.

originate from a slave or emancipated background, Jewett presumes that they represent "tenement churches," probably from the districts of Trastevere or Via Appia/Porta Capena.[169] This assumption is supported by the additional observation that in both groups no one person appears to have assumed leadership: "None of the five names appears to be playing the role of patron for the group, the social structure probably differed from what we have assumed was a normal house church."[170]

Jewett finds one more piece of evidence for "tenement churches"—this time in Thessalonica—in 2 Thess 3:10.[171] In contrast to house churches with their "love patriarchalism," in such insulae churches it appears that a system of love communalism provided the material and financial support for sacramental meals. The original Sitz im Leben for 2 Thess 3:10 is probably this "tenement church" system, which depended on the support of the Christian group itself in providing for the agape meals. In tenement churches that did not have a patron, these meals would have been endangered without the material and financial contributions of the individual members.[172]

Even though Jewett's thesis may seem quite attractive in some ways, many critical questions come to mind. Archaeological investigations in Ostia Antiqua indicate that Jewett is correct in pointing out that not all but rather only a small minority of Christians lived in their own homes. All of the others lived either with the owners in these houses or in rented apartments or tenement houses.[173] But it was precisely the existence in such cramped space that demanded alternative venues where enough room was available for the assembly of larger groups.[174] The mention of the patroness Phoebe and of

---

[169] Jewett, "Tenement Churches and Communal Meals," 28–31.
[170] Ibid., 30.
[171] Ibid., 33–42. Cf. also 1 Thess 2:9; 4:9–12.
[172] Cf. the analysis of the communion problem in Corinth by Hofius on pp. 174–77.
[173] Cf., e.g., Meeks, *First Urban Christians*, 40–50; Malherbe, *Social Aspects*, 63; regarding the general conditions in the Roman Empire, cf. Frier, *Landlords*, 3–47; Packer, "Housing" and *Insulae;* McKay, *Römische Häuser*, 6–176.

Balch and Osiek have pointed out, however, that there is no archaeological evidence for "four- to five-story, low rent apartment housing (*insulae*) in pre-Neronian Rome, its port of Ostia, or seemingly elsewhere" (*Families*, 21–23). Although Jewett (and other NT scholars) often refer to archaeological evidence for insulae in Ostia, it is all from the time of Trajan or even later, and so fifty years after Paul. Accordingly, their relevance regarding the conditions of Pauline house churches is questionable. Literary evidence for insulae in the pre-Neronian period, however, does exists (cf., e.g., Strabo, *Geogr.* 5.3.7, C235; Seneca, *Ira* 3.35.5; Martial, *Epigr.* 1.117; 7.20; Juvenal, *Sat.* 3.6–7; 3.198–202; 3.215–220). Nevertheless "these apartment houses were just beginning to be built in Roman cities in Paul's decades, and it is likely that most or at least many Pauline ekklesiai occurred in atrium houses," according to Balch and Osiek, *Families*, 24. If Balch and Osiek are proven correct, then Jewett's thesis becomes superfluous.

[174] Jewett, "Tenement Churches and Communal Meals," 26, correctly points out that, on the average, these tiny rooms were at most 10 sq. m. in size.

the patron Gaius in Rom 16:1, 23 underscores just how important such Christians were, who could provide meeting space, lodging, and support for others in such restricted living conditions.

Jewett's thesis stands or falls with his claim that sufficient space could have been created by "using space rented by Christian neighbors in upper floors, clearing away the temporary partitions between cubicles to create room for the meeting." Unfortunately, he doesn't offer any archaeological evidence in support of this claim. How the temporary partitions in these rooms were supposed to be cleared away is not clear. It is unlikely that this was possible. The rooms on upper floors of the insulae were separated into tiny cubicles by temporary partitions, but this does not mean that these partitions were portable. These "temporary" walls were constructed either with blocks made of tufa stone[175] or with wood.[176] Because they were temporary, few are still intact today. But where these tufa stone walls have been uncovered by archaeological excavation and are visible today, they do not give the impression that they were portable, that they could have been cleared away every evening or even once a week to make room for Christian meetings. That the wooden walls were portable is doubtful as well, because small families lived in these cubicles.[177]

Our reservations concerning Jewett's thesis are also supported by archaeological investigations of tenement houses in Ostia. After extensive study of these buildings, J. E. Packer summarizes the evidence: "The majority of Ostian flats were not homes in the modern sense of the word. They were not equipped to take care of all the physical needs of their inhabitants, and, save for the larger apartments . . . , they were probably not used to entertain friends."[178] Real life in urban settings was lived outside these apartments. The absence of kitchens in most of these tenement houses and the documented widespread existence of shops are both indications that these shops "supplied the inhabitants of the surrounding buildings with partially or completely prepared food and drink. . . . In ancient Ostia almost all the requirements of the vast majority of citizens were taken care of outside

---

[175] Caseggiato degli Aurighi (III, x, 1), erected ca. 140–150 C.E.; Packer, *Insulae*, 177–82, with floor plan, 106. Packer's description of the second floor mentions "later tufa block walls," with which the rooms were subdivided (p. 181). Cf. his "plate" 46, fig. 188; in the picture the tufa stone walls are clearly visible. "The use of temporary partitions is very characteristic of lower-class housing at Ostia" (Frier, *Landlords*, 4–5). They were also used on the "ground floor" of Caseggiato del Temistocle (V, xi, 2), erected ca. 117–134 C.E. (Packer, *Insulae*, 193–95, with floor plan, 110), and on the first floor of Casa di Diana (I, iii, 3–4), erected ca. 150 (ibid., 127–34, with floor plan, 94); the "Trajanic construction" is supposed to be typical (III, i, 12–13), "consisting of two rectangular 'rooms' . . . , each subdivided by flimsy partitions into two or three tiny apartments" (Frier, *Landlords*, 4).

[176] Cf. Frier, *Landlords*, 18.

[177] Packer, Bull. Comm. 81, (1968–1969), 127–48, 146 (quoted by Frier, *Landlords*, 14 n. 29); following him, Frier, ibid., 15.

[178] Packer, *Insulae*, 73.

the home."[179] If these people wanted to gather, they did so in the forum or, during bad weather, in the colonnades, but not in their houses.[180]

We have already observed that it was possible to meet as a church in a workshop. Lampe and more recently Murphy-O'Connor have considered whether the house church of Aquila and Prisca could have met in their tent-making workshop.[181] But it cannot be concluded on this basis alone that love communalism was practiced in their house church without the support of a householder. It was the householder Aquila who made space available for assembly. With him as the head of the household, we can assume that *oikos* structures were also in place in his workshop house church, as was common in any Jewish household throughout the Diaspora.

The previously quoted study of Lampe demonstrates very clearly that for our period the urban Christians of Rome were not exclusively poor people.[182] There were at least a few who were wealthy enough to afford to own or at least to rent their own homes. Lampe proves that even in the beginning many σεβόμενοι belonged to the church in Rome. It is known that, in contrast to proselytes, the God-fearers who sympathized with the Jews usually did not have a slave origin but more often came from socially well-to-do backgrounds; some had even as high as a knightly rank.[183] In addition, Paul assumes different social levels in the Roman congregation. In Rom 12:8, 13 he exhorts the wealthy to give alms for the poor. He distinguishes also between "the wise and the foolish" (1:14), whose differing education is an indication of different social status. He wanted to gain the church in Rome as a base for his mission to Spain, which also implies that he was assuming that among the Roman Christians were wealthy brothers who could afford to equip him with the necessities for such a mission: food, supplies, money, and companions (e.g., someone who knew Latin).

The example of Phoebe illustrates clearly that even an emancipated slave was sometimes able to attain independence and affluence, including house ownership.[184] Jewett's suggestion that the individuals in both groups in Rom 16:14, 15 are from a slave origin is in itself not sufficient evidence to conclude that the groups are tenement churches. One or more of them could

---

[179] Ibid., 73–74; so also McKay, *Römische Häuser*, 83.

[180] It can also be asked how comfortable it would have been to "celebrate" communion in such rooms as Jewett suggests. The rooms were lit poorly or not at all (Frier, *Landlords*, 15, 18) and just as poorly ventilated (McKay, *Römische Häuser*, 77–94). One can assume a joyless existence for most people who had to live in such buildings, "where they had no direct sunlight, only the bare minimum of living space and no fresh air. Public places offered opportunity and room for relaxation; but by night the 'locked in' existence must have been a nightmare for the majority of the population" (p. 85).

[181] This, of course, implies a somewhat larger shop.

[182] Lampe, *Stadtrömischen Christen*, 52, 53–65.

[183] *CII* 1:256, 462; *CII* 1:5; Josephus, *Ant.* 18.82; 20.195. Cf. K. Kuhn and Stegemann, "Proselyten," 9:1265–67; Gülzow, *Christentum*, 22–23.

[184] Klauck, *Hausgemeinde*, 30–31.

have been a homeowner, a προϊστάμενος (cf. 1 Thess 5:12; Rom 12:8; see pp. 190–210) or an ἐπίσκοπος (Phil 1:1). It is also possible that they belonged to another house church that met in someone's home, which would speak more for a patriarchal rather than an egalitarian ethos.[185] Our problem is that the texts simply do not give us enough information about these groups to justify drawing the kinds of conclusions that Jewett does.[186] Another observation speaks against his view as well: There is no indication in the Pauline Epistles for a purely egalitarian Christianity. The "egalitarian" baptismal tradition in Gal 3:26–28, 1 Cor 12:13, and Col 3:11 does not exclude either an *oikos* structure or leadership offices in a house church setting (see pp. 190–210).

The same is true for Thessalonica. Again, convincing textual evidence in support of Jewett's thesis is missing. On the contrary, the evidence appears to point in the direction of house churches in the traditional sense rather than toward tenement churches. As we have seen, a certain social stratification can be observed in Thessalonica, with the majority originating from the middle and lower levels. But at least a small minority of well-to-do, socially distinguished individuals were present as well; indeed, we know the name of one patron (see Acts 17:1–9) who made his home available to the congregation for meetings.[187]

The first Christians gathered in domestic house communities wherever possible, and it certainly is no coincidence that our sources speak only of *house* churches and not of Christian assemblies κατὰ συνοικίας or κατὰ νήσεις (= insulas). As Jewett correctly emphasizes, we need to keep in mind that the term οἶκος can mean an insula (an apartment in a tenement building). But even then Jewett's thesis is confronted by the dilemma that in none of the instances that he translates as tenement churches is the term οἶκος used.

Colossae

An additional house church in an undisputed Pauline epistle is that in connection with Philemon. Where it is to be located geographically is difficult to determine. In addition to references in Philemon, Onesimus and

---

[185] So Jewett, "Tenement Churches and Communal Meals," 29–31. The residential areas of the first Roman Christians formed a half circle in the city. Every area was accessible from the other by foot. E.g., the Field of Mars was easily reached from Trastevere over a bridge (cf. Lampe, *Stadtrömischen Christen*, 31).

[186] Jewett assumes that the five individuals mentioned in Rom 16:14, 15 are all leading personalities in the group. Five leaders imply a somewhat larger group, at least fifteen to twenty people. To accommodate them, a small space of 10 sq. m. is simply not enough.

[187] It is interesting to observe that Jewett supported this position already in 1986 (*Thessalonian Correspondence*, 103, on 1 Thess 5:12–13): "In all likelihood the leaders in question were patrons and patronesses of the house churches in Thessalonica as well as the socially prominent members of the congregation."

Archippus are mentioned in Col 4:9 and Col 4:17 respectively. For this reason it is assumed that Philemon's house church was in or near Colossae.[188]

The small letter to Philemon, particularly the prescript, informs us further regarding the house church in a number of ways. At the very beginning of the letter we find the third occurrence of the stock phrase ἡ κατ' οἶκον ἐκκλησία (Phlm 1–2). Paul writes, "To Philemon . . . , to Apphia our sister, to Archippus . . . and to the church in your house [τῇ κατ' οἶκον σου ἐκκλησίᾳ]." Even though this letter is one of the most personal of all the Pauline Epistles, it is not simply the private correspondence of one friend to another. Instead it is addressed to a church, a small house church that meets in the home of Philemon.[189] The problem that Paul deals with in Philemon is obviously not merely a private matter between Paul and Philemon alone but concerns the house church as a whole, as the reacceptance of Onesimus[190] depends on the willingness of the entire household to take him back. "Paul's Letter to Philemon is a pithy sample of practical, evangelical counsel concerning an urgent household problem."[191] This letter illustrates the important role that a household played in the social life, the worship, and the theological understanding of the Pauline mission.

Much has been written about the identity of Apphia and Archippus.[192] Most probable is the assumption that Apphia was the wife and Archippus a friend of Philemon.[193] Otherwise not much can be said.

The topic of the letter is Onesimus, Philemon's runaway slave, who, after fleeing, came to faith in Christ through Paul (v. 10). From this we can conclude that the extended family of Philemon did not consist only of Christians, as at least one member of the household—namely, the slave Onesimus—was originally not a believer (an indication that the conversion

---

[188] For background information on the city of Colossae, cf. Arnold, "Colossae"; E. Green, "Kolossä"; Hemer, *Letters*, 178–82. Philemon and Apphia are not mentioned in Colossians, and according to Col 2:1 Paul did not ever visit the city. In addition, the house church of Nympha is mentioned in Colossians; one belonging to Philemon is not.

[189] Cf. esp. the blessings (vv. 3, 25) in the plural, by which the entire house church is included. From this it can also be indirectly concluded that the letter was supposed to be read at one of their assemblies (Cf. Klauck, *Hausgemeinde*, 42).

[190] Cf. Hainz, *Ekklesia*, 200; so also Stuhlmacher, *Philemon*, 31. Whether Onesimus was a runaway slave who escaped from his master or, more likely, one who had placed himself under the protection of a friend of the householder is difficult to determine. According to Roman law, it was possible for a slave, if he was involved in a conflict with his master and was convinced his master had unfairly accused him, to place himself under the protection of a friend of the householder in order to ask the friend to intercede on his behalf. Cf. Lampe, "Keine 'Sklavenflucht'"; following him, Dunn, *Colossians and Philemon*, 304–5.

[191] Elliott, "Philemon," 145.

[192] Cf. literature by Ollrog, *Paulus*, 43 n. 198. Lightfoot, *Colossians, Philemon*, 306, saw Archippus as the grown son of Philemon.

[193] So Lightfoot, *Colossians, Philemon*, 304; Lohmeyer, *Kolosser und Philemon*, 171; Friedrich, "Philemon," 191; Lohse, *Kolosser und Philemon*, 267–68.

of slaves was not forced upon them).[194] Archippus was not a member of the immediate family but rather a friend of the householder with a special relationship to the house church. These observations are important because they show that house church and family were not always identical.

One additional aspect of the domestic dimension of the letter is the use of family terminology "to express the intimate bonds which unite fellow believers in Christ."[195] Timothy is introduced as "our brother" (v. 1). Paul and Philemon are "brothers" (vv. 4, 20). On the basis of this relationship, Paul can ask his brother Philemon to view his slave "no longer as a slave, but rather as much more: as a beloved brother" with whom they are both united in faith, and to welcome him back. By virtue of his commitment to Christ, the pagan Onesimus has become a "child" of Paul and Paul his "father," who can now call him "my very heart." "In this community of faith, all members—male and female, free and unfree—are children of one divine Father, just as all are owned and possessed by one Lord and Master (3,25)."[196]

The family metaphor was very important to Paul (see pp. 162–64). It is interesting to observe that, parallel to the household setting of the Christian assembly, we notice the use of household language to describe the relationships of Christians to each other. The correlation of the two could be coincidental. "Christians may not have had anywhere else to meet. . . . But just possibly the practical necessity for their use blended with a further, theologically based consideration. For, given the family character of the Christian community, the homes of its members provided the most conducive atmosphere in which they could give expression to the bond they had in common."[197]

Paul suggests a solution to an old problem of the ancient *oikos* on the basis of the "new" family. A new standard in the area of relationships and responsibility is implied for the family, which is understood as a community of sisters and brothers in Christ. Here the effective power is no longer the privilege of the *pater familia* but rather brotherly and sisterly love, no longer the principle that a certain transgression deserves a just punishment but rather Christian love and forgiveness.[198]

But there is a tension here as well. This understanding of church as the new family of God, in which the members are all children of God and ἀδελφοί in relationship with one another and are to accept one another in

---

[194] So Chrysostom, *Ta heuriskomena panta,* PG 62:704; cf. also Stuhlmacher, *Philemon,* 31 n. 44.
[195] Elliott, "Philemon," 148.
[196] Ibid.
[197] Banks, *Paul's Idea,* 56.
[198] According to Lampe, "Keine 'Sklavenflucht,'" 137, the letter to Philemon shows very well "how the apostle understands the renunciation of the rights belonging to a Christian suggested in 1 Cor 6: Philemon is supposed to love instead of punishing (legally allowed); he should love instead of demanding his material rights (legally unquestionable)." Cf. also Laub, *Begegnung,* 63–83, esp. 71–74.

love (1 Cor 13), implies a new way of relating to one another that was in tension with the conventional ethos of the ancient *oikos*. For example, once Onesimus is no longer slave but becomes Philemon's brother in Christ, Philemon is no longer merely his earthly master but also an equal who could potentially be even exhorted by his brother. Here we observe an element of uncertainty and a potential for conflict built into the house church from the very beginning (on conflict see pp. 173–77).

Philemon is also recognized as "coworker" (v. 1) and Archippus as "fellow soldier." With this title Paul describes, among others, Aquila and Prisca (Rom 16:3). Whether one can derive from this a certain leadership structure in this house church is a question that we will address later (see pp. 190–210).

It is also insinuated that Philemon has access to resources that allow him to show hospitality and charity toward his fellow believers (vv. 4, 7).[199] We can observe a number of indicators regarding his social status. Philemon appears to be quite wealthy.[200] He heads and owns a relatively large house (he has a guest room and space for the entire church to gather in his house) with at least one slave and most likely more. The strong insinuation by Paul that Philemon ought to send Onesimus back to him (vv. 8–14) implies that this would not impose an unbearable burden upon Philemon or his household. Philemon performed services for the congregation and the Pauline mission, including the provision of an assembly place in his house, the food for the agape meal and the Lord's Supper, and a coworker for Paul's missional outreach.[201]

In verse 22 we notice yet another aspect of the significance of houses for the Pauline mission. Paul asks Philemon to prepare quarters for him—surely in his own house. Evidently, Paul is hoping to travel to the Lycos valley some time in the near future to live with Philemon as his guest and to use his house as a base of operations for missional outreach.[202] This appears to be an integral part of the customary missional practice of the apostle (cf., e.g., Acts 18:1–7; Rom 16:23; and see below).[203]

Laodicea

The fourth example of the stock expression ἡ κατ' οἶκον ἐκκλησία is found in a disputed letter of Paul, namely, in Col 4:15: "Give my greetings to the brothers in Laodicea, and to Nympha and the church in her house

---

[199] Stuhlmacher, *Philemon*, 71.
[200] E. and W. Stegemann, *Urchristliche Sozialgeschichte*, 254, consider it possible that Philemon belonged to the upper class in the city.
[201] He thus fulfilled three criteria for the higher social status that Theissen suggests. Cf. Theissen, *Social Setting*, 73.
[202] Verse 22b indicates what motivates Paul to such a journey in spite of his imprisonment.
[203] With Klauck?, *Hausgemeinde*, 44.

[τὴν κατ' οἶκον αὐτῆς ἐκκλησίαν]."[204] Here we observe a woman as a homeowner who makes her house available to the congregation (perhaps even as the overseer or leader of the church in her house).[205] At any rate, with Nympha (along with Prisca, Phoebe, Junia, and Lydia) we have further indication of the concrete involvement of women in Pauline house churches.

The house church of Nympha is probably in Laodicea, about 9.3 miles from Colossae.[206] The greeting to Laodicea in 4:15a stands in close relationship to the instruction to exchange the letters and to have them read in 4:16; Nympha and her church are thus brought into connection with Laodicea.

If Nympha's house church can be located in Laodicea, we would have a house church within the overall local church in that area. In Col 4:16 Christians in Laodicea are mentioned as an ἐκκλησία. This "church" is most likely not identical with Nympha's house church. Colossians 4:16 distinguishes between the brothers in Laodicea and those in her house church. This "church" is best understood as the whole church at that location.[207]

A Plurality of House Churches within the Whole Church at One Location

Preliminary Questions on Language Usage and Text Criticism

How is the prepositional phrase κατ' οἶκον to be understood in our context? As we have seen, this fixed idiomatic expression is found in four different places in the *corpus paulinum*.[208] Some exegetes suggest translating the formula as "the church that establishes itself in a houselike manner."[209] Klauck supports this distributive translation with lexical argumentation.[210] He lists Josephus and several papyri[211] and appeals to the authority of Moulton-Milligan, W. Bauer, and G. Delling.[212]

---

[204] Regarding the city of Laodicea, cf. Rudwik and Hemer, "Laodizea"; F. F. Bruce, "Laodicea"; Hemer, *Letters*, 178–82. Regarding the text-critical problem with the name Nympha, see pp. 120–21.

[205] So Klauck, *Hausgemeinde*, 45; see pp. 210–25, the excursus on leadership responsibilities of women. A woman as householder (after the death of her husband) is documented; cf. Philostratus, *Gymn.* 272:30–31.

[206] Hierapolis has also been suggested. This city is nearby and Christians are also mentioned there (4:13).

[207] So also Klauck, *Hausgemeinde*, 46.

[208] Rom 16:3, 5; 1 Cor 16:19; Phlm 1–2; Col 4:15.

[209] Klauck, *Hausgemeinde*, 19; Stuhlmacher, *Philemon*, 71.

[210] For the distributive use of κατά, cf. Gerth and Kühner, *Ausführliche Grammatik*, 1:480.

[211] Josephus, *Ant.* 4.74; cf. also 4.163; Klauck, *Hausgemeinde*, 20 n. 23.

[212] Klauck, *Hausgemeinde*, 19. Moulton and Milligan (MM) quote P.Ryl. II 76.10,12, where, in the context of an inheritance matter, κατ' οἶκον means "according to households." Bauer-Aland[6], 1130 (BDAG 698), with reference to Diodor

Gielen, however, attempts to demonstrate with philological arguments that κατ' οἶκον is not to be understood in a distributive sense but rather in terms of location.[213] She rejects the distributive usage of κατά because it does not make sense in the context of the greetings list. In none of the four texts is a statement made regarding the manner of church assembly (in a houselike manner or in a series of individual houses) as such; rather, concrete individuals are named together with a church. The extension of the prepositional phrase κατ' οἶκον with a possessive pronoun locates the church in the house of the aforementioned persons. According to Gielen, because of this limitation to a very specific single house, the distributive interpretation can no longer be considered a possibility. Her assumption is supported by the observation that in Koine, κατ' οἶκον is documented as a standing phrase for ἐν οἴκῳ.[214] In addition, there are references already in classical Greek for the use of κατά with the accusative in the sense of location. In time it eventually became interchangeable with ἐν.[215]

Characteristically, the advocates of the distributive interpretation end up using the locational sense in their actual translation of the expression.[216] Indeed, this locational translation is the most common in the majority of recent commentaries.[217] It must be asked, however, how a distributive understanding of the phrase could be expressed in a translation in any way other than locationally and whether a locational translation necessarily excludes a distributive nuance (see below).

The locational translation, then, of the expression κατ' οἶκον as it appears four times in the *corpus paulinum* cannot, from a purely grammatical perspective, be read distributively but instead must be read locationally. In response to Gielen's arguments, it is true that in our four passages κατά with accusative implies an individualization and is therefore to be translated not distributively but locationally.[218] But if κατά with the accusative implies indi-

---

17,28,4; cf. Acts 2:46. PGrLa IV 299, 14–15, 20–21. Cf. Delling, "Zur Taufe" (1970), 301 n. 72, 306 n. 84.

[213] Gielen, "Zur Interpretation," 109–25, here 110–12. With her also Schöllgen, "Hausgemeinden."

[214] Gielen, "Zur Interpretation," 112.

[215] Cf. Schwyzer, *Griechische Grammatik*, 2:476–77.

[216] Klauck, *Hausgemeinde*, 21, 24, 41, 44; Stuhlmacher, *Philemon*, 29; Banks, *Paul's Idea*, 31, translates the expression in 1 Cor 16:19 as "together with the church in their house." Cf. also Lampe, *Stadtrömischen Christen*, 161. He translates the expression as "the church with them at home" and provides a few references (n. 135a); also White, *Building God's House*, 103 n. 7, "at home."

[217] Cf. Gielen, "Zur Interpretation," 111 n. 10, for a list of the commentaries. Bauer-Aland[6], 824, suggests "Hausgemeinde" (cf. BDAG 511–12, "the congregation in the house"). Käsemann (*Römer*, 392), Schlier (*Römerbrief*, 442), and Wilckens (*Römer*, 3:12–16, 132) all follow Bauer-Aland.

[218] Bauer[5], 803, c., d.; Bauer-Aland[6], 825, c., d. (BDAG 511–12). Cf. also Hoffmann/v. Siebenthal (§184,k): κατά with accusative is not only distributive but also locational.

vidualization, it must be asked, individualization of what? Considering the fact that Paul distinguishes between, on the one hand, an *ecclesia* as a whole (ἐκκλησία τοῦ θεοῦ ἐν Χριστῷ) and, on the other, concrete local churches that are spread out in different cities (Corinth, Rome, etc.), the expression κατ' οἶκον is nothing other than an individualization of the church as a whole into separate congregations.[219] Paul also distinguishes similarly in his Letter to the Romans on another level. He speaks, on the one hand, of the whole local church in Rom 1:7 (at least essentially even though not terminologically) and, on the other, of an individualization of this church as a whole in 16:5.[220] Here he juxtaposes the whole local church in Rome to the concrete house church of Prisca and Aquila. As soon as one speaks, however, of partial churches, they can be understood distributively: every local church in comparison with the church as a whole, every house church in comparison with the whole local church is a partial church and as such the partition of the whole church—in other words, a "distribution." The local church in relation to the church as a whole is the distribution of the church as a whole per location; the house church is, again, the distribution of the local church per house. Seen in this way, even though the expression κατ' οἶκον, from a pure grammatical perspective, can only be interpreted locationally, it needs to be understood distributively as well. If our analysis is correct, then it follows that the stock expression as Paul uses it in the four passages is an implicit reference to a plurality of house churches within the local church as a whole.[221]

How are we to understand the expression ἐκκλησία ὅλη (Rom 16:23; 1 Cor 14:23)? One of the key questions in our discussion is whether this phrase stands in opposition to ἐκκλησία κατ' οἶκον. In recent research scholars tend to agree that the early Christian movement was characterized by the coexistence of two church forms: the house church and the whole church at any given location.[222] This means that, in the various cities, alongside the local church as a whole there existed house churches in which most of the activities and life of the church took place. Central to this view is the observation that Paul appears to distinguish between

---

[219] For the relationship of the church as a whole to the local or house church in Paul, see pp. 160–62.

[220] For the relation of Rom 16 to the Letter to the Romans as a whole, see pp. 120–21. For the definition of the terms "local church," "church as whole," etc., see pp. 27–28.

[221] For a discussion of the possible origin of the stock expression κατ' οἶκον (Acts 2:46, 5:42), cf. Gehring, *Hausgemeinde*, 277–79.

[222] Among others, Stuhlmacher, *Römer*, 225; Theissen, *Social Setting*, 89; Dunn, *Romans*, 2:910–11; O'Brien, *Colossians, Philemon*, 257; Meeks, *First Urban Christians*, 75–76; Banks, *Paul's Idea*, 37–42; Branick, *House Church*, 22–27; Lampe, *Stadtrömischen Christen*, 161, 301–10; Gnilka, *Philemonbrief*, 17–33; Hainz, *Ekklesia*, 195 n. 4, 230, 346; Klauck, *Hausgemeinde*, 33–41.

meetings of the ἐκκλησία κατ' οἶκον and meetings of the ἐκκλησία ὅλη.[223] "The qualification 'whole'... would be unnecessary if the Christians at Corinth only ever met as a single group and *implies* that smaller groups also existed in the city."[224] The distributive interpretation of the expression κατ' οἶκον is also used as evidence in support of the view that churches were established "in a houselike manner," which in itself implies the coexistence of house churches alongside one another.[225]

Gielen has recently contested this view as well.[226] First, she points out that the formula appears exclusively in greeting lists that tell us nothing about the activities of these house churches. Everything adduced by other scholars about the organization and activities of alleged house churches applies not to the ἐκκλησία κατ' οἶκον but to common οἶκοι or οἰκίαι, which cannot be demonstrated to have served as regular meeting places for not only the household members but, beyond them, for actual churches in the full sense of the word. In addition, Gielen claims that for every local church there is only one ἐκκλησία κατ' οἶκον documented. Accordingly, Paul never addresses the recipients of his letters as a partial church but always as the whole church in that city, and nowhere does he indicate explicit knowledge of regular meetings of a part of the whole local church.

Gielen also contends that for Paul ἡ κατ' οἶκον ἐκκλησία and ἐκκλησία ὅλη do not stand in opposition to one another but instead that in both cases (Rom 16:23; 1 Cor 14:23) he uses ὅλη for text-pragmatic, semantic, and rhetorical reasons.[227] In the expression ἡ κατ' οἶκον ἐκκλησία she finds, rather, the whole local church, which for her means that house churches did not coexist as separate entities within the whole local church.[228] She does not deny that individual families and house fellowship groups played an important role in early Christian mission and church life. According to Gielen, however, it cannot be demonstrated that they became crystallization points of independent separate communities with regular meetings that grew significantly beyond the parameters of a house fellowship.

The following speaks against Gielen's view: First, a local gathering of the whole church is documented for Corinth alone (Rom 16:23; 1 Cor 11:20; 14:23), but the expression ἡ κατ' οἶκον ἐκκλησία is not documented for Corinth.[229] This means that we clearly have at least one local

---

[223] Cf. 1 Cor 14:23; Rom 16:23. Meeks, *First Urban Christians*, 75–76; O'Brien, *Colossians, Philemon*, 257; Banks, *Paul's Idea*, 38; Hainz, *Ekklesia*, 195, 346 with note; Klauck, *Hausgemeinde*, 34–35.

[224] Cf. O'Brien, *Colossians, Philemon*, 257; so also Banks, *Paul's Idea*, 38; Hainz, *Ekklesia*, 195, 346 with note; Klauck, *Hausgemeinde*, 34–35.

[225] Klauck, *Hausgemeinde*, 12, 21; Stuhlmacher, *Philemon*, 71 (see p. 7, n. 42, and p. 145).

[226] Gielen, "Zur Interpretation." Compare with Schöllgen, "Hausgemeinde," 78–80.

[227] Gielen, "Zur Interpretation," 110–18.

[228] Ibid., 118.

[229] With Lampe, *Stadtrömischen Christen*, 161.

church for which the expression was not used. Second, her thesis stands and falls (which she herself admits) with the uncertain assumption that Rom 16 was originally an independent letter. "The interpretation of ἡ κατ' οἶκον ἐκκλησία as the local church is not possible if Rom 16 was an original part of the Letter to the Romans, as those asked to greet others cannot simultaneously be the ones being greeted."[230] The intended subject of ἀσπάσασθε (16:3–5) is thus the local church in Rome. In verse 5 Paul asks the local church in Rome to greet the church that meets in the house of Prisca and Aquila, using the stock expression ἡ κατ' οἶκον ἐκκλησία. Here the expression would be at least in opposition to the phrase "all in Rome who are loved of God and called to be saints" (1:7)—that is, in opposition to the local church.

The result of our analysis of the linguistic and text-critical issues is the following: The locational and the distributive interpretations of the Pauline expression κατ' οἶκον do not mutually exclude one another, even though from a purely grammatical perspective it must be determined as locational. The thesis that the expression refers only to the local church cannot be demonstrated convincingly. Consequently, it is legitimate to understand the two expressions ἡ κατ' οἶκον ἐκκλησία and ἐκκλησία ὅλη as being in opposition to one another and to assume that the coexistence of house churches alongside the local church as a whole does not have to be excluded a priori as a possibility for exegetical reasons. Our earlier results (see pp. 130–55) have not been called into question through Gielen's criticism. There a plurality of house churches was demonstrated with certainty for Rome, probably for Thessalonica, and possibly for Ephesus, Philippi, and Laodicea, and the coexistence of a number of house churches alongside the local church as a whole was demonstrated for Corinth.[231]

It thus becomes clear that the relationship between the whole church and individual house churches will need to be one of the central questions in our study, partly because of past exegetical debate of the problem and partly because of disputes throughout church history. To this day the issue regarding the relationship of the individual churches to the local church as a whole or of the local church to the universal church has still not been clarified (for a definition of terms, see pp. 160–62.

Our question is therefore the following: how does Paul define the relationship between the individual church and the local church as a whole and between the local church and the universal church?

---

[230] Gielen, "Zur Interpretation," 123 n. 70.
[231] So Wieland, *Altar,* 27–33. Against Afanassieff, "L'assemblée eucharistique," esp. 4, 7–14, 16–19, 22, 25, who denies the coexistence of house churches and the local church as a whole for the entire early Christian movement, including for the primitive church in Jerusalem, as well as for the entire Pauline mission (following him, Provencher, "Vers une théologie," esp. 12–14). For discussion and rebuttal of his arguments, cf. Gehring, *Hausgemeinde,* 281 n. 277.

Paul's Ecclesiological Assertions

Broadly speaking, there are two sets of ecclesiological assertions in Paul's writings (and in the rest of the NT), which appear to be in tension with one another. How these two are to be reconciled has been a difficult ecclesiological problem from the earliest days.[232] The solution articulated by the Roman Catholic or Orthodox churches always emphasized the unity of the church as a whole both locally and universally.[233] For them the unity of the whole church has a greater priority than the individual congregation. Most Protestants take the opposite view: the dignity of the individual congregation is placed above that of the church as a whole.[234] These two different perspectives are understandable particularly in light of the tension between the two themes in Paul's own ecclesiology.

About the Universal Church

Ecclesiological assertions that transcend the local assembly are quite rare in Paul's writings, but they do occur (regarding Col 1:18 and Eph 4, see below). In particular, emphasis on the unity of the church is found in the expression ἐκκλησία τοῦ θεοῦ (ἐν Χριστῷ Ἰησοῦ) as the general term for the church as a whole.[235] This formulation may be linked back to a translation of קהל אל[236] (cf. 1QM 4:10; 1QSa 1:25em) and is viewed as the first self-designation of the primitive church. In the Jerusalem church the term was used because its meaning corresponded with that church's eschatological self-understanding. The primitive church understood itself as the vanguard of the end-times church of salvation, elected by God and called into existence through the Christ event, and as the crystallization point of the new eschatological Israel.[237] The term was evidently adopted by the Hellenists and by Paul in continuity with the Jerusalem church and passed on to local groups outside Jerusalem as well.[238]

---

[232] For a good overview, cf. Valeske, *Votum Ecclesiae*, esp. his extensive interdenominational ecclesiological bibliography in part 2, 67–106.

[233] Cf., for an example of orthodox ecclesiology, Afanassieff, "L'assemblée eucharistique"; for Catholic ecclesiology, cf. Provencher, "Vers une théologie." Cf. also Wikenhauser, *Kirche*; Schlier, "Einheit"; *Katechismus der katholischen Kirche*, 243–45; ecumenically sensitive is Döring, *Grundriss*, 170–71, 178–89. As a Catholic exception, cf. Hainz, *Ekklesia*, 229–55. Cf. the balanced view by Merklein, "Ekklesia Gottes."

[234] Cf. Roloff, *Kirche*, 96–98. As an exception, cf. K. Schmidt, "ἐκκλησία," *TDNT* 3:506–8.

[235] With a different view, Hainz, *Ekklesia*, 229–55.

[236] Cf. Stuhlmacher, *Gerechtigkeit Gottes*, 210–11 n. 2; in part against Schrage, "Ekklesia."

[237] Cf. also Roloff, "ἐκκλησία," *EDNT* 1:411–12.

[238] Cf. Stuhlmacher, *Grundlegung*, 357; people of God, 2 Cor 6:16, Rom 9:25–26; temple of God, 1 Cor 3:16–17, 2 Cor 6:16; Israel of God, Gal 6:16, Rom 11:13–32. The terms "people of God" and "Israel of God" imply a universal understanding of the ἐκκλησία τοῦ θεοῦ.

Some passages refer to Paul's persecution of the ἐκκλησία τοῦ θεοῦ (Gal 1:13; 1 Cor 15:9; Phil 3:6, without τοῦ θεοῦ). Here Paul appears to be using the term to mean the totality of all Christians worldwide, as he moves beyond a local sense. Accordingly, this has been understood as a reference to the universal church. In Gal 1:22–23, however, the term ἐκκλησία seems to refer to the churches in Judea (= Palestine).[239] In 1 Cor 10:32 Paul gives the directive not to cause anyone to stumble, whether Jews, Greeks, or the "church of God."[240] He is not speaking of the local church here but of the church as a whole, which coexists alongside two other independent groups (Jews and Greeks) as a third group, namely, the eschatological people of God, or the "church."[241] With "church of God" Paul cannot be speaking only of the local church in Corinth because the rule applies to all Christian behavior in general.

In 1 Cor 4:17 Paul teaches that there are instructions of Christ that he has taught everywhere in all the churches. This means that ethical norms and behavioral patterns exist that apply to all of the individual churches as a unit (cf. 1 Cor 11:16; 14:33–34). But it must also be noted that Paul uses the plural here, so the passage cannot be counted as an incontestable reference for the idea of the church as a whole. First Corinthians 12:28 is particularly important in this context. Here more than just the local church in Corinth is intended with ἐν τῇ ἐκκλησίᾳ. Paul speaks of a fundamental church structure that God instituted in all churches everywhere, that is, in the church as a whole.[242] The plural "apostles" also does not fit well with the concept of an individual church.[243] It should also be pointed out, however, that Paul may have adopted (Antioch) tradition here, although the extent of the tradition is unclear.[244] Apart from this, even assuming that ἐν τῇ ἐκκλησίᾳ is traditional, Paul did use the expression most likely because it corresponded with his own understanding of the church.

The Christian church in Jerusalem, the "church of God" par excellence, also functions for Paul as a reminder of a great movement. His mission perspective begins in Jerusalem (Rom 15:19) and is focused on Zion, the gathering place of the salvation church (Rom 11:26–27). From the beginning of his apostolic ministry, Paul was intent on holding together the church consisting of Jews and Gentiles (cf. the apostles' council; Rom 3:30; 15:7–12). The collection that Paul gathered for the poor in Jerusalem (Rom

---

[239] At this point Paul appears to render the words of the Christians almost literally. Bammel, "Gal 1:23."

[240] Cf. also 1 Cor 6:4; 11:22, which belong together with 10:32.

[241] Cf. K. Schmidt, "ἐκκλησία," *TDNT* 3:501–36, here 506–8.

[242] Cf. Harnack, *Entstehung,* 18–19, 155–73; Linton, *Problem,* 141; K. Schmidt, "ἐκκλησία," *TDNT* 3:506–7; Branick, *House Church,* 29. Against Hainz, *Ekklesia,* 252–53.

[243] Even Hainz, *Ekklesia,* 254 admits that here we have "a universal implication."

[244] Merklein, *Das kirchliche Amt,* 245; following him, A. Zimmermann, *Die urchristlichen Lehrer,* 108–10.

15:22–28; 1 Cor 16:1–3; 2 Cor 8:1–4; 9:2, 12) was for him a dramatic gesture intended to underscore the unity of the Gentile church with the mother church in Jerusalem and her central significance.[245]

Excursus: Paul's Understanding of the Body of Christ and the Family of God

An important expression of the unity and the worldwide dimension of the church is Paul's talk of the body of Christ (cf. 1 Cor 12:12–31; Rom 12:4–8). With this image a new ecclesiological accent in the history of early Christianity is set, and it can be seen as the central idea of Pauline ecclesiology.[246] Even though the question of the origin of this concept has yet to be fully clarified, three sources have been determined: the Lord's Supper tradition, the so-called Adam-Christ typology, and the concept of Jesus as the Messiah/Son of Man.[247] In particular, the idea of the world-encompassing body of Christ as a pneumatic reality rooted in the Adam-Christ typology, into which one is baptized (1 Cor 12:13) and which is equated with the church (1 Cor 12:12–31; Rom 12:4–8), implies a uniform and worldwide dimension of the ἐκκλησία τοῦ θεοῦ. For Paul the ἐκκλησία is really the body of Christ.[248] In 1 Cor 12:12–31 new believers are baptized into the body of Christ, which already existed before and independent of them.[249] The image of the body of Christ grew out of the statement regarding the believer's identity "in Christ" and appears for Paul to be a function of the christologically reflected notion of the people of God. From the two most important texts, it can be observed that two components work together in the understanding of the body of Christ: the concept of sacramental participation in the eucharistic body of Christ and the concept of an organism in which the members cooperate with one another.[250] "The local church is therefore the body of Christ because it gains participation in the body of the Lord in the eucharistic meal" (1 Cor 10:17).[251] The body of Christ results from participation in the bread. In this one bread Christ shares himself and the produce of his work on the cross with believers; the bread thereby has a unity-building function. "The reception of this bread by the believers causes them to be united with Christ as the one and only Savior and thus to be united with one another."[252]

---

[245] Stuhlmacher, *Grundlegung*, 357.

[246] The expression occurs in only three places in the undisputed Pauline Letters: 1 Cor 10:16–17; 12:12–26; Rom 12:5.

[247] Stuhlmacher, *Grundlegung*, 358. Cf. the excursus of Lang, *Korinther*, 175–81.

[248] Roloff, *Kirche*, 100–31; Stuhlmacher, "Kirche," 310.

[249] Cf. also the Pauline references to the one new man formed by Christians (compare 1 Cor 6:16–17; 12:12–13; Gal 3:28; Col 3:15 with Gen 2:22–24).

[250] Roloff, *Kirche*, 100.

[251] Ibid., 102.

[252] Ibid., 104.

This unity also has a social component. For Paul the church, the local gathering of Christians, is to be understood as the community of the body of Christ. This community comes into existence through the eucharistic celebration, and in this community the behavior of its members should not be incongruent with this celebration (1 Cor 11:17–34). Accordingly, Paul can describe the congregation as a new family of God. A whole series of terms from family language are adopted by Paul and applied to the Christian church.[253] Attention was drawn above to the family terminology used by Paul in his letter to Philemon to describe the loving relationship that unites siblings in Christ. For Paul this terminology has its foundation precisely in the relationship between believers, Christ, and God. God is the Father not only of Jesus Christ but of the believers as well (1 Thess 1:1, 3; 3:11, 13; 2 Thess 1:1–2; 2:16; Gal 4:6). Believers are for Paul children of God (Rom 8:16–17; cf. also Gal 4:4–5; 1 Thess 1:10) and, in relation to one another, brothers and sisters (cf., e.g., 1 Cor 8:11–13; 15:58; Rom 15:14; Phil 3:1; 4:1). "Let us do good to all people, especially to those who belong to the family of believers [πρὸς τοὺς οἰκείους τῆς πίστεως]" (Gal 6:10).[254] The central significance that the word "love" has in Paul's understanding of church confirms this view (cf. Phil 1:8; 2:12; 1 Cor 12:25–26; 13:4–8; 16:24; 1 Thess 3:12; Rom 12:9–10; Gal 5:22; 6:2; Col 3:12–14). The whole ἐκκλησία is supposed to show "how the new creation actually looks, the new creation that emerges from the reconciliation event" (2 Cor 5:7; Col 1:18; cf. later also Eph 3:10).[255] Although Paul never speaks explicitly of the "new family of God," the family of the faith (Gal 6:10) is this new creation and therefore the new family of God.[256]

In 1 Cor we see the high ecclesiological value that Paul places on unity among Christians as the body of Christ in the local church of Corinth. Apparently this unity transcends the local situation in Corinth. In Rom 12:5, with its first person plural, Paul includes himself and all of his churches in this unity with Christ. Colossians also confirms that this unity is understood as transcending the local situation. Colossians 1:18 makes clear that there are not many bodies of Christ but only one body whose head is Christ.

In summary, Paul sees the unity of all local congregations in one church as a whole, but this is difficult to demonstrate in his writings terminologically. Whenever he uses the term ἐκκλησία, even though rarely, in the larger

---

[253] Cf. Banks, *Paul's Idea*, 49–54, for a list of the terms and a good discussion. This does not call into question the fact that the body of Christ is the central idea of Pauline ecclesiology. On the contrary: the two metaphorical expressions belong together in Paul's understanding of the church. Roloff also sees this. But he applies the phrase "*koinonia* as a social entity" to the family aspect of Paul's ecclesiology.

[254] Later Eph 2:18–19 says that believers are members of the family of God (οἰκεῖοι τοῦ θεοῦ).

[255] Stuhlmacher, "Kirche," 311.

[256] Paul is not the first to emphasize this. His language reminds us of that of Jesus; cf. Mark 3:34–35; 12:30–31. It is possible that Paul knew the Jesus tradition and was theologically committed to it. The view that Paul described the church as

context transcending the local congregation, he intentionally follows the lead dictated by the tradition handed down to him (cf., as mentioned, Gal 1:12, 1 Cor 12:28). That he did not use the term more often for the (universal) church as a whole could be related to the fact that in his letters, in which he was addressing specific problems, it was important to him to emphasize the high dignity of the individual congregation as an *ecclesia* of God; but this does not exclude the possibility that, in his understanding of the church, all Christians everywhere are united into one comprehensive unit. This is certainly implied by the use of "church of God" (cf. 1 Cor 1:2; 2 Cor 1:1): the one ἐκκλησία exists in the Christian congregations that exist locally.

About the Individual Local Church

The second ecclesiological assertion made by Paul is the emphasis on each individual congregation with its dignity and justification to be an independent church. It is undisputed that Paul uses ἐκκλησία primarily in reference to the individual local church (see below).[257]

In a series of passages that reflect early Christian usage, particularly in the prescripts of the Pauline Epistles, we find the expression ἐκκλησία τοῦ θεοῦ (ἐν Χριστῷ Ἰησοῦ).[258] When Paul uses this expression, most often he has in mind the concrete gathering of Christians who live at a specific location.[259] For instance, in 1 Cor 1:1–2 Paul speaks to the Corinthian church as the "church of God in Corinth," in whose local existence the characteristics of the coming worldwide church of God appears in concrete form, that is, as a local church that represents this universal church of God in its totality.[260] The Pauline understanding of church attributes a high value to the local worship assembly. It is always "church" whenever individuals gather together ἐν ἐκκλησίᾳ (1 Cor 11:18).[261] Fundamental for the ἐκκλησία is the συνέρχεσθαι ἐν ἐκκλησίᾳ: ἐν ἐκκλησίᾳ implies the local assembly of the church, which comes into existence through the act of gathering. Every local Christian assembly in which God is worshiped and Jesus Christ is proclaimed is a church for Paul, an ἐκκλησία τοῦ θεοῦ.[262] This applies to the

---

the family of God has recently been contested by Schöllgen, "Hausgemeinde," 81–83. For a rebuttal of his arguments, cf. Gehring, *Hausgemeinde*, 288 n. 304.

[257] Cf. Hainz, *Ekklesia*, 230; Koester, *Idee der Kirche*, 240–42; K. Schmidt, "Kirche"; cf. also Banks, *Paul's Idea*, 27–31.

[258] 1 Cor 1:2; 2 Cor 1:1; cf. also 1 Cor 10:32; 11:22; 15:9; Gal 1:13; in the plural: 1 Cor 11:16, 22; 1 Thess 2:14; 2 Thess 1:4.

[259] Where ἐκκλησία appears alone as an ecclesiological term, it should be understood as the abbreviation of the original expression ἐκκλησία τοῦ θεοῦ even though the genitive of origin *(genitivus auctoris)* is always implicit. Cf., e.g., 1 Thess 1:1; 2 Thess 1:1; Rom 16:1; Col 4:16; Phil 4:15; K. Schmidt, "ἐκκλησία," *TDNT* 3:506–8.

[260] Roloff, "ἐκκλησία," *EDNT* 1:412–13.

[261] Hainz, *Ekklesia*, 230–31.

[262] Of course, there remains church outside the tangible gathering as well (cf. 1 Cor 14:23, "if the whole church comes together"). Cf. Hainz, *Ekklesia*, 231.

whole church at any location (cf. 1 Cor 11:20; 14:23; Rom 16:23). And it likewise applies to the house churches, such as those of Prisca and Aquila. Through the addition of ἡ ἐκκλησία ὅλη in 1 Cor 14:23, an important distinction is made between the gatherings ἐν ἐκκλησίᾳ in which the whole church gathered at one location and those in which only a part of the local church met in assembly. Paul does not indicate that there is any fundamental difference between these two.[263] Both are gatherings ἐν ἐκκλησίᾳ. Both are also gatherings ἐν οἴκῳ. Where is the whole worldwide church tangibly evident according to Paul? The universal church is tangible κατ' οἴκους, that is, in the gatherings of the individual local churches. Therefore, an integral element of the Pauline understanding of church is that the whole is present in the individual parts. Even in the smallest house church, ἡ ἐκκλησία τοῦ θεοῦ is present in its full sense.

If our exegesis is correct, it appears that Paul advocates greater rights for the individual church as opposed to the whole worldwide church.[264] But in the NT, Eph 4 and John 17 present a counterbalance to this emphasis.

SOCIAL STRATA IN PAULINE HOUSE CHURCHES

The sociohistorical method for investigating the NT was first introduced about seventy-five years ago in the context of form criticism, but it did not progress beyond a rudimentary stage of development.[265] Not until the 1970s did scholars begin again to show interest in sociohistorical questions. Since then a wide variety of studies have focused on the social circumstances of the early Christian movement. But the sociohistorical method remains to this day a relatively young branch of NT research. It still does not have reliable methodologies that have been fine tuned over time or a set of unified research categories upon which scholars have agreed. This applies especially to our complex of questions regarding the social strata of the Pauline house churches. Nevertheless, considerable progress has been made in the area of sociohistorical research.[266] In particular, the methods of prosopographic examination have been refined, and an attempt has been made to better define the categories and terms. In order to investigate the social stratification of early Christian congregations, one would need to define the criteria with which these social levels can be determined. Characteristic of older and more general sociological research was adoption of the standard criteria for determining social strata of a specific society or group—economic level, status, and power—whereby it was recognized that status had to be understood

---

[263] Hainz, *Ekklesia*, 230–31.
[264] So also Hainz, *Ekklesia*, 229–55, esp. 251. For a view different from mine, cf. Branick, *House Church*, 117–22.
[265] Cf. Holmberg, *Sociology*, 1–2, 21–23, for further discussion.
[266] Cf., e.g., ibid.; Schmeller, *Brechungen*, 16–49, 114.

as a multidimensional phenomenon.[267] Different times and cultures, however, can weigh these criteria differently.[268] For this reason the discussion of the social levels of any group must be seen in relation to its own specific society with its system for social stratification.

Roman Society

In the case of the NT, the specific society that forms the social background is that of the first-century Roman Empire. Roman society and its social stratification were characterized by a steep pyramid.[269] According to G. Alföldy and other historians, a middle class in the modern sense did not exist. The term was coined by present-day social analytical scientists and is a reference to a group's income level, but it is difficult to apply it to ancient society when distinguishing between different groups.[270]

At the very top of the social pyramid we find the *imperator*, his family, and the so-called *ordines*—the senators, knights, and so forth. They alone formed the upper class and together constituted about 0.5 percent (about a hundred thousand persons) of the total population (between fifty and eighty million). All the rest belonged to the so-called lower class—freemen, freedmen, and slaves—both in cities *(plebs urbana)* and in the country *(plebs rustica)*. Noble birth was the primary criterion for ensuring membership in the upper class in the first-century Roman world.

Although Alföldy's description of Roman society is more or less accurate, it is of little assistance in determining the social levels of the early Christian movement. In our context, the statement that the majority of Christians in Pauline churches originated from the lower class is of virtually no significance—99.5 percent of the population were at that level! For this and other reasons, the attempt to divide Roman society into only two strata has been criticized by K. Christ and F. Vittinghoff.[271] "Alföldy's position may be correct as far as the formulated awareness of the ancient participants themselves goes, but leaves us moderns without much of an instrument to see and understand the social differences within the vast majority of this society. It seems that

---

[267] Esp. Meeks, *First Urban Christians*, 53–55, 68–73. Cf. also E. and W. Stegemann, *Urchristliche Sozialgeschichte*, 62–68.

[268] E.g., our contemporary Western culture considers income level to be a more important criterion in determining social status than some other modern or ancient cultures have.

[269] Cf. esp. Alföldy, *Römische Sozialgeschichte* and *Römische Gesellschaft*; MacMullen, *Roman Social Relations*; Verner, *Household*, 47–54; Meeks, *Moral World*, 32–39; Esler, *Community*, 171–75.

[270] Alföldy, "Römische Gesellschaft: Struktur und Eigenart," 53–54; cf. also *Römische Sozialgeschichte*, 85–132.

[271] Christ, "Grundfragen," esp. 169–76, and *Geschichte*. Christ points out that Alföldy paid too little attention to principles of local history in his research. Cf. also Vittinghoff, "Gesellschaft," 163–277; Alföldy's defense against this criticism, "Römische Gesellschaft: Eine Nachbetrachtung."

Alföldy's ... distinction needs to be supplemented by a stratificatory classification that allows for a fuller representation of social differences."[272]

Other scholars have pointed out the difficulty with distinguishing only between the categories of rich and poor in Roman society.[273] For instance, Meeks has suggested that significant differences can be observed in wealth, power, and status among the *plebs* also, even though these differences were graduated and not always clearly defined. Criteria for a higher status at this level were also Roman and city citizenship; offices in smaller cities; above all, inherited wealth invested in land rather than trade; and family and origin (the older and the nearer to Rome the better; Greek upbringing was superior to "barbarian"; military office or status as veteran in a colony; and freedom by birth).[274] It also should be pointed out that many in this group, particularly the free farmers, tradesmen, and craftsmen with citizenship rights and property, did not view themselves as lower-class people.[275] Therefore it appears legitimate to classify them as a kind of middle class.[276] Some scholars even place individuals according to criteria such as wealth, social standing, and higher education at the low end of the upper class.[277] In light of these and other insights, K. Christ suggests an alternative model.[278] At the peak of society in the Roman Empire during the emperor period, we find imperial leadership, which is to be distinguished from the imperial upper class with a regional and local upper class just below. According to Christ, a middle class existed even though it was most likely somewhat nonhomogeneous, consisting of wealthy freemen, even individual slaves from the *familia Caesaris,* free farmers, tradesmen, craftsmen, and soldiers with property and partially with citizenship. The lower classes were similarly heterogeneous.

Pauline House Churches

The social makeup of early Christian churches became a focus of research as early as the turn of the twentieth century. In this older research, scholars arrived quite quickly at a consensus: the majority of Christians originated socially from the lower class. A. Deissmann was the main advocate of

---

[272] Holmberg, *Sociology,* 24.

[273] A number of things speak in favor of distinguishing according to the criterion of "in the *oikos*" and "outside the *oikos.*" Cf. esp. Judge, *Social Pattern,* 30–39, who points out that the very poorest people were those outside the protection provided by the system of patronage (see p. 177).

[274] Meeks, *Moral World,* 34.

[275] Holmberg, *Sociology,* 24.

[276] Cf., e.g., Christ, "Grundfragen," esp. 169–76, and *Geschichte;* Vittinghoff, "Gesellschaft," 163–277.

[277] Cf., e.g., Schöllgen, *Ecclesia sordida?* 12–15, who follows Christ and Vittinghoff. Cf. also the discussion of the entire problematic in E. and W. Stegemann, *Urchristliche Sozialgeschichte,* 58–94.

[278] Christ, "Grundfragen," 174–76.

this view.[279] In more recent research, more scholars appear to be embracing the opposite view. Some have even suggested that a consensus has been reached, in particular regarding the social stratification of Pauline congregations. Meeks and Malherbe have called this the "new consensus," which maintains that the social structure of Pauline churches essentially reflects that of the surrounding urban society.[280] With only minor exceptions, particularly at the top of society, all levels are represented analogously to their urban environment: "A Pauline congregation generally reflected a fair cross-section of urban society." The typical Christian is a free artisan or small trader.[281]

Theissen made a significant contribution to the "new consensus" as early as 1974–1975 with several articles in which he examined the social stratification of the Corinthian church.[282] His point of departure was the insight from 1 Cor 1:26–28 that at least some of the members of the congregation in Corinth were educated and powerful and originated from the upper classes. He then attempted to identify more clearly the individuals with elevated social status by applying certain criteria (as mentioned above, holding of office, house ownership, service rendered to the congregation, and travel). Theissen concluded that members of the urban elite were the most influential and powerful in the Corinthian congregation.[283] According to him, this applies as well to all other Pauline churches.

Schöllgen, however, has fundamentally criticized the "new consensus" for the following reasons.[284] First, because of a lack of adequate

---

[279] Deissmann, *Christentum*, 19, 23, 40. Cf. for a good overview of the general state of research on the topic up to the 1970s, Grimm, *Untersuchungen*, 19–37; for later contributions, Holmberg, *Sociology*, 28–76; E. and W. Stegemann, *Urchristliche Sozialgeschichte*, 249–51.

[280] Meeks, *First Urban Christians*, 73; Malherbe, *Social Aspects*, 31; Judge, *Social Pattern*, 49–61. Following Judge but with certain revisions and including both positions: Theissen, *Social Setting*, 70–72; Kreissig, "Zur sozialen Zusammensetzung"; Gülzow, *Christentum*, 28; Hengel, *Eigentum*, 44; Grimm, *Untersuchungen* (cf., on one hand, the section "Personen von Rang und Stand im Frühchristentum" [pp. 126–48] and, on the other, his comment that "the masses of typical believers belonged most likely to the lower classes" [313]). With him also Klauck, *Hausgemeinde*, 47.

[281] Meeks, *First Urban Christians*, 73.

[282] Theissen, "Legitimation und Lebensunterhalt"; "Soziale Schichtung"; "Soziale Integration"; "Starken und Schwachen."

[283] Theissen, *Social Setting*, 69–70.

[284] Schöllgen, "Was wissen wir?" This article contains critical comments on Meeks, in *First Urban Christians*, esp. on the first two chapters. In reality, however, it is a criticism of the entire Anglo-Saxon research as represented by Meeks, Malherbe, Filson, etc. Schöllgen is not the only one to question the "New Consensus." Cf. the research report by Judge, "Social Identity," esp. 208 ("We are still far from being in a position to attempt final conclusions"); E. and W. Stegemann, *Urchristliche Sozialgeschichte*, 249–71; Lampe, *Stadtrömischen Christen*, 38, 52, 93, 112–13; Gager, *Kingdom*, 96–98, 106–8 (cf., however, the convincing criticism of Gager by Holmberg, *Sociology*, 60–64).

source material, it will never be possible to produce useful results enabling us to determine the social structure of a specific society. Second, this difficulty becomes even more acute in the investigation of Christian sources. The question of the social structure of early Christian congregations cannot be sufficiently answered at the present state of research because of the barren nature of the material. According to Schöllgen, this applies to the entire pre-Constantinian period.[285] Schöllgen lists a number of objections to the "new consensus"; the most important are summarized here.

1. The prerequisite for demonstrating structural congruence with the overall society is a clear picture of the sociohistorical background for the early Christian churches. The problem is that we know too little about the social conditions of these churches. "For none of these cities does there as yet exist a detailed investigation of their social structure, not to mention whether such investigations have produced satisfying results. In light of the difficulties that other investigations have encountered that had similar objectives—investigations of cities for which we have much more data available than for the often insignificant locations of the Pauline churches—it appears highly unlikely that useful results will be produced for all or even a majority of these cities."[286] The construct of a more or less homogenous "ancient urban society" must be questioned. The small cities of Galatia with their old entrenched populations, on the one hand, and the relatively recently established Corinth with the legal system of a Roman colony, on the other hand, represent in legal, cultural, and social terms very different urban social structures.[287] They cannot readily be pressed into the category of "ancient city."

2. One additional methodological mistake made by Meeks is the implicit assumption that all Pauline congregations have identical social stratification. The few references that we have indicate rather that the individual congregations had quite different social structures, "as is to be expected in light of the different economic situations of each of their home cities"[288] (compare, e.g., 2 Cor 8:2 and the poverty of the Macedonian congregations with the abundance found in the Corinthian church). This means that each church should be examined individually regarding its social stratification. If Schöllgen is correct, then the thesis that all Pauline churches reflect the same social levels cannot be demonstrated because the Corinthian church (and the Roman?) is the only one for which there is any hope of attaining dependable results.

---

[285] Schöllgen, "Was wissen wir?" 78.
[286] Schöllgen, "Was wissen wir?" 72–73. For a summary of his investigation of Carthage, cf. *Ecclesia sordida?* 98–154. See the overview of these cities by Meeks, *First Urban Christians*, 40–50.
[287] Schöllgen holds to the north Galatian theory, which is, however, contested. Cf. Scott, *Paul*, 181–215.
[288] Schöllgen, "Was wissen wir?" 73.

3. Some of the most important direct and indirect evidence that Meeks lists in the prosopographic section of his study's second chapter for determining the social status of individual people is much less forceful than he assumes. First, the term οἶκος is not a reference to the size of the house and therefore cannot be used as a criterion for higher status. A family who lived in an *oikos* could have found accommodation in a smaller house or a rented apartment. Second, travel is not a certain indication of wealth. Not always one's own means were used to finance travel. Besides, it was possible to travel on foot by taking advantage of ancient hospitality.[289] Third, manual labor was a characteristic not only of craftsmen but of almost all urban vocations. Fourth, even if one considers Meeks's prosopographic results accurate regarding about the thirty or so individuals he examined, we cannot be sure that they can be considered representative for all Pauline churches. In order to draw conclusions about the social conditions of Pauline churches in general, one would have to prove that the individuals examined were somehow representative. But in the Pauline Epistles and in the book of Acts, overwhelmingly it is people of special capacity who are referred to by name, whereas the average member remains unmentioned. In other words, one might be able to draw conclusions regarding the social status of the leadership of these churches, but the mass of Pauline Christians remain sociohistorically in the dark.[290]

To summarize Schöllgen's main argument: we know too little about the social conditions of ancient cities and about Pauline congregations in these cities to arrive at dependable results about the social stratification of these congregations. His criticism is so fundamental that it categorically rejects the validity of sociohistorical investigation of the NT period.

B. Holmberg has, however, pointed out, "This negative judgment on the possibility of New Testament social history as such results from the type of demands Schöllgen makes on it."[291] It is undoubtedly true that the Christian sources and the social data in them are so scarce that we will never be able to carry out a complete analysis of the social structure of Christian congregations, at least if we apply Schöllgen's standards. But still it is possible (even Schöllgen admits this) to reach dependable results regarding the social stratification of the congregation in the city of Corinth. It is also possible to say something about the social status of those in leadership of the other Pauline churches. Even these two points alone are more than nothing. As a result of the careful prosopographic investigations of Judge, Theissen, and Meeks, at least the following insight appears to be worthy of consideration as well: "Their results confirm that the early Christian movement in Asia Minor, Greece, and Italy in the middle of the first century was not exclusively a movement among the poorest strata of society. This is important in-

---

[289] *Did.* 11:1, 13; cf. Harnack, "Lehre."
[290] Schöllgen, "Was wissen wir?" 76.
[291] Holmberg, *Sociology*, 68–69; Schmeller, *Hierarchie*, 55.

formation that has repercussions on our whole understanding of first-century Christianity."[292]

For our study it is not important whether the "new consensus" formulated by Meeks and Malherbe is correct. For us it is the existence of a group of leading individuals and their often demonstrable high status that are very interesting. Among them were the patrons—the homeowners or renters. It is the size of *their* houses that is significant for our study. That something can be said about this is contested by no one, not even Schöllgen. On the basis of evidence in reliable texts, we can be certain that such householders existed and that they made their homes available to the congregation for assembly. Here again it is not necessary to prove that these householders belonged to the upper levels of society. Even the questions whether they were homeowners or renters and how large their houses were are all intriguing but not decisive for our study. Whether they were homeowners like Gaius or Phoebe, with relatively large homes, or like Aquila and Prisca, with their smaller (rented?) house with workshop, or not, our texts reveal to us that Christians met for worship in their *oikos*, whatever kind it was.

THE WORSHIP SERVICES IN PAULINE HOUSE CHURCHES

A Separation of the Service of the Word and the Celebration of Communion

As we have seen, house churches coexisted within the local church as a whole in Corinth. In 1 Cor 14:23 a gathering of the whole church is implied: Ἐὰν οὖν συνέλθῃ ἡ ἐκκλησία ὅλη ἐπὶ τὸ αὐτό. In Rom 16:23 similar terminology is used: ἀσπάζεται ὑμᾶς Γάϊος ὁ ξένος μου καὶ ὅλης τῆς ἐκκλησίας. What was the content of this worship service of the whole church? Was it different from those in the house churches? Did Corinthian Christians gather, as in Jerusalem, in houses for a communion service and as the whole church for a preaching and teaching service? Did the Corinthians meet separately for a service of the word that did not include communion?[293] What happened in the other Pauline churches regarding such issues?

Whether Paul was thinking of one and the same worship service in 1 Cor 11 and 14 or different assemblies with varying content is one of the key questions here. In 1 Cor 11 an assembly with communion is mentioned. The content of the meeting in 1 Cor 14 appears to be a word service with teaching and preaching. As the program as such of the worship service was

---

[292] Holmberg, *Sociology*, 69.

[293] This question has generated much discussion over the years, and as yet no consensus has been reached. Cf. Schenk, "Einheit," for a research report up to 1970, who advocates, with A. Schweitzer and Cullmann and against C. Weizsäcker, a united worship service; Salzmann (*Lehren*, 50–81) speaks for the coexistence of the Lord's Supper and a word service in Corinth.

not the focus of Paul's discussion in 1 Cor 11–14, we need to reconstruct for ourselves a picture of the Corinthian worship service from the random data provided.

A number of linguistic arguments speak in favor of a unified type of service. First of all, it is striking that Paul uses parallel wording in 1 Cor 11 and 14: συνέρχεσθαι in 11:17–18, 20, 33–34 and in 14:23, 26; twice together with ἐπὶ τὸ αὐτό (11:20; 14:23).[294] Still, 11:33 mentions an assembly for eating, and 1 Cor 14 an assembly for prayer. An additional linguistic parallel is formed by the word family οἰκοδομεῖν, οἰκοδομή (compare the meal theme in 8:1, 10; 10:23 with 14:4, 5, 12, 17, 26). A further connection has been seen in the repetition of εὐχαριστία or a related form of the word in 14:16–18, which could indicate the embedding of the Lord's Supper "in the events of a charismatic worship service."[295] One could, however, object that Paul does not limit these terms to the Lord's Supper or the worship service as such (cf., e.g., 1:14).

Against the coexistence of the Lord's Supper and a service of the word speaks the presence of non-Christians at the assembly (14:24—ἄπιστος ἢ ἰδιώτης; cf. also 16:22–23), for one would not expect that they would be allowed access to the communion service after the instruction given in 1 Cor 10. To give the nonbaptized fellowship in the blood and body of Christ (10:16) would be premature and is theologically illegitimate (12:13). Conversely, it would have been quite natural for nonbelievers to be present for a word service with an evangelistic emphasis. In addition, according to one possible interpretation (see below), the have-nots came too late for the love feast (11:21), and the "affluent" are exhorted by Paul to hold off with the meal until the "poor" come later (11:33). We thus encounter another difficulty if the celebration meal followed the word service, which is what most scholars who advocate a united worship assembly assume. The difficulty remains even if it is assumed that the words of institution were spoken before the word service. It is highly unlikely that the Corinthian Christians would not have held off on the bread word until the poor had arrived. To perform such a liturgical rite before everyone had arrived at the meeting is something Paul surely would have vehemently opposed, and yet there is no trace of any such opposition in his letter to the Corinthians.

This difficulty can be resolved, however, if one assumes along with Klauck that there was considerable diversity and overlap in early Christian worship services.[296] In particular, if one accepts our view that a plurality of house churches existed, then it appears quite likely that in those small groups the members at times would celebrate the Lord's Supper alone and at other times assemble merely for a word service.

---

[294] See pp. 86–89 for the demonstration that συνέρχεσθαι and ἐπὶ τὸ αὐτό are technical terms for the worship assembly of the church.
[295] Schlier, "Herrenmahl," 211.
[296] Klauck, *Hausgemeinde,* 37.

On different evenings during the week, they could have done different things. Along with communion and teaching or preaching services, there were baptismal celebrations, evangelistic messages, and catechetical instruction, all of which required their own setting.[297] One can assume the same content for the worship meetings in house churches as for the assemblies of the whole church.... After all, the large meetings also took place in a house and would have continued what began in the smaller house church gatherings. On the whole, ... the transitions from house church to the whole local church and back were quite fluid. Only the two poles were stationary: the individual family here and the fully developed local church as a whole there. The reality of the first Christian congregations was often lived out in an "in-between" sphere that is difficult to define.[298]

The Celebration of Communion in the Corinthian House Churches

In establishing the church in Corinth, Paul taught the Christians there (1 Cor 11:2) to celebrate the κυριακὸν δεῖπνον (11:20) in a certain fashion. He impressed upon their minds a specific text, which was to be normative for the celebration (11:23–35). In particular, Paul placed a high value on the congruence of the meal and the celebration (cf. 10:17; 12:12–13). As far as Paul was concerned, a celebration meal that contradicted Christian fellowship was no longer really the Lord's Supper. The meal celebration, as Paul introduced it (after the Jerusalem and Antioch model), was held most likely as an actual meal embedded in the overall celebration of communion (the Lord's Supper).[299] The meal celebration could have followed the proclamation of the word. Paul probably envisioned his letter (1 Corinthians) being read at the beginning of the meal celebration: the conclusion of his letter (16:20–24; cf. *Did.* 10:6) clearly indicates a transition from the reading of his letter into the Lord's Supper.[300]

Everyone brought along what food he or she could for the meal. Paul apparently took for granted that not only the more affluent but also the poorer Christians, who were not able to bring anything, would be able to eat to their satisfaction from the food brought by others. From 10:14–22 and 11:17–34 it can be concluded that, after Paul's departure from Corinth, abuse in the context of the Lord's Supper began to occur that contradicted the instruction that he had already given on the matter during his first visit in Corinth. The κοινωνία among the guests at the Lord's table was being

---

[297] Klauck, ibid., points out correctly that the baptism of households implies that the celebration of baptism was connected with the physical house in some way.

[298] Klauck, *Hausgemeinde,* 38–39. With a different view, Afanassieff, "L'assemblée eucharistique."

[299] Stuhlmacher, *Grundlegung,* 366. Cf. also suggestions for a different order and background by Klinghardt, *Gemeinschaftsmahl,* and Klauck, *Herrenmahl,* 318–19.

[300] Bornkamm, "Anathema"; Wolff, *Der erste Brief,* 437–38; Salzmann, *Lehren,* 58–59.

destroyed by a twofold division—a rupture that was both theological and sociological—between the different groups in the congregation (1:10–17, 26–29). It was particularly during the celebration of the Lord's Supper, of all things, that the congregation split into two groups, the rich and the poor. While some enjoyed their food, others hardly had anything to eat and were thus humiliated. Paul severely rebukes this behavior (11:19–22).

For the reconstruction of the Corinthian situation after the apostle's departure, the interpretation of the two verbs προλαμβάνειν and ἐκδέχεσθαι in 11:21, 33 is of great importance. Usually προλαμβάνειν is understood in the sense "to anticipate; to go ahead; to be or do beforehand," and ἐκδέχεσθαι as "to wait for someone or something."[301] Many scholars have thus come to the following understanding of the text:[302] Although Paul initially introduced a regular meal surrounded by the celebration of the Lord's Supper in Corinth, the Christians there moved the words of institution to the end of the meal and oversacramentalized this liturgical act. In addition, the rich and the free, who were able to come to the meal earlier, ate their meals ahead of the others. As a result, nothing was left to eat for the unfree and poorer manual laborers, who could not leave their master's house or their place of work any earlier and were not able to bring much or any of their own food. The wealthy members of the church apparently assumed that, in the end, all that really mattered was for all to be able to take bread and wine as spiritual nourishment and, in so doing, to be able to participate in the power of the Spirit, which was present in the elements. After all, the have-nots who came late *were* able to participate wholly in the celebration of the Lord's Supper. The wealthy had obviously completely overlooked the fact, however, that their poorer fellow Christians were still hungry and, even worse, had to sit there and watch their richer fellow believers not only eat until they were satisfied but, in some cases, even to watch them drink until they were drunk.

This reconstruction, however, is not without its problems. What sense does it make to wait for the others with your food if everyone is to eat their own food (11:21)? If the have-nots were not able to bring their own food, it is of no help for them if the wealthy merely wait for them with their food. Waiting also implies sharing. O. Hofius has therefore suggested another view.[303] For him ἐκδέχεσθαι means "to receive as a guest" ("gastlich aufnehmen") instead of "to wait." In addition, he suggests that προλαμβάνειν be understood in the sense "to undertake" (one's own meal) ("sich sein eigenes Mahl vornehmen"), "to take in" (one's own meal) ("zu sich

---

[301] This is the way the word is used by Paul, the NT, and the Apostolic Fathers (cf., e.g., 1 Cor 16:11).

[302] Bornkamm, "Herrenmahl," 138–76, here 141–42; a list of additional representatives of this view by Hofius, "Herrenmahl," 207 n. 26; now also Salzmann, *Lehren*, 55–67.

[303] Hofius, "Herrenmahl," 203–43.

nehmen").³⁰⁴ According to this view, the Christians in Corinth did not proclaim the bread and wine words after the meal and thereby oversacramentalize the Lord's Supper; rather they kept the original order introduced by Paul. The abuse and thus the object of Paul's criticism was that all who were able to bring their own food ate it in one room together with the others. Thus some went hungry, and the others feasted right before the very eyes of the hungry. This is why the μὴ ἔχοντες were humiliated by the rich.³⁰⁵ This interpretation is linguistically and factually possible even though the suggested meaning of ἐκδέχεσθαι remains somewhat unusual both for the NT and for the Apostolic Fathers. Historically, it is certainly the less complicated reconstruction of the two.³⁰⁶

B. Winter's research seems to support Hofius's reconstruction. Independently of Hofius he comes to similar exegetical results on the basis of the sociohistorical background of the ancient *oikos* with particular consideration of the system of patronage.³⁰⁷ He translates προλαμβάνω as "devour" (derived from the root meaning, "receive") without a temporal connotation for προ and gives inscription evidence in support of this possibility.³⁰⁸ Consistently with this he translates ἀλλήλους ἐκδέχεσθε as "to share with the others" ("to receive one another" in the sense of sharing) instead of "to wait."³⁰⁹

According to Winter, the problem in 11:17–34 originates with the socioeconomic differences among Christians in Corinth, which become apparent at the κυριακὸν δεῖπνον. For him a part of the problem was that during the meal there existed a clear division not only between the rich and the poor³¹⁰ but between the secure and the insecure. The secure were those who could provide for themselves (e.g., the householders, independent tradesmen) and those who were a part of a household (e.g., members of the family, slaves, clientele, friends) and were provided for by someone else, for instance, the patron of their house. In contrast, the insecure were those who could not provide for themselves and were under the protection of a patron.

---

³⁰⁴ Ibid., 218–19, 220–21.
³⁰⁵ Ibid., 219–20.
³⁰⁶ With Stuhlmacher, *Grundlegung*, 369. However, with a different view, Wolff, *Der erste Brief*, 256–81. For yet another view, cf. Salzmann, *Lehren*, 55 n. 72.
³⁰⁷ Winter, "Lord's Supper" and "Secular and Christian." Following him, Blue, "House Church at Corinth." Others have also acknowledged Winter's article. Cf. Fee, *1 Corinthians*, 542; Nicholson, "Houses." For clear proof of the system of patronage in Corinth at this time, see pp. 193–95, esp. the literature listed in n. 414.
³⁰⁸ Cf. *SIG* 1170 1:5, 7, 9–10; Winter, "Lord's Supper," 75–77 for further examples. His translation can be understood to be much like that of Hofius, however, as an intensification of Hofius's "zu sich nehmen." Cf. also MM 542; Bauer-Aland⁶, 1405–6 (BDAG 864).
³⁰⁹ Winter, "Lord's Supper," 79–80. Here again Winter's translation is very similar to Hofius's "gastlich aufnehmen."
³¹⁰ Many others, esp. Theissen, *Social Setting*, 145–74.

They are "those who had no houses, in the sense that they were not connected to the essential social unit of the first century, the household, and thereby lacked the social security that provided a guarantee whether a man was a household slave or a freedman, of food, clothing and other benefits."[311] In the ancient world such individuals, even those who were free, were in a worse position than many slaves, who at least could count on the provision of their householder. In case of famine, for instance, such people were most vulnerable and usually the early victims. In 1 Cor 11, then, we have the following situation: while the secure were devouring their meal, the insecure had nothing to eat and, even worse, were forced to watch as the others were able to eat until satisfied.

Winter then asks how it could have come to such a blatant violation of the instructions Paul had given during his long stay in Corinth (Acts 18:11; 1 Cor 11:2) regarding the ever so important Lord's Supper. How was it possible for such conditions to prevail at the Lord's Supper only a short time after Paul's departure? Had something gone wrong in the meantime? According to inscriptional sources, Tiberius Claudius Dinippus, an affluent patron in Corinth, held the office of *curator annonae* three times.[312] One was elected to *curator annonae* (*annona,* annual grain supply) only during a time of already occurring or threatening famine. The person holding this office had the task of fighting the famine. Winter points out that the curatorship of Dinippus probably fell during the time of a severe famine during the reign of Gallio as governor of Achaia (51–52 C.E.). If this is correct, this famine would have occurred shortly after Paul's departure from Corinth.[313] Such a famine would have severely depressed the economy in Corinth, with the consequence that those who normally had enough food now would have been dependent on the charity grain distributed by the *curator annonae*. The distinction between those who had enough and those who depended on charity must have affected the situation in house churches at the meal celebration. Apparently the secure (the haves) had no mercy on the insecure (the have-nots). Paul's reaction is to condemn this behavior: in accordance with the gospel, the secure are to *share* with the insecure.[314]

---

[311] Winter, "Lord's Supper," 81. Cf. also Judge, *Social Pattern,* 60.

[312] Cf. West, *Latin Inscriptions,* nos. 86–90; Kent, *Inscriptions,* nos. 158–63; Winter, "Secular and Christian."

[313] As previously mentioned, however, the dating of Paul's visit in Corinth is disputed. Compare Winter with Murphy-O'Connor, *St. Paul's Corinth,* 137–60; Hengel, "Ursprünge," 15–38, esp. 16–18; for an extensive discussion, cf. Riesner, *Frühzeit,* 139–89.

[314] "To refuse to receive at the Lord's Dinner . . . in the fullest sense of the word, those whom Christ has unreservedly received, both denies the reality of the Gospel to break down all barriers, and brings to light in the banquet of the new age those socioeconomic divisions that belong to the age that is passing away" (Winter, "Lord's Supper," 82).

If Winter's suggestion regarding a famine in Corinth is historically accurate, then he has made an intriguing and significant contribution to research on this topic. One difficulty remains, however: the exact date of Paul's visit in Corinth (see above). In addition, the problem that nowhere in the letters to the Corinthians is such a situation clearly reflected would suggest a need for caution.[315] Things may well have happened that way—but for now we cannot be entirely certain.

Concerning tension during the communion celebration in 1 Cor 1:10–12 Paul complains about the existence of parties. It is not surprising that the houses that offered Paul and Apollos their hospitality during the development of the mission in Corinth then became house churches and continued to give their allegiance to the two missionaries responsible for their spiritual existence. Their homes apparently became the meeting places for the party of Paul and of Apollos respectively. It is quite likely that each house church was lead by a householder or teacher/leader who, precisely as a representative of either Paul or Apollos, enjoyed the loyalty of his followers. It is also evident that the plurality of house churches in coexistence with the whole local church in Corinth initially led to difficulty. For this reason some have correctly seen house churches as fertile soil and a cause for such division. "The existence of several house churches in one city goes far to explain the tendency of party strife in the apostolic age."[316] A loyalty to a certain house often brought with it a subtle potential for such division within the church as a whole in a given city.

Whether this party strife affected the celebration of the Lord's Supper is difficult to determine with certainty. In 1 Cor 11 Paul speaks of αἱρέσεις and not of σχίσματα. How one is to understand these two terms is disputed. Αἱρέσεις is often interchangeable with σχίσματα. But if 11:19a is translated with "there *have* to be divisions among you" because here Paul has taken up an unknown Jesus saying referring to the last judgment (cf. Justin, *Dial.* 35.3),[317] then the two terms can no longer be understood as synonyms. Seen in this way, the situation in Corinth could no longer be viewed from a sociohistorical perspective because the division then would extend far beyond mere difficulties originating from the house church setting. In light of this, I have decided not to address the sociohistorical dimensions of party strife here but instead in the next chapter, in the context of an exegetical analysis of Titus 1:11.

---

[315] Winter, "Secular and Christian," 93–94, points out the indirect evidence for famine in 1 Corinthians. Cf. also Fee, *1 Corinthians*, 328–29. Without question, for the people in Corinth (cf. *1 Clem.* 56:9) and elsewhere in the ancient world, famine was an ever present threat; cf. Garnsey, *Famine*.

[316] Filson, "Significance," 110. Following him, e.g., Malherbe, *Social Aspects*, 92–112; Klauck, *Hausgemeinde*, 39; Meeks, *First Urban Christians*, 76; White, *Building God's House*, 103–10 n. 31; Blue, "In Public," 176–89.

[317] Jeremias, *Unbekannte Jesusworte*, 74–75; following him, Stuhlmacher, *Grundlegung*, 368. With a different view, Wolff, *Der erste Brief*, 260–61.

The Service of the Word in Pauline House Churches

In 1 Cor 14, Paul apparently has a service other than the meal celebration in mind, as it is out of the question that nonbelievers (14:22–23) would have been allowed to participate in the Lord's Supper (see above). Moreover, the Lord's Supper is not mentioned in 1 Cor 14.[318] That non-Christians would come to the service is a hypothetical possibility that Paul takes into account in this context (cf. the conjunctive "and"), but this does not imply that he is saying they would only randomly "pop in" every now and then. It is a very real expectation of Paul's that nonbelievers would attend the services with some kind of regularity; otherwise the example loses its persuasive power.

The following elements are indications that the topic is a worship service in 1 Cor 14: the song, the prayer in tongues, the prophetic speech, and the instruction/teaching (14:26–33).[319] It also can be assumed that prayer in understandable language was an integral part of the service (cf. 11:4–5). The reading of Scripture to the congregation could also be insinuated by the term διδαχή, even though it is not explicitly mentioned by Paul in 1 Cor 14.[320] If non-Christians were allowed to attend the word service, it can be assumed that at least at times the message had an evangelistic focus.[321]

To supplement our discussion of the worship services in Pauline house churches, we also need to look at other references in the rest of Paul's epistles. The concluding exhortation in 1 Thess 5:16–22 could have been given in the context of the worship service (cf. the reminder not to dampen the Spirit and not to treat prophecy with contempt) even though the application transcends the worship service and reaches out into daily life. In Rom 12:3–8, Paul places service, teaching, and exhortation alongside prophecy. Here he is also thinking of the worship service although, again, service extends beyond the worship assembly. In 1 Thess 5:27 Paul challenges the recipients of his letter to have it read "to all the brothers." It is clear here that the letter was to be read in each of the individual house churches.[322] This is also an indication that, first, the path was already being prepared for the view that the Pauline letters had the character of "Scripture" and, second, that word services took place in house churches.[323] In Laodicea (Col 4:16) Pauline letters were also read to the congregation at meetings in houses. In Col 3:16 the worship service is mentioned (cf. Eph 5:19), which obviously

---

[318] For additional arguments, cf. Salzmann, *Lehren*, 60–61.
[319] For an extensive proof, cf. ibid., 67–72.
[320] So also Hahn, "Der urchristliche Gottesdienst," 61. Cf. Salzmann, *Lehren*, 73.
[321] For an extensive discussion of the possible patterning of the Christian service after that of the synagogue, cf. Salzmann, *Lehren*, 75–77.
[322] With a different view, T. Holtz, *Der erste Brief,* 274.
[323] Bornkamm, "Anathema," suggests that the reading of 1 Corinthians could have taken the place of the sermon (not every time, of course, but only when it arrived).

took place in various house churches.³²⁴ Here teaching and the singing of psalms, hymns, and songs are mentioned.³²⁵ It is also significant for our study that at least one worship service is documented (Acts 20:7–12) as held in the evening (every Sunday?), including a communion celebration with preaching and/or teaching at a Christian assembly in the upper room of a larger three-story building in Troas.³²⁶

THE HOUSE IN THE PAULINE MISSION

Center and Coworker Missional Outreach

What are the main characteristics of Pauline missional outreach?³²⁷ Paul, who had been shaped by his own mission experiences in Syria and Cilicia (Gal 1:21) as well as at the side of Barnabas in the context of the Antioch mission, ultimately became independent of the church of Antioch and went on to develop his own innovative mission enterprise.³²⁸ Called by God in Christ Jesus to preach the gospel among all Gentiles,³²⁹ he was deeply convinced of the necessity to reach the entire world.³³⁰ Supported by the initial agreement of the apostles' council, he launched out from the missional region of Antioch in southern Asia Minor. In several significant cities in Galatia, Macedonia, and Greece, in one city in each province, usually in the respective capital—Thessalonica, Corinth, Ephesus—he proclaimed the gospel and established churches. In doing so, he followed the commercial routes of world trade. Accordingly, his mission initially embraced urban centers. From both the book of Acts and the Pauline Epistles, it is clear that Paul practiced "cell planting" *(Schwerpunktmission)* missional outreach in

---

³²⁴ Cf. Klauck, *Hausgemeinde*, 46.

³²⁵ Cf., for an extensive discussion of a different view, Salzmann, *Lehren*, 82–89. Cf. also Hahn, "Der urchristliche Gottesdienst," 61.

³²⁶ For discussions regarding the exact day (eve of the Sabbath or the first day of the week), cf. Pesch, *Apostelgeschichte*, 2:190–91; Roloff, *Apostelgeschichte*, 297–98. For proof that "bread breaking" means Christian communion, see pp. 79–86. Regarding the historicity of the "we" report in Acts 20, cf. Salzmann, *Lehren*, 38–40; Pesch, *Apostelgeschichte*, 2:188–91; Roloff, *Apostelgeschichte*, 297.

³²⁷ Cf. Bornkamm, *Paulus,* 27–120; Hahn, *Verständnis,* 80–94; Hengel, "Zwischen Jesus und Paulus" and "Ursprünge"; Stuhlmacher, "Weg," 121–26; Kasting, *Anfänge,* 53–123; Becker, "Paulus," 102–59. For a new perspective, cf. Stuhlmacher, "Matt 28:16–20."

³²⁸ This happened after the so-called Antioch incident and applies in particular to Paul's second mission journey.

³²⁹ Rom 1:5, 13; 11:25; 16:26; Gal 3:8. (Cf. also Rom 1:1–7, 14–17; 9:1–5; 10:14–21; 11:1–32; 15:14–29; Stuhlmacher, "Weg," 122).

³³⁰ Harnack, *Mission,* 1:79–81. There is strong evidence that Paul's choice of routes for his mission was influenced by the missional prophecy in Isa 66:18–21 (cf. Riesner, *Frühzeit,* 216–25; more extensively, Scott, *Paul,* 135–80).

these centers.³³¹ The references to Paul's extended stays in the cities of Corinth and Ephesus confirm this picture.³³²

Paul believed that his main objective was to establish small cells, that is, bases of operations in these cities, and to develop missional outreach from these support bases. From these bases outward, the city itself and then the surrounding area were to be reached with the gospel.³³³ For this reason Paul did not stay in these cities until the development of each cell into a full-fledged church had been completed but only as long as necessary for each to become self-reliant.³³⁴ These churches were trained by Paul to take responsibility for their own community life and the missional outreach in their city and to the surrounding area. The resources he used to accomplish this were a first and oftentimes a second visit to the city, his letters, and the employment of coworkers in establishing and looking after these congregations.

Building on this perspective and drawing from insights gained from the research of Paul's use of coworkers, W. H. Ollrog attempts to shed further light on the uniqueness of the Pauline missional approach.³³⁵ Paul is able to accomplish the objectives of such a massive missional enterprise by further developing a staff of coworkers, an idea with which he had become familiar in Antioch. He chose a few select men to be a part of his team (e.g., Timothy, Titus, Silvanus), who were then made responsible for looking after congregations, the organization of collections, the delivery of letters, and so forth. In addition to these permanent coworkers, there were a number of temporary ones. They were sent out by the Pauline congregations and were available to Paul in particular for the mission in the surrounding areas of the city centers mentioned above.³³⁶ These churches, established by Paul, expressed their sense of missional responsibility by making such "ambassadors" (2 Cor 2:25–30; Phil 2:25) available to the Pauline mission. Through the congregants who were released from local responsibilities and sent out, these churches participated in the missional outreach of the apostle. This is the

---

³³¹ Altogether Luke counts eighteen cities as travel objectives and stations for Paul (cf. Acts 13:5–21:8, esp. 16:4–5). For the most part, these stays were for the founding, the building up, or the encouragement of the different mission churches, with small cells of Christians in scattered households. In his letters Paul confirms these references in Acts. His letters are almost all written to churches in important cities. The statement in Rom 15:19b can only be understood on the basis of a cell-planting concept of mission in these cities (cf. Bornkamm, *Paulus*, 73; Meeks, *First Urban Christians*, 9–10).

³³² 1 Cor 16:18; Acts 18:18; cf., for Athens, also 1 Thess 3:1–2, 6.

³³³ Ollrog, *Paulus*, 157–60. Cf. Dibelius, *Paulus*, 63–77; Goppelt, *Apostolische und nachapostolische Zeit*, 61, 63; Conzelmann, *Geschichte*, 76–77; Eichholz, *Theologie*, 25; Kasting, *Anfänge*, 107.

³³⁴ Sometimes he was forced to leave abruptly, earlier than he had intended (cf. Philippi, 1 Thess 2:1; Thessalonica, 1 Thess 1:6, 2:13–20, 3:1–13).

³³⁵ Ollrog, *Paulus*, 111–61.

³³⁶ 1 Cor 16:15–18; Phil 2:25–30; 2 Cor 8:18–19. Stephanas, Fortunatus, Achaicus, and Epaphroditus are among them.

first time that the practice of "center mission" *(Zentrumsmission)* becomes historically tangible in the early Christian movement.

"Center mission" is defined differently here[337] than in the past.[338] The term implies a series of young congregations networked with and equal to one another in the (capital) cities, that is, *centers*, which then became bases of operation for the Pauline mission. They formed these bases by sending workers to Paul to help with missional outreach for a limited time. "Center mission" is the opposite of the centrally organized mission of the Antioch church. There the base of operation was one single congregation, which, as the "mother church," sent out traveling missionaries on mission journeys, who went from location to location as itinerant preachers, staying for a brief time at each and then finally returning to the mother church.

The innovative elements of the Pauline model, according to Ollrog, are the turning away from the traveling-missionary or mission journey approach and to the formation of "center missions"; the development of a system of coworkers; the self-understanding of the Pauline churches as independent missional congregations.

Although Paul's approach to missions was in many ways innovative at the local level, he retained important elements of the pre-Easter radical itinerary mission for his own missionary practice at a regional and worldwide level.[339] This is evident, for instance, in his renunciation of marriage as well as the right to have personal belongings and a permanent residence.[340] In addition, Paul continued the practice of partner mission for his own missional outreach, something he had learned earlier in Antioch; as a traveling missionary, he almost always took someone along with him.[341]

Ollrog's view is enlightening, and there is much in his analysis with which we can readily agree. Certainly, the concept of a mission based on a system of coworkers sent out by individual congregations was an innovative addition to the missional approach Paul had learned in Antioch. Ollrog has also made a significant contribution to NT research in pointing out the connection between coworkers and the center mission concept as well as the significance of the individual congregation in making coworkers available for the Pauline mission. It must be asked, however, whether Ollrog has drawn sufficient attention to the significance of houses for the Pauline missional outreach.

---

[337] Dibelius, *Paulus*, 61–77, esp. 62–63; Goppelt, *Apostolische und nachapostolische Zeit*, 61, 63; Eichholz, *Theologie*, 25–26; Kasting, *Anfänge*, 107; Conzelmann, *Geschichte*, 76–77.

[338] Ollrog, *Paulus*, 126.

[339] Rom 15:19–21, 23.

[340] 1 Cor 7:7; 13:3; Acts 20:33, 35.

[341] Barnabas from Antioch (Acts 11:30; 13:2–3; 15:1–2; Gal 2:1); Silas on the first mission journey (Acts 15:40; 1 Thess 1:1; 2 Thess 1:1; 2 Cor 1:1); Timothy on the second (Phil 1:1; Col 1:1; Phlm 1).

Missional Outreach from House to House

Ollrog has correctly recognized that the local churches were the basis of the Pauline mission. They provided workers for the mission endeavor. These local churches, however, consisted of one or more house churches. The houses in which they gathered were the source and the basis of the co-workers for the mission in that city and the surrounding area. They were, in fact, much more than that: they were the starting point for the entire local and regional missional enterprise. Paul himself describes his work as that of a gardener who only planted while others did the watering (1 Cor 3:6). Even if these metaphorical statements do not mean that Paul merely did evangelistic ministry, they indicate that he "saw his ministry primarily in the establishment of small cells out of which full-fledged congregations would later develop."[342] Theses small cells, however, were house churches. In the Pauline mission, houses served not only as meeting places for the worship services but also as missional support bases that provided the manpower for missional outreach to the city and beyond.[343] Some of these coworkers were the householders themselves (cf. Stephanas from Corinth or Prisca and Aquila); others were household members, such as slaves or clientele (cf. those from the household of Stephanas in Corinth), who were released for ministry by their householders. The prime example of this is the house of Philemon in Colossae; his house church was able to contribute to the Pauline mission in and around Ephesus through Onesimus.[344] Providing manpower in this way was made possible by the economic and social resources of the ancient *oikos*.

Hospitality, Letters, and Travel

As in Jesus' mission and in the early church in Jerusalem, so also in Pauline missional outreach, the sedentary householders and the urban house churches stand in a complementary relationship to the traveling missionaries (Paul and his permanent coworkers) and their mission enterprise.[345] Some of the specific characteristics of ancient hospitality, a phenomenon that was integrally linked to the ancient *oikos*, were of great significance in the context of Paul's mission.[346] Hospitality was important not only for the Christian missionaries but also for Jewish and Christian individuals who traveled in

---

[342] Vogler, "Bedeutung," 790.
[343] So also Judge, "Early Christians," 127.
[344] Phlm 13; Col 4:7–8. With Stuhlmacher, "Weg," 123. Ollrog, *Paulus*, 101–6, does not see the significance of the *oikos* in the overall scheme of missional outreach.
[345] Cf. Phil 4:15; 2 Cor 11:9; 1 Thess 1:7–8; 3:1–3; Gal 4:13; 1 Cor 1:11; 4:17; 5:9; 7:1; 16:11; 16:12; 2 Cor 2:12; 7:5–7; 8:6, 10, 16–17; 18–20, 22–24; 9:2, 3–5; 12:17–18; 13:1; Rom 16:1–2.
[346] Harnack, *Mission and Expansion*, 219–24; Riddle, "Early Christian Hospitality"; Rusche, *Gastfreundschaft*, 1–47; Stählin, "ξένος," *TDNT* 5:1–36; Mathews, "Hospitality"; Reck, *Kommunikation*, 88–89; Leutzsch, *Bewährung*, 59–71 (cf. esp. 159 n. 52 for additional literature on hospitality).

the context of their business. The numerous public inns were, for the most part, avoided by Jews and Christians alike because of their bad reputation.[347] Travelers resorted therefore to private hospitality; Jews and Christians usually sought out lodging in the private homes of their fellow believers.[348] Acts 21:4–8 show how hospitality was expected and given as matter of course.[349] With this backdrop Paul's exhortations to practice hospitality take on a deeper dimension.[350]

Letter writing also belonged to the customs associated with hospitality. This practice was widespread, and with time a fairly fixed set of conventions evolved. One example is the letter of recommendation, with its standardized form and technical language, which implicitly addressed the hospitable responsibilities of the householder.[351] Typical expressions are προσδέχομαι and προπέμπω, which, in their function as literary signals, reveal elements of Christian hospitality as exercised in the house church. In Rom 16:2, for example, the request is made of the saints in Rome to "receive" Phoebe (cf. also Phil 2:29). She delivered Paul's letter (presumably the original Letter to the Romans),[352] which he dictated during his last stay in Greece, in Corinth, as a guest in the house of Gaius (cf. Rom 16:22–23) and sent to Rome from there (Acts 20:3). It is possible that Phoebe read and commented on the letter in the various house churches in Rome.[353] Accordingly, it is important to Paul that she be given respect and all the assistance she needs. Just as she offered Paul and other Christians her hospitality in the church in her house in Cenchreae, the urban house churches in Rome are to receive her and give her their hospitality. "Paul's old house church network from the Aegean was now providing entry into the new house church networks in Rome, through the exercise of letter-writing and hospitality."[354]

In addition, these οἶκοι and the hospitality of their owners may well have made possible Paul's trips as well as those of his coworkers in that they

---

[347] Cf., e.g., B. Valentin in Clement, *Stromata* 2.114.3–6; Friedländer, *Darstellungen,* 351; Stählin, "ξένος," 18 n. 135; Mathews, "Hospitality," 27–28, 200; Lampe, "Zur gesellschaftlichen und kirchlichen Funktion," 533–42, here 538.

[348] Malherbe, *Social Aspects,* 66.

[349] Most of the NT references to hospitality are found in Acts (cf., e.g., 9:43; 10:48; 16:15; 18:3, 20; 28:14; Mathews, "Hospitality," 172: μένειν can only be understood as a technical term in the context of hospitality). Cf., however, 3 John 5–10 (see pp. 281–87, the excursus on house churches in 2 and 3 John); Gal 1:18; 1 Cor 16:6–7; and the passages yet to be mentioned here.

[350] Cf., e.g., Rom 12:13; 16:2; also Heb 13:2; 3 John 8.

[351] Kim, *Form,* 9–97, 119–42; Stowers, *Letter Writing,* 51–70; Malherbe, *Social Aspects,* 94–103; P. Marshall, *Enmity,* 9–117. Esp. 1 Cor 16:15–16, 17–18; Phil 2:29–30; 4:2–3. 1 Thess 5:12–13 and Rom 16:1–2 are examples of such letters of recommendation.

[352] With Stuhlmacher, *Römer,* 217; Cranfield, *Romans,* 2:780; cf. Schlier, *Römerbrief,* for additional exegetes of this opinion.

[353] Jewett, "Paul, Phoebe"; following him, Halteman Finger, *Paul,* 26, 75.

[354] White, *Building God's House,* 106.

gave them the necessary material and financial resources needed for their travel. These resources were provided, most likely through collection, by the entire church (much as in Philippi). Many members probably earned their money somehow in the context of the ancient *oikos*. We need to steer clear, however, of an all-too-schematic reconstruction here. We cannot assume that every homeowner also became the patron of a house church *and* of missional outreach. It could have been that some of the householders did their part by making their home available to the congregation as a meeting place and then other affluent members or the entire church contributed for travel costs and so forth. Not everyone who was wealthy was also automatically a homeowner. Nevertheless, the well-to-do would have contributed the major portion, and householders certainly belonged to that affluent group.

Interestingly, all of this was organized through letter correspondence. With the letter Paul had Phoebe deliver to Rome, he was also making preparations for his trip to Rome and from there on to Spain. He was hoping not only that he would receive hospitality in Rome (room and board, etc.) but that the house churches in Rome would materially and financially "assist him on his journey" to Spain as well (Rom 15:24; cf. Acts 15:3; 1 Cor 16:6, 11; 2 Cor 1:16).[355] Οἶκοι offered Paul, his coworkers, and other itinerant missionaries overnight quarters as well as room and board for longer stays. As we have already seen, Paul wrote Philemon, among other things, to ask him to prepare a guest room. He most likely received such a guest room in the home of Gaius as well.

Paul's correspondence, an integral part of his mission, was made possible by a network of houses scattered throughout the entire region. Every one of the letters he sent needed one or more carriers, who were dependent on a "sending" *oikos* for the resources necessary to start the trip and, along the way, on the hospitality of several additional houses for lodging and resources to continue the trip.[356] Both Stephanas and Epaphroditus (Phil 2:25) traveled on behalf of their congregations to visit Paul.[357] Stephanas delivered a letter with questions from the Corinthian church to Paul (1 Cor 7:1; 8:1; 12:1). In 1 Cor 16:17 it says that he along with Fortunatus and Achaicus would visit Paul in Ephesus. Epaphroditus brought Paul material support from the church in Philippi (Phil 4:10–18). As we have seen, Stephanas was definitely a homeowner in Corinth (1 Cor 1:16; 16:15).[358] It can be as-

---

[355] With Dodd, *Romans,* 228–29; against Mathews, "Hospitality," 234.

[356] So also White, *Building God's House,* 105–6. Cf. 1 Cor 16:3; Rom 16:1–2; Col 4:11; Acts 19:27.

[357] With Ollrog we can assume that Stephanas and Epaphroditus served for short stints in missional outreach on behalf of their congregation (cf. Ollrog, *Paulus,* 63–72, 73–79, 98–99). Cf. esp. the characterization of Epaphroditus as συνεργὸς καὶ συστρατιώτης (Phil 2:25; cf. also 2:30, ὑμῶν ὑστέρημα = the church's responsibility of sending temporary mission helpers). An almost literal correspondence to Phil 2:30 is found in 1 Cor 16:17, referring to Stephanas, Fortunautus, and Achaicus.

[358] Cf. 1 Cor 16:15 and the corresponding references in 16:16; 16:18b.

sumed that his self-reliance as a householder made it possible for him to travel to Paul and to stay with him.[359] Regarding Epaphroditus, there is no indication that he was either affluent or a property holder.[360] It is difficult to determine on the basis of his name if he was free, slave, or freedman. This uncertainty, however, does not effect our thesis. "If Epaphroditus was a freedman, we would need to assume that he had somehow become wealthy, which would have enabled him to finance his absence from home and his journey to Paul as well as the stay with him. Because there is no indication one way or another, it would also have been possible that he traveled with permission or on behalf of his master."[361] In summary, it can be said that the travel of congregation members and their ministry involvement in the Pauline mission would not have been possible without the assistance of Christian houses.[362] In this way as well, houses played a crucial role, in particular for the "center mission" that Paul further developed for his mission enterprise.

The Intentional Recruitment of Householders

In the book of Acts, Luke particularly emphasizes the success of the mission in the synagogue among God-fearers and Gentiles.[363] It appears that this group was of special importance for the expansion of Christianity. This was true for Diaspora Judaism as well and is partially related to the fact that, for the most part, God-fearers belonged to the more affluent social classes (see pp. 150–51). As a result, they were in a position to support the synagogue community financially.[364] When large numbers of God-fearers converted to Christianity, the church benefited from this phenomenon as well.

Both Luke (Acts 17:4b, 12, 34) and Paul (1 Cor 1:26) confirm that from the beginning wealthy members of this group belonged to Pauline congregations. First Corinthians 1:26 needs to be read not only theologically but also sociologically. Sociologically, the verse implies that at least some σοφοί, δυνατοί, and εὐγενεῖς belonged to the congregation (see pp. 165–71

---

[359] Cf. Theissen, *Social Setting*, 87–88, 91–92: Stephanas belonged to a category of people who were perhaps so independent financially that they did not need to work and thus had time and money for travel.

[360] Cf. Lambertz, *Sklavennamen*, 49, 73–87, 88; the discussion in Gielen, *Tradition*, 97.

[361] Gielen, *Tradition*, 97.

[362] So also ibid., 98.

[363] Cf. Acts 13:14–51; 14:1–6; 17:1–9, 10–15, 17; 18:1–12, 19. This is considered a Lukan "scheme" and therefore not historical by many scholars (cf. Schmithals, *Paulus und Jakobus*, 44–49; Bornkamm, "Missionary Stance"; Löning, *Saulustradition;* Meeks, *First Urban Christians*, 26). Cf., however, Rom 1:16; 10:14–21; 1 Cor 9:20–21; 2 Cor 11:24–25; Stuhlmacher, *Vorgeschichte*, 99 n. 5; Wilson, *Gentiles*, 250; Holmberg, *Paul*, 11–13; Jervell, "Paul." The missional success among God fearers can also be seen as historically reliable (cf. Thraede, "Frau," 8:229; Gülzow, *Christentum*, 24).

[364] Theissen, *Social Setting*, 103–4; Gülzow, *Christentum*, 13, 24.

on social stratification). This affluent minority appears to have had a very active, influential role in the life of the church.

First Corinthians 1:14, 16 also has central importance for our study. In a section dealing with party strife, Paul emphatically reminds the group loyal to him that he himself only baptized a few Corinthians.[365] It is interesting to note, however, that every one of the persons baptized by Paul was a significant personality: Crispus, head of the synagogue and homeowner; Gaius, homeowner and host of the whole church; Stephanas and his entire household, firstfruits. This information is quite remarkable in light of 1:26. Even though the social makeup of the congregation shows that the majority of the members came from lower social strata, those whom Paul baptized were all from upper levels. First Corinthians 1:26 thus indicates that in his missional outreach in Corinth Paul initially had the most success among the upper class. It is my contention that this was intentional on his part, that at the beginning of his mission in Corinth, he purposely targeted the more affluent individuals.[366] It appears that Paul was particularly well qualified for such an approach by virtue of his own social background and status: he was of Roman citizenship as well as a citizen of the city of Tarsus, and highly educated (in Jerusalem).[367] All of this certainly would have opened doors socially for Paul, which in turn would have facilitated his missional outreach to the upper-class Jewish and God-fearing population. "He thus possessed an unusually well balanced set of social qualifications, a combination shared with only a very small minority of persons in the eastern Mediterranean. This fact he demonstrated when it suited him by moving freely in the best circles in that society."[368]

It is also remarkable that in all three cases it was householders whom Paul baptized. Thus Paul himself underscores, at least for Stephanas and Gaius, the significance of their houses for missional outreach in Corinth.

Although Paul directly reveals his house-to-house missional approach only in Corinth, we have no reason to doubt that he practiced this as he established churches in other cities as well. The perspective given here by Paul

---

[365] For the following, cf. Gielen, *Tradition*, 80–82.

[366] So also Popkes, *Adressaten*, 73–76. This is not to say that Paul targeted the upper class exclusively in his missional outreach.

[367] Regarding Tarsan and Roman citizenship, cf. Acts 9:11, 30; 16:37–38; 21:39; 22:3, 25–27; 23:27, 39. Cf. Lüdemann, *Das frühe Christentum*, 249–50; Hengel, "Der vorchristliche Paulus," esp. 188–93, 193–208; Riesner, *Frühzeit*, 129–39. Paul and Luke are in agreement regarding Paul's pharisaic background, his education as a pharisaic scribe in Jerusalem, and his zeal for the law. Cf. Phil 3:4–11; Rom 11:1; Acts 22:3–5; 23:6. In addition, Paul's exegesis of the OT also indicates a high level of theological education. Cf. Oepke, "Probleme," 443.

[368] Judge, *Social Pattern*, 58. Regarding Paul's citizenship and status, cf. also Grimm, *Untersuchungen*, 112–13; Theissen, *Social Setting*, 102–3; Banks, *Paul's Idea*, 150. This view of Paul's citizenship, status, and education is disputed; cf. Stowers, "Social Status," 59–82, esp. 74; W. Stegemann, "War der Apostel Paulus?"; E. and W. Stegemann, *Urchristliche Sozialgeschichte*, 256–61. See previous note.

regarding the Corinthian situation is more or less confirmed in Acts 18:1–8 (see above on Acts 18). As we have seen, Paul apparently took a similar approach in Thessalonica in that he won Jason, a homeowner, to faith in Christ (see above on 17:1–9). In Philippi we saw (Acts 16) that he was able to recruit two householders at the very beginning of his ministry there. How and when Philemon came to faith we do not know; the possibility cannot be excluded that he was reached for Christ by Paul in this same manner as well.

This thesis is supported by the so-called *oikos* formula in the book of Acts (10:1–2, 22/11:12b–14; 16:14–16; 16:30–34; 18:8).[369] The *oikos* formula corresponds exactly with the Pauline statement in 1 Cor 1:16 regarding the baptism of Stephanas and his entire house. In all four references to the *oikos* formula, the householders are characterized as well-to-do on the basis of, first of all, their home ownership, but also because of their occupation. Except for the jail keeper in Philippi, all of them emerged from the synagogue setting, and Cornelius and Lydia are explicitly referred to as God-fearers.[370]

The *oikos* formula confirms therefore that it was typical of the Pauline missional approach in any given city to initially target individuals from higher social levels. In this way Paul was able to win homeowners, along with their entire households, for the gospel and to set up a base of operations in their house for local and regional mission.[371] The baptism of entire households surely accelerated the spread of the gospel. Another positive aspect of this phenomenon is the corporative solidarity effective as a result of the conversion of an entire household at once.[372] From the very beginning of one's spiritual journey, each individual experienced the built-in support of his or her decision for Christ in the rest of the newly converted household.[373] Each new Christian was immediately integrated in a community of faith that provided significant assistance for further growth as a believer.

The Missional Attraction of House Churches

There is one more aspect on which we need to focus our attention concerning the local significance of the house for Pauline missions. Paul was not

---

[369] See pp. 121–22 for the antiquity of the *oikos* formula (he or she was baptized or came to faith with his or her [entire] house).

[370] Gielen, *Tradition*, 83–84. Cf. also Matson, *Household Conversion*.

[371] Cf., regarding the social setting of the Pauline sermon, Malherbe, *Paul*, 7–12, who also discusses the other options, e.g., the synagogue, marketplace, street (Acts 17:16–34), hall (Acts 19:9–10), or workshop that Paul uses for evangelistic ministry and preaching. Meetings in public buildings were evidently the exception. Cf. Stowers, "Social Status," 59–82. He, however, sees no connection between Paul's preaching ministry in the synagogue and in houses. Cf. Gielen's criticism of Stower, *Tradition*, 84 n. 95.

[372] Cf. Sandnes, *New Family*.

[373] Still, the baptism of members of the household dependent on the householder could mean that they may not have had a personal faith of their own. Cf. Meeks, *First Urban Christians*, 77.

always under way. As mentioned, an integral part of his center missional outreach usually consisted of a prolonged stay in someone's house at a given location (cf. Corinth, Ephesus). These houses played an important role in the context of Paul's evangelistic ministry by naturally opening the door to a whole network of relationships. Householders were able to create an immediate audience for Paul by inviting their friends, relatives, and clientele. As the guest of the head of the household, Paul was automatically an insider and as such enjoyed the trust not only of the householder but of the entire household and everyone connected with it as well. Thus, within a very short time after becoming the guest in someone's home, Paul had a relatively large number of high-quality contacts for one-on-one conversations and his evangelistic meetings.[374]

The house was not only significant as a meeting place and as a source of evangelistic contacts. "Because the mission originally started in the Diaspora synagogues, Gentiles encountered the gospel from the very beginning in most cities not as one lonely voice but rather in the context of a practicing faith community. The congregation most likely participated in the evangelistic meetings that Paul held, and conversely the worship service was also evangelistically oriented and fruitful (1 Cor 14:24–25). Early Christians shared their faith from person to person and from house to house."[375] According to 1 Thess 1:9–10 and Rom 11:25–26, the Pauline gospel had a universal scope. It was not simply a matter of reaching "all" Israel but the "full number of the Gentiles" as well. Contained in the message itself is the motivation to proclaim it to everyone everywhere. Not only Paul but every Christian sensed a calling to be "light in the world" and "salt of the earth" (cf. 1 Thess 1:6–8; Rom 10:14–18; Phil 1:14–18; Col 4:2–6).[376] This means not only that Paul used the house as a base of operations for missional outreach but that the Christian house itself as a sociological entity became evangelistically active in a twofold manner. Whereas Paul and his coworkers place the main ministry emphasis on evangelistic proclamation, households had an evangelistic impact on others around them through their personal confession of faith and through the attraction of their community life together (cf. Rom 12:1–2; 1 Thess 4:10–11; 1 Cor 6:1–11; 2 Cor 6:14–7:1; Phil 2:12–16; Col 4:2–6).[377]

This is illustrated well in Rom 12:1–2.[378] As Christians belong fully to Christ after baptism, Paul challenges them to offer their bodies as a sign of their new worship to God. This worship is to test and approve what God's will is for daily life in the world. For Paul this will of God is summarized by the great commandment in Lev 19:18, defined exclusively by the salvation

---

[374] Cf. also P. Marshall, *Enmity*, 143.
[375] Goppelt, *Apostolische und nachapostolische Zeit*, 60.
[376] Regarding Phil 1:14, cf. Ernst, *Briefe*, 46
[377] Cf. Stuhlmacher, "Kirche," 311. On the evangelistic proclamation, cf. Ollrog, *Paulus*; following him, Vogler, "Bedeutung," 791.
[378] Cf. Käsemann, "Gottesdienst"; following him, Stuhlmacher, "Christliche Verantwortung," esp. 168–70.

act of Jesus Christ. The love of Christ enables the Christians truly to love their neighbors. The practice of this self-sacrificial love, as it was experienced and lived out in the house churches, made these groups very attractive in their surrounding environment. A similar pattern has already been observed in the primitive church in Jerusalem. This is one very significant reason for the rapid spread of the gospel in the first century.

By their very existence, house churches were of great importance for the expansion of the early Christian movement (cf. 1 Thess 1:8; 4:12; Rom 1:8; 12:17; 2 Cor 4:2; 8:21). With them a phenomenon entered the Greco-Roman world that demanded the attention of their environment.[379] Their unaffected way of relating, their brotherly love, their sense of togetherness as members of the body of Christ, from which a mutual concern for one another grew (or was supposed to grow; cf. 1 Cor 11–14)—all of this stimulated the interest of their fellow citizens and presumably led them to ask the members of these house churches why they were the way they were.[380]

In addition, "the extreme sociological and ethnoreligious barriers characteristic of the ancient world between Jew and Gentile, free and unfree, man and woman, upper and lower, educated and uneducated . . . were shattered in favor of a new bonding of all to Christ as the Lord (Gal 3:27; 1 Cor 1:26; 12:12)."[381] As a result of this soteriological principle of equality established in baptism, Christian house churches were able to compete evangelistically with other religious groups[382] that were likewise open to people from all sociological and ethnoreligious backgrounds.[383] But in comparison to those who were not open to all (e.g., the synagogue), Christian house churches had a decisive advantage.

Many scholars point to the astounding capacity of Pauline house churches to integrate people from different backgrounds.[384] Some suggest that this "brotherly love" was uniquely revolutionary.[385] If asked to give the reason for the phenomenal success of the early Christian mission, it would have to be related to the powerful attraction of this brotherly love. The message to love one another, which is anchored in the Pauline doctrine of the

---

[379] Vogler, "Bedeutung," 790; cf. also Bömer, *Die wichtigsten Kulte und Religionen,* 172, 178–79.

[380] Our texts show that this concern was not always without tension (cf. Corinth; see pp. 173–77).

[381] Stuhlmacher, *Philemon,* 74.

[382] With Stuhlmacher, *Grundlegung,* 355–56.

[383] According to the temple law of Philadelphia in Asia Minor in the first century B.C.E., "men and women, free and slaves" gathered together in the house of Zeus (Dittenberger, *Sylloge,* 985). The same group of people had access to the mystery cults in Asia Minor (cf. Berger and Colpe, *Religionsgeschichtliches Textbuch,* 274–76). Cf. also the extensive work of Schmeller, *Hierarchie,* 19–95.

[384] Weiser, "Evangelisierung im 'Haus,'" 75–76; Laub, "Sozialgeschichtlicher Hintergrund," 268–69; Lührmann, "Neutestamentliche Haustafeln," 93; Klauck, *Hausgemeinde,* 41; Theissen, *Social Setting,* 107–8.

[385] Cf., e.g., Gager, review of books, 179.

justification of all through faith in Christ alone, did not remain mere theory but was experienced in practice and lived out in exemplary fashion in the house churches. Galatians 3:28 was not simply an ideal but reflects the reality of these communities, as Theissen has plainly demonstrated at least for Corinth.[386] Jews and Gentiles, men and women, slaves and free alike came together in the house churches and sat at one table. Social tensions that became evident (cf., e.g., 1 Cor 11) arose as a consequence of this principle, but they do not negate it. Pauline house churches were both a training ground *in* brotherly love for Christians and a showcase *for* brotherly love to non-Christians.[387]

In their function as urban and regional operational bases, houses were the foundation upon which Paul built his center-focused city and international mission enterprise. Private houses provided a venue for worship and communion services. They offered a meeting place for prayer, evangelistic proclamation, and instruction or teaching; as such, they were the physical prerequisite for all church life.[388] For this reason an integral part of Paul's missional approach was to win one or more householders to faith in Christ, preferably at the very beginning of his outreach in a city. Both the undisputed Pauline Letters and the book of Acts confirm this view. Indeed, Judge identifies forty affluent upper- or higher-class individuals in Acts and the Pauline Epistles who supported the activities of Paul in a variety of ways with their houses. Even if one is not inclined to view the historical value of the book of Acts as favorably as Judge, a remarkably large number of names can be documented in an obviously reliable text in Acts and the undisputed Pauline Letters. Judge also emphasizes that it belonged to Paul's missional approach to win householders to the faith. The reason Judge suggests for this is quite stimulating: Paul "found that the most effective way of countering the opposition of the synagogues was to create an alternative platform on the strength of this connection. His mission now has the patronage of eminent persons; he preaches under their auspices; they provide him with a retinue of assistants and with an audience, including their social dependents."[389]

Leadership Structures and Organizational Formation

The Sociohistorical Approach

Why do references to those who carried out functions and held responsibility in the church seldom occur in the undisputed Pauline Letters, and why are clear statements about their activities, positions, and number almost totally absent? For instance, it is striking that Paul not once mentions elders

---

[386] Theissen, "Social Stratification in the Christian Community," in *Social Setting*, 69–119, esp. 107–8.
[387] Cf. Judge, "Social Identity," 215–17.
[388] Gielen, *Tradition*, 94; cf. Elliott, *Home*, 188–89.
[389] Judge, "Early Christians," 127–31, here 127.

in his undisputed letters. This is seen as the main argument in support of the view that Paul did not value organizational forms much and therefore did not establish any official leadership structures in his churches. Instead, Pauline churches would have had a charismatic organizational structure: there were volunteer workers but no office holders.[390]

This view has been contested for exegetical, sociological, and historical reasons. It has been suggested that an exclusive and narrow concentration on theology and ideology, along with the failure to consider sociological factors, has lead to this conclusion.[391] The problems inherent in this position have been addressed repeatedly, and extensive scholarly literature is available (see nn. 390 and 391). This section will examine the most important references to leadership structures in Pauline house churches. One of our main questions will be: can the ancient *oikos* serve as an appropriate model for explaining organizational formation and the emergence of leadership structures in Pauline congregations? Much seems to speak in favor of embracing this approach.

It seems that the sociohistorical approach is a welcome and necessary supplement to the more or less one-sided theological perspective of the past, particularly in answering the questions regarding the organization of the early Christian church.[392] This method of using sociohistorical models to describe the early church is not entirely new.[393] It was used sporadically in the 1960s by only a few and then in the 1980s by quite a number of scholars.[394] Each of the sociohistorical models with which early Christianity can be compared—for instance, the synagogue, the collegia, or the Essene community (cf. Acts 4:8, 23; 6:12; 22:5; 23:14; 25:15)—had official organizational structures.[395] Thus we should expect the same to have been true of the first Christian congregations.

---

[390] This view has been the consensus in Protestant research for almost a century. For an extensive discussion of the state of research until 1932, cf. Linton, *Problem;* until 1972, cf. Brockhaus, *Charisma,* 7–94; until 1992, cf. Burtchaell, *Synagogue,* 1–179.

[391] Cf. Brockhaus, *Charisma;* Holmberg, *Paul;* Chapple, "Local Leadership"; Burtchaell, *Synagogue;* A. Clarke, *Secular and Christian;* Campbell, *Elders;* Schmeller, *Hierarchie.*

[392] Cf. Holmberg, "Sociological versus Theological"; more extensively in *Paul.*

[393] Harnack, *Entstehung,* 17, 31–32. Before that, Hatch, *Organization* (1901), 213. Cf. an overview of available literature in H. Beyer, "ἐπίσκοπος," *TDNT* 2:608; Adam, "Entstehung," 104–13, here 104–6; Linton, *Problem,* 104–6.

[394] Cf. Judge, *Social Pattern,* 18–48; later Klauck, *Hausgemeinde;* Meeks, *First Urban Christians,* 75–84; Burtchaell, *Synagogue.*

[395] It has often been observed that the Jerusalem church with its presbyterial organization form was analogous to, or maybe even patterned after, the synagogue. Apparently collegia existed in all cities of the Roman Empire as well as in Palestine; see Kloppenborg, "Edwin Hatch," esp. 213. Studies from Bardtke, Dombrowski (literature by Kloppenborg, "Edwin Hatch," 227 n. 55), and esp. Weinfeld, *Organizational Pattern,* intend to show that even the organization of the Qumran community was significantly influenced by the Greco-Roman association. With an influence on Christian churches via Qumran, an indirect Hellenistic influence would thus be implied.

It has often been argued that the Jewish synagogue was the model after which the Pauline churches were patterned, including their organizational forms. One of the most recent attempts to demonstrate this is the work of J. T. Burtchaell.[396] His thesis is that, among other things, the first Christians patterned their organizational structures after the Jewish synagogue. Out of three offices—synagogue ruler, elder, and synagogue assistant—developed the Christian triad of *episkopos,* presbyter, and deacon. In part other names were used in order to avoid using official names used by other groups. Nevertheless, the overseers and leaders of the Pauline churches should be understood as essentially analogous to the synagogue offices.

How can it be explained, then, that in his undisputed letters Paul never mentions elders and hardly ever any other leadership functions even though in the very next generation, apparently without noteworthy controversy, office holders appear? Burtchaell rejects the old consensus and offers a new hypothesis: it is not because they did not exist. It can be assumed that from the very beginning office holders did exist in the Pauline churches; we hear nothing about them simply because they were not important.[397] The explanation for this is that initially these office holders were not the ones who had the real authority but rather the independent charismatics, such as apostles, prophets, teachers, and evangelists.[398] The charismatics led the churches; the bishops, the elders and the deacons only presided.[399] Not until the second century C.E., after the repression of the charismatics, did the institutional forces finally gain power.

Even if one is willing to recognize the strong influence of the Jewish synagogue in this process, there are a number of points in Burtchaell's hypothesis that cause concern. First, the *argumentum e silentio* is used repeatedly to support his hypothesis. Indeed, Burtchaell consistently paints with broad strokes without adequate differentiation, particularly when he portrays the Jewish synagogue as being much too uniform.[400] Second, it could be that the Jerusalem church patterned itself after the synagogue but that the churches in Antioch and in the Pauline mission did not. As we have seen, it is possible that the Jerusalem church did not orient itself to the synagogue regarding the office of elder, as this office did not exist in the synagogue. Third, it must be asked whether the distinction between leading and presiding is legitimate. For instance, "overseer" is a title that implies the carrying of

---

[396] Burtchaell, *Synagogue.*

[397] Ibid., 188, 349.

[398] Burtchaell apparently considers the apostles charismatics.

[399] Ibid., 350–51.

[400] This question is very difficult to answer. The sources are fragmentary, many are significantly younger than the period we are interested in, and they demand a local-history approach. Rajak and Noy, "ARCHISYNAGOGOI," have seriously questioned the work of Schürer, G. Vermes, Krauss, and Schrage, which many scholars, including Burtchaell, have considered authoritative (Schürer, *History,* 2:415–54; Krauss, *Synagogale Altertümer;* following him, Schrage, "συναγωγή," *TDNT* 7:798–841).

responsibility. What sense does it make to call someone an overseer if in reality he did not exercise any responsibility?[401] Besides, the hypothesis that there was a clear distinction between charismatics, who had authority in the Christian church, and bishops, elders, and deacons is not supported by the texts (see below). In addition, Burtchaell does not adequately consider the possibility that Christian leadership structures emerged from the household setting of the early Christian church.[402]

It appears that the comparison with the ancient *oikos*, as yet somewhat neglected by scholars, ought to be quite fruitful in shedding light on early Christian organizational forms.[403] Our examinations above have shown that, from the primitive church in Jerusalem to the Pauline churches and beyond, the ancient household, or rather the householder, provided early Christians with a meeting place and patronage support.[404] The extended family was often the core of the congregation and explains the rapid expansion of the Christian movement. Hence it is quite natural to ask whether the structures of the household influenced or even determined the leadership structures of the church partially or, in some cases, even extensively.[405]

Was the ancient household perhaps the matrix of the new Christian community?[406] This community met for the most part in an *oikos*. In the ancient world the *oikos* not only consisted of physical space but also was a clearly defined social environment. For the church to meet in this context meant allowing itself to be more or less influenced by this environment. This applies particularly to its organizational forms and leadership structures. "It is clear that the local Christian church's structure, which grew out of its external household setting, also significantly determined its inner life and organization."[407]

---

[401] Cf. further criticism by Klauck, book review; Campbell, *Elders*, 114–18, 203–4.

[402] Although Burtchaell mentions the house church every now and then, he appears to understand it more in the sense of a building in which people gathered, not as the faith community within the social structure of the ancient household.

[403] The ancient *oikos* has seldom been considered an analogy or a model for the organization of the early church. As the exception, cf., in addition to Campbell, *Elders*, also the little-noticed work of Chapple, "Local Leadership," and H. Maier, *Social Setting*, 1991.

[404] More and more scholars have seen this. Cf. Michel, "οἶκος," *TDNT* 5:119–33, here 130; Judge, *Social Pattern*, 1–77; Rordorf, "Was wissen wir?" 110–28, here 111. Stuhlmacher, "Exkurs: Urchristliche Hausgemeinden," in *Philemon*, 70–75; Vogler, "Bedeutung," 786–787; Klauck, *Hausgemeinde*, 99–102; Meeks, *First Urban Christians*, 75–77; White, "Domus"; Roloff, *Kirche*, 72, 142, 293. Similarly A. Schlatter, *Paulus*, 76.

[405] This does not exclude the possibility that theological considerations were also influential. It is quite possible that in this regard it was a "mysterious combination." Cf. Lampe, *Stadtrömischen Christen*, 346–48.

[406] Campbell, *Elders*, 118: "The household was more than a model; it was the matrix of the new congregation."

[407] Rordorf, "Hausgemeinde," 77. So also Klauck, *Hausgemeinde*, 101; Gnilka, *Philipperbrief*, 17; Meeks, *First Urban Christians*, 76, 84.

As previously observed, all of the evidence seems to indicate that the first Christians, from Jerusalem to Illyricum, gathered primarily in private homes. Because they met in houses, it can be assumed that they also had some kind of leadership at the house church level. The most natural thing, even from the earliest days, would have been for the host to fill this role. This would have been the Jewish housefather, in the Greco-Roman world the οἰκοδεσπότης, or *pater familias,* who made his home available to meet the needs of the congregation. This means that the leadership structures of the house church did not have to be created out of nothing. "The church in the house came with its leadership so to speak 'built in.' "[408]

Only those who were relatively wealthy were able to own (or rent) a house large enough to accommodate assembly needs of the congregation. Such affluent individuals were correspondingly educated. The position of the householder, his responsibility and protective duties, and his authority over his social dependents (family members and slaves) are all significant in this context. This far-reaching legal, economic, and religious independence and power of the ancient *oikos,* which grew out of the position of the head of the household, led E. Dassmann to the conclusion that the householder having "had special authority in the house church was only natural."[409] Because the first Christians met in private homes, house church leaders provided by the structure of the ancient *oikos* were available from the very beginning.[410] These were individuals who served the believers meeting in their homes as leaders in a pastoral and patronal sense. The householders were clearly predestined to carry out pastoral tasks—the Jewish and Greco-Roman housefathers, with their education and experience as teachers in their own families, were relatively well equipped for a teaching, leading responsibility in the church and, as a result of their experience in the financial management of their own houses, for an administrative task.[411] The religious authority and the social position of the head of the

---

[408] Campbell, *Elders,* 126.

[409] Dassmann, "Hausgemeinde," 82–97, here 89–90; Filson, "Significance," 111–12; Vogler, "Bedeutung," 792; Klauck, *Hausgemeinde,* 32; Holmberg, *Paul,* 106; Malherbe, *Social Aspects,* 64, 67. For a criticism of this view, cf. Schöllgen, "Hausgemeinden."

On the position of the householder, cf. Badian, *Foreign Clientelae,* 1–14; Judge, *Social Patterns,* ch. 3; Strobel, "Begriff"; Theissen, *Social Setting,* 154–55; Gülzow, "Soziale Gegebenheiten," 192–93, 198–99; Gaudemet, "Familie," 331–33; Malherbe, *Social Aspects,* 69; Saller, *Personal Patronage;* Vittinghoff, "Gesellschaft," 163–277, esp. 169, 175–77; Meeks, *First Urban Christians,* 76; Winter, *Seek the Welfare,* 11–78.

[410] Cf. Vogler, "Bedeutung," 792.

[411] Filson, "Significance," 111. He observes that the host of a house church "was . . . almost inevitably a man of some education, with a fairly broad background and at least some administrative ability . . . they were likely candidates for leadership." On Jewish housefathers, see A. Klostermann, *Schulwesen,* 4–10; Ebener, *Elementary Education,* 17–19; Safrai, "Home"; Goppelt, *Apostolische und nachapostol-*

household are also good reason to assume that he or she participated in presiding over the Lord's Supper. Much seems to support the likelihood "that, analogously to the Jewish and in part to the pagan mealtime customs, the housefather—specifically, the host in whose house they met—presided over the meal" (see pp. 217-19).[412]

The leadership role of the householder was also well established in the system of patronage and sanctioned as a custom common throughout the empire.[413] This system was understood and accepted both by those who exercised this authority and by those who benefited from it. Through their position as patrons or householders, they also enjoyed a certain honor socially and were thus equipped for leadership tasks involving community affairs.[414]

Schöllgen draws attention, however, to recent scholarship that has concluded that the extended family with the powerful householder at its head, familiar from earlier periods, was the exception for the first century.[415] In response, it must be pointed out first that it is disputed in which regions and to what extent this development actually took place. Scholars agree only that a general tendency toward the disintegration of the extended family is observable for our period. Apparently this development began as early as the pre-NT period and continued into the Mishnaic period. Second, for our thesis it suffices to conclude that the extended family with its powerful head still existed even as the exception. My contention is that those who were able to make their homes available to the church as a meeting place were in the minority; large numbers of such individuals were not required.

In addition, analogies in the history of religion support our view. Two examples are sufficient illustration. The first is from a Jewish context. As the house synagogues provide a parallel to the Christian house churches, so the

---

ische Zeit, 133 ("Many were involved in teaching in the church from householders to apostles"). This custom appears to be universal in the ancient world. Cf. Dürr, "Heilige Vaterschaft"; Hermisson, *Studien*, 103–8; Marrou, *Geschichte*, 31–46, 341–43; Barclay, *Educational Ideals*, 49–77; Blomenkamp, "Erziehung," 6:503–59, here 510.

[412] Klauck, *Herrenmahl*, 349–50; cf. also *Hausgemeinde*, 43; F. Maier, *Paulus*, 28; D. Smith, "Social Obligation"; Ysebaert, *Amtsterminologie*, 87.

[413] Cf. Saller, *Personal Patronage;* MacMullen, *Roman Social Relations*, 61, 125; cf. Danker, *Benefactor*, for the significance of the system of patronage in the NT.

[414] Cf. Elliott, *Home*, 189–90. For the system of patronage in general and specifically for its significance in the Corinthian church at the time of Paul, cf. Chow, *Patronage*, esp. chs. 2 and 3. Recognition of the significance of patronage for the early Christian mission is not new. Cf. Judge, *Social Pattern*, ch. 3, and "Early Christians." Judge's insights are being adopted by more and more scholars; cf., e.g., Holmberg, *Paul*, 104–7; Elliott, *Home*, 188–99; C. S. Hill, "Sociology," 260–61; Chapple, "Local Leadership," 217–55; White, *Building God's House*, 77–85, 140–48; Meeks, *First Urban Christians*, 1993; A. Clarke, *Secular and Christian*, 9–39.

[415] Dassmann and Schöllgen, "Haus II," 13:805–6, 811–12, 815–29, 843–53. See pp. 210–25, the excursus on leadership responsibilities of women in Pauline house churches, esp. nn. 535 and 559, for further literature on this new research.

patrons of these synagogues offer an analogy to the householders of the house churches. Evidence of this has been found in connection with the synagogue in Stobi, though not until the third century C.E.[416] A certain Claudius Tiberius Polycharmus financed the remodeling of his own house in order that the Jewish community would be able to use the lower floor for assembly while he and his family lived in the upper story. In appreciation of his gift, he was given the title ὁ πατὴρ τῆς Στόβις συναγωγῆς.[417]

The similarities to the Christian patrons in our second example (a religious association) are even more striking. An inscription originating from the early second or late first century B.C.E. tells of a certain Dionysius. The extensive study of this inscription done by S. C. Barton and G. H. R. Horsley demonstrates that he made his house available to the religious association as a meeting place.[418] In addition, the members of his house formed the core of this community. Dionysius himself did not have official leadership status in the group, but as the "host-benefactor" he played a special role in the life of the religious association.[419] Barton and Horsley point out a series of similarities between the religious association and Christian house churches, in particular regarding the significance of the patron: "Hence, the initiative taken by Dionysius . . . to widen access to the cult located in his οἶκος is analogous to the initiative of those men and women of means amongst the early Christians who . . . opened their houses to the gatherings of believers."[420] As we will see, both of these examples provide important analogies to the role of the householder in Pauline house churches.[421]

References to Leadership Structures in Pauline House Churches

Those who hold to the widespread opinion that Paul established his churches without institutional order and entirely open to the free working of the Spirit have overlooked the central importance Paul placed on the office of

---

[416] Cf. Hengel, "Synagogenschrift"; on Stobi, Delos, and other synagogues in connection with houses and patrons, cf. White, "Domus," 241–378, 437–74, and *Building God's House*, 62–77.

[417] This title was also used in synagogues in Rome. Here and there it was "given to rich members of the congregation, who invested their social and financial power for the benefit of the group" (Hengel, "Synagogenschrift," 122).

[418] Barton and Horsley, "Hellenistic Cult Group," 7–41, here 8–10. For a differing opinion, cf. Stowers, "Cult."

[419] Barton and Horsley, "Hellenistic Cult Group," 22.

[420] Ibid., 28.

[421] In my opinion, the association does not form an alternative model to the significance of the private domestic house in early Christian missions. We know of cases in which associations "were formed in close conjunction with specific households" (Meeks, *First Urban Christians*, 77). Cf., e.g., *CIL* 6.9148 "Collegium quod est in domu Sergiae Paullinae"; the cultic association of Agdistis in Philadelphia and further examples by White, *Building God's House*, 26–59; Klauck, *Hausgemeinde*, 83–92.

apostle.[422] "The institutionalization of leadership functions within the individual congregation was not an urgent necessity as long as Paul himself, as 'a called apostle of Jesus Christ' (1 Cor 1:1; cf. Rom 1:1; Gal 1:1; etc.), led the churches. His letters are actually nothing other than the media for exercising this leadership function from a distance."[423] In 1 Cor 4:15 Paul calls himself the only true "father" of the church in Corinth. In ancient society his authority to portray himself to the congregation through the image of fatherhood has a legal connotation. Paul exercised his authority by educating, teaching, and exhorting.[424] In light of this, the suggestion that, because there is no indication of institutionalization in Corinth, Paul left everything up to the free working of the Spirit is inadmissible and finds no support in the text.[425]

In addition, the lack of clear signs of institutionalization is not proof that absolutely no leadership functions existed in the Pauline churches. There are many references indicating that from the very beginning there were individuals in Paul's churches in addition to him who carried responsibility partly with clear-cut titles and ongoing functions. Almost all of the elements of what later became the Christian office were already present: duration, authority, title, and legitimization through a letter of recommendation, special status, and payment.[426]

Thessalonica

In his first letter to the Thessalonians (5:12-14) only a few months after the founding of the church about 50 C.E., Paul mentions a specific group of individuals with ongoing leadership functions and a clearly recognizable special status in the group.[427] All exegetes are in agreement regarding the meaning of κοπιάω, "to exert oneself, to work hard," and νουθετέω, "to exhort, to warn."[428] Paul uses the term κοπιάω elsewhere as well in order to

---

[422] Cf., on the topic of the leadership structures in general, Brockhaus, *Charisma*, 95-127; Holmberg, *Paul*, 96-123; Roloff, *Kirche*, 132-43. With a somewhat different view from ours is Banks, *Paul's Idea*, esp. 139-48.

[423] Roloff, "Ansätze," 124; cf. also Roloff, *Der erste Brief*, 172 n. 315.

[424] Holmberg, *Paul*, 78; following him, Roloff, "Ansätze," 125.

[425] Cf. also F. Maier, *Paulus*, 68, 73, 78.

[426] Brockhaus, *Charisma* (1991), 123; cf. 24-25 n. 106 for his definition of "office" and a list of the criteria for the Christian office. Cf. also the definition of "office" in Roloff, *Kirche*, 139: "An office exists if a function that is necessary for establishing and maintaining the church is exercised by the same individuals with a certain regularity and duration over time."

[427] 1 Thess 5:12; cf. 1 Tim 5:17 with similar terminology for the presbyter. As representatives of the Protestant consensus, cf., e.g., Dibelius, *Thessaloniker, Philipper,* 26; Dobschütz, *Thessalonicher-Briefe*, 215-59; Laub, *Eschatologische Verkündigung*, 85. In support of the view here, cf. also Chapple, "Local Leadership," 209. Cf. also the dispute between Harnack and Dibelius/Dobschütz; Harnack, regarding 1 Thess 5:12, decides against them for the interpretation "office holder" (κόπος, esp. 7-10). The church there is very young; cf. Acts 17; 1 Thess 3:1-6; Kümmel, *Einleitung*, 183.

[428] On κοπιάω, Bauer-Aland⁶, 901 (BDAG 558). On νουθετέω, Bauer-Aland⁶, 1101 (BDAG 679).

describe his preaching and teaching ministry (e.g., 1 Thess 3:5; Gal 4:11; 1 Cor 3:8; Phil 2:16). He seldom uses the term for the ministry of others, but when he does, it is in the context of church ministry (e.g., 1 Cor 16:15–16; Rom 16:6, 12; and also here 1 Thess 5:12—cf. ἐν ὑμῖν).[429] Even though Paul understands the task of exhorting (νουθετέω) as the responsibility of all Christians (cf. 1 Thess 5:14), here he refers to those "who exhort you" as a specific group who does this task with a certain regularity. Hence their task is to be distinguished from the general responsibility of all Christians quantitatively but not necessarily qualitatively. The observation that together the three participles in verse 12 have only one article and that τὸ ἔργον αὐτῶν in verse 13 is singular clearly indicates that not just functions but a specific group of individuals is intended, for whom Paul demands the recognition and respect of the congregation.[430] He thereby acknowledges their special status in the group and strengthens their position by giving his clear recommendation. Here it becomes evident that Paul's request that these individuals be respected, without referring to their title, can be seen to support our hypothesis that initially a person's status as office holder did not appear worth mentioning and that over time the office holders naturally emerged out of the house church setting (for the sociohistorical approach, see above).

In contrast to κοπιάω and νουθετέω, the meaning of προΐσταμαι in verse 12 as well as in Rom 12:8 is disputed. Some exegetes prefer the first possible translation, "be at the head, lead, rule, direct, administrate"; others favor the second, "be concerned about, care for, give aid."[431] The rigid alternative between "caretaker" and "ruler," however, is unnecessary. In classical Greek as well as in the NT, both connotations are intended by the term.[432] One does not need to choose between leading and helping; the help that is given here is the protection and material support of a patron.[433] The following translation of the term unites all of these elements: "to act as patron or protector."[434] This is supported by the observation that the three

---

[429] Cf. Chapple, "Local Leadership," 216, for proof that κοπιᾶν is used by Paul as a semitechnical term for this type of activity; Paul was confident that the Thessalonians clearly understood the word.

[430] Greeven, "Propheten" (1977), 348; Schürmann, "Die geistlichen Gnadengaben," 362–412, here 399 n. 132; Brockhaus, *Charisma,* 107–8 (that the text speaks of "active persons, not of activities"); Chapple, "Local Leadership," 211–15.

[431] Bauer-Aland⁶, 1415–16 (BDAG 870–71), mentions both possibilities without deciding for one or the other.

[432] Cf. esp. P.Tebt. II 326 (ca. 266 C.E.); *SIG* 700 (ca. 118–117 B.C.E.); Greeven, "Propheten" (1977), 346 n. 74; Reicke, "προΐστημι," *TDNT* 6:700–703; following him, Brockhaus, *Charisma,* 106; Chapple, "Local Leadership," 218–19.

[433] Michel, *Römer,* 379; Wilckens, *Römer,* 3:15; Dunn, *Romans 9–16,* 2:731.

[434] Important commentaries support the translation "protecting patron": Dobschütz, *Thessalonicher-Briefe,* 216; Dibelius, *Thessaloniker, Philipper;* Best, *Thessalonians.* Cf. also Greeven, "Propheten" (1977), 346 n. 74; Chapple, "Local Leadership," 217–32, here 221–22; Meeks, *First Urban Christians,* 134; following him, Branick, *House Church,* 85–88, 91.

parallel participles in 1 Thess 5:12—derived from κοπιάω, νουθετέω, and προΐσταμαι—denote functions of one single role, indeed the role of the protecting patron. In Rom 12:8 the two terms parallel to προϊστάμενος, namely μεταδιδούς and ἐλεῶν, make the option for the translation "protecting patron" even more sensible.[435] The adverb σπουδῇ also fits well with the role of the patron (cf. Gal 2:10, where ἐσπούδασα describes Paul's efforts for the poor). The triad of participles in 1 Thess 5:12 finds its echo in the word pair ἀντιλήμψεις / κυβερνήσεις in 1 Cor 12:28, where "help" is probably also to be understood as material assistance.[436]

Such individuals provided Paul with such assistance many times in the context of his mission by making their houses available as a meeting place and by offering hospitality, good standing, and protection. Helpful in translating the multifaceted term προΐσταμαι in our context is the verbal substantive derived from it—προστάτις, which means "protector" (Rom 16:2). Paul justifies his request to support Phoebe by pointing out that she served many as their protector (see p. 143, esp. n. 137). As we have seen, the help that Phoebe provided for Paul and others was given as hospitality in the context of a patronage relationship. It can be assumed that she took on leading responsibilities in her house church.[437] It can also be expected that those who served as patrons in other Pauline congregations, including in Thessalonica, were viewed as leaders in their house churches.

Their leadership responsibility is not simply identical, however, with the duties of a patron. G. Heinrici correctly pointed out long ago that both participles κοπιῶντες and νουθετοῦντες imply a different task from that of the ancient patron.[438] In the patron-client relationship a different ethos was in effect from what Paul had in mind for the Thessalonians. The clientele received various *beneficia* from the patron, and in return he was given *gratia* in the form of honor and the personal loyalty of his clients. In contrast, the relationship of the Christian προϊστάμενοι to the Thessalonian church was characterized by the relationship of both to Christ. The patron is therefore ἐν κυρίῳ, in consequence of which he is no longer to seek his own honor but rather the honor of the Lord by serving the church. Conversely, the members of the church are no longer clients of the προϊστάμενοι but rather ἀδελφοί in the Lord. For this reason the translation "patron" is not to be understood in the formal or legal sense, referring to the patron's secular rights and powers. Once again it has become clear that the ancient *oikos* and the Christian ecclesia are not identical.

"The caretaking authority that these individuals possessed and exercised as προϊστάμενοι implies an element of leadership and is not conceivable

---

[435] So Bengel, *Gnomon*, 554: "qui alios curat et in clientela habet."
[436] Brockhaus, *Charisma*, 109 nn. 76, 78; following him Holmberg, *Paul*, 100–101.
[437] On the question of the leadership position of Phoebe, see pp. 210–25, the excursus on leadership responsibilities of women.
[438] G. Heinrici, "Christengemeinde," esp. 516–20.

without the element of duration. These were therefore ongoing leadership functions."⁴³⁹ In 1 Thess 5:12–13 Paul draws attention to a group of individuals who worked hard for the church, cared for it, and instructed, exhorted, and led it. Over time this effort would have given them a special status within the congregation. "A position of authority grows out of the benefits that persons of relatively higher wealth and status could confer on the community."⁴⁴⁰ From this it becomes clear that authority and service stand in close correlation to one another.⁴⁴¹

As early as 1909, Ernst von Dobschütz listed, regarding our passage (1 Thess 5:12), ten different functions of προϊστάμενοι in his commentary on the letters to the Thessalonians: "Providing the meeting place for the worship service; perhaps maintaining the necessary order at the meeting; praying, reading, and singing; providing room and board for the traveling brothers; providing support for the poor; putting up bond (cf. Jason, Acts 17:19); representation in court; at times perhaps a trip on behalf of the congregation—in short, all the duties that later fell to the church leader."⁴⁴²

Without explicitly mentioning it, Dobschütz described the duties of the patron of a local house church. B. Holmberg points out that most of these functions imply a certain degree of wealth and status: a house that was large enough to serve as a meeting place for the church; time and leisure to care for the needs of others; and the financial means necessary to do all this.⁴⁴³ The description fits quite well for the householder. Thus it appears likely that the προϊστάμενοι in Thessalonica were, at least in part, householders and leaders of house churches.⁴⁴⁴

We can also assume that even in the earliest months individuals existed in the church in Thessalonica who, as a result of their service and status, were viewed as church leaders. Considering that 1 Thessalonians was written to such a young church, which was not characterized by inner-congregational conflict, some scholars have assumed that these conditions—above all, the budding organizational forms of a young congregation—can be generalized and applied to the other Pauline churches.⁴⁴⁵

One question regarding such a reconstruction, however, needs to be raised. How did all this develop in such a short time? If it is assumed that Paul did not appoint leaders, if such authority grows out of ongoing service,

---

⁴³⁹ Brockhaus, *Charisma*, 108. Cf. also Ysebaert, *Amtsterminologie*, 74.
⁴⁴⁰ Meeks, *First Urban Christians*, 134.
⁴⁴¹ Brockhaus, *Charisma*, 124. Serving is characteristic of the function that is mentioned here. But this does not exclude the possibility that the serving person also exercises a leading function in the congregation. Cf. also Holmberg, *Paul*, 102.
⁴⁴² Dobschütz, *Thessalonicher-Briefe*, 216.
⁴⁴³ Holmberg, *Paul*, 102–3.
⁴⁴⁴ So Schürmann, "'. . . und Lehrer,'" 135.
⁴⁴⁵ Laub, "Paulus," esp. 17, 32.

if a longer period of time must be assumed before the congregation would recognize such individuals as leaders, how could all this already be in place after a few short months?

The model of the ancient *oikos* and the assumption that house churches existed in Thessalonica go a long way to explain how this could have happened. For the congregation that met in a house, a leadership structure was already in place from the very beginning, built into the social infrastructure of the ancient *oikos* in advance. As seen previously, the legal, economic, and religious power of the ancient *oikos*, power that grew out of the position of the householder, all suggest that the leadership of a house church would naturally gravitate to the head of the household.[446]

This is also a possible explanation for why leadership structures were already in place in Thessalonica after such a short time. Our hypothesis is supported by the observation that Acts 17:1–9 reports on such a man by name in Thessalonica. According to Luke, Jason provided Paul hospitality and patronal protection during the first days of the existence of the church in Thessalonica. It is very likely that he and others continued to provide this service and that they, as the προϊστάμενοι τῆς ἐκκλησίας, made their homes available to the congregation as gathering places.

Colossae

The hypothesis of the emergence of leadership structures from the house setting is confirmed by what we know of Philemon's house church in or near Colossae. There the homeowner and host Philemon is called "fellow worker," and Archippus, a friend of the house, a "fellow soldier." Both terms are titles that were used by Paul as references to some special effort in the mission or in building a church.[447] "At any rate, an inner structuring of the house church can be seen in the text. Structures are in development and evolving out of the natural setting [of the ancient *oikos*]. Figures and functions are beginning to crystallize."[448]

This leads to the question whether Paul installed leaders or let them emerge from the household setting. Did these leaders have an office, or did they do their tasks as voluntary activities? Again the rigid distinction between installed office holders and voluntary co-laborers is an inappropriate alternative.[449] They were not full-fledged office holders (this is not to be expected after such a short time), nor were they merely voluntary coworkers. Their position "is neither official nor incompatible with office, but informal

---

[446] Cf. p. 194, n. 409; also Hainz, *Ekklesia*, 346: "One can assume that a certain leading function fell to the homeowners on the basis of their natural position in the ἐκκλησία that met in their house."

[447] Hainz, *Ekklesia*, 203; esp. Ollrog, *Paulus*, 63–72, 74–75, 90–92. Cf. 1 Thess 3:2; Rom 16:3, 9, 21; 1 Cor 3:9; Phil 2:25; 4:3; 2 Cor 1:24; 8:23.

[448] Klauck, *Hausgemeinde*, 43. So also Hainz, *Ekklesia*, 346–48.

[449] Brockhaus, *Charisma*, 107.

and *tending towards office.*"⁴⁵⁰ The view that we should not set up a false alternative here is confirmed by the observation that Luke himself used ambivalent language in this regard. In Acts 14:23 he indicates that Barnabas and Paul install presbyters through the laying on of hands in every congregation, yet in 20:28 he speaks of an installation through the Holy Spirit.⁴⁵¹

In addition, it is important to recognize that three factors most likely interacted with one another in the overall process: Paul as the founder and "father" of the congregation, the local congregation itself, and the leader in question. The main initiative came from one of the parties, but all three needed to agree at some point that the said function was authentic and useful or, in the words of Paul, a χάρισμα from God to his church.⁴⁵² Even if Paul did not install leaders in any of his churches, those who were active as leaders in an individual congregation received confirmation in that role from both Paul and the congregation. In a house church it would have been quite natural, perhaps even taken for granted, that the householder would gravitate toward or be given a leading role.⁴⁵³ "It is fair to argue that in Paul's presence, as in his absence, household leadership emerged 'from below' in the community and was legitimated 'from above' by the apostle."⁴⁵⁴

Corinth

Conclusions simliar to those for Thessalonica can be drawn for the house of Stephanas from the short note in 1 Cor 16:15–16. Here Paul challenges the Corinthians to submit (ὑποτάσσεσθαι) to the house of Stephanas and all other individuals who in the same way work hard for the church. It is clearly evident in this context that Stephanas and some others in the Corinthian church had a special position and exercised a leading role. This is related partly to the fact that they were from the congregation's founding generation. This is underscored in a twofold manner. First, Paul refers to Stephanas and the members of his household with the honorific title ἀπαρχὴ τῆς Ἀχαίας. That this designation was a common title of

---

⁴⁵⁰ Chapple, "Local Leadership," 254 (italics added); cf. H. Beyer, "ἐπίσκοπος," *TDNT* 2:619; M. MacDonald, *Pauline Churches,* 53; Holmberg, *Paul,* 112–13. Some (but not all) of the criteria that Brockhaus views as essential for office are observable in 1 Thess 5:12: continuity, recognition by the church, and special position. Nevertheless their position cannot yet be called an office.

⁴⁵¹ Even if one does not consider these references historically reliable, they are at least proof that Luke did not view the two as rigid alternatives.

⁴⁵² Holmberg, *Paul,* 109.

⁴⁵³ Branick, *House Church,* 91–92: "The fact that Paul never explicitly mentions any such special leaders at Christian assembly is significant. Nowhere even remotely do we find any concern for a 'validly ordained' . . . minister. . . . It is precisely in the absence of such a concern on the part of Paul, that we should presume a presiding role for the host, man or women, the head of the household who becomes the patron of the assembly."

⁴⁵⁴ H. Maier, *Social Setting* (1991), 39. Here he follows—as does Holmberg (*Paul,* 119)—Laub ("Paulus," 34–35), who calls this "eine originäre Über- und Unterordnung."

honor in the early church can be seen in Rom 16:5. Before and after the name, an honoring attribute is always added. As "first fruits of Achaia" they are Christians from the very first days of the mission who were involved from the start in spreading the gospel and building the church. Second, they were baptized by Paul himself (1 Cor 1:16), which also means that Paul led them to Christ. For all these reasons they enjoyed special status in that region of the mission.[455]

In addition, Paul not only acknowledges the special status of Stephanas and his people but emphasizes it with the addition "and they devoted themselves to the service of the saints" (1 Cor 16:15). Paul was thereby soliciting appreciation and recognition for them and was admonishing the believers to submit to these individuals (16:16). This group of individuals has earned this submission and this recognition, just as the leadership in the Thessalonian church did, by serving the congregation and working hard for it: "submit to such as these and everyone who joins in the work and labors at it."[456] Surely a part of Stephanas's service referred to here included making his house available as a meeting place and, as patron of a house church, providing and caring for the group.[457] It is quite clear, then, that Stephanas and his people played a leading role in the Corinthian church.[458] It would be premature, however, on the basis of this single passage, to suggest that by the time 1 Corinthians was written, office holders already existed in the Corinthian church. But that an office would emerge from this is already evident at this stage in the development.[459]

Even though the organizational forms were in flux, Paul still expected that certain members of the Corinthian congregation would attempt to resolve the internal conflicts (6:1–5). We can assume that there were individuals in a position to expel from the congregation members who were behaving immorally (5:1–5). Paul does not give clear instructions on how this is to be done; he apparently assumes the congregation is capable and trusts its leadership to take the correct steps to take care of the problem. Paul is like a father to them (4:14; cf. also 1 Thess 2:5–12, esp. 7; Gal 4:19) and wants to raise "his children" to be self-reliant. He expects them to grow up and become adults who are able to take care of their own affairs (1 Cor 3:1–4). In such a situation it can be assumed that leadership structures emerge fairly rapidly in order to deal with such conflicts, problems, and other matters. At any rate, it has been clearly demonstrated that Paul was anything but

---

[455] Cf. also Rom 16:5. Lietzmann, *Korinther,* 89; Dodd, *Romans,* 237; Conzelmann, *Der erst Brief,* 357; similarly Banks, *Paul's Idea,* 142.

[456] These two terms—"joins in the work" and "labors at it"—belong to the specific missional terminology of Paul.

[457] Campenhausen, *Kirchliches Amt,* 72.

[458] In addition to Stephanas, Fortunatus and Achaicus appear to have belonged to the leadership in the Corinthian church. Cf. 1 Cor 16:17–18.

[459] Cf. Roloff, *Kirche,* 139 n. 130; Brockhaus, *Charisma,* 110–12; Hainz, *Ekklesia,* 98–101; Chapple, "Local Leadership," 444.

indifferent to the question of leadership; rather he was "deeply concerned with the nature of the leadership which did exist in the community."[460]

In addition to the "hard working" authorities in the early days, there is also reference to concrete tasks with formal titles.[461] In 1 Cor 12:28 Paul mentions the "office triad" of apostles, prophets, and teachers. The designations of prophet and teacher are somewhat older than the titleless leadership functions in Thessalonica. They most likely originated from the early Palestinian church[462] and were handed on from there to the church in Antioch, as can be observed in reliable texts in Acts.[463] Here Paul apparently has the Antioch model in mind. There Spirit-filled prophets and teachers directed the life of the church. Following this model, Paul speaks about the church as the body of Christ or as a charismatic corporation in which the Spirit-gifted apostles, prophets, and teachers carry leadership responsibilities (see p. 110).[464]

These titles were evidently used quite early in Pauline churches. As early as the composition of 1 Corinthians (ca. 55 C.E.), prophets were an integral part of the worship service in Corinth as a clearly defined group of individuals.[465] A concrete reference to such activity by teachers does not exist. The mention of teachers in 1 Cor 12:28 is an indication, however, that they were well known in Corinth. In addition, the function of teaching (κατηχῶν) is documented for the church in Galatia.[466] There Paul asserts that an instructor has the right to expect material and financial support from the church.[467] It could have been members of the local congregation who had committed themselves more or less to a full-time teaching ministry and were therefore in need of support from the church. It could also have been teachers who traveled, as Paul and others, from city to city and for this reason depended on the support. Either way we can conclude from all this that we

---

[460] A. Clarke, *Secular and Christian*, 132. Clarke delivers convincing arguments that leadership structures existed in Corinth and that Paul was very much interested in them (pp. 130–32).

[461] Much has been written on 1 Cor 12–14 and the so-called charismatic church order. We will not enter this discussion here, as it goes beyond the parameters of our study. Cf. Brockhaus, *Charisma,* part 3, who, along with Bultmann, Schweizer, Roloff, Käsemann, and Ridderbos, does not see "charisma" and "office" as being mutually exclusive. Cf. also with him Roloff, *Kirche,* 138–39, and *Apostolat,* 126.

[462] Dautzenberg, *Urchristliche Prophetie;* Aune, *Prophecy.*

[463] Acts 11:28; 13:1; 21:10; also Matt 10:41; Rev 11:18; 16:6; 18:20. Cf. Schürmann, "Die geistlichen Gnadengaben," 389; Brockhaus, *Charisma,* 97 n. 11.

[464] Compare 1 Cor 12:12–31 and Rom 12:4–8 with Acts 13:1–2. With Stuhlmacher, "Kirche," 309.

[465] Greeven, "Propheten" (1977), 305–61, here 309–15. Compare 1 Cor 12:8–10; 14:37 with 1 Cor 11:5.

[466] Gal 6:6; cf. also 1:12; Rom 6:17; 12:7; 16:17; 1 Cor 4:17; 14:26; Col 2:7.

[467] Brockhaus, *Charisma,* 101–3, convincingly demonstrates this. Cf. also H. Beyer, "κατηχέω," *TDNT* 3:638–40. For an overview of the various exegetes on this passage, cf. Schlier, *Galater,* 275 nn. 2 and 3; Oepke, *Galater,* 150.

are dealing with a somewhat formal, ongoing, and more or less full-time function in the church.[468]

The apostolate is more complicated. There is no uniform usage of the term "apostle" in the NT. Even before Paul's time two different meanings for the term existed:[469] the "appearance" apostolate and the "congregation" apostolate.[470] Both are very old and designate leadership functions with high authority. In 1 Cor 12:28 the term "apostle" is most likely a reference to the appearance apostolate.[471] Accordingly, then, Paul is the only such apostle in Corinth.

From the same text we learn that other, less exceptional gifts also existed: especially ἀντιλήμπψεις and κυβερνήσεις. These signify assistance, leading, and administration—in other words, abilities that are needed for church leadership. The authority of these individuals was based primarily on their own service and labor in and for the church (cf. 1 Cor 16:15–16). This suggests that their function was much like that of the προϊστάμενοι in 1 Thess 5:12 and Rom 12:8.[472] This supports the assumption that the function of the homeowner and host of the house church was identical with that of the προϊστάμενοι and to be understood coming under the κυβερνήσεις.[473] This strengthens the hypothesis that the προϊστάμενοι can be viewed partially as "overseers" of house churches and as "prestructures" of the office of overseer that we find more fully developed in Philippi.[474]

Philippi

In the introduction to the Letter to the Philippians (Phil 1:1), ἐπίσκοποι and διάκονοι are mentioned. Unfortunately, nothing more is said about these functions.[475] Nevertheless, the passage has great significance for our question on leadership structures in the Pauline churches. If we consider that the only mention of ἐπίσκοποι in any undisputed Pauline letter occurs in the

---

[468] Greeven, "Propheten" (1977), 325–26; Brockhaus, *Charisma*, 101–3; Roloff, *Kirche*, 139.

[469] Cf. Brockhaus, "Exkurs zum doppelten Apostelbegriff," in *Charisma*, 112–23.

[470] An appearance apostle is one who had experienced a postresurrection appearance of Jesus. Examples of congregation apostles are Silvanus and Timothy (1 Thess 2:7); Andronicus and Junia (Rom 16:7); cf. 2 Cor 8:11 and 11:5. Cf. also Stephanas as a temporary church apostle in 1 Cor 16:15–18; Phil 2:25–30; 2 Cor 8:18–19; here reference is made to "church envoys."

[471] Wolff, *Der erste Brief*, 305–6; Barrett, *1 Corinthians*, 293; Fee, *1 Corinthians*, 620. With a different view, F. Maier, *Paulus*, 69.

[472] Bourke, "Reflections," 493–511, here 501; Holmberg, *Paul*, 100–103.

[473] So also Hainz, *Ekklesia*, 346.

[474] So also Schürmann, "'. . . und Lehrer,'" 135.

[475] For this reason those who have not shown much openness for an episcopal church order in Pauline congregations have attempted to minimize the significance of this reference to ἐπίσκοποι. But one cannot ignore it—it is there, moreover, in a text that does not have a text-historical variant of note. For a discussion of the different attempts to explain the text, cf. Best, "Bishops," esp. 372 n. 1; Schenk, "Philipperbrief," 25.4:3280–3313, here 3286.

one that was written to the church that, in Paul's view, was in many ways an exemplary congregation, it becomes all the more important.

In spite of the text's brevity, some information can be gleaned from it. First, it is quite clear that multiple individuals exercised a leadership function in the church in Philippi. Moreover, this function is unmistakably designated as an office.[476] Paul uses ἐπίσκοποι and διάκονοι as technical terms. He assumes that the church knows what they mean and that he therefore does not need to explain them.[477] In addition to the saints, he particularly mentions the ἐπίσκοποι and the διάκονοι because they have a special position and function in the congregation.[478] Hence in Philippi, even more clearly than in Thessalonica and in Corinth, we have concrete reference to a formal, ongoing leadership function and an obviously special position for those who carry out the function.[479]

It is striking that, when discussing our passage, most commentators exercise a remarkable reluctance to reflect on the social setting of the overseer function of the ἐπίσκοποι in the Philippian church.[480] If we ask, however, what or whom the ἐπίσκοποι in Philippi led, everything seems to indicate that they were overseers of the churches that met in their homes, much like Stephanas in Corinth; in other words, they were leaders of individual house churches.[481] Together as a group such overseers could have formed the leadership team or council for the whole local church in that city.[482]

Everything that we know about house churches in Jerusalem, Antioch, and the Pauline cities supports the above assumption. House churches appear as the point of departure for the development of the local church in these cities. As already demonstrated, missional outreach targeting householders was an intentional aspect of Paul's evangelistic approach. The

---

[476] Cf., e.g., Lohmeyer, *Briefe*, 12; O'Brien, *Philippians*, 48–49.

[477] Ysebaert, *Amtsterminologie*, 63.

[478] Gnilka, *Philipperbrief*, 40. Here one could argue that Paul is referring to a voluntary activity (e.g., the sending of gifts to Paul, Phil 4:10–12) but not to an office. Cf. H. Beyer, "ἐπίσκοπος," *TDNT* 2:616: "If Paul were intending merely to greet those who had collected and sent the love-offering, he would have said so, and not used two words commonly employed by the Greeks as titles. As the words stand, they refer to those whose responsibility is that of ἐπισκοπεῖν and διακονεῖν."

[479] Brockhaus, *Charisma*, 124; Chapple, "Local Leadership," 578–87.

[480] The hypothesis that *episkopoi* were generally overseers of house churches who jointly led the local church is not at all new. Indeed, it can be traced all the way back to Baur (cf. *Pastoralbriefe*, 83–84). For the exception to the above-mentioned reluctance, cf. Roloff, *Der erste Brief*, 171–77; Pilhofer, *Philippi*, 140–47.

[481] Cf. Hainz, "Anfänge," 105; following him, Dassmann, "Hausgemeinde," 89. So also Roloff, *Der erste Brief*, 171–73; Chapple, "Local Leadership," 558–73.

[482] Cf. Schürmann, "'. . . und Lehrer,'" 135 n. 122; Roloff, *Kirche*, 142; Rohde, *Urchristliche und frühkatholische Ämter*, 45, who all presume this for the early Christian and the Pauline churches in general. Cf. also Dassmann, "Hausgemeinde," 89–90; so also Gnilka, *Philipperbrief*, 32, 34; F. F. Bruce, "St. Paul," 282–83; more recently Chapple, "Local Leadership," 558; following him, Campbell, *Elders*, 125. With a different view, Hainz, *Ekklesia*, 346–47.

church in Corinth offers the best illustration. As previously observed, from the very beginning the leadership of the house churches was in the hands of men and women of means, homeowners such as Stephanas, Gaius, and Crispus. These were the type of people Paul attempted to reach for Christ early in his mission in a given city in the hope that they would make their house available as a base of operations for outreach. This was most likely his approach in Thessalonica (see Acts 17 and Jason, above). It can be assumed that in Philippi he also recognized the importance of energetic, influential individuals for his mission and for the establishment of local congregations.[483] Luke reports that, right at the start of his ministry in Philippi, Paul was able to win two well-to-do householders to Christ (see Acts 16, Lydia and the jailer, above) in order that their houses might become centers for further missional work. After his departure and in his absence, he most likely left the householders in charge of these house churches.

Our text (Phil 1:1) does not give a clear indication of the actual tasks of the διάκονοι and the ἐπίσκοποι. Considering both the central significance of the Lord's Supper and the house church setting in the Pauline mission—particularly in Philippi—much seems to support the following reconstruction. Up until the composition of the Letter to the Philippians, the number of Christians in Philippi apparently so grew that multiple houses were necessary as ongoing places of assembly. This would be a plausible explanation for the plural number of overseers in 1:1.[484] Each house church needed someone to preside over the celebration of the Lord's Supper and to provide support and leadership for the worship service.[485] The householders who made their homes available would have been likely candidates for such a responsibility. There is much in support of the view that the ἐπίσκοποι in 1:1 were hosts and leaders of house churches in Philippi.[486]

The διάκονοι may well have been the assistants of the ἐπίσκοποι.[487] It is not certain, however, that two different offices are intended. Several interpretations are possible: "those who lead and serve" or "those who serve by leading." At any rate, Paul is willing to use the term διάκονος for his own ministry as well as for the ministry of others. While the householders (ἐπίσκοποι) and the hosts of the house churches presided over communion, the διάκονοι presumably oversaw the meal service at the worship assembly, the preparation for the Lord's Supper, and were responsible for the collection

---

[483] Cf. esp. Filson, "Significance," 111–12; cf., in addition to the already mentioned scholars, Augsten, *Natural Motivation,* 53; Schürmann, "'... und Lehrer,'" 107–47, here 135 n. 121.

[484] Hainz, *Ekklesia,* 346–47; Roloff, *Der erste Brief,* 172–73.

[485] Cf. Roloff, *Kirche,* 142, who sees here in the overseers of Phil 1:1 the institutionalization of the gifts of helps and administration mentioned in 1 Cor 12:28.

[486] Cf. Dassmann, "Hausgemeinde," 82–97, here 89–90; following him, Roloff, *Ansätze,* 123, and *Kirche,* 142; Chapple, "Local Leadership," 558–90.

[487] Cf. already Chrysostom; following him, Hawthorne, *Philippians,* 7–9; Collange, *Philippians,* 38–39.

as well as the administration of the gifts.⁴⁸⁸ This assumption is supported by the original meaning of the term. The word implies a clear picture of table service. It could be that the deacons were originally members of the household—for example, servants or slaves of the householder who led the house church. There are no traces of such a ministry yet in the church meal portrayed in 1 Cor 11, "but it is bidding them to come."⁴⁸⁹ In Philippi such a ministry appears indeed to have already developed.

The question of who presided over the Christian communion has often been discussed.⁴⁹⁰ This is difficult to determine with final certainty. From the perspective of the ancient *oikos*, however, it would appear quite natural, at least in the Corinthian church, for the householder hosting the congregation in his house to have taken on this responsibility. This practice would have been analogous to the Jewish, and partially to the pagan, meal customs. The householder provided the meeting place and at times perhaps the food for the regular meal in the context of the Lord's Supper. He would normally have presided over the regular meal and would have decided when to begin. When Paul writes to the Corinthians about abuse regarding the Lord's Supper, he appears to be addressing those who were responsible for the meal. They were the only ones who could have insured the order during the worship service for which Paul is pleading (1 Cor 11:33–34). But not only the hosts would have been responsible for this. It could have been Paul or Peter, the congregation apostles, prophets, or teachers who took on or were given the task of presiding over the Lord's Supper as guests of honor. Hence the householder presiding over communion cannot be assumed to be the general and binding norm.⁴⁹¹ Nevertheless, we agree with A. Schreiber: "The hosts exercised a leadership function at least in form in that they provided space, invited, greeted, and surely took on a special role during the Eucharist celebration."⁴⁹² As we have seen, this can also be assumed for the church in Philippi and most likely for the other Pauline congregations as well.⁴⁹³

Much has been written about the origin of the word ἐπίσκοπος. The term occurs quite often in classical Greek and also in the LXX. It apparently grew out of the context of administration and service.⁴⁹⁴ From this scholars

---

⁴⁸⁸ On the householders and hosts, Schreiber, *Gemeinde*, 135; Klauck, *Hausgemeinde*, 43. On the διάκονοι, Roloff, *Kirche*, 143.

⁴⁸⁹ "aber es ruft nach ihnen" (Goppelt, *Apostolische und nachapostolische Zeit*, 128).

⁴⁹⁰ That Christian *episkopoi* in general did this was already suggested long ago by Sohm, *Die geschichtlichen Grundlagen*, 55–57. Cf. also Müller, "Kirchenverfassung," 3:970.

⁴⁹¹ Cf. Acts 20:11. Here Paul, in the congregation on a visit, was allowed to preside over the Lord's Supper. Cf. Roloff, *Der erste Brief*, 173.

⁴⁹² Schreiber, *Gemeinde*, 135.

⁴⁹³ Cf. Roloff, *Der erste Brief*, 173; Branick, *House Church*, 91–92; Ysebaert, *Amtsterminologie*, 87.

⁴⁹⁴ Roloff, *Kirche*, 142, favors the profane origin of the designation. Cf. Goppelt (*Apostolische und nachapostolische Zeit*, 128–29), however, who rejects

have concluded that a leader designated with this title would have been involved primarily in administration and service and that he would not have taken on any spiritual or pastoral responsibilities. This distinction, however, appears to be too modern, as the Essene מבקר evidently carried responsibilities in both areas. He not only had administrative tasks but also was engaged in a teaching role.[495] Accordingly, it need not be assumed that the overseers in Philippi were only administrative functionaries in the church with bookkeeping responsibilities.[496] It could be that they also carried out pastoral duties that had a spiritual quality.

Some have attempted to explain the phenomenon of episcopal leadership structures in the Philippian church by dating the Letter to the Philippians late. In that case, Phil 1:1 would document a later development of offices in the Pauline churches. This development hypothesis is attractive, and a number of things seem to speak in favor of it. For instance, it would explain why Paul seldom mentions individuals carrying functional responsibilities and doesn't mention ἐπίσκοποι at all until Philippians (1:1). The notion of development also fits well with the hypothesis that leadership structures emerged from below, out of the household setting. Moreover, we also see the development toward more formal organizational forms in Jerusalem even though there it was more in the direction of a presbyterial church order. The thesis must remain nothing more that a hypothetical possibility, however, as the place and the date for the composition of the Letter to the Philippians remain disputed. For instance, if Paul wrote the letter in Ephesus and not in Rome, it could have been composed before 1 Corinthians, and this would rob the development theory of its foundation.[497]

After a discussion of all references to leadership structures in Pauline churches, B. Holmberg suggests the following:

> In most of Paul's churches we have a group of persons who teach, guide, transmit divine revelations, expound the scriptures and formulate God's will in concrete, everyday life, and here we find the prophets and teachers.... Beside this group we find another, not so clearly defined, consisting of people with sufficient initiative, wealth, and compassion to care for the sick and poor, to receive traveling missionaries and other Christians, to be able to accommodate the worshippers and the communal meals of the church in their own houses, sometimes traveling on behalf of the church and generally taking administrative responsibility.[498]

---

the profane origin with good arguments. For a discussion of the state of research with his own position, cf. Chapple, "Local Leadership," 546–57.

[495] CD 13, 14. This would support the connection between ἐπίσκοπος and rqbm. Cf. Schürmann, "Die geistlichen Gnadengaben," 397 n. 124.

[496] With Roloff, *Kirche,* 142.

[497] Cf. Kümmel, *Einleitung,* 242, 291; Brockhaus, *Charisma,* 125–26. Cf. Marshall and Donfried (*Theology,* 121–22), who for good reasons favor Rome.

[498] Holmberg, *Paul,* 118.

With this summary Holmberg has more or less accurately portrayed the situation. He leaves us with the impression, however, that virtually none of those in the second group were involved in any kind of teaching ministry. At this point it must be asked whether he is working with much too modern categories in distinguishing so sharply between the two groups. Why would the householder, as the leader of a house church, not have taught or spoken prophetically? Aquila and Prisca exemplify such homeowners and house church leaders who exercised a teaching ministry (cf. Acts 18:1–3, 24–26). As we have seen, the προϊστάμενοι in Thessalonica were both at the same time; as protecting patrons, they carried not only patronal but also pastoral responsibilities.[499] Moreover, in Caesarea, Philip was simultaneously homeowner and evangelist (Acts 21:8). And Stephanas was both homeowner and congregational apostle (cf. 1 Cor 16:15–18), which is a clear indication that an identity as householder and a charismatic ability are not mutually exclusive.[500]

It was also the common duty not only of the Jewish housefather to give instruction to his children but also of householders in general in the entire ancient world (see p. 194, esp. n. 411). Accordingly, it would be expected that a well-to-do homeowner who in general had a higher education than the other members of his household would have accepted teaching responsibilities for the group that met in his home.

Excursus: Leadership Responsibilities of Women

The relatively heavy involvement of women, often wealthy and from higher social levels, in the Pauline mission has been increasingly acknowledged in NT research.[501] One sociohistorical reason for this high involve-

---

[499] Cf. 1 Thess 5:12. "Since Paul's statement refers to one group whose activity has three important dimensions, and not to three groups, the leaders are those in whom patronal (προΐστασθαι) and pastoral (νουθετεῖν) ministries are combined, and who display an evident commitment (κοπιᾶν) to both" (Chapple, "Local Leadership," 255).

[500] It is striking, however, that the ministry of the word is not documented for Stephanas. This could be related to the fact that Paul's letters were written to address specific problems, and we should not expect him to deal with all issues exhaustively.

[501] Cf. esp. Gülzow, "Soziale Gegebenheiten," esp. 200–206; Harnack, *Mission and Expansion*, 217–39. Cf., e.g., also Thraede, "Frau," 8:230; Ollrog, *Paulus*, 9–62; Lohfink, "Weibliche Diakone"; Dautzenberg, "Zur Stellung" (for further literature, p. 182); Weiser, "Rolle der Frau"; Schüssler Fiorenza, *In Memory*, 205–41; Schotroff, "Wie berechtigt ist"; Heine, *Frauen*, 91–116; E. and W. Stegemann, *Urchristliche Sozialgeschichte*, 332–46; Witherington, *Women*, 76–127; Baumert, *Frau*, 159–92; Grenz and Kjesbo, *Women*, 98–141; Eisen, *Amtsträgerinnen*; Osiek, "Family" and "Women." Such involvement of women applies also for the entire Christian mission movement, for which the expansion of Judaism among affluent women prepared the way. Cf., e.g., Brooten, *Women Leaders*, and literature in n. 411.

ment is to be found in the central role that house churches played in the expansion of early Christian missions.[502] The significance the house church setting had in providing leadership opportunities for women has also been pointed out by a number of scholars.[503] Nevertheless, the set of questions concerning this issue remain difficult to answer partly because of the scarcity of reliable sources, partly because of a complicated textual situation. An examination of the pertinent references by Luke and Paul in particular consideration of the house church setting will help us draw our own conclusions about the leadership responsibilities of women in the Pauline mission.

Approximately one-fourth of the coworkers mentioned in the undisputed Pauline Epistles are women.[504] If we add Nympha, mentioned in Colossians, and Lydia, in Acts, there are a total of twelve women: Euodia, Julia, Junia, Lydia, Mary, Nympha, Persis, Phoebe, Prisca, Syntyche, Tryphaena, and Tryphosa.

We meet Euodia and Syntyche in Phil 4:2-3, two women who, according to Paul, "fought for the gospel."[505] For Harnack the two women are "joint founders of the church in Philippi" along with Lydia, and they "were highly respected (perhaps as overseers of two house churches, as was Nympha in Colossae)."[506] It cannot be convincingly demonstrated from the information found in our text that they actually were founders of the Philippian church. In fact, verse 3 appears to prohibit that interpretation. Neither does the text clearly indicate that they were house church leaders.

Nympha (see pp. 155–62) appears in Col 4:15 as either a widow or a single woman who owned a house (or her husband had not come to faith?).[507] From everything we know about the ancient *oikos,* we can assume that Nympha, who would have had a certain amount of authority simply because of her position as homeowner and householder, had influence in the life of the congregation that met in her house in Laodicea.[508] In the ancient world religious matters within the household were the woman's classic sphere of influence. "On occasion women of course took their part in all

---

[502] Stuhlmacher, *Philemon,* 70–74; Klauck, *Hausgemeinde.*

[503] Klauck, *Hausgemeinde;* Swidler, *Biblical Affirmations,* 296; Weiser, "Rolle der Frau," 166–67, 172–75; Dautzenberg, "Zur Stellung," esp. 193–221; Banks, *Paul's Idea,* 118–27; Verner, *Household,* 127–80; Schüssler Fiorenza, *In Memory,* 226–33; Beck, "Women"; Branick, *House Church,* 58–97; Blue, "Acts," 178–86.

[504] Purely from the perspective of numbers, the involvement of women in the overall Pauline mission was much lower than that of men. Some may feel that it is much too low from a modern point of view. From an ancient point of view, however, it would have drawn attention for being unusually high.

[505] For the different positions regarding the identity and significance of both women, cf. Heine, *Frauen,* 97; Baumert, *Frau,* 185; Witherington, *Women,* 111–12; commentaries on the passage.

[506] Harnack, *Mission and Expansion,* 221, n. 1.

[507] In that case it would be difficult to maintain that Nympha was a homeowner.

[508] For inscriptional and documentary references to women as householders, cf. G. Horsley, *New Documents,* 2:25–32.

manner of public rites, but it is in the household that they are the conspicuous worshippers."[509] This, however, does not yet mean that Nympha had taken on the *spiritual* leadership of the church.[510] Religio-historical comparison certainly provides a helpful parallel (i.e., the religious role of women in the ancient *oikos*). Nevertheless, as will be seen, some differentiation has to be made in the Pauline house churches. Unfortunately, in the case of Nympha the text in Col 4:15 does not give us any further information that would enable us to obtain a clear-cut answer to our question.

Acts 16 relates the story of how a house church was established in Lydia's home (see pp. 131–32). Luke also portrays Lydia as the first Christian in Macedonia. Can we elevate her to leader of the church in her house on this basis alone?[511] It is a very real possibility (cf. Acts 16:40). She appears to have led the house church particularly in the early days. On the other hand, she is not mentioned by name in the letter to the Philippians. Still, we need to recognize that with his report Luke also wants to say that, in spite of his Jewish training, Paul is willing to establish a church with a group of women.[512] By implying that, in contrast to the synagogue (*m. Meg.* 4:3), women alone were allowed to found a Christian church, Luke indirectly points to a difference in the status of women in the two religious groups at that time.[513] And Lydia, yet new to the faith, appears to transcend social barriers by insisting that the male Jewish missionaries accept her hospitality. "Perhaps Luke means us to see here a portrait of a woman who grasped from the first that whatever barriers being a Gentile and a single woman might erect regarding housing non-Christians (particularly Jews) in her home, these barriers were no longer obstacles to Christians, even Christian males whom she had just met."[514]

The majority of the women discussed above are found in the list of greetings in Rom 1:1–16. In addition, the mother of Rufus, "who was also a mother to me," and the sister of Nereus (Rom 16:13–16) are mentioned. There is also reference to a (missionary?) couple, Julia and her husband, Philologus. Mary, Paul's "dear friend" Persis, Tryphaena, and Tryphosa

---

[509] Rose, "Religion," 95–116, here 98; following him, Thraede, "Frau," 8:206; Klauck, *Hausgemeinde*, 46. So also Schüssler Fiorenza, *Zu ihrem Gedächtnis*, 225–27. Cf. also the literature in n. 535.

[510] Cf., e.g., Klauck, *Hausgemeinde*, 45–46, and Banks, *Paul's Idea*, 124, who both consider it possible that Nympha had a leadership position in her house church.

[511] So Schüssler Fiorenza, *Zu ihrem Gedächtnis*, 228; Jervell, *Apostelgeschichte*, 422, 428 n. 132.

[512] So long as Paul was still present, he would have had the lead. After his departure Lydia could have taken it over. If Lydia had older sons, slaves, and clientele, then men would have belonged to the church in her house. It also should be asked which responsibilities an older son of Lydia or, for that matter, the jailer would have carried.

[513] Cf. Thomas, "Place of Women," 117–20, here 117.

[514] Witherington, *Women*, 149; cf. also Ramsay, "Denials," who suggests that Lydia was able to receive men into her house without violating local customs because her house was large enough to accommodate the men in separate room(s).

worked hard "in (the service of) the Lord" (κοπιᾶν; see pp. 197–99). From these references alone we can deduce that Paul had personal contact with many women and had high respect and appreciation for all of them.[515]

Even more interesting for our study, however, are the references to other women in this list of greetings. Junia and her husband, Andronicus, have much in common with Paul.[516] They are Jews and came to faith before he did. Like Paul they suffered for Christ, and they were in prison (possibly with him). They both are considered "outstanding among the apostles."[517] In this context the title is not necessarily used in the sense of the office of apostle as in one of the Twelve or Paul (1 Cor 1:1; 15:5, 8–9).[518] As we have seen, there were appearance apostles (Gal 1:17; 1 Cor 15:7) but also congregation apostles, that is, church envoys (2 Cor 8:23) in early Christianity (see p. 205). Whether Andronicus and Junia belonged to the group of appearance apostles is no longer possible to determine.[519] That they became Christians before Paul and were "outstanding among the apostles" could speak in favor of that view (Gal 1:17 with Rom 16:7).[520] It is quite certain, however, that they were involved with Paul in the mission to the Gentiles; otherwise they would not have been imprisoned.[521] Thus Junia was at least a congregation apostle[522] who held a missionary office.[523] Nowhere do we hear that Junia was involved in a missional preaching ministry, but the possibility that

---

[515] These and other observations show, according to Cranfield, *Romans*, 2:789, "the falsity of the widespread and stubbornly persistent notion that Paul had a low view of women."

[516] There should be no more doubt that in Rom 16:7 the feminine form Junia is the correct one. The masculine form Junias does not occur in the literature anywhere. The older accented manuscripts read Ἰουνίαν, which is clearly the the woman's name. For further arguments, cf. Cranfield, *Romans*, 2:788; Wilckens, *Römer*, 3:135; Stuhlmacher, *Römer*, 219; Lohfink, "Weibliche Diakone," 327–29; Brooten, "Junia"; Lampe, "Junia/Junias."

[517] Not "well known to the apostles" (Meyer) but, rather, "outstanding among the apostles"; cf. Rengstorf, "ἐπίσημος," *TDNT* 7:267–68; Sanday and Headlam, *Romans* (1902), 423: "The Passage was apparently so taken by all patristic commentators."

[518] With a different view, Heine, *Frauen*, 96: Junia and Andronicus "are not beneath the apostle Paul in any way." Cf. similarly Brooten, "Junia." More balanced is Cranfield, *Romans*, 2:789, who considers the couple apostles in a broader sense: they are "itinerant missionaries who were recognized by the churches as constituting a distinct group among the participants in the work of spreading the gospel."

[519] So, e.g., Eisen, *Amtsträgerinnen*, 50–55.

[520] About their becoming Christians before Paul, the argument would apply that the resurrected Lord appeared to them before he appeared to Paul, which has made them eye witnesses of Jesus Christ. And if they were only temporary envoys of a congregation, their designation as outstanding would not fit them well. They could have belonged to the group of the ἀπόστολοι πάντες, which Paul mentions in 1 Cor 15:7. This would fit well with the πρὸ ἐμοῦ γέγοναν.

[521] Wilckens, *Römer*, 3:135; Cranfield, *Romans*, 2:789.

[522] Cranfield, *Romans*, 2:789.

[523] Stuhlmacher, *Römer*, 219.

she preached the gospel cannot be ruled out. Her membership in (or at least affiliation with) the circle of apostles would make good sense for mission-strategic reasons. Under the conditions existing in ancient society, women would have been extremely difficult to reach for Christ without the active involvement of women on the missional-outreach team.[524]

Concerning the other couple, Prisca and Aquila (see pp. 134–38), what were Prisca's leadership responsibilities?[525] As already pointed out, the mention of Prisca before her husband could indicate that she was more important in some way, either because of her special service in Christian ministry or because of a higher social status. This in itself is not yet conclusive evidence that she had some kind of leadership responsibility in the church. It is undisputed, however, that she was engaged in missional outreach, that she went on mission journeys with her husband, and that she helped Paul with his mission work, among other things by making her house available to the congregation as a meeting place in several different locations. Prisca did so together with Aquila independently of Paul; this can be deduced from the date of her conversion, which was prior of Paul's. One should not conclude, however, that they were somehow equal to, or on the same authoritative level as, Paul, the apostle to the Gentiles, simply because they worked together with him later.[526] Paul's personal calling, as he describes it in Gal 2:7, could not simply be passed on to his coworkers.[527] His apostolic and missional calling was unique and nontransferable (1 Cor 3:10; 9:1).

In Rom 16:3, Prisca and Aquila are called συνεργούς μου. This designation has a titular character.[528] According to Ollrog's analysis, however, what Paul really meant with the title συνεργός can only be determined on the basis of the context. Paul understood the word, according to Ollrog, in terms of the charge to work or partner together. For Ollrog the correct translation is "coworker": "the mission partner commissioned by God to do missional ministry who in so doing becomes Paul's fellow laborer."[529] Ollrog leaves the question open whether the designation became that of an office during Paul's lifetime. Whether we can say, as Ollrog does, on the basis of this observation, that in missional outreach with Paul Prisca did not play a subordinate role is difficult to determine.[530] Depending on the context, the connotation of συνεργός as "companion" and "assistant" in the sense of a

---

[524] Ibid. Cf. Clement of Alexandria, *Strom.* 3.53.3: the wives of the apostles "were able to take the teachings of the Lord into the women's quarters without defamation."

[525] Cf. Harnack, "Über die beiden Rezensionen."

[526] This tendency can be observed in both Heine, *Frauen,* 51–52, 96–97, and Schüssler Fiorenza, *In Memory,* 219–20.

[527] With Baumert, *Frau,* 185.

[528] Cf. Ollrog, *Paulus,* 63–79, 91–92.

[529] Ibid., 91.

[530] Ibid., 26.

subordinate laborer cannot be ruled out.⁵³¹ One needs to keep in mind the difference between συνεργὸς θεοῦ and συνεργός μου. To be called συνεργός μου by Paul certainly appears to be an expression of subordination.

It is also striking that Prisca is always mentioned in connection with her husband. It can also be assumed that Prisca and Aquila were familiar with Paul's perspective as he expressed it in 1 Cor 11:2–16.⁵³² Again, the fact that they were Jews is significant here. All of this leads us to assume that "the nature of their involvement did not fundamentally violate the otherwise established cultural and ecclesiological parameters"⁵³³ even though our texts never explicitly state this.⁵³⁴ The observation alone that Prisca is mentioned first and that the married couple made their house available to the church as a meeting place does not necessarily indicate that Prisca took on the leading role in the house church in a spiritual, ecclesiological sense. On the one hand, everything that we know about their cultural and ecclesiological background points in the direction of Aquila acting as the housefather in this house church.⁵³⁵ That the housefather was to lead the church does not stand in contradiction with Gal 3:26–28, but the passage does have implications regarding how he was to do this.⁵³⁶ On the other hand, it would be completely wrong to assume that merely because Prisca was a woman, she had nothing to say about the life and thought of the church meeting in her home.⁵³⁷

---

⁵³¹ Ollrog, "συνεργός," *EDNT* 3:303–4, is too narrow, not allowing for a broader set of connotations. Cf. Bertram, "συνεργός," *TDNT* 7:871–76.

⁵³² The interpretation of this passage, however, is not at all an easy task (see pp. 221–23).

⁵³³ Baumert, *Frau*, 185. Cf. also Theissen, *Psychologische Aspekte*, 163, who emphasizes that the early Christian missional movement outside Palestine "was not in conflict with society but rather well integrated within it."

⁵³⁴ Cf. Schüssler Fiorenza, *Zu ihrem Gedächtnis*, 222, who points out that neither Prisca nor Junia is designated as a "wife." It is neither their traditional status nor their role as wives that are in focus but rather their efforts to spread the gospel. It can be asked whether their traditional status is not the focus of attention simply because it is assumed.

⁵³⁵ This applies esp. to women in the Jewish world. For the position of women in the ancient world, cf. Oepke, "γυνή," *TDNT* 1:776–84; Leipoldt, *Frau;* Thraede, "Frau"; for the OT and Judaism, cf. Str-B 3:468–69, 558–62, 610, 614; Jeremias, *Jerusalem*, 395–413.

⁵³⁶ Cf. P. Marshall, *Enmity*, 135–36, for "the softening process" of the Pauline gospel on the ancient *oikos*. Cf. also pp. 142–46 nn. 62, 77: Paul uses the language "of servitude or subordination" and not "of patronage or leadership." Here he follows Judge, "Paul," esp. 196–97. This view is very close to "love patriarchalism" (cf. Theissen, *Social Setting*, 107–10; with reference to E. Troeltsch, 268 n. 87). Cf. also Banks, *Paul's Idea*, 67–76, 127–38. See p. 247 for further discussion.

⁵³⁷ This is also confirmed by the comparison with the religiohistorical background at the time. In the Jewish Diaspora, women were given titles such as "synagogue ruler," "elder," and an even higher honorific, "mother of the synagogue." In a similar way both Prisca and Lydia could have felt responsible for their Christian house church. We no longer know for sure, however, what influence and what

This is clearly illustrated by the story in Acts 18:1–3, 24–26. The Jewish-Christian Apollos of Alexandria is invited into the couple's house and given basic instruction regarding Christian doctrine.[538] This implies that Prisca was involved in teaching him (Acts 18:26).[539] That Prisca is mentioned first here could even mean that she had the primary teaching responsibility. On the other hand, some exegetes emphasize that Prisca and Aquila worked as a team and that Prisca exercised her teaching gift under the authority of her husband.[540] In addition, this did not take place in the public realm of the church but in the private atmosphere of the home.[541] Nevertheless, that the congregation met in the private context of the home for worship services meant that the line between private and public was not at all clear-cut.[542] The fact remains: Prisca exercised a teaching function not only among women but at least once for a man as well.[543] Whether she taught during the worship service or a church meeting our texts do not say.

Regarding the leadership and teaching functions taken on by these women, one could object that all this occurred in a missional pre-ecclesial, not a fully developed ecclesial, situation. On the basis of this distinction, it has been pointed out that the exegetical result of the above examination does not really contribute to the clarification of whether women carried leadership and teaching responsibility in the church. Regarding Phoebe, however, the argument that her ministry took place in a pre-ecclesial context no longer applies. The church in Corinth cannot be classified as a missional pre-ecclesial situation, for Paul spent eighteen months in the city, preaching, teaching, and building up the church. Cenchreae was a harbor town adjacent to Corinth and located just 4.3 miles southeast of the city.[544] During the Roman period the two cities were connected with a paved street.[545] Hence

---

power these Jewish women exercised in the life and worship of the synagogue community. Cf. Brooten, *Women Leaders,* 149–51, who has attempted to demonstrate that these titles were functional.

[538] Here προσλαμβάνω means "to take aside" or "to receive into his (domestic) community." Bauer-Aland[6], 1436 (BDAG 883); Delling, "προσλαμβάνω," *TDNT* 4:15.

[539] The text history of the narrative shows that this is indeed to be understood in this way (cf. the changes made in the Western text, which are intended to make the narrative less offensive in this regard). Discussed extensively in Heine, *Frauen,* 53–54.

[540] Cf. Witherington, *Women,* 154.

[541] In addition, one must ask how this is to be understood in connection with 1 Cor 14:33b–36 (see below, n. 581).

[542] Cf. Barton, "Paul's Sense."

[543] Even those who do not consider Acts 18:24–26 historically reliable must at least admit that Luke did not have any hesitation to portray a woman exercising a teaching ministry as if it were perfectly normal. That Prisca gave Apollos instruction is also an indication that she was educated. "As the latter was a cultured Greek, the woman who was capable of instructing him must have been herself a person of culture" (Harnack, *Mission and Expansion,* 222).

[544] Scranton et al., *Topography.*

[545] Riesner, "Kenchreä."

Corinth was easily and quickly accessible from Cenchreae and vice versa. Klauck even speaks of the church in Cenchreae as a branch of the Corinthian church.[546]

Everything that we know about Phoebe is found in Rom 16:1–2. As we have seen, she was the protecting patroness of the church in Cenchreae.[547] It can be assumed that she made her house available to the congregation as a meeting place and so served as their hostess. For Meeks she therefore belonged to the leadership team of the church in Cenchreae.[548] As already demonstrated, two texts in which the same verb occurs (προΐστημι in Rom 12:8; 1 Thess 5:12) indicate that Phoebe had a leading function at least in the Cenchreaen church. Also the reference to her as διάκονος τῆς ἐκκλησίας in Cenchreae sounds official and reminds us of the office mentioned in Phil 1:1.[549] It can be assumed that those who read Philippians evidently knew what was meant with the term (it is not explained) and therefore that διάκονος was not an exceptional but a formal function (1 Cor 11:23; Col 1:7; 1 Thess 3:2; 2 Cor 6:4).[550] The expression διάκονος with a genitive designating a congregation is unique in Paul's writings and implies a recognized and ongoing ministry in the church.[551] Nevertheless, the content of the task that διάκονος describes is difficult to determine (see pp. 207–8).[552] Phoebe's task should be understood in connection with her title προστάτις. The significance and duration of the ministry that she performed in the church by virtue of her προστασία (see pp. 142–43, 199) appears to have led to her being called διάκονος.

A. Lemaire points out that here διάκονος as well as συνεργός both signify a missionary with preaching and church leadership responsibilities.[553] The term is also used for preaching and teaching in extrabiblical sources, and therefore it appears quite clear "that the *diakonoi* of the Pauline churches

---

[546] Klauck, *Hausgemeinde*, 31.

[547] On the term προστάτις, see p. 143, n. 147, and p. 199.

[548] Meeks, *Zur Soziologie*, 131. Cf. (one-sided) Schüssler Fiorenza, *In Memory*, 47–48, who sees in Phoebe the leader of the entire church in Cenchreae. A plurality of house churches in Cenchreae is not documented, however, anywhere in our texts. Against Klauck, *Hausgemeinde*, 31, without giving any reasons, she claims that Rom 16:1–3 does not refer to a house church. Cf. Ysebaert, *Amtsterminologie*, 127–28; Banks, *Paul's Idea*, 123, 143.

[549] Dodd, *Romans*, 234–35: "We may assume that, whatever the 'deacons' were at Philippi, that Phoebe was at Cenchreae." So also Lohfink, "Weibliche Diakone," 320–38, here 324–26. Paul does not use the feminine διακόνισσα (not documented until the second century). For this reason we cannot exclude the possibility that women could have been among the διάκονοι in Philippi. That women held offices only shortly after this is demonstrated in 1 Tim 3:11 and 5:9–16.

[550] Cf. Beyer, "διάκονος," *TDNT* 2:93; Michel, *Römer*, 377; Brockhaus, *Charisma*, 100; following them, Ollrog, *Paulus*, 31 n. 136.

[551] Lohfink, "Weibliche Diakone," 326.

[552] Cf. also the excursus in Gnilka, *Philipperbrief*, 32–40, esp. 39, who assumes it was possible for a deacon to exercise a teaching ministry.

[553] Lemaire, "Von den Diensten" and "Ministries."

had recognized and official functions as missionary preachers and teachers."[554] The dilemma remains, however, that a teaching or preaching ministry for a female deacon is not documented in any of our NT texts. In fact, there are no clear references indicating that a woman "preached," that is, engaged in the public explanation of Scripture or evangelistic proclamation.[555] There are, however, references to women speaking prophetically during the worship service (cf., e.g., 1 Cor 11:5) and teaching (in a private context? Acts 18:26; see above). Προφητεύειν was certainly public and also qualified as teaching. Prayer in the ancient world was also done out loud, and the entire congregation said "Amen" in closing (cf. 1 Cor 11:5; 14:16).

Is it possible to determine more precisely which leadership responsibilities Phoebe had? Because she was a woman, many commentators suggest that, in consideration of the social and ecclesiological context, we can assume she had tasks connected with caring for others personally or in the context of table service but not any public functions.[556] It has also been pointed out that it was not common in the Greco-Roman world for a woman to take on leadership functions in public.[557] According to recent research results, however, this can no longer be maintained. The public activity of a woman in social and especially in religious life was more common in the Hellenistic world than, for example, in Jewish Palestine.[558] Over the years the restriction of women to the domestic realm, common in ancient Greece, had been affected by a kind of "emancipation" that more or less affected the entire Roman Empire.[559] In addition, the present state of research no longer assumes uniformity throughout the empire.[560] Regarding our questions we need to distinguish between the local histories of cities such as a Roman Corinth and a Macedonian Philippi.[561] Moreover, as mentioned above in the context of the house church that met in Phoebe's home, it would have been very difficult to separate public tasks of hers from those that would have been private.[562]

Apparently Phoebe was either a widow or a single woman who somehow gained ownership of a house. From what we know about the position of such a woman in the urban culture of Corinth, she most likely took over the

---

[554] Schüssler Fiorenza, *In Memory*, 47.

[555] With Baumert, *Frau*, 187; cf. in contrast Acts 14:3, 9, 21, 25, etc.

[556] Cf., e.g., Käsemann, *Römer*, 395–96; Michel, *Römer*, 473.

[557] Cf., e.g., Baumert, *Frau*, 159–92, esp. 186–87.

[558] Against Baumert, ibid., who assumes a much too uniform macroculture. Cf. Stambaugh, "Social Relations"; MacMullen, "Women"; following them, Schüssler Fiorenza, *In Memory*, 231–33; Banks, *Paul's Idea*, 125; cf. also the literature in the following note.

[559] Cf., e.g., the short discussion of this emancipation and further literature in Dautzenberg, "Zur Stellung," 193–214. Cf. Thraede, "Frau," 8:201, 215–16.

[560] Cf., e.g., G. Horsley, *New Documents*, 2:32, who points out that Roman law was not applied uniformly in all of the different provinces.

[561] Cf., e.g., Witherington, *Women*, 5–23.

[562] Cf., e.g., Osiek, "Family," 1–24, here 12–14.

responsibilities of the absent housefather.⁵⁶³ Accordingly, in the church in her house she would have taken on a number of organizational responsibilities. Does this mean that she became the leader of the house church in a spiritual, ecclesiological sense? Does it mean, for instance, that in the house church in her house Phoebe presided not only over the regular meals in her home but over the agape meal as well as the Lord's Supper, or did she ask one of the men present at the assembly to do so? It was not uncommon in a Greek and Jewish context to ask "guests of honor" to preside at the meal.⁵⁶⁴ Historically, the question regarding presiding over the Lord's Supper does not become acute until much later. When it does, it is always clear that a man had the lead. It could be that in isolated cases a woman such as Phoebe took on this task. Whether Phoebe actually did the text does not say. Normally, whenever a housefather was present, he presided.⁵⁶⁵ This view is supported by the observation that in the NT and post-NT texts there is no indication of any kind of conflict regarding this issue (cf., e.g., 1 Cor 11:14). This speaks against the opinion, at least regarding the question who presided over the Lord's Supper, that initially a period of pneumatic freedom for women existed in the Pauline mission and that not until later did a theology dominated by the interests of men gain control of the life of the church.⁵⁶⁶

It could also be that Phoebe had a teaching ministry in the house church in Cenchreae as householder and deaconess.⁵⁶⁷ As we have seen, it is possible that she not only delivered the letter to the Romans but also read and explained it to the house churches in Rome. It would not be surprising if Phoebe, who most likely knew Paul (and his theological thinking) quite well from her time with him in Cenchreae, assumed such a responsibility in Rome, perhaps even during the worship service. It is also possible that she, as Prisca in Ephesus, introduced new Christians (not only women) to the basic tenets of the Christian faith in the context of the church in Cenchreae. Our texts do not, however, explicitly confirm this. It could also be that Phoebe gave the Epistle to the Romans to the local householder and that he read it to the church. But even then the congregation might have asked Phoebe to explain what Paul meant regarding

---

⁵⁶³ Cf. Witherington, *Women*, 5–23; Johansson, *Women*, 19; Hardy, "Priestess," 60; Stambaugh, "Social Relations," 75–99, here 76; Osiek, "Women," 311. Cf. also the literature in n. 535. Cf. also Banks, *Paul's Idea*, 124, on Nympha. In Philostratus, *Gymn.* 23, a woman as head of the household after the death of her husband is documented.

⁵⁶⁴ Cf. Baumert, *Frau*, 189.

⁵⁶⁵ In the Jewish world, the tasks for the father and mother during the Passover meal—forms that by this time had long since solidified—could not simply be interchanged. Regarding the Jewish background for the Christian communion celebration, see pp. 79–86.

⁵⁶⁶ Schüssler Fiorenza, *In Memory*, 205–84 (see pp. 231–32).

⁵⁶⁷ Cf. Banks, *Paul's Idea*, 123, who considers it possible that Phoebe "was engaged in teaching and leading in her local church in Cenchreae."

difficult passages, and her answer to those questions could be understood as a kind of teaching.

The answer to the question concerning the leadership responsibilities of women in the Pauline mission is not only found by analyzing historical-exegetical observations such as those made above; it also needs to be deduced from Paul's own theology. Central to Paul's theological thought in this context is the baptismal formula found in Gal 3:27–28:[568] "For all of you who were baptized into Christ have clothed yourselves with Christ. There is neither Jew nor Greek, slave nor free, male nor female, for you are all one in Christ Jesus." For many scholars this passage is the *locus classicus* of Paul's teaching about women, the point of departure from which he develops his theology. Others contest this, however.[569]

Whereas the older exegesis insisted that the subordination, the distinction, and in part the depreciation of women in comparison to men in the church were to be viewed as normative, some more recent exegesis maintains that in Gal 3:27–28 Paul emphasizes that men and women are "equal, but different."[570] But even these exegetes arrive at different conclusions in their examination of Gal 3:27–28. Scholars agree, however, that this formula stands in strong contrast to the surrounding social environment, in which generally women enjoyed neither sociological nor soteriological-religious equality with men. In the synagogue, for instance, the free Jewish men thanked God daily that they were not created as a pagan, a slave, or a woman (cf. *t. Ber.* 7:18). It was not much different among Hellenistic men, who also had three reasons to be thankful: that they were not born as an animal, as a woman, or as a barbarian.[571] In contrast to this basic attitude of Greeks and Jews, the men and women new to the Christian faith were told at their baptism that "for them the previous religious rights and privileges based on creation, birth, and social position were abolished and everyone in the church has been given one and the same relationship to God as his children through Christ."[572] The soteriological equality of all believers before

---

[568] Cf. also 1 Cor 12:13; Col 3:9–11. With Stuhlmacher, *Grundlegung,* 220, 353–54. Cf. Gehring, *Hausgemeinde,* 206–7, for our proof.

[569] Cf., for discussion of the positions, Hauke, *Problematik,* 339–45; Schüssler Fiorenza, *In Memory,* 205–7. For a good discussion regarding hermeneutical issues associated with the exegesis of Gal 3:28 and other Pauline passages, cf. Yarbrough, "Hermeneutics."

[570] Even though accented differently, cf., e.g., Jewett, "Sexual Liberation" 55–87, here 75–76; Stendahl, *Bible,* 33; Clark, *Man and Woman,* 137–63; Hauke, *Problematik,* 339–92; Banks, *Paul's Idea,* 126; Neuer, *Man and Woman,* 102–29; Ellis, *Pauline Theology,* 53–86, esp. 78–84. For literature of the older view, cf. Rohde, *Galater,* 164–66.

[571] Cf. Stuhlmacher, *Grundlegung,* 220; Heine, *Frauen,* 94. This common attitude can be observed, e.g., in Thales (Diogenes Laertius, *Clar. phil.* 1.33), Socrates (Diogenes Laertius, *Clar. phil.* 1.33), and Plato (Plutarch, *Mar.* 46.1). Cf. F. F. Bruce, *Galatians,* 187.

[572] Stuhlmacher, *Grundlegung,* 220.

God through Jesus Christ has taken the place of previous religious and social rights. With their baptism new Christians were transformed into a new existence and transferred into the new community of the church of Christ (2 Cor 5:17; Col 3:9–11).

For many exegetes this passage, however, does not speak against different functions of women and men in the church. Granted, it emphasizes the equal soteriological identity and value of all,[573] but it allows for the possibility of other kinds of differences.[574] The necessity of different (leadership) responsibilities for men and women in the church is based on a difference in kind anchored in OT creational order. Emerging from that creational order is the subordination of the woman toward the man (Gen 1 and 2). The creation theology argumentation of Paul in 1 Cor 11:2–16, especially verses 3, 7, and the assertions he makes in 14:33b–36 (cf. 1 Tim 2:12–14) are given as the main references documenting that this is the apostle's view.[575]

This view, however, is not without its problems. For text-critical reasons and for reasons of exegetical theology, many scholars do not view 14:33b–35 as genuinely Pauline but rather as a later addition to the text.[576] It also

---

[573] Cf., however, Banks (*Paul's Idea*, 111–14), who emphasizes correctly that, on the one hand, in Gal 3:26–28 Paul underscores that fellowship with God dare no longer be made dependent on national, social, and sexual differences. "But this should not lead us into a false impression of what he is asserting. Paul's stress is not so much on the equality of Jews and Greeks, free and slave, men and women as upon their unity in Christ. . . . Paul is no advocate of a universal, classless, and unisex society—he merely affirms that these differences do not effect one's relationship with Christ and members in the community. There is an egalitarian strain in Paul's pronouncement, but it is secondary" (p. 114). Cf. also Col 3:11; Ellis, *Pauline Theology*, 84.

[574] Cf. Clark, *Man and Woman*, 137–63; Hauke, *Problematik*, 339–40; balanced, Ellis, *Pauline Theology*, 53–86. With a different view, Heine, *Frauen*, 91–116; Schüssler Fiorenza, *In Memory*, 205–41; Funk, "Mann und Frau," 283. Delling, *Paulus' Stellung*, 97, 108, accuses Paul of being a woman hater and making the woman a second-class human being.

[575] Cf. 1 Cor 12:13–14, 17–18; Rom 12:4–8, which also point to differing spiritual gifts and hence different tasks in the body of Christ. They are not to be understood, however, as specified for one sex and not the other. Nevertheless Hauke, *Problematik*, 340–41, lists them as a partial proof that there are different tasks for men and women in the Christian church.

[576] Cf. the discussion and literature in Fee (*1 Corinthians*, 699–708), who also decides against the text being genuine and classifies it as a later addition. Cf. also the discussion and literature in Hauke (*Problematik*, 358–63), who considers the passage genuine. He follows the work of Swedish NT scholars who as yet have received little attention in the German and Anglo-Saxon world (cf. ibid., 359–60 n. 2 for a short research report on the passage). Cf. also Conzelmann (*Der erst Brief*, 290 nn. 55, 58), who considers the verses a gloss for literary-critical reasons. Cf. Wolff (*Der erste Brief*, 341–43), who points out that vv. 34–35 cannot be rejected as genuine on the basis of text-critical arguments. Text criticism only demonstrates the uncertain placement of v. 34–35 and thus the tension and the attempt to resolve the tension of the present text with its context. Besides, in none of the NT manuscripts is the text (vv. 34–35) missing. Even Marcion knew of it. Only a few unimportant

must be asked how κεφαλή in 11:3 is to be interpreted—as "head" or as "origin"?[577] Only if 14:33b–35 is not a later addition, if the command to be silent is a prohibition to teach or even a prohibition to speak at all, and if κεφαλή in 11:3 must be translated as "head" or as "origin" in the sense of subordination can the impossibility of a leadership or a teaching ministry for women during the worship service be maintained in terms of exegetical theology with any certainty as Paul's position here.[578]

If one considers 14:33b–35 genuinely Pauline, the problem arises that Paul argues passionately in 11:3–16 that women should wear a head covering when they pray and speak prophetically during the worship service but according to 14:33b–35 suddenly they are to be silent in church. G. Dautzenberg offers this solution: "In this passage [11:2–26] Paul wants to reprove women's misconduct in appearing with their heads uncovered. He simply mentions, without condoning it, that women prophesy. He addresses this problem later in 14:33b–36, and there he prohibits women from speaking."[579] This solution, however, is not satisfying. If women are not allowed to prophesy, then why make all the fuss regarding the prohibition of the uncovered head in order that they may prophesy honorably? Others suggest that the apparent tension between the two passages can be resolved by assuming that 14:33b–35 is not an absolute prohibition to speak. According to this view, Paul was only forbidding women from interrupting by asking questions, or he was perhaps merely prohibiting that a women teach authoritatively in the context of a teaching discussion (cf. 14:35, "inquiring" and "asking" as references to a teaching discussion). The parallel passage in 1 Tim 2:12 also speaks explicitly of "teaching" (διδάσκειν) and not of speaking in general. This interpretation is difficult, however, because the Greek term for "remaining silent" (σιγάω) in 1 Cor 14:34 can be understood as refraining from all verbal communication.[580] The Greek term λαλέω in verse 34 also means "speaking, talking, saying" in general and therefore is possibly limited to "teaching" alone. Understood in this way, it would include prayer

---

manuscripts (D F G a b vg^{ms}) add it after 14:40. An influence through 1 Tim 2:11–12 cannot be clearly demonstrated because of differences in language (cf. Dautzenberg, *Urchristliche Prophetie*, 257–59).

[577] For the view "origin," cf. Bedale, "Meaning of κεφαλή"; following him, F. F. Bruce, *1 and 2 Corinthians*, 103; for the view "head," cf. Grudem, "Meaning of Kephale." Cf. also Schlier, "κεφαλή."

[578] Barrett, *1 Corinthians*, 248–49: "Paul does not say that man is the lord . . . of the woman; he says that he is the origin of her being. In this he is directly dependent on Gen ii.18–23. . . . That *God is head of Christ* is understood in a similar way." According to Barret, because Paul clearly taught a form of subordination of the Son to the heavenly Father (cf. 1 Cor 3:23; 15:28; Phil 2:6), we can assume that if one has its origin in the other, this also implies subordination, and accordingly we can say of 1 Cor 11:3, "Thus a chain of originating and subordinating relationships is set up: God, Christ, man, woman."

[579] Dautzenberg, *Urchristliche Prophetie*, 266.

[580] Cf. Bauer-Aland⁶, 1498–99 (BDAG 922); 1 Cor 14:28, 30.

as well as speaking prophetically.⁵⁸¹ If Paul is totally forbidding women from speaking during the worship service in 1 Cor 14, then this would be in extreme tension with 11:3–16. The attempt suggested by A. Schlatter that the tension can be resolved by assuming that the prayer and prophecy of women in 1 Cor 11 refer to domestic prayer meetings or partial congregational meetings whereas 1 Cor 14 focuses on worship services involving the whole church is untenable for the reason that, as already observed,⁵⁸² the domestic meetings of only a part of the church at any one location are to be considered full-fledged house churches in which services of the word and the Lord's Supper were celebrated.⁵⁸³ In Rome an assembly of the whole church is not even documented. But even in Corinth, where a meeting of the whole church is recorded, the Christians celebrated worship services not only ἐπὶ τὸ αὐτό but also in the individual house churches. Besides, in light of Paul's overall argumentation, verses 5, 10, and 13 of 1 Cor 11 are embedded in the context of the worship service (cf. 11:10, 16, 18, 20). The head covering regulation points clearly to the worship service as its context. From 11:17 the worship service is implied in the instructions regarding the Lord's Supper, which is prepared for directly before the beginning of chapter 11. The mention of angels in 11:10 also implies a worship service setting. "Judaism, particularly in the Qumran writings, already knows of the presence of the 'messengers of God' during worship celebration."⁵⁸⁴

If we can assume that 14:34–35 is genuine, then it can be asserted with C. Wolff and G. D. Fee that the following solution, though not without its problems, has at least fewer difficulties than the previously suggested interpretations.⁵⁸⁵ In 14:33b–36 Paul is merely prohibiting women from any speaking that is not empowered by the Spirit, perhaps in an attempt to stop the disruptive asking of questions (cf. 14:34b, 35).⁵⁸⁶ Prayer and prophetic speaking by women are not included in the prohibition. E. E. Ellis's solution

---

⁵⁸¹ Cf., however, Wolff, *Der erste Brief,* 343–45, who decides that our passage is genuine and along with many other exegetes (cf. Wolff, 344 n. 554) does not understand "remain silent" in an absolute sense and qualifies "speaking" in 1 Cor 14:33b–36 as "asking questions or talking in a disruptive manner," even though the same term is used earlier in the same section as glossolalia or prophetic speech. There, however, the pneumatic character of this speech is clearly emphasized (cf. vv. 27–28, 29, also 39), but not in v. 33b–36. Besides, 33a ends the section in which the order of the Spirit-empowered speaking is addressed, so that from 33b on another problem regarding order is the focus.

⁵⁸² See the section "A Plurality of House Churches within the Whole Church at One Location," pp. 155–65.

⁵⁸³ Schlatter, *Korintherbriefe,* 180. It also needs to be emphasized here that the worship service back then surely did not run like ours today with rigid forms regarding the sermon. The service of the word could have contained a teaching discussion that was in the place of our present sermon (cf. Hauke, *Problematik,* 369–75).

⁵⁸⁴ Ibid., 367. Hauke follows Dautzenberg, *Urchristliche Prophetie,* 267 n. 47.
⁵⁸⁵ Wolff, *Der erste Brief,* 341–54; Fee, *1 Corinthians,* 708.
⁵⁸⁶ So also Banks, *Paul's Idea,* 123.

offers a certain supplement and yet at the same time a restriction to this view.[587] He considers 14:34–35 to be a culturally motivated prohibition that Paul supports on the basis of a creation theology argument and that is directed exclusively at the charismatically gifted wives of the prophets, out of respect toward their husbands during the worship service.[588] He suggests the following paraphrased translation: "Prophets, let your wives be silent in the assemblies. For it is not permitted for them to speak in the interchange between the prophets."[589] This suggested solution, however, does not address the above-mentioned problem that in 14:30 the prophets are told not to speak at the same time but rather after one another, and it is difficult to determine why the term σιγάω in verse 34 should be translated differently than in verse 30.

Assuming that 14:33–36 originated with Paul, H. Ridderbos points out that in the argumentation two different motives are connected closely with one another: "(a) what 'the law' says or what is inferred from the history of the beginning, and (b) what was considered unbecoming for a woman according to standards current in Paul's day. The latter he denotes with the words 'it is shameful' [cf. also 1 Cor 11:5–13]. . . . On the other hand, it is clear, that there is also a relativizing element in this appeal to custom . . . as the (sub-*ordinated*) position of woman with respect to man is to be given expression in a manner that must be considered appropriate for a certain time and culture."[590] In the Corinthian situation Paul is apparently intent on motivating the Corinthians as well as his other churches to remain within the general cultural parameters regarding the behavior of women at that time. Perhaps some of the women (wives?) allowed themselves to be too strongly influenced by the current emancipation movement (see above) and took more "freedom" than was the case in other churches.

Our exegetical analysis indicates that women, even though it was the exception, assumed leadership and teaching responsibilities in the Pauline house churches (see above; cf. also Col 3:16). The uncertainty in the text history and the extremely disputed interpretation of 1 Cor 14:33b–35 should warn against viewing this text as an eternal prohibition even in a culture in which women speaking in a public assembly is not seen as shameful behavior.[591] In my opinion, Paul viewed women and men as soteriologically

---

[587] Ellis, "Silenced Wives" and *Pauline Theology*, 67–71.

[588] Γυνή can indicate "wife" or merely "woman" (cf. Rom 7:2). Cf. the Western text for 14:34, which Ellis considers a correct interpretation (*Pauline Theology*, 69); cf. also Rom 7:2; Col 3:18–4:1; (Eph 5:21–6:9).

[589] Ibid., 71. Cf. also his solution to 1 Tim 2:9–15 (pp. 71–78); Köstenberger, *Women*.

[590] Ridderbos, *Paul*, 462–63.

[591] Fee, *1 Corinthians*, 708; cf. also the discussion of the complicated history of interpretation for 1 Cor 14:33b–35 and the different suggested solutions. Cf. also Wolff, *Der erste Brief*, 341–48, for a discussion of the topic. Schrage (*Die konkreten Einzelgebote*, 126) is of the opinion that a satisfying solution is yet to be found.

equal in Christ[592] and allowed the women in Corinth to publicly pray and prophesy (11:2–6) even though in the same section he asserts the creation theology subordination of the woman to the man and then restricts this permission in 14:33b–36 (for wives?) for whatever reason.[593] Accordingly, 14:34 alone cannot be used as an exegetical basis for excluding women from leadership offices or teaching ministries within the church.

CONCLUSIONS

Much of this chapter's discussion was centered on the relationship between the house church and the whole church at any given location in the overall Pauline mission. Associated with it was the question of the ecclesiological implications of this relationship. The plurality of house churches led to the issue concerning leadership and organizational structures in these house churches, and so the question whether and how the infrastructure of the ancient *oikos* influenced the organization of house churches became the focus of our examination.

As in the Jerusalem church, we again observed a plurality of house churches within the local church as a whole in Corinth. With all probability a multiple number of house churches existed in Rome as well. In light of the size of the city and because of the large number of groups, it is highly unlikely that the Christians there regularly met together in one place. There are also good indications of a plurality of house churches in Thessalonica, Ephesus, Philippi, and Laodicea.

The question concerning the existence of a multiple number of house churches alongside the whole local church led to the question how Paul defined the relationship between the individual congregation and the whole local church as well as that between the whole church at any one location and the entire worldwide church. On the basis of a plurality of house churches within the local church as a whole, which can be documented for the Pauline mission and for the primitive church in Jerusalem, and in light of the emphasis that Paul put on the dignity of the individual congregation, it appears that he maintains the priority of the individual congregation over the whole worldwide church.[594]

For the first time in our study, a hint of one of the shadow sides of the house church in its significance for the Pauline mission became discernible.

---

[592] Cf. F. F. Bruce (*Galatians*, 188–90), who draws attention to the fact that Gal 3:28 prohibits all discrimination not only on a racial and social but also on a sexual basis.

[593] In that case the text-historical uncertainty can be explained by a gloss written in the margin by Paul himself. Cf. Ellis, "Silenced Wives"; following him, Barton, "Paul's Sense," 229–30.

[594] As previously mentioned, however, cf. Eph 4 and John 17 for a balance.

The existence of several house churches in one city appears to have been a source for the formation of opposing parties and thereby a reason for intra- and intercongregational social tension among the Pauline Christians (in Corinth). This raises the question whether this constitutes a fundamental weakness of the house church model. The next chapter will address this issue more extensively.

Overall the significance of the house church in the Pauline mission must be seen as positive. In their function as operational bases for local church life and for the local/urban and regional missional outreach, much as in Jerusalem, in Antioch, and, in essence, even before Easter in the ministry of Jesus starting in Capernaum, houses represented the architectural, social, personal, and economic foundation for Paul's center-oriented, church-establishing mission as well as his supraregional outreach.

The private homes of wealthy members served Paul, his coworkers, and the other Pauline Christians as gathering points, as meeting rooms for fellowship, prayer, instruction, and the Lord's Supper. The homeowners made such worship services possible through their patronal hospitality, that is, by providing a place for assembly and, if needed, materials—for example, for the agape meal and the Lord's Supper. These patrons and patronesses offered the congregation and the itinerant missionaries protection in the face of the urban authorities and assumed leadership responsibility for the political affairs of the church. Often the hosts of a house church grew into a church leadership role because of their natural position, education, gifts, and talents. Thus house churches were a kind of training ground for future leaders for church and mission.

This view was confirmed by our findings based on an examination of the leadership structures of the Pauline house churches. In his undisputed letters Paul used a whole series of terms that point to leadership functions in his churches. A variety of names and descriptions imply instructional, leadership, administrative, and material support. Someone or some group had to provide a gathering place, lead the meetings and preside over the meals, and organize food for the poor. Someone had to be responsible for organizing the church and representing it with the authorities and, if needed, with other congregations in the city. In Paul's absence someone had to assume the task of teaching and leading. In the early days the group that would have been best qualified for such a role would have been the householders. In light of the position they enjoyed in an *oikos* society, it would have been quite natural for them to emerge as leaders and perhaps as teachers. After all, the church met in their home. This is not to suggest that the householders were the only ones who would have come into question as able to assume such leading and teaching functions in a house church. As in the primitive church in Jerusalem, there were other gifted members of the church who were not homeowners and yet could have taken and did take a leading role, including slaves and at times itinerant preachers, prophets, and others.

The fact that Paul does not mention installing leaders in the house churches in his undisputed letters is significant in our context. Even though he was not indifferent to leadership issues, Paul appears not to have concerned himself with the question of the official installation of leaders. This could be related to the fact that it was not necessary because leadership structures were already built in to the ancient *oikos* and hence leaders emerged from below, from the household setting itself. "We are, therefore, led to suspect that the social forces of the time and culture did in fact provide for their [the house church leaders'] emergence. The group that comes to mind as the one that could easily emerge in this manner with these responsibilities are the heads of households, men and women of means with the ability to manage the affairs of the church."[595]

Houses served also as missional bases of operation. They provided the mission with co-laborers for outreach in the city and surrounding area. Houses offered Paul, his assistants, other itinerant missionaries, and fellow believers room and board during their missional stay at any one location. At the same time, houses made a significant contribution to the mission of Paul and his coworkers in their function as assembly places for missional proclamation, catechetical baptismal instruction, and Christian teaching. A hospitality-providing network of οἶκοι was the basis that made possible Paul's letter-writing ministry, so very important for his work of church planting and building. In addition, houses made missionary travel possible in that they provided the necessary material and financial support for the trips. The house with its workshop and its network of relationships (extended family, clients, and association and business contacts) offered natural evangelistic contacts and conversation opportunities. Moreover, not only individuals but also entire households were baptized, and this was one of the most significant factors contributing to the rapid spread of the gospel. An additional advantage of this phenomenon was the built-in corporative solidarity during and after conversion, which provided natural, effective support for the new believers. Finally, house churches were also training grounds and display platforms for Christian brotherly love, with a strong integrating and missional impact. One of the main factors for the powerful contribution made to the Pauline mission by house churches is their size. Because of the limited number of people that the triclinium of a Greek or Roman house could accommodate comfortably, the groups remained small by necessity. This meant that they remained family-like, personal, friendly, and attractive to outsiders. Because the groups were small, it was easy to keep track of relationships and hold one another accountable. In their function as missional bases of operation for the city and surrounding area, house churches were the foundation of Paul's center-oriented mission. This is most likely the reason an integral part of his missional approach was to win entire houses to the faith

---

[595] Branick, *House Church*, 91.

at the very beginning of his missional outreach in a given city, and the key was first reaching the householder for Christ.

Paul thoroughly integrated his missional outreach with the social conditions of the ancient *oikos* and vice versa; the ancient *oikos* was closely integrated with the mission as well. "With the integration of the 'house' into the church, a very important principle became fruitful for missional outreach. The believers remain . . . in the world and consider themselves obligated to the historical and created social stations through which life in this world is sustained . . . (1 Cor 7:20–24). Because they live together *with* other people *within* the social order and according to its rules and yet they live *differently* than the others, they become witnesses—through their words, their life, and their suffering."[596] The Pauline, indeed the entire early Christian movement was able to organize itself as an independent entity not "*alongside* private Christian households but, rather, exclusively *in* them."[597] By remaining in their οἶκοι, it became clearer there than perhaps anywhere else that the first Christians were "in the world but not of the world." This is undoubtedly one of the more important reasons why the house church was of such great significance for early Christian missions.

---

[596] Goppelt, *Apostolische und nachapostolische Zeit*, 60–61. A conflict between the church and the world is latent here, a topic addressed in the next chapter.

[597] Lampe, "Zur gesellschaftlichen und kirchlichen Funktion," 537 (italics added); cf. also Laub, *Begegnung*, 52.

CHAPTER FIVE

The Continuing Influence of Oikos Structures

HOUSEHOLD CODE IN COLOSSIANS AS *OIKOS* ORDER

The Present State of Research (Col 3:18–4:1)

The present state of research on Col 3:18–4:1 is very complex and diverse.[1] Even though this passage has been examined from virtually every perspective, NT scholars still have not come to any kind of consensus regarding its interpretation.[2] Just after the turn of the century Dibelius and slightly later his student Weidinger contended that this and other household codes were somewhat Christianized versions of an ethical code borrowed from the Stoics.[3] Dibelius believed the reason the young Christian movement borrowed such material was rooted in their need to establish everyday routines because of the delay of the second coming. In contrast, J. E. Crouch argued that the Stoic influence was negligible in comparison to that of ancient Jewish values.[4] In the 1970s Lührman, K. Thraede, and D. L. Balch independently

---

[1] For a brief discussion of the introductory questions concerning authorship, etc., of Colossians and my position regarding these issues, cf. Gehring, *Hausgemeinde*, 385. The present study assumes that the Letter to the Colossians at least still reflects the historical situation of Paul's (later) life and ministry. It thus represents a bridge between the Pauline and the post-Pauline periods.

[2] Luther called this form of exhortation "Haustafel" ("household code") (cf. *Small Catechism*). Most scholars place the following passages more or less in this category: Col 3:18–4:1; Eph 5:21–6:9; 1 Pet 2:11–3:7; 1 Tim 2:8–6:2a; Titus 2:1–10. Col 3:18–4:1 is considered the oldest NT "Haustafel" tradition. The present state of research for the household codes has often been discussed in recent times and does not need to be repeated here; cf. Lührmann, "Neutestamentliche Haustafeln"; Laub, "Sozialgeschichtlicher Hintergrund"; Strecker, "Die neutestamentlichen Haustafeln"; Gielen, *Tradition;* Lips, "Haustafeln"; Balch, "Household Codes," *ABD* 3:318–20; a brief review in Gehring, *Hausgemeinde*, 385–93. Cf. also the numerous excursuses on household codes in reputable commentaries on Colossians, Ephesians, 1 Peter, and the Pastoral Letters.

[3] Dibelius, *Kolosser, Epheser, Philemon,* 91–92; Weidinger, *Haustafeln,* 5–6, 18–19.

[4] Social duties listed in reciprocal terms and the distinction between superior and subordinate individuals are non-Stoic features that are characteristic of Hellenistic Jewish codes.

rejected both of these hypotheses and suggested that the household codes are related instead to stereotypical Hellenistic texts discussing household management *(oeconomica)*, in particular those written by Aristotle.[5]

That Col 3:18–4:1 contains traditional material from early Christian paraenetic instruction has often been observed.[6] From the very beginning, house churches were established around a family, and therefore there was a need for special instruction on the family. In spite of the expectation that the coming of Christ was quite near, potentially long-lasting social forms emerged early on as a result of the integration of church life and *oikos* structures. The parallels found in the Hellenistic household management texts cannot explain the paraenetic character and content of the individual admonitions in the household codes.[7] Among other things, this led H. von Lips to suggest that the NT domestic codes should be categorized differently than the *oeconomica*.[8] Instead of being identified as a *Gattung*, the household codes are better classified as a topos.[9] According to Lips, the domestic codes in 1 Peter, Titus, and Colossians all follow a similar pattern, which he calls a "paraenetic scheme" reflecting these areas of life: church, house, and public.[10] The categorization of the household codes as paraenesis could indicate that the early Christian contribution to their formulation was much greater than is generally assumed. In fact, the tradition behind Col 3:18–4:1 may well have originated from within the missional context of the Pauline house churches.[11]

The Household Ethic: A Regression

A number of scholars, some in harsh tones, others in resignation, point to the household code in the Letter to the Colossians as a prime example of Christian tradition that stifled "true" freedom, originally a fundamental

---

[5] Lührmann, "Wo man nicht mehr," esp. 76–78, and "Neutestamentliche Haustafeln"; Thraede, "Zum historischen Hintergrund"; Balch, *Let Wives*.

[6] Cf. already Weidinger, *Haustafeln;* Gielen, *Tradition*, 3–4, 105–6.

[7] Cf. Verner, *Household*, 22, 84–86; Balch, "Household Codes" (1988), 27; following them, Gielen, *Tradition*, 55–66.

[8] Cf. Lips, "Haustafeln"; Popkes, *Paränese*, 123–25, 165–67; Gehring, *Hausgemeinde*, 388–93, for a brief summary of their arguments.

[9] In German scholarship *Gattung* is the term used for a multiple number of texts with a common form and a common Sitz im Leben. "Topos" is the term used to categorize certain individual parts of a paraenesis according to themes without these texts displaying a common form characteristic of a *Gattung*. Cf. Lips, "Haustafeln," 265; Bradley, "TOPOS."

[10] The term "scheme" is used for texts that are structured either in their form and/or in their content.

[11] Cf. Gielen, *Tradition*, 100–103. She attempts to demonstrate that the Christian householders were the ones responsible for adopting the *oeconomica* and that its reception in the form of the Christian household codes took place in the context of Christian houses in the Pauline mission. Cf. also Gehring, *Hausgemeinde*, 390.

value of the early Christian movement, from developing into its full potential. One group of scholars, usually from a feminist theological persuasion, maintains that the household codes reintroduced patriarchal structures that significantly encouraged, legitimized, and solidified the suppression and exploitation of women.[12] The other group, most often sympathetic toward revolutionary ideals, emphasizes that, by embracing the household codes with their conservative ethic based on ancient philosophical tradition, the early Christian movement missed an opportunity to initiate a socioethical revolution.[13]

E. Schüssler Fiorenza is typical of the first group. For her, Gal 3:28 represents the key text. Like most scholars, she assumes that 3:28 did not originate from Paul. For Schüssler Fiorenza this tradition originated rather from an alternative vision of a pre-Pauline early Christian missional movement.[14] In contrast to patriarchal structures characteristic of much of ancient society, which empowered men to exploit women, 3:28 envisions a Christian community in which patriarchal marriage—and patriarchal relationships in general between men and women—are no longer practiced. Schüssler Fiorenza understands the expression "neither male nor female" to mean that in the church the polarity between the sexes and the roles based on that polarity are to be abandoned. Galatians 3:28 calls the church to be one in Christ, which means that all social, cultural, religious, national, and biological differences between the sexes, indeed all power structures of any kind, are to be overcome.[15]

The view taken by S. Schulz is typical for the second group. Like Schüssler Fiorenza, Schulz assumes that 3:28 did not originate from Paul's pen but from the baptismal tradition of an enthusiastic-gnostic Christian community whose revolutionary motto was "Here there is neither Jew nor Greek, slave nor free, male nor female."[16] On the basis of this threefold scheme in 3:28, Schulz concludes that in this community the social differences between Jews and Gentiles were overcome, slavery was abolished in the church not only during the worship service but in everyday life as well, and the creational-order differences between man and woman were totally eradicated. The practice of this motto would have led to a socioeconomic revolution if Paul had not turned against it. First Corinthians 7:20–24 clearly demonstrates that Paul fundamentally misunderstood his own gospel by not drawing the necessary consequences from his doctrine of justification regarding the legal position of slaves in everyday life and their emancipation.

---

[12] Trible, "Das patriarchalische Prinzip," esp. 94; Schüssler Fiorenza, *In Memory*, 205–342; and "Ehe." Cf., even more radically, Meeks, "Image."

[13] Cf. S. Schulz, *Gott*, 154–203, esp. 193–200; *Mitte*, 90–91, 98, 105–6, 279, 290, 304, 330, 341, 349, 379; *Neutestamentliche Ethik*, 416–21.

[14] Schüssler Fiorenza, *In Memory*, 208–9.

[15] Ibid., 263–72.

[16] S. Schulz, *Gott*, 160–99.

Paul's followers also adopted this position. Indeed, according to Schulz, the introduction of the household codes demonstrates that they even sanctioned it theologically by adding a static creational-order dimension. In so doing, these "early Catholic" believers demanded of themselves and particularly of Christian slaves a nonresistant compliance to the existing social reality.

Is this criticism of the household codes justified? Is there really a contradiction between the older tradition in Gal 3:28 and Paul's position? What is the relationship between the household codes and 3:28–29 (cf. also Col 3:10)? Did the author of Colossians really make a mistake by introducing the household code and turning back to creation order? The next section will investigate the household code in Colossians regarding these questions and at the same time attempt to learn as much as possible about house churches from the code.

The first question we need to address regards Gal 3:27–28. As we observed, Schüssler Fiorenza and Schulz both see a contradiction between the older tradition in 3:27–28 and Paul, who allegedly does not draw all the necessary consequences inherent in this tradition. This contradiction exists, however, only if one interprets 3:27–28 the way Schüssler Fiorenza and Schulz do. On the basis of NT evidence, it cannot be convincingly demonstrated historically that Christian groups with the alleged egalitarian or revolutionary ethos ever really existed. Galatians 3:27–28 can also be understood quite differently. In my opinion, it has been clearly demonstrated that 3:28 is not the enthusiastic battle cry of some revolutionary Christ-Spirit congregation committed to the abolition of slavery nor the theological statement of a pre-Pauline congregation intent on dismantling patriarchal social structures in hopes of establishing an egalitarian community. Instead it is a pre-Pauline baptismal text that Paul adopted in confessing the new existence of the church in Christ.[17]

First of all, no one disputes that Paul is referring to the unity of all Christians in Christ in 3:27–28. This unity certainly transcends all religious, social, and sexual differences, all of which are foundational for this present world; however, it does not abolish them.[18] The following observations support this view. First, in Rom 10:12 Paul asserts that there is no soteriological difference between Jews and Gentiles in spite of the remaining differences between the two groups he lists in Rom 9–10. Second, Paul also uses the verb ἐνδύειν elsewhere in the context of a corporative sphere of existence—that is, where he speaks of the incorporation of the individual into Christ or of an individual's status in Christ (2 Cor 5:3; cf. Col 3:10). Third, in our context the meaning of the expression "in Christ" is decisive. This expression occurs

---

[17] Cf. Becker, *Galater,* 45. For a rebuttal of Schulz's position, cf. Stuhlmacher, *Philemon,* 47–48.

[18] Cf. Rohde, *Galater,* 165; H. Beyer and Althaus, *Galater,* 31; following Ellis, *Pauline Theology,* 80; cf. also Dunn, *Galatians,* 207; with a somewhat different view, Schlier, *Galater,* 174–75.

very often in the Pauline Letters and denotes the new existence of the individual and the entire Christian community (1 Thess 4:16; 1 Cor 4:15; 15:22; 2 Cor 5:17; Rom 6:23; 12:5). It describes the church's objective state of salvation.[19] Accordingly, Gal 3:28 means that in the eyes of God regarding salvation there is no difference; every person, whether man or woman, slave or free, Jew or Gentile, can become a child of God by faith in Christ Jesus (cf. Gal 3:20).[20]

The author of Colossians obviously does not see a contradiction between asserting, on the one hand, that in God's eyes (soteriologically) religious and social differences among people are nullified, and maintaining, on the other, the continued existence of creational differences among Christians in the family and in the church.[21] Nor did Paul see a contradiction between these two statements even though a tension exists (compare, e.g., 1 Cor 7:17–24; 11:2–16 with Gal 3:27–28). That Paul did not intend an unvarying monotony in the sense of a complete obliteration of the creational differences between individuals, including their sexuality, is illustrated with his use of the image of the body of Christ in 1 Cor 12. The unity of the body does not exclude the existence of individual members each with different tasks. Moreover, Paul differentiates between creational dissimilarities (e.g., between men and women) and social differences (e.g., between masters and slaves), as the following exegesis of the household code in Colossians will demonstrate.

Structural Analysis of Col 3:18–4:1

The exhortation in Col 3:18–4:1, which is addressed to women and men, children and fathers, and slaves and masters, in that order, begins without a connecting transition and represents a self-contained and complete section.[22] Colossians 4:2 could be connected seamlessly with 3:16–17 through the topics of prayer and worship service, whereas the behavior of the community members is the focus of the household code. The following observations can be made regarding the overall structure of the code. All of the addressees have in common *oikos* membership—therefore the designation "household code." It is also striking that the set of instructions for the slaves is much longer than the other two; it appears to be the main emphasis of the household code.

---

[19] Ridderbos, *Paul*, 46.
[20] Cf. Rohde, *Galater*, 164–65; H. Beyer and Althaus, *Galater*, 31.
[21] Rohde, *Galater*, 165; Ellis, *Pauline Theology*, 84–85; cf., however, F. F. Bruce, *Galatians*, 189–90.
[22] Lohse, *Kolosser und Philemon*, 220. Cf. the reputable commentaries on the passage; Schroeder, "Haustafeln," 79–171; Rengstorf, "Neutestamentliche Mahnungen" and *Mann und Frau*, 7–52; Müller, "Haustafel," 267–316; Gielen, *Tradition*, 104–203.

Exegetical Analysis of Col 3:18–4:1

Husbands and Wives (3:18–19)

The household code in Colossians begins with the instructions for women and men as married couples. "Wives submit to your husbands, as it is fitting in the Lord. Husbands, love your wives and do not be harsh with them" (3:18a–19). Corresponding with this is the fact that the relationship of the married couple constitutes the foundation for the ancient *oikos* and the interpersonal relationships within it.[23] It is striking that just as the wives are addressed first here, the exhortation is directed toward the subordinate members first in the other two cases as well. In this case, however, not only is the exhortation to submit to their husbands (ὑποτάσσεσθε τοῖς ἀνδράσιν) directed toward the wives; the husbands are commanded clearly and in apodictic form to love their wives (ἀγαπᾶτε τὰς γυναῖκας).[24] This command to the husbands to love is the nonnegotiable counterbalance to the obligation of the wives regarding submission.[25] At the same time, the exhortation to the men to love also applies to the women, and the submission required of the women is also expected from the men. The positive exhortation to the men is amplified by a negative extension that prohibits an opposite attitude and behavior: καὶ μὴ πικραίνεσθε πρὸς αὐτάς.[26]

Precisely how the two expressions ὑποτάσσεσθε τοῖς ἀνδράσιν and ἀγαπᾶτε τὰς γυναῖκας are to be understood is disputed among scholars. Among other things, the interpretation depends on the amount of influence the ancient Greek household management texts had on the formation of the household code in Colossians. Moreover, one does not dare forget that the household code in Colossians has a Hellenist-Jewish background.[27] Because I assume with Lips that the household code is not a *Gattung* but represents merely a topos of early Christian paraenetic instruction, it follows that the household management texts *(oeconomica)* may not be viewed as the hermeneutical key but rather only as an analogy that assists us to better understand the NT household codes.[28] Therefore the household code is not to

---

[23] Cf. Thraede, "Ärger," 63; following him, Gielen, *Tradition*, 129.

[24] This command to the men to love their wives was not unique in the ancient world. Cf., e.g., Callicratides; Plutarch; Aristotle, *[Oec.]* 3; proof texts in Gielen, *Tradition*, 129–35.

[25] Cf. Schweizer, *Kolosser*, 164; following him, Gielen, *Tradition*, 137; cf. also Schrage, "Zur Ethik," 12.

[26] Cf. Gnilka, *Kolosserbrief*, 218; Lohse, *Kolosser und Philemon*, 226; Schweizer, *Kolosser*, 165.

[27] Cf. Gnilka, *Kolosserbrief*, 217 (cf. Josephus, *Ag. Ap.* 2.201; Philo, *Spec.* 2.124).

[28] Lips, "Haustafeln"; cf. the extensive discussion in Gehring, *Hausgemeinde*, 386–400. Compare Gielen (*Tradition*, 129, 137) with Müller ("Haustafel," 292–304) and Thraede ("Zum historischen Hintergrund," 365), who consider the household management texts as such a hermeneutical key.

be interpreted as a self-contained tradition but rather in the context of the letter to the Colossians itself, particularly in the context of paraenesis in Colossians.[29] In contrast with a number of other scholars, it is therefore my conviction that the Colossian household code should not be interpreted in isolation from Colossians.

One additional key to interpreting the Colossian household code is the determination of the meaning of the expression "to submit." K. H. Rengstorf suggests that it means "to submit to *the* order as such."[30] For him this is based on an ontological creational order. E. Schweizer considers it a voluntary yielding as Christ himself practiced in his relationship to the Father (1 Cor 15:28).[31] J. Gnilka understands it rather as a universally valid order effective throughout ancient society.[32] On the basis of an alleged debate regarding the appropriate ordering of interpersonal relationships, Gielen points out that such a unified prescribed order did not exist even in the ancient world.[33] Along with K. Müller she suggests that the expression means "to yield to *an* order" (i.e., the acceptance of the leadership role of the man, but in the manner prescribed by the moderate household management texts). In the context of the Colossian household code, this would mean choosing a moderate form of patriarchalism, as opposed to more emancipated or stricter forms of ancient Greek household management, as the hermeneutical background for understanding our text. Other exegetes draw a distinction based on anthropological arguments between the relationship man/woman and parents/children, on the one hand, and the relationship masters/slaves, on the other. They would argue anthropologically that the relationship parent/child has greater (universal and eternal) validity than the relationship master/slave, which developed on the basis of (more or less temporal) social factors in part no longer in effect. "More central than the relationship parent/child is that of man/woman and the super- and subordination connected with it, which, as opposed to slavery, are anchored in creation."[34] Today most exegetes contend that the household code does not assert that slavery belongs to creational order. The question precisely how marriage and family are to be understood in our context can only be answered, however, after the expression ὡς ἀνῆκεν ἐν κυρίῳ is interpreted.

---

[29] Cf. Lohse, *Kolosser und Philemon;* Schweizer, *Kolosser;* Gnilka, *Kolosserbrief;* Lindemann, *Kolosserbrief;* Schrage, "Zur Ethik," 12–14; they include not only the Hellenistic models but also the context of the letter in interpreting the household code in Colossians. Because Colossians stands in the Pauline tradition, Pauline theology as a whole also should be seen as the hermeneutic background and taken into account in the interpretation of the Colossian household code.

[30] Rengstorf, *Mann und Frau,* 29.
[31] Schweizer, *Kolosser,* 164.
[32] Gnilka, *Kolosserbrief,* 217.
[33] Gielen, *Tradition,* 58–60, 137. Cf., however, Gen 1 and 2.
[34] Hauke, *Problematik,* 349.

Regarding the second expression, "love your wives," it is disputed whether the love demanded of the man is to be specifically understood in a Christian or simply in a conventional sense.[35] As just observed, it has often been argued that the household code in Colossians is to be interpreted as a self-contained traditional unit, which would prohibit the interpretation of the imperative ἀγαπᾶτε within the parameters established in Colossians regarding Christian love.[36] On the basis of the hermeneutical position stated above, however, we must do just that. In Colossians agape is represented as the most important character trait of the new man made possible through Christ and his Spirit (cf. 1:4, 8, 13; 2:2; 3:12, 14). This love "is not simply a matter of affectionate feeling or sexual attraction; it involves his [the husband's] active and unceasing care for her well-being."[37] The immediate context for the household code in Colossians also needs to be considered (3:5–17). There all Christians are exhorted to practice heart-felt compassion, kindness, humility, gentleness, and patience in interpersonal relationships. This prohibits the Christian husband, even as the head of the household, from mistreating any person, least of all his wife.

In Col 3:18b the justification for the exhortation to the woman is given: ὡς ἀνῆκεν ἐν κυρίῳ. In a general sense the term ἀνῆκεν refers to that which is "fitting."[38] But it is that which is fitting "in the Lord." The words ἐν κυρίῳ change nearly everything. They indicate that the members of a Christian household, and thus the Christian church as well, are supposed to live "according to the will of Christ." Above all, with this is introduced a new dimension that is missing in the corresponding Stoic recommendation to live this way because nature demands it.[39] For, according to 1:15–20, Christ the Lord is the mediator of creation and salvation. And so ἐν κυρίῳ has ramifications for all the natural order (as creation).

As we have seen, for many of the ethical assertions of the Christian household codes, we find parallels in the Stoic, Hellenist-Jewish household management sources. One cannot therefore conclude, however, that the possible adoption of such secular household management instructions and their adaptation via the expression "in the Lord" represent a superficial

---

[35] Schrage, "Zur Ethik," 13 n. 2; Schroeder, "Haustafeln," 123–27. *Ad loc.* Lohse, *Kolosser und Philemon;* Schweizer, *Kolosser;* Gnilka, *Kolosserbrief;* Lindemann, *Kolosserbrief;* Mussner, *Epheser,* who all argue for the Christian sense.

[36] Cf. Thraede, "Zum historischen Hintergrund," 365 n. 34; following him, Gielen, *Tradition,* 136.

[37] F. F. Bruce, *Colossians, Philemon, Ephesians,* 164.

[38] Cf. Bauer-Aland⁶, 131 (BDAG 78–79); Schlier, "ἀνέχω," *TDNT* 1:359; BDF §358.2; with many scholars, Gnilka, *Kolosserbrief,* 217: "The phrase 'as is fitting' (ἀνῆκεν) reminds us of the Stoic καθῆκον." Cf. Müller, "Haustafel," 292–97, 299–303; with him Thraede, "Ärger," 86, and "Zum historischen Hintergrund," 364–65; following them, Gielen, *Tradition,* 139–40.

[39] Cf. F. F. Bruce, *Colossians, Philemon, Ephesians,* 162 n. 172: "The Stoic way of life could be summed up as ὁμολογουμένως ζῆν, 'to live in harmony (with nature).' Conduct in accordance with nature was καθῆκον, 'fitting' (cf. Eph 5,4)."

christianization of them.⁴⁰ "The added words, simple as they are, transform the whole approach to ethics."⁴¹ Of the fourteen occurrences of κύριος in the Letter to the Colossians, seven are found in the Colossian household code. The expression ἐν κυρίῳ occurs four times in Colossians (3:18, 20; 4:7, 17). It appears about forty times in the *corpus paulinum,* often in the context of family relationships (cf., e.g., 1 Cor 7:22, 39; Eph 6:1; Phlm 16). This relationship "does not supersede earthly relationships but subsumes them and lifts them on a higher plane."⁴² The expression "in the Lord" offers the motivation for Christian behavior, and the other references to the Lord show that the entire thought-life and behavior of believers is to be yielded to the Lord Jesus Christ (cf. Col 3:17).⁴³ The Colossian household code makes it clear how this obedience to Christ should be evident specifically in the family.

By the time the Letter to the Colossians was written, the *oikos* had long been an established social unit in ancient society. The Christian church, however, had not—it was God's *new* creation (Col 3:9–11). In the church, conditions existed in which the new creation could be put into practice. In the church, women were to be valued just as highly as men, slaves as their masters, Gentiles as Jews (3:11, cf. also Gal 3:27–28). The structure of the family in the *oikos* society of the ancient world was set in its ways, however, and it was not at all the intention of the church to destabilize that society.⁴⁴ This would have happened, however, if the Christian movement had radically changed the *oikos* structures.⁴⁵ Moreover, because of its theological commitment to Christ as mediator of creational order and thus to family structures, the church was not interested in the disempowerment of marriage and family (cf. Col 1:15–20).⁴⁶

The authority of the husband, the father, and the head of the household continued to be exercised, but now only as it was "fitting unto the Lord." Women, children, and slaves of the household continued to respect

---

⁴⁰ Cf., e.g., Schrage, "Zur Ethik," 12; Rengstorf, *Mann und Frau,* 46.

⁴¹ F. F. Bruce, *Colossians, Philemon, Ephesians,* 162. In this context Lohse, *Kolosser und Philemon,* 321, speaks of a fundamental transformation of the household codes as a result of this *kyrios* motif.

⁴² F. F. Bruce, *Colossians, Philemon, Ephesians,* 164. Here he follows Moule, *Origin,* 54–63; cf. also Schrage, "Zur Ethik," 15.

⁴³ Cf. Lohse, *Kolosser und Philemon,* 218–19; Schrage, "Zur Ethik," 19–21; Schweizer, "Traditional Ethical Patterns," 203–4; following them, O'Brien, *Colossians, Philemon,* 219.

⁴⁴ Cf. also Meeks, *First Urban Christians,* 106.

⁴⁵ Cf. F. F. Bruce, *Colossians, Philemon, Ephesians,* 163: "The structure, hierarchical as it was, was left unaltered, apart from the introduction of the new principle, 'as is fitting in the Lord'—which was to be more revolutionary in its effect than was generally foreseen in the first Christian century."

⁴⁶ This is easiest to imagine if we consider Jewish Christians who, even before their conversion to the Christian faith, had believed in God as creator and now discovered that they could confess Christ himself as creator as well.

this authority also, as was "fitting unto the Lord." This does not mean that in God's eyes women were inferior to men.[47] The dignity of the woman in general and the wife specifically is maintained through the expression "in the Lord." Moreover, with reference to 1 Cor 15:28, E. Kähler has pointed out that, in and of itself, ὑποτάσσεσθαι does not imply degrading subservience.[48] Paul refers to a hierarchial order of creation (1 Cor 11:3, 7–9) in which the husband is the "head" of his wife.[49] Therefore, the argument in the Colossian household code is definitely Pauline. According to Col 1:15–20, Christ is mediator not only of salvation but of creation as well.[50] Thus, in the Colossian household code, marriage and family as the foundational structure of the *oikos* are understood as instituted by God and Christ Jesus in creation.

Immediately before the Colossian household code, it is written, "And whatever you do, whether in word or deed, do it all in the name of the Lord Jesus" (Col 3:17). This establishes the parameters for interpreting the household code in Colossians. If everything is to be done in the name of the Lord, then all efforts to maintain right family relationships are included. "The household codes intend to subordinate all of Christian life to the lordship of Christ, including that part of it lived in the order and structures of the world."[51] In this context A. Weiser refers to an "evangelization of the ancient household." By this he is not suggesting a christianization of a piece of secular literary tradition but the complete permeation of ancient family relationships by the gospel.[52] With the expression "in the Lord," the paraenetic instruction, including what is expressed in ancient *oikos* terminology and corresponds with extra-Christian content, is placed under the lordship of Christ.[53]

Children and Fathers (3:20–21)

The instruction for the children is placed before that for the fathers. They are to obey the parents in everything, as this is fitting in the Lord.[54]

---

[47] Cf. most well-known commentaries; J. Foster, "St. Paul"; Caird, "Paul."

[48] Cf. Kähler, "Zur 'Unterordnung'"; Kähler follows Schrage, "Zur Ethik," 12, 15. Cf. also Lohse, *Kolosser und Philemon*, 224 n. 7; on ὑποτάσσεσθαι in general, Bauer-Aland[6], 1689–90 (BDAG 1042); Delling, "ὑποτάσσω," *TDNT* 8:41–45.

[49] Cf. Eph 5:21, however, in which the mutual submission of the married couple one to another is prescribed.

[50] Cf. the wisdom tradition (esp. Sir 1:4; 24:3–5, 9–10; 43:26) and the (wisdom) teachings on creation in Gen 1 and 2. Also cf. the discussion of the background of the hymn in Colossians in Schweizer, "Church" and "Kirche"; Witherington, *Jesus*, 266–72.

[51] Schrage, *Ethik*, 258. Schrage does not view the household code in Colossians as God's creational order.

[52] Cf. Weiser, "Evangelisierung im 'Haus,'" 79–80. Cf. in this direction also Schrage, "Zur Ethik," 19; Laub, *Begegnung*, 91; Mussner, *Epheser*, 153; Ernst, *Briefe*, 382; F. F. Bruce, *Colossians, Philemon, Ephesians*, 171.

[53] Schrage, *Ethik*, 258.

[54] Cf. G. Kittel, "ὑπακούω," *TDNT* 1:224–25. In Eph 6:2–3 the fourth commandment is quoted according to Ex 20:12 LXX almost word for word in addition

Most likely the children referred to here are those who are somewhat older and still being raised by the parents.[55] This exhortation implies (cf. the expression "in the Lord") that there were children in the community who were baptized and who therefore belonged to Christ. From passages such as Acts 16:33 (see pp. 121–22), we know that entire households were baptized as one unit. Our passage here is indirect evidence for the assumption that believing children were included in the house churches, as this letter was read to the community.[56]

With his central position in mind, the householder is addressed a second time, this time regarding his responsibility as father. Corresponding to his responsibility to love his wife, the father is to avoid provoking his children. The reason given is that otherwise the children will become discouraged. The psychological sensitivity that is expressed here is surprisingly modern.[57] It is striking as well to note that the emphasis is not on the authority or the rights and privileges of the father in the home but on his responsibilities and duties.[58] This implies that the father, like the women and children, is to fulfill a specific function in the *oikos*. If this function is neglected or misused, the entire household suffers. It is too seldom emphasized in present-day NT exegesis that the household codes clearly maintain that in the *oikos* the special dignity of the husband is found in the fact that he is called to fatherhood—in other words, he is called to be the father, which means being the kind of father God intended him to be.[59]

Interesting in this context is also the comparison with the household code in Ephesians. Ephesians 6:4b includes the addition "instead, bring them up in the training and instruction of the Lord." Here the responsibility of the father to give Christian catechism to the children is addressed.[60] The significance of the house (church) as the place for Christian education and catechetical instruction thereby becomes evident.[61] In the end, as parents raise their children in the Christian faith, they are also making a significant contribution to building the church (cf. also Eph 6:4).[62] Whether

---

to Col 3:20 as further motivation for obedience with the promise "that it may go well with you and that you may enjoy long life on the earth" (cf. Deut 5:15).

[55] Cf. Lohse, *Kolosser und Philemon*, 226; following him, Mussner, *Epheser*, 162. Older children may have also been included here, but most likely they would have been married and lived in their own houses. Cf. E. Sachers, "Potestas patria"; Gielen, "Exkurs 2," in *Tradition*, 146–48; Dunn, *Colossians, Philemon*, 249–50.

[56] Cf. Schweizer, *Kolosser*, 165–66; Gnilka, *Kolosserbrief*, 220; following him, Dunn, *Colossians, Philemon*, 250.

[57] Cf. Schweizer, *Kolosser*, 166; Dunn, *Colossians, Philemon*, 252. But cf. Plutarch *[Lib. ed.]* 7, 10, 12, 16, 2010 (2.4C, 7E, 8F, 9A, 12C, 14A).

[58] Cf. Rengstorf, *Mann und Frau*, 35; following him, Schrage, *Ethik*, 260; Dunn, *Colossians, Philemon*, 251.

[59] Rengstorf, *Mann und Frau*, 35.

[60] Cf. C. Wright, "Family," 2:769.

[61] Cf. also 1 Cor 14:35.

[62] With Lampe, "Zur gesellschaftlichen und kirchlichen Funktion," 539.

catechetical instruction occurred during the worship service in a more or less public setting or at home as private instruction is not explicitly indicated in our text. But because the household code is intended as instruction for the family, it can be assumed that the catechism was also given to the children in the private sphere of the home.[63]

It is important to emphasize that the Colossian household code clearly demonstrates that early Christians viewed the family as an essential life unit ordained by God.[64] Fathers, mothers, and children are all exhorted to care for one another in the states ordered for them in creation. Marriage and the family were extremely important for the early Christian movement, and by taking this view, they strengthened the household, which played such a key role in early Christian missional outreach. Therefore the strengthening of the family simultaneously strengthened the house church model for the missional building up of the church as a whole. A well-functioning household can only exist upon the foundation of a healthy, intact family.[65] Hence a house church could only be established if a well-functioning family existed. It thus becomes clear that a close connection exists between the family as ordained in creation and the NT house church.[66] This insight has significant consequences for present-day missional outreach and church development (see pp. 300–311).

Slaves and Masters (3:22–4:1)

The household code closes with an extensive exhortation to slaves and masters. This admonition is striking if only for its length in comparison with the others, which is again another argument for the topos view taken above.[67] "Slaves, obey your earthly masters in everything; and do it, not only when their eye is on you and to win their favor, but with sincerity of heart and reverence for the Lord. Whatever you do, work at it with all your heart, as working for the Lord, not for men, since you know that you will receive an inheritance from the Lord as a reward. Serve the Lord Christ. Anyone who does wrong will be repaid for his wrong, and there is no favoritism" (3:22-25). This so-called slave admonition consists of two parallel and mu-

---

[63] This would correspond with our present knowledge of Jewish and Greco-Roman families (see pp. 197–99).

[64] Cf. esp. Col 3:18, 19, 20, 21. Cf. also 1 Tim 5:3, 4, 8. This is true also for the household code in Ephesians.

[65] Here it needs to be emphasized that this was true for the ancient world as a whole and thus was not just a "Christian" phenomenon.

[66] This topic, family and house church, which this study has repeatedly touched upon, deserves its own investigation and discussion. Cf. Barton, "Living as Families"; Osiek and Balch, *Families*.

[67] For Caird, *Apostolic Age,* 103 (with Deissmann), this admonition reflects the social structure of these churches, which implies that there were more slaves than masters in the church. This is plausible. On the other hand, Meeks (*First Urban Christians,* 64) points out that this argument is not final: "The contents of the admonitions would certainly be more readily approved by owners than by slaves."

tually corresponding exhortations (v. 22 with v. 24a; v. 24b with v. 25). Between the actual exhortation in 3:22a and the corresponding motivation stands an extensive, well-structured elaboration. The slave admonition forms the heart of the Colossian household code not only because of its length but even more so because of its content.

This section has been called the slave admonition for a reason—the main emphasis of the household code is placed on the exhortation to the slaves, probably because this group best portrays the position of all Christians in their relationship to Christ (cf. 1 Peter).[68] The relationship of Christ to all believers in general is illustrated with the help of *oikos* structures, that is, the interpersonal relationship between slave and master.

The slave admonition in Col 3:22a calls for an all-inclusive obedience (κατὰ πάντα) and implies a relationship of complete dependence on the master.[69] The household code in Colossians does not question the legal position of the slave in the ancient household. The expression κατὰ σάρκα does not have a negative connotation.[70] Instead it limits the master's sphere of power regarding interpersonal relationships within his own *oikos* and draws attention to the contrast with the sphere of power of the Lord in heaven (4:1).[71]

Such statements are found not only in the Colossian household code but in the Letter to Philemon as well. For this reason most commentators point to the case of the slave Onesimus (cf. Col 4:9).[72] It is possible that questions similar to those addressed in Philemon also became acute in the Colossian house churches. What does it mean that the house slave is now "brother" not only in the flesh but also in the Lord (Phlm 16)?[73] Our passage instructs the slave not only to do the minimum in his service to his earthly master in order to avoid punishment or receive his wages—that is, not only to act according to outward appearances in order to merely please men. Rather the Christian slave is to perform his duties with a sincere heart, with reverence for the Lord. "Christian slaves are above all else servants of Christ and they are to work first and foremost so as to please him. Not fear of an earthly master, but reverence for the Lord Christ should be their primary motive."[74] Echoing Col 3:17, this is underscored once again in verse 23.

Verse 24 reminds the slaves that they will receive judgment and reward from the Lord, who measures their performance (3:1). In heaven the eternal

---

[68] Cf. Gielen, *Tradition*, 107–21, 160–98, esp. 160; similarly though not as detailed, Schweizer, *Kolosser*, 164.
[69] O'Brien, *Colossians, Philemon*, 226.
[70] Cf. Gnilka, *Kolosserbrief*, 221; following him, Gielen, *Tradition*, 161.
[71] Cf. O'Brien, *Colossians, Philemon*, 226–27; F. F. Bruce, *Colossians, Philemon, Ephesians*, 293.
[72] Cf. Philemon; Schweizer, *Kolosser*, 167; F. F. Bruce, *Colossians, Philemon, Ephesians*, 167–68; O'Brien, *Colossians, Philemon*, 226; the discussion of Onesimus on pp. 152–54.
[73] Cf. Schweizer, *Kolosser*, 167.
[74] O'Brien, *Colossians, Philemon*, 227.

inheritance is already laid aside (cf. 1:5, 27; 3:1–4).[75] Therefore τῷ κυρίῳ Χριστῷ δουλεύετε. This sentence is not to be understood in an indicative but rather in an imperative sense (particularly in view of ἐργάζεσθε, v. 23). Here one can ask whether the admonition (v. 24b) is also implicitly directed toward the masters, perhaps even toward the entire household.[76] The same applies to verse 25: it addresses at least the masters as well.[77]

The admonition to the slaves finds its necessary counterpart in the instruction to the masters: "Masters, provide your slaves with what is right and fair, because you know that you also have a Master in heaven" (4:1).[78] As was the case for the prior pair of exhortations, here the admonition to the masters is inseparably coupled with the instruction to the slaves (3:22a). The two can only be correctly interpreted in connection with one another.

The masters are not asked to release their slaves. Nevertheless, they are instructed to conscientiously carry out their duties toward their slaves. In contrast to the Roman law regarding the *patria potestas*, the Christian household code here in Colossians does not emphasize the householder's unlimited power of disposal but his duties. These duties are defined on the basis of love. All misuse of the master's rights toward his slaves is prohibited. As the Christian masters are now responsible for their behavior to the Lord, the principle "What is right and fair" takes on new meaning.[79] From now on the masters will be held accountable to the Master of all masters for how they treat their slaves (4:1b). With this a totally new dynamic has entered the relationship between master and slave.[80] "He who sees a brother in Christ in his slave can no longer view him as a slave in the old sense."[81] Because they both owe the Lord obedience, they now have the correct standard for relations with one another, which is brotherly love. Just because love is not mentioned in the admonition to the masters does not mean that the masters are not responsible for acting in love; rather it is a reminder that rights and privileges are not to be separated from love, that love renounces *its* rights but does not renounce right and wrong as such, that even regarding the treatment of their slaves earthly masters will stand before a heavenly Judge, and that as masters they also have a Master.[82] Insofar as they fulfill their duties as householders in this manner, they serve their Master in heaven. Seen in this light, they themselves are slaves of Christ (cf. v. 24b).

---

[75] Cf. ibid., 228–29; F. F. Bruce, *Colossians, Philemon, Ephesians*, 167–69.

[76] Cf. Schweizer, *Kolosser*, 168; Gielen, *Tradition*, 191–93.

[77] Schweizer, *Kolosser*, 168; Lohse, *Kolosser und Philemon*, 230, leaves the question open; cf. O'Brien, *Colossians, Philemon*, 230–31, for a discussion of the various opinions among exegetes.

[78] Schweizer, *Kolosser*, 168.

[79] For the meaning of the principle in the ancient world, cf. G. Schrenk, "δίκαιος," *TDNT* 2:182–87; Stählin, "ἴσος," *TDNT* 3:343–55; Crouch, *Origin*, 117–19; Schweizer, *Kolosser*, 168–69; Lohse, *Kolosser und Philemon*, 229–30.

[80] Cf. Lohse, *Kolosser und Philemon*, 231.

[81] Mussner, *Epheser*, 165.

[82] Schrage, "Zur Ethik," 15; cf. also *Die konkreten Einzelgebote*, 266.

Household Code in Ephesians as a Rule of Order

Structural Analysis of Eph 5:21–6:9

The household code in Ephesians consists of 5:21–6:9.[83] In contrast to the code in Colossians, that in Ephesians does not begin quite so abruptly. Instead a series of participles beginning with 5:19 provide for a much softer transition. In addition, a general instruction addressing all members rather than merely a specific group (5:21) is inserted; this, however, is already an integral part of the Ephesian household code as such. Because verse 21 is addressed to all community members and because of its structural position in the overall paraenesis, it becomes a kind of heading for the code thereby takes on the function of a *Leitsatz*, or guiding principle, for the entire Ephesian household code.[84] The end of the code is clearly designated by the term τοῦ λοιποῦ (6:10), typically used in transition and here indicating the beginning of a new (final) section.

A number of observations can be made regarding the overall structure of our passage. All of those being addressed have one thing in common: *oikos* affiliation. Thus, just as in Colossians, the Ephesian paraenetic instruction also deserves the designation "*household* code." As in Col 3:18–4:1, the Ephesian code addresses in three pairs the six groups that constituted an ancient *oikos* (women/men; children/fathers; slaves/masters) with reciprocal, apodictic instructions in the same sequence as in Colossians. These six groups are distinctly highlighted through the repetition of the address typical for the household codes and characterized by the use of the definite article and nominative plural. As in Colossians, in all three pairs the instructions are first given to the subordinate group: women, children, and slaves.

In contrast with the Colossian code (nine verses), the Ephesian code has more than double that, with a total of twenty-two. Particularly striking is the expansion of the first pair of instructions for married couples from two verses in Colossians (3:18–19) to twelve in Ephesians (5:22–33), more than half of the entire Ephesian household code. Thus it is already evident even before our exegetical analysis that, in contrast to the Colossian code with the prominence it gave to the slave/master admonition, the primary accent in the Ephesian code has been placed on the instruction for married couples.

---

[83] The present study draws clear conclusions on the household code as a rule of order for the church on pp. 247–54 and 257–60. For a brief discussion of the introductory questions on Ephesians concerning authorship, etc., and my position regarding these issues, cf. Gehring, *Hausgemeinde*, 413–14.

[84] All community members are indicated by the masculine participle (with Schnackenburg, *Epheser*, 248).

Exegetical Analysis of Eph 5:21–6:9

This section will not attempt an exhaustive exegesis of the Ephesian household code but rather will focus on the discussion of the issues that appear to be relevant for our study of the house church, with particular attention given to content not common with the Colossian code.

Husbands and Wives (5:21–33)

One striking difference from the Colossian code is found in the very first verse (Eph 5:21), the so-called *Leitsatz* of the household code in Ephesians.[85] All members of the community are to submit to one another out of reverence for Christ. In the Greek text verse 21 is also closely linked with the previous section through a participial construction. Grammatically, ὑποτασσόμενοι is the last of four coordinated participles all dependent on the verb πληροῦσθε in verse 18b. The broader implication here is that the precondition for being able to put the admonitions regarding the Christian household (up to Eph 6:9) into practice is to allow oneself to be filled with the Spirit.[86] Also, the participle ὑποτασσόμενοι has a grammatical impact on the following text as well: it is understood that the verb for verse 22 is to be supplied from this participle. In light of all this, it is not surprising that many view verse 21 as the heading for the Ephesian code; one exegete has suggested "Obedient Christian Existence in Reverence to Christ."[87]

From the very onset of the Ephesian code, then, the principle of mutual submission[88] one to another is to transform the social structures of the ancient *oikos*.[89] Submission in this sense can thus be understood as the comprehensive expression for Christian behavior in community.[90] The entire Ephesian household code should be interpreted with this in mind. This principle is rooted in the obligation of all Christians to live in reverence to Jesus Christ.

In contrasting the Ephesian household code to the one in Colossians, a few additional observations can be made. First, characteristic of the Ephesian code is a stronger emphasis on love (cf. esp. Eph 5:25, 28), not only in a formal sense but in terms of content as well. As in the Colossian code, the submission of the woman to her husband is "firmly anchored in the love of the husband for his wife."[91] Here as well the charge to the husbands to love

---

[85] For an informative discussion of the possible tradition behind the Ephesian code, cf. Sampley, *"And the Two."*

[86] This has been observed by a number of exegetes. Cf. Baumert, *Frau*, 193.

[87] Schlier, *Epheser*, 250.

[88] Cf. Gal 5:13; Phil 2:3b; 1 Pet 5:5b; the introductory admonition in Eph 4:1–3.

[89] Cf. Ernst, *Briefe*, 382; following him, Mussner, *Epheser*, 156.

[90] Cf. Kamlah, "ὑποτάσσεσθαι," 238: submission is understood here as *the* characteristic of early Christian household codes, Following him, Schnackenburg, *Epheser*, 250.

[91] Mussner, *Epheser*, 152; cf. also Baumert, *Frau*, 205.

their wives forms the nonnegotiable counterweight of the admonition to the wives regarding submission. Even though the husband is called "the head of the wife" (v. 23a; cf. 1 Cor 11:3), the predicate "head" is integrally linked with the phrase "as Christ is head of the church" (v. 23b). As a result, the term "head" is given a special semantic nuance.[92]

Second, the Ephesian code also anchors its ethical instruction ἐν κυρίῳ. Here, however, the love between husband and wife is even more solidly grounded "in the Lord Jesus Christ." This is due to the fact that the marriage admonition of Ephesians is to be understood as "mimesis" ethic—to practice love and submission in marriage is seen as imitating the example of Jesus Christ.[93] The bond between husband and wife is portrayed in analogy to the relationship of Christ, the "head," to the church, his "body."[94] Just as Christ, in his death on the cross, gave his everything for the church (cf. Mark 10:42–45), the love of the husband for his wife is also supposed to be radically sacrificial.[95] Once the husband understands his task in the marriage in light of the christological conditions outlined above, "he will consider it both a privilege and a grave responsibility. Even more than an enlightened monarch in his relation to his subjects, he is then 'the first servant' of his wife. In short, a headship qualified, interpreted, and limited by Christ alone is proclaimed, not an unlimited headship that can be arbitrarily defined and has to be endured."[96] Here again there is no evidence for a "gentrification" (*Verbürgerlichung*) of this early Christian community. On the contrary, what we see here is again an "evangelization" of the ancient household in an even more vigorous form than we have already witnessed in the Colossian code.

This view is confirmed by the soteriological, christological, and creation theology assertions made in the Ephesian household code. The concept of "being in Christ" (cf., e.g., 1 Cor 7:39c; 8:6) is crucial to understanding the correlation between Christ and creation in Paul's writings. If creation is "in Christ," then it follows that it is sanctified through Christ—in other words, drawn into the order of salvation. Here Ephesians appears very much to be in alignment with Pauline tradition. In Eph 1:21–23 Christ is described as being the "head over everything" as a result of his salvific work, particularly in his resurrection (cf. Col 1:15–20 as well). He is the head of not only

---

[92] Barth, *Ephesians*, 620, speaks of a "subordination to love" on the part of the wife. "Only this and nothing else is preached in Eph 5:21–33. Where there is no love Paul does not expect submission."

[93] Cf. Schrage, "Zur Ethik," 15–17; following him, Mussner, *Epheser*, 153.

[94] The ecclesiological assertions in the Ephesian code are not merely examples for the instruction on marriage but rather the actual objective of the passage. Nevertheless the "head-body" and the "bride-groom" ecclesiologies will not be discussed here (cf. Gehring, *Hausgemeinde*, 417 n. 177; the reputable commentaries on the subject).

[95] Cf. Barth, *Ephesians*, 618; Rengstorf, *Mann und Frau*, 131–45; following him, Mussner, *Epheser*, 153.

[96] Barth, *Ephesians*, 618–19.

the new but also of the old creation.⁹⁷ All of created life, including marriage, has been put under his authority. This applies all the more for *Christian* marriage, which has been placed into the domain of the church, for which Jesus Christ has been appointed "head."

Because creational order has been renewed in Christ, he is also its founder and guarantor. According to Eph 5:25–33, marriage corresponds to the intimate relationship between Christ and the church, which itself represents the mystery of perfect unity referred to in Gen 2:24. If the relationship between Christ and the church is an image and a prototype for marriage, it follows that Christ, as the representative of this image, also guarantees the correspondence—that is, that the correspondence really exists. He who answers for the actual image also answers for the correspondence.⁹⁸ According to Eph 5:21–31; 6:1–7, Christ is therefore not only savior but also the founder and guarantor of the order of creation, which is observed exemplarily in the church: in and through Christ created life is sanctified—in marriage, in the family, in the household, and in the church. It therefore becomes evident that Ephesians ascribes a special dignity to the *oikos:* the basic structure of the *oikos* has been ordained by God. This perspective can be traced all the way back to the Jesus tradition (compare 1 Cor 6:16 with Mark 10:7–8/Matt 19:4).

Slaves and Masters (6:5–9)

For the most part, the instructions to the slaves correspond with Col 3:22–4:1. What is unprecedented is that in both, the obedience of the slaves toward their earthly masters is understood entirely as an exercise in obedience toward Christ.⁹⁹ In comparison with Colossians, here the expression "slaves of Christ" (v. 6b) catches our attention. In Gal 1:10 Paul contrasts between someone who desires to be a servant of Christ and one who merely wants to please men. It could be that, by using the phrase "slaves of Christ," the author of Ephesians is reaffirming the Pauline perspective that all Christians, including the masters, should be servants of Christ (see n. 68). In both cases the burden of the slaves' obligation to obey their masters is lightened by adding the motivation that God rewards a person for doing good, whether he is slave or free.

Exegetes have drawn attention to another difference between the Colossian and Ephesian codes. Whereas Col 3:22–23 clearly differentiates the earthly masters from the Master Jesus Christ, Eph 6:5b appears to associate them more closely with one another: "obey your earthly masters . . . as you would obey Christ."¹⁰⁰ The slaves are no longer admonished to fear

---

⁹⁷ Cf. Schlier, *Epheser*, 89.
⁹⁸ Cf. Käsemann, *Jesu letzter Wille*, 142–43. Cf. also P. Brunner, "Theologie," 226–29.
⁹⁹ Mussner, *Epheser*, 164.
¹⁰⁰ Cf. Schweizer, "Weltlichkeit," 409–10.

God alone (Col 3:22) but rather to obey their earthly masters "with respect and fear."[101] According to some scholars, this passage appears to encourage the misunderstanding that serving God can be identified with the service of the more affluent, higher social classes (cf. also 1 Pet 2:18–25). The danger of such a misunderstanding is clearly averted, however, through the emphasis on "earthly" in verse 5a and the comment in verse 9b, "since you know that he who is both their Master and yours in heaven."[102]

In the brief instruction to the masters, they are admonished to treat their slaves "in the same way" without clearly defining what "the same" actually means. Does it refer to the doing of good in verse 8, or maybe to verses 6b, 7a, that they, like slaves of Christ, should do the will of God from their heart and serve wholeheartedly? In light of the fact that slaves and masters are put in the same category with regard to their position before Christ (v. 9b), it can be assumed that the author is requiring a corresponding behavior from the masters. "What is recommended for the slaves also applies mutatis mutandis for the masters. They have the authority but are not to misuse it in a harsh or threatening manner; rather they are to exercise it according to the will of their mutual Master, that is, with gentleness and goodness."[103] With the expectation that they will do the will of the Master, it is surely implied that the Christian masters are at the same time to be servants of Christ. An important theological insight of Paul's is thereby underscored. This may well be the reason the motif "there is no favoritism with the Master in heaven" is applied to both groups in the Ephesian household code in contrast to Colossians (cf. 3:25).[104]

The Development of Household Ethics from the Christian *Oikos*

On the basis of our exegesis, it is now possible to address the concerns of Schüssler Fiorenza and S. Schulz reviewed earlier. For Schüssler Fiorenza the household codes represent an example of a revival of patriarchal subjection even though Christians had other options from which to choose, such as the early Christian missional movement (cf. Gal 3:28) and models in the surrounding environment, all of which would have been much more humane and egalitarian.[105]

First of all, one can ask whether it is legitimate to so generally conclude that the household code tradition is in fact a revival of patriarchal subjection. The Colossian code contains a number of elements critical of ancient patriarchal structures. Whereas Aristotle argues that the appropriate relationship

---

[101] Cf., even more unreserved, Titus 2:9.
[102] Cf. esp. Schweizer, "Weltlichkeit," 409–10.
[103] Schnackenburg, *Epheser*, 271; F. F. Bruce, *Colossians, Philemon, Ephesians*, 401–2.
[104] Cf. Mitton, *Ephesians*, 70-71.
[105] Cf. Gehring, *Hausgemeinde*, 394–96, for a review of her points. For a criticism of Schüssler Fiorenza, cf. Balch, "Early Christian"; Campbell, *Elders*, 154–55.

between master and slave is one of "tyranny" and not of "justice," Col 4:1 admonishes the masters to treat their slaves in a manner that is "right and fair" (see our exegesis above).[106] The emphasis in the Colossian code is placed not on the authority of the householder but on his duties (see n. 57). In the Ephesian code *all* members of the community are instructed to practice mutual submission (Eph 5:21).

Second, to a great extent Schüssler Fiorenza follows Thraede, who refers to ancient authors such as Columella, Antipater, and Plutarch in an attempt to demonstrate that household structures were widely debated back then.[107] According to Thraede, the writings of these authors show that these structures were not at all set in stone but rather quite fluid. At the time Colossians was written, there existed widespread a number of more liberal, humane forms of marriage and family with genuine gender equality.[108]

Balch, however, has criticized this view.[109] Without wanting to deny the historicity of such a debate, Balch points out that one must distinguish between these authors' theoretical discussions and their practical recommendations:[110] "The Roman Stoics Antipater, Musonius Rufus, and Hierocles as well as the Middle Platonist Plutarch demonstrate that the subordination of wives was general, contemporary Hellenistic *practice*. Some writers held the Stoic *theory* of the natural equality of the sexes while encouraging the Aristotelian practice of the subordination of wives to husbands."[111] One should not use the isolated text from Columella as evidence for the view that the traditional social roles were no longer in effect or that the wife was considered socially or politically equal to her husband. Columella is merely an indication that the wives of affluent husbands often did not fulfill their duties.[112] "Those Hellenistic philosophers discussed above, whom modern authors have interpreted as egalitarians, in practice

---

[106] Cf. Aristotle, *Eth. nic.* 5.1134b.9–18; 8.1060a.23–8.1661a.10. Cf. also 1 Pet 2:19–23; 3:1; 1:18; 4:3; Balch, "Household Codes," *ABD* 3:319.

[107] Thraede, "Ärger," 51–63, 68–69, 85–86; "Zum historischen Hintergrund," 359–68, here 365; "Frau." Cf. also Müller, "Haustafel," 277–319; Gielen, *Tradition*, 129–35. Columella, *Rust.* 12.pref.5 and 7–10; 12.2.6; cf. Thraede, "Frau"; for his references to Columella, cf. esp. 203, 206, 210, 217, 239. Cf. Antipater, *Für und wider die Ehe* (Arnim and Gaiser), 254.23–257.10; Thraede, "Ärger," 58–59. Cf. Plutarch, *Mulierum virtutes; Conjugalia praecepta; Amatorius*; Thraede, "Ärger," 60, 85; and "Frau," 8:215.

[108] Thraede, "Ärger," 44, 81, and "Frau."

[109] Balch, *Let Wives*, 143–49. Cf. also, critical of Thraede, Laub, *Begegnung*, 95.

[110] Cf. also in Lutz, Musonius Rufus, "That Women Too Should Study Philosophy," *Or.* 3.38.26–3.40.2, 3.42.10–15, 17; "Should Daughters Receive the Same Education as Sons," *Or.* 4.46.13–32; "Sexual Indulgence," 12.86.38–13.88.4. Cf. also Hierocles, 22–23; 503.12–16.

[111] Balch, *Let Wives*, 147 (italics added). Cf. Plutarch, *Conj. praec.* 142D, E; also Schrage, "Zur Ethik," 13. This passage is not an isolated incident; cf. Plutarch, *Lyc.* 14.1; *Ant.* 10.

[112] Balch, *Let Wives*, 144.

urged the subordination of wives, and their practical philosophical views are properly *compared,* not *contrasted,* with the *practical,* paraenetic domestic codes in the New Testament."[113]

The Colossian household code did not intend to give theoretical instruction but rather wanted to regulate practice. It addresses concrete questions, such as how a husband and wife are to live in relationship with one another. One cannot look for the identity of early Christians somewhere beyond their own sexuality, beyond the created polarity of man and woman. In the ancient world the choice between ascetical, matriarchal, and patriarchal domestic structures existed only theoretically.[114] As those wanting to remain faithful to Pauline tradition, it is highly unlikely that the Ephesian Christians could have felt called to withdraw from the world into some sort of ascetical community lifestyle.[115] Neither were matriarchal structures a real possibility. This would have merely reversed the roles of submission without doing away with them. Structures thus would have continued to be in effect that still had the potential of being every bit as repressive. For the early Christians there remained only one form of domestic life to embrace: that within the *oikos* structure, which came quite naturally because of the house church setting of their assemblies, and which was congruent with their theology.[116]

The NT household codes are not the result of a decision made by early Christians to choose any one of the already existing social forms common during that period.[117] First of all, there is no evidence in our texts that the authors of either Ephesians or Colossians were aware of any such debate, let alone that they took part in it. It seems more likely that the domestic codes are expressed in more humane terms because they were developed theologically and permeated by Christology (see pp. 236–38).[118] It appears that the domestically oriented paraenesis of the household codes is also an expression of the central significance of the *oikos* as the foundational social structure for the beginnings of early Christianity.[119] The domestic

---

[113] Ibid., 147 (italics added). When comparing the NT household codes with patriarchal forms common in the surrounding environment, scholars agree that they indeed belong to the more moderate category (cf., e.g., Gielen, *Tradition,* 129–44).

[114] D'Arms, "Roman Convivium," also concludes, on the basis of his research of that period, that the patriarchal hierarchy remained intact in society as a whole in spite of equalitarian rhetoric.

[115] For this reason the Therapeutae mentioned by Philo cannot be considered evidence for the fact that the Pauline house churches had other choices regarding domestic structures, as Schüssler Fiorenza suggests (*Zu ihrem Gedächtnis,* 267–69, 309–16). The Pauline communities neither were nor wanted to be ascetic. Cf. Schrage, "Zur Ethik," 6.

[116] It is possible that a house church that met in a home where there was no housefather could have had matriarchal structures (see pp. 210–25, the excursus on leadership responsibilities of women in Pauline house churches).

[117] Against Gielen, *Tradition,* 129–44.

[118] Against Thraede, "Zum historischen Hintergrund," 359–61, 367 nn. 1–10; "Ärger," 122.

[119] Laub, "Sozialgeschichtlicher Hintergrund," 254.

codes are best characterized as "admonitions within the only conceivable structures of those days past."[120]

On the basis of our exegesis, we can go even one step further: in Christ, mediator of creation, neither Paul nor the churches in Colossae and in Ephesus had the freedom to choose other social structures in the place of marriage and family. They were theologically obligated to choose these, as both had been handed down to them through the creation traditions found in Scripture, primarily in wisdom literature. In their minds, their only choice was to faithfully interpret this creation tradition for their community in devotion to that tradition, to the church, and to God.[121] This is one more reason the Pauline churches attributed such great significance to the *oikos* as the seminal cell of the church, and it is why they did not hesitate to adopt and adapt (i.e., "evangelize") the contemporary patriarchal household order into Christian form.

What of the concerns raised by S. Schulz? Taking a revolutionary point of departure, Schulz is convinced on the basis of Gal 3:28 that early Christianity advocated and offered complete liberation. In contrast, Paul (1 Cor 7) and the domestic codes represent a regression.[122] But as we have already determined, early Christians could not choose just any social model, and they were not interested in developing totally new models.[123] Early Christians had no intention of instigating a social revolution. The early Christian movement was not one that consciously and primarily aimed at effecting social and economic change even though its proclamation had social and economic consequences.[124] When it came to slavery, an institution sanctioned by Roman law and from the beginning an integral part of Greco-Roman and Jewish society, early Christians strove neither for the acceptance nor for the abolition of it. "Christianity certainly did not adopt more radical critiques of society . . . , or pursue utopian dreams by encouraging slave rebellions, all of which could have resulted in the demise of Christianity within a few generations."[125]

Furthermore, it is historically inappropriate to accuse the Pauline communities of being too tolerant toward slavery, one of the cruelest and most brutal institutions ever known. It is unfair because it assumes a widely held modern anthropological consciousness that was virtually nonexistent in ancient society.[126] Just as historically inappropriate is the allegation that slaves

---

[120] Lührmann, "Wo nicht mehr," 81; cf. also 63 n. 31.

[121] Thraede has a sense for the christological problem here. Cf. "Zum historischen Hintergrund," 359–61, 367 nn. 1–10, and "Ärger," 122.

[122] Cf., for further criticism of Schulz, Eichholz, *Theologie*, 278–80; Schweizer, "Zum Sklavenproblem"; Stuhlmacher, "Historisch unangemessen."

[123] Cf. Lohse, *Kolosser und Philemon*, 231–32.

[124] Cf. Lührmann, "Neutestamentliche Haustafeln," 91.

[125] Cf. Dunn, *Colossians, Philemon*, 246; cf. also Stuhlmacher, "Historisch Unangemessen," 298.

[126] With Stuhlmacher, "Historisch Unangemessen," 298. Cf. Yarbrough, "Hermeneutics," who correctly points out that "the self-congratulatory appeal of modern

were generally treated cruelly throughout the entire ancient world.[127] The primary concern of the ancient household management literature was not only the authority of the householders but also their high duty to care for and protect, which was to affect the way they carried out all of their tasks for the overall good of the entire *oikos*.[128] S. Schulz either ignores or fails to recognize that freedom remains abstract as long as it does not simultaneously guarantee the economic foundation for that freedom; under the conditions of the ancient world, this meant the management of one's own house.[129] In his novel Petronius creates the figure of Trimalchio, who becomes an example of the social and economic possibilities for advancement that existed in the ancient world for liberated slaves. It is important to note, however, that this advancement took place within the system and not outside it.

The first Christians were more concerned about the question—particularly once it became clear that the second coming of Christ was not necessarily imminent—how the economic means could be secured to keep on living as a family and/or as a house church. In the Colossian household code, concrete ethical questions are the primary focus. What are believers to do and not to do as husbands and wives, as masters and slaves, as parents and children in a small economic faith community that belonged to the church of Christ and wanted to live in obedience to the Lord? What are the consequences of Christian faith for a small domestic economic unit that needs servants in order to continue its existence? What does it mean for household management that slaves are now brothers in a spiritual sense? All of these and more are concrete and pressing issues addressed in the domestic codes. The continued existence of house churches in this world was at stake.

It could be that the Colossian code intends to correct the misunderstanding caused by an overspiritualizing denial of the world and wants to call believers back to the simple duties of daily life in the family (cf. 1 Thess 5:14; 2 Thess 3:11–13). Even though the author of Colossians exhorts the church members to "set their hearts on things above, not on earthly things," his concept of life under the leadership of Christ above is actually a life that is to be lived down here on earth: in marriage, in family, and in the daily duties of

---

Westerners overlooks that modern liberal economic and labor structures are in essential respects too reminiscent of the ancient institution of slavery to condemn the Bible's world order" (pp. 189–90). He asserts that in a sense the modern equivalent to slavery still exists in the form of those who work for a living, which means virtually everyone, although it is true that we are not "slaves" in the traditional, restricted sense. Nevertheless, "a few still reign, and most still serve them with the best efforts of their productive years. The alternative is to suffer the consequences—at best welfare or the dole, otherwise life on the streets" (p. 187).

[127] Cf. Judge, *Social Pattern*, 38, 60; see pp. 176–77.
[128] Laub, "Sozialgeschichtlicher Hintergrund," 258; F. Wagner, *Bild*.
[129] Lührmann, "Neutestamentliche Haustafeln," 90 n. 40. The necessary and desirable abolition of slavery in the United States was in itself not sufficient, as it did not solve the social and economic problems encountered by former slaves.

our work.[130] The lordship of Christ *in* the world (cf. Col 1:15–20)—and this means in all areas of human life, including the *oikos*—is the focus of the Letter to the Colossians and its household code.[131]

In the context close to our household code, Col 3:11 says, "Here there is no Greek or Jew, circumcised or uncircumcised, barbarian, Scythian, slave or free, but Christ is all, and is in all." There is a tension here between freedom, which is freely given in Christ, and "slavery," in which the Christian slave was supposed to continue to serve his master (cf. 1 Cor 7:21–24).[132] It is all about the realization of the new creation within the context of the still existing old creation. Thus the theological question is how a person, as a member of the community of Christ, or a group, as a house church and as new creation (compare Gal 3:28 with Col 3:11), can live credibly inwardly and outwardly in the context of the old world as it continues to exist.[133] The authors of Ephesians and Colossians decided against a revolution of the external social circumstances and for a spiritual transformation from the inside out.

In Colossians—historically for the first time, as far as we can discern—the question of what it means de facto for Christian families to live under the banner "here there is no Greek or Jew . . ." becomes the focus of systematic reflection. The author of Colossians integrated Col 3:11 with the domestic code in 3:18–4:1. He was very much aware that the two were in tension with one another, a tension between living a new existence and simultaneously having to remain in the old.[134] Here it is acknowledged that one is no longer of the world but nevertheless must still live in the world. Christians are not to live in denial of the world. Instead they should prove themselves in the world. The model advocated by the household code represents an extraordinary intellectual and missional achievement that attempts to avoid the two extremes: the complete rejection of social contact with the world, on the one hand, and a total and uncritical assimilation into society, on the other.

Paul protests implicitly and explicitly against an overly enthusiastic attitude that ignores the structures of this world and considers ways of life from the past antiquated in light of the eminent dawning of a new world (cf. Rom 13:1–3; 1 Cor 11:2–4; 14:40).[135] The pairs slave/free, male/female in Gal 3:28, a text foundational for the Pauline churches, demonstrate that the

---

[130] Schweizer, "Traditional Ethical Patterns," 204; following him, O'Brien, *Colossians, Philemon,* 219.

[131] Cf. Schrage, "Zur Ethik," 6; Lohse, "Christologie," 249–52.

[132] Cf. O'Brien, *Colossians, Philemon,* 226. Regarding 1 Cor 7:21–23, cf. the discussion of the possibilities with his own position as well as a critique of Schulz in Stuhlmacher, *Philemon,* 45–48. Cf. also Wendland, "Sklaverei"; Gülzow, *Kirche* and *Christentum;* Laub, *Begegnung;* Gnilka, "Exkurs: Sklaven," in *Philemonbrief,* 54–56.

[133] Schrage, "Zur Ethik," 5; Stuhlmacher, "Historisch unangemessen," 298.

[134] Cf. Bieritz, "Rückkehr?" 120, who sees a remaining tension here that was engraved into the emerging Christian church and her self-understanding.

[135] With Schrage, "Zur Ethik," 5.

oikos was in view from the very beginning.[136] The negative formulation of 3:28 leaves different possibilities open. The Pauline interpretation of 3:28 in 1 Cor 7 appears surprisingly conservative to us with its assertion that socially everything should remain as it is.[137] On the one hand, in 1 Cor 7 it is clear that the foundation of the *oikos* can be shaken through the conversion of one of the spouses (vv. 12–13); on the other hand, Paul does not draw this conclusion. On the contrary, he proceeds quite cautiously and places a high value on preserving the marriage in Christ and thereby preserving the *oikos*.[138]

In Lührmann's opinion, modernity's tendency to focus on the issue of ancient slavery as an unjust institution and on the apparent passivity of the household code toward its social injustice actually distracts our attention from another important fact.[139] The integration, even that of the slaves, which is referred to in Gal 3:28 (cf. also 1 Cor 12:13), became more or less a reality in Christian house churches (see pp. 187–90).[140] This is documented with a slightly different accent in the Colossian and Ephesian household codes. In light of ancient social history, one must agree with F. Laub: "The household and church code tradition with its slave paraenesis is evidence of an extraordinary dynamic for community formation and a powerful force for social integration within the early Christian churches."[141] We dare not overlook that, contrary to the ancient household management literature, in the household codes the slave appears as a full member of the church in that he is addressed as a responsible individual.[142] Even though the motif of submission now and again unquestionably shines through, it was

---

[136] The expression "male/female" does not perfectly correspond with the terminology in the household codes, but it is an intentional allusion to Gen 1:27. The pair "slave/free" is also not the same social relationship as the "master/slave" of the domestic codes but is rather a description of status.

[137] Lührmann, "Neutestamentliche Haustafeln," 92. Bartchy, μᾶλλον χρῆσαι, 162–65, has drawn attention to the connection between Gal 3:28 and 1 Cor 7. Jew/Greek (1 Cor 7:18, 20), slave/free (1 Cor 7:21–23), and the relationship husband/wife are the actual topics of the section.

[138] Cf., however, 1 Cor 7:15. In this context it becomes clear that for Paul marriage has great importance but that belonging to the church has greater importance. The church's new existence in Christ is of eternal value and dare not be jeopardized, not even for the preservation of a (mixed) marriage.

[139] Lührmann, "Wo man nicht mehr," 67. Lührmann is perhaps the first scholar to view the household codes from this perspective. Following him, Laub, *Begegnung*, 92; but he exaggerates somewhat in representing this integration as something totally new and specifically Christian ("Sozialgeschichtlicher Hintergrund," 268–69, 271). Cf. Bömer, *Wichtigsten Kulte*, esp. 3:229–34.

[140] So also Stuhlmacher, *Philemon*, 74, and "Historisch unangemessen," 298.

[141] Laub, *Begegnung*, 92.

[142] In the household management tradition, the slave is considered capable of this only in a limited sense. Cf., e.g., Aristotle, *Pol.* 1.1259b.21–1260b.24. It also does not speak to the slave about his ethical religious responsibility but rather attempts to skillfully motivate him to do what is right. Cf. Xenophon, *Oec.* 13.9–12; 14.9.

not primarily the authority structures of the *oikos* that brought and held house churches together.[143] It was rather a love that overcame all social barriers—brotherly love based on a soteriology anchored in the sacrificial death of Christ on the cross enabling a salvation that is available to all people, including slaves. The fact that Christian house churches usually attracted and integrated a large variety of people is primarily and integrally related to the inner structure of this new faith (Col 3:11; Gal 3:27–28). Simply meeting in a house church, that is, in the *oikos* structures of a private domestic house, did not automatically lead to the reconciliation of all those from such diverse backgrounds.[144]

From the very beginning, the Pauline proclamation of the crucified one and with it his teaching on justification by faith were designed to lead to community formation and not just individual religious self-realization.[145] It can even be asked not only whether Pauline ecclesiology was open for the social formation of the church according to the *oikos* model[146] but whether this was a consequence of his proclamation from the very beginning.[147] The letters to the Colossians and the Ephesians certainly view it as a consequence (see pp. 257–60).

This decision to adopt the *oikos* structure also had a positive consequence for the relationship between church and society. The ancient *oikos* reflected the status order of that period, which was composed of all the different social classes. As a result of the decision to adopt the *oikos* order, the house church corresponded structurally with the rest of ancient society. Thus Christianity settled into virtually all, rather than just a few, social classes and avoided becoming socially one-sided or even isolated.[148] "It also had the bonus of demonstrating the good citizenship of the young churches, facilitating communication with the rest of society, and making possible an apologetic and evangelistic impact which should not be discounted."[149] This

---

[143] Regarding community formation, however, the later household tradition reveals a growing interest in order and authority, i.e., in hierarchically ordered structures relating to social-ethics issues (cf. 1 Tim 6:1, 2; Titus 2:9; 1 Pet 2:18; *1 Clem.* 21:6–9; 1:3; Ign. *Pol.* 6:1; *Did.* 4:11; *Barn.* 19:7; see the discussion of the Pastoral Letters on pp. 260–81).

[144] Exclusively men gathered in the house Mithraea; usually members of the same social class gathered together in the *collegia*. The social makeup of house synagogues was somewhat more varied, but even there the inclination was toward gatherings of compatriots or vocational colleagues, which always tends to have an excluding effect.

[145] Cf. Lührmann, "Neutestamentliche Haustafeln," 93.

[146] Cf. the *oikos* terminology by Paul and, above, the excursus on the Pauline understanding of the body of Christ and the family of God (see pp. 162–64), which demonstrated that for Paul σῶμα Χριστοῦ and *familia Dei* belong together. Cf. also Vielhauer, "'Oikodome'"; I. Kitzberger, *Bau der Gemeinde*.

[147] So, e.g., Lührmann, "Neutestamentliche Haustafeln," 93.

[148] Cf. Popkes, "Forschugshinweise"; Pokorný, *Kolosser*, 177–80.

[149] Dunn, *Colossians, Philemon*, 245.

decision not only had a positive effect on the spread of the Christian message. It enabled tradition, continuity, and duration for the church as a whole. By embracing the *oikos* structure, the church became capable of long-term survival and was able to make the transition from one generation to the next.[150] In retrospect, we know that the approach taken here was the one to which the future of the church belonged.[151]

This perspective has been hotly disputed, however, by a number of scholars. Schöllgen, in particular, has criticized the position held by Laub, who maintains that the *oikos* model was "advanced and became a foundational interpretive model for all of early church history."[152] Schöllgen must admit that the case made by Laub and others possesses a fairly compelling inner logic in its explanation of early Christian church development.[153] With the ancient *oikos* as the guiding pattern, we have an all-encompassing perspective that unites all other theological and sociohistorical explanatory models. Nevertheless, in the end, he does not find Laub's arguments in support of an "Oikos-Church" convincing.

According to Schöllgen, the early church most certainly did not adopt the ancient household "as the formative model for her ecclesiology, church development, and social relationships among believers."[154] For him there are only two alternatives. On the one hand, we have the undisputed fact that Christian communities met in private homes, and this constitutes a merely technical assertion; on the other hand, the consequence of this fact was that "the choice of the gathering place was formational for the self-understanding and the organizational structures of the individual churches to such an extent that the ancient *oikos* can be seen as *the* formational model for ecclesiology."[155]

The main thrust of Schöllgen's argumentation is found in the results of his examination of *oikos* metaphor in the context of ecclesiological assertions made in the NT. He concludes that, for the first two Christian generations, there is no evidence in our sources for the logical development of

---

[150] Cf. Lührmann, "Neutestamentliche Haustafeln," 93–94; following him, Popkes, "Forschungshinweis," 12. This is particularly clear in the Ephesian domestic code and later even more so in the Pastoral Epistles (see pp. 260–81).

[151] Cf. Klauck, *Hausgemeinde,* 47; Laub, *Begegnung,* 89; O. Brunner, "Das 'ganze Haus'" (1956), 38; following him, Laub, "Sozialgeschichtliche Hintergrund," 257. *Oikos* structures remained significant for the first three centuries. It was not until Constantine that all this changed (see pp. 1–16 on the history of scholarship). Cf. Ratzinger, *Volk und Haus,* 159–87, for the effect of the notion of the house of God as articulated in Augustine's ecclesiology on church history.

[152] Schöllgen, "Hausgemeinden," esp. 76; following him, Wagener, *Ordnung,* 36–38.

[153] Cf. Klauck, *Hausgemeinde,* 21–81; Dassmann, "Hausgemeinde," 82–84; Vogler, "Bedeutung," 785–87.

[154] Schöllgen, "Hausgemeinde," 76.

[155] Ibid., 80.

church organization in alignment with the ancient *oikos* model.[156] House and family metaphors are certainly quite common in Paul's writings, but they did not function as an ecclesiological model for him. They served merely as a means for defining the individual aspects of the believer's relationship to God or the relationship of the community members one to another. Nor are the household codes evidence for the view that these communities understood themselves as *oikos* churches. They intended to establish guidelines for family structures but were not concerned about church order. In addition, the codes did not use *oikos* vocabulary metaphorically. Not until the third generation, in the Pastoral Epistles with their οἶκος θεοῦ as leitmotif, can an "*oikos* ecclesiology" be documented.

Schöllgen supports his case partially on the basis of a position, developed by Gielen, that is not convincing (see pp. 155–65). Schöllgen certainly is correct, however, in stressing that an *oikos* ecclesiology is first clearly documented in the Pastoral Letters. Neither can it be disputed that the body of Christ and not the ancient *oikos* represents the primary guiding metaphor for the development of Paul's ecclesiology.[157] By maintaining, however, that either the *oikos* played a key role in the formation of NT ecclesiology or acknowledgement of the existence of house churches is a mere technical assertion, Schöllgen creates a false alternative. Between those two options is a broad spectrum of different possibilities. The arguments suggesting that family metaphors played a totally subordinate role in the formation of Pauline ecclesiology are not at all compelling. As already demonstrated, the body of Christ and the family of God belong together in Paul's understanding of the church (see pp. 162–64). In the ancient world the Hellenistic view that *oikos* structures served as a model for public life in the πόλις was fairly widespread. Quite early on, this may have prepared the logical step to expand the application of domestic *oikos* ethics, as we encounter them in the Colossian household code, to the life of the church as well as to church organizational structures. In present-day scholarship it is the *communis opinio* that the Colossian household code represents a traditional piece, that is, that it was already in circulation much earlier than the epistle and could have served as a foundation for the above-mentioned development. It is true that the domestic codes are primarily concerned with family structures, but it should not be overlooked that they also regulate family structures in the church. This applies with certainty, at the very latest, to the Ephesian code, which is also evidence that the *oikos* order was expanded into a church

---

[156] Schöllgen, ibid., does not dispute the factual significance of converted families for early Christian missions; he stresses rather that it is simply not documented that "the emergent church therefore *understood* itself as the constant continuation of this family" (italics added).

[157] Ibid., 77. Lührmann ("Neutestamentliche Haustafeln," 93) does not dispute this either. He is merely saying that the Pauline ecclesiology was open for this development.

order. It is also incorrect to say that *oikos* vocabulary was not used in an ecclesiological context in the NT (cf. Eph 2:19–24; 4:12, 16; see n. 170). In addition, there is one final difficulty with Schöllgen's position: he fails to offer an alternative model.[158]

House Church, Local Church, and Church Order in Colossians and Ephesians

A look at the relationship between the church as a whole and the individual congregation is appropriate here also. In Colossians ἐκκλησία occurs as a designation for the individual church (cf. Col 4:15), but also for the church as a whole (1:18; 4:16—see above). From this we may conclude that Colossians "takes into account the existence of different forms of assembly and at one and the same time views all of these as *church*."[159] As in the undisputed Pauline Letters, the concept of the church as a whole is in the making (cf. Col 4:16, apostle letters are being exchanged; 4:10–14, the request to pass on greetings and information via an internal process), even though no institutional organizational structures or offices for the church as a whole are mentioned.[160] In Ephesians the state of affairs is different. There the term ἐκκλησία is reserved exclusively for the whole or universal church and never used for the local individual gathering of Christians. Organizational structures for the church as a whole are evident (cf. Eph 4:7–16), even though the letter appears to be relatively uninterested in the concrete formation of constitutional order as such.[161]

Characteristic for these two epistles are several fundamental statements regarding the nature of the church. Both letters establish a close relationship between Christ and the church and in so doing integrally associate Christology with ecclesiology.[162] The basis for this in tradition history is the Pauline understanding of the church as the body of Christ (1 Cor 12:27; Rom 12:5). The relationship between Christ and the church is defined, on the one hand, with Christ being directly identified with the body, that is, the church (cf. Col 1:24), and on the other hand with Christ as the head of the church (Col 1:17–18; 2:19; Eph 1:22; 4:15; 5:23).[163] In all of these cases the term "church" no longer refers to the individual congregation but rather to

---

[158] He rejects the hypothesis that associations served as a model for Christian community organization (Schöllgen, "Hausgemeinde," 74–75).

[159] Roloff, *Kirche*, 231 (italics added).

[160] One cannot conclude a total lack of church offices on the basis of an absence of any reference to them (with Roloff, *Kirche*, 231; against Lohse, "Christusherrschaft," 274). Cf. nevertheless Col 4:17, where Archippos, portrayed as bearer of a διακονία, was most likely active as a teacher in a number of churches.

[161] Cf. Roloff, *Kirche*, 246.

[162] Cf. Roloff, "ἐκκλησία," *EDNT* 2:414.

[163] Cf. Roloff, *Kirche*, 227–31, for a discussion of the cosmic connection of the ecclesiology of Colossians.

the church as a whole, to some extent in a universal sense as an all-embracing global entity (cf. also Eph 3:10, 21; 4:4–6; 5:22, 25, 27, 32). Nevertheless, it must be stressed that at the time Colossians and Ephesians were written, wherever this one church gathered, its members met together in homes, that is, in house churches, whether as individual congregations or as the whole church for that location. Precisely there, in those small groups, Jews and Gentiles, masters and slaves were to live together in unity in Christ (cf. Col 3:11; Eph 2:11–20; 4:1–3).

With the Colossian household code we encounter for the first time a model that is intended as a set of rules within a Christian household community.[164] As a set of rules for the *oikos*, the code applies not only to one but also to all Christian families. Even as early as the Colossian code, it is no longer conceivable that a different set of rules could be allowed to be in effect in each of the various house churches. Proof of this is the fact that in the Colossian code all household members are always addressed in this plural, which implies that the rules are directed not only toward the one master, wife, and so forth, in one household, but rather toward all masters, wives, and so forth, that is, all members in all households and all house churches, everyone in the entire church as a whole at that location.[165] It is obviously expected that all Christian οἶκοι are to remain within the parameters of these guidelines. At the latest, after the number of Christians at one location has grown and the whole church has begun to gather together ἐπὶ τὸ αὐτό, it would have become necessary to formulate a set of general rules for such issues. From that time on, it would no longer have been feasible for one house church to behave in one way and another in a quite different manner.

This applies in particular to the code in Ephesians. First, both the address in the plural as well as the heading in Eph 5:21 point in the same direction. Ephesians 5:21 is directed toward all members of the church, as the participle ὑποτασσόμενοι demonstrates. Second, the expansion of the Ephesian code in comparison to the one in Colossians is an indication that the question of household order was such a fundamental problem that it could not be treated comprehensively enough in such a short text. The code is expanded so that a basic behavioral pattern becomes evident. The Colossian code was obviously so convincing that in the Ephesian code this order was made binding not only for the individual households but also for the church as a whole. Here the *oikos* order applies explicitly to all house-

---

[164] I agree, however, with Klauck (*Hausgemeinde*, 47) that here the thrust of the appeal of the Colossian code is directed not only at each individual Christian household as such but at the different social stations that are spread horizontally throughout all households. The code applies to the Christian *oikos* as a whole as well as to the behavior of the Christians (masters, women, slaves, children) in a household, which does not consist only of believers (so also Rengstorf, "Neutestamentliche Mahnungen," 137; following him, Lührmann, "Neutestamentliche Haustafeln," 94 n. 60; with a different view, Schroeder, "Haustafeln," 88–89).

[165] So also Laub, "Sozialgeschichtlicher Hintergrund," 262.

holders, all women, all children, and all slaves. Thus it appears legitimate to speak of a church code.

Is it possible, however, to speak of a church order here? The result of the research earlier in this study on the significance of house churches in early Christian missional outreach gives reason to assume that the household structures of the domestic codes had an impact on church order. Verner observes, however, that the comparison between domestic and church structure in Ephesians and the Pastorals points in the opposite direction.[166] Accordingly, in the Ephesian code the church would form a conceptual model for the structure of the family (Eph 5:21). For M. Barth as well, Christ is described here as "the model and cause of the action and attitude expected . . . , rather than mere exemplification."[167] For this reason it would appear best not to postulate that church order was directly derived from *oikos* structures. Verner's suggestion, however, does not have to be understood as an alternative but can just as well be seen as a complementary argumentation. "Both are offered: instruction on marriage and on the mystery of the church in inseparable mixture. Both illuminate one another reciprocally. The church possesses her image in marriage."[168] Particularly in Eph 5:31–32 marriage appears to be a model of the relationship between Christ and the church.[169]

Furthermore, one needs to bear in mind that in Ephesians the church is described as the temple of God or rather, in architectural *oikos* terminology, as the house of God, which is the honorary title for the temple.[170] Ephesians 4:12–16 particularly is a classical example of architectural imagery fused with the Pauline concept of the church as the body of Christ.[171] In Eph 2:19–22 an array of connections can be observed: "you are . . . fellow citizens with God's people and *members of God's household, built* on the *foundation* of the apostles and prophets, with Christ Jesus himself as the chief *cornerstone*. In him the whole *building* is joined together and rises to become a holy *temple* in the Lord. And in him you too are being *built* together to become a *dwelling* in which God lives by his Spirit."[172] Klauck correctly

---

[166] Verner, *Household*, 182 n. 184: "The author of the Pastorals . . . conceptualizes the church as a great household . . . in the Ephesian *Haustafel* the reverse process has occurred, i.e., the household relationship of husband and wife has been conceptualized on the model of Christ and the church (Eph 5:22ff)."

[167] Barth, *Ephesians*, 614, 635.

[168] Gnilka, *Epheserbrief*, 274. Cf. also Roloff, *Kirche*, 236.

[169] This is, however, also disputed. Cf. Schnackenburg, *Epheser*, 259–61.

[170] Cf. also Klauck, *Hausgemeinde*, 64–66, who points out the architectural and domestic metaphorizing of the *oikos* concept in the NT. For Ephesians the ground for such a metaphorical transposition was already prepared in the undisputed Pauline Letters (compare 1 Cor 3:16; 6:19 with 1 Cor 3:9, "you are God's building [οἰκοδομή]"; cf. also Gal 6:10). Cf. also Vielhauer, "'Oikodome,'" 53–144; Pfammatter, *Kirche*, 5–139; Kitzberger, *Bau der Gemeinde*, 34–157.

[171] So also Stuhlmacher, "Kirche," 313.

[172] Cf. Klauck, *Hausgemeinde*, 65. On the term "household member" as angel, representative of the heavenly church, cf. Roloff, *Kirche*, 239 n. 41.

stresses, "Such theological models certainly are not therefore primarily developed from or for the house church. On the other hand, however, it is not entirely without significance that such house/household images were so often used for the theological conceptualization and description of Christian communities that gathered almost exclusively in houses."[173] Neither is it without significance that this usage is found in Ephesians, a letter that connects domestic *oikos* terminology integrally with the church. If, metaphorically speaking, the church is the temple of God, or rather the house of God, it is only a short step from there to understanding it in a metaphorical sense as the family of God.[174] Much appears to speak in favor of understanding the Ephesian household code as church order,[175] even though this is not yet fully developed terminologically. At any rate, it can be said that the model "οἶκος equals οἶκος θεοῦ" is already intimated (foreshadowed?) in Ephesians (cf. 1 Tim 3:15). J. Dunn summarizes succinctly, "The model of the well-run household provided precedent for the well-run church."[176]

CHRISTIAN *OIKOS*, CHURCH, AND LEADERSHIP STRUCTURES IN THE PASTORAL EPISTLES

The question here is whether a reflection of the household setting can also contribute to a deeper understanding of the Pastoral Epistles, something we would expect on the basis of the significance of the *oikos* for the entire Christian movement up until this time. This focus may also shed light on some features in these letters that have previously gone unnoticed in previous NT research.

Oikos Order as Church Order

As in Ephesians, the church and our understanding of it are the main topic in the Pastorals. The interest of the author is paraenetic, that is, that the community of believers might know "how people ought to conduct themselves in God's household, which is the church of the living God, the pillar and foundation of the truth" (1 Tim 3:15). Out of this paraenetic instruction emerges a clear ecclesiological image of the church as the *oikos* church.[177] For this reason scholars have correctly declared 1 Tim 3:15 to be the central ecclesiological passage for all three of the Pastoral Letters.[178] In contrast to

---

[173] Klauck, *Hausgemeinde*, 66.
[174] Cf. Roloff, *Kirche*, 239.
[175] So Stuhlmacher, "Kirche," 313.
[176] Dunn, *Colossians, Philemon*, 245
[177] Cf. 1 Tim 2:1–15; 5:1–22 and Titus 2:1–15; 1 Tim 3:1–13; 4:11–16 and Titus 1:5–9; 2 Tim 2:14–3:9 and Titus 3:8–11; 1 Tim 6:20–21 and 2 Tim 1:11–14.
[178] Brox, *Pastoralbriefe*, 157; following him, Klauck, *Hausgemeinde*, 67. So also Verner, *Household*, 127; Roloff, *Kirche*, 253.

Ephesians (Eph 2:19; cf. also Gal 6:10), here οἶκος θεοῦ is not only understood metaphorically, with the church perceived as the house of God merely in an architectural or sociological sense. The understanding of the church here goes beyond the metaphorical: the church is characterized, even in its concrete organizational structures, by the perception of itself as a household, with "household" understood in terms of the ancient *oikos*.[179] For the Pastorals the church really is the household or the family of God.[180] Viewed in this way, "house or family of God" becomes the model for responsible behavior as well as for church order and leadership structures, and thus the central, all-guiding image for the self-understanding and organization of the church.[181]

Much supports this perspective. First of all there are the numerous terminological inferences to parallels between house and church.[182] That these parallels are not coincidental is demonstrated by the observation that in the Pastorals terminological and substantial correspondence exists between assertions about house and family, on the one hand, and those about church organizational structures, on the other (cf. virtue-and-vice catalogs, duty codes, instructions regarding the behavior of individual groups).[183] Notice,

---

[179] For a proof of this, cf. Verner, *Household*, 27–180; Lips, *Glaube-Gemeinde-Amt*, 96–97, 121–50; following him, Klauck, *Hausgemeinde*, 66–68; following them, Campbell, *Elders*, 194–96; cf. also Lührmann, "Neutestamentliche Haustafeln"; Laub, "Sozialgeschichtlicher Hintergrund"; Dassmann, "Hausgemeinde," 96. Cf. also Roloff, *Kirche*, 253–54, who points out that old Jewish-Christian terminology for the temple now and again shines through here; cf. also 2 Cor 6:16. Cf. a critique of this view, Weiser, "Kirche," 111–12; cf. in general, regarding NT usage of "house of God," Michel, "οἶκος," *TDNT* 5:125–27.

[180] So most exegetes today. Cf. the list of scholars by Lips, *Glaube-Gemeinde-Amt*, 97 n. 17.

[181] In the meantime, many scholars have acknowledged this. Cf., e.g., Michel, "οἶκος," *TDNT* 5:125–31; Lips, *Glaube-Gemeinde-Amt*, 142–43; Lührmann, "Neutestamentliche Haustafeln," 95 ("Out of household codes emerged church order"). Klauck, *Hausgemeinde*, 67; Verner, *Household*, 83–111, 127; Dassmann, "Hausgemeinde," 95–96, who speaks of an "οἶκος ecclesiology"; Roloff, *Kirche*, 250–53; Wagener, *Ordnung*, 61–65; Campbell, *Elders*, 194. As a model for responsible behavior, cf. Popkes, *Paränese*, 98.

[182] Cf. Lips, *Glaube-Gemeinde-Amt*, 122. Notice, e.g., the parallel use of προϊστάναι in one's own house and in the church (compare 1 Tim 3:4–5, 12 with 5:17) and that διδάσκειν is placed parallel to αὐθεντεῖν ("to rule"; cf. 1 Tim 2:12). Slaves are admonished not to disrespect their masters (1 Tim 6:2), and the same is expected from the church in relation to the authorities (1 Tim 4:12; Titus 2:15); compare Titus 2:9 with 2 Tim 2:21 also.

[183] For individual exegetical proofs, cf. Lips, *Glaube-Gemeinde-Amt*, 123–38. He does an analysis of the following texts: virtue/vice catalogues (1 Tim 1:9–10; 2:2; 6:4–6; 2 Tim 2:21; 3:2–4; Titus 1:10–12; 2:12; 3:1–3); instruction on the behavior of individual groups (1 Tim 2:8–10; 3:4, 11; 5:11–13; 6:1–2, 17–18; Titus 1:6; 2:2–6, 9–10); and qualifications and behavior of office holders (1 Tim 1:12; 3:2–4, 8–10; 4:12; 5:1–5, 17; Titus 1:5–6, 7–8; 2:7; 2 Tim 2:2, 24). Following him, Klauck, *Hausgemeinde*, 67.

for example, the designations for offices in the Pastorals (elder, overseer, deacon) and their duties (manage, direct [1 Tim 3:5; 5:17], care for [1 Tim 3:5], command [1 Tim 1:3; 4:11; 5:7; 6:13, 18], rebuke [Titus 3:15]), and various terms for teaching and training (cf., e.g., 2 Tim 3:16; Titus 2:11–12). These are all expressions adopted from the ancient *oikos* and integrally connected with the duties of the householder.[184] Corresponding to this is the duty of the individual church member to learn and to submit himself or herself (cf., e.g., 1 Tim 2:11–12; 4:11–16; 2 Tim 2:14; 3:7, 14, 16–17; Titus 3:14).

In addition, the system of order in the church is in alignment with the ancient *oikos* regarding the formation of member groups. Hence rules are established for men/women, the elderly/youths, masters/slaves, and widows (see n. 183). Everyone is supposed to behave according to general social norms common in the *oikos* for such groups. In comparison with the Colossian and Ephesian domestic codes, a number of noteworthy shifts can be observed. The individual household groups are no longer addressed or admonished in their mutual responsibility as pairs but according to their position in the congregation along with other church-specific individuals and groups, such as overseers, elders, deacons, and so forth. In contrast to the household codes, the rules in the Pastorals are clearly more comprehensive, encompassing the entire church. It thus becomes evident that here we have before us a church code, or church order.[185]

The designation of the church as οἶκος θεοῦ is therefore to be understood quite literally. Here the image of the house is fused with the notion of *familia Dei*.[186] If one understands the church as the house of God, then it logically follows that a *pater familias*, God himself, would be at its head.[187] In 2 Tim 2:20–21 the members of the church are described as objects in a large house (μεγάλη οἰκία).[188] God is called δεσπότης (head of the household, 2 Tim 2:21). He has appointed a local church leader (ἐπίσκοπος, overseer) as an οἰκονόμος (house administrator or manager; Titus 1:7).[189] This overseer is supposed to carry out the function of the householder (1 Tim 3:5) in the church of God (ἐκκλησία θεοῦ), in that he directs/manages, commands/leads, rebukes/corrects, and so forth (see above).[190] That he has the

---

[184] Cf. Lips, *Glaube-Gemeinde-Amt*, 130–42; following him, Klauck, *Hausgemeinde*, 67.

[185] Church code = "Gemeindetafel" understood as topos (Lips).

[186] Cf. also Roloff, *Der erste Brief*, 178, and "ἐκκλησία," *EDNT* 1:415: "The image of the house easily flows into that of the household: the Church is the *familia dei*." With a different viewpoint, Michel, "οἶκος," *TDNT* 5:125–26.

[187] So also Dassmann, "Hausgemeinde," 96.

[188] Cf. Roloff, *Kirche*, 259–61.

[189] Cf. Michel, "οἶκος," *TDNT* 5:149–51; H. Kuhli, "οἰκονόμος," *EDNT* 2:498–500.

[190] Reicke, "προΐστημι," *TDNT* 6:700–703. Regarding προΐστασθαι, see pp. 198–201. Cf. also Roloff, *Der erste Brief*, 307.

ability to do so is something he was supposed to have demonstrated in his own *oikos* (1 Tim 3:4).[191] It is evident here that an analogy can be made between the function of the householder and the church office holder.[192]

The most important function of an overseer as οἰκονόμος θεοῦ is clearly specified in Titus 1:9 through the explicit reference to his teaching duties. "Here the subject that dominates the ecclesiology of the Pastorals—the church as the *familia Dei*, whose householder is the bishop—becomes transparent in its main theological core. This is, to be exact, the service of stewardship of the gospel, definitely a Pauline motif (1 Cor 4:1). . . . The norm that defines the οἰκονομία of the bishop is the teaching of the gospel because it alone enables him to order and to form the community life of the church, that is, the household of God entrusted to him."[193]

On the basis of all the evidence compiled above, it appears legitimate to speak, with E. Dassmann, of an *oikos* ecclesiology in the Pastorals (see n. 181). How does this ecclesiological concept compare with that of the undisputed letters of Paul? As we have already noticed, the notions of the family of God and of the house of God are both clearly an important part of Paul's understanding of the church (see pp. 62–64). The passage in 1 Cor 3:10–17 particularly comes to mind; it strongly reminds us of the church metaphor in the Pastorals.[194] In the Pastorals, however, the notion of the body is much less prominent. In fact, σῶμα Χριστοῦ is not even mentioned explicitly. The understanding of the church as the body, in which the cooperation of the individual members with each other and the good of the whole are emphasized and in which Christ is viewed as the head of the body, is a different church structure from the one that is conceptualized according to a model based on the ancient *oikos*. Granted, much like the *oikos*, the structure of the body implies a certain hierarchy, particularly regarding the importance of the functions. It is also true that, as with the household, the σῶμα has only one κεφαλή and it must lead. But the structure of the body emphasizes the aspect of mutual relationships more strongly. From the notion of the body alone, one cannot develop a linear, hard-and-fast structure of authority; rather the individual member acquires authority as a result of exercising his or her spiritual gift(s). In comparison, the church order based on the concept of the house of God has fixed, irreversible structures of authority.[195]

In Ephesians the notion of the body is often united with the concept of the house (see above). In 2 Tim 2:19–22 there is an indirect reference to

---

[191] Similar behavior is expected of the deacons (1 Tim 3:12).
[192] Roloff, "ἐκκλησία," *EDNT* 1:415; following him, Oberlinner, *Pastoralbriefe*, 1:124 n. 49. Cf. also Laub, "Sozialgeschichtlicher Hintergrund," 263–64; Schöllgen, "Hausgemeinde," 89–90.
[193] Roloff, *Der erste Brief*, 178. Cf. also Luke 12:42–45.
[194] Cf. Weiser, "Kirche," 111.
[195] Cf. Lips, *Glaube-Gemeinde-Amt*, 141–43.

members of the church as members of a household and not of a body. Here, as in Ephesians, the church is understood as an independent entity. Roloff stresses that "if one considers the assertions about the church as a system of order, a protective space, and a stable place of truth, then the church takes on all the features of an institution."[196] As an institution, the church is entirely in the world, but precisely because the Christian church did not withdraw from the world, it retained, first, the possibility of persuasively testifying to the remaining presence of the truth of God in the world[197] and, second, the hope of transcending its own generation.[198] Nevertheless, the impact this text has had on church history shows that the one-sided emphasis of the ecclesiological assertions made in the Pastorals without sufficient consideration of other NT passages, particularly Pauline, has led to the transgression of fundamental boundaries, to ecclesiological institutionalism, and to the restriction of freedom for those baptized in Christ.[199]

The emergence of such *oikos* language in the Pastorals is best explained by assuming a house church setting, in which here again private domestic houses belonging to a few wealthy members of the congregation served as gathering places for the church.[200] It cannot be completely ruled out that in individual cases the house of the overseer itself was large enough to provide the meeting place for the whole church at that location. It is more probable, however, that the churches as a whole at these locales significantly exceeded a single household numerically and the capacity of a single house spatially.[201]

The assumption of a house church setting for the church in the Pastorals is supported by the observation that there are indirect references in the letters indicating the existence of a number of affluent Christians.[202] The instructions for the slaves (1 Tim 2:9) imply that members of the church were wealthy enough to own such slaves. Admonitions such as 1 Tim 2:9 for women, that they dress modestly and not wear expensive jewelry, or 6:9–10 for those who fall away from the faith because they are obsessed with money,

---

[196] Roloff, *Kirche,* 260; following him, Weiser, "Kirche," 112–13. Roloff also emphasizes that this need not be considered regression in comparison to the undisputed Pauline Letters, as the church already has institutional qualities there. "An institutionalization was unavoidable for a church that wanted to exist beyond its own origin" (Roloff, *Kirche,* 260), and it is a good thing that the Pastorals recognized this as their task. Cf. Holmberg, *Paul,* 166–67.

[197] Cf. Stuhlmacher, "Kirche," 313–14; Roloff, *Kirche,* 259.

[198] Cf. Lührmann, "Neutestamentliche Haustafeln," 83–97.

[199] Cf. Stuhlmacher, "Kirche," 314, and "Christliche Verantwortung," 185–86.

[200] So also Klauck, *Hausgemeinde,* 66–68; Dassmann, "Hausgemeinde," 82–97, esp. 85–87; H. Maier, *Social Setting,* 44–46; following him, Campbell, *Elders,* 194–95. With a different view, Malherbe, *Social Aspects,* 98–100. See Schöllgen, "Hausgemeinde," 84, for his criticism of this view; Gehring, *Hausgemeinde,* 443 n. 297, for a response.

[201] Cf. Klauck, *Hausgemeinde,* 67.

[202] Cf. Spicq, *Épîtres pastorales,* 424–25; Verner, *Household,* 180–86; extensively, Kidd, *Wealth,* 75–109.

are all evidence of an affluent group within the church. The same is most likely true for 1 Tim 6:17–19. Verse 18 particularly is expressed in the language of patronage: the rich ought to "do good, to be rich in good deeds [ἐν ἔργοις καλοῖς], and to be generous and willing to share." In another passage in the Pastorals, the expression καλὸν ἔργον also implies material help (Titus 3:14). There seems to be much support for the view that a number of the church leaders were from a higher social class.[203] They are warned not to love money. Granted, the love of money does not necessarily prove a person is wealthy, for it can also be a problem for poorer people. The leader should instead be φιλόξενος (v. 2). As we have already observed, hospitality was not only offered to travelers. It was also an integral part of community life in the house church (see pp. 182–85). "The inclusion of hospitality among the characteristics of a bishop may be interpreted as an indication that overseers invited the community into their homes. This virtue probably implied a form of patronage."[204]

Potential leaders are also encouraged to seek leadership responsibilities, with the reasoning that this is a καλὸν ἔργον (1 Tim 3:1). It has been suggested that this expression originated from the secular world and was used as motivation for potential candidates for public office in a city at a time when city offices were not necessarily sought after because of the very high financial burden placed on such office holders.[205] "Whether or not this is in fact the case, the saying would fit very well into that context, because it reflects the general concept of public office that one commonly finds in the Hellenistic municipalities, namely, that office holding is a public service to be undertaken by the well-to-do."[206]

It has been assumed that 1 Tim 3:1–3 and Titus 1:5–6 describe the profile of a qualified overseer as a hospitable *pater familias* who is supposed to have his domestic affairs in order.[207] This assumption is confirmed by the observation that one criterion of an overseer is that he have a good reputation with outsiders (1 Tim 3:7). This makes good sense. For a faith community that wants to be attractive to outsiders[208] and therefore also highly values public respect,[209] a householder who is held in high esteem in the local urban society is a good candidate for a leading position within that group. Conversely, a potential disadvantage of the house church also becomes evident. If the patron had a bad reputation in the city, this would have had a negative effect on the missional outreach of the entire house church.

---

[203] So, e.g., D. MacDonald, *Legend*, 71–72; Countryman, *Rich Christian*, 181 n. 42.
[204] H. Maier, *Social Setting*, 46.
[205] Barrett, *Pastoral Epistles*, ad loc.
[206] Verner, *Household*, 151. Following him, H. Maier, *Social Setting*, 45; Campbell, *Elders*, 195.
[207] Countryman, *Rich Christian*, 167.
[208] Cf. Roloff, *Kirche*, 257.
[209] Cf. Stuhlmacher, "Kirche," 313.

The description of an ideal deacon in 1 Tim 3:12 as someone who not only manages his children well but also his own household most likely includes servants in that household.[210] Slave ownership is again evidence that these individuals belonged to a fairly high social class. The author is not saying, however, that a relatively high social position is a prerequisite for church office. It is simply "a casual assumption he makes about them. Thus it is not the author's special program or prejudices that are reflected here, but the actual situation in the churches. He apparently accepts this situation without question and pursues his own aims within it."[211] As we have observed in the primitive church in Jerusalem and in the Pauline churches, here again it would also be wrong to conclude from the above that there were no leadership patterns other than the householder type in the churches referred to in the Pastorals. Nevertheless, in the Pastoral Letters there appears to be, to a large extent, the general pattern of leadership emerging from the *oikos* structures. "It is probable that such patrons carried out important administrative tasks which contributed to them prevailing over other possible patterns. The host who possessed the wealth and initiative to invite the church into his or her own home had important leadership responsibilities, probably occasioned by the patronage he or she offered."[212]

The kinds of service that the affluent church members could perform are well illustrated in 2 Tim 1:16 (cf. 4:19). Here we have the description of the activities of a certain Onesiphorus. He and his house are represented as being fairly wealthy. He is praised for having often refreshed Paul with his hospitality. Furthermore, he made mission journeys and performed services for the church. This is all evidence that he was probably relatively well off. Whether Onesiphorus was an actual historical figure or not, we can agree with H. O. Maier: "The description of him provides a window through which we can see the kinds of activities the well-to-do were probably expected to perform for the community."[213]

In the Pastoral Epistles, then, we encounter Christians who are supposed to exemplify a household, well ordered through God and in Christ, to a pagan, urban society. In their families and in their house churches, they are expected to be an illustration of order and an example of quiet civil loyalty and faithfulness inwardly and outwardly. According to the Pastorals, it is precisely this behavior that makes them so effective in their missional outreach (cf. 1 Tim 2:4; 3:15; Titus 3:8).[214] Thus one of the strengths of the house church in terms of its significance for early Christian missions again

---

[210] With Theissen, *Social Setting*, 85; Delling, "Zur Taufe" (1965), 285–311, here 294; following them, Verner, *Household*, 133; H. Maier, *Social Setting*, 45.

[211] Verner, *Household*, 133.

[212] H. Maier, *Social Setting*, 47.

[213] Ibid., 45. For Klauck, *Hausgemeinde*, 68, it is possible that "authentic information pertaining to an old house church in Paul's vicinity" is coming through in this text.

[214] Cf. Stuhlmacher, "Weg," 126.

becomes evident, similar to what we have observed in the primitive Jerusalem church and in the Pauline churches.[215]

On the other hand, the Pastorals also reveal a shadow side, a potential weakness of the house church structure. As we have already noticed, quite a number of scholars have drawn attention to the problematic in the context of the Corinthian church.[216] Even as early as Corinth it becomes evident that the existence of several house churches within the church as a whole at that location caused serious difficulties. In Rome as well, it is conceivable that the background to Rom 14–15 was conflicts between house churches.[217] As early as 1939 Filson emphasized, "The existence of several house churches in one city goes far to explain the tendency of party strife in the apostolic age."[218] Loyalty to a certain house could have produced a subtle potential for such division within the whole church in a given city.

Apparently the fact that, at the time of the writing of the Pastorals, a multiple number of house churches already existed at a location was also a structural weak point in the local church as a whole. As is well known, the church of the Pastorals was being jeopardized by a heresy; Titus 1:11 issued a warning against false teachers who taught things they ought not to for the sake of dishonest gain and who were evidently capable of destroying entire houses. "They are the kind who worm their way into homes and gain control over weak-willed women" (2 Tim 3:6).[219] In both of these letters one has the impression that the danger came from without. If a house church leader is weak and no one else is there, the house church stands alone, more or less unprotected against the dangers of such a heresy.[220]

---

[215] For a discussion of the pros and cons of viewing Christian "Bürgerlichkeit" as *the* ethos of the Pastorals as Dibelius did, see the excursus in Gehring, *Hausgemeinde*, 447–49. Cf. esp. Towner, *Goal*, 249–57.

[216] So, e.g., Malherbe, *Social Aspects*, 70; Klauck, *Hausgemeinde*, 35; Vogler, "Bedeutung," 794; following them, Dassmann, "Hausgemeinde," 88–89.

[217] Cf. Stuhlmacher, *Römer*, 199, regarding Rom 14:9.

[218] Filson, "Significance," 110. Virtually all scholars who have studied the house church follow him. Cf., e.g., Malherbe, *Social Aspects*, 92–112; Klauck, *Hausgemeinde*, 39; Meeks, *First Urban Christians*, 76; White, *Building God's House*, 103–10 n. 31; Blue, "In Public," 176–89.

[219] This passage does not refer directly to house churches but, rather, merely to houses. Nevertheless it is clearly evident that at least Christian families are being jeopardized by the heresy. Furthermore, it can be asked why the false teachers infiltrated precisely these homes in an attempt to convert them. One plausible explanation is that they targeted houses that were centers or gathering places for other Christians, i.e., house churches, in order to reach all the more. As already seen, the transition between such Christian families and house churches was fluid. In addition, it can be assumed that there existed a multiple number of house churches at the time of the Pastorals (cf., e.g., 1 Tim 3:5–6; 2 Tim 3:6–7; Titus 1:11). That such churches would have been isolated from one another and hence unprotected from such dangers is also a reasonable assumption.

[220] That they had bad experiences with weak church leaders (in this case the potential weakness of the leader is connected with his immaturity in the faith), or rather wanted to avoid them, is demonstrated by 1 Tim 3:6.

It was also possible for heretics or believers with fanatical tendencies to pose a threat to the church from within.[221] Householders themselves could be potential false teachers or fanatics. The house church was endangered at this point, especially where the members of the household were loyal exclusively to their own householder. If the head of the household (and/or teacher) was a person with a dominant or charismatic personality, he could influence an entire house church and intentionally guide the group in his own (one-sided) theological direction, which may be contrary to that of the church as a whole. In time, this inevitably led to an unhealthy dependence on the leadership in the house church and possibly even to division in the whole church at that location.[222] In an *oikos* society it would have been quite natural for a householder to exercise such influence, as he could have easily taken advantage of the feelings of loyalty that, according to the ethic of the ancient *oikos*, the members of his household owed him as their patron, and in this way he could have misused them in an attempt to force his own agenda upon the church that met in his house.

The dangers from both within and without called for a house church structure with a stronger consolidation of the leadership and organization of the whole church in that area. Ultimately, this is most likely the reason the author of the Pastorals drew that very conclusion. He placed a high value on the qualifications of the individual church leader and strengthened the local church as a whole (see below). The local and regional superstructures were also solidified, as the instructions to Timothy and Titus demonstrate. Without such structures firmly in place, particularly in locations that had a multiple number of house churches, the church as a whole in that area would not have been in a position to deal appropriately with such tendencies and problems. As long as Paul, the apostle of Jesus Christ, and his coworkers continued to lead the churches, this was more or less ensured. After his departure, however, new structures had to be created in order to stabilize these churches for the long term.

Leadership Structures

As already noticed, the Pastoral Epistles contain a number of references to leadership functions in the church.[223] Elders are mentioned three times (1 Tim 4:14; 5:17–19; Titus 1:5), overseers twice (1 Tim 3:1–7; Titus 1:7–9), and deacons (1 Tim 3:8–13) and widows (1 Tim 5:2–16) once. Fur-

---

[221] Cf. Vogler, "Bedeutung," 791.
[222] So already Achelis, *Christentum* (1925), 97. Cf. also Klauck, *Hausgemeinde*, 38–39.
[223] Leadership structures take up such a large part of the Pastorals that it is not possible to give extensive attention to them here and still remain within the parameters of this study. Cf. the reputable commentaries, e.g., the excursuses on the topic in Roloff, *Der erste Brief*, 169–89, 263–81. This discussion will limit itself to issues that appear relevant to our house church focus.

thermore, instructions on leadership are given to Timothy and Titus.[224] Three passages are particularly important for our study: Titus 1:5–9, 1 Tim 3:1–10, and 1 Tim 5:17–20. The texts are not without difficulty and pose a number of intriguing questions relevant to our study.

Titus 1:5–9 raises the issue of the identity of the elder. Are elders older men who are then appointed to another office, or are they bearers of the office of elder as a result of their appointment? An overseer is also mentioned.[225] Here the question is why the author uses both terms, "overseer" and "elder," as if their meanings were identical.

Regarding 1 Tim 3:1–10, it is striking that the two offices mentioned here also occur in Phil 1:1.[226] But here "overseer" is singular, there plural, whereas "deacon" is plural in both passages. Furthermore, in contrast to Titus 1,[227] here there is no reference at all to elders.

First Timothy 5:17–20 provokes the question whether the expression οἱ καλῶς προεστῶτες is a reference to all the elders or has a group within the whole body of elders in mind. Are those who do the work of preaching and teaching a further subgroup of elders, or are they identical with οἱ προεστῶτες and hence some kind of "overseers," or is this simply another expression for the group of elders as a whole? With which group, if any, should we associate the overseer? In what way is the honor that such elders deserve a double one?

The key question here is the nature of the relationship between the overseer and the elder. The solutions to this issue offered by scholars can be divided into four groups.[228] First, a large number of exegetes identify the two terms with one another and then attempt to explain the remaining difficulties.[229] The central proof text for this position is Titus 1:5–9. As we have seen, the author uses the two terms there as if they were interchangeable titles (cf. also Acts 20:17, 28; 1 Pet 5:1–2; *1 Clem.* 44:1, 5). The major difficulty with this interpretation is the fact that in the Pastorals the term "overseer" occurs in the singular and the term "elder" in the plural. Those who see the two as identical understand "overseer" in the singular as generic.[230] Against the generic interpretation of ἐπίσκοπος it could be argued that this usage does not occur with the other offices.[231]

---

[224] Cf. Roloff, *Kirche*, 263–65.

[225] In order to avoid misunderstanding, the term "overseer" will be used here instead of "bishop" as the translation of ἐπίσκοπος because it is not as restricted regarding its possible meaning.

[226] Cf. also *Did.* 15:1–2 and *1 Clem.* 42:4.

[227] Cf. also the letters of Ignatius.

[228] Cf., for the following, Campbell, *Elders*, 179–93.

[229] Cf., e.g., Lightfoot, *Philippians*, 95; Dibelius and Conzelmann, *Pastoralbriefe*, 40–47; H. Beyer, *TDNT* 2:617; Kelly, *Pastoral Epistles*, 13; Fee, *1–2 Timothy, Titus*, 84; Ysebaert, *Amtsterminologie*, 60–61, 69–73.

[230] Cf. Kelly, *Pastoral Epistles*, 13; Fee, *1–2 Timothy, Titus*, 84, 128; Spicq, *Épîtres pastorales*, 450–55.

[231] Cf., e.g., Bornkamm, "πρέσβυς," *TDNT* 6:667 n. 95.

Second, other scholars have decided in favor of the solution that the elders in the Pastorals are not office holders, that they are simply older members of the church who were held in high esteem and the overseers were chosen from this group of older men.[232] According to this view, there were only two church offices in the Pastorals: overseers and deacons, as in Phil 1:1.[233] J. Jeremias has drawn attention to the difficulty in 1 Tim 5:17 that results if one understands "elder" as a designation of office: "According to 5:18, the word 'honor' (v. 17) surely includes payment, which would mean that verse 17 is saying that the 'hardworking' elders should receive double the wage of the other elders. This would distinguish two different salary levels for the elders according to their performance! This does not appear very likely."[234] If, on the other hand, "elders" does not indicate a title of office but is rather the designation of age (as in 5:1), the difficulty is resolved. "Then verse 17 makes complete sense: those elderly men who have been appointed to an office [the office of overseer] . . . are to receive double the payment—that is, in comparison to the elderly and widows who are supported by the congregation! The difficulty in Titus that the designations of office of presbyter and *episkopos* (1:7) appear to be interchangeable is resolved as well in that *presbyteros* in Titus 1:5 is also a designation of age and not of office."[235]

Much is valid in this position. In particular, this view of the elders, as we have come to understand better against the background of the Jewish and Greco-Roman world, corresponds to a large extent with the findings of our study up to this point. There is one difficulty, however, in that καταστήσης (καθίστημι) in Titus 1:5 would have to be understood in an absolute sense and 1:5 would be saying that Titus was to appoint elders as overseers, that is, that he was to appoint overseers from the available group of elders.[236] The normal use of the verb in a corresponding context would not leave it up to the reader to infer the office to which one is being appointed.[237] Furthermore, Jeremias's interpretation of the "double" payment for the overseer in contrast to the widows becomes difficult because, according to 1 Tim 5:3–16, only the truly needy widows are to be supported financially. Nor

---

[232] Cf., e.g., Sohm, *Die geschichtlichen Grundlagen*, 96; Jeremias, *Timotheus und Titus*, 23, 41–42, 69–70; Harvey, "Elders," 330; Campbell, *Elders*, 194–96.

[233] Cf. Jeremias, *Timotheus und Titus*, 20–21. Regarding rqbm, cf. Nauck, "Probleme"; G. Holtz, *Pastoralbriefe*, 81–82; Roloff, *Der erste Brief*, 173 n. 325. This is if one does not count the widow as an office. Cf. Jeremias, *Timotheus und Titus*, 20.

[234] Jeremias, *Timotheus und Titus*, 36. In contrast, Kelly (*Pastoral Epistles*, 125) interprets that "the executive officers should receive twice as much as the rest, presumably because they devote more of their time and energies to their functions."

[235] Jeremias, *Timotheus und Titus*, 41. G. Holtz, *Pastoralbriefe*, 124–25, follows Jeremias regarding 1 Tim 5:17.

[236] Neither Jeremias nor Harvey ("Elders," 329–30) appears to be aware of this.

[237] Campbell, *Elders*, 185, has drawn attention to this. Cf. also Bauer-Aland[6], 792; (BDAG 492). Cf., as an exception, *1 Clem.* 43:1 and esp. 44:2 and 54:2.

does the text indicate anywhere that the church had established any kind of general support for the elderly.[238]

Third, many exegetes believe that the terms "elder" and "overseer" originate from different backgrounds.[239] According to this view, the term "elder" emerged from Jewish-Christian churches, whose usage was patterned after the Jewish synagogue.[240] In contrast, we encounter the term "overseer" first among the Gentile Christians, who adopted it from their Hellenistic environment.[241] There ἐπίσκοπος meant quite generally "anyone who had authority to oversee or inspect anything or anyone else."[242] With the passing of time, however, certainly sometime before the composition of the Pastorals, these two terms became interchangeable designations for the same local church leader. A later development is evident in the Pastorals, however, in which a single overseer emerges from the ranks of the elders to become the head of the local church. In reality, it is the monarchical bishop who is being addressed in the two apostolic delegates Timothy and Titus.[243] According to A. T. Hanson, the strongest argument for this view is to be found in the broad scope of the authority that Timothy and Titus are supposed to exercise. They rebuke; they are authorized to ordain clerics and to appoint church office holders. This reminds one of the authority that Ignatius delegated to the bishops of his time.[244] For Hanson the real objective of the author of the Pastorals is to offer a handbook for such monarchical church leaders and to encourage the church to accept these leaders.

One question needs to be asked regarding this perspective. As we know from his undisputed letters, by means of his subsequent letters and by sending a coworker as his representative, Paul himself exercised authority in the churches he established.[245] From this Campbell concludes, "If the Pastorals are really from long after Paul's death, it seems likely that they are drawing on the authoritative image Paul and his delegates were remembered to have had as a way of urging what they have to say upon the churches."[246] Accordingly, the churches would have been encouraged by the Pastorals to view the authority of their own leaders in much the same way. But so understood, the

---

[238] So Roloff, *Der erste Brief,* 308 n. 422.
[239] Cf. Hanson, *Pastoral Epistles,* 31–38; Bornkamm, "πρέσβυς," *TDNT* 6:651–83.
[240] Cf. also Brox, *Pastoralbriefe,* 159; Gnilka, *Philipperbrief,* 34.
[241] Cf. Dibelius and Conzelmann, *Pastoralbriefe,* 44–45; Gnilka, *Philipperbrief,* 38; G. Holtz, *Pastoralbriefe,* 81.
[242] Hanson, *Pastoral Epistles,* 32.
[243] Cf. Käsemann, "Amt," 129, who, along with Hanson and others, considers Timothy and Titus fictional apostolic delegates. He believes the Pastorals intended to legitimize the monarchical bishop in retrospect.
[244] Hanson, *Pastoral Epistles,* 33.
[245] Cf., e.g., Holmberg, *Paul,* 79–81; see pp. 196–210, for an extensive proof.
[246] Campbell, *Elders,* 188.

Pastorals still do not represent a handbook for the monarchical bishop in the style of the second and third centuries.

Another important critique of this viewpoint is that it takes one aspect of the position of the apostolic delegates as it is represented by the Pastorals and makes it absolute. But the Pastorals also highlight other aspects, such as the tasks of both delegates, that extend beyond the individual congregation (Titus 1:5). Furthermore, nowhere in the Pastorals is a title of office used in reference to either one of the addressees.[247]

Fourth, a position also supported by many scholars, though dissimilarly accented, is that the Pastorals document the process of an amalgamation of two different types of church order originating from two diverse streams of Christian tradition. This process included the amalgamation (*Verschmelzung*) of the presbyter model with the bishop-deacon (or episcopal) model.[248] Roloff offers the most mature development of this view.[249]

According to Roloff, the presbyter model represents a Christian adaptation of contemporary Jewish models originating from both Jewish community and Jewish synagogue government.[250] There public esteem, along with maturity and experience evidenced by advanced age, were the main qualifications for the office of elder. The presbyterial order was adopted very early by the primitive church in Jerusalem. In contrast, Paul does not mention elders anywhere in his undisputed letters. This is because leadership responsibilities are to be developed exclusively from his teachings on spiritual gifts; the functions that certain individuals take on in the church are determined by, or grow out of, their spiritual gifts. "The basic notion of an honorific position, which is inherent to the office of elder, stands in diametric opposition to the basic idea of *charisma*."[251] On the other hand, bishops and deacons (Phil 1:1) are defined clearly on the basis of their functions and as such are fully reconcilable with the Pauline doctrine of *charisma*.[252]

For Roloff as well, very early in the Pauline mission, those who made their houses available to the congregation as gathering places were the ones who emerged with the task, and into the position, of the overseer (ἐπίσκοπος).[253] The multiplication of house churches at a larger location

---

[247] For further criticism of this and other similar viewpoints, cf. Lips, *Glaube-Gemeinde-Amt*, 106–8.

[248] Cf., e.g., Roloff, *Der erste Brief*, 170; Merkel, *Pastoralbriefe*, 91–92; for a somewhat different accent, cf. Quinn, *Titus*, 84; also Schnackenburg, "Episkopus"; following him, Gnilka, *Philipperbrief*, 34; Dibelius and Conzelmann, *Pastoralbriefe*, 47; following Dibelius, Bornkamm, "πρέσβυς," *TDNT* 6:668. Cf. also a further listing of the representatives of this view in Lips, *Glaube-Gemeinde-Amt*, 112 n. 103.

[249] Cf. Roloff's valuable and extensive excursus "Die gemeindeleitenden Ämter," in *Der erste Brief*, 169–89.

[250] Ibid., 171.

[251] Ibid.

[252] Ibid.

[253] Ibid., 172–73.

logically led to a multiple number of overseers. "This is apparently the developmental stage presupposed in Phil 1:1."[254] The author of the Pastorals attempts, then, to fuse the two church orders, the house church overseers with the council of elders, so as to retain the advantages of both orders, albeit with the overseer-deacon model slightly favored. This is indicated by the fact that in 1 Tim 5:17 the author singles out the elders who are doing a good job of exercising their function as overseers (καλῶς προεστῶτες), particularly by teaching and preaching. His real intention in doing so is to extend the office of overseer (which until now had been limited in its use and scope to the house church) to the whole local church on a citywide level as a general office of church leadership. The fact that the Pastorals speak of ἐπίσκοπος exclusively in the singular shows that from now on the local church as a whole is to be led by *one* overseer as its "house father" in close correlation with its organization as the household of God (1 Tim 3:15).

Roloff's analysis, too, has much to commend it. The independent emergence of leadership structures in early Christian churches from the house church setting has also been one of the findings of our study. This is a plausible explanation for the existence of a multiple number of overseers at one location as well as for Paul's extensive silence on issues regarding leadership structures (see pp. 196–210). It also appears that Roloff has aptly pinpointed the extension of the office of house church overseer to the local church as a whole as the real concern of the author of the Pastorals and has correctly identified the correlation between the *one* overseer and the *oikos* order of the church.[255]

Campbell, however, has criticized some of Roloff's findings.[256] In particular, Campbell fundamentally questions the notion of an amalgamation proposed by Roloff (and others). First, he attempts to demonstrate "that there did not exist two opposed forms of church government needing to be reconciled.... From Jerusalem to Corinth, the churches were nurtured in homes, received oversight from their familial ἐπίσκοποι, who were naturally known by the collective title of πρεσβύτεροι."[257] Roloff's thesis presupposes, on the basis of a single passage (Phil 1:1), that two church orders existed—one Pauline-episcopal, the other Jewish Christian-presbyterial—that needed to be reconciled with one another. "How do we know that the appearance of ἐπίσκοποι and διάκονοι in Philippi does not represent the adoption by a Pauline church of titles developed elsewhere"[258]—for

---

[254] Ibid., 173.
[255] So also Lips, *Glaube-Gemeinde-Amt,* 142–43; Lohse, "Entstehung," 67; Dassmann, "Hausgemeinde," 96; Laub, "Sozialgeschichtlicher Hintergrund," 261–65; Schöllgen, "Hausgemeinde," 89.
[256] Campbell, *Elders,* 190–92.
[257] Ibid., 193.
[258] Ibid., 191.

example, from a Jewish-Christian setting in Antioch or Jerusalem? Campbell's main objection, however, is directed against the alleged infiltration of the presbyterial order into the Pauline churches: "We wonder why a Pauline church [in Ephesus!—author] did not have overseers and deacons in the first place, or how and why it lost them, and why this invasion of elders took place."[259]

Second, according to Campbell, it must be asked why the author went to such trouble to reconcile these two systems. No one else appears to have had difficulty with equating the two. Luke simply has Paul appoint elders (Acts 14:23) and then refers to them as overseers (20:28).[260] According to this evidence, one could get the impression that the two terms really were interchangeable and seen to be merely verbal distinctions without a substantial difference. "The clumsy alterations of the singular and plural in the Pastorals . . . demand an alternative solution."[261]

Campbell offers the following resolution. He begins quite accurately with the criticism that all previously suggested solutions appear unsatisfactory "because they all neglect to take seriously the household setting of the churches, and its effect on the development of the ministry."[262] For him, as for us, the household setting represents the Sitz im Leben of the paraenetic-ecclesiological instruction of the Pastoral Epistles.

Campbell continues with this observation: "The most significant development in the ordering of these churches in the period after the death of Paul is the emergence of a single ἐπίσκοπος over the church in a certain place. This appears to have taken place not all over at once but at different times in different places."[263] In addition to the Pastorals, he lists as evidence for his thesis James, the Lord's brother in Jerusalem; the letters of Ignatius; and finally the Pauline mission.[264] With the passage of time, both the household setting of the Pauline mission and the leadership style of the apostle himself (cf. his self-understanding as father of his churches and the way he exercised authority through his visits, letters, and the dispatching of coworkers) would have led to the emergence of a monarchical ἐπίσκοπος.[265] Furthermore, the metaphorical use of the expression "house of God" as a

---

[259] Ibid., 192.

[260] Cf. also 1 Pet 5:2; *1 Clem.* 44. Schnackenburg, "Episkopus," however, lists Acts 20:17–28 as an example of an amalgamation.

[261] Campbell, *Elders*, 192.

[262] Ibid., 193. With a different view, Oberlinner, *Pastoralbriefe*, 1:125 n. 51, who follows Schöllgen, "Hausgemeinde," 85. See, however, my criticism of Schöllgen, pp. 255–57.

[263] Campbell, *Elders*, 195. For Campbell (p. 179), the Pastorals were written ca. ten years after the death of Paul (ca. 70–75 C.E.).

[264] Campbell, *Elders*, offers an extensive proof for this in chs. 4, 5, and 7. That Ignatius assumes *monepiskopoi* for the churches in Asia Minor is an indication that at that time there existed such an office in Antioch.

[265] Cf. also Holmberg, *Paul*, 79–81.

description of the church must have quite organically led to the idea of one single head as the leader of the church.²⁶⁶

On the basis of these observations, Campbell proposes this scenario: "The Pastoral Epistles are written, not to effect an amalgamation of overseers and elders, but to legitimate the authority of the new overseer."²⁶⁷ The whole church in that city is being asked to accept one single leader with the title ἐπίσκοπος, which is in effect a *monepiskopos*. He is to function as the leader of all those who were already acting as the ἐπίσκοποι in their own house churches and were known collectively as πρεσβύτεροι in the context of the local church as a whole in that city.

Campbell supports his position in the following manner: Titus 1:5–9 refers to the appointment of elders κατὰ πόλιν. He understands this expression not only in the sense of "in all the cities" but in the sense of "at the city level." In an earlier chapter, Campbell attempted to demonstrate that Luke distinguishes between different levels: κατ' οἶκον as the house church level, where the leader was called ἐπίσκοπος, and κατ' ἐκκλησίαν, the level of several house churches together, where the leaders of these house churches were collectively called πρεσβύτεροι.²⁶⁸ Furthermore, for Campbell the term πρεσβύτεροι is not a title of office but a title of honor, and this still applies for the church of the Pastorals. On these premises, regarding Titus 1:5 he says, "What is going on here is the elevation of one of the πρεσβύτεροι to be ἐπίσκοπος at city level—κατὰ πόλιν. The title πρεσβύτεροι would still apply to such ἐπίσκοποι when considered collectively, just as it had to the household ἐπίσκοποι. Both κατ' οἶκον and κατὰ πόλιν, the individual leader is ὁ ἐπίσκοπος. Viewed together the several leaders are οἱ πρεσβύτεροι."²⁶⁹

First Timothy 5:17 reads, "The elders who *direct* the affairs of the church well are worthy of *double* honor, especially those whose work is *preaching* and *teaching*." Who are the "elders" referred to here? Campbell is of the opinion that they are not house church "overseers," but rather the new *monepiskopoi* κατὰ πόλιν. He comes to this conclusion mainly because of the "double honor" that they are supposed to receive. Because τιμή here, regardless of any other connotation, is definitely to be understood in a financial sense (compare 5:18 with 1 Cor 9:9, 14), it is unlikely that a householder would need to be paid for services performed in the house church meeting in his or her home. Householders are *"ex hypothesi* well-to-do people. Patrons received loyalty from their clients, but hardly money. On the

---

²⁶⁶ Campbell, *Elders*, 196; here Campbell is following Dassmann, "Hausgemeinde," 95–96. This thesis is also advocated by Roloff, *Der erste Brief,* 169–71, which Campbell does not mention at this point, and it has also been confirmed by the results of my research (pp. 260–68). In contrast to Roloff, however, I would not say that this development first started with the church of the Pastorals but, rather, much earlier.

²⁶⁷ Campbell, *Elders*, 196. Similarly Käsemann, "Amt," 129.

²⁶⁸ Campbell, *Elders*, 164–72, 193.

²⁶⁹ Ibid., 197.

other hand ἐπισκοπή in the new sense may well have been a full-time job, which even a well-to-do person might hesitate to take on for nothing." The double honor means that although all elders are to be honored, the new monarchical overseers "who are giving their time . . . to preaching and teaching are *doubly worthy* of honor, receiving not only obedience but financial support."[270]

Again, there is very much in Campbell's analysis with which one can wholeheartedly agree. It is evident that he has succeeded in fleshing out the implications of the house church setting for this context. His interpretation of κατὰ πόλιν as the citywide level is plausible and ought to be viewed as an exegetical advancement. His perspective on the double honor is commendable as well.[271] Campbell may also be right in assuming that, in substance, elders already existed in the Pauline mission even though they may not have been explicitly called that.[272] It has already been demonstrated above that the Pauline churches had leadership structures as well as leading individuals (see pp. 196–210)[273] and that they emerged from the household setting of the Pauline mission. Our observation that a presbyterial church order had already proven itself in Jerusalem and was also in use in the non-Pauline missions (cf. 1 Pet 5:1–3) appears to be supported by Campbell's findings. Luke reports that Paul and Barnabas appointed elders in Acts 14:23, but this might be anachronistic, as Paul does not mention elders anywhere in his undisputed letters. But even then it could be "that Luke has used a term current in his own time to refer to leaders who may possibly have been known by other designations in the earlier period."[274] Finally, from *1 Clem.* 44:1–4 we know that a presbyterial church structure was employed in Corinth and in Rome during the last decade of the first century. The polemic of *1 Clement* against the dismissal of presbyters and *episkopoi* in Corinth (cf., e.g., 44:1-3) clearly documents this for the city. On the basis of the research of K. Beyschlag, it can be safely assumed that the presbyter model existed in the original structure in Rome and that Paul simply does not mention this in Rom 12.[275]

Campbell may also be correct in assuming that the Pastorals are not advocating the amalgamation of two church constitutions but rather merely the advancement of one person out from the rank of elders and the legitimi-

---

[270] Ibid., 202–3.

[271] This idea is not new; cf. similarly Brox, *Pastoralbriefe*, 199; Knight, *Pastoral Epistles*, 232; Fee, *1–2 Timothy, Titus*, 89. On τιμή, cf. Bauer-Aland⁶, 1629–30 (BDAG 1005): the term can mean either honor or payment.

[272] Cf. Gnilka, *Philipperbrief*, 32.

[273] This has been seen by an increasing number of scholars. Cf., e.g., Roloff, *Der erste Brief*, 172 n. 315, who refers to Holmberg, *Paul*, 193–94.

[274] I. H. Marshall, *Acts*, 241; so also F. F. Bruce, *Acts*, 326; following him, Campbell, *Elders*, 166.

[275] Beyschlag, *Clemens Romanus*, 348–50; following him, Stuhlmacher, "Evangelium-Apostolat-Gemeinde," 39; with a nuanced view, Campenhausen, *Kirchliches Amt*, 91.

zation of this new overseer in the church as a whole in the city. Along with Campbell one is inclined to question the notion of a fusion supposedly first put into effect at the time of the Pastorals. Even Roloff admits that Titus 1:5–9 is the only reference that appears to indicate that the author intended to bring the two constitutions together with one another, and that even here it is uncertain.[276]

Indeed, one needs to ask if an amalgamation took place at all. Perhaps the two formed a unit quite early, possibly from the earliest days. The household setting of the early Christian churches appears to support this possibility. Roloff himself assumes that the house church backdrop explains the emergence of leadership structures in the Pauline mission and that, as a rule, householders as house church leaders are to be identified with the overseers (cf. Phil 1:1).[277] But even an overseer, understood in this way, stands in tension with the Pauline teaching on *charisma* as the determining factor for church leadership structures. For the most part, the house church leaders, as householders, would have subconsciously retained certain views about their leadership role that were more than likely patterned after an ancient *oikos* mentality. The members of their churches, who were, to some degree and often to a large extent, a part of their own household, servant staff, and clientele, would have shared these views. If the leaders enjoyed a certain high esteem in the church and society on the basis of their seniority and affluence, then their position in the congregation did not depend solely on the responsibilities they held there, nor only on their charismatic gifts.[278] Even though Paul never calls these house church leaders elders, they appear to share many of the characteristics of such elders and de facto acted, and were viewed to be, very much like them. That the house church leaders at one time were indeed called elders should not surprise us either, particularly in light of their Jewish-Christian, or synagogal,[279] and Greco-Roman background.[280] Add to this the fact that Paul and his coworkers most certainly knew of the presbyter model in the Jerusalem church under the leadership of the Lord's brother, James. In light of this, the Pauline mission can be considered an earlier stage of the development that we encounter in the Pastorals. Thus the hypothesis of an amalgamation of the two constitutions is no longer necessary. It is difficult, however, to determine with any certainty exactly what happened, as many of the details of these events remain more or less in the dark. For the purposes of our study, this issue can remain unresolved.

---

[276] Roloff, *Der erste Brief*, 175.

[277] Ibid., 172–73.

[278] With Holmberg, *Paul*, 58–123; Campbell, *Elders*, 191.

[279] Cf. at least the presence of the honorific πρεσβύτερος (see pp. 100–105).

[280] The combination of administrative and patriarchal elements is documented for the government councils of Roman cities. Cf. Dibelius and Conzelmann, *Pastoralbriefe*, 46.

Even though Campbell's reconstruction has much to commend it, there are some difficulties with it. As already seen (see pp. 103–5), his thesis that the leaders of the house churches were already called overseers in the primitive church in Jerusalem is not convincing, the major difficulty being that this cannot be documented anywhere in the texts at our disposal. In addition, one must ask whether the Pastorals really do refer to the monarchical overseer. "The notion of the supreme rule of a single bishop does not find sufficient support either in the theology of office or in what the [Pastoral] letters say about the competencies to which the overseers are actually entitled."[281] More cautious and yet probably more accurate than Campbell is the position taken by Roloff, that the author of the Pastorals intended to extend the office of overseer, which up until that time had only applied to the house church, as a church leadership office to the whole citywide church.[282]

One further question concerns Campbell's view that the title of elder is a designation of honor, not office. The results of our study seem to indicate that, at least in this regard, Campbell and Harvey appear to be right. In the government of the contemporary Jewish community and synagogue, there was no office of elder but only the honorific title "elder" (see pp. 103–5). Campbell concludes from this that in the Pastorals the title of elder is also merely a designation of honor. Still, that it is used as a title of honor in contemporary Jewish and Greco-Roman society does not prove that the designation, as we see it being used in Jerusalem (cf. Acts 21:18) or in the church of the Pastorals, was patterned after the Jewish or the Greco-Roman model. We cannot exclude a priori the possibility of a uniquely Christian usage of the terminology as an actual designation of office. It is possible in both Jerusalem and the Pastorals that, regarding the development of the office of elder, the Christian contribution was far greater than is commonly assumed. This is especially plausible in light of the house church setting of early Christianity. The house churches had members who, as householders and hosts, because of their natural authority and their independence and influence, carried special responsibility for the life of the community that met in their home. It appears natural that with time the house church leaders in a given city would have also formed a kind of council responsible for networking between the individual house churches and for the cohesion of the church as a whole at that location. We do not know just how these house church leaders went about their work in the service of the local church at its citywide level. Nevertheless, E. Dassmann states it well: "As

---

[281] Schöllgen, "Hausgemeinde," 84. Exegetical research is still divided on this issue. Most scholars tend not to see a *monepiskopos* (let alone a monarchical *episkopos*) in the Pastorals. Nevertheless the tendency toward it cannot be overlooked (cf. Lips, *Glaube-Gemeinde-Amt*, 142–43; Lohse, "Entstehung," 67; Roloff, "Amt IV," *TRE* 2:509–33.

[282] Roloff, *Der erste Brief*, 175–76.

soon as one of these 'elders' or *episkopoi* began acting as the leader of the group, became the speaker for all, and began coordinating the activities and the sermons for the worship service and ensuring confessional unity, the circumstance would have existed that could be described as that of one bishop presiding in a council of presbyters."[283]

It is also possible that a certain development led up to the circumstances we encounter in the Pastorals. It could be, for instance, that early Christians, first in Jerusalem then perhaps in the Pauline mission as well, used the title "elder" as a designation of age or honor much in the way it was used in the surrounding environment. Then over a period of time it became progressively more and more a designation of office. Such a development seems to correspond well with what we read in Acts (cf. 15:2, 4, 6, 22–23, 41; 16:4; 21:18). A household setting for the primitive church in Jerusalem has already been demonstrated above (see pp. 79–86). There also the position of the elders, in contrast to the apostles, appears to grow progressively stronger over time to the point that the apostles are no longer mentioned at all.[284] At the end of this process, we find a presbyterial council with James, the Lord's brother, at its head (see pp. 100–102). In the Pauline mission as well, we notice (with Campbell and Chapple) functions and titles that are "neither official nor incompatible with office" but rather "informal and tending toward office."[285] In the Pastorals this tendency toward office appears to have reached a certain completion.

It is my view that the state of affairs including a council of presbyters has presumably already been reached in the Pastorals. Here "elder" has ultimately become a designation of office, although this does not exclude the possibility that in some passages the term resonates with an age/honor undertone and, in some cases, overtone (cf. 1 Tim 5:1, πρεσβύτερος as a designation of age).[286] The following points support the usage of the term "elder" as a designation of office in the Pastorals. First, there are a multiple number of elders in the congregation (Titus 1:5). Together they form a college (πρεσβυτέριον, 1 Tim 4:14). The group of elders is to be understood as the body that gives church leadership.[287] An even stronger argument is found in 1 Tim 4:14. Here an official function of the presbyterial college as a leadership council becomes evident, namely, its involvement in the ordination of Timothy.[288] Furthermore, elders are appointed in Titus 1:5[289]—καθίστημι

---

[283] Dassmann, "Hausgemeinde," 90.
[284] Cf. Rohde, "πρεσβύτερος," *EDNT* 3:149.
[285] Campbell, *Elders*, 122.
[286] Cf. Oberlinner, *Pastoralbriefe*, 1:248.
[287] Cf. Lips, *Glaube-Gemeinde-Amt*, 111; so also Bornkamm, "πρέσβυς," *TDNT* 6:666, and many more (cf. the list offered by Lips, 108–11).
[288] With Oberlinner, *Pastoralbriefe*, 1:248; Roloff, *Der erste Brief*, 258–59; with a different view, Kelly, *Pastoral Epistles*, 108; G. Holtz, *Pastoralbriefe*, 111.
[289] Cf. Bornkamm, "πρέσβυς," *TDNT* 6:666; Lips, *Glaube-Gemeinde-Amt*, 108–9.

designates the appointment to a church office.²⁹⁰ As already demonstrated, it is unlikely that καθίστημι is being used absolutely in this passage. In Titus 1:6 characteristics of an elder are also listed as for the overseer in Titus 1:7–8 without distinguishing between the two. That the elders are not mentioned in 1 Tim 3 is probably due to the fact that the author's main interest lies in recommending the office of overseer as *the* leadership office for the local church as a whole.²⁹¹ The overall argument that the term "elder" is a designation of office is supported by the observation that the elders in the Jerusalem church were understood as office bearers (see pp. 95–105).²⁹² It can be assumed that, at the latest with the Pastorals, the Pauline churches had in place the presbyterial church order embraced originally by Jewish Christianity.²⁹³

Thus it is possible that both happened in the Pastorals: the legitimization of one single overseer for the whole church in one city (Campbell) *and* the new formation of the office of overseer by expanding the term to apply to the whole church in one city (Roloff), whereby the title "elder" was used as a designation of office (Roloff and others) and retained for the presbyterial college. Seen in this light, the legitimization, new formation, and expansion of the office of overseer would have emerged out of an already existing presbyterial organization of the church at the citywide level, on the one hand, and out of an already existing episcopal-patriarchal structure at the house church level, on the other hand. We then would have a presbyterial church order with an overseer at the head of the presbyterial college,²⁹⁴ much like the presbyter model familiar to us from the primitive church in Jerusalem (cf. Acts 15:4, 6, 22).²⁹⁵ Whether the overseer was viewed as the chairman of the presbyterial college—as *primus inter pares*—or was distinguished from the college of elders, clearly of higher authority, and regarded largely as the only leader of the church is still disputed among scholars and can remain unresolved here.²⁹⁶ The results of our study lead one to think that such presbyterial structures with the *office* of elder were not a mere copy of Jewish tradition. If Harvey and Campbell prove to be right, in the ancient world seniority was not specifically Jewish, nor did there exist in the synagogue community an office of elder that could have been adopted by the

---

²⁹⁰ Bauer-Aland⁶, 792 (BDAG 492); Bühner, "καθίστημι," *EDNT* 2:225; G. Holtz, *Pastoralbriefe,* 207.
²⁹¹ Cf. Roloff, *Der erste Brief,* 176.
²⁹² So also Bornkamm, "πρέσβυς." *TDNT* 6:662–72, esp. 662–63; Gnilka, *Philipperbrief,* 34.
²⁹³ So also Lips, *Glaube-Gemeinde-Amt,* 109.
²⁹⁴ This thesis is certainly not new. Cf. the list of the supporters of this view and a discussion by Lips, *Glaube-Gemeinde-Amt,* 112–14 nn. 104–7.
²⁹⁵ Cf. Stuhlmacher, "Weg," 126.
²⁹⁶ Lips, *Glaube-Gemeinde-Amt,* 113, favors the model *primus inter pares* and gives extensive proof. Cf. also Schöllgen, "Hausgemeinde," 84–86, for a contrasting view.

early Christian church. Accordingly, presbyterial structures with the office of elder can be considered a uniquely Christian innovation.²⁹⁷

Excursus: House Churches in 2 and 3 John

The second and third epistles of John definitely belong to a sociohistorical, exegetical study of the significance of the house church in early Christian missions.²⁹⁸ Very few passages in the NT supply as much subject matter for our topic as the passages in these two letters; they provide a lucid, concrete illustration of how house churches functioned. Here again the vital importance of the house church for early Christian missional outreach is unambiguously confirmed.

Even a brief look at the history of research shows that understanding the historical situation of the Johannine epistles is extremely difficult.²⁹⁹ To this day, scholars have not come to a consensus on the reason for the dispute between the "elder" (πρεσβύτερος, 2 John 1) and Diotrephes.³⁰⁰ Surely this is due to the fact that exegetes must come to grips with the quandary that the source material at our disposal is very coincidental and sparse. As a result, there is very little that we can know with precision and certainty.³⁰¹ As early as 1977 Malherbe pointed out that paying closer attention to the household setting would contribute to a better understanding of the epistles of John.³⁰² Other exegetes have supported Malherbe's view, even though some have criticized it in part or slightly revised certain aspects.³⁰³ Although every

---

²⁹⁷ So already H. Beyer, *TDNT* 2:615: "so that for the fulfillment of its [the early Christian] mission new offices had to be created, or developed out of the matter itself." Cf. also Karrer, "Ältestenamt," and the criticism of his analysis by Campbell, *Elders*, 161–62.

²⁹⁸ Regarding the historical question, cf. Hengel, *Johanneische Frage*, 110–12, and his debate esp. with R. Brown, *Community*, 93–144, and *Epistles of John*, 69–115. With Hengel we will assume that one author wrote all three letters of John. Cf. also Klauck, *Die Johannesbriefe*, 158. For further discussion of issues of introduction, cf. Kümmel, *Einleitung*, 390–92, 396–98; Strecker, *Johannesbriefe*, 11–28; Schnackenburg, *Johannesbriefe*, 1–48, 295–303.

²⁹⁹ Cf. R. Brown, *Epistles of John*, 14–46; Hengel, *Johanneische Frage*, 1–6.

³⁰⁰ Scholars have suggested different explanations for the conflict: doctrine, authority, and power. Cf. M. Leutzsch, *Bewährung*, 108–14, for an extensive discussion. Cf. also R. Brown, *Epistles of John*, 728, 732–39; the brief overview by Klauck, *Die Johannesbriefe*, 161–62.

³⁰¹ Hengel, *Johanneische Frage*, 5.

³⁰² Cf. Malherbe, "Inhospitality," esp. 92, 94 (citation is to the reprint in *Social Aspects*). Malherbe suggests "that we attempt to understand Diotrephes in light of the main subject of III John, which is the extension of hospitality to fellow Christians."

³⁰³ Following Malherbe, White, *Texts*, 24. Cf. also R. Brown, *Epistles of John*, 69–115, 728–39, and his criticism of Malherbe. Cf. also Hengel, *Johanneische Frage*, 124–50; Klauck, *Zweite und dritte Johannesbrief*, 65–67, and *Die Johannesbriefe*, 155–63; M. Leutzsch, *Bewährung*, esp. 90–115—all with different emphases.

historical reconstruction must remain hypothetical, and this is most certainly true of the Johannine Epistles, this section will attempt to illuminate the situation from the sociohistorical perspective of the ancient *oikos* on the basis of texts containing references to houses or house churches.

The central figure for our purposes is represented by Diotrephes (cf. 3 John 9–10). Even though the information about him is limited to these two verses, his person offers insight into the situation of the church of that time. Although the author of 3 John, "the elder," wrote to the church (2 John),[304] Diotrephes refused to receive him,[305] did not practice hospitality toward several itinerant Christians from other churches, and expelled from the congregation those who acted differently than he did. From 3 John one can see that the presbyter's admonition (2 John 10–11) led to a variety of reactions in the church as a whole.[306] Diotrephes ended up disobeying the elder whereas Gaius followed his advice.

As already repeatedly noted, the first believers gathered for worship primarily in the private homes of well-to-do Christian families. Guest rooms in such church centers were made available as living quarters for traveling fellow believers and missionaries. "Not to receive opposing itinerant missionaries into your home also meant refusing them access into the house church, and thus they were not able to speak at the gatherings, which would have been their best opportunity to propagate their doctrine and, in a worst-case scenario, to lead members of the church astray."[307]

Apparently Christians from different house churches were under way as itinerant missionaries and church delegates. Equipped with only the bare necessities, these messengers of Christ depended on the hospitality of Christian houses.[308] These traveling Christians led a life strongly reminiscent of the mission discourse found in the very old Jesus tradition (see

---

[304] With many other exegetes, the assumption here is that 2 John was written before 3 John (cf., e.g., cautiously, Klauck, *Die Johannesbriefe*, 125–26, and his discussion of the different positions).

[305] More and more scholars advocate the same translation of ἐπιδέχεσθαι for both 3 John 9 and 3 John 10, i.e., "receive"; cf., independent of one another but with similar arguments, Leutzsch (*Bewährung*, 90–115, esp. 101, 109–10) and Mitchell ("'Diotrephes'"); cf. also Klauck, *Zweite und dritte Johannesbrief*, 102. Some translate ἐπιδέχεσθαι in v. 9 differently than in v. 10, with "anerkennen" ("acknowledge, recognize"); cf., e.g., Schnackenburg, *Johannesbriefe*, 326. The translation decision one makes here has far-reaching consequences for the entire exegesis, esp. of 3 John 5–10, and for understanding the dispute between the elder and Diotrephes.

[306] Cf. Klauck, *Die Johannesbriefe*, 154; Hengel, *Johanneische Frage*, 146–50.

[307] Klauck, *Die Johannesbriefe*, 157; R. Brown, *Epistles of John*, 676. For the ancient and biblical understanding of a greeting in this context, cf. Hengel, *Johanneische Frage*, 145–46; also see pp. 56–57.

[308] Cf. 3 John 7. On hospitality, cf. Hiltbrunner, "Gastfreundschaft"; Malherbe, *Social Aspects*, 94–103; Klauck, "Exkurs 3: Gastfreundschaft," in *Zweite und dritte Johannesbrief*, 95–96; see pp. 182–85.

pp. 48–53).[309] According to 3 John 7, these itinerant preachers went out "for the sake of the Name," that is, to testify of God's rule in Christ Jesus, the one sent by God.[310] Because they adhered to the instructions of Jesus in Matt 10:5, 8–9, and 10 and embarked on their journey more or less destitute, they depended on the support of locally resident Christians. The "greeting" regulation in 2 John 10–11 is apparently a reference to Matt 10:12–13 par. In 2 and 3 John, therefore, we encounter itinerant preachers who are still strictly following the mission discourse instructions of Jesus.[311]

It was in relation to these traveling brothers that a conflict arose. The elder received word that Diotrephes had rudely rejected some of the itinerant missionaries. In contrast, Gaius had received them and even equipped them again for their return trip. Because the presbyter could not understand Diotrephes' behavior, he wrote a letter to the church, but in vain, as Diotrephes would not accept it (3 John 9). In an ensuing letter to Gaius (3 John), the presbyter accused Diotrephes of a "tyrannical disposition."[312] Diotrephes' motive for acting this way remains unclear.[313] Presumably, Diotrephes unequivocally opposed the elder and aggressively took action against the members of the church who wanted to abide by the presbyter's requests. Whether Diotrephes belonged to the false teachers mentioned in 1 John is difficult to determine, but it is likely. It is interesting to note that, despite the severity of his words, the elder did not want to categorically end the relationship with Diotrephes.[314]

In the same letter the presbyter attempted to motivate Gaius to continue his hospitality (3 John 8). This presupposes that Gaius had his own house, probably in the near vicinity of Diotrephes' residence. It is disputed whether the group that gathered in Gaius's home could already be considered a house church before the writing of 3 John and the conflict with Diotrephes.[315] The mention of the house of Gaius and his friends (3 John

---

[309] Cf. Stuhlmacher, "Weg," 129–31; Schnackenburg, *Johannesbriefe*, 325.

[310] "The Name" appears to have become a fixed designation for Christ. Compare Acts 5:41 with 4:17; 5:28, 40; 8:12; 9:10; 1 Pet 4:14, 16. The usage most likely is connected to the sayings of Jesus, such as Matt 10:22, 40–42; 18:5; 19:29. Cf. also Rom 1:5.

[311] In contrast to the coworker missional outreach of Paul (see pp. 179–81) and the Antiochene regional mission with its post-Easter modifications (see pp. 109–13), in the Johannine circle the regulations for the pre-Easter mission were adhered to in relatively pure form. Cf., however, Schmeller, *Brechungen*, 76–78, who, against Theissen, considers an overly strict distinction between itinerant charismatics and church organizers to be poor stereotyping.

[312] Klauck, *Die Johannesbriefe*, 161 n. 46; cf. 3 John 9.

[313] Cf., for the discussion of possibilities from their own standpoints, R. Brown, *Epistles of John*, 732–39; Klauck, *Die Johannesbriefe*, 162–63; and Leutzsch, *Bewährung*, 114–15.

[314] Cf. the announcement of a future visit and the presbyter's intent to dialogue with Diotrephes (3 John 10).

[315] Cf. R. Brown, *Epistles of John*, 730–38, and his discussion of, and arguments against, the position of Malherbe, "Inhospitality."

15) supports the view that the group represented a kind of house church even before the conflict arose.[316] At any rate, Gaius does not appear to be a part of the group that was dominated by Diotrephes, as there is no indication of any tension between the two or of any kind of confrontation. Furthermore, Gaius appears able to act independently of Diotrephes: in contrast to him, he adheres to the instructions of the elder. If the house of Gaius did not serve as a gathering place for an independent house church before the incident,[317] then it certainly was inherent "in the logic of the events that his house would develop into a new community center where other brothers and already existing friends . . . could find a new gathering place."[318] Evidently, in any case, Gaius and presumably other community members represent householders who were able to, and actually did, receive traveling brothers into their homes. In such houses and in due time, there apparently emerged a multiple number of house churches in the area.

Diotrephes' behavior insinuates as well that he had just taken over or already had the leadership in the church in his house. One should not yet see in him the monarchical bishop, as some have assumed.[319] Nevertheless, Hengel is by no means exaggerating when he states that Diotrephes is "probably the head of a house church who, as the homeowner, could exercise his rights as a householder in the house that served as a Christian place of assembly."[320] His authority was initially not ecclesial in nature but, rather, socially anchored in his position as head of the household.[321] It is evident, however, that development was moving in the direction of official church structures.[322] As we saw in the Pauline house churches, the distance from householder to church leader (and church office) is not great.[323] By rejecting the missionaries, Diotrephes usurped the position of the presbyter as

---

[316] So also Malherbe, *Social Aspects*, 104–5. Cf. also Hengel, *Johanneische Frage*, 126: "It is possible that Gaius was the leader of his own house church."

[317] The observation that the church addressed in the letter was not clearly designated supports the view that his house did not yet function as a meeting place for a house church.

[318] Klauck, *Die Johannesbriefe*, 160, 163; so also R. Brown, *Epistles of John*, 731–32. Brown and Klauck also consider the possibility that the preservation of 3 John may be connected with Gaius. If he became the host of a house church, the letter addressed to him could have been preserved by that church as a founding document belonging to the heritage of the Johannine community.

[319] So, e.g., quite early, Harnack, *Über den dritten Johannesbrief*, 21; Bauer, *Rechtgläubigkeit*, 93–98; Käsemann, "Ketzer," 173–74. Cf. the extensive discussion in R. Brown, *Epistles of John*, 733–35; Klauck, *Die Johannesbriefe*, 161–62, and "Exkurs 4: Diotrephes," in *Zweite und dritte Johannesbrief*, 106–9; Strecker, *Johannesbriefe*, 365–67; Leutzsch, *Bewährung*, 106–15.

[320] Hengel, *Johanneische Frage*, 128; so also Malherbe, *Social Aspects*, 109.

[321] So also Malherbe, *Social Aspects*, 110.

[322] Cf. Schnackenburg, *Johannesbriefe*, 329.

[323] So also R. Brown, *Epistles of John*, 738; Hengel, *Johanneische Frage*, 128–29; Klauck, *Zweite und dritte Johannesbrief*, 160–61.

the final authority and, in so doing, distanced himself from the leadership practice of the Johannine church as a whole (1 John 2:27).[324]

Furthermore, Diotrephes' actions are an indication that he was (or wanted to be) more than just leader of a church in his own house. One has the impression that he was the head of the local church as a whole or at least had aspirations of becoming such. Once again we encounter a situation in which the whole church and the house churches must be distinguished from one another: on the one hand, the house church in the home of Gaius (and presumably house churches in the homes of other church leaders) and, on the other, the whole church at that location or in that area.[325] The individual house churches appear to be well integrated with the whole church and under its leadership. This view requires that ἐκκλησία in 3 John 9 refer to the whole church at that location or in that area, although in the immediate context (3 John 6) the term is unmistakably used for an individual congregation. For good reasons, Malherbe advocates the whole-church position.[326] In particular, the contemporary practice of sending a letter to the whole church in one city or area would tend to support this view.[327]

The problems evident in the Johannine epistles receive further discussion in the *Didache*. There (*Did.* 11:1–6; 12:1–4) we observe another kind of itinerant Christian preacher, that is, false prophets who took advantage of the hospitality of local believers and at times even misused or abused it.[328] Apparently, they had hopes of living free from the cares of everyday life, all at the expense of the house churches. The *Didache* community developed clear guidelines for discerning false prophets and against the misuse and abuse of hospitality. [329]

One additional question is raised in 3 John regarding the possible cultic function of a house. White points out that both the regulation in 2 John and the actions of Diotrephes (barring itinerant Christians from the gathering in his home) demonstrate that "admission to the house of assembly in this community, and especially for Diotrephes, had become a much more formalized concept."[330] There is no indication whatsoever that Diotrephes' house had

---

[324] Cf. R. Brown, *Epistles of John*, 738; Klauck, *Die Johannesbriefe*, 161.

[325] There are at least two Christian groups in the area: one that is associated with Gaius, and the other with Diotrephes (so also Malherbe, *Social Aspects*, 105).

[326] Malherbe, *Social Aspects*, 103–12.

[327] This would also be true even if 3 John were written to Gaius, as the content of the letter applies to the church as a whole (cf. v. 15 and also the Letter to Philemon). Cf., however, the criticism of Malherbe by R. Brown, *Epistles of John*, 730–38.

[328] Cf. also Niederwimmer, *Didache*, 214–16, 223–25.

[329] One other possibile way of regulating the practice of hospitality and protecting it from misuse and abuse was to write letters of recommendation, with which traveling Christians could introduce themselves to the house churches located on their routes; 3 John can be viewed as an example of such a letter of recommendation. Cf. Malherbe, *Social Aspects*, 103–4; Leutzsch, *Bewährung*, 18–30.

[330] White, *Texts*, 24.

in any way been structurally altered in an attempt to convert it into a more official kind of church building reserved for worship assembly; it was still a dwelling place used for domestic purposes and privately owned by the person who served as the leader of the *house church* that gathered in it. Nevertheless, according to White, a development seems to be emerging here on the way in which this group is beginning to understand its gathering and its gathering place. "The doors and walls of the house itself had begun to define the limits of the cultic community in assembly. Admission to the house was symbolic of admission to the fellowship of the church."[331] For White this documents a development in the direction of the *church house* and an architectural definition of cultic space.[332]

Although there is much in White's analysis with which one can readily agree, one can ask if he is not slightly overchallenging the text here. It is correct that the church takes on a more formalized structure. It is moving in the direction of an official organization with a kind of legal order. As already noted, Diotrephes, in rejecting the itinerant preachers and expelling from the church other believers who were not willing to conform to his way of thinking, exercised his social power as householder and possibly his official, ecclesial power as the leading individual of the faith community that met in his home. He refused to care for the traveling teachers in his home and to give them living quarters. Perhaps he distinguished as well between members and nonmembers. In doing so, he acted within social, ecclesial, and legal organizational parameters. In my opinion, however, his actions did not constitute the cultic use of his house.

From our brief consideration of the Johannine Epistles, we can draw a number of important conclusions regarding the missional function and significance of NT house churches. Today scholars readily agree that early Christianity was indebted to itinerant missionaries for the rapid expansion of the movement.[333] At the time of the letters of John, missional outreach presumably consisted primarily of individual conversations with personal friends and acquaintances and invitations to the worship gatherings in the house churches.[334] Moreover, these Christian itinerant preachers were important information carriers. Third John, which was most likely delivered by the Demetrius referred to in verse 12, was probably read and interpreted to the congregation by him as well. In addition, he was supposed to strengthen the personal relationship of the presbyter with the recipients of the letter. In this way, the itinerant missionaries delivering the letter had the function—

---

[331] Ibid.

[332] Here White uses a term he coined: *domus ecclesiae*. For a discussion and definition of the terms "house church" and "church house" in the current study, see pp. 18–19.

[333] Cf., e.g., Malherbe, *Social Aspects,* 62–69; Stambaugh and Balch, *Social World,* 37–62.

[334] Hengel, *Johanneische Frage,* 133. Cf. the description of his conversion through an elderly teacher in Justin, *Dial.* 3.1–3.

this is especially evident in the Johannine Letters—of strengthening the house churches and fostering cohesiveness between them. Hengel is not overstating the case when he describes the itinerants, at least on a human level, as "the guarantors of the unity of the church."[335]

The letters of John unequivocally document that well-functioning house churches were indispensable for missional outreach in that they provided for the missionaries, cared for them if necessary, and, in preparation for further travel, equipped and supplied them with food, clothing, and finances (cf. 3 John 6).[336] The situation was quite precarious for traveling believers who were refused the hospitality of a Christian household. Even if a Christian church existed in the next town or city, it could have been dangerous to continue on (particularly by night).[337] The itinerant Christians of the Johannine Letters were also not willing to let pagans take them in (3 John 7).[338] As already seen, commercial hostels did not offer a suitable alternative regarding room and board (assuming there even was one in the near vicinity).[339] Apart from the bad reputation of these hostels, the lack of funds could have hindered the missionaries from making use of this option. This is why the author of 3 John placed such a high value on the reception of traveling missionaries. He identified as a serious crisis a situation in which the hospitable acceptance of such missionaries by locally resident fellow Christians was not ensured, because he knew that the success of all missional outreach was largely dependent on their reception.

---

[335] Hengel, *Johanneische Frage*, 134. Hengel correctly points out that these traveling Christians can also be a dangerous threat to the small house church groups (2 John 10) isolated from one another and perhaps without strong leadership, which again underscores a weakness of the house church model (see pp. 267–68).

[336] Cf. Klauck, *Zweite und dritte Johannesbrief*, 96: "The early Christian missional movement would have been unimaginable without the practice of hospitality among believing brothers and sisters (Rom 16:1f)."

In 3 John 6 προπέμπειν means not merely "send" but "equip for travel," as in Acts 15:3; 1 Cor 16:6, 11; 2 Cor 1:16; Titus 3:13; cf. Schnackenburg, *Johannesbriefe*, 324 n. 4; Klauck, *Zweite und dritte Johannesbrief*, 90.

[337] In addition to wild animals, there was the danger of falling into the hands of a band of robbers (cf. Luke 10:25–37; *Mek. Exod.* 2). On the danger of traveling by night, cf. Isaac, *Limits*, 182 n. 115; Krauss, *Talmudische Archäologie*, 68 nn. 196–97.

[338] It is not entirely clear whether the itinerant Christians in 3 John 7 would have been given anything from the pagans or if they would have accepted anything from them even it had been given. Both options would have been possible; presumably, both happened often. Cf. Hengel, *Johanneische Frage*, 128 n. 108; with a different view, Klauck, *Zweite und dritte Johannesbrief*, 92.

[339] Regarding the bad reputation of these hostels/hotels, see pp. 182–85.

CHAPTER SIX

The Ecclesiological and Missional Function and Significance of House Churches

FUNCTION AND SIGNIFICANCE FROM JESUS TO PAUL

As in ancient society generally, the *oikos* represented the basic unit for community life for the early Christian movement. Houses were more or less the architectural, social, and economic foundations of urban and interregional missions and incubators of local church life. In an embryonic sense, this was true in the earliest days of Jesus' village and regional missional ministry, even more so in the city outreach of the primitive church in Jerusalem, in the city and regional mission of Antioch, and in the worldwide center-oriented missional outreach of Paul. The following section will summarize once again the ecclesiological and missional functions and significance of the house from an architectural, socioeconomic, and ecclesiological point of view, this time giving special attention to the overall strengths and weaknesses of the house church model.[1]

The House as a Building (Architectural Significance)

We have observed how believers utilized private houses for worship and ministry in a variety of different ways in early Christian missions. Three basic options should be distinguished: (a) A room, usually the triclinium of a private domestic house, was made available at specific times for religious purposes without architectural changes to the structure of the house (*house church*). (b) A room (or several rooms) in a private domestic house was used exclusively for religious purposes with perhaps an architectural adaptation of the house. (c) An architecturally adapted house (*church house*) or a public building (*hall church*) belonged to a private individual but was used exclusively for religious purposes.[2] Even though all three types existed during the

---

[1] For a summary of the significance of houses in these periods, see above, the section "Conclusions" in each chapter.

[2] For the definition of the three terms "house church," "church house," and "hall church," see the research report, pp. 18–19.

NT period, the last two were the exception (White). The existence of the last two types during our time frame cannot be documented with certainty archaeologically because of a lack of positive evidence. Of course, the existence of the first type cannot be archaeologically documented *per definitionem,* as it was not physically changed or remodeled and thus left no archaeological evidence of Christian usage. An exception to the rule is the house of Peter in Capernaum, which was possibly used before 70 C.E. for Christian meetings (see pp. 31–42). We also must keep in mind that particularly wherever synagogue communities converted either partially or as a whole to the messianic faith, entire (public) buildings could have been dedicated for worship and ministry use. Here again we do not have entirely convincing evidence. Perhaps one confirmation of this view can be seen in the emergence of early house churches that are often described as filial or contrast groups to the synagogue.[3] Only the first type of house church can be exegetically documented with certainty in the NT, but then repeatedly: to begin with, before Easter in the ministry of Jesus (the house of Peter in Capernaum), next in the primitive church in Jerusalem (the house with the upper room; the house of Mary, mother of John Mark), and finally in the Pauline mission (e.g., the houses of Aquila, Gaius, Philemon, and Lydia).[4] Much later (starting with the third century) we see a growing tendency toward buildings owned by the congregation and used exclusively for religious purposes. Then with Constantine we see the beginning of a period characterized by large basilical church buildings. In remote, unchristianized regions all three types of house church continued to exist well into the fourth and fifth centuries C.E.

One important result of our examination can be seen in that we were able to demonstrate credibly the historic reliability of the pertinent NT references to houses and house churches in the missional outreach of Jesus and in the Jerusalem church. As mentioned, the majority of studies on early Christian house churches up until now have taken for granted that we stand on firm ground historically only with the references to house churches in the undisputed Pauline Epistles.

From an architectural point of view, the house offered certain strengths by providing space used in a variety of ways for missional outreach. To begin with, it should be pointed out that houses differ architecturally from one another. For the time period of the early Christian mission, Palestinian, Greek, and Roman types of private house come into question.[5] They were easily adapted, and they provided Christians with a low-cost venue for assembly. With relatively little effort it was possible to establish a Christian presence in

---

[3] Cf., in Philippi, Acts 16:13–15, 30–32; in Corinth, Acts 18:1–8; cf. also James 2:2–3.

[4] See pp. 31–42, 62–74, and 119–30 for documentation.

[5] See pp. 45–46, 69–70, and 140–41 for descriptions of the types of ancient house in question.

the everyday life of ancient cities. At least in the early days, the triclinium (often in conjunction with the courtyard [cf. Capernaum, Mark 2–4] or atrium) provided an ideal room for teaching and preaching ministries, catechetical instruction for baptism, and other missional activities. The triclinium was also a room well suited for prayer meetings, table fellowship, and the celebration of the Lord's Supper (cf. the primitive church in Jerusalem). Because of the physical limitations of the triclinium, the numerical size of the first house churches was relatively small (on average, twenty to forty persons; in very few exceptional cases, up to a hundred). Hence by necessity these first Christian communities were small, family-like groups in which individual pastoral care, intimate personal relationships, and accountability to each other were possible. "One reason for the house church's powerful impact on its environment is found in the fact that it was not possible to grow beyond the parameters of a small group due to lack of space."[6]

The house also provided other rooms that could be made available for missional outreach, such as guest rooms that served as quarters for travelers or for missionaries who stayed for longer periods of ministry at one location (e.g., Jesus in Capernaum; Paul in Corinth with Prisca and Aquila). The workplace was often located in the house and was also put to effective missional use. For instance, Paul took advantage of workplaces (e.g., in the house of Aquila) to generate opportunities for evangelistic conversations with business contacts.

At the same time, however, the private house also had its architectural limitations and weaknesses. The relatively small capacity of the triclinium was not only a positive factor, as by necessity it limited the potential number of participants for the worship service. Once the congregation outgrew the capacity of the living room, another homeowner with a large enough house had to be found who was also willing to make his home available to the church—something that, of course, could not be taken for granted. An additional architectural weakness of a private house can be seen in its lack of features that were important for worship services and other activities in the life of the church. For instance, most houses did not have a built-in facility for baptism. Some Palestinian houses containing *miqva'ot* may have been the exception to this rule.[7] Perhaps this is the reason that in the NT we hear relatively often of the baptism *of* a house but never a baptism *in* a house.

The architectural anonymity of a private house must be viewed with ambivalence. On the one hand, without an intentional Christian alteration, a private house did not outwardly testify to the faith. On the other hand, the anonymity could provide a certain protection in times of persecution, in which the private home became a hiding place for missionaries and church members (cf. Acts 12:12–14). This anonymity, however, was neither easy,

---

[6] Klauck, *Hausgemeinde,* 100.
[7] Cf. Avigad, *Discovering Jerusalem,* 139–43, for the archaeological evidence for ritual baths in Jerusalem; Netzer, "Ancient Ritual Baths," for Herodian Jericho.

nor always possible, to preserve (e.g., in Jerusalem; cf. Acts 8:3). As White points out, the renovation of a house or building would have caught the attention of the surrounding neighborhood, as such a project would have had to be financed and then tackled by a team of craftsmen and manual laborers.[8] If they had not noticed before, others would now begin to realize that this was a meeting place for Christians.

The House as a Community (Socioeconomic Significance)

As noted earlier, Klauck, Meeks, and White have all correctly pointed out that Christians were not the first and only religious group to meet in private homes. For example, members of the cult of Mithras, the mystery associations, and particularly the Jews in their house synagogues followed this pattern as well. Here the total (Mithras) or partial (Judaism) independence from historically established holy sanctuaries in specific locations is evident. The Christians also chose a socially and legally accepted form for their religious assemblies. In particular, the example of the mystery cults illustrates "how natural it would have been in those days for others in society to view and to accept the Christians as another religious association."[9]

From the very beginning and then continuing throughout the first, second, and third phases of the movement, an integration of the Christian community with the social and economic infrastructure of the ancient *oikos* can be observed. The household codes, as found in Colossians and Ephesians, represent the socioethical correspondence to *oikos* structures of earlier congregations against the backdrop of the *oeconomica* (household management literature—Lührmann). Even in the earliest days, with the firm expectation of the imminent return of Christ, potentially lasting social structures emerged in house churches. Because families formed the core of house churches from the onset, they needed special instruction and exhortation, which for us has become historically tangible in the household codes of Colossians and Ephesians. Hence it is not necessary to understand the household codes either as a reaction to the crisis that arose in the second (and third) generation as a result of the delay in the second coming or as a protest reaction against the eschatological enthusiasts. The categorization of the household codes in the paraenetical context of church, house, and public (Lips) as well as their definition as topos and not *Gattung* speak for a stronger Christian contribution to their formation than is normally assumed. The household code in Colossians could have emerged early on as "tradition" with a possible origin from within the missional context of the Pauline house churches (Gielen).[10]

The integration of *oikos* structures also had a positive consequence in the relationship between church and public. With the decision to adopt *oikos*

---

[8] White, *Building God's House*, 146–47.
[9] Stuhlmacher, *Philemon*, 72.
[10] See p. 230.

structures, the house churches corresponded closely with the ancient society around them, as the ancient *oikos* reflected the social order of that time (status, station, rank, position, class, profession), composed of almost all the different social strata. As a result, the composition of the early Christian movement was not limited to specific groups in the population. Christians were therefore positioned to reach all levels of society with the gospel. This becomes evident in Colossians and Ephesians but particularly in the Pastoral Letters. Christians are encouraged to reflect a household ordered by God in Christ in their own families and house churches, where they were to project an image of order inwardly and outwardly and live an exemplary life with the goal of reaching others with the gospel. The integration of the house church within the *oikos* had a positive effect not only for the spread of the gospel; it also enabled continuity, duration, and tradition. With the integration into *oikos* infrastructures, the Christian church became capable of long-term survival and was given the potential to transition from one generation to the next (Lührmann).

Another socioeconomic factor in early Christian missions was patronage. Most scholars agree that the role it played in missional outreach and church development cannot be overemphasized. By making their houses available for Christian assembly, householders provided and guaranteed the material and organizational foundation for church development. Early Christians took advantage of the social network in the household, profession, guild, and association of the householder to promote missional outreach and congregational development. The contacts of the *pater familias* with powerful individuals in urban government and society were often quite useful, particularly in times of crisis (cf. Jason, Acts 17). The publicly respected householder was able to provide legal protection and a certain social legitimacy for the faith community that met in his home. The extended family, including slaves, clients, and friends, as well as the contacts of the householder with his professional colleagues and business partners offered an entire network of relationships. Once accepted by the householder, Paul, his coworkers, and many other Christians became trusted insiders within this network of relationships and as a result were able to quickly reach out and touch the lives of large numbers of people for Christ (Judge, Hock, Meeks).

The socioeconomic system of ancient patronage served also to support the local and interregional mission. This can be observed even before Easter in Jesus' village and regional missional outreach from Capernaum into the entire area of the so-called evangelical triangle.[11] Here a complementary relationship existed between the itinerant missionaries and the sedentary followers of Jesus, in which a kind of patronage played a important role. The significance of the system of patronage becomes all the more obvious in the Pauline mission. Householders, men and women of means, enabled the mis-

---

[11] Capernaum, Bethsaida, Chorazin.

sion journeys of Paul and his coworkers through their hospitality and other material support (e.g., by covering travel costs). Moreover, the ancient *oikos* served as a source of candidates for the Pauline missional enterprise. Both householders (Stephanas from Corinth) and the members of their households made themselves available to the local and regional mission. The house and household were a training ground for co-laborers and leaders for missional outreach. Household heads, their slaves, and their clients were all able to develop their organizational, administrative, and (particularly the housefathers) their teaching skills even before their conversion to Christianity in the context of the ancient *oikos,* so that by the time they came to faith, they were in many ways ready-made house church leaders.

With the catchword "hospitality" we are reminded of yet another benefit of the ancient *oikos* for mission. The early Christian houses and house churches were places where Christian hospitality was practiced by and for Christians and non-Christians alike in a very concrete way. In house churches it was possible for both Christians and non-Christians to experience the safety and security of the *familia Dei*. Closely connected with this was early Christian brotherly love, which was able to unite radically different social groups into one community. Our investigation has clearly confirmed the results of recent research indicating that the members of the first Christian churches cannot be categorized exclusively as having originated from one social level but rather came from nearly all existing strata (see pp. 165–70). Both the makeup of the Pauline churches and the household code tradition in Colossians, Ephesians, and the Pastoral Letters reflect a high level of social stratification, which demonstrates that house churches embraced individuals from many different social backgrounds: householders and slaves, Jews and Gentiles, men, women, and even believing children. The growth of the Christian movement affected nearly every social level.

The only way that this could lead to lasting success was to develop a sense of unity that would be able to prevail even against the unavoidable conflict arising from the different behavioral patterns of each of these social groups.[12] In all three phases of early Christian missions, the house church provides one very important explanation for how it was possible for Christianity to succeed in integrating individuals from such different social backgrounds into one cohesive unit. Galatians 3:27, Col 3:11, and the Christian household codes are evidence for the exceptional community-building power and capability for social integration of the early Christian house churches. The concept of church as the family of God became the social model and affected the way Christians related to each other. Christian brotherly love, theologically rooted in the Pauline doctrine of justification by faith, transcended all social barriers, including those separating masters from slaves

---

[12] Schöllgen, "Hausgemeinde," 74.

and Jews from Gentiles. Through the penetrating power of the gospel, even the *oikos* structures underwent a partial transformation. In the small, family-like setting of the house church, individuals from extremely different social backgrounds were united into one new community. Inwardly, early house churches provided Christians with a training ground for practicing brotherly love and had a powerful integrating effect. Outwardly, house churches were display cases illustrating brotherly love to non-Christians, and as such they had a dynamic missional impact.

There is one further characteristic of ancient patronage that can be seen as a positive factor in early Christian missions. In those days it was generally expected that the subordinate members of the household would accept the religion of the head of the house. Although this was easier to enforce in smaller families than in larger ones and although a relaxation of this practice can be observed during the imperial period, there is some indication in the NT that not only individuals but entire houses were baptized (cf. the *oikos* formula in Acts). This obviously accelerated the spread of the gospel. One additional positive aspect of this phenomenon is the solidarity that grew out of this, which was effective even during, but particularly after, conversion. Seekers and new believers were supported from the very beginning in their decision for Christ by the rest of the household. Still, one possible consequence of the baptism of all or most of the subordinates in the household was that some may not have made a personal commitment to Christ or had any faith of their own.

Our study also revealed that the integration of the church and missional outreach into the ancient household had other drawbacks from a socioeconomic point of view. The missional impact of the householder, for instance, was not automatically positive. If the patron of a house church was appreciated and respected in the neighborhood and city, then this usually had a positive effect on the reputation and missional outreach of the church as well. If, however, the opposite was true of the householder, it became a liability for the church, in some cases even limiting its missional fruitfulness in that city. In light of this, the instructions given in the Pastoral Epistles appear all the more understandable.

An uncritical integration of the social order of the *oikos* into the house church often led to social problems as well. Because of the strong social position of the householder, it was possible for unhealthy, overreliant relationships to develop. Pagan *oikos* structures such as the client system could continue to exist under a Christian cloak. Moreover, there existed the danger that an overly dependent relationship could develop with individual leaders who had powerful, charismatic personalities. Just because someone was wealthy and educated did not guarantee his or her positive theological and spiritual development. Householders who fell into error were often capable of dragging their entire house church down with them, which could then lead to tension and conflict within the local church as a whole at that location (cf. the Pastoral Letters).

Simply gathering in a house did not automatically lead to the reconciliation of individuals from diverse backgrounds in the church. Meetings in a house Mithraeum were exclusively for men; the members of *collegia* were most often from the same social level. The membership in house synagogues was a bit more socially diverse, but even here there was the tendency toward community formation according to profession and nationality, which also led to exclusiveness. As a rule, Christian house churches integrated a large diversity of individuals from a variety of backgrounds. This is primarily related to, and grew out of, the inner structure of this new faith (Gal 3:27–28). Christ had enabled salvation for everyone; consequently, a diversity of people was supposed to live in loving unity one with the other. This is the reason Paul fought so hard against the separation of house churches according to nationality in Antioch. The Corinthian example also illustrates how social differences can negatively affect the house church. Even though the assembly in a house had increased potential for becoming and sustaining an accepting, loving, and supporting community, it did not always guarantee this.

The House as a Church (Ecclesiological Significance)

Our study has shown that, in all three phases of early Christian mission, the house served as the basic foundation for all church life. Even before Easter it can be observed that the house of Peter in Capernaum, the "cradle of the emerging church,"[13] was the operational base for the missional outreach of Jesus, a place where Jesus exercised his teaching and healing ministry, and an assembly place for the *familia Dei* consisting of Jesus and his disciples. Houses also served as bases of operations and meeting places for prayer, table fellowship, and teaching in the missional outreach of Jesus' disciples. Later, in the primitive church in Jerusalem, houses were used for assembly, community formation and fellowship, prayer, teaching, and the celebration of the Lord's Supper. It is legitimate here to speak of house churches as churches in the full sense, as all of the ecclesiological elements that constitute the church are observable. The house churches enabled the celebration of a specifically Christian worship service. Christians met in the temple for prayer, the teaching of the word, and the proclamation of the gospel, but it was only in houses that the celebration of the Lord's Supper was possible. This use of houses is continued then in Antioch and in all phases of the Pauline mission.

One important question addressed during our study was the relationship between the house church and the local church, with all its ecclesiological implications. In the NT the relationship between house church and local church varied from city to city and area to area. On the one hand, we

---

[13] Loffreda, "Tradizionale casa," 38.

find references in Acts to several houses that served as meeting places in Jerusalem; on the other hand, two centers are particularly singled out (esp. Acts 1:12–14; 12:10b–17)—the first place of assembly of the Jerusalem church in the upper room, and the other in the house of Mary, mother of John Mark. It is possible that these two house churches were the meeting places for the Hebrew- and the Greek-speaking congregations respectively. As a result of the rapid growth of the primitive church in Jerusalem, the number of house churches multiplied even in the earliest days (Acts 2:42–47; 5:42). Opposite these house churches we find the whole Jerusalem church, which met regularly in the temple. A plurality of house churches within the whole local church can already be observed in the primitive church in Jerusalem.

It is almost certain that a plurality of house churches existed in Rome, each with a different orientation (Rom 16). Because of the size of the city and the large number of groups there, it is highly unlikely that all Roman Christians met regularly at one place as the whole local church (Klauck, Lampe). Christians met in different private homes in Corinth as well. Paul, however, places a high value on a regular assembly of the whole local church there; accordingly we can assume that it happened. It can be asked whether the regular gathering of the whole church was to celebrate the Lord's Supper. It appears that the transition between house church and local church regarding the content of the worship service was fluid (Klauck). In any case, we can be certain that a plurality of house churches existed alongside the whole local church in Corinth. There are indications of a plurality of house churches as well in Antioch, Thessalonica, Ephesus, Philippi, and Laodicea.

The existence of a plurality of house churches led to the question how Paul theologically defined the relationship between the individual congregation and the local church and between the whole church at any one location and the whole worldwide church. How are the two series of ecclesiological assertions to be resolved in Paul's understanding of the church: the unity of the whole worldwide church, on the one hand, and, on the other, the position of the individual congregation? Does the unity of the whole church have priority over the individual congregation or vice versa? The decisive ecclesiological passages in the undisputed Pauline Letters speak for the priority of the individual congregation over the whole worldwide church.[14] In particular, the plurality of house churches within the whole local church as it can be demonstrated for the Pauline mission is an empirical expression of this priority. The emphasis that Paul himself placed on the dignity of the individual congregation documents it theologically as well (see pp. 164–65).[15]

An additional question emerged from our study, whether the structure of the ancient *oikos* had any influence on the organization of the house church and on the development of leadership structures. There are a number

---

[14] This is, however, not to be understood absolutely.
[15] As mentioned, Eph 4 and John 17 provide a balance.

of indications in the Jerusalem church that wealthy homeowners enjoyed special authority as the householders and hosts of the churches that met in their houses due to their social position in the group. After all, the community assembled in the social context of *their* houses with their own built-in authority patterns. We can assume that at least some of these hosts became leaders of these house churches. It is possible that in time some of those who formed the circle of seven around Stephen and later those who were designated elders were elected from this group of house church leaders and thus formed a kind of house church board or council. We do not, however, have certain evidence of this (see pp. 95–105). The book of Acts gives the impression that in the beginning the term "elder" was merely a designation of age or possibly an honorific title but in time indeed became a title of office (cf. esp. Acts 15:4, 6, 22, 41; 16:4; 21:18).

In the Pauline mission, then, it becomes very clear how household structures influenced the organization and leadership structures of house churches. It was most likely the Hellenists that brought the house church organizational forms (from Jerusalem) to Antioch, as we were able to determine an organizational transition from the primitive church in Jerusalem to the mission church in Antioch.[16] In both locations early Christians met in small house churches. This organizational structure was then transferred from Antioch to the worldwide Pauline center-oriented mission enterprise. As we saw, it was an integral part of Paul's missional approach to attempt to win one or more houses over to the Christian faith early in his mission at that location, and so the conversion of the head of the household was top priority (see pp. 185–87).[17] This was due in part to the significant role these householders played in Pauline missional outreach; among other things, they made worship services possible by providing the congregation with a place to assemble.

We discovered considerable evidence for concrete leadership structures in the Pauline house churches. Paul used a number of terms in his undisputed letters that indicate leading, teaching, administrative, and supportive functions of men and women (see pp. 196–210). Particularly in the absence of Paul and his full-time coworkers, the group that was most likely to assume responsibilities—such as providing a meeting place, leading the assembly and (communion) meals, church organization, representation of the church toward city officials and possibly other churches—was that of the householders. Because of their position in ancient society, it would have been natural for them to emerge into leadership and perhaps teaching roles in the church that met in their home. This is not to say, however, that the homeowners were the only ones who took on leadership responsibilities in

---

[16] Cf. Gehring, *Hausgemeinde*, 196–98 and 212–14.

[17] This approach (householder evangelism) is something we saw realized, at least in a preliminary form, even before Easter in the ministry of Jesus and his disciples (see pp. 53–60).

house churches. Surely there were other gifted members of the congregation who also assumed leading, teaching roles.

In the undisputed Pauline Letters, nothing is said about the official installation of church leaders through Paul or anyone else. This could be related to the fact that it did not appear necessary because leadership structures were already built in to the ancient household. Consequently, leaders emerged from below, out of the house church setting (see pp. 196–210). The acceptance and the recognition of these leaders both by the congregation itself and by Paul, however, were the preconditions for this type of house church leadership structure (Holmberg).

As we saw, ἐπίσκοποι are plainly documented as a designation of office for the Pauline mission churches (Phil 1:1 in the plural!). Given the plurality of house churches at any one location with householders as their hosts and leaders, it can be assumed that the overseers mentioned in Phil 1:1 were the leaders of house churches in the city of Philippi.[18] This view is later confirmed in the Pastoral Letters. The house church setting provides a plausible explanation for the presence of a plural number of ἐπίσκοποι at one location, a title that had become a formal designation for office by the time the Pastoral Letters were written.

In some respects the architectural and particularly the social image of the ancient *oikos* becomes the determining image for ecclesiology, church development, leadership structures, and the social relationships of Christians in community. The well-organized household became the model for a well-organized church. This is related in particular to the fact that many house churches were small, close-knit groups with a nuclear family as their core. Consequently, it was quite natural that household patterns impressed themselves upon the social reality of the congregation. The house churches of the Pastoral Letters understood themselves essentially as the "household or family of God," and it is therefore fully legitimate to speak here of an *oikos* ecclesiology. It seemed quite logical and natural that one single overseer should lead the house church, just as the household was led by one housefather, and this is indeed the conclusion to which the Pastoral Letters came. The metaphorical use of the expression "house of God" as the description of the church led to the notion of one single overseer as congregational leader (first as the leader of a house church, then as the leader of the whole church at that location [Dassmann]). Here it is evident that leadership structures and offices emerged from the household setting.

In the Pastoral Letters we see the extension of the office of overseer from the basis of existing episcopal-patriarchal structures to the level of the house churches, on the one hand, and from the basis of the existing presbyterial organization to the city level, on the other hand. At the very latest with the writing of the Pastoral Letters, the title "elder" is to be under-

---

[18] For a discussion, see pp. 205–10 and 268–81.

stood as the designation of a formal office. One important result of our study is the finding that the presbyterial structure with an office of elder, as it was in effect in the Pastoral Letters and possibly already in the primitive church in Jerusalem, could not have been a mere copy of Jewish tradition. If Harvey and Campbell have correctly understood the ancient and particularly the Jewish use of the title "elder" as an honorific, then no such office existed either in a communal or in a synagogal form. This would mean that the Christian contribution was much greater than is generally assumed in the development of the office of elder.

These organizational structures are also an indication that the church of the Pastoral Letters already shows signs of institutionalization. This is not necessarily negative (see below). Institutionalization is unavoidable for an organization that wants to continue existing and growing beyond its first generation (Roloff). It was precisely the formation of church leadership and organizational structures that led to the stabilization of the church. As these leadership structures emerged from the household setting, it can be said that the integration of the church into the *oikos* insured long-term stability and enabled the continued transmission of the gospel into the future. Thus house churches became tradition bearers of the Christian faith for generations to come. Hence they made possible the tradition, continuity, and duration of the church.

We also uncovered in the house church model, however, structural weaknesses that can lead to divisiveness, disunity, and the formation of splinter groups within the local church as a whole. As in the early days in the life of the Corinthian church, the existence of several house churches in one city became a problem indeed for the churches in the Pastoral Letters. Not only could an unhealthy dependence on a house church leader with a strong, charismatic personality develop (see pp. 291–95). In addition to this danger from within, house churches encountered one from without. An isolated house church, in particular one with weak leadership, was quite vulnerable to those attempting to lead members of the church astray spiritually and theologically (Titus 1:11). All of these dangers, which were inherent to the house church setting, demanded a consolidation of organizational and leadership structures at the level of the local church as a whole. Ideally, these dangers can be countered with a local and supralocal organizational infrastructure, including the formalization of offices for specific leadership functions. The Pastoral Letters testify most unambiguously to such a development.

The early Christian house churches also exhibited a number of weaknesses from an ecclesiological perspective. The main problem lies in the one-sidedness of an *oikos* ecclesiology, which could lead to narrow understanding and practice in the life, organization, and theology of the church. It can become particularly critical if ecclesiology and church order are developed exclusively from the Pastoral Letters without sufficient consideration given to other ecclesiological assertions in the NT, especially those found in the other Pauline Letters. The NT as a whole did not elect the *oikos* as its primary ecclesiological image, and thus it exercises a healthy caution toward these potentially negative tendencies. The *oikos* as a theological concept must be integrated into NT ecclesiology and at the same time confined by it.

Colossians and Ephesians clearly demonstrate that early Christianity firmly believed that God instituted marriage and family as a part of the creational order. This view can be traced all the way back to Jesus tradition. The basic structure of the family has proven itself as the incubator and nucleus of the mission church.[19] The important theological question is thereby raised whether marriage and family, as a part of God's instituted creational order, are necessary elements of church development (see below). Nevertheless, the church of Jesus Christ as a whole is not called οἶκος but rather ἐκκλησία, λαὸς θεοῦ, and/or σῶμα Χριστοῦ. The ἐκκλησία transcends the earthly, temporal institutions of marriage and family into the broad and eternal realm of salvation history. The hope of eschatological consummation exists for the church but not for the οἶκος.

The House Church Model for Today

It is not within the parameters of this NT study to extensively address the issue of the ecclesial and missional significance of the house church model for the present. This section therefore will not provide exhaustive coverage of the present-day house church situation. Neither is the question of the possibilities today for realizing the house church model in all different contexts the focus of our examination.[20] Instead only a few observations and suggestions will be made.[21]

First of all, one needs to distinguish geographically regarding the present-day significance of the house church. Today house churches can be found in nearly every country of the world, and their significance in the third

---

[19] For a short discussion of the significance of house churches throughout history, cf. Lorenzen, "Christliche Hauskirche," 341–434; more extensive, E. Wright, "Critical Examination," 77–143.

[20] Cf., e.g., Weber, "Hauskirche" (for a criticism, cf. Bieritz and Kähler, "Haus III," 14:487–88); C. Williams, *Kirche*, esp. 189–226; Clark, *Building*; Olsen, *Step*, 72–138; P. and P. Anderson, *House Church*, 131–73; A. Foster, *House Church*, 59–126; Frankemölle, *Kirche von unten*; Bäumler, *Kommunikative Gemeindepraxis*, 109–15; Seitz, *Erneuerung*; R. and J. Banks, *Home Church*, esp. 102–42; Möller, *Konzepte*; Birkey, *House Church*, 87–156, and "House Church"; Herbst, *Missionarischer Gemeindeaufbau*, esp. 406–9; F. and C. Schwarz, *Theologie*, 117–48; Strunk, *Schritte*, esp. 164–78; E. Wright, "Critical Examination"; Rebell, *Zum neuen Leben*; Blohm, "Dritte Weise"; Eickhoff, *Gemeinde*, esp. 189–206; Gorman, *Community*; Arn and Schwarz, *Gemeindeaufbau*; Pompe, *Der erste Atem*.

[21] On these questions, cf. Bieritz, "Rückkehr?"; Lorenzen, "Christliche Hauskirche," with additional literature.

world, in the former communist Eastern block, in the Western world,[22] and from one Western country to another will most likely vary.[23] The question of the persecution and oppression of Christians needs to be considered in our attempt to determine the present importance of the house church model, as recent examples from Russia, Egypt, and China demonstrate. Moreover, the time span separating the NT from our present situation must be kept in mind, and here again we need to distinguish geographically: the ancient *oikos* as extended family including slaves, hired laborers, and clients, with its fundamental significance for society and economy, does not exist as such anymore, at least not in the Western world. Our term for family is no longer synonymous with that of the ancient household. We cannot and do not want to call back to life the ancient *oikos* as the setting for present-day church ministry, thereby giving absolute power to the householder over all the other members of the household. We certainly do not want to reinstate slavery, albeit an integral element of Roman society, nor the norms of that time for the appropriate public behavior of women.

By no means, however, do the findings of our study confirm that the NT house churches have no ecclesiological or missional significance at all for today on the assumption that the distance between life and thought in early Christian congregations and our situation is simply too great not only because of the progression of time but also because of a massive change in our emotional and intellectual consciousness. Granted, the church of Jesus Christ does not dare to stagnate or, worse, regress by attempting to merely imitate first-century conditions.[24] The church has the responsibility to continue to move forward according to, and in the freedom of, the gospel of Jesus Christ. It is its duty to discern and articulate how believers can live up to the gift and responsibility of the gospel in our present situation.[25] The gospel of the crucified and resurrected Christ never becomes old fashioned or out-of-date but rather remains ever a source of guidance for the future. "As God's call, which is intended both to be comforting and to lead to repentance, the gospel makes faith in Jesus Christ possible and at the same time establishes certain parameters for church life and thought."[26]

---

[22] Compare the ecclesial situation in the United States, which is totally dominated by "free" churches, with that in Germany, which is controlled predominantly by state churches.

[23] Cf. the short descriptions in Lorenzen, "Christliche Hauskirche," 333–52, here 344; Cowan and Lee, *Dangerous Memories*, 33–60; Birkey, "House Church," 75–77.

[24] Gnilka, *Philemonbrief*, 32, correctly warns against a literal, automatic, and monolinear transfer of the NT questions and answers into those of the present. We cannot simply return to the situation of the early Christian house churches. Cf. Klauck, *Hausgemeinde*, 12.

[25] Stuhlmacher, "Volkskirche," 151–70, here 163.

[26] Ibid., 163.

In light of the minority situation in which Christianity once again finds itself (in the first world as well), it can be said that "the church today has entered into a situation that, of course, is no longer chronologically identical with life in the primitive church in Jerusalem and the house churches of Corinth or Rome but nevertheless and by all means is structurally identical."[27] The main problem facing Christian communities that decide to get serious about becoming an "inviting congregation"[28] "is not whether our doctrinal confessions, baptism, communion, and life in Christian community in the spirit of God's love are sufficient today as they were back then [of course they are] but rather how believers, as members of the body of Christ held together by the love of Christ, can best fulfill their commission to praise God and to credibly make Christ alive in our world."[29] Whether this can *only* be realized today in the context of a house church (or in a home group) is not the point. At the same time, however, it would not be wise to rule out a priori a possible significance of the house church model for the present with the argument "But that was such a long time ago; things are so different now."

What are the objections to the ecclesial and missional significance of the house church model for today? It appears that most of the weaknesses of this model apply worldwide, whether the third world, the West, or any other area of the world is in focus. First, the quantitative limitation needs to be mentioned. As in the NT period, so today the size of the living room in a private home sets a limit to the potential growth of a house church. We also dare not underestimate the psychological value of larger meetings. The worship service in a large setting (or any kind of big meeting) generates a dynamic that stimulates church growth. In addition, there is the danger today as well that the house church could become an incubator for conflict. Closely related to this is the potential for division. The tendency of the house church toward divisiveness within the local church remains a problem that can hinder the outward representation of church unity in Christ and consequently cause the missional testimony of those who are supposed to be "reconciled in Christ" to appear inconsistent. The danger of one-sidedness also needs to be mentioned, which can occur when an unhealthy dependence on the leading personality emerges, particularly if one forces his or her own (narrow/extreme) theological and spiritual convictions upon the group meeting in one's house. Furthermore, just as there is the tendency for established churches to allow ecclesiology to suppress Christology, in a house church the temptation is to attribute a higher value to the personal fellowship with each other than to the relationship of each individual to Jesus Christ. Connected with this is the additional danger of the formation of an elitist attitude.[30] Particularly in an

---

[27] Ibid., 164; so also Lohfink and Pesch, *Tiefenpsychologie*, 109–12.
[28] Sorg (a former bishop of the Protestant state church in Germany), "Einladende Kirche."
[29] Stuhlmacher, "Volkskirche," 164–65.
[30] Popkes, "Gemeinschaft," who demonstrates that this is a potential danger for every fellowship group or close-knit community.

isolated house church, a self-contented exclusive attitude can develop that is indifferent to the needs of the church as a whole and the world and therefore uninterested in any kind of service outside the group. Today there are plenty of examples in the Christian church of small groups, be it a house church or a home Bible study group, that gather together only those who already like one another and are all of the same opinion.

All of these objections point to weaknesses of the house church model that need to be taken seriously, but none of them represents an insurmountable problem. What are the strengths of the house church model, giving due consideration to the above-mentioned weaknesses and the geographical differences? We will begin with the worldwide perspective, which will lead us to the possible significance of the house church for the Western world. As mentioned, Christians have gathered for fellowship and worship in private homes and apartments, particularly in places where they have been and are being persecuted for social, family, religious, and ethnic reasons. In such situations of persecution, house churches provide even today a less public and therefore less dangerous venue for Christian fellowship, Bible study, prayer, and communion (cf., e.g., China).

In the third world and in some industrialized countries, the house church model offers a financially attractive alternative to large church facilities. More often than not the private houses of individual members of the congregation represent an effective, low-cost missional-strategic solution. They are highly flexible and can be used as meeting places for worship and instruction as well as for missional proclamation, for evangelistic discussion groups, and for individual counseling—all in the personal context of the family (this of course is the ideal). Worship and fellowship are thus solidly anchored in the everyday life of the congregation. Because Christian church members meet where they and others also live out their daily lives, entering the church does not involve entering (what is perhaps perceived to be) uniquely sacred space. As a result of the absence of this physical hurdle, an outsider is not as likely to be so hesitant in attending the worship service.[31] In light of the well-known missiological problem that mainline churches are, as a rule, no longer reaching the unchurched, it is precisely here that house churches have great potential.[32]

---

[31] Granted, there are personal and emotional hurdles as well, but these can be overcome through friendly reception into the house church.

[32] See pp. 308–11 for the reference to the concept of "church planting" as it is being practiced in Great Britain. The problem in mainline churches is not only true of most of Europe but also of the United States today. Leonard Sweet shared these statistics at a seminar ("Leadership and the Church in Contemporary Culture," George Fox Evangelical Seminary, Portland, Oreg., May 16, 2002): 75 percent of the churches in the United States today are declining, 24 percent are growing, but only because of "transfer" Christians from other congregations; only 1 percent of the churches are growing as a result of reaching unchurched non-Christians.

For those who give the sermons and lead the evangelistic groups, the house church provides a chance to develop individual leadership abilities that in turn are necessary for missional outreach and building up the church. Thus the house church contributes to the development of leaders for church and missional ministry in a low-risk setting. In addition, the house church model also provides something of universal cultural relevance: the freedom for cultural diversity, founded on the family as a God-created unit of community. Even though the extended family presently exists only in a few regions of the world, to this day the immediate family still represents a universal phenomenon. Today the same as ever, Christian brotherly love offers the possibility of social integration inwardly and a missional impact outwardly. Ideally, social differences will be overcome in house churches today as well, which in turn can be attractive outwardly. The practice of Christian hospitality with an evangelistic orientation is also easier in a house church than in a large church facility. The integration into the family-like community of a house church can fulfill the universal need of all humankind to be at home, to belong, to be in a family with a sense of safety and security.[33] In some cultures the enabling of corporate solidarity during and after conversion is of great missional significance.[34] Seen in this light, the house church represents a very flexible model architecturally, financially, and socially, which could be very useful across both geographical and cultural boundaries.

The house church model can also make a significant contribution in the industrialized countries of the West. The house church is small and personal, providing a setting in which accountability to each other can develop. The house church thus has the potential of overcoming the anonymity of a larger church. Particularly in Western society, where the living and working climates are often quite impersonal, house churches provide "the opportunity for intimate and accountable fellowship, in which personal encounters, human warmth, and trusting, long-lasting relationships can be experienced."[3] This will become even more important "in the upcoming age of mass media, which will radically isolate people from one another."[36] The house church

---

[33] Even apart from the house church model, one needs to ask here whether the image of the *familia Dei* needs to be emphasized more strongly in the ecclesiology and the worship service practice of mainline churches in Europe and the United States. As we have seen, the family of God is certainly not the only ecclesiological image used in the New Testament, but it is a very important one. Cf. Sorg, "Zwischen Säkularität und Religiosität," esp. 70; following him, Stuhlmacher, "Volkskirche," 155. The question remains, however, whether the church will succeed in becoming more family-like without any kind of small-group structure. Actually, ever since Constantine and the introduction of larger sacred buildings used only for religious purposes, the church has had difficulty adequately integrating the biblically based family elements of the *ecclesia* into the overall understanding and life of the church.

[34] Cf. the results of the recent study by Sandnes, *New Family*.

[35] Lorenzen, "Christliche Hauskirche," 349.

[36] Stuhlmacher, "Kirche," 312; so also Seitz, "Distanz und Liebe"; cf. also Sweet, *FaithQuakes*, 21–39.

can also serve as an effective agent against the tendency to separate doctrine from everyday life, a contribution that should not be underestimated. House church leaders know the individuals in their congregation and are therefore more able to prepare their sermons and Bible studies to meet the real and felt needs of the members of their group. Because the group is small, it is easier to keep abreast of where people are personally, vocationally, and spiritually. Hence it is possible for the house church leader, on the basis of such feedback, to discern more accurately what was understood and whether it has been put into practice. A person who belongs to a small group cannot distance himself or herself from the group for there exists a healthy accountability one to another that usually leads to more authenticity. The life of a house church is the actual life of its members.[37]

Obviously, there are many questions and issues to consider for which good, well-reflected solutions need to be found, for example, the question of the relationship between the house church and the local church. Just as important is the issue of the relationship of the house church to the concept of office as understood (differently) by major denominations. As we have seen, even as early as in NT times an organizational structure with clearly defined leadership including offices was introduced. As a result, the church was able to counteract the potential divisiveness of house churches and their tendency to develop into splinter groups. Today as well, house church models that are the most vital on a long-term basis and thus the most convincing are the ones that are well integrated into such suprastructures,[38] that is, under the authority and safeguard of a local church or major denomination.[39] The organization of the house church at the level of the individual and the local church will vary depending on the cultural, political, and denominational setting. It also must be asked whether each house church should be led by an ordained office holder or whether here the leadership can be assumed by laypeople, and then the question of the theological and practical training of such persons becomes acute. The question of leadership structures is also connected with that of the administration of the sacraments, which, depending on the model, does not necessarily have to be assumed by the leadership of the house church alone.[40] In this case, however, the question is whether such a group would then be considered a house church in the full sense. Therefore one could ask whether the concept of the home group could be understood as a modified form and partial application of the house church model. The

---

[37] Cf. Lorenzen, "Christliche Hauskirche," 350.

[38] Cf., e.g., the "integrierte Gemeinde" in Munich. For a short portrayal of these groups, cf. Hampe, "Integrierte Gemeinde," esp. 105–6, for their integration in the organizational structures of the Catholic church.

[39] Cf. the report by H. Schulz, "Territoriale Gemeinde." The advantages of integrating the house church or small group into a larger organized "community" or local church are well developed by Clark, *Haus*, 43–78.

[40] For alternative solutions, see the literature suggestions in n. 20.

advantages of the home group model have been tested in the church growth movement in many Western countries with very good results both in qualitative and in quantitative terms.[41]

To illustrate the significance of the house church model for today, here are presented two representative examples. In China the house church became a tradition bearer for the Christian faith early in the pioneer mission, but particularly in times of persecution, especially after 1949 and during the cultural revolution (1966–1976).[42] Although most missionaries were forced to leave China after the communist party seized power under the leadership of Mao Tse Tung and they were thus compelled to abandon the Chinese Christians, the Protestant congregations thereafter experienced the greatest growth in their history.[43] The Protestant Christians in China tried to make the best of their situation. They organized themselves throughout the country as a legally recognized association under the name Three-Self Movement and continued to meet in urban and rural areas in private homes.[44] In the traumatic years from 1966 to 1976, Christian assembly was forbidden, and all church buildings were closed or transformed into factories, storage halls, or schools.[45] Chinese Christians were able to meet only in houses if at all.[46]

---

[41] Cf., e.g., Schweitzer, *Hauskreis offensiv;* Herbst, *Missionarischer Gemeindeaufbau,* 406–9; Eickhoff, *Gemeinde,* 189; Neighbour and Jenkins, *Where Do We Go?* and also further literature in n. 20. In the United States the expression "Growing larger by focusing smaller" has been coined. "Qualitative" refers here to the spiritual growth of the individual, and "quantitative" to the numerical growth of the congregation as a whole.

[42] Cf., e.g., the overviews and reports in Ting, *Chinese Christians;* Wang, "House Church"; Towery, *Christen.* Towery was a longtime missionary in Taiwan and Hong Kong, knows the Chinese language and way of life, and has traveled extensively throughout China.

[43] Cf. G. Brown, *Christianity,* 79–99, for a presentation of the events during the 1950s that led to the expulsion of the missionaries from China. Estimations of growth vary depending on the source. Cf. Wang, "House Church," 178–80, for a balanced discussion. In 1949 the number of Protestant Christians in China was estimated at anywhere from 700,000 to 1,000,000, scattered in 70,000 congregations of different denominations, for the most part in house churches with an average size of 10 members. Today the official count is ca. 13,000,000 Protestant Christians. But most Protestants meet unofficially; estimates range all the way up to 60,000,000 (cf. *idea Spektrum,* "Liebe Leser" and "Nachrichten").

[44] The congregational assembly in a house was already a traditional form of the worship service in China even before the communist takeover. (cf. Peifen, "Church Life," 104; E. Wright, "Critical Examination," 130–31).

[45] Among the 65,000,000 victims of the Mao period were large numbers of Christians (cf., regarding the figure 65,000,000, the most recent study, Courtois, *Schwarzbuch,* reviewed in Altwegg, "Hundert Millionen Tote"). Pastors, Christian teachers, and others were transported to concentration camps, tortured, and in many cases killed (cf. Lawrence, *Church,* 109–28; E. Wright, "Critical Examination," 128).

[46] Cf. Towery, *Christen,* 64.

Bishop K. H. Ting describes his experience during this period: "Our seminary became the headquarters of the Red Guard in Nanjing. We were not able to continue in the usual manner. We started meeting for tea in order to pray and read the Bible with one another. We noticed that the kind of meeting was quite satisfying. In such groups everyone served everyone else. As bishop I felt somewhat uncomfortable in such groups, but I learned to allow others to serve me. Small house meetings have become an important characteristic of Chinese Christianity."[47] Back then the Chinese Christians learned in a concrete and practical sense what it really means that all baptized are one in Christ Jesus. "The educated and the farmer sat side by side and learned from one another."[48] Overcoming social differences is apparently characteristic of house churches in China even to this day.

Even after the restoration of the church in China, many Protestant Christians still meet in house churches.[49] Two main forms of worship service exist: in the large facilities of a local church and in private houses.[50] Assembly in house churches is common particularly in suburban and rural areas. An observation important for our study is that house churches and local churches very often cooperate quite well with one another.[51] The main worship service takes place on Sunday in a large church building often with as many as one thousand to five thousand seats. In larger cities there are usually two or three such churches, and in some even more (e.g., in Shanghai, twenty-three; in Peking, twenty). Virtually all of the baptisms take place during the main worship services. Communion is celebrated once a month as a part of the main service and weekly in some house churches. Other than this the major part of church life takes place, today the same as ever, in house churches, for example, Bible study groups, prayer, sharing, fellowship, and evangelism. Most of the unchurched are introduced to Christ in the natural context of personal relationships initially developed in the house church setting. On Easter of 1981, for instance, forty-eight individuals were baptized during the main worship service of the local church in Nanjing; most of them came to faith in Christ in house churches.[52] Missionaries are sent out by the Three-Self Movement into areas where as yet no house churches exist. These

---

[47] Quoted ibid.

[48] Ibid.

[49] This has been explained in different ways. It is reported that even to this day local communist functionaries persecute Christians and arrest their leaders. On March 16, 1997, e.g., eight house church leaders were arrested in Zhengzhou in the province of Henan (cf. *idea Spektrum*, "Nachrichten"). But the situation is different from region to region. In some areas Christian ministry is possible without risk of persecution; in others it is not. In some cases, Christians in China have continued to meet in homes because the house church offers certain advantages that worship in large meetings does not.

[50] Regarding the following, cf. Peifen, "Church Life," 104–5; Towery, *Christen*, 64–66, 140–66; E. Wright, "Critical Examination," 130–32.

[51] Cf. Towery, *Christen*, 66.

[52] Cf. Peifen, "Church Life," 105–6; Towery, *Christen*, 70.

evangelists find living quarters in the area and stay for three to six months with the objective of starting a house church there. It is primarily in this manner that Christianity has been spread throughout China.[53]

Chinese Christians themselves recognize the advantages of the house church model from many years of experience. They make these points: House churches are small and therefore more manageable in terms of the pastoral care needed in the group. They allow for the relatively rapid development of intimate personal relationships and provide a meeting place for prayer. They make it easier to share life experiences, to care for and to serve one another. The leaders of such house churches know their people personally and can better prepare their sermons and Bible studies to meet the needs of the members of their group.[54] Wherever Christians are still being oppressed, persecuted, and arrested, house churches provide an existential advantage: a place of assembly that is relatively safe.

The second example is taken from a Western country. In Great Britain a house church movement has existed since the 1970s. The movement is, however, theologically and organizationally quite fluid and, as a coalition of congregations from varying backgrounds, extremely stratified and therefore very difficult to describe in a few short sentences.[55] This discussion is therefore limited to a single phenomenon in the British scene—church planting—as practiced for over twenty-five years in the Anglican state church.[56] The objective of the church-planting model is to maintain church unity locally and within the state church but at the same time to enable a flexible response to the challenges posed to the church by a society that is progressively becoming more differentiated.[57] In particular, an attempt is made to address the missiological problem that mainline churches are no longer reaching unchurched individuals and groups and to consider the potential of house churches and home groups in this context.

Characteristic of a church planting are the following elements: It grows out of an intentional evangelistic thrust. With the consent of the local church leadership, the congregation commissions a team of Christians (usually lay leaders and workers) to plant a sister congregation or perhaps to

---

[53] Stefan Müller, interview by author in Tübingen, Germany, February 1994. Müller is a German evangelist who has spent many years in China as well as in Mongolia and is intimately familiar with the situation there. For documentation of this approach for earlier periods, cf. E. Wright, "Critical Examination," 130–31; G. Brown, *Christianity*, 22–44.

[54] Cf. Peifen, "Church Life," 105–6.

[55] For an overview, cf. Hollenweger, "House Church"; N. Wright, "Restoration," who points out that the designation "house church movement" no longer applies. Most of these groups "have erected some of the most sophisticated buildings that can be found today" (p. 4). For extensive coverage, cf. Walker, *Restoring*.

[56] Cf. the collection of statistics by G. Lings in Carey, *Planting*, 161–78.

[57] Cf. the attempt at a definition of church planting by Carey, ibid., 11–17; Harris et al., *Breaking*, 5–8.

renew a neighboring church that is in danger of closing down. From the very beginning, pastoral-leadership structures are established for the project by the sending congregation and the team being sent. The objective can be sociologically or geographically defined—for example, to serve an identifiable group (young adults, families, the socially challenged, a minority group) or to reach a neighborhood with the gospel of Jesus Christ. Instead of erecting a church building, a private home is used, or a school, a community center, or a room in a restaurant is rented as space for assembly. Working together with church members who live in the area, the team starts to develop small groups and home Bible studies, to plan a social project together with the residents of the area, and to celebrate regular worship services that are especially tailored for the target group.

Although church planting needs to be distinguished from the house church movement in Great Britain and does not represent a purely house church approach, it is still of considerable interest for our study. Particularly in the initial phase, private homes and then, in the following phases, Christian families play a very important role in the development of the church-planting project as an integral part of the core group.[58] Many examples since 1985 demonstrate that church planting represents a very effective model for reaching the unchurched with the gospel.[59] This approach enjoys the full support of the leadership of the Anglican Church.[60] This model has also attracted attention in Germany.[61]

Past and present speak a clear message: By no means should the house church model be overlooked today as a viable option for church growth; it is a tried and tested approach. The worldwide ecclesial and missional contribution of a small group, be it a house church in the full sense or a home group for Bible study, fellowship, prayer, and/or social involvement, training for lay leaders, or evangelistic discussion, cannot be valued too highly.

For all these models the well-functioning, intact Christian family is of decisive significance for its contribution to the successful building of the church. Today it is evident that the family is still the natural cell for the establishment of missional house churches, just as it was in the past. As this study has demonstrated, the metaphorical language of family in the NT was

---

[58] Cf. Harris et al., *Breaking*, 15–21; Carey, *Planting*, 101–10, esp. 105–6; 139–46, esp. 140.

[59] This is also the expressed goal (cf. Carey, *Planting*, 14, 24–25). Cf. also the report in Harris et al., *Breaking*, 15–33, esp. 21–22; Carey, *Planting*, 37–157; Warren, *Building* (Warren is the Church of England's national officer for evangelism).

[60] All of the bishops support it, including the then archbishop of Canterbury, George Carey: "Church planting, along with other initiatives, has great potential as an exciting and positive resource for the church, and the fulfiling of that potential is my hope and my prayer" (keynote speech at the fourth national day conference on church planting in the Church of England, Holy Trinity Brompton, London, May 22, 1991, in Carey, *Planting*, 21–32, here 32).

[61] Cf. the report by Schlaudraff, "Gemeinde."

directly related to the real life of the church, which was fundamentally dependent on the family as a developmental resource, for material and financial support, and for living and meeting space. This study also revealed that the central significance of the family in the NT is directly associated with early Christianity's firm belief that marriage and family are an integral part of God's created order. Thus, for reasons of mission theology as well, we as Christians are obligated to view critically any and all attempts to minimize or undermine the central importance of marriage and family as a fundamental form of Christian life.

As early as 1526 Martin Luther stressed the importance of the house church in his paper *Deutsche Messe und Ordnung des Gottesdiensts* on the "third kind" of worship service for those "who seriously want to be Christians and to proclaim the gospel with their actions and their words."[62] These "would need to enter their name (in a list) and gather together (in a home) in a small group for prayer, to read (the Scripture), for baptism, to receive the sacraments, and to do other Christian services." But he regretted very much that he "did not yet have individuals who were doing this and did not see many who felt compelled to do so in the future."[63]

In recent times more and more theologians and church leaders are pointing to the significance of small groups for mission and church development.[64] Professor Dr. M. Seitz from the University of Erlangen believes that the church in Germany is on its way to becoming a minority group and that small groups will gain more and more significance for Christian ministry and church development.[65] The former bishop of Württemberg, Theo Sorg, feels similarly. According to him, the church of the future can no longer afford to be a large administrative institution primarily providing social services and performing baptisms, weddings, and funerals. "We need to become a church of small house churches, of involved, committed groups, a church with attractive worship services and missional events and activities, a church in which spiritually sensitive individuals make themselves available to others, a church in which opportunities for connecting, personal conversations, and dialogue are being offered, a church in which the gospel of Jesus Christ can manifest its invitational character."[66]

Leonard Sweet, a Christian historian and futurist, points out that the house church model has already taken on additional significance in the United States today because of the seismic postmodern shift that has affected

---

[62] Aland, *Kirche*, 89–90.
[63] Ibid.
[64] Cf., in addition to the authors listed below, e.g., Klauck, *Hausgemeinde*, 99–102; Clark, *Building*, esp. 60–66; Lampe, "Zur gesellschaftlichen und kirchlichen Funktion"; partially critical, Bieritz and Kähler, "Haus III," 14: 487–89; Eickhoff, *Gemeinde*, 189–206; Rordorf, "Hausgemeinde," 76–85.
[65] Seitz, "Distanz und Liebe." Cf. also Seitz, *Erneuerung*, 20–21, 66–67, 77, 169; Stuhlmacher, "Kirche," 312, and "Volkskirche," 166.
[66] Sorg, "Einladende Kirche," 13; cf. also Sorg, "Perspektiven," esp. 10.

our culture in the last twenty-five years. According to Sweet, "the best way into the postmodern home is through the family."[67] He states that three of the most significant developments in education, medicine, and religion during this period were "mushrooming movements toward home schools, home births, and *home churches*." This is due to "the cultural phenomenon of *cocooning*, a postmodern desire to seek refuge in the inner circle of the home for relief from the harsh, nightmarish outside world."[68] C. F. George, a nationally recognized church consultant, confirms the view taken by Seitz, Sorg, and Sweet.[69] George introduces the concept of the so-called metachurch, which is essentially a congregation not merely *with* but *of* small groups. He says that if a congregation wants to be ready to reach new, unchurched populations and effectively minister to believers in the twenty-first century, it needs to be large enough to celebrate and yet small enough to care. Sweet and George are only two examples of the many church leaders and scholars in the United States today who have recognized the importance of the house church, that is, small groups, from an empirical perspective. In light of the results of our study of the past and present significance of early Christian house churches, their views appear to have a rock-solid foundation.

---

[67] Sweet, *FaithQuakes*, 29.
[68] Ibid., 21 (italics added).
[69] George, *Prepare*.

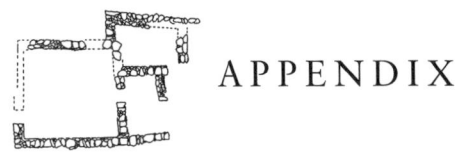 APPENDIX

Floor Plans and Reconstructions

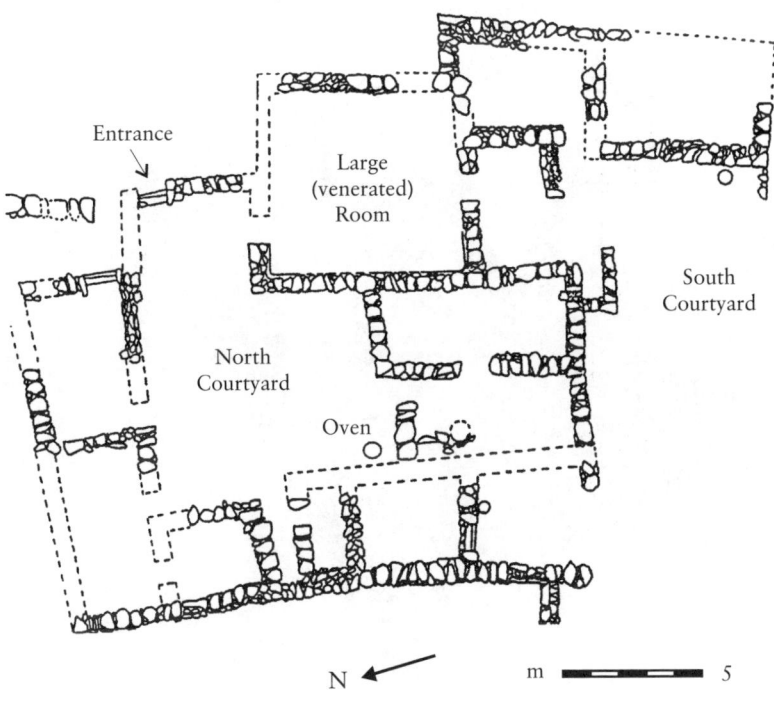

Fig. 1. Floor Plan of St. Peter's House in Capernaum (1st cent. C.E.)
Based on V. Corbo, *Gli edifici della città,* fig. 9

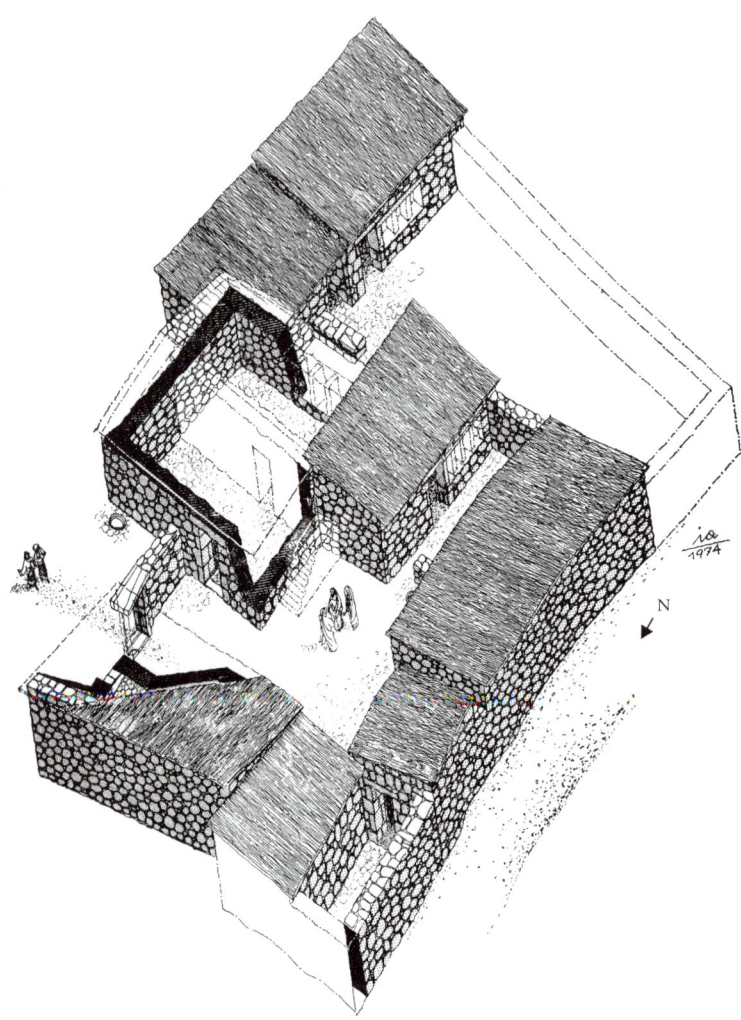

Fig. 2. Isometric Reconstruction of St. Peter's House in Capernaum (1st cent. C.E.)
Based on V. Corbo, *Gli edifici della città*, fig. 10

Appendix / Floor Plans and Reconstructions • 315

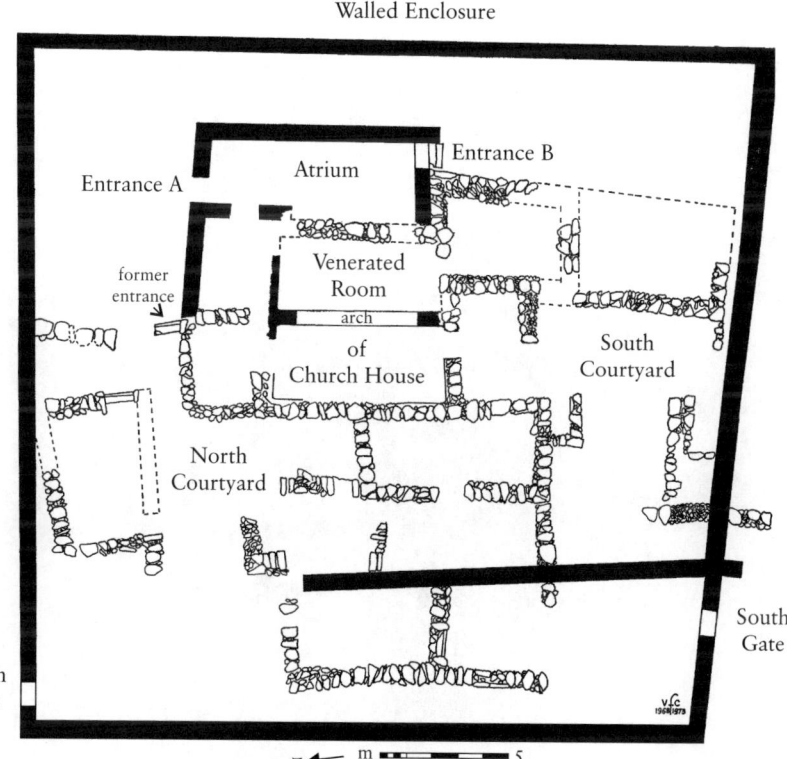

Fig. 3. Floor Plan of the Church House (Domus Ecclesiae) in Capernaum
Based on V. Corbo, *Gli edifici della città,* fig. 7

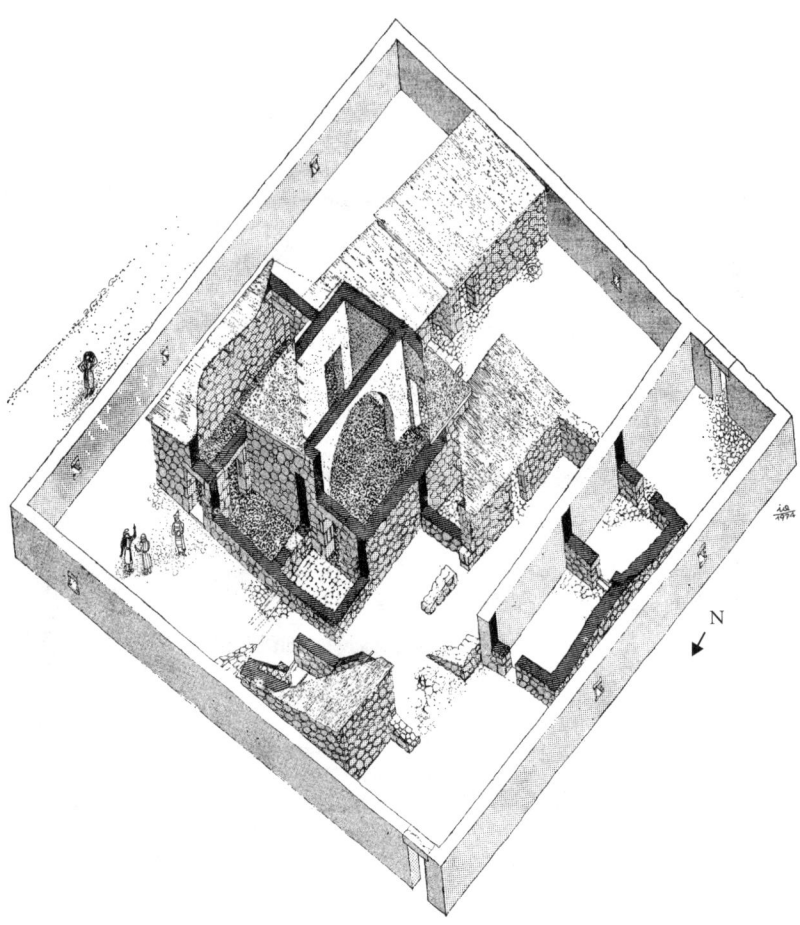

Fig. 4. Isometric Reconstruction of the Church House in Capernaum (4th cent. C.E.) Based on V. Corbo, *Gli edifici della città*, fig. 8

Appendix / Floor Plans and Reconstructions • 317

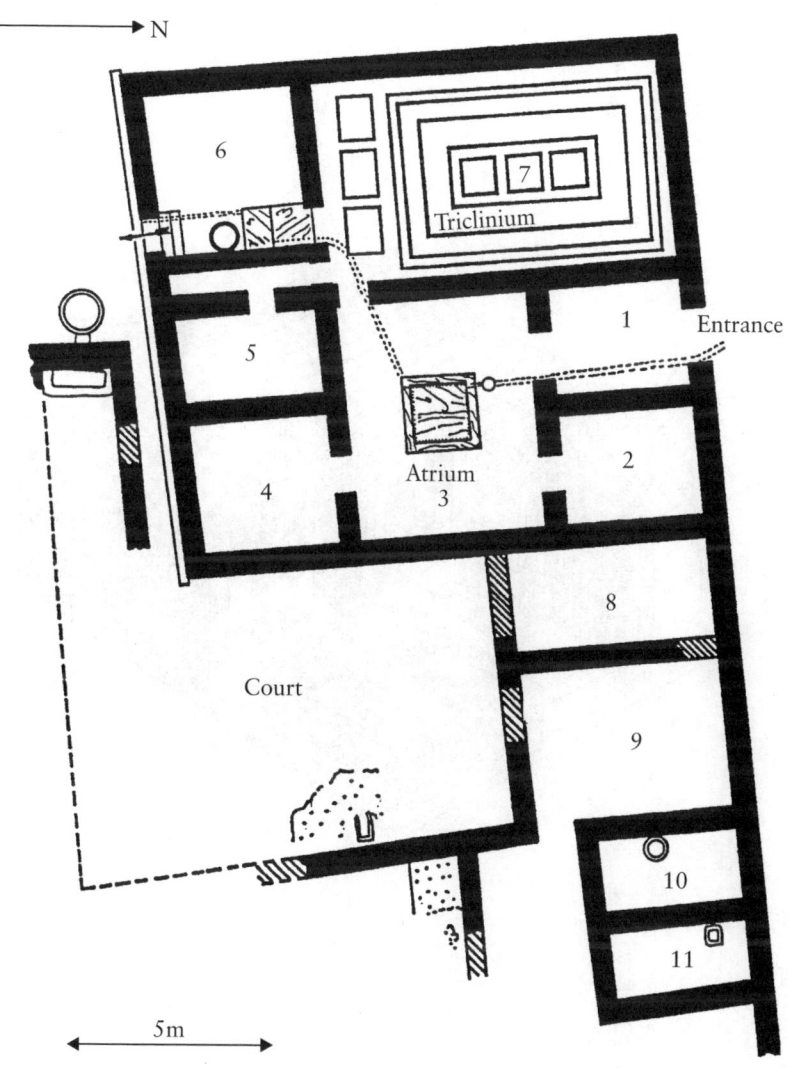

Fig. 5. Floor Plan of the Roman Villa at Anaploga
Based on J. Murphy-O'Connor, *St. Paul's Corinth,* fig. 6

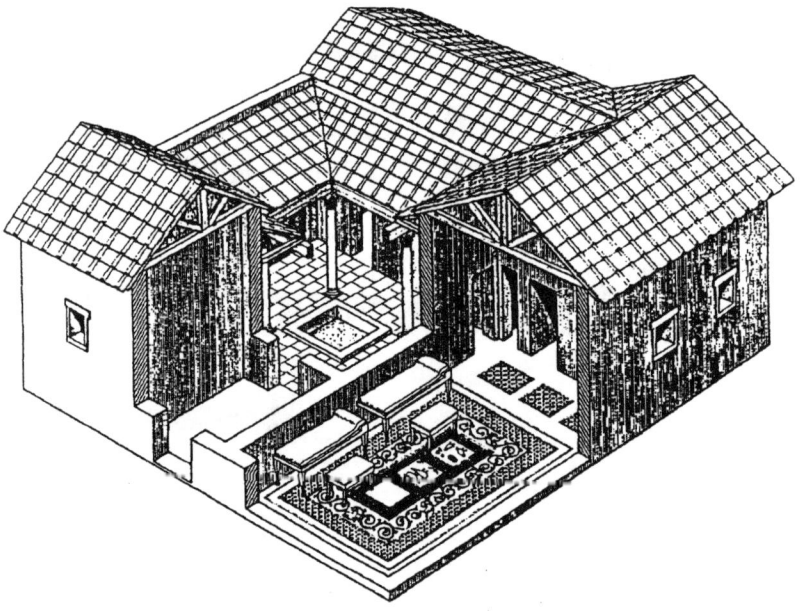

Fig. 6. Reconstruction of the Roman Villa at Anaploga
Based on the drawing by L. Ritmeyer, Ritmeyer Archaeological Design, Jerusalem

Appendix / Floor Plans and Reconstructions • 319

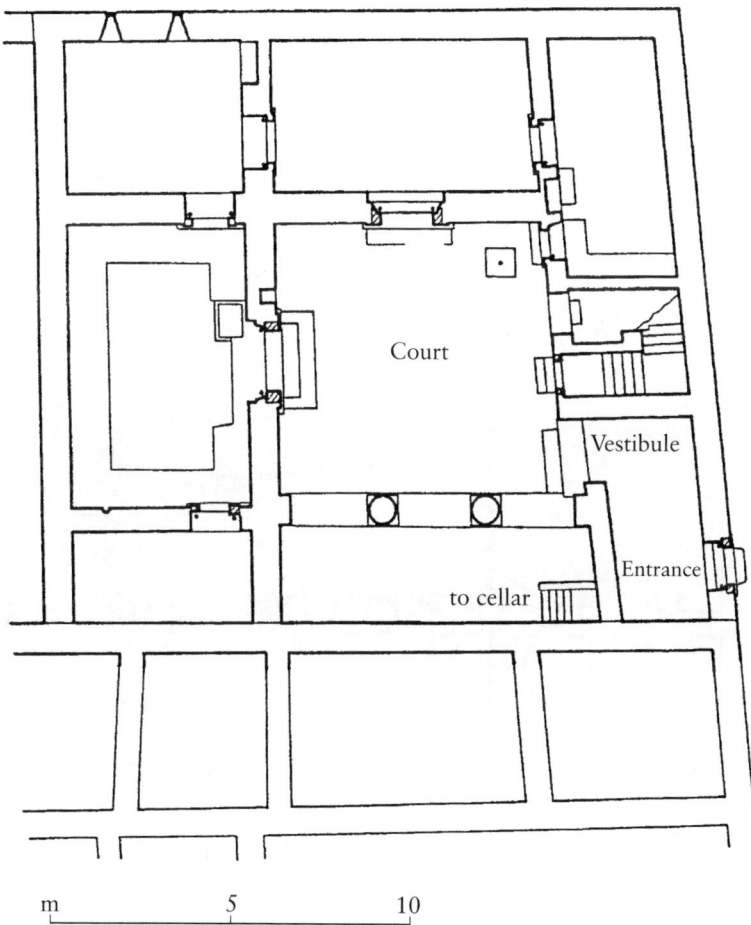

Fig. 7. Reconstruction of the House Plan (Dura) before Adaptation
Based on C. H. Kraeling, *The Christian Building*, pl. 4

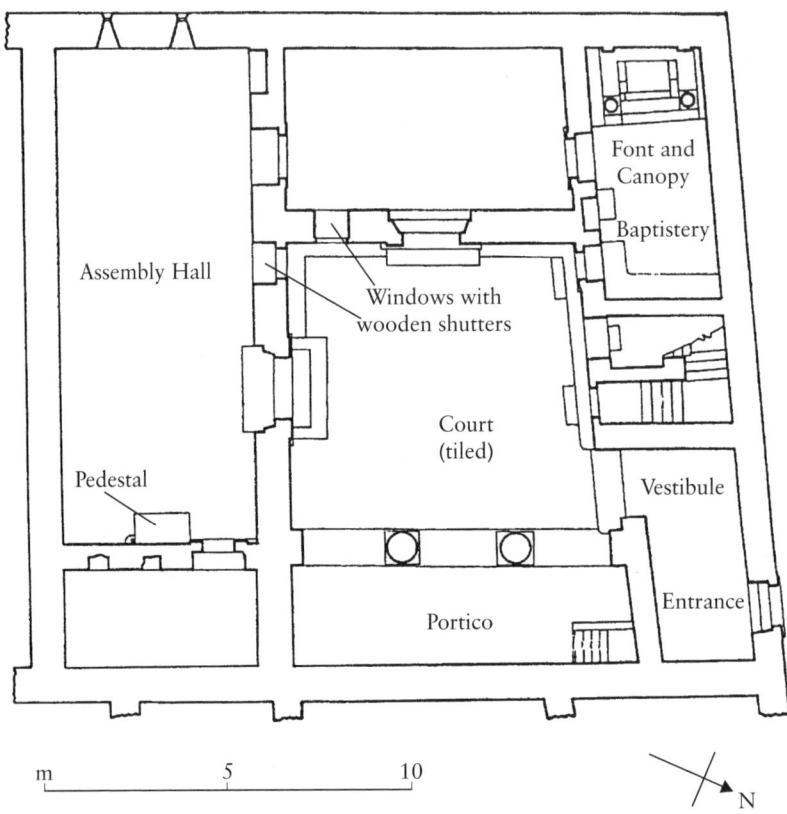

Fig. 8. Reconstruction of the Church House in Dura
Based on C. H. Kraeling, *The Christian Building*, pl. 5

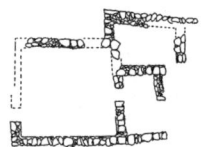

Bibliography

PRIMARY SOURCES

Old Testament and Jewish-Hellenistic Literature

Der babylonische Talmud. Translated by L. Goldschmidt. 12 vols. Berlin: Judischer, 1929–1936.
Biblia Hebraica Stuttgartensia. Edited by K. Elliger and W. Rudolph. Stuttgart: Deutche Bibelgesellschaft, 1987.
The Book of Enoch. Edited by R. H. Charles. 2d ed. Oxford: Clarendon, 1912. (Ethiopic Apocalypse.)
Die Esra-Apocalypse (IV. Esra). Edited by B. Violet. 2 vols. GCS 18, 32. Leipzig: J. C. Hinrichs, 1910–1924.
Josephus. Translated by H. S. J. Thackeray et al. 10 vols. LCL. Cambridge: Harvard University Press, 1926–1965.
Josephus. *De bello judaico.* Edited and translated by O. Michel and O. Bauernfeind. 3 vols. in 4. Darmstadt: Wissenschaftliche Buchgesellschaft, 1959–1963.
———. *Opera.* Edited by B. Niese. 10 vols. 2d ed. Berlin: Apud Weidmannos, 1955.
Josephus. *The Works of Flavius Josephus.* Edited and translated by W. Whiston. 4 vols. 9th ed. Grand Rapids: Baker Book House, 1982.
Midrash Rabbah. 2d ed. Translated by H. Freedman and M. Simon. 13 vols. in 10. London: Soncino, 1951.
Die Mischna: Text, Übersetzung, und ausführliche Erklärung. 6 vols. Edited by G. Beer and O. Holtzann. Berlin: de Gruyter, 1912–.
The Palestinian Talmud. Translated by J. Neusner. Chicago: University of Chicago, 1984.
Philo of Alexandria. Translated by F. H. Colson and G. H. Whitaker. 10 vols. and 2 supplemental vols. LCL. Cambridge: Harvard University Press, 1929–1962.
Philo of Alexandria. *Opera Quae Supersunt.* Edited by L. Cohn and P. Wendland. 7 vols. Berlin: de Gruyter, 1896–1930.
———. *Die Werke Philos von Alexandria in deutscher Übersetzung.* Edited by L. Cohn et al. 7 vols. Breslau: M. & H. Marcus, 1909–1962.
Die Psalmem Salomos. Edited by S. Holm-Nielsen. 2d ed. JSHRZ 4/2. Gütersloh: Gerd Mohr, 1977.
Pseudo-Phocylides. *Über das Phokylideische Gedicht.* Edited by J. Bernays. Berlin: Hertz, 1856.

Septuaginta. Edited by A. Ralfs. Abridged ed. in 1 vol. Stuttgart: Dt. Bibelges., 1979.
Talmud Babli. 12 vols. Wilna: n.p., 1895–1908.
Talmud Jeruschalmi. New York: n.p., 1949. Reprint of the Krotoschiner edition.
The Tosefta. Translated by J. Neusner. 6 vols. New York: Ktav, 1977–1986.

Christian Sources

Die Apostolischen Väter. Edited by J. A. Fischer. 10th ed. Darmstadt: Wissenschaftliche Buchgesellschaft, 1993.
Die Bekenntnisschriften der evangelisch-lutherischen Kirche. 10th ed. Göttingen: Vandenhoeck & Ruprecht, 1986.
Clement of Alexandria. *Stromata.* Vol. 2. Edited by O. Stählin and L. Früchtel. 3d ed. GCS 52. Berlin: Akademie-Verlag, 1960.
Epiphanius. *Epiphanius' Treatise on Weights and Measures: The Syriac Version.* Edited by J. E. Dean. SAOC 11. Chicago: University of Chicago, 1935.
———. *Panarion haer[esium].* Edited by K. Holl. 3 vols. GCS 25, 31, 37. Leipzig: J. C. Hinrichs, 1915–1933.
Eusebius. *Die Chronik des Hieronymus.* Vol. 7 of *Eusebius Werke.* Edited by R. Helm. GCS 47. Berlin: Akademie-Verlag, 1956.
———. *Kirchengeschichte.* Edited by H. Kraft. Munich: Kösel, 1967.
———. *Kirchengeschichte.* Edited by E. Schwarz. Kleine Ausgabe. 5th ed. Berlin: Akademie-Verlag, 1952.
Eutychius. *Annales.* Cols. 889–1156 in vol. 111. PG. Edited by J.-P. Migne. 162 vols. Paris: J.-.P Migne, 1857–1886.
Itinerarium Egeriae. Pages 112–13. CSEL 34. Vienna, 1898.
Jerome. *Commentarius in Ecclesiasten.* Cols. 1061–1174 in vol. 23. PL. Edited by J.-P. Migne. 217 vols. Paris: J.-P. Migne, 1844–1864.
———. *Epistula 103.* In *Sancti Eusebii Hieronymi Epistulae: Pars II, Epistulae LXXI–CXX.* Edited by I. Hilberg. 2d ed. CSEL 50. Vienna: Verlag der Österreichischen Akademie der Wissenschaften, 1996.
———. *De viris illustribus.* Cols. 631–766 in vol 23. PL. Edited by J.-P. Migne. 217 vols. Paris: J.-P. Migne, 1844–1864.
John Chrysostom. *Homilies on the Acts of the Apostles.* Edited by H. Browne. Translated by J. Walker and R. Sheppard. Library of the Fathers. Oxford: Parker, 1851.
Justin Martyr. *Die ältesten Apologeten.* Edited by E. J. Goodspeed. Göttingen: Vandenhoeck & Ruprecht, 1914.
Novum Testamentum Graece. Edited by E. and E. Nestle, K. Aland, et al. 27th ed. Stuttgart: Deutsche Bibelstiftung, 1993.
Origen. *Gegen Celsus.* Edited by P. Koetschau. 2 vols. GCS 2, 3. Leipzig: Hinrichs, 1899.

Greco-Roman Authors and Collections

Antipater. *Für und wider die Ehe: Antike Stimmen zu einer offenen Frage.* Text by H. von Arnim. Translated by K. Gaiser. Stoicorum veterum fragmenta

3. *Dialog mit der Antike* 1. Munich: Heimeran, 1974. *Für und wider die Ehe: Antike Stimmen zu einer offenen Frage.*
Apuleius. *Metamorphosen: Lateinisch und deutsch*. Edited and translated by R. Helm. Darmstadt: Wissenschaftliche Buschgesellschaft, 1956.
Aristotle. *Oeconomica*. Edited by B. A. van Groningen and A. Wartelle. Paris: Les Belles Lettres, 1968.
———. *Opera*. Edited by I. Becker. 5 vols. Die königliche preussische Akademie der Wissentschaften. Berlin: de Gruyter, 1831–1870.
———. Aristotle. *Politeia*. Edited by A. Dreizehnter. Munich: W. Fink, 1970.
Columella. *De re rustica libri duodecim*. Edited and translated by W. Richter. 3 vols. Munich: Artemis, 1981–1983.
———. *On Agriculture*. Translated by H. B. Ash. 3 vols. LCL. Cambridge: Harvard University Press, 1941.
Dio Chrysostom. *Orationes*. Edited by G. de Budé. Leipzig: B. G. Teubneri, 1906.
Diogenes Laertius. Translated by R. D. Hicks. 2 vols. LCL. Cambridge: Harvard University Press, 1959.
Dionysius of Halicarnassus. *Antiquitatum romanarum Quae Supersunt*. Edited by A. Kiessling. 4 vols. Teubner. Leipzig: B. G. Teubneri, 1860–1870.
Hierocles [disciple of Musonius]. *C. Musonii Rufi Relequiae*. Edited by O. Hense. Vol. 4 of *Ioannis Stobaei anthologium*. Edited by C. Wachsmuth and O. Hense. Leipzig: Teubner, 1905.
Juvenal. *Satiren lateinisch-deutsch*. Edited and translated with comments by Joachim Adamietz. Sammlung Tusculum. Zurich: Artemis and Winkler, 1993.
Lactantius. *Opera Omnia*. CSEL 19. Prague: F. Tempsky, 1890.
Martial. *Epigrammata*. Edited by D. R. Shackleton Bailey. Teubner. Stuttgart: B. G. Teubner, 1990.
Musonius Rufus. *Musonius Rufus: "The Roman Socrates." Or. III, IV, XII*. Edited and translated by C. Lutz. YCS 10. New Haven: Yale University Press, 1947.
Paulus Orosius. *Historiarum adversum paganos libri VII*. Edited by Carolus Zagemeister. CSEL 5. Vienna: C. Geroldi filium, 1882.
Philostratus. *De gymnastica*. Page 23 in vol. 1 of *Flavii Philostrati opera*. 2 vols. Edited by C. L. Kayser. Bibliotheca scriptorum Graecorum et Romanorum Teubneriana. Leipzig: Teubner, 1870–1871.
Philostratus and Eunapius. *The Lives of the Sophists*. Edited by M. von Albrecht. Stuttgart: n.p., 1963.
Plutarch. *Demetrius and Antony, Pyrrhus and Caius Marius*. Vol. 9 of *Plutarch's Lives*. Translated by B. Perrin. 11 vols. LCL. Cambridge: Harvard University Press, 1950.
———. *Moralia*. Translated by F. C. Babbitt et al. 16 vols. LCL. Cambridge: Harvard University Press, 1927–1969.
Vitruvius. *On Architecture*. Translated by F. Granger. 2 vols. LCL. Cambridge: Harvard University Press, 1931–1943.
———. *Zehn Bücher über Architektur*. Translated with footnotes by C. Festerbusch. 3d ed. Darmstadt: Wissenschaftliche Buchgesellschaft, 1981.
Xenophon. *Oikonomos*. Translated with commentary by K. Meyer. Westerburg: Kaesberger, 1975.

———. *Opera Omnia*. Vol. 2. Edited by E. C. Marchant. 2d ed. Oxford: Clarendon, 1967.

Major Reference Works

Aland, K. *Synopsis Quattuor Evangeliorum*. 13th rev. ed. Stuttgart: Deutsche Bibelgesellschaft, 1986.
Computer-Konkordanz zum Novum Testamentum Graece von Nestle-Aland^{26} und zum Greek New Testament. Edited by Institut für Neutestamentliche Textforschung and Rechenzentrum der Universität Münster. 3d ed. Berlin: De Gruyter, 1990.
Gerth, B., and R. Kühner. *Ausführliche Grammatik der griechischen Sprache*. 2 vols. Vol. 1, *Elementar- und Formlehre*. Vol. 2, *Satzlehre*. 3d ed. Hannover: Hahnsche Buchhandlung, 1966.
Gesenius, W. *Hebräisches und aramäisches Handwörterbuch über das Alte Testament*. Revised by F. Buhl et al. 17th ed. Berlin: Springer, 1962.
Hoffmann, E. G., and H. von Siebenthal. *Griechische Grammatik zum Neuen Testament*. Rieher: Immanuel, 1985.
Liddell, H., G. R. Scott, and H. S. Jones. *A Greek-English Lexicon*. Oxford: Clarendon, 1968. 9th ed. with revised supplement, 1996.
Lisowsky, G., and L. Rost. *Konkordanz zum hebräischen Alten Testament*. 2d ed. Stuttgart: Privileg. W(u)rtt. Bibelanstalt, 1966.
Maier, J. *Die Qumran-Essener: Die Texte vom Toten Meer*. 2 vols. UTB.W 1862. Munich: E. Reinhardt, 1995.
Metzger, B. M. *A Textual Commentary on the Greek New Testament*. 2d ed. Stuttgart: Deutsche Bibelgesellschaft, 1994.
Morgenthaler, R. *Statistische Synopse*. Zurich: Gotthelf-Verlag, 1971.
Schwyzer, E. *Griechische Grammatik*. Edited by A. Debrunner. 2 vols. Munich: Beck, 1950.
Theologisches Handwörterbuch zum Alten Testament. Edited by E. Jenni, with assistance from C. Westermann. 2 vols. Zurich: Theologischer, 1971–1976.

Commentaries

Barrett, C. K. *A Critical and Exegetical Commentary on the Acts of the Apostles*. Vol. 1. ICC. Edinburgh: T&T Clark, 1994.
———. *The First Epistle to the Corinthians*. HNTC. New York: Harper & Row, 1968. Repr., Peabody, Mass.: Hendrickson, 1993.
———. *The Pastoral Epistles in the New English Bible with Introduction and Commentary*. Oxford: Clarendon, 1963.
Barth, M. *Ephesians*. Vols. 1–2. AB 34. New York: Doubleday, 1974.
Bauernfeind, O. *Die Apostelgeschichte*. THKNT 5. Leipzig: A. Deichert, 1939.
Baur, F. C. *Die sogenannten Pastoralbriefe des Apostel Paulus aufs neue kritisch untersucht*. Stuttgart: J. G. Cotta'schen Verlagshandlung, 1835.
Becker, J. *Der Brief an die Galater*. 4th ed. NTD 8. Göttingen: Vandenhoeck & Ruprecht, 1990.

Benoit, P. *L'évangile selon saint Matthieu.* 4th ed. BiJer. Paris: Cerf, 1972.
Best, E. *The First and Second Epistles to the Thessalonians.* 2d ed. BNTC 10. London: Black, 1972.
Beyer, H. W., and P. Althaus. *Der Brief an die Galater.* 12th ed. NTD 8. Göttingen: Vandenhoeck & Ruprecht, 1970.
Blomberg, C. L. *Matthew.* NAC 22. Nashville: Broadman, 1992.
Brown, R. *The Epistles of John.* AB 30. New York: Doubleday, 1982.
Brox, N. *Die Pastoralbriefe.* 4th ed. RNT 7/2. Regensburg: Verlag Friedrich Pustet, 1969.
Bruce, F. F. *1 and 2 Corinthians.* NCB. London: Oliphants, 1971.
———. *1 and 2 Thessalonians.* WBC 45. Waco: Word, 1982.
———. *The Book of the Acts.* NICNT. Grand Rapids: Eerdmans, 1988.
———. *The Epistle to the Colossians, to Philemon, and to the Ephesians.* NICNT. Grand Rapids: Eerdmans, 1984.
———. *The Epistle to the Galatians.* 2d ed. NIGTC. Grand Rapids: Eerdmans, 1990.
Cadbury, H. J., and K. Lake. *The Acts of the Apostles.* Vols. 4 and 5. Part 1 of *The Beginnings of Christianity.* Edited by F. Foakes-Jackson and K. Lake. London: Macmillan, 1920. Repr., Grand Rapids: Baker, 1979.
Calvin, J. *The Acts of the Apostles.* Translated by J. N. Fraser and W. J. C. McDonald. 2 vols. Edinburgh: Saint Andrew, 1965–1966.
Collange, J. F. *The Epistle of St. Paul to the Philippians.* London: Epworth, 1979.
Conzelmann, H. *Die Apostelgeschichte.* 2d ed. HNT 7. Tübingen: Mohr, 1972.
———. *Der erste Brief an die Korinther.* 12th ed. KEK 5. Göttingen: Vandenhoeck & Ruprecht, 1981.
Cranfield, C. E. B. *The Epistle to the Romans.* 2 vols. 6th ed. ICC. Edinburgh: T&T Clark, 1990.
Davids, P. H. *The Epistle of James.* Exeter: Paternoster, 1982.
Dibelius, M. *An die Kolosser, Epheser, an Philemon.* HNT 3/2. Tübingen: J. C. B. Mohr (P. Seibeck), 1912.
———. *An die Thessalonicher I–II, an die Philipper.* 2d ed. HNT 2. Tübingen: J. C. B. Mohr (P. Seibeck), 1937.
———. *Die Pastoralbriefe.* 2d ed. HNT 13. Tübingen: Mohr, 1931.
Dibelius, M., and H. Conzelmann. *Die Pastoralbriefe.* 4th ed. HNT 13. Tübingen: J. C. B. Mohr (P. Siebeck), 1966.
Dibelius, M., and H. Greeven. *An die Kolosser, Epheser, an Philemon.* 3d ed. HNT 12. Tübingen: Mohr, 1953.
Dobschütz, E. von. *Die Thessalonicher-Briefe.* 7th ed. KEK 10. Göttingen: Vandenhoeck & Ruprecht, 1909. Repr., 1974.
Dodd, C. H. *The Epistle of Paul to the Romans.* MNTC. New York: R. Long and R. R. Smith, Inc., 1932.
Dunn, J. D. G. *The Epistle to the Colossians and to Philemon: A Commentary on the Greek Text.* NIGTC. Grand Rapids: Eerdmans, 1996.
———. *The Epistle to the Galatians.* BNTC 9. Peabody, Mass.: Hendrickson, 1993.
———. *Romans.* 2 vols. WBC 38. Waco: Word, 1988.
Easton, B. S. *The Gospel according to St. Luke.* Edinburgh: T&T Clark, 1926.

Ernst, J. *Die Briefe an die Philipper, an Philemon, an die Kolosser, an die Epheser.* RNT 8. Regensburg: Pustet, 1974.
———. *Das Evangelium nach Lukas.* RNT 3. Regensburg: Pustet, 1976.
———. *Das Evangelium nach Markus.* RNT 2. Regensburg: Pustet, 1981.
Fee, G. D. *1–2 Timothy, Titus.* Good News Commentary. San Francisco: Harper & Row, 1984. Revised ed. NIBCNT 13. Peabody, Mass.: Hendrickson, 1988.
———. *The First Epistle to the Corinthians.* NICNT. Grand Rapids: Eerdmans, 1987.
Filson, F. V. *A Commentary on the Gospel according to St. Matthew.* 2d ed. BNTC 7. London: A. and C. Black, 1971.
Fitzmyer, J. A. *The Gospel according to Luke.* 2 vols. New York: Doubleday, 1981.
Friedrich, G. "Der Brief an Philemon." In H. W. Beyer et al., *Die kleineren Briefe des Apostels Paulus.* 10th ed. NTD 8. Göttingen: Vandenhoeck & Ruprecht, 1965.
Furnish, V. F. *Second Corinthians: Translated with Introduction, Notes, and Commentary.* AB 32A. New York: Doubleday, 1984.
Gaechter, P. *Das Matthäus-Evangelium.* 2d ed. Innsbruck: Tyrolia, 1964.
Gnilka, J. *Der Epheserbrief.* HTKNT 10/2. Freiburg: Herder, 1971.
———. *Das Evangelium nach Markus.* 2 vols. EKKNT 2/1, 2. Zurich: Benziger, 1978–1979.
———. *Der Kolosserbrief.* HTKNT 10/1. Freiburg: Herder, 1980.
———. *Das Matthäusevangelium.* 2d ed. 2 vols. HTKNT 16/12. Freiburg: Herder, 1986–1988.
———. *Der Philemonbrief.* HTKNT 10/4. Freiburg: Herder, 1982.
———. *Der Philipperbrief.* 4th ed. HTKNT 10/3. Freiburg: Herder, 1987.
Goppelt, L. *Der erste Petrusbrief.* KEK 12/1. Göttingen: Vandenhoeck & Ruprecht, 1978.
Grundmann, W. *Das Evangelium nach Lukas.* 8th ed. THKNT 3. Berlin: Evangelische Verlagsanstalt, 1977.
———. *Das Evangelium nach Markus.* 7th ed. THKNT 2. Berlin: Evangelische Verlagsanstalt, 1977.
———. *Das Evangelium nach Matthäus.* 4th ed. THKNT 1. Berlin: Evangelische Verlagsanstalt, 1975.
Guthrie, D. *The Pastoral Epistles.* 2d ed. TNTC 14. Leicester: Inter-Varsity, 1990.
Haenchen, E. *Die Apostelgeschichte.* 16th ed. KEK 3. Göttingen: Vandenhoeck & Ruprecht, 1977.
Hanson, A. T. *The Pastoral Letters.* Cambridge: University Press, 1966.
Hauck, F. *Das Evangelium des Lukas.* THKNT 3. Leipzig: A. Deichert, 1934.
Hawthorne, G. F. *Philippians.* WBC 43. Waco: Word, 1983.
Heinrici, G. *Der zweite Brief an die Korinther.* 7th ed. KEK 6. Göttingen: Vandenhoeck & Ruprecht, 1890.
Holtz, G. *Die Pastoralbriefe.* 5th ed. THKNT 13. Leipzig: Evang. Verl.-Anst., 1992.
Holtz, T. *Der erste Brief an die Thessalonicher.* EKKNT 13. Zurich: Benziger, 1986.

Jeremias, J. *Die Briefe an Timotheus und Titus.* NTD 9. Göttingen: Vandenhoeck & Ruprecht, 1975.
Jervell, J. *Die Apostelgeschichte.* KEK 3. Göttingen: Vandenhoeck & Ruprecht, 1998.
Jülicher, A. *Der Brief an die Römer.* 3d ed. SNT 2. Göttingen: n.p., 1917.
Käsemann, E. *An die Römer.* HNT 8a. Tübingen: Mohr, 1973.
Kelly, J. N. D. *A Commentary on the Pastoral Epistles.* HNTC. Peabody, Mass.: Hendrickson, 1987.
Klauck, H. J. *Der zweite und dritte Johannesbrief.* EKKNT 23/2. Zurich: Benziger, 1992.
Klostermann, E. *Das Matthäusevangelium.* 3d ed. HNT 4. Tübingen: Mohr, 1938. 4th ed., 1971.
Knight, G. W., III. *The Pastoral Epistles.* NIGTC. Grand Rapids: Eerdmans, 1992.
Lampe, P. "Der Brief an Philemon." Pages 205–32 in N. Walter, E. Reinmuth, P. Lampe, *Die Briefe an die Philipper, Thessalonicher, und an Philemon.* NTD 8/2. Göttingen: Vandenhoeck & Ruprecht, 1998.
Lane, W. L. *The Gospel according to Mark.* NICNT. Grand Rapids: Eerdmans, 1974.
Lang, F. L. *Die Briefe an die Korinther.* NTD 7. Göttingen: Vandenhoeck & Ruprecht, 1986.
Lietzmann, H. *An die Korinther I–II.* 4th ed. HNT 9. Tübingen: J. C. B. Mohr, 1949.
———. *An die Römer.* 5th ed. HNT 8. Tübingen: Mohr, 1971.
Lightfoot, J. B. *Colossians and Philemon.* London: Macmillan, 1875.
———. *St. Paul's Epistle to the Philippians.* London: Macmillan, 1868.
Lindemann, A. *Der Kolosserbrief.* ZBK.NT 10. Zurich: Theologischer Verlag, 1983.
Lohmeyer, E. *Die Briefe an die Kolosser und an Philemon.* 13th ed. KEK 9/2. Göttingen: Vandenhoeck & Ruprecht, 1964.
———. *Der Brief an die Philipper.* 14th ed. KEK 9/1. Göttingen: Vandenhoeck & Ruprecht, 1974.
———. *Das Evangelium des Markus: Mit Ergänzungsheft.* 17th ed. KEK 1/2. Göttingen: Vandenhoeck & Ruprecht, 1967.
———. *Das Evangelium des Matthäus.* 4th ed. KEK Sonderband. Göttingen: Vandenhoeck & Ruprecht, 1967.
Lohse, E. *Die Briefe an die Kolosser und an Philemon.* 14th ed. KEK 9. Göttingen: Vandenhoeck & Ruprecht, 1968.
Lona, H. E. *Der 1 Clemensbrief.* KAV 2. Göttingen: Vandenhoeck & Ruprecht, 1998.
Marshall, I. H. *1 and 2 Thessalonians.* NCB. London: Marshall, Morgan and Scott, 1983.
———. *The Acts of the Apostles.* TNTC. Leicester: InterVarsity, 1980.
———. *The Gospel of Luke.* NIGTC. Grand Rapids: Eerdmans, 1978.
Martin, R. P. *2 Corinthians.* WBC 40. Waco: Word, 1986.
———. *Colossians and Philemon.* NCBC. London: Oliphants, 1974.
Merkel, H. *Die Pastoralbriefe.* NTD 9/1. Göttingen: Vandenhoeck & Ruprecht, 1991.

Michel, O. *Der Brief an die Römer.* 5th ed. KEK 4. Göttingen: Vandenhoeck & Ruprecht, 1978.
Mitton, C. L. *Ephesians.* NCB. London: Oliphants, 1976.
Morris, L. *The First and Second Epistles to the Thessalonians.* 2d ed. Grand Rapids: Eerdmans, 1991.
Mussner, F. *Apostelgeschichte.* 2d ed. NEB.NT 5. Würzburg: Echter, 1988.
———. *Der Brief an die Epheser.* ÖTK 10. Gütersloh: Mohn, 1982.
———. *Der Jakobusbrief.* Freiburg: Herder, 1975.
Niederwimmer, K. *Die Didache.* 2d ed. KAV 1. Göttingen: Vandenhoeck & Ruprecht, 1993.
O'Brien, P. *Colossians, Philemon.* WBC 44. Waco: Word, 1982.
———. *The Epistle to the Philippians.* NIGTC. Grand Rapids: Eerdmans, 1991.
Oberlinner, L. *Die Pastoralbriefe.* 4 vols. HTKNT 11/2. Freiburg: Herder, 1994–1996.
Oepke, A. *Der Brief des Paulus an die Galater.* 2d ed. THKNT 9. Berlin: Evangelische Verlagsanstalt, 1957.
Pesch, R. *Die Apostelgeschichte.* 2 vols. EKKNT 5/1, 2. Zurich: Benziger, 1986.
———. *Das Markusevangelium.* 2 vols. 2d ed. HTKNT 2/1, 2. Freiburg: Herder, 1976–1977.
Pokorný, P. *Der Brief des Paulus an die Kolosser.* THKNT 10/1. Berlin: Evangelische Verlagsanstalt, 1987.
Polhill, J. B. *Acts.* NAC. Nashville: Broadman, 1992.
Preuschen, E. *Die Apostelgeschichte.* HNT 4/1. Tübingen: J. C. B. Mohr, 1912.
Quinn, J. D. *The Letter to Titus.* AB 35. New York: Doubleday, 1990.
Ramsay, W. M. *A Historical Commentary on St. Paul's Epistle to the Galatians.* 2d ed. London: Hodder & Stoughton, 1900.
Rengstorf, K. H. *Das Evangelium nach Lukas.* 17th ed. NTD 3. Göttingen: Vandenhoeck & Ruprecht, 1978.
Robinson, T. H. *The Gospel of Matthew.* New York: Doubleday, 1928.
Rohde, J. *Der Brief des Paulus an die Galater.* THKNT 9. Berlin: Evangelische Verlagsanstalt, 1989.
Roloff, J. *Die Apostelgeschichte.* NTD 5. Göttingen: Vandenhoeck & Ruprecht, 1981.
———. *Der erste Brief an Timotheus.* EKKNT 25. Neukirchen-Vluyn: Neukirchener, 1988.
Sanday, W., and A. C. Headlam. *A Critical and Exegetical Commentary on the Epistle to the Romans.* ICC. Edinburgh: T&T Clark, 1895. 5th ed. Edinburgh: T&T Clark, 1902.
Schille, G. *Die Apostelgeschichte des Lukas.* 2d ed. THKNT 5. Berlin: Evangelische Verlagsanstalt, 1984.
Schlatter, A. *Der Evangelist Matthäus: Seine Sprache, sein Ziel, seine Selbständigkeit.* 2d ed. Stuttgart: Calwer, 1933.
———. *Das Evangelium des Lukas aus seinen Quellen erklärt.* Stuttgart: Calwer, 1931.
———. *Die Kirche der Griechen im Urteil des Paulus.* 3d ed. Stuttgart: Calwer, 1983.
———. *Die Korintherbriefe.* Vol. 6 of *Schlatters Erläuterung zum Neuen Testament.* 5th ed. Stuttgart: Calwer, 1928.

Schlier, H. *Der Brief an die Epheser.* 7th ed. Düsseldorf: Patmos, 1971.
———. *Der Brief an die Galater.* 5th ed. KEK 7. Göttingen: Vandenhoeck & Ruprecht, 1971.
———. *Der Römerbrief.* HTKNT 6. Freiburg: Herder, 1977.
Schmithals, W. *Die Apostelgeschichte des Lukas.* ZBK.NT 3/2. Zurich: Theologischer Verlag, 1982.
Schnackenburg, R. *Der Brief an die Epheser.* EKKNT 10. Neukirchen-Vluyn: Neukirchener, 1982.
———. *Die Johannesbriefe.* 7th ed. 2 vols. HTKNT 13/3. Freiburg: Herder, 1984.
Schneider, G. *Die Apostelgeschichte.* HTKNT 5/1, 2. Freiburg: Herder, 1980–1982.
———. *Das Evangelium nach Lukas.* 2 vols. ÖTK 3/1. Gütersloh: Mohn, 1977.
Schniewind, J. *Das Evangelium nach Markus.* 12th ed. Göttingen: Vandenhoeck & Ruprecht, 1977.
———. *Das Evangelium nach Matthäus.* 12th ed. Göttingen: Vandenhoeck & Ruprecht, 1968.
Schürmann, H. *Das Lukasevangelium.* 2 vols. HTKNT 3. Freiburg: Herder, 1969–1993.
Schweizer, E. *Der Brief an die Kolosser.* 2d ed. EKKNT 12. Zurich: Benziger, 1980.
———. *Das Evangelium nach Markus.* 15th ed. NTD 1. Göttingen: Vandenhoeck & Ruprecht, 1978.
———. *Das Evangelium nach Matthäus.* 14th ed. NTD 2. Göttingen: Vandenhoeck & Ruprecht, 1976.
Spicq, C. *Les épîtres pastorales.* 4th ed. Paris: Livrairie Lecoffre-Gabalda, 1969.
Stählin, G. *Die Apostelgeschichte.* 7th ed. NTD 5. Göttingen: Vandenhoeck & Ruprecht, 1975.
Strecker, G. *Die Johannesbriefe.* KEK 14. Göttingen: Vandenhoeck & Ruprecht, 1989.
Stuhlmacher, P. *Der Brief an Philemon.* 3d ed. EKKNT 18. Zurich: Benziger, 1989.
———. *Der Brief an die Römer.* NTD 6. Göttingen: Vandenhoeck & Ruprecht, 1989.
Suhl, A. *Der Brief an Philemon.* ZBK.NT 13. Zurich: Theologischer, 1981.
Taylor, V. *The Gospel according to St. Mark.* 2d ed. London: Macmillan, 1966.
Towner, P. H. *1–2 Timothy and Titus.* IVP NT. Downers Grove, Ill.: InterVarsity, 1994.
Vincent, M. R. *A Critical and Exegetical Commentary on the Epistle to the Philippians and to Philemon.* ICC 11. Edinburgh: T&T Clark, 1897. 5th ed., Edinburgh: T&T Clark, 1955.
Weiser, A. *Die Apostelgeschichte Kapitel 1–12.* 2 vols. ÖTK 5/1. Gütersloh: Mohn, 1981.
Wellhausen, J. *Das Evangelium Lucae.* Berlin: Reimer, 1904.
———. *Das Evangelium Marci.* 2d ed. Berlin: Reimer, 1909.
———. *Das Evangelium Matthaei.* 2d ed. Berlin: Reimer, 1914.
Wikenhauser, A. *Die Apostelgeschichte.* RNT 5. Regensburg: Pustet, 1956.
Wilckens, U. *Der Brief an die Römer.* 3 vols. EKKNT 6/3. Zurich: Benziger, 1978–1982.

Wolff, C. *Der erste Brief des Paulus an die Korinther.* THKNT 7. Berlin: Evangelische, 1996.
Wolter, M. *Der Brief an die Kolosser, Der Brief an Philemon.* ÖTK 12. Gütersloh: Mohn, 1993.
Wright, N. T. *The Epistle of Paul to the Colossians and to Philemon.* TNTC. Grand Rapids: Eerdmans, 1986.
Yates, R. *The Epistle to the Colossians.* Epworth Commentaries. London: Epworth, 1993.
Zahn, T. *Die Apostelgeschichte des Lucas.* 2 vols. 3d and 4th ed. KNT 5. Leipzig: Leichert, 1927.

Other Secondary Literature

Abrahamsen, V. A. "The Rock Reliefs and the Cult of Diana at Philippi." Diss., Harvard Divinity School, 1986.
Achelis, H. *Das Christentum in den ersten drei Jahrhunderten.* 2 vols. 1912. 2d ed. Leipzig, 1925. Repr., 2 vols. in 1. Aalen, Germany: Scientia, 1975.
Adam, A. "Entstehung des Bischofsamts." *Wort und Dienst* 5 (1957): 104–13.
Adamson, J. B. *James—The Man and His Message.* Grand Rapids: Eerdmans, 1989.
Adan-Bayewitz, D. "Kefer Hannanya." *Israel Exploration Journal* 37, no. 2/3 (1987): 178–79.
———. "Manufacture and Local Trade in the Galilee of Roman-Byzantine Palestine: A Case Study." PhD diss., Hebrew University, Jerusalem, 1985.
Adan-Bayewitz, D., and I. Perlman. "Local Pottery Provenience Studies: A Role for Clay Analysis." *Archaeometry* 27, no. 2 (1985): 203–17.
Adler, L. *Religion der geheiligten Zeit: Die biblischen Festzeiten und das Judentum.* Basel: E. Reinhardt, 1967.
Afanassieff, N. "L'assemblée eucharistique unique dans l'église ancienne." *Kleronomia* 6 (1974): 1–34.
Aguirre, R. "La casa como estructura base del cristianismo primitivo: Las iglesias domesticas." *Estudios eclesiásticos* 59 (1984): 27–51.
Akurgal, E. *Ancient Civilizations and Ruins of Turkey: From Prehistoric Times until the End of the Roman Empire.* 3d ed. Istanbul: Haset Kitiabevi, 1973.
Aland, K., ed. *Kirche und Gemeinde.* Vol. 6 of *Luther deutsch: Die Werke Martin Luthers in neuer Auswahl für die Gegenwart.* Stuttgart: Klotz, 1966.
———. *Die Säuglingstaufe im Neuen Testament und in der alten Kirche: Eine Antwort an Joachim Jeremias.* 2d ed. TEH NF 86. Munich: C. Kaiser, 1963.
———. "Der Schluss und die urspüngliche Gestalt des Römerbriefes." Pages 284–301 in *Neutestamentliche Entwürfe.* Edited by K. Aland. TB 63. Munich: Kaiser, 1979.
Alföldy, G., ed. *Die römische Gesellschaft: Ausgewählte Beiträge.* Wiesbaden: Steiner, 1986.
———. "Die römische Gesellschaft: Eine Nachbetrachtung über Struktur und Eigenart." Pages 69–81 in *Die römische Gesellschaft: Ausgewählte Beiträge.*

———. "Die römische Gesellschaft: Struktur und Eigenart." Pages 41–68 in *Die römische Gesellschaft: Ausgewählte Beiträge*.
———. *Römische Sozialgeschichte*. 3d ed. Wissenschaftliche Paperbacks 8. Wiesbaden: Steiner, 1984. ET: *The Social History of Rome*. Baltimore: Johns Hopkins University, 1988.
Allen, R. *Missionary Methods: Saint Paul's or Ours?* Grand Rapids: Eerdmans, 1962.
Allison, D. C. "The Pauline Epistles and the Synoptic Gospels: The Pattern of the Parallels." *New Testament Studies* 28 (1982): 1–32.
Allmen, D. von. *La famille de Dieu: La symbolique familiale dans le paulinisme*. OBO 41. Fribourg: Éditions universitaires, 1981.
Alt, A. "Galiläische Probleme." Pages 343–63 in vol. 2 of *Kleine Schriften zur Geschichte des Volkes Israels*. 3 vols. Munich: Beck, 1953.
Altwegg, J. "Hundert Millionen Tote: Vom 'Klassen-Genozid' Stalins bis zum Terror Pol Pots—im Kommunismus wurde der Massenmord zur Regierungsform." *Frankfurter Allgemeine Zeitung* 275 (November 26, 1997): 10–11.
Anderson, P. A., and P. M. Anderson. *The House Church*. Nashville: Abingdon, 1975.
Andresen, C. *Von den Anfängen bis zur Hochscholastik*. Vol. 1 of *Geschichte des Christentums*. ThW 6. Stuttgart: Kohlhammer, 1975.
Applebaum, S. "Economic Life in Palestine." Pages 631–700 in *The Jewish People in the First Century*. Edited by S. Safrai and M. Stern. CRINT I/2. Assen: Van Gorcum, 1976.
———. *Judaea in Hellenistic and Roman Times: Historical and Archaeological Essays*. SJLA 40. Leiden: Brill, 1989.
Arn, W., and C. A. Schwarz. *Gemeindeaufbau: Liebe in Aktion*. 2d ed. Neukirchen-Vluyn: Aussaat-Verl., 1994.
Arnold, C. E. "Colossae." *ABD* 1:1089–1090.
Aune, D. E. *Prophecy in Early Christianity and the Ancient Mediterranean World*. Grand Rapids: Eerdmans, 1983.
Austgen, R. J. *Natural Motivation in the Pauline Epistles*. Notre Dame: University of Notre Dame, 1966.
Avi-Yonah, M. "Ancient Synagogues." Pages 95–109 in *The Synagogue: Studies in Origins, Archaeology, and Architecture*. Edited by J. Gutmann. New York: Ktav, 1975.
———. "The Development of the Roman Road System in Palestine." *Israel Exploration Journal* 1 (1950/1951): 54–60.
———. *The Holy Land from the Persian to the Arab Conquests: An Historical Geography*. Grand Rapids: Baker, 1966.
———. "Synagogues." *EAEHL* 4:1129–38.
Aviam, M. *Survey of Sites in the Galilee*. Jerusalem: n.p., 1995.
Avigad, N. *Discovering Jerusalem*. Nashville: Thomas Nelson, 1983.
———. "How the Wealthy Lived in Herodian Jerusalem." *Biblical Archaeology Review* 2 (1976): 22–35.
———. "Jerusalem in Flames: The Burnt House Captures a Moment in Time." *Biblical Archaeology Review* 9 (1983): 66–72.

Bachmann, M. *Jerusalem und der Tempel: Die geographisch-theologischen Elemente in der lukanischen Sicht des jüdischen Kultzentrums*. BWA(N)T 109. Stuttgart: Kohlhammer, 1980.

Badian, E. *Foreign Clientelae (264–70 b.c.)*. Oxford: Clarendon, 1958.

Bagatti, B. *The Church of the Circumcision*. Translated by E. Hoade. 2d ed. Jerusalem: Franciscan Printing Press, 1984.

Balch, D. L. "Early Christian Criticism of Patriarchal Authority: 1 Peter 2:11–3:12." *Union Seminary Quarterly Review* 39 (1984): 161–74.

———. "Household Codes." *ABD* 3:318–20.

———. "Household Codes." Pages 25–30 in *Greco-Roman Literature and the New Testament*. Edited by D. L. Aune. SBLSBS 21. Atlanta: Scholars Press, 1988.

———. *Let Wives Be Submissive: The Domestic Code in 1 Peter*. SBLMS 26. Chico, Calif.: Scholars Press, 1981.

Balch, D. L., and C. Osiek. *Families in the New Testament World: Households and House Churches*. Louisville: Westminster John Knox, 1997.

Baldi, D. *Enchiridion Locorum Sanctorum*. Jerusalem: Franciscan Printing Press, 1955.

Balz, H. "φοβέω." *TDNT* 9:189–219.

Bammel, E. "Gal 1:23." *Zeitschrift für die neutestamentliche Wissenschaft und die Kunde der älteren Kirche* 59 (1968): 108–12.

Banks, R. *Going to Church in the First Century: An Eyewitness Account*. Parramatta, N.S.W.: Hexagon, 1985.

———. *Paul's Idea of Community: The Early House Churches in Their Cultural Setting*. 2d rev. ed. Peabody, Mass.: Hendrickson, 1994.

Banks, R., and J. Banks. *The Home Church: Regrouping the People of God for Community and Mission*. Sutherland, N.S.W.: Albatross Books, 1986. Rev. ed., *The Church Comes Home: Building Community and Mission through Home Churches*. Peabody, Mass.: Hendrickson, 1998.

Bar-Adon, P. "Another Settlement of the Judean Desert Sect at 'En el Ghuweir on the Shores of the Dead Sea." *Bulletin of the American Schools of Oriental Research* 227 (1977): 1–25.

Barclay, W. *Educational Ideals in the Ancient World*. London: Collins, 1959.

Bardtke, H. *Die Handschriften am Toten Meer: Die Sekte von Qumran*. Berlin: Evangelische Haupt-Bibelgesellschaft, 1958.

Bartchy, S. S. μᾶλλον χρῆσαι: *First-Century Slavery and the Interpretation of 1 Corinthians 7:21*. SBLDS 11. Missoula: Society of Biblical Literature, 1973.

Barton, S. C. "Living as Families in the Light of the New Testament." *Interpretation* 52.2 (1998): 116–224.

———. "Paul's Sense of Place: An Anthropological Approach to Community Formation in Corinth." *New Testament Studies* 32 (1986): 225–46.

Barton, S. C., and G. H. R. Horsley. "A Hellenistic Cult Group and the New Testament Churches." *Jahrbuch für Antike und Christentum* 24 (1981): 7–41.

Bauckham, R. "James and the Jerusalem Church." Pages 415–80 in *The Book of Acts in Its Palestinian Setting*. Edited by R. Bauckam. Vol. 4 of *The Book of Acts in Its First Century Setting*. Edited by B. W. Winter. Grand Rapids: Eerdmans, 1995.

Bauer, W. *Rechtgläubigkeit und Ketzerei im ältesten Christentum*. 2d ed. BHT 10. Tübingen: Mohr, 1964.
Bauernfeind, O. "ἁπλότης." *TDNT* 1:386–87.
Baur, F. C. "Die Christuspartei in der korinthischen Gemeinde, der Gegensatz des petrinischen und paulinischen Christentums in der ältesten Kirche, der Apostel Petrus in Rom." *Tübinger Zeitschrift für Theologie* 4 (1831): 61–206.
———. *Paulus, der Apostel Jesu Christi: Sein Leben und Wirken, seine Briefe, und seine Lehre*. 2 vols. Leipzig: Fues's (L. W. Reisland), 1866–1867.
Baumert, N. *Frau und Mann bei Paulus: Überwindung eines Missverständnisses*. Würzburg: Echter, 1991.
Baumgarten, J. M. "4Q502, Marriage or Golden Age Ritual?" *Journal of Jewish Studies* 34 (1983): 125–35.
Bäumler, C. *Kommunikative Gemeindepraxis: Eine Untersuchung ihrer Bedingungen und Möglichkeiten*. Munich: C. Kaiser, 1984.
Beck, R. "The Women of Acts: Foremothers of the Christian Church." Pages 294–96 in *With Steadfast Purpose: Essays on Acts*. Festschrift H. J. Jackson Flanders Jr. Edited by N. H. Keathley. Waco: Baylor University Press, 1990.
Becker, J. "Paulus und seine Gemeinden." Pages 102–59 in *Die Anfänge des Christentums*. Stuttgart: Kohlhammer, 1987.
Bedale, S. "The Meaning of κεφαλή in the Pauline Epistles." *Journal of Theological Studies* 5 (1954): 211–15.
Beebe, H. K. "Ancient Palestinian Dwellings." *Biblical Archaeologist* 31 (1968): 38–58.
———. "Domestic Architecture and the New Testament." *Biblical Archaeologist* 38 (1975): 89–104.
Bengel, J. A. *Gnomon Novi Testamenti*. Repr. of 3d ed., London: Williams & Norgate, et D. Nutt, 1862.
Benoit, P. "Le prétoire de Pilate à l'époque byzantine." *Revue biblique* 91 (1984): 161–77.
Berger, K. "Die sogenannten 'Sätze heiligen Rechtes' im NT: Ihre Funktion und Sitz im Leben." *Theologische Zeitschrift* 28 (1972): 305–30.
———. "Zu den sogenannten Sätzen heiligen Rechtes." *New Testament Studies* 17 (1970/1971): 10–40.
Berger, K., and C. Colpe. *Religionsgeschichtliches Textbuch zum Neuen Testament*. TNT 1. Göttingen: Vandenhoeck & Ruprecht, 1987.
Bertram, G. "συνεργός." *TDNT* 7:871–76.
Best, E. "Bishops and Deacons: Philippians 1:1." Pages 371–76 in *Studia Evangelica*. Edited by F. L. Cross. TUGAL 102. Berlin: Akademie, 1968.
———. *Following Jesus: Discipleship in the Gospel of Mark*. JSNTSup 4. Sheffield, Engl.: JSOT, 1981.
Beyer, H. W. "διάκονος." *TDNT* 2:88–93.
———. "ἐπίσκοπος." *TDNT* 2:608–20.
———. "κατηχέω." *TDNT* 3:638–40.
Beyer, K. *Die aramäischen Texte vom Toten Meer*. Göttingen: Vandenhoeck & Ruprecht, 1984.
———. *Semitische Syntax im Neuen Testament*. 2d ed. SUNT 1. Göttingen: Vandenhoeck & Ruprecht, 1968.

Beyschlag, K. *Clemens Romanus und der Frühkatholizismus: Untersuchungen zu I Clemens 1–7*. BHT 35. Tübingen: Mohr, 1966.
Bieritz, K. H. "Rückkehr ins Haus? Sozialgeschichtliche und theologische Erwägungen zum Thema 'Hauskirche.'" *Berliner Theologische Zeitschrift* 3 (1986): 111–26.
Bieritz, K. H., and C. Kähler. "Haus III." *TRE* 14:478–92.
Binder, H. "Paulus und die Thessalonicherbriefe." Pages 87–93 in *The Thessalonian Correspondence*. Edited by R. F. Collins. BETL 87. Leuven: Leuven University, 1990.
Birkey, D. "The House Church: A Missiological Model." *Missiology* 19, no. 1 (1991): 69–80.
———. *The House Church: A Model for Renewing the Church*. Scottdale, Pa.: Herald, 1988.
Bishop, E. F. F. "Jesus and Capernaum." *Catholic Biblical Quarterly* 15 (1953): 427–37.
Black, M. *An Aramaic Approach to the Gospels and Acts*. 3d ed. Oxford: Clarendon, 1967.
Blenkinsopp, J. "The Literary Evidence." Pages 201–12 in vol. 1 of *Excavations at Capernaum*. Edited by V. Tsaferis. Winona Lake: Eisenbrauns in assoc. with Pepperdine University, 1989.
Blinzler, J. "Die Heimat Jesu: Zu einer neuen Hypothese." *Bibel und Kirche* 25 (1970): 14–20.
Bliss, F. J. *Excavations at Jerusalem, 1894–1897*. London: Committee of Palestine Exploration Fund, 1898.
———. "Third Report on the Excavations at Jerusalem." PEFQS (1895): 9–25.
Blohm, J. *"Die dritte Weise": Zur Zellenbildung in der Gemeinde—Betrachtungen und Überlegungen zur Hauskreisarbeit unter Zugrundelegung einer empirischen Erhebung*. CThM.PT. Stuttgart: Calwer, 1992.
Blomenkamp, P. "Erziehung." *RAC* 6:503–59.
Blue, B. B. "Acts and the House Church." Pages 119–222 in *The Book of Acts in Its Graeco-Roman Setting*. Edited by D. W. J. Gill and C. Gempf. Vol. 2 of *The Book of Acts in Its First Century Setting*. Edited by B. W. Winter. Grand Rapids: Eerdmans, 1994.
———. "The House Church at Corinth and the Lord's Supper: Famine, Food Supply, and the *Present Distress*." *Chinese Theological Review* 5 (1991): 221–39.
———. "In Public and Private: The Role of the House Church in Early Christianity." PhD diss., University of Aberdeen, 1989.
Böcher, O. "Das sogenannte Apostoldekret." Pages 325–36 in *Vom Urchristentum zu Jesus*. Festschrift Joachim Gnilka. Edited by H. Frankemölle and K. Kertelge. Freiburg: Herder, 1989.
Boethius, A., and J. B. Ward-Perkins. *Etruscan and Early Architecture*. 2d ed. Harmondsworth: Penguin, 1978.
———. "Notes on the Development of Domestic Architecture in Rome." *American Journal of Archaeology* 24 (1934): 158–70.
Bömer, F. *Die wichtigsten Kulte der griechischen Welt*. Vol. 3 of *Untersuchungen über die Religion der Sklaven in Griechenland und Rom*. Edited by P. Herz. 2d ed. Forschungen zur antiken Sklaverei 14, 3. Stuttgart: Steiner, 1990.

———. *Die wichtigsten Kulte und Religionen in Rom und im lateinischen Westen*. Vol. 1 of *Untersuchungen über die Religion der Sklaven in Griechenland und Rom*. Edited by P. Herz. 2d ed. Forschungen zur antiken Sklaverei 14, 1. Stuttgart: Steiner, 1990.

Borchert, G. L. "Philippi." *ISBE* 3:834–36.

Boring, M. E. *Sayings of the Risen Jesus: Christian Prophecy in the Synoptic Tradition*. SNTSMS 46. Cambridge: Cambridge University, 1982.

Bormann, L. *Philippi: Stadt und Christengemeinde zur Zeit des Paulus*. NovTSup 78. Leiden: Brill, 1995.

Born, A. van den. "Haus." BL², 670–72.

Bornhäuser, K. *Das Wirken des Christus durch Taten und Worte*. Gütersloh: C. Bertelsmann, 1924.

Bornkamm, G. "Das Anathema in der urchristlichen Abendmahlsliturgie." Pages 123–33 in *Das Ende des Gesetzes*. Vol. 1. of *Gesamelte Aufsätze*. 5th ed. BEvT 16. Munich: Kaiser, 1966.

———. "Herrenmahl und Kirche bei Paulus." Pages 138–76 in *Studien zu Antike und Urchristentum*. Vol. 2. of *Gesammelte Aufsätze*. 3d ed. BEvT 28. Munich: Kaiser, 1970.

———. *Jesus von Nazareth*. 14th ed. UB 19. Stuttgart: Kohlhammer, 1988.

———. "The Missionary Stance of Paul in I Corinthians 9 and Acts." Pages 194–207 in *Studies in Luke-Acts*. Edited by L. E. Keck et al. 2d ed. Philadelphia: Fortress, 1980.

———. *Paulus*. UB 119. 7th ed. Stuttgart: Kohlhammer, 1993.

———. "πρέσβυς." *TDNT* 6:651–83.

Borsch, F. H. "Jesus, the Wandering Preacher?" Pages 45–63 in *What about the New Testament? Festschrift Christopher Evans*. Edited by M. D. Hooker and C. Hickling. London: SCM Press, 1975.

Bosch, D. J. *Transforming Mission: Paradigm Schifts in Theology of Mission*. 6th ed. Maryknoll, N.Y.: Orbis Books, 1993.

Bösen, W. *Galiläa als Lebensraum und Wirkungsfeld Jesu: Eine zeitgeschichtliche und theologische Untersuchung*. Freiburg: Herder, 1985. Reprinted as *Galiläa: Lebensraum und Wirkungsfeld Jesu*. Freiburg: Herder, 1998.

Botermann, H. "Der Heidenapostel und sein Historiker: Zur historischen Kritik der Apostelgeschichte." *Theologische Beiträge* 24 (1993): 62–84.

Bourke, M. M. "Reflections on Church Order in the NT." *Catholic Biblical Quarterly* 30 (1968): 493–511.

Bousset, W. *Kyrios Christos: A History of the Belief in Christ from the Beginnings of Christianity to Irenaeus*. Translated by J. E. Steely. Nashville: Abingdon, 1970.

Bowersock, G. W. *Augustus and the Greek World*. Oxford: Clarendon, 1965.

Bradley, D. G. "The TOPOS as a Form in Pauline Paraenesis." *Journal of Biblical Literature* 72 (1953): 238–46.

Branick, V. *The House Church in the Writings of Paul*. Wilmington, Delaware: Michael Glazier, 1989.

Braun, H. *Qumran und das Neue Testament*. 2 vols. Tübingen: Mohr, 1966.

Bringmann, K. "Sallusts Umgang mit der historischen Wahrheit in seiner Darstellung der Catilinarischen Verschwörung." *RMP* 114 (1971): 98–113.

Brockhaus, U. *Charisma und Amt: Die paulinische Charismenlehre auf dem Hintergrund der frühchristlichen Gemeindefunktionen*. Wuppertal: Brockhaus, 1972. Repr., Wissenschaftliche Tschenbücher 8. Wuppertal: Brockhaus, 1987.

Broek, R. van den. "Der Brief des Jakobus an Quadratus und das Problem der judenchristlichen Bischöfe von Jerusalem (Eusebius, HE 4:1–3)." Pages 56–65 in *Text and Testimony: Essays on New Testament and Apocryphal Literature*. Festschrift A. F. J. Klijn. Edited by T. Baarda et al. Kampen, Neth.: J. H. Kok, 1988.

Brooten, B. J. "Junia . . . hervorragend unter den Aposteln (Rom 16:7)." Pages 148–51 in *Frauenbefreiung: Biblische und theologische Argumente*. Edited by E. Moltmann-Wendel. Munich: Kaiser, 1978.

———. *Women Leaders in the Ancient Synagogue: Inscriptional Evidence and Background Issues*. Chico, Calif.: Scholars Press, 1982.

Broshi, M. "Excavations on Mount Zion, 1971–72: Preliminary Report." *Israel Exploration Journal* 26 (1976): 83–86.

———. "The Population of Western Palestine in the Roman-Byzantine Period." *Bulletin of the American Schools of Oriental Research* 236 (1979): 1–10.

———. "The Role of the Temple in the Herodian Economy." *Journal of Jewish Studies* 38, no. 1 (1987): 31–37.

Brown, G. T. *Christianity in the People's Republic of China*. 2d ed. Atlanta: John Knox, 1986.

Brown, R. E. *The Churches the Apostles Left Behind*. New York: Paulist Press, 1984.

———. *The Community of the Beloved Disciple*. New York: Paulist Press, 1979.

———. *Priest and Bishop: Biblical Reflections*. Paramus: Paulist, 1970.

Browne, H. *John Chrysostom: Homilies on the Acts of the Apostles*. Translated by J. Walker and J. Sheppard. Library of the Fathers. Oxford: J. H. Parker, 1851.

Bruce, F. F. "Laodicea." *ABD* 4:229–31.

———. *Men and Movements in the Primitive Church*. Exeter: Paternoster, 1979.

———. *The New Testament Documents: Are They Reliable?* Grand Rapids: Eerdmans, 1960.

———. *Paul: Apostle of the Free Spirit*. Exeter: Paternoster, 1977.

———. "St. Paul in Macedonia, 3: The Philippian Correspondence." *Bulletin of the John Rylands University Library of Manchester* 63 (1980/1981): 260–84.

Bruce, M., and G. E. Duffield, eds. *Why Not? Priesthood and the Ministry of Women*. Appleford: Marcham Manor Press, 1972.

Brunner, O. "Das 'ganze Haus' und die alteuropäische 'Ökonomik.'" Pages 33–61 in *Neue Wege der Verfassungs- und Sozialgeschichte*. Göttingen: Vandenhoeck & Ruprecht, 1956.

Brunner, P. "Theologie der Ehe als ökumenische Aufgabe." Pages 216–44 in *Bemühungen um die einigende Wahrheit: Aufsätze*. Göttingen: Vandenhoeck & Ruprecht, 1977.

Buchanan, G. W. "Jesus and the Upper Classes." *Novum Testamentum* 7 (1964): 195–209.

Bühner, J. A. "καθίστημι." *EDNT* 2:225–26.

Bultmann, R. *Exegetica: Aufsätze zur Erforschung des Neuen Testaments.* Edited by G. Dinkler. Tübingen: Mohr, 1967.
———. *Die Geschichte der synoptischen Tradition.* 9th ed. Göttingen: Vandenhoeck & Ruprecht, 1979.
———. *Jesus.* Tübingen: Mohr, 1926. 5th ed., 1988.
Burchard, C. *Der dreizehnte Zeuge.* FRLANT 103. Göttingen: Vandenhoeck & Ruprecht, 1970.
Burkitt, F. C. "The Last Supper and the Paschal Meal." *Journal of Theological Studies* 17 (1916): 291–97.
Burtchaell, J. T. *From Synagogue to Church: Public Services and Offices in the Earliest Christian Communities.* Cambridge: Cambridge University, 1992.
Burney, C. F. *The Poetry of Our Lord: An Examinaion of the Formal Elements of Hebrew Poetry in the Discourses of Jesus Christ.* Oxford: Clarendon, 1925.
Byatt, A. "Josephus and Population Numbers in First Century Palestine." *Palestine Exploration Quarterly* (1973): 51–60.
Cadbury, H. J. "Erastus of Corinth." *Journal of Biblical Literature* 50 (1931): 42–58.
———. "Lexical Notes on Luke-Acts, III: Luke's Interest in Lodging." *Journal of Biblical Literature* 45 (1926): 305–22.
———. "Luke—Translator or Author?" *American Journal of Theology* 24 (1920): 454.
———. *Style and Literary Method of Luke.* Cambridge, Mass.: Harvard University, 1920.
Caird, G. B. *The Apostolic Age.* London: G. Duckworth, 1955.
———. "Paul and Women's Liberty." *Bulletin of the John Rylands University Library of Manchester* 54 (1971/1972): 268–81.
Campbell, R. A. "Does Paul Acquiesce in Divisions at the Lord's Supper?" *Novum Testamentum* 33 (1991): 61–70.
———. "The Elders of the Jerusalem Church." *Journal of Theological Studies* 44 (1993): 511–28.
———. *The Elders: Seniority within Earliest Christianity.* Studies of the New Testament and Its World. Edinburgh: T&T Clark, 1994.
Campenhausen, H. von. *Kirchliches Amt und geistliche Vollmacht in den ersten drei Jahrhunderten.* 2d ed. BHT 14. Tübingen: Mohr, 1963.
Cannon, G. E. *The Use of Traditional Materials in Colossians.* Macon: Mercer University, 1983.
Capper, B. J. "The Community of Goods of the Early Jerusalem Church." *ANRW* 26.2:1730–74. Part 2. *Principat,* 26.2. Edited by H. Temporini and W. Haase. New York: de Gruyter, 1979.
———. "The Palestinian Cultural Context of Earliest Christian Community of Goods." Pages 323–56 in *The Book of Acts in Its Palestinian Setting.* Edited by R. Bauckam. Vol. 4 of *The Book of Acts in Its First Century Setting.* Edited by B. W. Winter. Grand Rapids: Eerdmans, 1995.
———. "PANTA KOINA: Earliest Christian Community of Goods in Its Hellenistic and Jewish Contexts." ThD diss., Cambridge University, 1986.
Carcopino, J. *Daily Life in Ancient Rome.* Translated by E. O. Lorimer. New Haven: Yale, 1959.

Carey, G., et al. *Planting New Churches*. Edited by B. Hopkins and T. Anderson et al. Guildford: Eagle, 1988.

Chapple, A. L. "Local Leadership in Pauline Churches: Theological and Social Factors in Its Development—a Study Based on 1 Thessalonians, 1 Corinthians, and Philippians." PhD diss., University of Durham, 1984.

Charlesworth, J. H. *The Old Testament Pseudepigrapha and the New Testament*. Cambridge: Cambridge University, 1985.

―――. "The Origin and Subsequent History of the Authors of the Dead Sea Scrolls." *Revue de Qumran* 10 (1980): 213–33.

Chin, M. "A Heavenly Home for the Homeless." *Tyndale Bulletin* 42, no. 1 (1991): 96–112.

Chow, J. K. *Patronage and Power: A Study of Social Networks in Corinth*. JSNTSup 75. Sheffield, Engl.: JSOT, 1992.

Christ, K. *Geschichte der römischen Kaiserzeit: Von Augustus bis Konstantin*. Munich: C. H. Beck, 1988.

―――. "Grundfragen der römischen Sozialstruktur." Pages 152–76 in *Geschichte und Geschichtsschreibung der römischen Kaiserzeit*. Vol. 2 of *Römische Geschichte und Wissenschaftsgeschichte*. Darmstadt: Wissenschaftliche Buchgesellschaft, 1983.

Clark, S. B. *Building Christian Communities: A Strategy for Renewing the Church*. Notre Dame, Ind.: Ave Maria, 1978.

―――. *Man and Woman in Christ: An Examination of the Roles of Men and Women in Light of Scripture and the Social Sciences*. Ann Arbor: Servant Books, 1980.

Clarke, A. D. *Secular and Christian Leadership in Corinth: A Socio-historical and Exegetical Study of 1 Cor 1–6*. Leiden: Brill, 1993.

Clarke, J. R. *The Houses of Roman Italy, 100 BC–AD 250: Ritual, Space, and Decoration*. Berkeley: University of California, 1993.

Claussen, C. *Versammlung, Gemeinde Synagoge: Das hellenistisch-jüdische Umfeld der frühchristlichen Gemeinden*. Göttingen: Vandenhoeck & Ruprecht, 2002.

Cohen, S. J. D., ed. *The Jewish Family in Antiquity*. BJS 289. Atlanta: Scholars Press, 1993.

Conzelmann, H. *Geschichte des Urchristentums*. 5th ed. GNT 5. Göttingen: Vandenhoeck & Ruprecht, 1983.

Corbo, V. C. "Capernaum." *ABD* 1:866–69.

―――. "The Church of the House of St. Peter at Capernaum." Pages 71–76 in *Ancient Churches Revealed*. Edited by Y. Tsafrir. Jerusalem: Israel Exploration Society, 1993.

―――. *Gli edifici della città*. Vol. 1 of *Cafarnao*. PSBF 19/1. Jerusalem: Franciscan Printing Press, 1975.

―――. *The House of St. Peter at Capharnaum: A Preliminary Report of the First Two Campaigns of Excavations, 1968*. Translated by S. Saller. PSBF.Mi 5. Jerusalem: Franciscan Printing Press, 1969.

―――. "Resti della sinagoga del primo secolo a Cafarnao." *Studia Hierosolymitana* 3 (1982): 313–57.

Corwin, V. *St. Ignatius and Christianity in Antioch*. New Haven: Yale, 1960.

Countryman, W. *The Rich Christian in the Church of the Empire: Contradictions and Accommodations*. New York: Edwin Mellen, 1980.

Courtois, S., ed. *Das Schwarzbuch des Kommunismus*. Munich: Piper, 1998.
Covolo, E. dal. "Una 'domus ecclesiae' a Roma sotto l'impero di Alessandro Severo?" *Ephemerides liturgicae* 102 (1988): 64–71.
Cowan, M. C., and B. J. Lee. *Dangerous Memories: House Churches and Our American Story*. Kansas City: Sheed & Ward, 1986.
Coyle, J. K. "Empire and Eschaton: The Early Church and the Question of Domestic Relationships." *Eglise et théologie* 12 (1981): 35–94.
Crosby, M. H. *House of Disciples: Church, Economics, and Justice in Matthew*. Maryknoll, N.Y.: Orbis Books, 1988.
Crouch, J. E. *The Origin and Intention of the Colossian Haustafel*. FRLANT 109. Göttingen: Vandenhoeck & Ruprecht, 1972.
Cullmann, O. *Das Gebet im Neuen Testament: Zugleich Versuch einer vom Neuen Testament aus zu erteilenden Antwort auf heutige Fragen*. Tübingen: Mohr, 1994.
D'Arms, J. "The Roman Convivium and the Idea of Equality." Pages 308–20 in *Sympotica: A Symposium on the Symposium*. Edited by O. Murray. Oxford: Clarendon, 1990.
Dalman, G. *Das Haus, Hühnerzucht, Taubenzucht, Bienenzucht*. Vol. 7 of *Arbeit und Sitte in Palästina*. BFChTh.M 48. Gütersloh: C. Bertelsmann, 1942.
———. *Jerusalem und sein Gelände*. Gütersloh: C. Bertelsmann, 1930.
———. *Orte und Wege Jesu*. 3d ed. BFCT 2/1. Gütersloh: C. Bertelsmann, 1924.
———. *Die Worte Jesu*. 2d ed. Darmstadt: Hinrichs, 1930. Repr., Darmstadt: Wissenschaftliche Buchgesellschaft, 1965.
Daniélou, J. *The Dead Sea Scrolls and Primitive Christianity*. New York: New American Library of World Literature, 1958.
Danker, F. W. *Benefactor: Epigraphic Study of a Graeco-Roman and New Testament Semantic Field*. St. Louis: Clayton Publishing House, 1982.
———. "The υἱός Phrases in the New Testament." *New Testament Studies* 7 (1960/1961): 94.
Dar, S. *Landscape and Pattern: An Archaeological Survey of Samaria, 800 B.C.E.–636 C.E.* 2 vols. Oxford: B. A. R., 1986.
Dassmann, E. "Hausgemeinde und Bischofsamt." Pages 82–97 in *Vivarium*. Festschrift T. Klauser. JAC.E 11. Münster: Aschendorff, 1984. Repr., pages 74–95 in *Ämter und Dienste in den frühchristlichen Gemeinden*. Hereditas Studien zur alten Kirchengeschichte 8. Bonn: Borengässer, 1994.
Dassmann, E., and G. Schöllgen. "Haus II." *RAC* 13:801–905.
Daube, D. "Responsibilities of Master and Disciples in the Gospels." *New Testament Studies* 19 (1972/1973): 1–15.
Dauer, A. *Paulus und die christliche Gemeinde im syrischen Antiochia: Kritische Bestandsaufnahme der modernen Forschung mit einigen weiterführenden Überlegungen*. BBB 106. Weinheim: Beltz Athenäum, 1996.
Dautzenberg, G. *Urchristliche Prophetie: Ihre Erforschung, ihre Voraussetzungen im Judentum, und ihre Struktur im ersten Korintherbrief*. BWA(N)T 104. Stuttgart: Kohlhammer, 1975.
———. "Der Verzicht auf das apostolische Unterhaltsrecht: Eine exegetische Untersuchung zu 1Kor 9." *Biblica* 50 (1969): 212–32.

———. "Zur Stellung der Frauen in der paulinischen Gemeinden." Pages 182–224 in *Die Frau im Urchristentum*. QD 95. Freiburg: Herder, 1983.
Davies, W. D. *The Setting of the Sermon on the Mount*. Cambridge: Cambridge University, 1963.
Deissmann, A. *Licht vom Osten: Das Neue Testament und die neuentdeckten Texte der hellenistisch-römischen Welt*. 4th ed. Tübingen: Mohr, 1923.
———. *Das Urchristentum und die unteren Schichten*. 2d ed. Göttingen: Vandenhoeck & Ruprecht, 1908.
Delling, G. *Paulus' Stellung zu Frau und Ehe*. BWA(N)T 56. Stuttgart: Kohlhammer, 1931.
———. "προσλαμβάνω." *TDNT* 4:15.
———. "ὑποτάσσω." *TDNT* 8:39–46.
———. "Zur Taufe von 'Häusern' im Urchristentum." *Novum Testamentum* 7 (1965): 285–311. Repr., pages 288–310 in *Studien zum Neuen Testament und zum hellenistischen Judentum: Gesammelte Aufsätze, 1950–1968*. Göttingen: Vandenhoeck & Ruprecht, 1970.
Derrett, J. D. M. *Jesus' Audience: The Social and Psychological Environment in Which He Worked*. London: Darton, Longman & Todd, 1973.
Dibelius, M. *Aufsätze zur Apostelgeschichte*. 5th ed. Edited by H. Greeven. FRLANT 60. Göttingen: Vandenhoeck & Ruprecht, 1968.
———. *Paulus*. Edited by W. G. Kümmel. 4th ed. SG 1160. Berlin: de Gruyter, 1970.
Dinkler, E. "Dura-Europos III." *RGG* 2:290–92.
Dittenberger, W. *Sylloge inscriptionum graecarum*. 3d ed. 4 vols. Lipsiae: Hirzelium, 1915–1924.
Dix, G. *The Shape of Liturgy*. London: Dacre Press, 1978.
Dixon, S. *The Roman Family*. Baltimore: Johns Hopkins University, 1991.
Dodd, C. H. *Der Mann, nach dem wir Christen heissen*. Limburg: Lahn-Verlag, 1975.
———. *New Testament Studies*. 3d ed. Manchester: University Press, 1967.
Dombrowski, B. W. "היחד in 1QS and τὸ κοινόν: An Instance of Early Greek and Jewish Synthesis." *Harvard Theological Review* 59 (1966): 293–307.
Dömer, M. *Das Heil Gottes: Studien zur Theologie des lukanischen Doppelwerkes*. BBB 51. Cologne: Hanstein, 1978.
Donfried, K. P. "The Cults of Thessalonica and the Thessalonian Correspondence." *New Testament Studies* 31 (1985): 342–44.
———, ed. *The Romans Debate*. 2d ed. Peabody, Mass.: Hendrickson, 1991.
———. "A Short Note on Romans 16." *Journal of Biblical Literature* 89 (1979): 441–49.
Döring, H. *Grundriss der Ekklesiologie: Zentrale Aspekte des katholischen Selbstverständnisses und ihre ökumenische Relevanz*. Darmstadt: Wissenschaftliche Buchgesellschaft, 1986.
Downey, G. *A History of Antioch in Syria from Seleucus to the Arab Conquest*. Princeton: Princeton University, 1961.
Duncan-Jones, R. *The Economy of the Roman Empire: Quantitative Studies*. Cambridge: Cambridge University, 1982.
Dungan, D. L. *The Sayings of Jesus in the Churches of Paul: The Use of the Synoptic Tradition in the Regulation of Early Church Life*. Philadelphia: Fortress Press, 1971.

Dunn, J. D. G. "The Incident at Antioch (Gal 2:11–18)." *Journal for the Study of the New Testament* 18 (1983): 3–75.
———. "The Relationship between Paul and Jerusalem according to Galations 1 and 2." *New Testament Studies* 28 (1982): 461–78.
———. *Unity and Diversity in the New Testament*. 2d ed. London: SCM Press, 1990.
Dürr, L. "Heilige Vaterschaft im Alten Orient." Pages 1–20 in *Heilige Überlieferung: Ausschnitte der Geschichte des Mönchtums und des heiligen Kultes*. Edited by Odo Casel. Münster: Aschendorff, 1938.
Ebner, E. *Elementary Education in Israel during the Tannaitic Period (10–220 C.E.)*. New York: Bloch, 1956.
Edwards, D. R. "First Century Urban/Rural Relations in Lower Galilee." Pages 169–82 in *SBL Seminar Papers, 1988*. SBLSP 124. Atlanta, Ga.: Scholars Press, 1988.
———. "The Socio-economic and Cultural Ethos of the Lower Galilee in the First Century: Implications for the Nascent Jesus Movement." Pages 53–73 in *The Galilee in Late Antiquity*. Edited by L. I. Levine. New York: Jewish Theological Seminary of America, 1992.
Ehrhardt, A. *The Acts of the Apostles: Ten Lectures*. Manchester: Manchester University, 1969.
Eichholz, G. *Die Theologie des Paulus im Umriss*. 9th ed. Neukirchen: Neukirchener, 1991.
Eickhoff, K. *Gemeinde entwickeln für die Volkskirche der Zukunft: Anregung zur Praxis*. Göttingen: Vandenhoeck & Ruprecht, 1992.
Eisen, U. E. *Amtsträgerinnen im frühen Christentum: Epigraphische und literarische Studien*. Göttingen: Vandenhoeck & Ruprecht, 1996.
Eiss, W. "Das Amt des Gemeindeleiters bei den Essenern und der christliche Episkopat." *Die Welt des Orients* 2 (1954–1959): 514–19.
Elbogen, I. "Eingang und Ausgang des Sabbats nach talmudischen Quellen." Pages 173–87 in *Festschrift zu Israel Lewy's siebzigtem Geburtstag*. Edited by M. Braun and J. Elbogen. Breslau: M. & H. Marcus, 1911.
———. *Der jüdische Gottesdienst in seiner geschichtlichen Entwicklung*. 3d ed. Frankfurt: J. Kauffmann, 1931. Repr., Hildesheim: G. Olms, 1967.
Elliger, W. *Ephesos, Geschichte einer antiken Weltstadt*. Stuttgart: Kohlhammer, 1985.
———. *Paulus in Griechenland: Philippi, Thessaloniki, Athen, Korinth*. SBS 92/93. Stuttgart: Katholisches Bibelwerk, 1978.
Elliott, J. H. *A Home for the Homeless: A Sociological Exegesis of 1 Peter, Its Situation and Strategy*. Philadelphia: Fortress, 1981.
———. "Philemon and House Churches." *The Bible Today* 22, no. 3 (1984): 145–50.
———. "Social-Scientific Criticism of the New Testament and Its Social World: More on Methods and Models." *Semeia* 36 (1986): 1–34.
———. "Temple versus Household in Luke-Acts: A Contrast in Social Institutions." *Hervormde teologiese studies* 47 (1991): 88–120.
Ellis, E. E. "New Directions in Form Criticism." Pages 299–315 in *Jesus Christus in Historie und Theologie*. Festschrift H. Conzelmann. Edited by G. Strecker. Tübingen: Mohr, 1975.

———. *Pauline Theology: Ministry and Society*. Grand Rapids: Eerdmans, 1989.
———. "The Role of the Christian Prophet in Acts." Pages 55–67 in *Apostolic History and the Gospel: Biblical and Historical Essays*. Festschrift F. F. Bruce. Edited by W. W. Gasque and R. P. Martin. Exeter: Paternoster, 1970.
———. "The Silenced Wives of Corinth (I Cor. 14,34–5)." Pages 213–20 in *New Testament Textual Criticism: Its Significance for Exegesis*. Edited by E. J. Epp and G. D. Fee. Oxford: Clarendon, 1981.
Esler, P. F. *Community and Gospel in Luke-Acts: The Social and Political Motivations of Lukan Theology*. SNTSMS 57. Cambridge: Cambridge University, 1987.
Falk, D. K. "Jewish Prayer Literature and the Jerusalem Church in Acts." Pages 267–301 in *The Book of Acts in Its Palestinian Setting*. Edited by R. Bauckham. Vol. 4 of *The Book of Acts in Its First Century Setting*. Edited by B. W. Winter. Grand Rapids: Eerdmans, 1995.
Falk, Z. W. *Introduction to Jewish Law of the Second Commonwealth*. Vol. 2. Leiden: Brill, 1978.
———. "Jewish Private Law." Pages 504–34 in *The Jewish People in the First Century*. Edited by S. Safrai and M. Stern. CRINT I/1. Assen: Van Gorcum, 1974–1976.
Farrer, A. M. "The Ministry in the New Testament." Pages 113–82 in *The Apostolic Ministry: Essays on the History and the Doctrine of Episcopacy*. Edited by K. E. Kirk. 2d ed. London: Hodder and Stoughton, 1947.
Ferguson, E. "Jewish and Christian Ordination." *Harvard Theological Review* 56 (1963): 13–20.
———. "Laying on of Hands: Its Significance for Ordination." *Journal of Theological Studies* 26 (1975): 1–12.
———. "Ordain, Ordination." *ABD* 5:37–40.
———. "When You Come Together: *Epi to auto* in Early Christian Literature." *Restoration Quarterly* 16 (1973): 202–8.
Fiechter, E. "Haus." PW 7:2523–46.
———. "Römisches Haus." PWSup 1:961–95.
Fiedler, P. "Haustafel." *RAC* 13:1063–73.
———. *Jesus und die Sünder*. BBET 3. Frankfurt: Lang, 1976.
Fiensy, D. A. "The Composition of the Jerusalem Church." Pages 213–36 in *The Book of Acts in Its Palestinian Setting*. Edited by R. Bauckham. Vol. 4 of *The Book of Acts in Its First Century Setting*. Edited by B. W. Winter. Grand Rapids: Eerdmans, 1995.
———. *The Social History of Palestine in the Herodian Period*. SBEC 20. Lewiston, N.Y.: Mellen, 1991.
Filson, F. V. *Geschichte des Christentum in neutestamentlicher Zeit*. Translated and revised by F. J. Schierse. Düsseldorf: Patmos, 1967.
———. "The Significance of the Early House Churches." *Journal of Biblical Literature* 58 (1939): 105–12.
Finegan, J. *The Archeology of the New Testament: The Life of Jesus and the Beginnings of the Early Church*. Princeton: Princeton University, 1969.
Finger, R. Halteman. *Paul and the Roman House Churches*. Scottdale, Pa.: Herald Press, 1993.

Finley, M. I. *The Ancient Economy*. London: Chatto and Windus, 1973.
———. *Die antike Wirtschaft*. 2d ed. DTV WR 4277. Munich: Deutsche Taschenbuch, 1980.
———. *Atlas der klassischen Archäologie*. Munich: List, 1979.
Finney, P. C. "Early Christian Architecture: The Beginning." Review Article. *Harvard Theological Review* 81 (1988): 319–39.
Fitzmyer, J. A. *Essays on the Semitic Background of the NT*. London: G. Chapman, 1971.
———. *Jewish Christianity in Acts in Light of the Qumran Scrolls: Essays on the Semitic Background of the New Testament*. London: G. Chapman, 1971.
Fjärstedt, B. *Synoptic Tradition in 1 Corinthians: Themes and Clusters of Theme Words in 1 Corinthians 1–4 and 9*. Uppsala: Uppsala University, Teologiska Institutionen, 1974.
Flusser, D. "Qumran and the Famine during the Reign of Herod." *Israel Museum Journal* 8 (1987): 7–16.
Foerster, G. "The Ancient Synagogues of the Galilee." Pages 289–319 in *The Galilee in Late Antiquity*. Edited by L. I. Levine. New York: Jewish Theological Seminary of America, 1992.
Foerster, W. "ἀνθρωπάρεσκος." *TDNT* 1:456.
———. "εἰρήνη." *TDNT* 2:400–417.
———. "Ἰησοῦς." *TDNT* 3:284–93.
Forestell, J. T. *Targumic Traditions and the New Testament*. Chico, Calif.: Scholars Press, 1979.
Foster, A. L. *The House Church Evolving*. Chicago: Exploration, 1976.
Foster, J. "St. Paul and Women." *Expository Times* 62 (1950/1951): 376–78.
France, R. T. "Mark and the Teachings of Jesus." Pages 101–36 in vol. 1 of *Gospel Perspectives: Studies of History and Tradition in the Four Gospels*. Edited by R. T. France and D. Wenham. Sheffield, Engl.: JSOT Press, 1980.
Frankemölle, H., ed. *Kirche von unten: Alternative Gemeinden—Modelle-Erfahrungen-Reflexionen*. Mainz: Grünewald, 1981.
Freyne, S. *Galilee from Alexander the Great to Hadrian, 323 B.C.E. to 135 C.E.* Notre Dame: University of Notre Dame Press, 1980.
———. *Galilee, Jesus, and the Gospels*. Philadelphia: Fortress Press, 1988.
———. "Urban-Rural Relations in First-Century Galilee: Some Suggestions from the Literary Sources." Pages 75–91 in *The Galilee in Late Antiquity*. Edited by L. I. Levine. New York: Jewish Theological Seminary of America, 1992.
Friedel, E. "Der neutestamentliche Oikos-Begriff in seiner Bedeutung für den Gemeindebau." Pages 89–106 in *Domine, dirige me in Verbo tuo: Herr, leite mich nach deinem Wort! Festschrift D. M. Mitzenheim*. Berlin: Evangelische Verlagsanstalt, 1961.
Friedländer, L. *Darstellungen aus der Sittengeschichte Roms in der Zeit von Augustus bis zum Ausgang der Antonine*. Vol. 1. Aalen, Germany: Scientia, 1979.
Frier, B. W. *Landlords and Tenants in Imperial Rome*. Princeton: Princeton University, 1980.
Funk, A. "Mann und Frau in den Briefen des Heiligen Paulus." *Una sancta: Rundbriefe für interkonfessionelle Begegnung* 32 (1977): 280–85.

Furnish, V. P. "Corinth in Paul's Time: What Can Archaeology Tell Us?" *Biblical Archaeology Review* 15 (1988): 14–27.
Gager, J. G. *Kingdom and Community: The Social World of Early Christianity*. Englewood Cliffs: Prentice-Hall, 1975.
———. Review of books by Grant, Malherbe, and Theissen. *Religious Studies Review* 5 (1979): 174–80.
Gamber, K. *Domus Ecclesiae: Die Ältesten Kichenbauten Aquilejas sowie im Alpen- und Donaugebiet bis zum Beginn des 5. Jahrhunderts liturgiegeschichtlich untersucht*. SPLi 2. Regensburg: Pustet, 1968.
———. "Die frühchristliche Hauskirche nach Didascalia apostolorum II 57:1–58:6." *Studia patristica* 10 (1970): 337–44.
Gamble, H., Jr. *The Textual History of the Letter to the Romans: A Study in Textual and Literary Criticism*. SD 42. Grand Rapids: Eerdmans, 1977.
Garland, D. E. "Matthew's Understanding of the Temple Tax (Mt 17:24–27)." Pages 190–209 in *SBL Seminar Papers, 1987*. SBLSP 123. Atlanta, Ga.: Scholars Press, 1987.
Garnsey, P. *Famine and Food Supply in the Graeco-Roman World: Responses to Risk and Crisis*. Cambridge: Cambridge University, 1988.
Garnsey P., and R. Saller. *The Roman Empire: Economy, Society, and Culture*. Berkeley: University of California Press, 1987.
Gaudemet, J. "Familie." *RAC* 7:286–358.
Gehring, R. W. *Hausgemeinde und Mission*. BWM 9. Giessen, Germany: Brunnen, 2000.
Geis, R. R. *Vom unbekannten Judentum*. HerBü 102. Freiburg: Herder, 1961.
George, C. F. *Prepare Your Church for the Future*. Grand Rapids: Revell, 1992.
Georgi, D. *Die Gegner des Paulus im 2. Korintherbrief: Studien zur religiösen Propaganda in der Spätantike*. WMANT 11. Neukirchen-Vluyn: Neukirchener Verlag, 1964.
Gerhardsson, B. *Anfänge der Evangelientradition*. Wuppertal: Brockhaus, 1977.
———. *Memory and Manuscript: Oral Tradition and Written Transmission in Rabbinic Judaism and Early Christianity*. 2d ed. ASNU 22. Lund, Sweden: C. W.K. Gleerup, 1964.
Gerkan, A. von. "Zur Hauskirche von Dura-Europos." Pages 143–49 in *Mullus*. Festschrift T. Klauser. Edited by A. Stuiber and A. Hermann. JAC.E 1. Münster: Aschendorff, 1964.
Gese, H. "Der Dekalog als Ganzheit betrachtet." *Zeitschrift für Theologie und Kirche* 64 (1967): 121–38.
Geus, C. de. "The Profile of an Israelite City." *Biblical Archaeologist* 49 (1986): 224–27.
Gevaryahu, H. M. I. "Privathäuser als Versammlungsstätten von Meistern und Jüngern." *Annual of the Swedish Theological Institute* 12 (1983): 5–12.
Gibson, M. D. "The House in Which the Last Supper Was Held." *Journal of Theological Studies* 17 (1916): 398.
Gielen, M. *Tradition und Theologie neutestamentlicher Haustafelethik: Ein Beitrag zur Frage einer christlichen Auseinandersetzung mit gesellschaftlichen Normen*. BBB 75. Frankfurt: Hain, 1990.
———. "Zur Interpretation der paulinischen Formel ἡ κατ' οἶκον ἐκκλησία." *Zeitschrift für die neutestamentliche Wissenschaft und die Kunde der älteren Kirche* 77 (1986): 109–25.

Giesekke, F. "Zur Glaubwürdigkeit von Apg 16:25–34." *TSK* 71 (1989): 348–51.
Gillman, J. "Paul's εἴσοδος: The Proclaimed and the Proclaimer (1Thes 2:8)." Pages 62–70 in *The Thessalonian Correspondence*. Edited by R. F. Collins. BETL 87. Leuven: Leuven University, 1990.
Gnilka, J. "Die neutestamentliche Hausgemeinde." Pages 229–42 in *Freude am Gottesdienst: Aspekte ursprünglicher Liturgie*. Edited by J. Schreiner. Stuttgart: Katholisches Bibelwerk, 1983.
———. *Die Verstockung Israels: Jes. 6:10 in der Theologie der Synoptiker.* SANT 3. Munich: Kösel-Verlag, 1961.
Goetz, K. G. "Ist der מבקר der Genizafragmente wirklich das Vorbild des christlichen Episkopats?" *Zeitschrift für die neutestamentliche Wissenschaft und die Kunde der älteren Kirche* 30 (1931): 89–93.
Goetzmann, J. "Haus, bauen." *TBLNT* 2/1: 636–45.
Goldhahn-Müller, I. *Die Grenze der Gemeinde: Studien zum Problem der Zweiten Busse im Neuen Testament unter Berücksichtigung der Entwicklung im 2. Jh. bis Tertullian*. GTA 39. Göttingen: Vandenhoeck & Ruprecht, 1989.
Goodman, M. *State and Society in Roman Galilee, A.D. 132–212*. Totowa, N.J.: Rowman & Allanheld, 1983.
Goodspeed, E. J. "Gaius Titius Justus." *Journal of Biblical Literature* 69 (1950): 382–83.
Goppelt, L. *Die apostolische und nachapostolische Zeit*. 2d ed. KIG 1. Göttingen: Vandenhoeck & Ruprecht, 1966. ET: *Apostolic and Post-Apostolic Times*. Translated by R. A. Guelich. Grand Rapids: Baker, 1980.
———. "Jesus und die 'Haustafel'-Tradition." Pages 93–106 in *Orientierung an Jesus, zur Theologie der Synoptiker*. Festschrift J. Schmid. Edited by P. Hoffmann, N. Brox, and W. Pesch. Freiburg: Herder, 1973.
Gorman, J. A. *Community That Is Christian: A Handbook on Small Groups*. Wheaton, Ill.: Victor Books, 1993.
Gowan, D. E. *Bridge between the Testaments: A Reappraisal of Judaism from the Exile to the Birth of Christianity*. 2d ed. PTMS 14. Pittsburgh: Pickwick Press, 1980.
Graham, W. J. "Origins and Interrelations of the Greek House and the Roman House." *Phoenix* 20 (1966): 3–31.
Grant, R. M. *Christen als Bürger im Römischen Reich*. Göttingen: Vandenhoeck & Ruprecht, 1981.
———. *Early Christianity and Society*. San Francisco: Harper & Row, 1977.
Green, E. M. B. "Kolossä." *GBL* 2:803–5.
Green, E. M. B., and C. J. Hemer. "Ephesus." *GBL* 1:319–21.
Green, M. *Evangelism in the Early Church*. Grand Rapids: Eerdmans, 1970.
Greeven, H. "Propheten, Lehrer, und Vorsteher bei Paulus: Zur Frage der 'Ämter' im Urchristentum." Pages 305–61 in *Das kirchliche Amt im Neuen Testament*. Edited by K. Kertelge. WdF 439. Darmstadt: Wissenschaftliche Buchgesellschaft, 1977.
Grelot, P. "Sur l'origine des ministères dans les églises pauliniennes." *Istina* 16 (1971): 453–69.
Grenfell B. P., and A. S. Hunt, eds. *Oxyrhynchus Papyri*. Part 1. London: Egypt Exploration Fund, 1898.

Grenz, S. J., and D. Muir Kjesbo. *Women in the Church: A Biblical Theology of Women in Ministry*. Downers Grove: InterVarsity, 1995.

Grimm, B. *Untersuchungen zur sozialen Stellung der frühen Christen in der römischen Gesellschaft*. Munich: B. Grimm, 1975.

Gross, W. H. "Haus." *KlPauly* 2:957–61.

Grudem, W. "The meaning of Kephale ('Head')." Pages 425–68 in *Recovering Biblical Manhood and Womanhood: A Response to Evangelical Feminism*. Edited by J. Piper and W. Grudem. Wheaton, Ill.: Crossway, 1991.

Gülzow, H. *Christentum und Sklaverei in den ersten drei Jahrhunderten*. Bonn: R. Habelt, 1969.

———. *Kirche und Sklaverei in den ersten zwei Jahrhunderten*. Kiel: Universitatsbibliotek Kiel, 1966.

———. "Soziale Gegebenheiten der altkirchlichen Mission." Pages 189–226 in *Die Alte Kirche*. Vol. 1 of *Kirchengeschichte als Missionsgeschichte*. Edited by H. Frohnes and U. W. Knorr. Munich: Kaiser, 1974.

Gunther, J. J. *Paul, Messenger and Exile: A Study in the Chronology of His Life and Letters*. Valley Forge: Judson Press, 1972.

Gutmann, J. *Ancient Synagogues: The State of Research*. Chico, Calif.: Scholars Press, 1981.

———, ed. *The Synagogue: Studies in Origins, Archaeology, and Architecture*. New York: Ktav, 1975.

Haenchen, E. *Der Weg Jesu: Eine Erklärung des Markusevangelium und der kanonischen Parallelen*. Berlin: Töpelmann, 1966.

Hahn, F. "Der urchristliche Gottesdienst." *Jahrbuch für Liturgik und Hymnologie* 12 (1967): 1–44.

———. *Das Verständnis der Mission im Neuen Testament*. WMANT 13. Neukirchen-Vluyn: Neukirchener Verlag des Erziehungsvereins, 1963.

Hainz, J. "Die Anfänge des Bischofs- und Diakonenamtes." Pages 91–107 in *Die Kirche im Werden*. Edited by J. Hainz. Munich: Paderborn, 1976.

———. *Ekklesia: Strukturen paulinischer Gemeinde-Theologie und Gemeinde-Ordnung*. BU 9. Regensburg: Pustet, 1972.

Hall, J. F. "Rome." *ABD* 5:830–34.

Hamman, A. *Die Ersten Christen*. Translated by K. Schmidt. Stuttgart: Reclam, 1985.

Hampe, J. C. "Die integrierte Gemeinde." Pages 99–107 in *Alternativ leben in verbindlicher Gemeinschaft: Evangelische Kommunitäten, Lebensgemeinschaften, junge Bewegungen*. Edited by I. Reimer. Stuttgart: Quell-Verlag, 1979.

Harder, G. "Hausgemeinde." *BHH* 2:661.

Hardy, E. R. "The Priestess in the Greco-Roman World." Pages 58–65 in *Why Not? Priesthood and the Ministry of Women*. Edited by M. Bruce and G. E. Duffield. Appleford: Marcham Manor Press, 1972.

Harnack, A. von. *Die Apostelgeschichte*. Vol. 3 of *Beiträge zur Einleitung in das Neue Testament*. Leipzig: J. C. Hinrichs, 1908.

———. *Beiträge zur Einleitung in das Neue Testament*. 7 vols. Leipzig: J. C. Hinrichs, 1906–1911.

———. *Entstehung und Entwicklung der Kirchenverfassung und des Kirchenrechts in den zwei ersten Jahrhunderten*. Leipzig: J. C. Hinrichs, 1910.

———. "κόπος (κοπιάν, οἱ κοπιῶντες) im frühchristlichen Sprachgebrauch." *Zeitschrift für die neutestamentliche Wissenschaft und die Kunde der älteren Kirche* 27 (1928): 1–10.

———. "Die Lehre von den zwölf Aposteln." TUGAL 2/1. Leipzig: Hinrichs, 1884.

———. *Die Mission und Ausbreitung des Christentums in den ersten drei Jahrhunderten.* 2 vols. 4th ed. Leipzig: J. C. Hinrichs, 1924. ET: *The Mission and Expansion of Christianity in the First Three Centuries.* Translated by J. Moffatt. New York: Harper, 1962.

———. "Probabilia über die Adresse und den Verfasser des Hebräerbriefes." *Zeitschrift für die neutestamentliche Wissenschaft und die Kunde der älteren Kirche* 1 (1900): 16–41.

———. *Über den dritten Johannesbrief.* TUGAL 15/3b. Leipzig: J. C. Hinrichs, 1897.

———. "Über die beiden Rezensionen der Geschichte der Prisca und des Aquila in act.Apost. 18:1–27." Pages 48–61 in *Das Magnificat der Elizabet.* SPAW 27. Berlin: de Gruyter, 1900.

Harper, G. M. "Village Administration in the Roman Province of Syria." *Yale Classical Studies* 1 (1928): 105–68.

Harris, P., et al. *Breaking New Ground: Church Planting in the Church of England—a Report Commissioned by the House of Bishops of the General Synod of the Church of England.* London: Church House Publishing, 1994.

Harvey, A. E. "Elders." *Journal of Theological Studies* 25 (1974): 318–31.

———. "The Workman Is Worthy of His Hire." *Novum Testamentum* 24 (1982): 209–21.

Hatch, E. *The Organization of the Early Churches.* Bampton Lectures for 1880. 6th ed., London: Longmans, 1901.

Hauck, A. "Kirchenbau." *RE* 10:774–94.

Hauck, F. "κοινωνία." *TDNT* 3:797–809.

Hauke, M. *Die Problematik um das Frauenpriestertum vor dem Hintergrund der Schöpfungs- und Erlösungsordnung.* 3d ed. Paderborn: Bonifatius, 1991.

Heine, S. *Frauen der frühen Christenheit: Zur historischen Kritik einer feministischen Theologie.* 3d ed. Göttingen: Vandenhoeck & Ruprecht, 1990.

Heinrici, G. "Die Christengemeinde Korinths und die religiösen Genossenschaften der Griechen." *Zeitschrift für wissenschaftliche Theologie* 19 (1876): 465–526.

Helly, B. "Politarchs, poliarques, et politophylaques." Pages 531–44 in vol. 2 of *Ancient Macedonia.* Salonika: Institute for Balkan Studies, 1977.

Hemer, C. J. *The Book of Acts in the Setting of Hellenistic History.* Edited by C. H. Gempf. WUNT 49. Tübingen: Mohr, 1989.

———. *The Letters to the Seven Churches of Asia in Their Local Setting.* JSNTSup 11. Sheffield, Engl.: JSOT Press, 1986.

———. "Lydia and the Purple Trade." Page 53–55 in vol. 3 of *New Documents Illustrating Early Christianity: A Review of the Greek Inscriptions and Papyri.* Edited by G. H. R. Horsley. North Ryde, N. S. W.: Macquarie University, 1983.

Hendrix, H. L. "Philippi." *ABD* 5:313–17.

———. "Thessalonica." *ABD* 6:523–27.

Hengel, M. *Eigentum und Reichtum in der früheren Kirche: Aspekte einer frühchristlichen Sozialgeschichte.* Stuttgart: Calwer, 1973. ET: *Property and Riches in the Early Church: Aspects of a Social History of Early Christianity.* Translated by J. Bowden. Philadelphia: Fortress, 1974.

———. "Entstehungszeit und Situation des Markusevangeliums." Pages 1–45 in *Markus-Philologie.* Edited by H. Cancik. Tübingen: Mohr, 1984.

———. "Der Historiker Lukas und die Geographie Palästinas in der Apg." *Zeitschrift des deutschen Palästina-Vereins* 99 (1983): 147–83.

———. "Jakobus der Herrenbruder—der erste 'Papst'?" Pages 71–104 in *Glaube und Eschatologie.* Festschrift W. Kümmel. Edited by E. Grässer and O. Merk. Tübingen: Mohr, 1985.

———. "Jesus als messianischer Lehrer der Weisheit und der Anfänge der Christologie." Pages 148–88 in *Sagesse et religion: Colloque de Strasbourg, octobre 1976.* Paris: Presses universitaires de France, 1979.

———. *Die Johanneische Frage: Ein Lösungsversuch mit einem Beitrag zur Apokalypse von J. Frey.* WUNT 67. Tübingen: Mohr, 1993.

———. *The Johannine Question.* Translated by J. Bowden. London: SCM Press, 1989.

———. *Judentum und Hellenismus: Studien zu ihrer Begegnung unter besonderer Berücksichtigung Palästinas bis zur Mitte des 2. Jh. v. Chr.* 3d ed. WUNT 10. Tübingen: Mohr, 1988. ET: *Judaism and Hellenism: Studies in Their Encounter in Palestine during the Early Hellenistic Period.* Translated by J. Bowden. Philadelphia: Fortress, 1974.

———. "Maria Magdalena und die Frauen als Zeugen." Pages 243–56 in *Abraham unser Vater: Juden und Christen im Gespräch über dem Bibel.* Festschrift O. Michel. Edited by O. Betz, M. Hengel, and P. Schmidt. Leiden: Brill, 1963.

———. *Nachfolge und Charisma: Eine exegetisch-religionsgeschichtliche Studie zu Mt 8:21f und Jesu Ruf in die Nachfolge.* BZNW 34. Berlin: A. Töpelmann, 1968.

———. *The Origins of the Christian Mission: In Between Jesus and Paul.* London: SCM Press, 1983.

———. "Probleme des Markusevangeliums." Pages 221–65 in *Das Evangelium und die Evangelien.* Edited by P. Stuhlmacher. Tübingen: Mohr, 1983.

———. "Proseuche und Synagoge: Jüdische Gemeinde, Gotteshaus, und Gottesdienst in der Diaspora und in Palästina." Pages 157–84 in *Tradition und Glaube: Das frühe Christentum in seiner Umwelt.* Festschrift K. G. Kuhn. Edited by G. Jeremias. Göttingen: Vandenhoeck & Ruprecht, 1971.

———. *Studies in the Gospel of Mark.* London: SCM Press, 1985.

———. "Die Synagogenschrift von Stobi." Pages 91–130 in vol. 1 of *Judaica et Hellenistica: Kleine Schriften.* Tübingen: Mohr, 1996.

———. "Die Ursprünge der christlichen Mission." *New Testament Studies* 18 (1971): 15–38.

———. "Der vorchristliche Paulus." Pages 177–291 in *Paulus und das antike Judentum.* Edited by M. Hengel and U. Heckel. WUNT, Reihe 1, 58. Tübingen: Mohr, 1991.

———. *War Jesus Revolutionär?* CwH 110. Stuttgart: Calwer, 1970.

———. *Zur urchristlichen Geschichtsschreibung.* 2d ed. Stuttgart: Calwer, 1984.

———. "Zwischen Jesus und Paulus: Die 'Hellenisten,' die Sieben, und Stephanus." *Zeitschrift für Theologie und Kirche* 72 (1975): 151–206.
Hengel, M., and A. M. Schwemer. *Paul between Damascus and Antioch: The Unknown Years*. London: SCM Press, 1997.
Hengel, M., and C. Markschies. *The "Hellenization" of Judaea in the First Century after Christ*. Philadelphia: Trinity, 1989.
Herbst, M. *Missionarischer Gemeindeaufbau in der Volkskirche*. 2d ed. Stuttgart: Calwer, 1988.
Hermann, R. "Das antike Vereinswesen, Haussynagogen, und die Hausgemeinden." ThD diss., University of Tübingen, forthcoming.
Hermansen, G. *Ostia: Aspects of Roman City Life*. Edmonton: University of Alberta Press, 1982.
Hermisson, H. J. *Studien zur altisraelitischen Spruchweisheit*. WMANT 28. Neukirchen-Vluyn: Neukirchener, 1968.
Hill, C. C. *Hellenists and Hebrews: Reappraising Division within the Earliest Church*. Minneapolis: Fortress Press, 1992.
Hill, C. S. "The Sociology of the New Testament Church to A.D. 62: An Examinaton of the Early New Testament Church in Relation to Its Contemporary Social Setting." PhD diss., University of Nottingham, 1982.
Hiltbrunner, O. "Gastfreundschaft." *RAC* 8:1061–1123.
Hirschfeld, Y. *The Palestinian Dwelling in the Roman-Byzantine Period*. SBF.CMi 34. Jerusalem: Franciscan Printing Press, 1995.
Hock, R. F. "Paul's Tentmaking and the Problem of Social Class." *Journal of Biblical Literature* 97 (1978): 555–64.
———. *The Social Context of Paul's Ministry: Tentmaking and Apostleship*. Philadelphia: Fortress Press, 1980.
———. "The Workshop as a Social Setting for Paul's Missionary Preaching." *Catholic Biblical Quarterly* 41 (1979): 438–50.
Hoffmann, P. *Studien zur Theologie der Logienquelle*. 3d ed. NTAbh NF 8. Münster: Aschendorff, 1982.
Hofius, O. "Herrenmahl und Herrenmahlparadosis." Pages 203–43 in *Paulusstudien von O. Hofius*. WUNT 51. Tübingen: Mohr, 1989.
Hollenweger, W. J. "The House Church Movement in Great Britain." *Expository Times* 92 (1980): 45–47.
Holmberg, B. *Paul and Power: The Structure of Authority in the Primitive Church as Reflected in the Pauline Epistles*. ConBNT 11. Lund, Sweden: LiberLäromedel/Gleerup, 1978.
———. "Sociological versus Theological Analysis of the Question concerning a Pauline Church Order." Pages 187–200 in *Die paulinische Literatur und Theologie*. Edited by S. Pedersen. Göttingen: Vandenhoeck & Ruprecht, 1980.
———. *Sociology and the New Testament: An Appraisal*. Minneapolis: Fortress Press, 1990.
Hopkins, I. W. J. "The City Region in Roman Palestine." *Palestine Exploration Quarterly* 112 (1980): 19–32.
Horbury, W. "The Temple Tax." Pages 265–86 in *Jesus and the Politics of His Day*. Edited by E. Bammel and C. F. D. Moule. Cambridge: Cambridge University, 1984.

Horsley, G. H. R. *New Documents Illustrating Early Christianity: A Review of the Greek Inscriptions and Papyri.* 6 vols. North Ryde, N. S. W.: Maquarie University, 1981–1992.

———. "Politarchs." *ABD* 5:384–89.

Horsley, R. A. *Galilee: History, Politics, People.* Valley Forge: Trinity Press International, 1995.

———. *Sociology and the Jesus Movement.* New York: Continuum, 1994.

Horst, P. W. van der. *Ancient Jewish Epitaphs: An Introductory Survey of a Millenium of Jewish Funerary Epigraphy (300 B.C.E.–700 C.E.).* CBET 2. Kampen, Neth.: Kok Pharos Publishing House, 1991.

———. "Jewish Funerary Inscriptions: Most Are in Greek." *Biblical Archaeology Review* 18, no. 5 (1992): 46–57.

———. "Das Neue Testament und die jüdischen Grabinschriften aus hellenistisch-römischer Zeit." *Biblische Zeitschrift* 36 (1992): 161–78.

Howard, W. F. *Accidence and Word Formation with an Appendix on Semitisms in the New Testament.* Vol. 2 of *A Grammar of New Testament Greek.* Edited by J. H. Moulton and W. F. Howard. Edinburgh: T&T Clark, 1929.

Hultgren, A. J. "Liebe Leser mit H. Herrmans, Landesbischof der Evangelisch-Lutheranischen Landeskirche Schaumburg-Lippe." *Idea Spektrum* 30/31 (1997): 3.

———. "Nachrichten: 'China' wurde nicht kritisiert—lutherische Vollversammlung in Hongkong ging mit einer Kontroverse zu Ende," 8.

———. *Paul's Gospel and Mission: The Outlook from His Letter to the Romans.* Philadelphia: Fortress Press, 1985.

Isaac, B. *The Limits of the Empire: The Roman Army in the East.* Oxford: Clarendon, 1990.

Jay, E. G. "From Presbyter-Bishops to Bishops and Presbyters." *Second Century* 1 (1981): 125–62.

Jeremias, J. *Abba: Studien zur neutestamentlichen Theologie und Zeitgeschichte.* Göttingen: Vandenhoek and Ruprecht, 1966.

———. *Die Abendmahlsworte Jesu.* 4th ed. Göttingen: Vandenhoeck & Ruprecht, 1967.

———. *Die Botschaft Jesu vom Vater.* CwH 92. Stuttgart: Calwer, 1968.

———. *Die Drei-Tage-Worte der Evangelien.* KuM 7. Hamburg: H. Reich, 1976.

———. "Die Einwohnerzahl Jerusalems zur Zeit Jesu." *Zeitschrift des deutschen Palästina-Vereins* 66 (1943): 24–31.

———. *Jerusalem zur Zeit Jesu: Eine kulturgeschichtliche Untersuchung zur neutestamentlichen Zeitgeschichte.* 3d ed. Göttingen: Vandenhoeck & Ruprecht, 1962.

———. *Jesus' Promise to the Nations.* 2d ed. Translated by S. H. Hooke. London: SCM, 1967.

———. *Die Kindertaufe in den ersten vier Jahrhunderten.* Göttingen: Vandenhoeck & Ruprecht, 1958.

———. *New Testament Theology: The Proclamation of Jesus.* Translated by J. Bowden. New York: Scribner's, 1971.

———. *Nochmals: Die Anfänge der Kindertaufe: Eine Replik auf Kurt Alands Schrift.* TEH NF 101. Munich: C. Kaiser, 1962.

———. "Paarweise Sendung im Neuen Testament." Pages 132–39 in *Abba: Studien zur neutestamentlichen Theologie und Zeitgeschichte*. Göttingen: Vandenhoeck & Ruprecht, 1966.

———. *Der Schlüssel zur Theologie des Apostels Paulus*. CwH 115. Stuttgart: Calwer, 1971.

———. *Die Sprache des Lukasevangeliums: Redaktion und Tradition im Nicht-Markusstoff des dritten Evangeliums*. Göttingen: Vandenhoeck & Ruprecht, 1980.

———. *Unbekannte Jesusworte*. 3rd ed. Gütersloh: Mohn, 1963.

Jervell, J. *Luke and the People of God: A New Look at Luke-Acts*. Minneapolis: Augsburg, 1972.

———. "Paul in the Acts of the Apostles: Tradition, History, Theology." Pages 68–76 in *The Unknown Paul: Essays on Luke-Acts and Early Christian History*. Minneapolis: Augsburg, 1984.

Jewett, R. "Paul, Phoebe, and the Spanish Mission." Pages 142–61 in *The Social World of Formative Christianity and Judaism*. Edited by J. Neusner. Philadelphia: Fortress Press, 1988.

———. "The Sexual Liberation of the Apostle Paul." *JAAR Supplements* 47, no. 1 (1979): 55–87.

———. "Tenement Churches and Communal Meals in the Early Church." *Biblical Research* 38 (1993): 23–43.

———. "Tenement Churches and Pauline Love Feasts." *Quarterly Review* (spring 1994): 43–58.

———. *The Thessalonian Correspondence: Pauline Rhetoric and Millenarian Piety*. Philadelphia: Fortress Press, 1986.

Johansson, N. *Women and the Church's Ministry: An Exegetical Study of I Corinthians 11–14*. Translated by C. J. de Catanzaro. Ottawa: n.p., 1972.

Johnson, L. T. *The Writings of the New Testament*. London: SCM Press, 1986.

Johnson, S. E. "The Jerusalem Church in Acts." Pages 129–35 in *The Scrolls and the New Testament*. Edited by K. Stendahl. London: SCM Press, 1958.

———. *Paul the Apostle and His Cities*. GNS 21. Wilmington, Del.: Glazier, 1987.

Jones, A. H. M. *The Cities of the Eastern Roman Provinces*. Oxford: Clarendon, 1971.

Judge, E. A. "The Decrees of Caesar at Thessalonica." *Reformed Theological Review* 30 (1971): 1–7.

———. "The Early Christians as Scholastic Community." *Journal of Religious History* 1 (1960): 4–15; 125–37.

———. "Paul as a Radical Critic of Society." *Interchange* 16 (1974): 191–203.

———. *Rank and Status in the World of Caesars and St. Paul*. University of Canterbury Publications 29. Canterbury: University of Canterbury, 1982.

———. "The Social Identity of the First Christians: A Question of Method in Religious History." *Journal of Religious History* 11 (1980): 201–17.

———. *The Social Pattern of the Christian Groups in the First Century*. London: Tyndale, 1960.

Ju-K'ang, T. *Peaks of Faith: Protestant Mission in Revolutionary China*. Leiden: Brill, 1993.

Just, A. A. *The Ongoing Feast: Table Fellowship and Eschatology at Emmaus*. Collegeville, Minn.: Liturgical Press, 1993.

Kadman, L. "Temple Dues and Currency in Ancient Palestine in the Light of Recent Discovered Coin-Hoards." *Israel Numismatic Bulletin* 1 (1962): 9–11.
Kähler, E. "Zur 'Unterordnung' der Frau im NT." *Zeitschrift für evangelische Ethik* 3 (1959): 1–13.
Kamlah, E. "ὑποτάσσεσθαι in den neutestamentlichen 'Haustafeln.'" Pages 237–43 in *Verborum Veritas*. Festschrift G. Stählin. Edited by O. Böcher and K. Haacker. Wuppertal: Brockhaus, 1970.
Kanatsoulis, D. *Die Politarchen der makedonischen Städte*. EEPSTh 7. Salonika: n.p., 1957.
Karrer, M. "Das urchristliche Ältestenamt." *Novum Testamentum* 32 (1990): 152–88.
Karris, R. J. Book review. *Journal of Biblical Literature* 104 (1985): 553–55.
Käsemann, E. "Amt und Gemeinde im Neuen Testament." Pages 109–34 in vol. 1 of *Exegetische Versuche und Besinnungen*. 6th ed. Göttingen: Vandenhoeck & Ruprecht, 1970.
———. "Gottesdienst im Alltag der Welt." Pages 198–204 in vol. 1 of *Exegetische Versuche und Besinnungen*. 6th ed. Göttingen: Vandenhoeck & Ruprecht, 1970.
———. *Jesu letzter Wille nach Joh 17*. 4th ed. Tübingen: Mohr, 1980.
———. "Ketzer und Zeuge: Zum johanneischen Verfasserproblem." Pages 168–87 in vol. 1 of *Exegetische Versuche und Besinnungen*. 6th ed. Göttingen: Vandenhoeck & Ruprecht, 1970.
———. *New Testament Questions of Today*. NTL. London: SCM Press, 1969.
———. *Der Ruf der Freiheit*. 5th ed. Tübingen: Mohr, 1981.
Kasker, A. "Diaspora." *TRE* 8:711–17.
Kasting, H. *Die Anfänge der urchristlichen Mission: Eine historische Untersuchung*. BEvT 55. Munich: Kaiser, 1969.
Katechismus der katholischen Kirche. Munich: Oldenbourg, 1993.
Katz, F. "Lk 9:52–11:36: Beobachtungen zur Logienquelle und ihrer hellenistisch-judenchristlichen Redaktion." ThD diss., University of Mainz, 1973.
Kauffman, P. E. *China, The Emerging Challenge: A Christian Perspective*. Grand Rapids: Baker Book House, 1982.
Keck, L. E. "On the Ethos of the Early Christians." *Journal of the American Academy of Religion* 42 (1974): 435–52.
Kee, H. C. "The Changing Meaning of Synagoge: A Response to Richard Oster." *New Testament Studies* 40 (1994): 281–83.
———. *Community of the New Age: Studies in Mark's Gospel*. Philadelphia: Westminster Press, 1977.
———. "Early Christianity in the Galilee: Reassessing the Evidence from the Gospels." Pages 3–22 in *The Galilee in Late Antiquity*. Edited by L. I. Levine. Cambridge: Harvard University, 1992.
———. "The Import of Archaeological Investigations in Galilee for Scholarly Reassessment of the Gospels." Paper presented at the annual meeting of the Society of Biblical Literature. Anaheim, Calif., November 20, 1989.
———. "The Transformation of the Synagogue after 70 C.E.: Its Import for Early Christianity." *New Testament Studies* 36 (1990): 1–24.

Kelber, W. H. *The Oral and the Written Gospel: The Hermeneutics of Speaking and Writing in the Synoptic Tradition, Mark, Paul, and Q.* Philadelphia: Fortress Press, 1983.
Kennard, J. S. "Was Capernaum the Home of Jesus?" *Journal of Biblical Literature* 65 (1946): 131–41.
Kent, J. H. *The Inscriptions, 1926–1950*. Corinth: Results of Excavations Conducted by the American School of Classical Studies at Athens 8/3. Princeton: American School of Classical Studies at Athens, 1966.
Kertelge, K. *Gemeinde und Amt im Neuen Testament*. Munich: Kösel-Verlag, 1972.
———, ed. *Mission im Neuen Testament*. QD 93. Freiburg: Herder, 1982.
———. *Die Wunder im Markusevangelium: Eine redaktionsgeschichtliche Untersuchung*. Munich: Kösel-Verlag, 1970.
Keys, D. "Das Wunder von Akaba: Der erste christliche Sakralbau . . . ." *Die Welt*, February 5, 1999, 13.
Kidd, R. M. *Wealth and Beneficence in the Pastoral Epistles*. SBLDS 122. Atlanta: Scholars Press, 1990.
Kiley, M. *Colossians as Pseudepigraphy*. BiSe 4. Sheffield, Engl.: JSOT Press, 1986.
Kim, Chan-Hie. *The Form and Structure of the Familiar Greek Letter of Recommendation*. Missoula: Society of Biblical Literature for the Seminar on Paul, 1972.
Kirsch, J. P. "Die christlichen Cultusgebäude in der vorkonstantinischen Zeit." Pages 6–20 in *Festschrift zum elfhundertjährigen Jubiläum des deutschen Campo Santo in Rom*. Edited by S. Ehses. Freiburg: Herder, 1897.
———. *Die römischen Titelkirchen im Altertum*. SGKA 9/1-2. Paderborn: F. Schöningh, 1918.
Kist, N. C. "Über den Ursprung der bischöflichen Gewalt in der christlichen Kirche in Verbindung mit der Bildung und dem Zustande der frühsten Christengemeinden." *Zeitschrift für historische Theologie* 2 (1832): 47–90.
Kittel, G. "ὑπακούω." *TDNT* 1:224–25.
Kitzberger, I. *Bau der Gemeinde: Das paulinische Wortfeld* οἰκοδομη/(ἐπ)οἰκοδομεῖν. FB 53. Würzburg: Echter, 1986.
Klauck, H. J. Book review. *Wissenschaft und Weisheit* 56 (1993): 95–96.
———. "Die Familie im Neuen Testament: Grenzen und Chancen." Pages 9–36 in *Familie leben: Herausforderungen für kirchliche Lehre und Praxis*. Edited by G. Bachl. Düsseldorf: Patmos, 1995.
———. *Gemeinde zwischen Haus und Stadt: Kirche bei Paulus*. Freiburg: Herder, 1992.
———. "Gütergemeinschaft in der klassischen Antike, in Qumran, und im Neuen Testament." *Revue de Qumran* 41 (1982): 47–79.
———. "Die Hausgemeinde als Lebensform im Urchristentum." *Münchener theologische Zeitschrift* 32 (1981): 1–15.
———. *Hausgemeinde und Hauskirche im frühen Christentum*. SBS 103. Stuttgart: Katholisches Bibelwerk, 1981.
———. "Haus/Haustafel." *NBL* 2 (1992), 57–59.
———. *Herrenmahl und hellenistischer Kult: Eine religionsgeschichtliche Untersuchung zum ersten Korintherbrief*. 2d ed. Neutestamentliche Abhandlungen 15. Münster: Aschendorff, 1986.

———. *Herrscher- und Kaiserkult, Philosophie, Gnosis.* Vol. 2 of *Die religiöse Umwelt des Urchristentums.* KStTh 9/2. Stuttgart: Kohlhammer, 1996.
———. "The House Church as a Way of Life." *Theology Digest* 30 (1982): 153–58.
———. *Die Johannesbriefe.* 2d ed. EdF 276. Darmstadt: Wissenschaftliche Buchgesellschaft, 1995.
———. "Kleine Gruppen fördern: Hausgemeinden damals und heute." *Bibel heute* 17 (1982): 175–77.
———. "Neue Literatur zur urchristlichen Hausgemeinde." *Biblische Zeitschrift* NF 26 (1982): 288–94.
———. *Stadt- und Hausreligion, Mysterienkulte, Volksglaube.* Vol. 1 of *Die religiöse Umwelt des Urchristentums.* KStTh 9/1. Stuttgart: Kohlhammer, 1995.
———. "Die urchristliche Hausgemeinde in der Apostelgeschichte des Lukas." *Im Land des Herrn* 42, no. 4 (1988): 31–38.
Klinghardt, M. *Gemeinschaftsmahl und Mahlgemeinschaft: Soziologie und Liturgie frühchristlicher Mahlfeiern.* TANZ 13. Tübingen: Francke, 1996.
Kloppenborg, J. S. "Edwin Hatch: Churches and Collegia." Pages 212–38 in *Origins and Method: Towards a New Understanding of Judaism and Christianity.* Festschrift J. C. Hurd. Edited by B. H. McLean. JSNTSup 86. Sheffield, Engl.: Sheffield Academic Press, 1983.
Klostermann, A. *Schulwesen im alten Israel.* Leipzig: Deichert, 1908.
Kluwe, E. "Haus und Herd in der griechischen Antike." *Altertum* 34 (1988): 77–86.
Knibb, M. A. *The Qumran Community.* Cambridge: Cambridge University, 1987.
Koch, D. A. *Die Bedeutung der Wundererzählungen für die Christologie des Markusevangelium.* BZNW 42. Berlin: De Gruyter, 1975.
Koester, W. *Die Idee der Kirche beim Apostel Paulus.* NTAbh 14/1. Münster: Aschendorff, 1928.
Kopp, C. *Die Heiligen Stätten der Evangelien.* 2d ed. Regensburg: Pustet, 1964.
Köstenberger, A. J., T. R. Schreiner, H. S. Baldwin, eds. *Women in the Church: A Fresh Analysis of 1 Timothy 2:9–15.* Grand Rapids: Baker, 1995.
Kraabel, A. T. "The Diaspora Synagogue: Archaeological and Epigraphic Evidence since Sukenik." *ANRW* 19.1:477–510. Part 2. *Principat,* 19.1. Edited by H. Temporini and W. Haase. New York: de Gruyter, 1979.
———. "The Roman Diaspora: Six Questionable Assumptions." *Journal of Jewish Studies* 33 (1982): 445–64.
———. "The Social Systems of Six Diaspora Synagogues." Pages 79–91 in *Ancient Synagogues: The State of Research.* Edited by J. Gutmann. Chico, Calif.: Scholars Press, 1981.
Kraeling, C. H. *The Christian Building.* Excavations at Dura-Europos: Final Report 8/2. New Haven: Dura-Europus Publications, 1967.
———. "The Jewish Community at Antioch." *Journal of Biblical Literature* 51 (1932): 130–60.
———. *The Synagoge.* Excavations at Dura-Europos: Final Report 8/1. New Haven: Yale University, 1956.
Kratz, R. *Rettungswunder: Motiv-, traditions-, und formkritische Aufarbeitung einer biblischen Gattung.* EHS.T 123. Frankfurt: Peter Lang, 1979.

Kraus, C. "Haus." *LAW* 1196–1208.
Krause, S. *Synagogale Altertümer*. Berlin: Harz, 1922.
———. *Talmudische Archäologie*. Vol. 1. Hildesheim: Georg Olm, 1966.
Krautheimer, R. "The Beginnings of Christian Architecture." *Review of Religion* 3 (1939): 144–59.
———. *Early Christian and Byzantine Architecture*. Baltimore: Penguin, 1965.
Krautheimer, R. et al., eds. *Corpus basilicarum christianarum Romae*. 5 vols. Vatican City: Pontificio instituto di archeologia cristiana, 1937–1977.
Kreissig, H. "Die Landwirtschaftliche Situation in Palästina vor dem Jüdäischen Krieg." *Acta antiqua* 17 (1969): 223–54.
———. "Zur sozialen Zusammensetzung der frühchristlichen Gemeinden im ersten Jahrhundert." *Eirene* 6 (1967): 91–100.
Kremer, J. *Pfingstbericht und Pfingstgeschehen*. SBS 63/64. Stuttgart: KBW, 1973.
Krentz, E. "Order in the 'House' of God: The *Haustafel* in 1 Peter 2:11–3:12." Pages 279–85 in *Common Life in the Early Church*. Festschrift G. F. Snyder. Edited by J. V. Hill. Harrisburg, Pa.: Trinity Press International, 1998.
Kretschmar, G. "Abendmahlsfeier I." *TRE* 1:229–78.
———. "Ein Beitrag zur Frage nach dem Ursprung frühchristlicher Askese." *Zeitschrift für Theologie und Kirche* 61 (1964): 27–67.
———. *Juden und Christen in der Antike*. Pages 26–40. Edited by J. van Amersfoort and J. van Oort. Kok-Kampen, Neth.: Kok, 1990.
Kroll, G. *Auf den Spuren Jesu*. 10th ed. Stuttgart: Verlag Katholisches Bibelwerk, 1988.
Kuhli, H. "οἰκονόμος." *EDNT* 2:1218–22.
Kuhn, H. W. "Et-Tell (Betsaida): Ausgrabung einer Wirkungstätte Jesu, besiedelt seit der frühen Bronzezeit." Pages 22–24 in *Gesellschaft von Freunden und Förderern der Universität München*. Ludwig-Maximilians-Universität München 72. Jahresbericht: n.p., 1993.
Kuhn, H. W., and R. Arav. "The Bethsaida Excavations: Historical and Archaeological Approaches." Pages 77–106 in *The Future of Early Christianity*. Edited by B. A. Pearson. Minneapolis: Fortress Press, 1991.
Kuhn, K. G. "Essener." *RGG* 2:701–3
———. "Qumran." *RGG* 5:745–54.
Kuhn, K. G., and H. Stegemann. "Proselyten." PWSup 9:1248–83.
Kümmel, W. G. *Einleitung in das Neue Testament*. 21st ed. Heidelberg: Quelle and Meyer, 1983.
———. *Verheissung und Erfüllung: Untersuchungen zur eschatologischen Verkündigung Jesu*. 3d ed. ATANT 6. Zurich: Zwingli-Verlag, 1956.
Kyrtatas, D. *The Social Structure of the Early Christian Communities*. London: Verso, 1987.
Lähnemann, J. *Der Kolosserbrief: Komposition, Situation, und Argumentation*. SNT 3. Gütersloh: Mohn, 1971.
Lambertz, M. *Die griechischen Sklavennamen*. Vienna: Selbstverlage des K. K. Staatsgymnasiums im VII. Bezirke, 1907.
Lampe, P. "The Eucharist: Identifying with Christ on the Cross." *Interpretation* 48, no. 1 (1994): 36–49.

———. "Junia/Junias: Sklavenherkunft im Kreise der vorpaulinischen Apostel (Röm 16,7)." *Zeitschrift für die neutestamentliche Wissenschaft und die Kunde der älteren Kirche* 76 (1985): 132–34.

———. "Keine 'Sklavenflucht' des Onesimus." *Zeitschrift für die neutestamentliche Wissenschaft und die Kunde der älteren Kirche* 76 (1985): 135–37.

———. "The Roman Christians of Romans 16." Pages 216–30 in *The Romans Debate*. Edited by K. P. Donfried. 2d ed. Peabody, Mass.: Hendrickson, 1991.

———. *Die stadtrömischen Christen in den ersten beiden Jahrhunderten: Untersuchungen zur Sozialgeschichte*. 2d ed. WUNT, Reihe 2, 18. Tübingen: Mohr, 1989. ET: *From Paul to Valentinus: Christians at Rome in the First Two Centuries*. Translated by M. Steinhauser. Minneapolis: Fortress, 2003.

———. "Zur gesellschaftlichen und kirchlichen Funktion der Familie in neutestamentlicher Zeit: Streiflichter." *Reformatio* 31 (1982): 533–42.

Lang, F. "Über Sidon mitten ins Gebiet der Dekapolis: Geographie und Theologie in Mk 7:31." *Zeitschrift des deutschen Palästina-Vereins* 94 (1978): 145–59.

Larsson, E. *Christus als Vorbild: Eine Untersuchung zu den paulinischen Tauf- und Eikontexten*. ASNU 23. Lund, Sweden: Kopenhagen, 1962.

Laub, F. *Die Begegnung des frühen Christentums mit der antiken Sklaverei*. SBS 107. Stuttgart: Katholisches Bibelwerk, 1982.

———. *Eschatologische Verkündigung und Lebensgestaltung nach Paulus: Eine Untersuchung zum Wirken des Apostels beim Aufbau der Gemeinde in Thessaloniki*. BU 10. Regensburg: Pustet, 1973.

———. "Paulus als Gemeindegründer (1Thess)." Pages 17–38 in *Kirche im Werden: Studien zum Thema Amt und Gemeinde im Neuen Testament*. Munich: Schöningh, 1976.

———. "Sozialgeschichtlicher Hintergrund und ekklesiologische Relevanz der neutestamentlich-frühchristlichen Haus- und Gemeinde-Tafelparänese— ein Beitrag zur Soziologie des Frühchristentums." *Münchener theologische Zeitschrift* 37 (1986): 249–71.

Laufen, R. "Die Doppelüberlieferung der Logienquelle und des Markusevangeliums." ThD diss., University of Bonn, 1978.

Laughlin, J. "Capernaum: From Jesus' Time and After." *Biblical Archaeology Review* 19 (1993): 54–61.

Lawrence, C. *The Church in China*. Minneapolis: Bethany House, 1985.

Leclercq, H. "Églises." DACL 4:2279–349.

Leipoldt, J. *Die Frau in der antiken Welt und im Urchristentum*. 2d ed. Leipzig: Koehler & Amelang, 1955.

Lemaire, A. "The Ministries in the New Testament." *Biblical Theology Bulletin* 3 (1973): 133–66.

———. "Von den Diensten zu den Ämtern." *Concilium* 8 (1972): 721–28.

Leon, H. J. *The Jews of Ancient Rome*. Philadelphia: Jewish Publication Society of America, 1960.

Leutzsch, M. *Die Bewährung der Wahrheit: Der dritte Johannesbrief als Dokument urchristlichen Alltags*. Stätten und Formen der Kommunikation im Altertum 2. Trier: Wissenschaftlicher, 1994.

Levine, L. I. *Ancient Synagogues Revealed.* Jerusalem: Israel Exploration Society, 1981.

———. "The Second Temple Synagogue: The Formative Years." Pages 7–31 in *The Synagogue in Late Antiquity.* Edited by L. I. Levine. Philadelphia: The American Schools of Oriental Research, 1987.

Lewis, L. A. "'As a Beloved Brother': The Function of Family Language in the Letters of Paul." PhD diss., Yale University, 1985.

Liechtenhan, R. *Die urchristliche Mission: Voraussetzungen, Motive, Methoden.* ATANT 9. Zurich: Zwingli-Verlag, 1946.

Lifshitz, B. *Donateurs et fondateurs dans les synagoges juives.* Paris: J. Gabalda, 1967.

Lindemann, A. "The Beginnings of Christian Life in Jerusalem according to the Summaries in the Acts of the Apostles (Acts 2:42–47)." Pages 202–18 in *Common Life in the Early Church.* Festschrift G. F. Snyder. Edited by J. V. Hill. Harrisburg, Pa.: Trinity Press International, 1998.

Lindsay, T. M. *The Church and the Ministry in the Early Centuries.* London: Hodder and Stoughton, 1902.

Linton, O. *Das Problem der Urkirche in der neueren Forschung: Eine kritische Darstellung.* Uppsala: Almqvist & Wiksells, 1932.

Lips, H. von, *Glaube-Gemeinde-Amt: Zum Verständnis der Ordination in den Pastoralbriefen.* FRLANT 122. Göttingen: Vandenhoeck & Ruprecht, 1979.

———. "Die Haustafeln als 'Topos' im Rahmen der urchristlichen Paränese: Beobachtungen anhand des 1.Petrusbriefes und des Titusbriefes." *New Testament Studies* 40 (1994): 261–80.

Loffreda, S. "Ceramica ellenistico-romana nel sottosuolo della sinagoga di Cafarnao." *Studia hierosolymitana* 3 (1982): 273–312.

———. *La ceramica.* Vol. 2 of *Cafarnao.* PSBF 19. Jerusalem: Franciscan Printing Press, 1974.

———. *Die Heiligtümer von Tabgha.* Jerusalem: Franciscan Printing Press, 1978.

———. *Recovering Capharnaum.* 2d ed. Jerusalem: Franciscan Printing Press, 1993.

———. "La tradizionale casa di Simon Pietro a Cafarnao a 25 anni dalla sua scoperta." Page 37–67 in *Early Christianity in Context: Monuments and Documents.* Festschrift E. Testa. Edited by F. Manns and E. Alliata. SBF.CMa 83. Jerusalem: Franciscan Printing Press, 1993.

———. *A Visit to Capharnaum.* Jerusalem: Franciscan Printing Press, 1978.

Lohfink, G. "Die christliche Familie—eine Hauskirche?" *Theologische Quartalschrift* 163 (1983): 227–29.

———. *Jesus and Community: The Social Dimension of Christian Faith.* Translated by J. P. Galvin. Philadelphia: Fortress, 1984.

———. "Weibliche Diakone im Neuen Testament." Pages 320–38 in *Die Frau im Urchristentum.* Edited by G. Dantzenberg, H. Merklein, and K. Müller. Freiburg: Herder, 1983.

Lohfink, G., and R. Pesch. *Tiefenpsychologie und keine Exegese: Eine Auseinandersetzung mit Eugen Drewermann.* SBS 129. Stuttgart: Katholisches Bibelwerk, 1987.

Lohse E. "Christologie und Ethik im Kolosserbrief." Pages 249–61 in *Die Einheit des Neuen Testaments*. Göttingen: Vandenhoeck & Ruprecht, 1973.

———. "Christusherrschaft und Kirche im Kolosserbrief." Pages 262–75 in *Die Einheit des Neuen Testaments*. Göttingen: Vandenhoeck & Ruprecht, 1973.

———. "Entstehung des Bischofsamtes in der frühen Christenheit." *Zeitschrift für die neutestamentliche Wissenschaft und die Kunde der älteren Kirche* 71 (1980): 58–73.

———. *Grundriss der neutestamentlichen Theologie*. 4th ed. ThW 5/1. Stuttgart: Kohlhammer, 1989.

———. *Die Ordination im Spätjudentum und im Neuen Testament*. Göttingen: Vandenhoeck & Ruprecht, 1951.

Löning, K. *Die Saulustradition in der Apostelgeschichte*. NTAbh NF 9. Münster: Aschendorff, 1973.

———. "Der Stephanuskreis und seine Mission." Pages 80–101 in *Die Anfänge des Christentums*. Edited by J. Becker. Stuttgart: Kohlhammer, 1987.

Lorenzen, T. "Die christliche Hauskirche." *Theologische Zeitschrift* 43 (1987): 333–52.

Lüdemann, G. *Das frühe Christentum nach den Traditionen der Apostelgeschichte: Ein Kommentar*. Göttingen: Vandenhoeck & Ruprecht, 1987.

———. *Studien zur Chronologie*. Vol. 1 of *Paulus, der Heidenapostel*. FRLANT 123. Göttingen: Vandenhoeck & Ruprecht, 1980.

Lührmann, D. "Neutestamentliche Haustafeln und antike Ökonomie." *New Testament Studies* 27 (1981): 83–97.

———. *Die Redaktion der Logienquelle*. WUANT 33. Neukirchen-Vluyn: Neukirchener, 1969.

———. "Wo man nicht mehr Sklave oder Freier ist: Überlegungen zur Struktur frühchristlicher Gemeinden." *Wort und Dienst* NF 13 (1975): 53–83.

Lynch, J. *Aristotle's School: A Study of a Greek Educational Institution*. Berkeley: University of California Press, 1972.

MacDonald, D. R. *The Legend and the Apostle: The Battle for Paul in Story and Canon*. Philadelphia: Westminster Press, 1983.

MacDonald, M. *The Pauline Churches: A Socio-historical Study of Institutionalization in the Pauline and Deutero-Pauline Writings*. SNTSMS 60. Cambridge: Cambridge University, 1988.

MacDowell, D. M. "The Oikos in Athenian Law." *Classical Quarterly* 83 (1989): 10–21.

MacMullen, R. *Christianizing the Roman Empire (A.D. 100–400)*. New Haven: Yale University Press, 1984.

———. "Market-Days in the Roman Empire." *Phoenix* 24, no. 4 (1970): 333–41.

———. *Roman Social Relations: 50 B.C. to A.D. 284*. New Haven: Yale, 1974.

———. "Women in Public in the Roman Empire." *Historia* 29 (1980): 208–18.

Maier, F. W. *Paulus als Kirchengründer und kirchlicher Organisator*. Würzburg: Echter, 1961.

Maier, H. O. *The Social Setting of the Ministry as Reflected in the Writings of Hermas, Clement, and Ignatius*. Dissertations SR 1. Waterloo, Ont.: Wilfrid Laurier University Press, 1991.

Maier, J. *Jüdische Auseinandersetzung mit dem Christentum in der Antike.* EdF 177. Darmstadt: Wissenschaftliche Buchgesellschaft, 1982.

———. *Die Qumran-Essener: Die Texte vom Toten Meer.* 2 vols. Basel: Reinhardt, 1995.

Maier, J., and K. Schubert. *Die Qumran-Essener.* Munich: Reinhardt, 1973.

Maisch, I. *Die Heilung des Gelähmten: Eine exegetisch-traditionsgeschichtliche Untersuchung zu Mk 2:1–12.* SBS 52. Stuttgart: KBW, 1971.

Malherbe, A. *Ancient Epistolary Theorists.* Atlanta: Scholars Press, 1988.

———. "God's New Family in Thessalonica." Pages 116–25 in *The Social World of the First Christians.* Festschrift W. A. Meeks. Edited by L. M. White and O. L. Yarbrough. Minneapolis: Fortress, 1995.

———. "The Inhospitality of Diotrephes." Pages 222–32 in *God's Christ and His People.* Festschrift N. A. Dahl. Edited by J. Jervell and W. A. Meeks. Oslo: Universitetsforlaget, 1977. Repr., pages 92–112 in *Social Aspects of Early Christianity.*

———. *Paul and the Thessalonians: The Philosophic Tradition of Pastoral Care.* Philadelphia: Fortress Press, 1987.

———. *Social Aspects of Early Christianity.* 2d ed. Philadelphia: Fortress Press, 1983.

Malina, B. J. *The New Testament World: Insights from Cultural Anthropology.* Atlanta: John Knox Press, 1981.

———. "The Social Sciences and Biblical Interpretation." *Interpretation* 36 (1982): 229–42.

Mancini, I. *L'archéologie judéo-chrétienne.* Notices historiques. Jerusalem: Franciscan Printing Press, 1977.

Manjaly, T. "The Pauline House Church: Some Pastoral Reflections." Pages 12–41 in *He Taught.* Festschrift S. S. Lyngdoh. Edited by G. Kottuppallil. Shillong, India: Vendrame institute publications, 1996.

Manson, T. W. *The Sayings of Jesus: As recorded in the Gospels according to St. Matthew and St. Luke.* London: SCM Press, 1971.

Mantle, I. C. "Roman Household Religion." PhD diss., University of Edinburgh, 1978.

Ma'oz, Z. "The Synagogue of Gamla and the Typology of Second-Temple Synagogues." Pages 35–41 in *Ancient Synagogues Revealed.* Edited by L. I. Levine. Jerusalem: Israel Exploration Society, 1981.

Marrou, H. I. *Geschichte der Erziehung im klassischen Altertum.* Freiburg: Alber, 1957.

Marshall, I. H. *Last Supper and Lord's Supper.* Didsbury Lectures 1980. Exeter: Paternoster, 1980.

———. *Luke: Historian and Theologian.* 3d ed. Downers Grove, Ill.: InterVarsity, 1988.

Marshall, I. H., and K. P. Donfried. *The Theology of the Shorter Pauline Letters.* Cambridge: Cambridge University, 1993.

Marshall, P. *Enmity in Corinth: Social Conventions in Paul's Relations with the Corinthians.* WUNT, Reihe 2, 23. Tübingen: Mohr, 1987.

Marxsen, W. *Einleitung in das Neue Testament.* Gütersloh: Mohn, 1978.

Maser, P. "Synagoge und Ekklesia: Erwägungen zur Frühgeschichte des Kirchenbaus." Pages 271–92 in *Begegnungen zwischen Christentum und Judentum in Antike und Mittelalter.* Edited by D. A. Koch and H. Lichtenberger.

Vol. 1 of *Schriften des Institutum judaicum delitzschianum*. Festschrift Heinz Schreckenberg. Edited by H. Lichtenberger. Göttingen: Vandenhoeck & Ruprecht, 1993.

———. "Synagoge und Ekklesia: Erwägungen zur Frühgeschichte des Kirchenbaus und der christlichen Bildkunst." *Kairós* 32/33 (1990/ 1991): 9–26.

Mathews, J. B. "Hospitality and the New Testament Church: An Historical and Exegetical Study." ThD diss., Princeton University, 1964.

Matson, D. L. *Houshold Conversion Narratives in Acts: Pattern and Interpretation*. JSNTSup 123. Sheffield, Engl.: Sheffield Academic Press, 1996.

McKay, A. G. *Römische Häuser, Villen, und Paläste*. Translated by H. Bideau. Revised and enlarged by R. Fellmann. Zurich: Atlantis-Verlag, 1980. Translation of *Houses, Villas, and Palaces in the Roman World*. London: Thames and Hudson, 1975.

Mealand, D. L. "Community of Goods and Utopian Allusions in Acts II–IV." *Journal of Theological Studies* 28 (1977): 96–97.

———. "Community of Goods at Qumran." *Theologische Zeitschrift* 31 (1975): 129–39.

Meates, G. W. *Lullingstone Roman Villa*. London: Heinemann, 1955.

———. *Lullingstone Roman Villa*. Ministry of Works Guide-Book. London: H. M. Stationery Off., 1962.

———. "Lullingstone Roman Villa." Pages 87–110 in *Recent Archaeological Excavations in Britain*. Edited by R. L. S. Bruce-Mitford. London: Routledge and Paul, 1956.

Meeks, W. A. *The First Urban Christians*. New Haven: Yale University, 1983.

———. "The Image of the Androgyne: Some Uses of a Symbol in Earliest Christianity." *History of Religions* 13 (1974): 165–208.

———. *The Moral World of the First Christians*. 2d ed. London: SPCK, 1987.

———, ed. *Zur Soziologie des Urchristentums: Ausgewählte Beiträge zum frühchristlichen Gemeinschaftsleben in seiner gesellschaftlichen Umwelt*. Historische Theologie 62. Munich: Kaiser, 1979.

Meeks, W. A., and R. L. Wilken. *Jews and Christians in Antioch in the First Four Centuries of the Common Era*. SBL 13. Missoula: Scholars Press for the Society of Biblical Literature, 1978.

Mell, U. *Neue Schöpfung: Eine traditionsgeschichtliche und exegetische Studie zu einem soteriologischen Grundsatz paulinischer Theologie*. Berlin: de Gruyter, 1989.

Merk, O. "Glaube und Tat in den Pastoralbriefen." *Zeitschrift für die neutestamentliche Wissenschaft und die Kunde der älteren Kirche* 66 (1975): 91–103.

Merklein, H. "Die Ekklesia Gottes: Der Kirchenbegriff bei Paulus und in Jerusalem." *Biblische Zeitschrift* NF 23 (1979): 48–70.

———. *Das kirchliche Amt nach dem Epheserbrief*. SANT 33. Munich: Kösel, 1973.

Meye, R. P. *Jesus and the Twelve: Discipleship and Revelation in Mark's Gospel*. Grand Rapids: Eerdmans, 1968.

Meyer, B. F. *The Early Christians: Their World Mission and Self-Discovery*. GNS 16. Wilmington: M. Glazier, 1986.

Meyer, E. *Ursprung und Anfänge des Christentums*. 3 vols. Stuttgart: Cotta, 1921–1923.

Meyers, E. M. "The Cultural Setting of Galilee: The Case of Regionalism and Early Judaism." *ANRW* 19.1:689–702. Part 2. *Principat*, 19.1. Edited by H. Temporini and W. Haase. New York: de Gruyter, 1979.

———. "Galilean Regionalism: A Reappraisal." Pages 115–31 in vol. 5 of *Approaches to Ancient Judaism*. Edited by W. Scott Green. BJS 32. Atlanta: Scholars Press, 1985.

———. "Galilean Regionalism as a Factor in Historical Reconstruction." *Bulletin of the American Schools of Oriental Research* 221 (1976): 93–102.

Meyers, E. M., and C. L. Meyers. "Finders of the Lost Ark." *Biblical Archaeology Review* 7 (1981): 24–40.

Meyers, E. M., and J. F. Strange. *Archaeology, the Rabbis, and Early Christianity*. Nashville: Abingdon, 1981.

Meyers, E. M., J. F. Strange, and D. E. Groh. "The Meiron Excavation Project: Archeological Survey in Galilee and Golan, 1976." *Bulletin of the American Schools of Oriental Research* 230 (1978): 1–24.

Michel, O. "Gnadengabe und Amt." *Deutsche Theologie* 9 (1942): 133–39.

———. "μικρός." *TDNT* 4:648–59.

———. "οἶκος." *TDNT* 5:119–33.

Milgrom, J. "The Temple Scroll." *Biblical Archaeologist* 41 (1978): 105–20.

Mimouni, S. C. "Pour une définition nouvelle du judéo-christianisme ancien." *New Testament Studies* 38 (1992): 161–86.

Minear, P. S. "Audience Criticism and Markan Ecclesiology." Pages 79–89 in *Neues Testament und Geschichte: Historisches Geschehen und Deutung im Neuen Testament*. Festschrift O. Cullmann. Edited by W. Baltensweiler and B. Reicke. Tübingen: J. C. B. Mohr, 1972.

———. "The Disciples and the Crowd in the Gospel of Matthew." *Anglican Theological Review* Supplementary Series 3 (1974): 28–44.

———. "Jesus' Audience according to Luke." *Novum Testamentum* 16 (1974): 81–109.

Mitchell, M. M. "'Diotrephes Does Not Receive Us': The Lexicographical and Social Context of 3 John 9–10." *Journal of Biblical Literature* 117, no. 2 (1998): 299–320.

Möller, C. "Gemeinde I." *TRE* 12:316–35.

———. *Konzepte-Programme-Wege*. Vol. 1 of *Lehre vom Gemeindeaufbau*. 2d ed. Göttingen: Vandenhoeck & Ruprecht, 1987.

Molthagen, J. "Die ersten Konflikte der Christen in der griechisch-römischen Welt." *Historia* 40 (1991): 53–57.

Monelli, A., and N. Monelli. "L'architettura cristiana delle origini: I primi trecento anni." *Bibbia e oriente* 37, no. 183 (1995): 49–57.

Moule, C. F. D. *The Origin of Christology*. Cambridge: Cambridge University, 1977.

———. "The Use of Parables and Sayings as Illustration Material in Early Christian Catechism." *Journal of Theological Studies* 3 (1952): 75–79.

Moulton, J. H., and G. Milligan. *The Vocabulary of the Greek Testament Illustrated from the Papyri and Other Non-literary Sources*. Peabody, Mass.: Hendrickson, 1997.

Müller, K. "Die Haustafel des Kolosserbriefes und das antike Frauenthema." Pages 263–319 in *Die Frau im Urchristentum*. Edited by G. Dautzenberg. QD 95. Freiburg: Herder, 1983.

———. "Kirchenverfassung, I: Im christlichen Altertum." *RGG*² 3:968–88.
Murphy-O'Connor, J. "The Cenacle—Topographical Setting for Acts 2:44–45." Pages 303–21 in *The Book of Acts in Its Palestinian Setting*. Edited by R. Bauckham. Vol. 4 of *The Book of Acts in Its First Century Setting*. Edited by B. W. Winter. Grand Rapids: Eerdmans, 1995.
———. "Corinth." *ABD* 1:1134–40.
———. *The Holy Land: An Archaeological Guide from Earliest Times to 1700*. Oxford: Oxford University, 1992.
———. "Prisca and Aquila." *Bible Review* (December 1992): 40–51, 62.
———. *St. Paul's Corinth: Texts and Archaeology*. 2d ed. Collegeville, Minn.: Liturgical Press, 1990.
Mussner, F. "Gab es eine 'galiläische Krise'?" Pages 238–52 in *Orientierung an Jesus: Zur Theologie der Synoptiker*. Edited by P. Hoffmann. Freiburg: Herder, 1973.
Nauck, W. "Probleme des frühchristlichen Amtsverständnisses." *Zeitschrift für die neutestamentliche Wissenschaft und die Kunde der älteren Kirche* 48 (1957): 200–220.
Neighbour, R. W., Jr., and L. Jenkins. *Where Do We Go from Here? A Guidebook for the Cell Group Church*. Houston: Touch Publications, 1990.
Nellessen, E. "Die Einsetzung von Presbytern durch Barnabas und Paulus (Apg 14:23)." Pages 175–93 in *Begegnung mit dem Wort. Festschrift Heinrich Zimmermann*. Edited by E. Nellessen. BBB 53. Bonn: Hanstein, 1980.
———. "Die Presbyter der Gemeinden in Lykaonien und Pisidien." Pages 493–98 in *Les Actes des Apôtres: Traditions, rédaction, théologie*. Edited by J. Kremer. BETL 48. Gembloux: J. Duculot, 1979.
Netzer, E. "Ancient Ritual Baths (Miqvaot) in Jericho." Pages 106–19 in vol. 2 of *The Jerusalem Cathedra*. Edited by L. I. Levine. Jerusalem: Yad Izhak Ben-Zvi Institute, 1982.
Neudorfer, H. W. *Der Stephanuskreis in der Forschungsgeschichte seit F.C. Baur*. Giessen, Germany: Brunnen, 1983.
Neuer, W. *Man and Woman in Christian Perspective*. Translated by G. Wenham. London: Hodder and Stoughton, 1990.
Neugebauer, F. "Die dargebotene Wange und Jesu Gebot der Feindesliebe." *Theologische Literaturzeitung* 12 (1985): 865–76.
Neuhäusler, E. *Anspruch und Antwort Gottes*. Düsseldorf: Patmos, 1962.
Neusner, J. *Formative Judaism: Religious, Historical, and Literary Studies*. Chico, Calif.: Scholars Press, 1982.
Nicholson, G. C. "Houses for Hospitality: 1 Cor. 1:17–34." *Colloquium* 19 (1986): 1–6.
Nock, A. D. *Conversion: The Old and the New in Religion from Alexander the Great to Augustine of Hippo*. Oxford: Clarendon, 1933.
Noordegraaf, A. "Familia Dei: De functie en de betekenis van de huisgemeente in het Nieuwe Testament." *Theologia reformata* 35 (1992): 183–204.
Normann, F. *Christos Didaskolos: Die Vorstellung von Christus als Lehrer in der christlichen Literatur des ersten und zweiten Jahrhunderts*. MBTh 32. Münster: Aschendorff, 1967.
Norris, F. W. "Antiochien I." *TRE* 3:99–103.
Nun, M. *Sea of Galilee: Newly Discovered Harbours from New Testament Days*. 3d ed. Ein Gev, Israel: Kinnereth Sailing, 1992.

Oberhummer, E. "Thessalonike." *PW* 2:143–48.
Oberlinner, L. "Ein ruhiges und ungestörtes Leben führen." *Bibel und Kirche* 46 (1991): 98–106.
Oepke, A. "γυνή." *TDNT* 1:776–89.
———. "παῖς." *TDNT* 5:636–54.
———. "Probleme der vorchristlichen Zeit des Paulus." *Theologische Studien und Kritiken* 105 (1933): 387–424.
"Oldest Church Found: Well, Maybe." *Biblical Archaeology Review* 24, no. 6 (1998): 22.
Ollrog, W. H. "Die Abfassungsverhältnisse von Röm 16." Pages 221–26 in *Kirche*. Festschrift G. Bornkamm. Edited by D. Lührmann and G. Strecker. Tübingen: Mohr, 1980.
———. *Paulus und seine Mitarbeiter: Untersuchungen zu Theorie und Praxis der paulinischen Mission*. WMANT 50. Neukirchen-Vluyn: Neukirchener, 1979.
———. "συνεργός." *EDNT* 3:303–4.
Olsen, C. M. *The Base Church: Creating Community through Multiple Forms*. Atlanta: Forum, 1973.
Osiek, C. "The Family in Early Christianity: 'Family Values' Revisited." *Catholic Biblical Quarterly* 58 (1996): 1–24.
———. "Women in House Churches." Pages 300–315 in *Common Life in the Early Church*. Festschrift G. F. Snyder. Edited by J. V. Hill. Harrisburg, Pa.: Trinity Press International, 1998.
Osiek, C., and D. L. Balch. *Families in the New Testament World: Households and House Churches*. Louisville: Westminster John Knox, 1997.
Oster, R. E. "Ephesus." *ABD* 2:542–49.
———. "Supposed Anachronism in Luke-Acts' Use of ΣΥΝΑΓΩΓΗ: A Rejoinder to H. C. Kee." *New Testament Studies* 39 (1993): 178–208.
O'Toole, R. F. "Philippian Jailor." *ABD* 5:317–18.
Overman, J. A. "Who Were the First Urban Christians?" Pages 160–68 in *SBL Seminar Papers, 1988*. SBLSP 124. Chico, Calif.: Scholars Press, 1988.
Packer, J. E. "Housing and Population in Imperial Ostia and Rome." *Journal of Roman Studies* 57 (1967): 80–95.
———. *The Insulae of Imperial Ostia*. MAAR 31. Rome: American Academy in Rome, 1971.
Papazoglou, F. "Politarques en Illyrie." *Historia* 35 (1986): 438–48.
Parker, S. T. "Brief Notice on a Possible Early 4th C. Church at 'Aqaba, Jordan." *Journal of Roman Archaeology* 12 (1999): 372–76.
Paschen, W. *Rein und Unrein: Untersuchung zur biblischen Wortgeschichte*. SANT 24. Munich: Kösel, 1970.
Pax, E. "Jüdische Familienliturgie in biblisch-christlicher Sicht." *Bibel und Leben* 13 (1972): 248–61.
Peifen, J. "Church Life at the Grass Roots." Pages 104–9 in *Chinese Christians Speak Out*. Edited by K. H. Ting. Beijing: New World Press, 1984.
Percival, J. *The Roman Villa: A Historical Introduction*. London: Batsford, 1976.
Percy, E. *Die Botschaft Jesu: Eine traditionskritische und exegetische Untersuchung*. Lund, Sweden: Gleerup, 1953.

Perdue, L. G., J. Blenkinsopp, J. J. Collins, and C. Meyers. *Families in Ancient Israel*. Louisville: Westminster John Knox, 1997.
Pesch, R. *Das Abendmahl und Jesu Todesverständnis*. Freiburg: Herder, 1978.
———. *Simon Petrus: Geschichte und geschichtliche Bedeutung des ersten Jüngers Jesu Christi*. PuP 15. Stuttgart: A. Hiersemann, 1980.
———. "Die sogenannte Gemeindeordnung Mt 18." *Biblische Zeitschrift* NF 7 (1963): 220–35.
———. "Voraussetzungen und Anfänge der urchristlichen Mission." Pages 11–70 in *Mission im Neuen Testament*. Edited by K. Kertelge. QD 93. Freiburg: Herder, 1982.
———. *Wie Jesus Abendmahl hielt*. 3d ed. Freiburg: Herder, 1979.
Petersen, J. M. "House-Churches in Rome." *Vigiliae christianae* 23 (1969): 264–72.
Peterson, E. "Die geschichtliche Bedeutung der jüdischen Gebetsrichtung." Pages 1–14 in *Frühkirche: Judentum und Gnosis*. Edited by E. Peterson. Rome: Herder, 1959.
Pfammatter, J. *Die Kirche als Bau: Eine exegetisch-theologische Studie zur Ekklesiologie der Paulusbriefe*. AnGr 110. Rome: Pontificia Universitas Gregoriana, 1960.
Pilhofer, P. *Philippi*. Vol. 1 of *Die erste christliche Gemeinde Europas*. WUNT 87. Tübingen: Mohr, 1995.
Pixner, B. "Church of the Apostles Found on Mt. Zion?" *Biblical Archaeology Review* 16, no. 3 (1990): 16–35.
———. "Das Essenerquartier in Jerusalem und dessen Einfluss auf die Urkirche." *Das Heilige Land* 113, no. 2/3 (1981): 3–14.
———. "Lukas und Jerusalem." Pages 372–81 in *Wege des Messias und Stätten der Urkirche: Jesus und das Judenchristentum im Licht neuer archäologischer Erkenntnisse*. Edited by B. Pixner and R. Riesner. 3d ed. Giessen, Germany: Brunnen, 1996.
———. "Searching for the New Testament Site of Bethsaide." *Biblical Archaeologist* 48 (1985): 207–16.
———. "Wege Jesu um den See Gennesaret." *Das Heilige Land* 119, no. 2/3 (1987): 1–14.
Plümacher, E. *Lukas als hellenistischer Schriftsteller*. SUNT 9. Göttingen: Vandenhoeck & Ruprecht, 1972.
Pöhlmann, W. *Der Verlorene Sohn und das Haus: Studien zu Lukas 15:11–32 im Horizont der antiken Lehre von Haus, Erziehung, und Ackerbau*. WUNT 68. Tübingen: Mohr, 1993.
Polag, A. *Die Christologie der Logienquelle*. WMANT 45. Neukirchen-Vluyn: Neukirchener, 1977.
Pölzl, F. X. *Die Mitarbeiter des Weltapostels Paulus*. Regensburg: Manz, 1911.
Pompe, H. H. *Der erste Atem der Kirche: Urchristliche Hausgemeinden—Herausforderung für die Zukunft*. Bausteine Gemeindeaufbau 2. Neukirchen-Vluyn: Aussaat, 1996.
Popkes, W. *Adressaten, Situation, und Form des Jakobusbriefes*. SBS 125/126. Stuttgart: Katholisches Bibelwerk, 1986.
———. "Forschungshinweis: 'Die Hausgemeinde im Urchristentum.'" *Theologisches Gespräch* 5/6 (1982): 11–12.
———. "Gemeinschaft." *RAC* 9:1100–1145.

---. *Paränese und Neues Testament.* SBS 168. Stuttgart: Katholisches Bibelwerk, 1996.
Powell, D. "Ordo Presbyterii." *Journal of Theological Studies* 26 (1975): 290-328.
Prete, B. "Il sommario di Atti 1:13-14 e suo apporto per la conoscenza della Chiesa delle origini." *Sacra doctrina* 18 (1973): 66-124.
Priest, J. F. "Mebaqqer, Priest, and the Messiah." *Journal of Biblical Literature* 81 (1962): 55-61.
Provencher, N. "Vers une théologie de la famille: L'église domestique." *Eglise et théologie* 12 (1981): 9-34.
Quinn, J. D. Book review. *Catholic Biblical Quarterly* 47 (1985): 178-80.
Radin, M. *The Jews among the Greeks and Romans.* Philadelphia: Jewish Publication Society of America, 1915.
Radl, W. "Befreiung aus dem Gefängnis." *Biblische Zeitschrift* 27 (1983): 81-96.
Räisänen, H. "Jesus and the Food Laws: Reflections on Mk 7:15." *Journal for the Study of the New Testament* 16 (1982): 59-100.
Rajak, T., and Noy, D. "ARCHISYNAGOGOI: Office, Title, and Social Status in the Greco-Jewish Synagogue." *Journal of Roman Studies* 83 (1993): 75-93.
Ramsay, W. M. "The Denials of Peter, Section III: The house in the New Testament." *Expository Times* 27 (1915/1916): 471-72.
---. *Pictures of the Apostolic Church.* London: Hodder and Stoughton, 1910.
Ratzinger, J. *Volk und Haus Gottes in Augustins Lehre von der Kirche.* MThS.S 7. Munich: K. Zink, 1954.
Ravarotto, E. "La 'casa' del vangelo di Marco è la casa di Simone-Pietro?" *Antonianum* 42 (1967): 399-419.
Rawson, B., ed. *Marriage, Divorce, and Children in Ancient Rome.* Oxford: Clarendon, 1991.
Rebell, W. *Zum neuen Leben berufen: Kommunikative Gemeindepraxis im frühen Christentum.* Munich: Kaiser, 1990.
Reck, R. *Kommunikation und Gemeindebau: Eine Studie zu Entstehung, Leben, und Wachstum paulinischer Gemeinden in den Kommunikationsstrukturen der Antike.* SBB 22. Stuttgart: Katholisches Bibelwerk, 1991.
Redlich, E. B. *S. Paul and His Companions.* London: Macmillan, 1913.
Reed, J. L. *The Population of Capernaum.* Occasional Papers of the Institute of Antiquity and Christianity 24. Claremont, Calif.: Institute for Antiquity and Christianity, 1992.
Reicke, B. *Diakonie, Festfreude, und Zelos in Verbindung mit der altchristlichen Agapefeier.* Wiesbaden: O. Harrassowitz, 1951.
---. *Glaube und Leben der Urgemeinde: Bemerkungen zu Apg. 1-7.* ATANT 32. Zurich: Zwingli, 1957.
---. *Neutestamentliche Zeitgeschichte: Die biblische Welt, 500 v.-100 n. Chr.* 3d ed. Berlin 1982.
---. "προΐστημι." *TDNT* 6:700-703.
---. "Die Verfassung der Urgemeinde im Lichte jüdischer Dokumente." *Theologische Zeitschrift* 10 (1954): 95-112.
Reicke, B., and A. Suhl. "Thessaloniki." *BHH* 3:1968-69.

Reinhardt, W. "The Population Size of Jerusalem and the Numerical Growth of the Jerusalem Church." Pages 237–65 in *The Book of Acts in Its Palestinian Setting*. Edited by R. Bauckham. Vol. 4 of of *The Book of Acts in Its First Century Setting*. Edited by B. W. Winter. Grand Rapids: Eerdmans, 1995.

———. *Das Wachstum des Gottesvolkes: Untersuchungen zum Gemeindewachstum im lukanischen Doppelwerk auf dem Hintergrund des Alten Testaments*. Göttingen: Vandenhoeck & Ruprecht, 1995.

Rengstorf, K. H. "ἐπίσημος." *TDNT* 7:267–68.

———. "μανθάνω." *TDNT* 4:390–461.

———. *Mann und Frau im Urchristentum*. Cologne: Westdt. Verlag, 1954.

———. "Die neutestamentliche Mahnungen an die Frau, sich dem Manne unterzuordnen." Pages 131–45 in *Verbum Dei manet in aeternum*. Festschrift O. Schmitz. Edited by W. Foerster. Witten, Germany: Luther-Verlag, 1953.

———. "ὀφθαλμοδουλία." *TDNT* 2:280.

Reumann, J. "One Lord, One Faith, One God, but Many House Churches." Pages 106–17 in *Common Life in the Early Church*. Festschrift G. F. Snyder. Edited by J. V. Hill. Harrisburg, Pa.: Trinity Press International, 1998.

Richardson, P. "Architectural Transitions from Synogogues and House Churches to Purpose-Built Churches." Pages 373–89 in *Common Life in the Early Church*. Festschrift G. F. Snyder. Edited by J. V. Hill. Harrisburg, Pa.: Trinity Press International, 1998.

Ridderbos, H. *Paul: An Outline of His Theology*. 2d ed. Translated by J. R. De Witt. Grand Rapids: Eerdmans, 1990.

Riddle, D. W. "Early Christian Hospitality: A Factor in the Gospel Transmission." *Journal of Biblical Literature* 57 (1938): 141–54.

Riesner, R. "Essener und Urkirche in Jerusalem." *Bibel und Kirche* 40 (1985): 64–76.

———. *Formen gemeinsamen Lebens im NT und heute*. 2d ed. Giessen, Germany: Brunnen, 1984.

———. *Die Frühzeit des Apostels Paulus: Studien zur Chronologie, Missionsstrategie, und Theologie*. WUNT 71. Tübingen: Mohr, 1994.

———. "Hauskirche." *GBL* 2:535.

———. "Das Jerusalemer Essenerviertel und die Urgemeinde: Josephus, Bellum Judaicum V 145; 11QMiqdasch 46:13–16; Apostelgeschichte 1–6; und die Archäologie." *ANRW* 26.2:1775–1922. Part 2. *Principat*, 26.2. Edited by H. Temporini and W. Haase. New York: de Gruyter, 1995.

———. *Jesus als Lehrer: Eine Untersuchung zum Ursprung der Evangelien-Überlieferung*. 3d ed. WUNT, Reihe 2, 7. Tübingen: Mohr, 1988.

———. "Jesus, the Primitive Community, and the Essene Quarter of Jerusalem." Pages 198–234 in *Jesus and the Dead Sea Scrolls*. Edited by J. H. Charlesworth. New York: Doubleday, 1992.

———. "Kenchreä." *GBL* 2:775.

———. "Korinth." *GBL* 2:815–19.

———. "Philippi." *GBL* 3:1196–99.

———. "Soziologie des Urchristentums: Ein Literaturüberblick." *Theologische Beiträge* 17 (1986): 213–22.

———. "Synogogues in Jerusalem." Pages 179–211 in *The Book of Acts in Its Palestinian Setting*. Edited by R. Bauckham. Vol. 4 of *The Book of Acts in Its First Century Setting*. Edited by B. W. Winter. Grand Rapids: Eerdmans, 1995.

———. "Thessalonich." *GBL* 3:1545–48.

Robert, L. "Documents d'Asie Mineure." *Bulletin de correspondance hellénique* 102 (1978): 405.

———. "Les inscriptions de Thessalonique." *Revue de philologie, de littérature, et d'histoire anciennes* 98 (1974): 180–264.

Robertson, D. S. *A Handbook of Greek and Roman Architecture*. Cambridge: University Press, 1943.

Robertson, E. H. "The House Church." Pages 366–71 in *Basileia*. Festschrift W. Freytag. Edited by J. Hermelink and H. J. Margull. 2d ed. Stuttgart: Evangelischer Missionsverlag, 1961.

Roetzel, C. *The Letters of Paul*. 2d ed. Atlanta: John Knox, 1982.

Robinson, D. M. "Haus." *PWSup* 7:224–78.

Rohde, J. "πρεσβύτερος." *EDNT* 3:148–49.

———. *Urchristliche und frühkatholische Ämter*. Berlin: Evang. Ver. Anst., 1976.

Roloff, J. "Amt IV." *TRE* 2:509–33.

———. "Ansätze kirchlicher Rechtsbildungen im Neuen Testament." Pages 83–142 in vol. 1 of *Studien zu Kirchenrecht und Theologie*. Edited by K. Schlaich. Heidelberg: FEST, 1987.

———. *Apostolat-Verkündigung-Kirche: Ursprung, Inhalt, und Funktion des kirchlichen Apostelamtes nach Paulus, Lukas, und den Pastoralbriefen*. Gütersloh: Mohn, 1965.

———. "ἐκκλησία." *EDNT* 1:410–15.

———. *Exegetische Verantwortung in der Kirche: Aufsätze*. Edited by M. Karrer. Göttingen: Vandenhoeck & Ruprecht, 1990.

———. *Das Kerygma und der irdische Jesus*. 2d ed. Göttingen: Vandenhoeck & Ruprecht, 1973.

———. *Die Kirche im Neuen Testament*. GNT 10. Göttingen: Vandenhoeck & Ruprecht, 1993.

Rordorf, W. "Die Hausgemeinde der vorkonstantinischen Zeit." Pages 76–85 in *Lex Orandi, Lex Credendi*. Festschrift W. Rordorf. Paradosis 36. Fribourg: Universitätsverlag, 1993.

———. "Was wissen wir über die christlichen Gottesdiensträume der vorkonstantinischen Zeit?" *Zeitschrift für die neutestamentliche Wissenschaft und die Kunde der älteren Kirche* 55 (1964): 110–28.

Rose, H. J. "The Religion of a Greek Household." *Euphrosyne* 1 (1957): 95–116.

Rösel, H. "Haus." *BRL2* 138–41.

Rost, L. "Archäologische Bemerkungen zu einer Stelle des Jakobusbriefes (Jak 2:2f)." *Palästina-Jahrbuch* 24 (1933): 53–66.

Rostovtzeff, M. *Die hellenistische Welt*. 3 vols. Stuttgart: Kohlhammer, 1955.

———. *The Social and Economic History of the Roman Empire*. 2 vols. Oxford: Clarendon, 1957.

Rudwik, M. J. S., and C. J. Hemer. "Laodizea." *GBL* 2:867–68.

Rüger, H. P. "Aramäisch." *TRE* 3:602–10.

Rusche, H. *Gastfreundschaft in der Verkündigung des Neuen Testaments und ihr Verhältnis zur Mission.* VIMW 7. Münster: Aschendorff, 1958.
Sachers, E. "Potestas patria." *RE* 22:1046–1175.
Safrai, S. "Home and Family." Pages 728–92 in vol. 2 of *The Jewish People in the First Century: Historical Geography, Political History, Social, Cultural, and Religious Life and Institutions.* Edited by S. Safrai and M. Stern. CRINT 1/2. Assen: Van Gorcum, 1976.
———. "Religion in Everyday Life." Pages 793–833 in vol. 2 of *The Jewish People in the First Century: Historical Geography, Political History, Social, Cultural, and Religious Life and Institutions.* Edited by S. Safrai and M. Stern. CRINT 1/2. Assen: Van Gorcum, 1976.
———. "The Synagogue." Pages 908–44 in vol. 2 of *The Jewish People in the First Century: Historical Geography, Political History, Social, Cultural, and Religious Life and Institutions.* Edited by S. Safrai and M. Stern. CRINT 1/2. Assen: Van Gorcum, 1976.
Saller, R. P. *Personal Patronage under the Early Empire.* Cambridge: Cambridge University, 1982.
Salzmann, J. C. *Lehren und Ermahnen: Zur Geschichte des christlichen Wortgottesdienstes in den ersten drei Jahrhunderten.* WUNT, Reihe 2, 59. 1994.
Sampley, J. P. *"And the Two Shall Become One Flesh."* SNTSMS 16. Cambridge: Cambridge University, 1971.
———. *Pauline Partnership in Christ: Christian Community in the Light of Roman Law.* Philadelphia: Fortress Press, 1980.
Sanders, E. P. *Jesus and Judaism.* Philadelphia: Fortress Press, 1985.
Sandnes, K. O. *A New Family: Conversion and Ecclesiology in the Early Church with Cross-cultural Comparisons.* SIGC 91. Bern: Lang, 1994.
Saxer, V. "Domus ecclesiae: οἶκος τῆς ἐκκλησίας in den frühchristlichen literarischen Texten." *Römische Quartalschrift für christliche Altertumskunde und Kirchengeschichte* 83 (1988): 167–79.
Schäfer, K. *Gemeinde als "Bruderschaft": Ein Beitrag zum Kirchenverständnis des Paulus.* Frankfurt: Lang, 1989.
Schedl, K. *Als sich der Pfingsttag erfüllte: Erklärung der Pfingstperikope Apg 2:1–47.* Vienna: Herder, 1982.
Schenk, W. "Die Einheit von Wortverkündigung und Herrenmahl in den urchristlichen Gemeindenversammlungen." *Theologische Versuche* 2 (1970): 65–92.
———. "Der Philipperbrief in der neueren Forschung." *ANRW* 25.4: 3280–3313. Part 2. *Principat*, 25.4. Edited by H. Temporini and W. Haase. New York: de Gruyter, 1987.
Schenke, L. *Die Wundererzählungen des Markusevangelium.* Stuttgart: Katholisches Bibelwerk, 1974.
———. "Zur sogenannten 'Oikosformel' im Neuen Testament." *Kairos: Zeitschrift für Religionswissenschaft und Theologie* 13 (1971): 226–43.
Schierse, F. J. "Zelle und Gruppenbildung im Urchristentum." Pages 111–28 in *Die Zelle in Kirche und Welt.* Edited by A. Spitaler. Graz: Styria, 1960.
Schille, G. *Anfänge der Kirche: Erwägungen zur apostolischen Frühgeschichte.* BEvT 43. Munich: Kaiser, 1966.
———. *Die urchristliche Kollegialmission.* ATANT 48. Zurich: Zwingli, 1967.

———. *Das vorsynoptische Judenchristentum.* AzTh Reihe 1, 43. Stuttgart: Calwer, 1970.
Schlatter, A. *Die Kirche Jerusalems vom Jahr 70 bis 130.* Gütersloh: C. Bertelsmann, 1898. Repr., pages 99–173 in *Synagoge und Kirche bis zum Barkochba-Aufstand.* Kleinere Schriften von Adolf Schlatter 3. Stuttgart: Calwer, 1966.
———. *Paulus der Bote Jesu.* Stuttgart: Calwer, 1934.
Schlaudraff, K. H. "Gemeinde pflanzen in der Volkskirche." *Für Arbeit und Besinnung: Zeitschrift für die Evangelische Landeskirche in Würtemberg* 22 (November 15, 1996): 820–24.
Schlier, H. "ἀνέχω." *TDNT* 1:359–60.
———. "Die Einheit der Kirche im Denken des Apostel Paulus." Pages 287–99 in *Die Zeit der Kirche: Exegetische Aufsätze und Vorträge.* Edite by H. Schlier. 3d ed. Freiburg: Herder, 1962.
———. "Das Herrenmahl bei Paulus." Pages 201–15 in vol. 3 of *Das Ende der Zeit: Exegetische Aufsätze und Vorträge.* Edited by H. Schlier. 2d ed. Freiburg: Herder, 1971.
———. "κεφαλή." *TDNT* 3:673–82.
Schmeller, T. *Brechungen: Urchristliche Wandercharismatiker im Prisma soziologisch orientierter Exegese.* SBS 136. Stuttgart: Katholisches Bibelwerk, 1989.
———. *Hierarchie und Egalität: Eine sozialgeschichtliche Untersuchung paulinischer Gemeinden und griechisch-römischer Vereine.* SBS 162. Stuttgart: Katholisches Bibelwerk, 1995.
Schmidt, J. "Philippi." *PW* 19:2206–44.
Schmidt, K. L. "ἐκκλησία." *TDNT* 3:501–36.
———. "Die Kirche des Urchristentums: Eine lexikographische und biblisch-theologische Studie." Pages 258–319 in *Festgabe für Adolf Deissmann zum 60. Geburtstag, 7. November 1926.* Edited by K. L. Schmidt. Tübingen: Mohr, 1927.
———. *Der Rahmen der Geschichte Jesu: Literarkritische Untersuchungen zur ältesten Jesusüberlieferungen.* 2d ed., Darmstadt: Wissenschaftliche Buchgesellschaft, 1964.
Schmithals, W. *Paulus und die Gnostiker: Untersuchungen zu den kleinen Paulusbriefen.* ThF 35. Hamburg-Bergstedt: Reich, 1965.
———. *Paulus und Jakobus.* FRLANT 85. Göttingen: Vandenhoeck & Ruprecht, 1963.
Schnackenburg, R. "Ephesus: Entwicklung einer Gemeinde von Paulus zu Johannes." *Biblische Zeitschrift* 35 (1991): 41–64.
———. "Episkopus und Hirtenamt: Zu Apg 20:28." Pages 66–88 in *Episcopus: Studien über das Bischofsamt.* Festschrift Kardinal Faulhaber. Regensburg: Pustet, 1949.
———. *Die Kirche im Neuen Testament.* 2d ed. QD 14. Freiburg: Herder, 1963.
———. "Lukas als Zeuge verschiedener Gemeindestrukturen." *Bibel und Leben* 12 (1971): 232–47.
———. *Die sittliche Botschaft des Neuen Testaments.* 2d ed. HMT 6. Munich: Max Hueber, 1962.
Schneider, G. "Philemon." *EDNT* 3:426.

Schneider, K. "Taberna." PW 4:1863–72.

Schöllgen, G. *Ecclesia sordida? Zur Frage der sozialen Schichtung frühchristlicher Gemeinden am Beispiel Karthagos zur Zeit Tertullians.* JAC.E 12. Münster: Aschendorff, 1985.

———. "Hausgemeinden, ΟΙΚΟΣ-Ekklesiologie, und monarchischer Episkopat." *Jahrbuch für Antike und Christentum* 31 (1988): 74–90.

———. "Probleme der frühchristlichen Sozialgeschichte: Einwände gegen Peter Lampes Buch über *Die stadtrömischen Christen in den ersten beiden Jahrhunderten.*" JAC.E 32 (1989): 23–40.

———. "Was wissen wir über die Sozialstruktur der paulinischen Gemeinden? Kritische Anmerkungen zu einem neuen Buch von W. A. Meeks." *New Testament Studies* 34 (1988): 71–82.

Schottroff, L. "Wie berechtigt ist die feministische Kritik an Paulus? Paulus und die Frauen in den ersten christlichen Gemeinden im römischen Reich." *Einwürfe* 2 (1985): 94–111.

Schrage, W. "Ekklesia und Synagoge." *Zeitschrift für Theologie und Kirche* 60 (1963): 178–202.

———. *Ethik des Neuen Testaments.* 5th ed. GNT 4. Göttingen: Vandenhoeck & Ruprecht, 1989.

———. *Die konkreten Einzelgebote in der paulinischen Paränese.* Gütersloh: Mohn, 1961.

———. "συναγωγή." *TDNT* 7:798–852.

———. "Zur Ethik der neutestamentlichen Haustafeln." *New Testament Studies* 21 (1974/1975): 1–21.

Schreiber, A. *Die Gemeinde von Korinth: Versuch einer gruppendymanischen Betrachtung der Entwicklung der Gemeinde von Korinth auf der Basis des ersten Korintherbriefes.* NTAbh NF 12. Münster; Aschendorff, 1977.

Schrenk, G. "δίκαιος." *TDNT* 2:182–91.

———. "πατήρ." *TDNT* 5:945–1014.

Schroeder, D. "Die Haustafeln des Neuen Testaments: Ihre Herkunft und ihr theologischer Sinn." ThD diss., University of Hamburg, 1959.

Schuler, C. "The Macedonian Politarchs." *Classical Philology* 55 (1960): 90–100.

Schulz, A. *Jünger des Herrn: Nachfolge Christi nach dem Neuen Testament.* Munich: Kösel, 1964.

———. *Nachfolgen und Nachahmen: Studien über das Verhältnis der neutestamentlichen Jüngerschaft zur urchristlichen Vorbildethik.* SANT 6. Munich: Kösel, 1962.

Schulz, H. M. "Die territoriale Gemeinde als Basisgemeinde: Zum Beispiel, Eschborn." Pages 111–21 in *Kirche von unten: Alternative Gemeinden—Modelle-Erfahrungen-Reflexionen.* Edited by H. Frankemölle. Mainz: Grünewald, 1981.

Schulz, S. *Gott ist kein Sklavenhalter: Die Geschichte einer verspäteten Revolution.* Zurich: Flamberg, 1972.

———. *Die Mitte der Schrift: Der Frühkatholizismus im Neuen Testament als Herausforderung an den Protestantismus.* Stuttgart: Kreuz, 1976.

———. *Neutestamentliche Ethik.* Zurich: Theologischer, 1987.

———. *Q: Die Spruchquelle der Evangelisten.* Zurich: Theologischer, 1972.

Schürer, E. *History of the Jewish People in the Age of Jesus Christ*. Edited by G. Vermes, F. Millar, and M. Black. 3 vols. in 4. Rev. ed. Edinburgh: T&T Clark, 1973–1987.

Schürmann, H. "Die geistlichen Gnadengaben in den paulinischen Gemeinden." Pages 362–412 in *Das kirchliche Amt im Neuen Testament*. Edited by K. Kertelge. WdF 439. Darmstadt: Wissenschaftliche Buchgesellschaft, 1977.

———. "Gemeinde als Bruderschaft." Pages 77–99 in *Ursprung und Gestalt: Erörterungen und Besinnungen zum Neuen Testament*. Edited by H. Schürmann. KBANT 2. Düsseldorf: Patmos, 1970.

———. "Das Gesetz des Christus (Gal 6:2)." Pages 282–300 in *Neues Testamemt und Kirche*. Edited by J. Gnilka. Freiburg: Herder, 1974.

———. *Traditionsgeschichtliche Untersuchungen zu den synoptischen Evangelien*. Düsseldorf: Patmos, 1968.

———. "' . . . und Lehrer': Die geistliche Eigenart des Lehrdienstes und sein Verhältnis zu anderen geistlichen Diensten im neutestamentlichen Zeitalter." Pages 107–47 in *Dienst der Vermittlung*. Edited by W. Ernst, K. Feiereis, and F. Hoffmann, EThSt 37. Leipzig: St. Benno, 1977.

———. "Die vorösterlichen Anfänge der Logientradition." Pages 342–70 in *Der historische Jesus und der kerygmatische Christus*. Edited by H. Ristow and K. Matthiae. Berlin: Evangel. Verlagsanst, 1960. Repr., pages 39–65 in *Traditionsgeschichtliche Untersuchungen zu den synoptischen Evangelien* (above).

Schüssler Fiorenza, E. "Ehe und Jüngerschaft." Pages 220–27 in *Frauenbefreiung: Biblische und theologische Argumente*. Edited by E. Moltmann-Wendel. 4th ed. Systematische Beiträge 12. Munich: Kaiser, 1986.

———. "You Are Not to Be Called Father: Early Christian History in a Feminist Perspective." Pages 151–79 in *Discipleship of Equals: A Critical Feminist Ecclesiology of Liberation*. New York: Crossroad, 1993.

———. *Zu ihrem Gedächtnis: Eine feministisch-theologische Rekonstruktion der christlichen Ursprünge*. Munich: Kaiser, 1988. ET: *In Memory of Her: A Feminist Theological Reconstruction of Christian Origins*. N.t. New York: Crossroad, 1983.

Schwank, B. "Gab es zur Zeit der öffentlichen Tätigkeit Jesu Qumran-Essener in Jerusalem?" Pages 115–30 in *Christen und Christliches in Qumran?* Edited by B. Mayer. ESt NF 32. Regensburg: Pustet, 1992.

———. "Qualis erat forma synagogarum Novi Testamenti?" *Verbum Domini* 33 (1955): 267–79.

Schwartz, D. R. "Non-joining Sympathizers (Acts 5:13–14)." *Biblica* 64 (1983): 550–55.

Schwarz, F., and C. A. Schwarz. *Theologie des Gemeindeaufbaus: Ein Versuch*. 3d ed. Neukirchen-Vluyn: Aussaat, 1987.

Schwarz, J. *Das heilige Land nach seiner ehemaligen und jetzigen geographischen Beschaffenheit*. Revised by I. Schwarz. Frankfurt: J. Kauffmann, 1852.

Schwarz, R. *Bürgerliches Christentum im Neuen Testament? Eine Studie zu Ethik, Amt, und Recht in den Pastoralbriefen*. ÖBS 4. Klosterneuburg, Austria: Österreichisches Katholisches Bibelwerk, 1983.

Schweitzer, O. *Hauskreis offensiv: Tips für missionarische Hauskreise.* Wuppertal: Brockhaus, 1984.
Schweizer, E. "The Church as the Missionary Body of Christ." *New Testament Studies* 8 (1961): 1–11.
———. *Gemeinde und Gemeindeordnung im Neuen Testament.* Edited by B. Mayer. 2d ed. ATANT 35. Zurich: Zwingli, 1962.
———. "Die Kirche als Leib Christi in den paulinischen Antilegomena." *Theologische Literaturzeitung* 86 (1961): 241–56.
———. "Traditional Ethical Patterns in the Pauline and Post-Pauline Letters and Their Development (List of Vices and House-Tables)." Pages 195–209 in *Text and Interpretation.* Festschrift M. Black and R. Wilson. Edited by E. Best. Cambridge: Cambridge University, 1975.
———. "υἱός." *TDNT* 8:334–97.
———. "Die Weltlichkeit des Neuen Testaments: Die Haustafeln." Pages 397–413 in *Beiträge zur alttestamentlichen Theologie.* Festschrift W. Zimmerli. Edited by H. Donner. Göttingen: Vandenhoeck & Ruprecht, 1977.
———. "Zum Sklavenproblem im Neuen Testament." *Evangelische Theologie* 32 (1972): 502–6.
Schwöbel, W. "Die Verkehrswege und Ansiedlungen Galiläas in ihrer Abhängigkeit von den natürlichen Bedingungen." *Zeitschrift des deutschen Palästina-Vereins* 27 (1904): 1–151.
Scott, J. M. *Paul and the Nations: The Old Testament and Jewish Background of Paul's Mission to the Nations with Special Reference to the Destination of Galatians.* WUNT 84. Tübingen: Mohr, 1995.
Scranton, R., et al. *Topography and Architecture.* Vol. 1 of *Kenchreai: Eastern Port of Corinth.* Leiden: Brill, 1978.
Scroggs, R. "The Sociological Interpretation of the New Testament: The Present State of Research." *New Testament Studies* 26 (1980): 164–79.
Seesemann, H. *Der Begriff* ΚΟΙΝΩΝΙΑ *im Neuen Testament.* BZNW 14. Giessen, Germany: A. Töpelmann, 1933.
Segert, S. *Die Gütergemeinschaft der Essener: A. Salach oblata.* Prague: n.p., 1955.
Seitz, M. "Distanz und Liebe zur Welt—von der Nachfolge unter den Bedingungen unserer Zeit." Lecture at a pastor's conference. Reichelsheim, Germany, March 6, 1997. Sound cassette.
———. *Erneuerung der Gemeinde: Gemeindeaufbau und Spiritualität.* Göttingen: Vandenhoeck & Ruprecht, 1985.
Selman, M. J. "Haus." *GBL* 2:529–33.
Shear, T. L. *The Roman Villa.* Corinth: Results of Excavations Conducted by the American School of Classical Studies at Athens 5. Cambridge, Mass: Harvard University, 1930.
Sherwin-White, A. N. *Roman Law and Roman Society in the New Testament.* Oxford: Clarendon, 1963. Repr., Grand Rapids: Baker, 1978.
Siegert, F. "Gottesfürchtige und Sympathisanten." *Journal for the Study of Judaism in the Persian, Hellenistic, and Roman Periods* 4 (1973): 109–64.
Smith, D. E. Book review. *Second Century* 8 (1991): 253–55.
———. "Social Obligation in the Context of Communal Meals: A Study of the Christian Meal in 1 Corinthians in Comparison with Graeco-Roman Meals." ThD diss., Harvard Divinity School, 1980.

Smith, J. Z. "The Social Description of Early Christianity." *Journal for the Study of Religion* 1, no. 1 (1975): 19–25.
Smith, R. W. "Chorazin." *ABD* 1:911–12.
Snyder, G. F. *Ante Pacem: Archaeological Evidence of Church Life before Constantine*. Macon: Mercer University Press, 1969.
Sobosan, J. G. "The Role of the Presbyter." *Scottish Journal of Theology* 27 (1974): 129–46.
Sohm, R. *Die geschichtlichen Grundlagen*. Vol. 1 of *Kirchenrecht*. Systematisches Handbuch der Deutschen Rechtswissenschaft, 8. Munich: Duncker & Humblot, 1923.
Solin, H. *Die Griechischen Personennamen in Rom: Ein Namenbuch*. 3 vols. Berlin: de Gruyter, 1982.
Sorg, T. "Einladende Kirche." *Theologische Beiträge* 22 (1991): 3–20.
———. "Perspektiven für unsere Kirche." *Lebendige Gemeinde* 2 (1994): 8–10.
———. "Zwischen Säkularität und Religiosität: Volkskirche in den neunziger Jahren." *Theologische Beiträge* 21 (1990): 65–77.
Spicq, C. "L'épître aux Hébreux: Apollos, Jean-Baptiste, les hellénistes, et Qumrân." *Revue de Qumran* 1 (1958/1959): 365–90.
Staerk, W. *Die jüdische Gemeinde des Neuen Bundes in Damaskus*. BFCT 27/3. Gütersloh: C. Bertelsmann, 1922.
Stager, L. E. "The Archaeology of the Family in Ancient Israel." *Bulletin of the American Schools of Oriental Research* 260 (1985): 1–35.
Stählin, G. "ἴσος." *TDNT* 3:343–55.
———. "ξένος." *TDNT* 5:1–36.
Stambaugh, J. E. "Social Relations in the City of the Early Principate: State of Research." Pages 75–99 in *SBL Seminar Papers, 1980*. SBLSP 19. Chico, Calif.: Scholars Press, 1980.
Stambaugh, J. E., and D. L. Balch. *The New Testament in Its Social Environment*. Philadelphia: Westminster Press, 1986.
———. *The Social World of the First Christians*. London: SPCK, 1986.
Stanton, G. N. "Form Criticism Revisited." Pages 13–27 in *What about the New Testament?* Festschrift C. Evans. Edited by M. D. Hooker and C. Hickling. London: SCM Press, 1975.
Stegemann, E., and W. Stegemann. *Urchristliche Sozialgeschichte: Die Anfänge im Judentum und die Christusgemeinden in der mediterranen Welt*. Stuttgart: Kohlhammer, 1995.
Stegemann, W. "Nachfolge Jesu als solidarische Gemeinschaft der reichen und angesehenen Christen mit den bedürftigen und verachteten Christen." Pages 89–153 in *Jesus von Nazareth: Hoffnung der Armen*. Edited by L. Schottroff and W. Stegemann. 2d ed. Stuttgart: Kohlhammer, 1981.
———. "Wanderradikalismus im Urchristentum? Historische und theologische Auseinandersetzung mit einer interessanten These." Pages 94–120 in *Der Gott der kleinen Leute*. Edited by W. Schottroff and W. Stegemann. Sozialgeschichtliche Auslegungen 2, Neues Testament. Munich: Kaiser, 1979.
———. "War der Apostel Paulus ein römischer Bürger?" *Zeitschrift für die neutestamentliche Wissenschaft und die Kunde der älteren Kirche* 78 (1987): 200–229.

———. *Zwischen Synagoge und Obrigkeit: Zur historischen Situation der lukanischen Christen.* FRLANT 152. Göttingen: Vandenhoeck & Ruprecht, 1991.

Stendahl, K. *The Bible and the Role of Women.* Philadelphia: Fortress Press, 1966.

Stowers, S. K. "A Cult from Philadelphia: Oikos Religion or Cultic Association?" Pages 287–301 in *The Early Church and Its Context.* Festschrift E. Ferguson. Edited by A. Malherbe. Leiden: Brill, 1998.

———. *Letter Writing in Greco-Roman Antiquity.* Philadelphia: Westminster Press, 1986.

———. "Social Status, Public Speaking, and Private Teaching: The Circumstances of Paul's Preaching Activity." *Novum Testamentum* 26 (1984): 59–82.

Strack, H. L. *Jesus, die Häretiker, und die Christen nach den ältesten jüdischen Angaben: Texte, Übersetzungen, und Erläuterungen.* Leipzig: J. C. Hinrichs, 1910.

Strange, J. F. "Beth-Saida." *ABD* 1:692–93.

———. "The Capernaum and Herodium Publications." *Bulletin of the American Schools of Oriental Research* 226 (1977): 65–74.

Strange, J. F., and H. Shanks. "Has the House Where Jesus Stayed in Capernaum Been Found?" *Biblical Archaeology Review* 8, no. 6 (1982): 26–37.

———. "Synagogue Where Jesus Preached Found at Capernaum." *Biblical Archaeology Review* 9, no. 6 (1983): 24–31.

Strecker, G. "Judenchristentum." *TRE* 17:310–25.

———. "Die neutestamentlichen Haustafeln (Kol 3:18–4:1 und Eph 5:22–6:9)." Pages 349–75 in *Neues Testament und Ethik.* Festschrift R. Schnackenburg. Edited by Helmut Merklein. Freiburg: Herder, 1989.

Streeter, B. H. *The Primitive Church.* London: Macmillan, 1929.

Strobel, A. "Der Begriff des 'Hauses' im griechischen und römischen Privatrecht." *Zeitschrift für die neutestamentliche Wissenschaft und die Kunde der älteren Kirche* 56 (1965): 91–100.

———. "Säuglings- und Kindertaufe in der ältesten Kirche: Eine kritische Untersuchung der Standpunkte von J. Jeremias und K. Aland." Pages 7–69 in *Begründung und Gebrauch der heiligen Taufe.* Edited by O. Perels. Berlin: Lutherisches Verlagshaus, 1963.

———. "Die Wasseranlagen von Hirbet Qumran." *Zeitschrift des deutschen Palästina-Vereins* 88 (1972): 55–86.

Strunk, R. *Schritte zum Vertrauen: Praktische Konsequenzen für den Gemeindeaufbau.* Stuttgart: Quell, 1989.

Stuhlmacher, P. "Christliche Verantwortung bei Paulus und seinen Schülern." *EvT* 28 (1968): 165–86.

———. "Evangelium-Apostolat-Gemeinde." *Kerygma und Dogma* 17 (1971): 28–45.

———, ed. *Das Evangelium und die Evangelien.* WUNT 28. Tübingen: Mohr, 1983.

———. *Gerechtigkeit Gottes bei Paulus.* 2d ed. Göttingen: Vandenhoeck & Ruprecht, 1965.

———. *Grundlegung: Von Jesus zu Paulus.* Vol. 1. of *Biblische Theologie des Neuen Testaments.* Göttingen: Vandenhoeck & Ruprecht, 1992.

———. "Historisch Unangemessen." *EK* 5 (1972): 297–99.
———. "Jesustradition im Römerbrief?" *Theologische Beiträge* 14 (1983): 240–50.
———. "Kirche nach dem Neuen Testament: G. Jeremias zum 60. Geburtstag." *Theologische Beiträge* 26 (1995): 301–25.
———. "Matthew 28:16–20 and the Course of Mission in the Apostolic and Postapostolic Age." Pages 17–43 in *The Mission of the Early Church to Jews and Gentiles*. Edited by J. Adna and H. Kvalbein. Tübingen: Mohr, 2000.
———. "Das neutestamentliche Zeugnis vom Herrenmahl." *Zeitschrift für Theologie und Kirche* 84 (1987): 1–35.
———. "Volkskirche—weiter so?" *Theologische Beiträge* 23 (1992): 151–70.
———. *Vorgeschichte*. Vol. 1 of *Das paulinische Evangelium*. FRLANT 95. Göttingen: Vandenhoek & Ruprecht, 1968.
———. "Weg, Stil, und Konsequenzen urchristlicher Mission." *Theologische Beiträge* 12 (1983): 107–35.
Stuhlmacher, P., and W. Class. *Das Evangelium von der Versöhnung in Christus*. Stuttgart: Calwer, 1979.
Sweet, L. *FaithQuakes*. Nashville: Abingdon Press, 1994.
Swidler, L. *Biblical Affirmations of Woman*. Philadelphia: Westminster, 1979.
Tajra, H. W. *The Trial of St. Paul: A Juridical Exegesis of the Second Half of the Acts of the Apostles*. WUNT, Reihe 2, 35. Tübingen: Mohr, 1989.
Tashjian, J. "The Social Setting of the Mission Charge in Q." PhD diss., Claremont University, 1987.
Taylor, J. E. "Capernaum and Its 'Jewish-Christians': A Re-examinaton of the Franciscan Excavations." *Bulletin of the Anglo-Israel Archaeological Society* 9 (1989/1990): 7–28.
———. *Christians and the Holy Places: The Myth of Jewish-Christian Origins*. Oxford: Clarendon, 1993.
———. "A Critical Investigation of Archaeological Material Assigned to Palestinian Jewish-Christians of the Roman and Byzantine Periods." PhD diss., University of Edinburgh, 1989.
Testa, E. "I 'Discorsi di Missione' di Gesù." *Studium biblicum franciscanum: Liber annuus* 29 (1979): 7–41.
Theissen, G. "Legitimation and Subsistence: An Essay on the Sociology of Early Christian Missionaries." Pages 27–67 *The Social Setting of Pauline Christianity: Essays on Corinth*. Edited and translated and with an introduction by J. H. Schütz. Philadelphia: Fortress Press, 1982. 2d ed., Edinburgh: T&T Clark, 1990.
———. *Psychologische Aspekte paulinischer Theologie*. FRLANT 131. Göttingen: Vandenhoeck & Ruprecht, 1983.
———. "Social Integration and Sacramental Activity: An Analysis of 1 Cor. 11:17–34." Pages 145–74 in *The Social Setting of Pauline Christianity: Essays on Corinth*. Edited and translated and with an introduction by J. H. Schütz. Philadelphia: Fortress Press, 1982. 2d ed., Edinburgh: T&T Clark, 1990.
———. *Social Reality and the Early Christians: Theology, Ethics, and the World of the New Testament*. Translated by M. Kohl. Minneapolis: Fortress Press, 1992.

———. *The Social Setting of Pauline Christianity: Essays on Corinth*. Edited and translated and with an introduction by J. H. Schütz. Philadelphia: Fortress Press, 1982. 2d ed., Edinburgh: T&T Clark, 1990.

———. "Social Stratification in the Corinthian Community: A Contribution to the Sociology of Early Hellenistic Christianity." Pages 69–119 in *The Social Setting of Pauline Christianity: Essays on Corinth*. Edited and translated and with an introduction by J. H. Schütz. Philadelphia: Fortress Press, 1982. 2d ed., Edinburgh: T&T Clark, 1990.

———. "The Sociological Interpretation of Religious Traditions: Its Methodological Problems as Exemplified in Early Christianity." Pages 175–200 in *The Social Setting of Pauline Christianity: Essays on Corinth*. Edited and translated and with an introduction by J. H. Schütz. Philadelphia: Fortress Press, 1982. 2d ed., Edinburgh: T&T Clark, 1990.

———. *Sociology of Early Palestinian Christianity*. Translated by J. Bowden. Philadelphia: Fortress, 1978.

———. "The Strong and the Weak in Corinth: A Sociological Analysis of a Theological Quarrel." Pages 121–43 in *The Social Setting of Pauline Christianity: Essays on Corinth*. Edited and translated and with an introduction by J. H. Schütz. Philadelphia: Fortress Press, 1982. 2d ed., Edinburgh: T&T Clark, 1990.

———. *Studien zur Soziologie des Urchristentums*. 3d ed. WUNT 19. Tübingen: Mohr, 1989.

———. "The Wandering Radicals: Light Shed by the Sociology of Literature on the Early Transmission of Jesus Sayings." Pages 33–59 in *Social Reality and the Early Christians: Theology, Ethics, and the World of the New Testament*. Translated by M. Kohl. Minneapolis: Fortress Press, 1992.

———. "We Have Left Everything . . . (Mark 10:28): Discipleship and Social Uprooting in the Jewish-Palestinian Society of the First Century." Pages 60–93 in *Social Reality and the Early Christians: Theology, Ethics, and the World of the New Testament*. Translated by M. Kohl. Minneapolis: Fortress Press, 1992.

Thiering, B. E. "Mebaqqer and Episkopos in the Light of the Temple Scroll." *Journal of Biblical Literature* 100 (1981): 59–74.

Thomas, W. D. "The Place of Women in the Church at Philippi." *Expository Times* 83 (1971/1972): 117–20.

Thompson, W. G. *Matthew's Advice to a Divided Community, Mt 17:22–18:35*. Rome: Biblical Institute Press, 1970.

Thornton, C. J. *Der Zeuge des Zeugen: Lukas als Historiker der Paulusreisen*. WUNT 56. Tübingen: Mohr, 1991.

Thraede, K. "Ärger mit der Freiheit." Pages 31–182 in *"Freunde in Christus werden . . .": Die Beziehung von Mann und Frau als Frage an Theologie und Kirche*. Edited by G. Scharffenorth and K. Thraede. Berlin: Burckhardthaus-Verlag, 1977.

———. "Frau." *RAC* 8:197–269.

———. "Zum historischen Hintergrund der 'Haustafeln' des Neuen Testaments." Pages 359–68 in *Pietas*. Festschrift B. Kötting. Edited by E. Dassmann and K. S. Frank. JAC.E 8. Münster: Aschendorff, 1980.

Thür, H. "Ephesos: Wohnen in einer antiken Grossstadt." *Bibel und Kirche* 53 (1998): 195–96.

Thurston, B. B. "τὸ ὑπερῷον in Acts 1:13." *Expository Times* 80 (1968): 21–22.
Tidball, D. *An Introduction to the Sociology of the New Testament.* Exeter: Paternoster, 1983.
Ting, K. H. *Chinese Christians Speak Out: Addresses and Sermons.* Beijing: New World Press, 1984.
Torrey, C. C. *The Composition and Date of Acts.* HTS 1. Cambridge: Harvard University Press, 1916.
Towery, B. *Christen in China.* Wuppertal: Oncken, 1987.
Towner, P. H. *The Goal of Our Instruction: The Structure of Theology and Ethics in the Pastoral Epistles.* JSNTSup 34. Sheffield, Engl.: JSOT Press, 1989.
Trautmann, M. *Zeichenhafte Handlungen Jesu: Ein Beitrag zur Frage nach dem geschichtlichen Jesus.* FB 37. Würzburg: Echter, 1980.
Trible, P. "Gegen das patriarchalische Prinzip in der Bibelinterpretation." Pages 93–117 in *Frauenbefreiung: Biblische und theologische Argumente.* Edited by Elisabeth Moltmann-Wendel. 4th ed. Systematische Beiträge 12. Munich: Kaiser, 1986.
Trilling, W. *Fragen zur Geschichtlichkeit Jesu.* 2d ed. Düsseldorf: Patmos, 1967.
———. *Das wahre Israel: Studien zur Theologie des Matthäusevangeliums.* ETS 7. Leipzig: St. Benno-Verlag, 1962. 2d ed., Munich: Kösel, 1964.
Trocmé, E. *The Formation of the Gospel according to Mark.* Translated by P. Gaughan. London: SPCK, 1975.
———. *Jesus and His Contemporaries.* SCM Press. London: SCM Press, 1973.
Tuckett, C. M. "Paul and the Synoptic Mission Discourse?" *Ephemerides theologicae lovanienses* 60 (1984): 376–81.
Turner, H. E. W. *Jesus, Master and Lord: A Study in the Historical Truth of the Gospel.* London: Mowbray, 1970.
Turner, H. W. *From Temple to Meeting House: The Phenomenolgy and Theology of Places of Worship.* RS 16. New York: Mouton, 1977.
Tzaferis, V., ed. *Excavations at Capernaum.* Vol. 1. Winona Lake, Ind.: Eisenbrauns, 1989.
———. "New Archaeological Evidence on Ancient Capernaum." *Biblical Archaeologist* 46 (1983): 198–204.
Urman, D. *The Golan.* Biblical Archaeology Review International Series 269. Oxford: B. A. R., 1985.
Uro, R. "Sheep among the Wolves: A Study on the Mission Instructions of Q." ThD diss., University of Helsinki, 1987.
Vaage, L. "Q: The Ethos and the Ethics of an Itinerant Intelligence." PhD diss., Claremont University, 1987.
Valeske, U. *Votum Ecclesiae.* 2 vols in 1. Munich: Claudius, 1962.
Vaux, R. de, *Archaeology of the Dead Sea Scrolls.* London: Oxford University, 1973.
Vazakas, A. "Is Acts I–XV. 35 a Literal Translation from an Aramaic Original?" *Journal of Biblical Literature* 37 (1918): 105–10.
Vermes, G. *The Dead Sea Scrolls in English.* 3d ed. Hamondsworth: Penguin, 1987.
———. *The Dead Sea Scrolls: Qumran in Perspective.* 2d ed. London: SCM, 1982.

Vermes G., and M. D. Goodman. *The Essenes according to the Classical Sources.* Sheffield, Engl.: JSOT, 1989.
Verner, D. C. *The Household of God: The Social World of the Pastoral Epistles.* SBLDS 71. Chico, Calif.: Scholars Press, 1983.
Vielhauer, P. *Geschichte der urchristlichen Literatur: Einleitung in das Neue Testament, die Apokryphen, und die Apostolischen Väter.* 2d ed. Berlin: de Gruyter, 1978.
———. "'Oikodome': Das Bild vom Bau in der christlichen Literatur vom Neuen Testament bis Clemens Alexandrinus." Pages 1–168 in vol. 2 of *Oikodome: Aufsätze zum Neuen Testament.* TB 65. Munich: Kaiser, 1979.
Vincent, J. J. *Disciples and Lord: The Historical and Theological Significance of Discipleship in the Synoptic Gospels.* Sheffield, Engl.: Academy Press, 1976.
Vitringa, C. *De synagoga vetere libri tres.* 2d ed. Weissenfels, 1726. ET: *The Synagogue and the Church.* Condensed by J. L. Bernard. London: B. Fellowes, 1842.
Vittinghoff, F. "Gesellschaft." Pages 161–369 in vol. 1 of *Handbuch der Europäischen Wirtschafts- und Sozialgeschichte.* Edited by F. Vittinghoff. Europäische Wirtschafts- und Sozialgeschichte in der römischen Kaiserzeit. Stuttgart: Klett-Cotta, 1990.
Vogler, W. "Die Bedeutung der urchristlichen Hausgemeinden für die Ausbreitung des Evangeliums." *Theologische Literaturzeitung* 11 (1982): 785–94.
Waele, F. J. de. "The Roman Market North of the Temple at Corinth." *American Journal of Archaeology* 34 (1930): 432–54.
Wagener, U. *Die Ordnung des "Hauses Gottes": Der Ort von Frauen in der Ekklesiologie und Ethik der Pastoralbriefe.* WUNT, Reihe 2, 65. Tübingen: Mohr, 1994.
Wagner, F. *Das Bild der frühen Ökonomik.* Salzburger sozialwissenschaftliche Studien 1. Salzburg: Stifterbibliothek, 1969.
Wagner, J. *Altchristliche Eucharistiefeiern im kleinen Kreis.* Trier: Deutschen Litergisches Institute, 1993.
Walker, A. *Restoring the Kingdom: The Radical Christianity of the House Church Movement.* London: Hodder and Stoughton, 1986.
Wallace-Hadrill, A. "Houses and Households: Sampling Pompeii and Herculaneum." Pages 191–227 in *Marriage, Divorce, and Children in Ancient Rome.* Edited by B. Rawson. 2d ed. Oxford: Clarendon, 1992.
———. *Houses and Society in Pompeii and Herculaneum.* Princeton: Princeton University, 1994.
Wang, J. "The House Church Movement: A Participant's Assessment." *Word and World: Theology for Christian Ministry* 17, no. 2 (1997): 175–82.
Wanke, J. *Die Emmauserzählung: Eine Redaktionsgeschichtliche Untersuchung zu Lk 24:13–35.* EThS 31. Leipzig: St. Benno, 1973.
Ward-Perkins, J. B. "Constantine and the Origins of the Christian Basilica." *Papers of the British School at Rome* 22 (1954): 69–90.
Warren, R. *Building Missionary Congregations: Towards a Post-modern Way of Being Church.* Board of Mission Occasional Paper No. 4. London: Church House Publishing, 1995.

Weber, H. R. "Die Hauskirche." *Das missionarische Wort* 11 (1958): 33–40.
Wechsler, A. *Geschichtsbild und Apostelstreit: Eine forschungsgeschichtliche und exegetische Studie über den antiochenischen Zwischenfall (Gal 2:11–14)*. BZNW 62. Berlin: de Gruyter, 1991.
Weidinger, K. *Die Haustafeln: Ein Stück urchristlicher Paränese*. UNT 14. Leipzig: J. C. Hinrichs, 1928.
Weigandt, P. "Zur sog. 'Oikosformel.'" *Novum Testamentum* 6 (1963): 49–74.
Weinberg, S. S. *The Southeast Building, The Twin Basilicas, The Mosaic House*. Corinth: Results of Excavations Conducted by the American School of Classical Studies at Athens 1/5. Princeton: American School of Classical Studies at Athens, 1960.
Weinfeld, M. *The Organisational Pattern and the Penal Code of the Qumran Sect: A Comparison with Guilds and Religious Associations of the Hellenistic-Roman Period*. NTOA 2. Göttingen: Vandenhoeck & Ruprecht, 1986.
Weingarten, H. "Die Umwandlung der ursprünglichen christlichen Gemeindeorganisation zur katholischen Kirche." *Historische Zeitschrift* 9 (1881): 441–67.
Weintraub, B. "Unearthing a Pioneer Church." *National Geographic Millennium Suppl.* 195, no. 2 (Feb 1999): n.p.
Weiser, A. "Evangelisierung im antiken 'Haus.'" Pages 119–48 in *Studien zu Christsein und Kirche*. SBAB 9. Stuttgart: Katholisches Bibelwerk, 1990.
———. "Evangelisierung im 'Haus.'" *Biblische Zeitschrift* NF 34 (1990): 63–86.
———. "Die Kirche in den Pastoralbriefen." *Bibel und Kirche* 46 (1991): 107–13.
———. "Die Rolle der Frau in der urchristlichen Mission." Pages 158–81 in *Die Frau im Urchristentum*. Edited by G. Dautzenberg. QD 95. Freiburg: Herder, 1983.
Weiss, J. *Earliest Christianity: A History of the Period A.D. 30–150*. 2 vols. Translated by F. C. Grant. New York: Harper and Row, 1959.
Weizsäcker C. *Das apostolische Zeitalter der christlichen Kirche*. 3d ed. Tübingen: Mohr, 1902.
Wendland, H. D. "Sklaverei und Christentum." *RGG* 6:101–4.
West, A. B. *Latin Inscriptions, 1896–1926*. Corinth: Results of Excavations conducted by the American School of Classical Studies at Athens 8/2. Cambridge: Harvard University Press, 1931.
Wetzel, K. "Hausgemeinde." *GBL* 2:534.
White, L. M. "Adolf Harnack and the 'Expansion' of Christianity: A Reappraisal of Social History." *Second Century* 5, no. 2 (1985/1986): 97–127.
———. Book review. *Journal of Biblical Literature* 103 (1984): 287–89.
———. *Building God's House in the Roman World: Architectural Adaptation among Pagans, Jews, and Christians*. Baltimore: Johns Hopkins University, 1990. Repr. as vol. 1 of *The Social Origins of Christian Architecture*. HTS 42. Valley Forge: Trinity, 1996.
———. "The Delos Synogogue Revisited: Recent Fieldwork in the Graeco-Roman Diaspora." *Harvard Theological Review* 80 (1987): 133–60.
———. "Domus Ecclesiae—Domus Dei: Adaptation and Development in the Setting for Early Christian Assembly." PhD diss., Yale University, 1982.
———. "Social Authority in the House Church Setting and Ephesians 4:1–16." *Restoration Quarterly* 29 (1987): 109–18.

———. "Sociological Analysis of Early Christian Groups: A Social Historian's Response." *Sociological Analysis* 47 (1986): 249–66.

———. *Texts and Monuments for the Christian Domus Ecclesiae in Its Environment.* Vol. 2 of *The Social Origins of Christian Architecture.* HTS 42. Valley Forge: Trinity, 1997.

———. "Visualizing the 'Real' World of Acts 16: Toward Construction of a Social Index." Pages 234–61 in *The Social World of the First Christians.* Festschrift W. A. Meeks. Edited by L. M. White and O. L. Yarbrough. Minneapolis: Fortress, 1995.

Wiedemann, T. E. J. *Adults and Children in the Roman Empire.* London: Routledge, 1989.

———. *Greek and Roman Slavery.* 3d ed. London: Routledge, 1992.

Wiefel, W. "Die jüdische Gemeinschaft im antiken Rom und die Anfänge des römischen Christentums." *Judaica* 26 (1970): 65–88.

———. "Der Synagogengottesdienst im ntl. Zeitalter und seine Einwirkung auf den entstehenden christlichen Gottesdienst." ThD diss., University of Leipzig, 1959.

Wieland, F. *Der Altar der vorkonstantinischen Kirche.* Vol. 1 of *Mensa und Confessio: Studien über den Altar der altchristlichen Liturgie.* VKHSM 2/11. Munich: J. J. Lentner, 1906.

Wikenhauser, A. *Die Apostelgeschichte und ihr Geschichtswert.* Münster: Aschendorff, 1921.

———. *Die Kirche als der mystische Leib Christi nach dem Apostel Paulus.* 2d ed. Münster: Aschendorff, 1940.

Wilckens, U. *Die Missionsreden der Apostelgeschichte: Form- und traditionsgeschichtliche Untersuchungen.* 2d ed. WMANT 5. Neukirchen-Vluyn: NeukirchenerVerlag des Erziehungsvereins, 1963.

Wilcox, M. *The Semitisms of Acts.* Oxford: Clarendon, 1965.

Wilken, R. L. *The Christians as the Romans Saw Them.* London: Yale University, 1984.

———. "Collegia, Philosophical Schools, and Theology." Pages 268–91 in *Early Church History: The Roman Empire as the Setting of the Primitive Christianity.* Edited by S. Benko and J. J. O'Rourke. London: Oliphants, 1972. German translation: "Kollegien, Philosophenschulen, und Theologie." Pages 165–93 in *Zur Soziologie des Urchristentums.* Edited by W. A. Meeks. Munich: Kaiser, 1979.

Wilkinson, J. "Christian Pilgrims in Jerusalem during the Byzantine Period." *Palestine Exploration Quarterly* 108 (1976): 75–101.

———. *Jerusalem Pilgrims before the Crusades.* Warminster: Aris and Phillips, 1977.

———. "Jerusalem under Rome and Byzantium, 63 BC–637 AD." Pages 81–91 in *Jerusalem in History.* Edited by K. J. Asali. London 1989.

Williams, C. W. *Kirche: Tendenz und Ausblicke.* Berlin: Burckhardthaus-Verlag, 1971.

Williams, S. R. "The Household in the Early Church with Comparative Selective Reference to the Roman Pagan Culture of the Roman World." B.Litt. diss., Oxford University, 1978.

Wilson, S. G. *The Gentiles and the Gentile Mission in Luke's Acts.* SNTSMS 23. Cambridge: Cambridge University, 1973.

Winter, B. W., ed. *The Book of Acts in Its First Century Setting.* 6 vols. Grand Rapids: Eerdmans, 1993–.

———. "The Lord's Supper at Corinth: An Alternative Reconstruction." *Reformed Theological Review* 37 (1978): 73–82.

———. "Secular and Christian Response to Corinthian Famines." *Tyndale Bulletin* 40 (1989): 86–106.

———. *Seek the Welfare of the City: Christians as Benefactors and Citizens.* Grand Rapids: Eerdmans, 1994.

Wiseman, J. "Corinth and Rome: 228 B.C.–A.D. 267." *ANRW* 7.1:438–548. Part 2. *Principat*, 7.1. Edited by H. Temporini and W. Haase. New York: de Gruyter, 1979.

Wiseman, J., and D. Mano-Zissi. "Excavations at Stobi." *American Journal of Archaeology* 75 (1971): 395–411.

Witherington, B., III. *Jesus the Sage: The Pilgrimage of Wisdom.* Minneapolis: Fortress Press, 1994.

———. *Women in the Earliest Churches.* Cambridge: Cambridge University, 1988.

Wright, C. J. H. "Family." *ABD* 2:761–69.

Wright, E. L. "A Critical Examination of the Origin and Development of House Churches and Their Significance for Contemporary Evangelism." ThD diss., New Orleans Baptist Theological Seminary, 1989.

Wright, N. G. "Restoration and the 'house church' movement." *Themelios* 16, no. 2 (1991): 4–8.

Wuellner, W. H. *The Meaning of "Fishers of Men."* NTL. Philadelphia: Westminster Press, 1967.

Yarbrough, R. W. "The Hermeneutics of 1 Timothy 2:9–15." Pages 155–96 in *Women in the Church: A Fresh Analysis of 1 Timothy 2:9–15.* Edited by A. J. Köstenberger et al. Grand Rapids: Baker, 1995.

Yates, R. "The Christian Way of Life: The Paraenetic Material in Colossians 3:1–4:6." *Evangelical Quarterly* 63 (1991): 241–51.

Yeivin, Z. "Ancient Chorazin." *Biblical Archaeology Review* 13, no. 5 (1987): 22–36.

———. "Chorazin." *NEAEHL* 1:301–4.

Ysebaert, J. *Die Amtsterminologie im Neuen Testamament und in der Alten Kirche.* Breda, Neth.: Eureia, 1994.

Zahn, T. "Die Dormitio sanctae Virginis und das Haus des Johannes Markus." *Neue kirchliche Zeitschrift* 10 (1899): 377–429. Also published as *Die Dormitio sanctae Virginis und das Haus des Johannes Markus.* Leipzig: Deichert, 1899.

———. *Einleitung in das Neue Testament.* 2 vols. 3d ed. Leipzig: Deichert, 1907. Repr., Wuppertal: Brockhaus, 1994.

Zimmermann, A. F. *Die urchristlichen Lehrer: Studien zum Tradentenkreis der διδάσκαλοι im frühen Urchristentum.* 2d ed. WUNT, Reihe 2, 12. Tübingen: Mohr, 1988.

Zimmermann, H. "Die Sammelberichte der Apostelgeschichte." *Biblische Zeitschrift* NF 5 (1961): 71–82.

Zingg, B. P. *Das Wachsen der Kirche: Beiträge zur Frage der lukanischen Redaktion und Theologie.* OBO 3. Fribourg: Universitätsverlag, 1974.

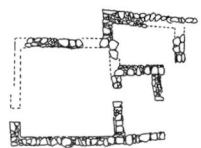

Index of Modern Authors

Achelis, H., 2
Aland, K., 65, 155
Alfödy, G., 166–67
Allmen, D. von, 5–6

Balch, D. L., 148, 229, 248
Banks, R., 6, 139, 221
Barrett, C. K., 66, 76, 79
Barth, M., 259
Barton, S. C., 196
Bauer, W., 65, 155
Baur, F. C., 1–2, 206
Benoit, P., 67
Blue, B. B., 15–16, 139
Bornkamm, G., 130, 180
Bosch, D. J., 27
Bösen, W., 31, 36
Bradley, D. G., 230
Brockhaus, U., 197, 202, 204
Brooten, B. J., 216
Broshi, M., 68
Brown, R. E., 284
Bruce, F. F., 71, 123, 128, 131, 132
Bultmann, R., 52, 204
Burtchaell, J. T., 192–93

Cadbury, H. J., 69, 70–71, 127
Campbell, R. A., 102, 103–5, 118, 271, 273–78, 279, 280, 299
Capper, B. J., 94
Carey, G., 309
Chapple, A. L., 210, 279
Christ, K., 166, 167
Clarke, A. D., 142
Cranfield, C. E. B., 213
Crouch, J. E., 229
Cullmann, O., 171

Dalman, G., 52
Dassmann, E., 194, 263, 278–79, 298
Deissmann, A., 4, 9, 167–68

Delling, G., 155
Dibelius, M., 92, 229
Dix, G., 3–4
Dobschütz, E. von, 200
Dombrowski, B. W., 77
Dungan, D. L., 42
Dunn, J. D. G., 152, 260
Durkheim, E., 23

Elliott, J. H., 6, 8
Ellis, E. E., 223

Farrer, A. M., 4
Fee, G. D., 223
Filson, F. V., 1–3, 4, 10, 11, 15, 20, 70, 138, 194
Frier, B. W., 150

Garnsey, P., 177
Gehring, R. W., 229, 230
George, C. F., 311
Gielen, M., 25, 26, 145, 156, 230, 235, 256, 291
Gnilka, J., 235

Haenchen, E., 42, 76, 79, 80, 81, 84, 92, 123–24, 127
Hahn, F., 50, 53
Hanson, A. T., 271
Harnack, A. von, 2, 13, 216
Harvey, A. E., 100, 104, 118, 280, 299
Hauck, A., 2
Hauck, F., 80–81
Hauke, M., 221
Headlam, A. C., 2
Heinrici, G., 199
Hemer, C. J., 69, 79
Hengel, M., 21, 31, 51, 53, 92, 100, 113, 136–37, 284, 287
Hermann, R., 21
Hirschfeld, Y., 68

Hock, R. F., 292
Hoffman, P., 51, 56, 57
Hofius, O., 174, 175
Holmberg, B., 170, 200, 209–10, 298
Horsley, G. H. R., 196
Horsley, R. A., 44, 45

Jeremias, J., 79, 80, 89–90, 98, 270
Jewett, R., 147–51
Judge, E. A., 3–4, 9, 15, 17, 20, 22–23, 143, 167, 170, 190, 292

Kähler, E., 238
Käsemann, E., 204
Kee, H. C., 30
Kirsch, J. P., 2
Kist, N. C., 1
Klauck, H. J., 5–6, 7–10, 15, 16, 19, 26, 71, 74, 135, 152, 155, 172, 217, 258, 259–60, 284, 291, 296
Kloppenborg, J. S., 191
Krause, S., 97
Krautheimer, R., 11, 12–13, 15, 18, 19
Kretschmar, G., 84
Kuhn, K., 138

Lake, K., 69, 71, 127
Lampe, P., 22, 26, 135, 136, 146, 147, 150, 152, 153, 296
Laub, F., 153, 253
Lemaire, A., 217
Levine, L. I., 30
Lewis, L. A., 6
Lips, H. von, 230, 234
Loffreda, S., 34, 39
Lüdemann, G., 122
Lührmann, D., 17, 53, 229, 253, 291, 292

Maier, H., 7, 266
Malherbe, A. J., 5, 20–21, 168, 171, 187, 281, 285
Maser, P., 11, 18
McKay, A. G., 143, 150
Meeks, W. A., 167, 168–71, 180, 187, 217, 291, 292
Michel, O., 3
Milligan, G., 9, 155
Moulton, J. H., 9, 155
Müller, K., 235
Murphy-O'Connor, J., 67–68, 135, 136, 141, 145, 150

Ollrog, W. H., 136, 180–82, 184, 214
Osiek, C., 148

Packer, J. E., 149
Pesch, R., 49, 66, 125
Pilhofer, P., 121
Polhill, J. B., 132

Ravarotto, E., 41
Reicke, B., 81
Rengstorf, K. H., 235
Richardson, P., 11
Ridderbos, H., 204, 224
Riesner, R., 5, 35, 66, 67, 71, 112
Roloff, J., 84, 97, 197, 204, 206, 264, 272–73, 277, 278, 280, 299
Rordorf, W., 4, 7, 15

Schenk, W., 171
Schlatter, A., 223
Schmidt, K. L., 31, 100
Schöllgen, G., 25, 26, 164, 168–70, 171, 195, 253–57
Schrage, W., 97
Schreiber, A., 208
Schulz, S., 231–32, 247, 250, 251
Schürer, E., 97
Schürmann, H., 48–49, 53
Schüssler Fiorenza, E., 131, 132, 215, 231, 232, 247, 248
Schweitzer, A., 171
Schweizer, E., 204, 235
Seitz, M., 310, 311
Sorg, T., 304, 310, 311
Stanton, G. N., 31
Stegemann, E., 143
Stegemann, H., 138
Stegemann, W., 125, 126, 143
Stuhlmacher, P., 7, 21, 62, 85, 89–90, 304
Sweet, L., 310–11

Taylor, J., 33–35
Theissen, G., 4, 44, 136–37, 139, 168, 170, 185, 190, 283
Thornton, C. J., 121, 122
Thraede, K., 229, 248
Ting, K. H., 307

Van de Velde, C. W. M., 39
Verner, D. C., 6–7, 259
Vitringa, C., 1
Vittinghoff, F., 166
Vogler, W., 5, 107

Wagner, J., 4
Wang, J., 306
Ward-Perkins, J. B., 11, 12
Weber, H. R., 23
Weidinger, K., 229
Weingarten, H., 1–2
Weiser, A., 238
Weiss, J., 2
Weizsäcker, C., 95, 171

White, L. M., 5, 9, 10–15, 16, 17, 18, 19, 22, 87–88, 124, 196, 286, 290, 291
Wieland, F., 2, 88
Winter, B., 175–77
Wolff, C., 221, 223

Yarbrough, R. W., 250–51

Zimmerman, H., 75

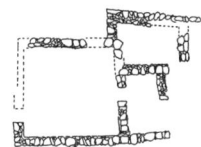

Index of Subjects

Achaicus, 184
Acts, book of, 13, 15–16, 19, 46, 95, 107, 170, 179, 190, 296, 297; on Antioch, 109–13; households in, 239; Jerusalem houses in, 62–79; in Pauline mission houses, 121–30
Adam-Christ typology, 162
Agdistis cult, 21, 196
agora. *See* marketplace
amicus, 41
Ananias, 107
Anaplago, Roman villa at, 317–18
Andronicus, 213
Anglican state church, 308–9
Antioch, 114, 161, 179, 192, 295, 296, 297; missional outreach of church of, 109–13, 117; population of, 112
Antipater, 248
Apollos, 177, 216
apostles, 213; history of term, 205; office of, 196–97; teachings of, 81–82, 84, 85
apostles' council, 179
apostolic delegates, 271–72
apostolic policy, 52
appearance apostles, 205
Apphia, 152
Aquila, 129, 134, 143–44, 145, 154, 159, 165, 171, 182, 210, 214–16, 290; house of, 142, 150, 289
Aramaic-speaking communities, 72–73, 103, 104
archaeological excavations. *See* excavation sites
Archippus, 152–54, 201
architecture: of early Christian assembly places, 10–15, 19; of houses, 288–91; of Pauline house churches, 140; variety in Greco-Roman world of, 18. *See also* floor plans; reconstructions
Areopagus, 15

Aristobulus, house of, 145
Aristotle, 230, 247–48
Asdod, 106
assembly places (Christian), architectural development of, 10–15, 19
associations, 21, 22, 24
atrium, 2, 135, 137, 140, 141, 290. *See also* courtyards; floor plans
aula ecclesiae, 14, 18

baptism, 131, 290, 294; in Antioch, 113; egalitarian tradition of, 151; by Paul, 121, 138, 186, 187, 188
Barnabas, 72–73, 115, 179, 202, 276; in Antioch, 109–10, 113
basilicas, 32; historical development of, 10–15, 19
bathhouses, 40, 290
behavior, moral, 203
Bethany, 89, 95; houses in, 43–44, 46, 59
Bethsaida, 38, 39, 41, 42
Bible study groups, 303, 305, 307
bishops, 25, 309; as heads of household, 4; in Pastoral Epistles, 263, 271–72, 278; use of term, 269
body: of Christ, 162–64, 257; in church structure, 263–64
book of Acts. *See* Acts, book of
"breaking bread," 79, 80–84, 96, 104, 162, 179
"brotherly love," 189–90, 293; in present day, 304
Byzantine basilicas, 32
Byzantis, 13, 14

Caesarea, 106, 108, 114, 115, 210
Capernaum, 46, 54, 59, 60; floor plans for, 37, 313, 315–16; house of Peter in, 31–35, 37–42, 289, 295; Jesus in, 35–46, 61, 115; population of, 39

capital cities, 181
caretaker, 198, 199–200
catechetical instruction, 239–40, 290
catechism, 38, 107
celebration of communion. *See* communion
cell planting, 179–80, 182
Cenacle, 68
Cenchreae, 183, 216–17; house churches in, 142–43
center mission, 181; travel and, 182–85
charisma, 272, 277
charismatics, 192, 204, 283
"child of peace," 56–57
children, household codes and, 238–40, 243
China: house churches in, 306–8; population of Christians in, 306
Chorazin, 38–39, 42
Christian liturgy, in house churches, 2
Christian office, 197
Christianity, in present day, 300–311
church: definition of, 257–58. *See also* local church; universal church; whole church
church envoys, 205
church house: architecture of, 288; definition of, 18. *See also aula ecclesiae*
"church of God," 161, 164
church order, 259–60; in Pastoral Epistles, 260–68
church planting, 303
church polity, 3
cities: disciples and, 55, 58; instructions for entrance into, 50–54; missional outreach in, 54
Clementis, 13, 14
clientela, 22
Codex D, 88
collegia, 20, 191, 254, 295
Colossae, 151–54, 182; leadership structures of, 201–2
Colossians: household codes in, 230, 232–42, 251–53, 258, 291, 293; research on, 229–30
Columella, 248
communion, 131, 150, 171–77, 207; in Antioch, 113; in house churches, 87
congregation apostles, 205
Constantine, 1, 4, 11, 289, 304
Constantinian basilica, 1, 10–11, 13
conversion, 128, 129–30, 133, 138
Corbo, Virgilio C., 32, 34

Corinth, 83–84, 159, 169, 170, 179, 180, 216–17; house churches in, 2, 9, 10, 134–42, 157, 158, 168, 171–77, 267, 295; leadership structures in, 202–5; Paul's ministry in, 128–30; population of church in, 139
Corinthians, 4
Cornelius, 93, 187; house of, 106, 108
corpus paulinum, 24, 155, 156, 237
courtyards, 45, 141, 290. *See also* atrium; floor plans
co-workers, 188, 214, 226, 274, 293, 297; in missional outreach, 180, 182, 183–84
creational order, 231, 233, 235, 237–38, 246, 300, 310
Crisogono, S., 13
Crispus, 129, 138, 186; house of, 207
cults, 12, 19, 21, 114, 196, 291–95; in Johannine epistles, 285–86
curator annonae, 176

Damascus, 106–7, 114
deaconess, 219
deacons, 192; in Pastoral Epistles, 262, 266, 268–69, 273, 274
Dead Sea Scrolls. *See* Q material
Decalogue, 94
Demetrius, 286
diakonoi, 217
Diaspora Judaism, 12, 21, 30, 73, 138, 150, 185, 188
Didache, 285
dietary policy, 52, 56
Dinippus, 176
Dionysus association, 21
Diotrephes, 281–86
disciples: appointment of, 37; in Jerusalem houses, 64, 66; pre-Easter use of houses by, 48–61
domestic houses, 29, 32; in Pastoral Epistles, 264. *See also* house churches; houses; private homes
domus ecclesiae, 13, 14, 18; in Capernaum, 34–35, 315–16
Dura, floor plans for, 319–20
Dura Europos, 2, 12, 13

Easter. *See* post-Easter period; pre-Easter period
ecclesia, 21, 304
Edict of Milan, 11
elders, 100, 101–5, 117–18, 215, 297, 298; in Johannine epistles, 281–84;

Index of Subjects • 389

in Pastoral Epistles, 262, 268–80; in Pauline Letters, 190–92
Emmaus, 95
Epaenetus, 144
Epaphroditus, 184, 185
Ephesians, 261, 263–64; household codes in, 239, 243–47, 253, 258–59, 291, 293
Ephesus, 159, 179, 180, 182, 225; house churches in, 143–44, 296
Epiphanius, Bishop of Salamis, 67
episcopal leadership, in Pauline church, 209
episcopal model, 280, 298; in Pastoral Epistles, 272, 273
episkopos, 192, 206, 270, 276, 279. *See also* elders
Erastus, 139, 141–42
Essenes, 20, 77, 82, 94, 209
et Tell, 39
ethics, household codes and, 236–37, 245, 251
ethnicity, in house churches, 113
Eucharist, 13, 208; in private homes, 3–4
Euodia, 211
Eutychius, 67
evangelical proclamations, 82
evangelical triangle, 38, 42, 46, 54, 61, 115, 292
evangelism: definition of, 91; in Jerusalem, 92–93; by Jewish Christians, 92
evangelists, Philip as, 106
excavation sites: of Bethsaida, 39; in Capernaum, 32–34, 37; in Corinth, 135; of house synagogues, 12; in Jerusalem, 65, 67; in Ostia Antiqua, 148, 149
exhortation, 197–98, 229; in Colossians, 233, 234; to slaves and masters, 240–41

false teachers, 267–68
familia Caesaris, 167
familia Dei, 47, 293, 295, 304; in Pastoral Epistles, 262–63
family, 300; household codes and, 234–40, 243, 248–50; missional outreach and, 240; in Paul's epistles, 5–6
family groups, 2
family life, 3
family metaphors, 153, 256
"family of God," 5, 163–64, 261, 298
famine, 176–77

fathers, household codes and, 238–40, 243
Feast of Tabernacles, 90
fellowship groups, 119
fellowships, 93–94; in present day, 303; in Rome, 145–46
floor plans, 149; for Capernaum, 37; of church house in Capernaum, 315–16; for Pauline house churches, 140; of Roman villa at Anaploga, 317; of St. Peter's house in Capernaum, 313
Fortunatus, 184

Gaius, 149, 171, 186; house of, 6, 139, 142, 183, 207, 289; in Johannine epistles, 283–85
Galatia, 169, 179
Galilean ministry, 36, 38
Galilee, 28
Gattung, 230, 234, 291
Gaza, 106
Gennesaret, 42
Gentiles: in Antioch, 109–13; in Thessalonica, 126–27
Gerasenes, 42
Gospel of Mark, 28, 31
Gospels, 29, 31, 40. *See also* Synoptic Gospels
Great Britain, church planting in, 303, 308–9
Greco-Roman world: cities in, 18; elders in, 277–78; house churches in, 12; households in, 7; patronage in, 22–23
Greece, 179
Greek, 57, 77; in Jerusalem, 113–14; in services, 88; words for house, 7–8, 9, 65, 74, 120–21, 156; words for leadership, 197–98. *See also* koinwia; oikia; oikoz; translation

hall church: architecture of, 288; definition of, 18–19
hall of Solomon, 15, 79, 82
hall of Tyrannus, 15
Haustafel, 229
head coverings, 222
Hebrew, in services, 88
Hellenistic associations, 21
Hellenistic-Roman world, households in, 7
Hellenists: in Antioch, 110; in Jerusalem church, 97–98; as link between Jerusalem church and Pauline missions, 113–16; missional outreach of, 105–7

390 • HOUSE CHURCH AND MISSION

heresy, 267–68
Hierocles, 248
home. *See* domestic houses; private homes
hospitality, 199, 201, 226–27, 293; in Johannine epistles, 282, 287; to missionaries, 182–83; in Pastoral Epistles, 265–66
hostels, 287
house churches, 258, 296; architecture of, 288–89; associations and, 21; basilical architecture and, 11–15, 19; book of Acts on Jerusalem, 63–79; book of Acts on Pauline mission, 121–30; in China, 306–8; *collegia* and, 20; conflict between, 10, 267; definitions of, 18, 26–27; elders and, 275–77; elements of, 65–66, 74; Filson's observations on, 3; in Great Britain, 308–9; in Johannine epistles, 281–87; leadership structures in Jerusalem, 95–105; liturgy development for, 13; models for, 19–24; organizational structures of, 296–99; overseers and, 272–73, 276; in Pastoral Epistles, 264–68; Paul and, 119–21; in Pauline mission, 130–55, 187–90, 225–28; plurality in Antioch of, 112; plurality in Jerusalem of, 86–89; post-1980 research on, 5–16; pre-1980 research on, 1–5; in present day, 300–311; renovations for, 13, 14; social order in, 293–95; in United States, 310–11; whole church and, 24–26; women and, 211–25; worship services in, 79–86, 295–96. *See also domus ecclesiae*
house fellowships. *See* fellowships
house missional rule, 54–55
"house of God," 261, 274–75, 298
house of Matthew. *See* Matthew
house of Peter. *See* Peter
"house of the church." *See domus ecclesiae*
house synagogues, 1, 10, 11, 18, 19, 21, 30, 82, 195–96, 291; excavation sites of, 12; in Jerusalem, 88–89; *oikos* and, 17–18; in Rome, 146
house teacher, 41, 98
house-to-house mission, 42–48, 89–92, 186
housefathers, 103, 194, 210, 219
household codes: children and, 238–40, 243; in Colossians, 230, 232–42, 251–53, 258; criticism of, 229–32; in Ephesians, 239, 243–47, 253, 258–59; ethics and, 236–37, 245, 251; family and, 234–40, 243, 248–50; fathers and, 238–40, 243; husbands/wives and, 234–38, 243, 244–46, 249; love and, 236; marriage and, 234–38, 240, 243, 244–46, 248–50; masters and, 240–42, 243, 246–47, 248, 293; mothers and, 240; *oikos* and, 233–47, 250, 253–57, 258, 291–94; in Pastoral Epistles, 262; patriarchal structures and, 231, 232, 247–49; research on, 229–30; slavery and, 233, 235, 240–42, 243, 246–47, 248, 251–53, 293
household management texts, 230, 234, 235, 251, 253, 290
"household of God," 7
householder evangelism, 59
householders, 97, 99–100, 103–4, 175, 193–95, 277, 292–94; as false teachers, 268; as fathers, 239; in Johannine epistles, 284; in Pastoral Epistles, 261, 262–63, 265; in Pauline mission, 184; recruitment of, 185–87; women as, 211, 219
households, 22; associations and, 20–21; in Christian movement, 6; Greco-Roman traditions of, 7; heads of, 4, 23, 41, 54, 58–59, 87, 188, 236, 268. *See also oikos*
houses: architectural significance of, 288–91; disciples' pre-Easter use of, 48–61; ecclesiological significance of, 295–300; Greek words for, 7–8, 9, 65, 74, 156; instructions for entrance into, 50–54; Jesus's ministry in, 28–30; Jesus's use of, 46–48; missional outreach in, 54–59; in Palestine, 45; in Pauline mission, 121–30, 179–90, 187–90, 227; in primitive church in Jerusalem, 62–79; socioeconomic significance of, 291–95; upper floors/rooms of, 68, 69–73. *See also* domestic houses; house churches; house synagogues; *oikia; oikos;* private homes
husbands, 246–47, 249; household codes and, 234–38, 243, 244–46, 249

Ignatius, 271, 274
imperator, 166

Index of Subjects • 391

industrial countries, house churches in, 303–5, 308–9
inner courtyard. *See* atrium; courtyards
inns, 183
instructions: household codes and, 233–34; on leadership, 269. *See also* missional instructions
insulae, 135, 140, 147, 149, 151
itinerant missionaries, 55, 59–60, 61, 104, 108, 114, 181, 184, 213, 227; in Johannine epistles, 282–87

James, 274; house of, 70–73, 78; leadership of church in Jerusalem by, 95, 99, 100–105
Jason, 187; house of, 124–25, 127–28, 132–34; as patron, 201
Jericho, 95
Jerusalem, 43; art and architecture in, 68; early Church in, 20; house churches in, 2, 9; houses in primitive church in, 62–79; plurality of house churches in, 86–89; population of, 86–87; primitive church in, 116–18, 160–62, 289, 290, 295, 296; worship service in house churches in, 79–86
Jesus: biblical knowledge of, 28; in Capernaum, 31, 35–46, 61, 115; ministry in houses of, 29–30; missional approach of, 46–48; poverty of, 42; as Son of Man, 90; teaching by, 28–29
Jewish Christians, 33, 67, 72–73, 81–82, 89, 106, 110, 112, 113, 127, 134, 216
Joanna, wife of Chuza, 69
Johannine epistles, house churches in, 281–87
Johannine Letters, 287
Johannine mission, 100
John, son of Zebedee, 91, 96
John Mark, 72–73
Joppa, 107
Joseph of Arimathea, 69, 96
Josephus, 20, 30, 155
Judaism, 44, 291; Hellenistic associations and, 21; house synagogues in, 3, 6, 10; women in, 215. *See also* Diaspora Judaism
Judas, house of, 107
Julia, 211, 212
Junia, 211, 213–14

Khirbet el Araj, 39
Khirbet Kerazeh, 39
kingdom message, 57
koinonia fellowship, 94, 163
koinwia, 80–81

Laodicea, 159, 178, 211, 225; house churches in, 154–55, 296
Last Supper, 66, 84, 96
Lateran basilica, 12, 13
Lazarus, 46, 59
leadership structures: in Jerusalem house churches, 95–105; in Pastoral Epistles, 268–81; in Pauline church, 190–93, 297–98; in Pauline house churches, 196–210; in present day, 305; women and, 210–25. *See also* organizational structures
Leitsetz, 243, 244
Letter to the Colossians. *See* Colossians
Letter to the Philippians, 205
letter writing, hospitality and, 183
living rooms, 136
local church, 27, 145–46, 164–65, 295–96; in Pastoral Epistles, 275; in Pauline mission, 182; in present day, 305; translation issues on, 155–59
local council, 98
Loffreda, Stanislao, 32, 34
Lord's Supper, 83–84, 85, 117, 154, 162, 171–79, 195, 207–8, 219, 223, 290, 295
love, household codes and, 236
Lucius, 111
Lukan redaction, book of Acts and, 63–64, 69–70, 75, 121–22, 123, 125–26, 128–29
Luke: on assembly of primitive church, 91; conversions by, 133; as Paul's companion, 122; primitive church in Jerusalem and, 62–67, 69–70, 74–78; on public and private meetings, 15–16
Lullingstone, 14
Luther, Martin, 310
LXX, 7–8, 208
Lydia, 121–22, 131–32, 187, 207, 211, 212; house of, 289

Macedonia, 125–26, 128, 169, 179, 212
Mark, Gospel of, 28, 31
marketplace, 15

marriage, 300; household codes and, 234–38, 240, 243, 244–46, 248–50
Mars Hill, 15
Martha, 59
Mary, mother of John Mark, 44, 89, 144, 211, 212, 289; house of, 68, 70–74, 78, 99–100, 103, 296
masters, 248, 293; household codes and, 240–42, 243, 246–47, 248
matriarchal structures, 249
Matthew, 32, 37, 100; house of, 43–44; taxes and, 36
mebaqqer, 103
Menahem, 111
miracle narratives, 32
mission, definition of, 27, 91
"mission journey," 115
missional, definition of, 27
missional discourse, 48–53
missional instructions, 50–61, 107
missional ministry, of Jesus, 42–43
missional outreach: of Antioch church, 109–13, 117; "cell planting" form of, 179–80; center mission and, 181; as community lifestyle, 93–95; elements of, 91; family's importance in, 240; of Hellenists, 105–7; houses' use in, 53–61; in Jerusalem, 89–91, 116–18; as one-on-one conversation, 92–93; Paul's use of houses in, 182–90; of Peter, 107–9; in post-Easter period, 91–92; women and, 214. *See also* Pauline mission
missional proclamation, 15
missionaries, Christian, 128, 131
missions, early Christian, 4; house churches in, 24–26
Mithraea, 295; house of, 254
Mithras, cult of, 12, 291
morality, 203
"mother church," 181
mothers, household codes and, 240
Mount of Olives, 43, 63–64, 67
Mount Zion, 66, 68
Musonius Rufus, 248

Narcissus, 145
Nazareth, 28, 36
New Testament, house churches' significance in, 9
Nicholas the proselyte, 111
Numfan, 120–21
Nympha, 211–12; house church of, 154–55

oeconomica, 230, 234, 291. *See also* household management texts
office: criteria for, 202; definition of, 197
office holders, 197–201, 198, 201–2, 299; in Pastoral Epistles, 262, 265, 269–71, 278; in Pauline church, 191–92
office triad, 204
oikia, 7–8, 9, 158
oikos, 25, 26, 29, 41, 42, 47, 153–54, 170, 171, 175, 250; church organization and, 20, 22–24, 63; conversion and, 129; First Corinthians and, 121; household codes and, 233–42, 243–47, 258–60; householders and, 193–94, 201; Jerusalem and, 78, 87, 92, 93, 96, 100, 101, 103–4, 116, 117; Johannine epistles and, 281–87; organizational structures and, 191, 298–300; in Pastoral Epistles, 260–68; Pauline house churches and, 119; in Pauline mission, 182–84, 184, 187; in Philippi, 124; significance of, 17–18; social order and, 253–57, 291–94; Western world and, 301
oikoz, 6–8, 9, 135, 158, 196, 227–28, 258. *See also* translation
Onesimus, 151–54, 182, 241
Onesiphorus, 266
ordines, 166
organizational structures: of house churches, 296–99; in Pastoral Epistles, 261–67; of Pauline churches, 190–96. *See also* leadership structures
Orphism, 19
Ostia Antiqua, 148–49
overseers, 192–93, 205, 206, 298; in Pastoral Epistles, 262, 268–71, 272–80

Palestine, 30
Palestinian church, 52
Palestinian houses, 45, 65, 290
paraenetic instruction, 230, 235, 238, 249, 260, 274
party strife, 3, 186
Passover, 74, 82, 84, 88
Pastoral Epistles, 7, 256, 294; leadership structures in, 268–81; *oikos* order as church order in, 260–68
Pastoral Letters, 256, 266, 292, 293, 294
pastoral ministry, 209, 210
pater familias, 22, 153, 194, 262, 265, 292

patriarchal structures: in Colossians, 235; household codes and, 231, 232, 247–49
patronage, 15, 21–22, 22–23, 167, 193–95, 226, 292–93, 298; in Pastoral Epistles, 265
patronal ministry, 210
patrons, 199–200
Paul: in Antioch, 109–11, 113, 179; on body of Christ, 162–64; book of Acts and, 121–30; in Corinth, 290; ecclesiological passages by, 296; elders and, 276; family in epistles of, 3, 5–6; on individual local church, 164–65; in leadership role, 197; on leadership structures, 273; Luke and, 62; missional outreach of, 179–80, 183–90; open door policy of, 16; passage on house churches by, 119–21; teachings on women by, 220–25; on unity of Christians, 232–33; on universal church, 160–62; on women's role in church, 213–15
Pauline church, 83; organizational structure of, 190–96; women in, 211–25
Pauline Epistles, 19, 62, 105, 116, 147, 151, 152, 164, 170, 179, 190; house churches in, 289; women in, 211
Pauline house churches, 6, 9, 10–11, 18, 95, 100, 189–90, 225–28; architecture of, 140; *collegia* and, 20; leadership structures in, 196–210; passages on, 119–30; social strata in, 4–5, 165–71
Pauline Letters, 95, 120–21, 122, 124, 130, 132, 139, 190, 205, 233, 257, 264, 296, 298–99
Pauline mission, 100; Hellenists and, 113–16; local church in, 182; patronage in, 292–93; in specific cities, 130–55
Pauline mission outreach: characteristics of, 179–81; householders and, 185–87, 297
Pauline sermon, 187
Pentecost, 66
peristyle houses, 135, 140
Persis, 211, 212
Peter, 91, 115; exclusion from city of, 100; house of, 31–33, 35, 37–42, 46–48, 59, 60, 289, 295, 312–14; in Jerusalem, 71–74; leadership of church in Jerusalem by, 95–100;

missional outreach of, 107–9; taxes and, 36
Philemon, 151–54, 187; house of, 182, 201, 289; Letter to, 241
Philip, 115, 210; as evangelist, 106
Philippi, 123–24, 126, 159, 184, 187, 225; house churches in, 131–32, 296, 298; leadership structures in, 205–10; missional outreach in, 121–22
Philologus, 212
philosophical schools, 20, 21
Phoebe, 142–43, 148–49, 150, 171, 183, 184, 199, 211, 216–20
plebs rustica, 166
plebs urbana, 166
Plutarch, 248
post-Easter period, 47; missional outreach in, 91
poverty, missionaries and, 55
prayer, 178, 218; in worship service, 81–84
pre-Easter period: disciples' use of houses in, 48–61; house churches in, 9; Jesus's use of houses in, 28–48; missional approach in, 116
pre-Lukan tradition, book of Acts and, 63–64, 69–70, 75, 121–22, 123, 125–26, 128–29
presbyter, 192
presbyter model, 280–81, 298; in Pastoral Epistles, 272, 273, 276, 277
presbyterial organization, 101
presbyteros, 270
Prisca. *See* Priscilla
Priscilla, 129, 134–35, 136–37, 143–44, 145, 154, 159, 165, 171, 182, 210, 211, 214–16, 290; house of, 142, 150
prison, 132; Paul in, 137
private homes, 27, 29, 194; architecture of, 288–91; as assembly places, 13–16; Eucharist in, 3–4; in missional outreach, 116–18; in Pastoral Epistles, 264; in Pauline mission, 226; present day use of, 302; and synagogues, 18. *See also* domestic houses; house churches; house synagogues; houses
proclamations, 15, 82, 125

Q material, 31, 35–36, 49–50
Qumran community, 20, 75, 77, 81, 191, 223

rabbinical scribes, 38
reconstructions: of Church House in Capernaum, 316; of house plan before Adaptation, 319; of Roman villa at Anaploga, 318; of St. Peter's house in Capernaum, 314
reliability of texts, 35, 36, 62, 86, 122, 124, 126, 129–30, 289
Rhoda, 69
ritual law, 114
road systems (Roman), 39
Roman society, 166–67; patronage in, 22–23. *See also* patronage
Roman soldiers, 132
Roman villa, floor plans for, 317–18
Rome, 159; house churches in, 2, 6, 9, 144–51, 157, 267, 296. *See also* Greco-Roman world

salvation, 51, 56–57, 90, 233
Sarapis cult, 19
Saul, 88
Scripture, 178
Sea of Galilee, 38, 39, 40
sedentary followers, 43–44, 60, 61, 104, 114, 182
service of the word, 171–73, 178–79
Sidon, 42
Silvanus, 180
Simeon, 111
Simon, house of, 107
Sitz im Leben, 274
slave admonition, 241–42, 246–47, 248
slavery, 250–53, 293, 301; abolition of, 231–32; household codes and, 233, 235, 251–53; in Pastoral Epistles, 264–66
slaves, 152–53, 176, 190, 208, 248, 293; household codes and, 240–42, 243, 246–47, 248
social order, *oikos* and, 253–57
"social" research, 23
social strata: in early Christianity, 3, 4–5, 22, 134, 136–37, 138–39, 147–48, 150, 154, 165–71, 186, 292; in Pastoral Epistles, 265–66
"sociological" research, 23–24
Son of Man, 162
Sopater, 127
Stephanas, 182, 184, 185, 186, 210, 293, 297; house of, 134, 138, 202–3, 207
Stephen, 105–6
Stobi, 196
Stoics, 229, 236, 248

synagogue ruler, 215
synagogue sermon, 131
synagogues, 54, 81, 96, 105, 122, 128, 129–30, 185, 188, 220, 271, 289; elders in, 101–3, 104–5, 118, 280; organizational structure of, 192; women in, 212. *See also* house synagogues
Synoptic Gospels, 28–29, 36, 43, 49
Syntyche, 211

tabernae, 135–36
table fellowship, 131, 295
Tarsus, 186
taxes, on temples, 32, 36, 37
teachers, 209, 267–68; in Pauline church, 204; women as, 216
teachings, of apostles, 81–82, 84, 85
Tell Hum, 32, 38, 40. *See also* Capernaum
temple taxes. *See* taxes
temples, 82–83; Christian gatherings in, 75. *See also* hall of Solomon
tenement churches, 147–48, 150–51
tenement houses, 147, 149
Thessalonica, 151, 159, 179, 187, 225; church at, 124–28; house churches in, 132–34, 148, 296; leadership structures in, 197–201
third world countries, house churches in, 303
Three-Self Movement, 306, 307
Timothy, 180; in Pastoral Epistles, 268–69, 271, 279
Titius Justus, 142; house of, 129, 130, 137–38, 145
titles, in Pauline church, 204
tituli, in Rome, 146
Titus, 180, 230; in Pastoral Epistles, 268–69, 271, 277
topos, 230, 234
Torah, 82, 85, 106
trade routes, 179; Capernaum and, 40
translation, issues of, 156–59
travel, in Pauline missional outreach, 183–85
triclinium, 288, 290, 317
Troas, 179
Tryphaena, 211, 212
Tryphosa, 211, 212
the Twelve, 100, 104, 108; establishment of, 96
Tyre, 42

United States, house churches in, 310–11
unity, of Christians, 232–33
universal church, 27, 160–62, 165, 257–58
upper floors/rooms, 65–67, 68, 69–73, 149, 179, 289

village-to-village outreach, 42–48
villas, 135, 140; floor plans for, 317–18
voluntary associations, 24. *See also* associations

whole church, 117, 161, 257–58; in Antioch, 112–13; in Corinth, 139, 142; definition of, 27; house churches and, 24–26; in Jerusalem, 83; in Pastoral Epistles, 275; in Rome, 146; translation issues on, 155–59

widows, in Pastoral Epistles, 268
witness regulations, 53
wives, 215; household codes and, 234–38, 243, 244–46, 248–49
women: household codes and, 231, 232; leadership responsibilities of, 210–25; in Pastoral Epistles, 264. *See also* wives
word service. *See* service of the word
workshop apartments, 135, 137, 140
worship service, 226, 295–96; in Antioch, 113; contents of, 26; in Jerusalem house churches, 79–86, 117; Martin Luther and, 310; in Pauline house churches, 171–79; in present day, 302–3; women in, 222–24

Zacchaeus, 59

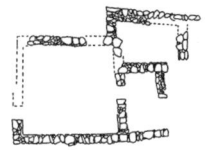

Index of Ancient Sources

OLD TESTAMENT

Genesis
1–2   235n.33, 238n.50
1:27   253n.136
2:18–23   222n.578
2:22–24   162n.249
2:24   246

Exodus
20:12   238n.54
30:13   36n.63

Leviticus
19:18   188

Numbers
11:25   57
35:30   53n.167

Deuteronomy
5:15   239n.54
17:6   53n.167
19:5   53n.167

Joshua
24:15   8n.44

1 Kings
17:19–21   65

2 Kings
2:15   57
4:10–11   65

Nehemiah
10:32–33   36n.63

Psalms
80   90
87   90

Isaiah
2:2–4   90n.161
52:7   51n.153, 57n.186
56:1–8   90n.160
66:18–21   179n.330

Daniel
6:11   65

Micah
4:1–4   90n.161

Nahum
2:1   51n.153, 57n.186

PSEUDEPIGRAPHA

3 Baruch
4:9–15   32n.31

1 Enoch
57   90n.161
90:33   90n.161

4 Ezra
13:13   90n.161

Psalms of Solomon
17:32–35   90n.161

APOCRYPHA

Sirach
1:4   238n.50
24:3–5   238n.50
24:9–10   238n.50
43:26   238n.50

NEW TESTAMENT

Matthew
4:13   35n.54
4:14   36
4:17   57n.189
4:23   30n.17, 38n.68
5:1–2   51n.153
5:23   43n.98
5:38–48   94
6:1–4   43n.98
6:5–6   43n.98
6:25–34   77n.88
7:15   43n.98
8:5–13   31, 107n.249
8:11–12   90n.161
8:20   42n.95
8:21–22   59n.199
8:28   42
8:34   29n.11
9:1   32, 36, 37
9:9   40
9:26   29n.11
9:27   32
9:27–31   32n.28, 37
9:28   29n.11
9:31–32   29n.11
9:35   30n.17, 38n.68
9:37–38   48n.129
9:37–10:16   50
10:1–40   49
10:5   283
10:5–6   90
10:7–16   48n.129
10:8–9   283
10:9–10   110
10:10   51n.152
10:11–12   108n.251
10:11a   51
10:12–13   58, 108, 283
10:22   283n.310

10:23   90, 94n.178
10:25   47
10:37   59n.199
10:40–42   283n.310
10:41   204n.463
11:5   57n.186
11:20–24   31
11:21   38
11:21–24   36n.58
11:23   35
11:25   4n.23, 47n.126
12:28   52n.159
12:30   52n.159
13:16f.   51n.153
13:36   37n.66
14:13   41n.89
15   90
15:21–28   107n.249
17:24–27   32, 36, 37
18:15–17   100, 101n.207
18:16   53n.167
19:4   246
19:29   283n.310
21:17   43
23:2–3   43n.98
23:9   47
24:4–5   43n.98
24.14   90
24:16   43
24:23–25   43n.98
24:26–27   43n.98
26:6   43
26:59–60   53n.167
27:57   69n.43
27:60   69n.43
28:16–20   89
28:16–28   90, 91

Mark
1:2   35n.54
1:6   52n.156
1:12   31
1:13   143n.140
1:15   57n.189
1:16–18   77n.88
1:20   40n.80
1:21   35n.56
1:21–39   38n.68
1:28   29n.11, 76n.81
1:29   32, 35, 41n.90
1:29–31   31, 37, 43
1:31   143n.140
1:32   29n.11

1:33   31, 32, 35, 37, 39n.79
1:37   39n.79
1:38–39   42
1:39   30n.17, 38n.68
1:40   29n.11
1:45   29n.11
2–4   290
2:1   31, 32, 35, 36, 37
2:2   39n.79
2:5   47n.126
2:13–15   40
2:15   35n.56
3:8   29n.11, 42n.96
3:20   31, 32, 35, 37
3:20–21   46n.120, 47, 60
3:21   59n.199
3:31–32   35n.56
3:31–35   46n.120, 47, 60
3:34–35   163n.256
4:10   37n.66
5:1   42
5:19–20   43
5:35   47n.126
6:1   43
6:4   59n.199
6:6   43
6:6–13   90n.156
6:6b–11   48n.129
6:7–9   55
6:7–13   49
6:10   55, 58
6:10b   52n.156
6:30   49
6:33   29n.11
6:53   42
6:56   43
7:14–15   37n.66
7:17   31n.20, 37n.66
7:18–23   37n.66
7:24   42n.96, 106n.244
7:31   42, 106n.244
8:1   29n.11
8:5   40
8:22   39
8:27   42, 43, 106n.244
9:14–27   37n.66
9:17   29n.11
9:28   35n.56
9:28–29   31n.20, 37n.66
9:30   43

9:32   76n.81
9:33   31, 32, 35, 37
10:2–9   37n.66
10:7–8   246
10:7–16   52n.161
10:10   31n.20
10:10–12   37n.66
10:13   29n.11
10:17–19   77n.88
10:24   47n.126
10:28–30   44n.108, 77n.88
10:29–30   46n.120, 47, 60
10:42–44   94
10:42–45   99, 245
10:45   98
10:46–52   95n.179
10:54   98
11:1   43
11:11   43
11:12   43
11:15   43
11:27   43
12:12–14   99
12:17   99
12:28–34   94
12:30–31   163n.256
13:14   43, 94n.178
14:3   43
14:3–9   95n.179
14:14   66, 70n.49, 96n.183
14:15   96n.183
14:22–25   84
14:28   33
14:36   85n.132
15:40–41   43n.99
15:42–47   43n.99
15:43   69n.43
15:45–46   69n.43
16:7–8   33

Luke
1:9   56
1:28–29   56
1:40–41   56
1:56   131n.70
1:79   57n.186
2:14   57n.186
4:14   29n.11
4:14–15   30n.17, 38n.68
4:14b   76n.81

Index of Ancient Sources • 399

4:16   30n.18
4:23   36n.58
4:37   76n.81
4:43   38n.68
4:43–44   30n.18
4:44   38n.68
5:17–26   30n.18
6:6–11   30n.18
6:20–21   51n.153, 57n.186
6:27–36   94
7:1–2   40
7:1–10   30n.18, 31
7:5   40
8:2–3   43n.99, 128n.53
8:3   69
8:37–39   43
9:1–6   48n.129, 49
9:2   55
9:3   51n.152, 55, 77n.88
9:4   55, 131n.70
9:10   39, 49, 52n.161
9:45   76n.81
9:57b–60   42n.95
9:58   59n.199
10:1–2   110
10:1–3   109
10:1–12   46n.120, 48, 51–55, 90n.156, 107
10:1–16   48n.129
10:1–20   49, 50n.142
10:2–12   50, 60
10:4   77n.88, 108
10:5   56, 58
10:5–6   57n.191, 59
10:5–7   108
10:7   131n.70
10:9   57, 108
10:11   57
10:13   38
10:13–15   31, 36n.58
10:15   35
10:17   52
10:17–20   48n.129, 109
10:23f.   51n.153
10:25–37   287n.337
10:29   110n.262
10:38   58n.196
10:38–39   43, 46n.119
10:38–42   43n.101, 44, 95n.179
10:40   143n.140
10:42   58n.196
11:3   77n.88

11:13–15   38
11:20   52n.159, 57n.189
11:23   52n.159
12:42–45   263n.193
13:10–17   30n.18
13:33   38n.68
15:3–7   90
17:3   100n.206
18:34   76n.81
19:1–10   43, 59
19:5   131n.70
21:21   43
22:12   66
22:25–27   98, 99
22:30   52n.156
22:41   63n.5
23:50–52   69n.43
24:5–53   63
24:13   63n.5
24:13–35   84, 95n.179
24:29–30   131n.70
24:36   56n.181
24:52   79n.93, 82n.111
24:53   81n.105
26:6   43

John
1:44   41n.90
2:12   31, 35n.54
4:1–42   107n.249
4:46   31
4:53   8n.45, 121n.11
6:17   31
6:17–59   35n.54
8:17   53n.167
10:23   65n.23
11:1   43, 46n.119, 58n.196
11:1–3   95n.179
11:18   43
11:19   44
11:31   44
12:1–9   44
12:2   58n.196, 95n.179, 143n.140
17   166, 225n.594, 296n.15
19:38   69n.43
19:40–42   69n.43
20:19   56n.181
20:21   56n.181
20:26   56n.181
21:1–14   33

Acts
1–6   90n.158
1–12   96
1–14   103
1:2   63n.5
1:12–14   100, 296
1:12–15   63–69
1:13   74, 96nn.183,184
1:13–14   71
1:14   80, 81
1:15   86n.136, 87n.142
1:15–17   66n.26
1:21–26   99
1:23–24a   64
1:24–25   81n.107
1:26   64, 66n.28
2:1   86n.136
2:1–3   66n.26
2:1–4   66n.28
2:1–41   91n.164, 108
2:3   64n.11
2:9   129
2:18   92n.167
2:36   94
2:41   80n.96, 86, 87nn.142,145
2:42   81, 83, 84, 87, 93
2:42–47   74–78, 79, 80, 93n.175, 296
2:44   86n.136
2:44–45   81
2:46   19n.105, 25n.136, 66, 81, 82nn.111,113, 83, 84, 87, 88n.147, 91, 156n.212, 157n.221
2:47   86, 94
3:1   81n.105, 82n.113, 96n.184
3:1–3   79n.93, 82n.111
3:1–10   91
3:1–26   108
3:3   96n.184
3:4   96n.184
3:11   65n.23, 79n.93, 82n.111, 96n.184
3:11–12   15
3:11–13   91n.164
3:48   15
4:1   96n.184
4:2   82n.111
4:3   96n.184
4:4   86, 87n.142
4:7   96n.184

4:8   191
4:10   91
4:11–12   91
4:13   96n.184
4:17   283n.310
4:19   96n.184
4:23   96n.184, 191
4:23–25   66nn.26,29
4:24–30   81n.107
4:29   123n.19
4:29b   92n.167
4:31   66, 66nn.26,29, 123n.19
4:32   66n.29, 77, 79, 80n.98, 93
4:32–35   76
4:32–37   81
4:36–37   73, 109
5:1–11   76, 98
5:4   78
5:6   98n.197, 99
5:10   99
5:11–16   76
5:12   65n.23, 82n.111
5:12–16   79
5:14   86, 93n.175
5:16   94
5:21   82n.111
5:25   82n.111
5:28   283n.310
5:36–37   110
5:40   283n.310
5:41   283n.310
5:41–42   75
5:42   15, 19n.105, 66, 74, 79n.93, 80n.98, 82, 87, 91, 157n.221, 296
6:1   64n.12, 84n.128
6:1–3   76n.83, 83n.119, 88
6:1–6   97–98, 105
6:1–7   71
6:2   100, 143n.140
6:4   80, 81n.105
6:7   86
6:8–10   105
6:10   98n.190
6:12   191
6:13   98n.190
6:14   106
6:15   64n.11
7:2–53   98n.190
7:59–8:3   106
8:1–3   95

8:3   88, 291
8:4–13   106
8:4–25   109
8:5   98n.190
8:12   283n.310
8:14   96n.184
8:17   96n.184
8:25   96n.184, 108, 123n.19
8:26–40   98n.190, 106
9:1–19   106
9:2   107
9:10   283n.310
9:10–19a   107
9:11   186n.367
9:30   186n.367
9:31–43   94n.178
9:32   108
9:32–43   108n.253
9:36–43   107
9:37   66n.26
9:39   66n.26
9:43   183n.349
10–12   90n.158
10:1–2   82n.111, 187
10:1–3   16, 104, 107n.249
10:1–48   108
10:3   64n.11
10:9   81n.107
10:22   82n.111, 187
10:23–48   93
10:36   56n.183
10:48   183n.349
11:1   94n.178, 108
11:12b–14   187
11:19   123n.19
11:19–21   112n.273
11:19–30   109
11:20   110
11:23   131
11:26   110, 112
11:27   64n.12
11:27–29   77n.88
11:27–30   111
11:28   204n.463
11:29   94n.178
11:29–30   110
11:30   101n.209, 181n.341
12:1–3   100
12:2   96
12:3–4   74
12:4–17   69n.44

12:5b   74
12:7   69
12:10b–17   69–74, 296
12:12   19n.105, 78, 80, 81n.107, 88n.147
12:12–14   25n.136, 290
12:16   96
12:17   78
13–14   110
13:1   111, 204n.463
13:1–2   113n.276, 204n.464
13:1–3   109, 112
13:2–3   181n.341
13:4–14:28   109
13:5   72
13:5–21:8   180n.331
13:7–12   128n.53
13:13   72
13:14–15   185n.363
13:15   131n.71
13:46   123n.19
13:46–50   127
14:1–6   185n.363
14:3   218n.555
14:9   218n.555
14:21   73, 218n.555
14:22   131
14:23   202, 274, 276
14:25   123n.19, 218n.555
15   109
15:1–2   181n.341
15:1–15   110
15:2   101n.209, 279
15:3   100, 184, 287n.336
15:4   101n.209, 105, 118, 279, 280, 297
15:6   101n.209, 105, 118, 279, 280, 297
15:13–21   72n.64
15:22   100, 105, 118, 280, 297
15:22–23   101n.209, 279
15:26   77n.88
15:32   131
15:37   72
15:38–40   110n.261
15:40   181n.341
15:41   105, 118, 279, 297
16   187, 207

16:4   105, 118, 279, 297
16:11–15   122, 131
16:11–40   121, 123, 127
16:13–15   19n.105, 289n.3
16:14–15   129
16:14–16   187
16:15   25n.136, 138, 183n.349
16:16–40   126
16:17   138
16:25–29   124
16:25–34   131, 132
16:29–34   124
16:30–34   19n.105, 187
16:31–34   129
16:32   123n.19
16:33   239
16:37–38   186n.367
16:40   131, 212
17   197n.427, 207, 291
17:1–9   126, 127, 128, 132, 151, 185n.363   201
17:1–15   124–25
17:4   133
17:4b   185
17:6   133
17:7   133
17:9   133
17:10   133
17:12   185
17:16–34   187n.371
17:17   15
17:19   200
17:22   15
17:34   128n.53, 185
18:1–3   210, 216
18:1–4   128–30
18:1–7   154
18:1–8   19n.105, 187, 289n.3
18:1–9   134n.87, 135n.91
18:1–12   185n.363
18:1–17   128n.56, 129, 130, 144n.145
18:2   136n.98
18:2–4   25n.136
18:3   136, 183n.349
18:5–8   128n.55
18:5–17   127

18:5b   128n.56
18:6   128n.56
18:7   137
18:7–8   128–30
18:8   138, 187
18:9–10   128n.56
18:9–11   128n.55
18:10   139
18:11   176
18:12–17   128n.55
18:18   129n.60, 136n.98, 180n.332
18:18–19b   143
18:19   129n.60, 136n.98, 185n.363
18:20   183n.349
18:24–26   210, 216
18:26   136, 136n.98, 143, 218
18:27   129n.60
19:1–3   144n.145
19:7   64n.11, 87n.142
19:8–41   127
19:9   15, 138n.107
19:9–10   187n.371
19:19   73
19:22   141
19:27   184n.356
20   104n.230
20:1–2   131
20:3   183
20:4   144n.145
20:7   75, 83, 84
20:7–8   33n.32, 66n.26
20:7–9   80n.98
20:7–12   82, 130   179
20:8–10   25n.136
20:11   75, 83, 208n.491
20:12   131
20:17   269
20:17–19   144n.145
20:17–28   274n.260
20:18   70
20:20   74n.73
20:28   202, 269, 274
20:33   181n.340
20:35   181n.340
21:4–8   183
21:8   25n.136, 98n.190, 210
21:8–9   106
21:10   204n.463
21:15–18   74, 78

21:18   101n.209, 104, 105, 118, 278, 279, 297
21:39   186n.367
22:3   186n.367
22:3–5   186n.367
22:5   191
22:25–27   186n.367
23:6   186n.367
23:14   191
23:27   186n.367
23:39   186n.367
24:5   85n.130
24:24   82n.111
24:26   82n.111
25:15   191
27:35   83
28:14   183n.349
28:16–18   16
28:22   85n.130
28:30   82n.111
28:30–31   146n.154

Romans
1:1   197
1:1–7   179n.329
1:1–16   212
1:3–4   107n.247
1:5   179n.329, 283n.310
1:7   146, 157, 159
1:8   189
1:13   179n.329
1:14   150
1:14–17   179n.329
1:16   185n.363
3:30   161
6:17   204n.466
6:23   233
7:2   224n.588
8:16–17   163
9–10   232
9:1–5   179n.329
9:25–26   160n.238
10:12   232
10:14–18   188
10:14–21   179n.329, 185n.363
11:1   186n.367
11:1–32   179n.329
11:13–32   160n.238
11:25   179n.329
11:25–26   188
11:26–27   161

12   276
12:1–2   188
12:3–8   178
12:4–8   162, 204n.464, 221n.575
12:5   163, 233, 257
12:7   204n.466
12:8   150, 151, 198, 199, 205, 217
12:9–10   163
12:12   64
12:13   150, 183n.350
12:17   189
13:1–3   252
14–15   267
15:7–12   161
15:14   163
15:14–29   179n.329
15:19   110n.262, 161
15:19–21   181n.339
15:19b   180n.331
15:22–28   161–62
15:23   181n.339
15:24   184
16   120, 296
16:1   129n.60, 145n.154, 149, 164n.259
16:1–2   130, 142, 182n.345, 183n.351, 184n.356, 217, 287n.336
16:1–3   217n.548
16:2   134, 183, 199
16:3   119, 130, 136nn.98,99, 144, 154, 155n.208, 201n.447, 214
16:3–5   159
16:3–16   144n.147
16:4   137
16:5   8n.45, 24n.131, 75, 119, 130, 135n.91, 144, 145, 155n.208, 157, 203
16:5–6   144
16:6   198
16:7   205n.470, 213
16:9   201n.447
16:10   145
16:10–11   146
16:11   145
16:12   198
16:13–16   212
16:14   147
16:14–15   119, 145, 150, 151n.186
16:15   147
16:16   80n.98
16:17   100n.206, 204n.466
16:21   127, 201n.447
16:22–23   183
16:23   9, 25, 119, 134, 138n.108, 139, 141, 142, 145n.154, 149, 154, 157, 158, 166, 171
16:26   179n.329

1 Corinthians
1:1   197, 213
1:1–2   164
1:2   145n.154
1:9   75
1:10–12   177
1:10–17   174
1:11   182n.345
1:12   129n.60
1:14   129, 138n.108, 139n.113, 186
1:16   8n.45, 121, 129, 138, 184, 186, 187, 203
1:26   142, 185, 186, 189
1:26–28   134, 168
1:26–29   174
1:26–31   4n.23
3:1–4   203
3:6   129n.60
3:8   198
3:9   201n.447, 259n.170
3:10   214
3:10–17   263
3:16   259n.170
3:16–17   160n.238
3:23   222n.578
4:1   263
4:6   129n.60
4:14   203
4:15   197, 233
4:17   161, 182n.345, 204n.466
5:1–5   203
5:9   182n.345
5:9–13   100n.206
6   153n.198
6:1–5   203
6:1–11   100n.206, 134n.86, 188
6:4   161n.240
6:16   246
6:16–17   162n.249
6:19   259n.170
7   250, 253
7:1   182n.345, 184
7:7   110, 181n.340
7:17–24   233
7:20–24   228, 231
7:21–24   252
7:22   237
7:39   237
7:39c   245
8:1   172, 184
8:6   245
8:10   172
8:11–13   163
9   49
9:1   214
9:4–18   52n.157
9:5   44n.108, 60n.201
9:6   109n.259, 110, 275
9:12–18   110
9:14   275
9:16–18   129n.59
9:20–21   185n.363
10:14–22   173
10:16   75, 83, 172
10:16–17   162n.246
10:17   162
10:23   172
10:32   161, 164n.258
11   171, 176, 190
11–14   172, 189
11:1–16   116n.283
11:2   173
11:2–4   252
11:2–6   225
11:2–16   215, 221, 233
11:2–26   222
11:3   238, 245
11:3–16   223
11:4–5   178
11:5   204n.465, 218
11:5–13   224
11:7–9   238
11:14   219
11:16   161, 164n.258
11:17   223
11:17–19   25n.136
11:17–26   113

11:17–34   163, 173, 175
11:18   145n.154, 164, 223
11:19–22   174
11:19a   177
11:20   75, 84, 86n.136, 139, 158, 166, 223
11:21   174
11:22   8n.45, 161n.240, 164n.258
11:23   217
11:23–25   84
11:23b–25   107n.247
11:26   84n.124
11:30   73
11:33   174
11:33–34   208
11:34   8n.45
12   233
12–14   204n.461
12:1   184
12:8–10   204n.465
12:12   189
12:12–13   173
12:12–31   162, 204n.464
12:13   151, 220n.568, 253
12:13–14   221n.575
12:17–18   221n.575
12:25–26   163
12:27   257
12:28   111, 161, 164, 199, 204, 205, 207n.485
13   154
13:3   181n.340
13:4–8   163
14   178
14:6   218
14:23   9, 25, 75, 86n.136, 139, 145n.154, 157, 158, 165n.262, 166, 171
14:23–25   16n.88
14:24–25   188
14:26   204n.466
14:28   222n.580
14:30   222n.580
14:33–34   161
14:33–36   224
14:33b–36   216n.541, 221, 222, 223, 225
14:35   8n.45, 239n.61
14:37   204n.465
14:40   222n.576, 252
15:3b–5   107n.247
15:5   90n.158, 213
15:5–7   90n.157
15:7   213
15:8–9   213
15:9   88n.149, 161, 164n.258
15:22   233
15:28   222n.578, 235, 238
15:58   163
16:1–3   162
16:1–4   134n.86, 144n.145
16:2   142n.133
16:3   184n.356
16:6   184, 287n.336
16:6–7   183n.349
16:11   174n.301, 182n.345, 184, 287n.336
16:15   8n.45, 121n.11, 134, 184
16:15–16   183n.351, 198, 202, 205
16:15–18   180n.336, 205n.470, 210
16:16   184n.358, 203
16:17   184
16:17–18   183n.351, 203n.458
16:18   180n.332
16:18b   184n.358
16:19   8n.45, 24n.131, 75, 119, 120, 130, 135n.91, 136n.98, 137n.102, 144, 146n.154, 155n.208, 156n.216
16:20   80n.98, 144
16:20–24   173
16:22   84n.124
16:22–23   172
16:24   163

2 Corinthians
1:1   146n.154, 164, 181n.341
1:16   184, 287n.336
1:19   129n.60
1:24   201n.447
2:12   182n.345
2:25–30   180
4:2   189
5:3   232
5:7   163
5:17   221, 233
6:4   217
6:10   110
6:14–7:1   188
6:16   160n.238, 261n.179
7:5–7   182n.345
8:1–4   162
8:2   169
8:10   182n.345
8:11   205n.470
8:14   134n.86
8:16–17   182n.345
8:18–19   180n.336, 205n.470
8:18–20   182n.345
8:21   189
8:22–24   182n.345
8:23   201n.447, 213
9:2   162, 182n.345
9:3–5   182n.345
9:12   162
9:13   75
11:5   205n.470
11:7–10   129n.59
11:7–13   52n.157
11:9   182n.345
11:24–25   185n.363
11:27   110
12:12   110n.262
12:17–18   182n.345
13:1   53n.167, 182n.345
13:11   100n.206
13:12   80n.98

Galatians
1:1   197, 204n.466
1:10   246
1:12   164
1:13   88n.149, 161, 164n.258
1:17   213
1:18   72n.64, 90n.158, 96, 183n.349
1:21   109n.259, 179
1:22   46, 88n.149, 94n.178
1:22–23   161
1:23   88n.149

2:1   72n.64, 181n.341
2:1–3   109n.259
2:1–24   110
2:7   214
2:9   72n.64
2:9–10   81n.102
2:10   199
2:11–14   112
2:12–13   113
3:8   179n.329
3:20   233
3:26–28   113, 116n.283, 151, 215, 221n.573
3:27   189, 293
3:27–28   220, 233, 237, 254, 295
3:27–29   232
3:28   116, 162n.249, 190, 225n.592, 247, 250, 252, 253
4:4–5   163
4:6   163
4:11   198
4:13   182n.345
4:19   203
5:13   244n.88
5:22   163
6:1   100n.206
6.2   163
6:6   204n.466
6:10   163, 259n.170, 261
6:16   160n.238

Ephesians
1:21–23   245
1:22   257
2:11–20   258
2:18–19   163n.254
2:19   261
2:19–22   259
2:19–24   257
3:10   163, 258
3:21   258
4   160, 166, 225n.594, 296n.15
4:1–3   244n.88, 258
4:4–6   258
4:7–16   257
4:12   257
4:12–16   259
4:15   257
4:16   257
5:4   236n.39
5:19   178

5:21   238n.49, 248, 258, 259
5:21–33   245n.92
5:21–6:9   224n.588, 229n.2, 243–47
5:22   258
5:22f.   259n.166
5:23   257
5:25   258
5:27   258
5:31–32   259
5:32   258
6:1   237
6:2–3   238n.54
6:4   239
6:10   243
6:18b   244

Philippians
1:1   25, 104n.230, 151, 181n.341, 207, 209, 269, 270, 272, 273, 277, 298
1:8   163
1:14   123n.19
1:14–18   188
2:3b   244n.88
2·6   222n.578
2:12   163
2:12–16   188
2:16   198
2:25   180, 201n.447
2:25–30   180n.336, 205n.470
2:29   183
2:29–30   183n.351
2:30   184n.357
3:1   163
3:4–11   186n.367
3:6   88n.149, 161
4:1   163
4:2–3   183n.351, 211
4:3   201n.447
4:10–12   206n.478
4:10–18   184
4:11–13   110
4:15   165n.259, 182n.345
4:16   127
4:22   8n.45

Colossians
1:1   181n.341
1:4   236

1:5   242
1:7   217
1:8   236
1:13   236
1:15–20   236, 237, 238, 245, 252
1:17–18   257
1:18   160, 163, 257
1:24   257
1:27   242
2:1   152n.188
2:2   236
2:7   204n.466
3:1   241
3:1–4   242
3:5–17   236
3:9–11   220n.568, 221, 237
3:10   232
3:11   151, 252, 254, 258, 293
3:12–14   163
3:15   162n.249
3:16   178, 224
3:16–4:1   233
3:17   237, 238, 241
3:18   237, 240n.64
3:18–19   234
3:18–25   116n.283
3:18–4:1   224n.588, 229–30, 243, 252
3:18b   236
3:19   240n.64
3:20   237, 240n.64
3:20–21   238–39
3:21   240n.64
3:22   247
3:22–4:1   240–42, 246
3:25   247
4:1   248
4:2   64, 233
4:2–6   188
4:7   237
4:7–8   182n.344
4:9   152, 241
4:10   73
4:10–14   257
4:11   184n.356
4:13   155n.206
4:15   8n.45, 24n.131, 119, 120, 130, 146n.154, 154–55, 211, 212, 257

4:16 155, 164n.259, 178, 257
4:17 152, 237, 257n.160

1 Thessalonians
1:1 146n.154, 163, 164n.259, 181n.341
1:3 163
1:6 180n.334
1:6–8 188
1:7–8 182n.345
1:8 189
1:9 133
1:9–10 188
1:10 163
2:1 180n.334
2:2 124, 126
2:5 129n.59
2:5–12 203
2:7 205n.470
2:9 148n.171
2:9–12 133n.80
2:13–20 180n.334
2:14 94n.178, 126, 127, 133, 164n.258
2:15–16 126
3:1–2 180n.332
3:1–3 182n.345
3:1–6 126, 197n.427
3:1–13 180n.334
3:2 201n.447, 217
3:5 198
3:6 129n.60, 180n.332
3:11 163
3:12 163
3:13 163
4:9–12 148n.171
4:10–11 188
4:11 133n.80
4:12 189
4:15 133
4:16 233
5:12 133, 151, 199, 202n.450, 205, 210n.499, 217
5:12–13 151n.187, 183n.351, 200
5:12–14 197, 198
5:14 251
5:16–22 178
5:26 80n.98
5:27 133, 178

2 Thessalonians
1:1 164n.259, 181n.341
1:1–2 163
1:4 164n.258
2:16 163
3:6 100n.206
3:6–12 133n.80
3:10 148
3:11–13 251
3:14–15 100n.206

1 Timothy
1:3 144n.145, 262
1:7 270
1:9–10 261n.183
1:12 261n.183
2:1–15 260n.177
2:2 261n.183
2:4 266
2:8–10 261n.183
2:8–6:2a 229n.2
2:9 264
2:9–15 224n.589
2:11–12 222n.576, 262
2:12 222
2:12–14 221
3 280
3:1–3 265
3:1–7 268
3:1–10 269
3:1–13 260n.177
3:2 104n.230
3:2–4 261n.183
3:4 263
3:4–5 261n.182
3:5 262
3:5–6 267n.219
3:6 267n.220
3:7 265
3:8–10 261n.183
3:8–13 268
3:11 217n.549, 261n.183
3:12 261n.182, 263n.191, 266
3:15 7, 260, 266, 273
4:11–16 260n.177, 262
4:12 261nn.182, 183
4:14 268, 279
5:1 98n.197, 270, 279
5:1–5 261n.183
5:1–22 260n.177
5:2–16 268

5:3 240n.64
5:3–16 270
5:4 240n.64
5:7 262
5:8 240n.64
5:9–16 217n.549
5:11–13 261n.183
5:17 197n.427, 261nn.182,183, 262, 270, 273, 275
5:17–19 268
5:17–20 269
5:18 270, 275
5:19 53n.167
5:19–20 100n.206
6:1–2 254n.143, 261n.183
6:2 261n.182
6:4–6 261n.183
6:9–10 264
6:13 262
6:17–18 261n.183
6:17–19 265
6:18 262
6:20–21 260n.177

2 Timothy
1:11–14 260n.177
1:16 266
1:18 144n.145
2:2 261n.183
2:14 262
2:14–3:9 260n.177
2:19–22 263
2:20–21 262
2:21 261nn.182,183
2:24 261n.183
3:2–4 261n.183
3:6 267
3:6–7 267n.219
3:7 262
3:14 262
3:16–17 262
4:2 100n.206
4:12 144n.145
4:19 136n.98, 266
4:20 141

Titus
1:5 268, 270, 272, 279
1:5–6 261n.183, 265
1:5–9 260n.177, 269, 275, 277
1:6 261n.183, 280

1:7   262
1:7–8   261n.183, 280
1:7–9   268
1:10–12   261n.183
1:11   177, 267, 299
2:1–10   229n.2
2:1–15   260n.177
2:2–6   261n.183
2:6   98n.197
2:7   261n.183
2:9   247n.101,
   254n.143, 261n.182
2:9–10   261n.183
2:11–12   262
2:12   261n.183
2:15   261n.182
3:1–3   261n.183
3:8   266
3:8–11   260n.177
3:10   100n.206
3:13   287n.336
3:14   262, 265
3:15   262

Philemon
1   130, 153, 154,
   181n.341
1–2   24n.131, 119, 152,
   155n.208
1–3   104
2   8n.45, 75, 130,
   146n.154
3   152n.189, 153
4   153, 154
7   154
8–14   154
10   152
13   182n.344
16   237, 241
20   153
21–22   119, 130
22   154
25   152n.189, 153

Hebrews
10:28   53n.167
13:2   183n.350
13:6   123n.19
13:22   131n.71

James
2:2–3   11, 289n.3

1 Peter
2:11–3:7   229n.2
2:18   254n.143
2:18–25   247
4:14   283n.310
4:16   283n.310
5:1–2   269
5:1–3   276
5:2   274n.260
5:5   98n.197
5:5b   244n.88
5:14   80n.98

1 John
1:3   81n.102
1:6–7   81n.102
2:27   285
5:19–20   100n.206

2 John
1   281
10   287n.335
10–11   282, 283

3 John
5–10   183n.349,
   282n.305
6   285, 287
7   282n.308, 283, 287
8   183n.350, 283
9   283, 285
9–10   282
10   283n.314
12   286

Revelation
2:1–7   144n.145
11:8   204n.463
16:6   204n.463
18:20   204n.463
22:20   84n.124

DEAD SEA SCROLLS

1 QS
5:12   86n.135
8:12   86n.135

1QM
4:10   160

1Qsa
1:25em   160

RABBINIC
LITERATURE

Babylonian Talmud
Baba Batra
133b   65n.18

Baba Qamma
36b   36n.63

Bekorot
50b   36n.63

Gittin
58a   89n.152

Ketubbot
105a   89n.152

Jerusalem Talmud
Berakot
8a   30n.13
30b   30n.13

Gittin
58a   30n.13

Ketubbot
35c   30n.13, 89n.152
105a   30n.13

Megillah
73d   30n.13, 89n.152

Sanhedrin
21b   65

Mekilta Exodus
2   287n.337

Midrash Rabbah
Genesis Rabbah
31:11   45n.114

Qoheleth Rabbah
1:8   33n.34
7:27   33n.34
38a   33n.34

Mishnah
'Abot
4:15b   56n.181

Berakot
3:6d   45n.114
8:12c   45n.114

Megillah
4:3   212

Šabbat
1:4   65

Šeqalim
1:1   36n.63
1:3   36n.63
2:1   36n.63

Tosefta
Berakot
7:18   220

Makkot
3:8   38

PAPYRI

Ryland Papyri II
76.10   155n.212
76.12   155n.212

Tebtunis Papyri II
326   198n.432

OTHER ANCIENT AND MEDIEVAL WRITINGS

1 Clement
1:3   254n.143
21:6–9   254n.143
42:4   269n.226
43:1   270n.237
44   274n.260
44:1   269
44:1–4   276
44:2   270n.237
44:5   269
54:2   270n.237

Acts of John
106–110   80n.98

Apuleius
Metamorphoses
9.24–25   136n.95

Aristotle
Ethica nichomachea
5.1134b.9–18   248n.106
8.1060a.23–8.1661a.10
   248n.106

Oeconomica
3   234n.24

Politica
1.1259b.21–1260b.24
   253n.142

Barnabas
19:7   254n.143

Clement of Alexandria
Stromata
2.114.3–6   183n.347
3.53.3   214n.524

Columella
De re rustica
12. pref. 5, 7–10,
   248n.107
12.2.26   248n.107

Didache
4:11   254n.143
10:6   173
11:1   170n.289
11:1–6   285
11:5   55n.177
11:13   170n.289
12:1–4   285
15:1–2   269n.226

Diogenes Laertius
*De clarorum
   philosophorum vitis*
1.33   220n.571

Eusebius
Onomasticon
174.23   39n.73

Ignatius
To Polycarp
6:1   254n.143

Jerome
Epistulae
103   66n.28

*De situ et nominibus
   locorum hebraicorum*
194   39n.73

Josephus
Against Apion
2.201   234n.27

Jewish Antiquities
4.74   155n.211
4.163   155n.211
7.202   63
15.121–122   67
18.20–22   77n.86
18.82   150n.183
20.169   63
20.195   150n.183
20.200   101n.210

Jewish War
2.122–127   77n.86
2.229   30n.13
3.194–196   36n.63
5.70   63
5.185   65n.23
7.45   111n.267
7.218   36n.63

Justin
Apologia i
67.4   80n.98

Dialogus cum Tryphone
3.1–3   286n.334
35.3   177

Martyrium Justini
3.1   146n.161
3.3   146n.161

Juvenal
Satirae
3.6–7   148n.173
3.198–202   148n.173
3.203–207   136n.95
3.215–220   148n.173

Martial
Epigrammata
1.117   148n.173
7.20   148n.173
12.32   136n.95

Musonius Rufus
Oratio
3.38.26–3.40.2   248n.110
3.42.10–15,17   248n.110
4.46.13–32   248n.110
12.86.38–13.88.4   248n.110

Origen
Contra Celsus
8.22   66n.28

Paulus Orosius
Historiae adversus paganos
7.6.15–16   129n.59

Philo
De specialibus legibus
2.62   30n.13

De vita Mosis
2.216   30n.13

Hypothetica
11.14–13   77n.86

Legatio ad Gaium
132   30n.13

Quod omnis probus liber sit
76–77   77n.86
85–87   77n.86

Philostratus
De gymnastuca
23   219n.563
272.30–31   99n.201, 155n.205

Plutarch
Antonius
10   248n.111

Conjugalia praecepta
142D,E   248n.111

De liberis educandis
2.4C   239n.57
2.7E   239n.57
2.8E   239n.57
2.9A   239n.57
2.12C   239n.57
2.14A   239n.57

Lycurgus
14.1   248n.111

Marius
46.1   220n.571

Seneca
De ira
3.35.5   148n.173

Strabo
Geographica
5.3.7   148n.173

Suetonius
Divus Claudius
25.4   129n.59

Xenophon
Oeconomicus
13.9–12   253n.142
14.9   253n.142